JOHANNES MAYER (1933–2023) assumed le
Community's publishing house, Verlag Ura
three-decade tenure at the Stuttgart-based c
with Verlag Freies Geistesleben in 1996—he o
numerous significant works on religion, philosophy and art. Following the merger, Mayer founded his own publishing venture, Johannes Mayer Verlag, which he ran until its acquisition by Info3 in 2013, just before his 80th birthday. Beyond publishing, Mayer was a dedicated researcher of the enigmatic figure Kaspar Hauser. In collaboration with Peter Tradowsky, he compiled an extensive compendium in 1984, drawing on archival materials inherited from historian and Hauser expert Hermann Pies. His scholarly pursuit led him to the Stanhope archives in England, where he meticulously examined historical documents for years. The fruits of this research were published in German in 1988 as a seminal volume on the subject.

LORD STANHOPE

The Adversary of Kaspar Hauser

Johannes Mayer

Translated by Terry M. Boardman

TEMPLE LODGE

Temple Lodge Publishing Ltd.
Hillside House, The Square
Forest Row, RH18 5ES

www.templelodge.com

First published in English by Temple Lodge in 2025

Originally published in German under the title *Philip Henry Lord Stanhope, Der Gegenspieler Kaspar Hausers* by Verlag Urachhaus, Stuttgart, in 1988

A CIP catalogue record for this book is available from the British Library

ISBN 978 1 915776 41 9

Cover by Morgan Creative featuring portrait of Philip Henry Stanhope,
4th Earl Stanhope (1781–1855) by unknown painter
Typeset by Symbiosys Technologies, Visakhapatnam, India
Printed and bound by 4Edge Ltd., Essex

Contents

Introduction

'One of the strangest figures...'

Fritz Klee, next to Hermann Pies certainly the most important Kaspar Hauser researcher, wrote in his book *Neue Beiträge zur Kaspar-Hauser Forschung* ('New Contributions to Kaspar Hauser Studies'), which appeared in 1929:

> This book deliberately does not go into the question of Stanhope. To clarify what role that mysterious Englishman played in Germany and especially in the life of Kaspar Hauser would be a task in itself...It may be said regarding the ambiguous behaviour of Lord Stanhope, who at first showed such a striking affection for Hauser and later rejected him so utterly, that there is insufficient clarity about this man, about his various travels and his visits to princely courts.

Georg Friedrich Kolb expressed himself in a similar vein as did almost all those who have engaged with the question of Kaspar Hauser. 'One of the strangest figures in the whole Kaspar Hauser drama,' according to Kolb, 'is the mysterious Lord Stanhope.' Similarly, Adolf Bartning, who declared that 'in the environment of Kaspar Hauser' Stanhope 'certainly played the strangest role, which to this day has not been clarified'. Finally, there is the witness of Georg Friedrich Daumer, Kaspar Hauser's contemporary, who remarked that the Englishman 'transformed himself from a real or apparent friend, even an affectionate enthusiast for Kaspar Hauser, into his greatest enemy, persecutor and accuser'. 'It is on England,' said Daumer, 'and its high and wealthy aristocracy that the dark shadow of suspicion falls, a suspicion that cannot be dismissed and which is for me grounded in quite particular circumstances and experiences.'

As much as there has been agreement in seeing Stanhope as primarily responsible for bringing about the decisive turning point in Kaspar Hauser's life, just as little has it been possible to underpin this fact through a more exact knowledge of the complicated life of the Englishman let alone through an interpretation of his possible motives. That this latter point has remained outstanding may have been due to the fact that without further research in Stanhope's home country there was little to say that had not already been said by Hermann Pies and others.

I was drawn to research such a significant figure in the drama of Kaspar Hauser not only because this 'mysterious Englishman' had for 150 years been accorded the same all too brief and partly completely false commentaries, but rather because I was prompted by the question of why and how he came to play his utterly destructive role in the life of the foundling.

The details of his life, which he purposely concealed and the facets of which are illuminated by nothing particularly brilliant, varied or distinguished, are, however, permeated by a hidden inner tension and dynamic, which increasingly fascinated me as the years went by. So, I began to work my way into the closed existence of this unknown character, looking for his trail through the years and even the days of his life. To a far greater extent than is normally necessary in cases of biographies of well-known personalities, I felt I had to go into the minutiae of his daily life, also paying particular attention to all those contemporaries whom he met or whose acquaintance he sought. These details often cast a penetrating light on Stanhope himself, on his times and on the Kaspar Hauser issue, even though at first glance they did not seem to have played any significant role.

I avoided everything of a casual, decorative and novelesque nature. Illustrative elements, however, are, as a rule, based on letters and other contemporary sources. They were found primarily in more than 1000 previously unpublished letters, notes and written comments from England and France, which, as far as they are of significance to this study, are indicated in the reference section. The letters written in German appear in the original form with allowances for modern spelling.

In his home country Philip Henry, the 4th Earl Stanhope, merits a few sentences in the 'Dictionary of National Biography' alongside his significant predecessors and descendants, on account of his occasional contributions to parliamentary debates and his proposals for reform, mainly of the Corn Laws and the Poor Laws. Botanists may be familiar with the fact that a species of Guatamalan orchid—the *Stanhopea oculata*—carries his name; he was the President of the Medico-Botanical Society at the time [1829–1837—*Ed.*]. Publishers and printers may know of the 'Stanhope press', a very effective machine developed by Philip Henry's father. Only the first Earl Stanhope achieved real fame; a splendid monument to him was erected in a prominent position in Westminster Abbey in London in recognition of his military victories. The choir stalls, designed and constructed in 1833–4 by Edward Blore include two altarlike monuments, on the left in memory of Isaac

Newton and keeping respectful company with it on the right, one to James Stanhope (1673–1721), a general raised to the rank of earl in 1717 and who, during the reign of George I (1714–27), had a famous political career. As Secretary of State, Minister and First Lord of the Treasury, he had a further impact on his country's history, since in a most difficult situation he had 'saved the crown for the House of Hanover' as the 4th Earl once told his son.

The plinth of the shrine carries all the names of the Stanhope family line, which became extinct with James Richard, the 7th Earl (1880–1967). Under the dates of the 4th Earl are those of his son, also named Philip Henry (1805–75), well-known in England as an historian. Ten streets, bridges and squares in London bear the family name.

In Germany the name Stanhope was only to some extent known to those familiar with the story of Kaspar Hauser, especially from the account by Anselm von Feuerbach in his book *Beispiel eines Verbrechens am Seelenleben des Menschen* ('Example of a Crime against the Soul Life of Man'). In the book Feuerbach honoured 'His Lordship' before all the world at a time when he considered the lord to be acting in the interest of Kaspar Hauser, particularly as the Englishman had even been the foundling's foster father for a period.

This short section of his biography—1831 to 1833—has also been accessible in the past through a few letters and documents. But beyond the meagre facts known about this period, there was complete ignorance about Stanhope's appearance in Nuremberg and Ansbach. Understandably, Stanhope himself did not consider himself obliged to leave behind the story of his life.

One could have allowed things to rest there, had not Stanhope's ever increasing interventions in the life of Kaspar Hauser for whatever motives, not been of such overriding significance and attracted the most divergent interpretations, which were, subsequently, only of interest to those for whom, from a critical point of view, Stanhope's behaviour must have appeared incomprehensible. Gottlieb von Tucher was the first to have his doubts; then followed Daumer and finally, Feuerbach, when it was already too late. Since that time, there have been countless others who could no longer believe in the 'foster father's' humanitarian engagement, who noticed a conspiratorial element in his behaviour, which they found objectionable, and who finally began to reconsider Stanhope's role. But they did not get much further with it. In 1834 Daumer's mother, after a very unloving comment of Stanhope's about Kaspar Hauser, called him Hauser's 'murderer', which does not fit the actual facts of the case, but which nevertheless contains some truth in the eyes of those with a deeper sensibility. At that time, Stanhope unexpectedly began to manifest the attitude which did not harmonise with the behaviour he had shown up to that point and which displayed its true face when he now started to become, even publicly, the tireless and vindictive opponent of Kaspar Hauser. The reason he gave for this change in attitude was his 'great disappointment' over the 'ungrateful fraud', something which careful examination shows does not correspond with the facts, as will be demonstrated.

What then were the actual motives for the Briton's attraction to and repulsion from Kaspar Hauser, and calling to mind the few proven facts of the case, what was the purpose and background of this whole course of events?

All the prerequisites for a satisfactory answer to these questions seem at first to be lacking. Stanhope himself took systematic care of this since he had 'made it a rule not to write down anything at all which could be detrimental for the discovery of the story, should the papers by any misfortune fall into unsafe hands'. It lies in the nature of things that all those involved in such matters—not just Stanhope—would take care to eliminate all hard evidence against themselves. This attitude has unfortunately created painful gaps in the family archives. In particular, an accurate travel diary of Philip Henry's would be of the greatest interest, but just such a revealing document no longer exists—a loss which is hard to understand if it had only included positive impressions and observations which he had recorded during his undertakings. But the documentary sources have dried up in other directions too. His contemporaries appear to have taken no further notice of the 4th Earl. There is scarcely any other diary or journal in which he is either enthusiastically praised or condemned. Without noteworthy correspondence, and as an unknown in literary circles as in almost all other areas of public life, this perpetual traveller appears as a superficial, charmingly spoken personality with aims and intentions that remain in the background. His métier was the politics that went on beyond the headlines. His interests had to do with certain relations between Great Britain and Austria and the way these might impinge on France and the German states. In this context, one motive and one driving force in this restless life becomes perceptible which already touched the orbit of Kaspar Hauser's life early on and which it is therefore worth trying to reconstruct.

Kaspar Hauser was an incomparable and sensational historical phenomenon which, despite its apparent outward lack of consequence, cast a powerful spell on its contemporaries. Overwhelmingly, people felt a positive sympathy for him. Not a few, however, with quite different feelings, could refrain from letting him feel their deep-rooted dislike, and so it has been characteristically said of him that in a very quiet way he had a deep effect on people's consciousness. Since this phenomenon is still the case today, a certain timelessness can be attributed to it. More interesting than the friendly and well-disposed people therefore, whose enthusiasms are easier to understand, are Hauser's enemies, whose motives and verbal attacks, in the face of a destiny such as that of Kaspar Hauser, which is as moving today as it was then, remain almost incomprehensible. If among many others, such as the Berlin Police Chief Johann Friedrich Merker, there was *one* great opponent in Hauser's life, it was Stanhope, who created in Hauser the greatest hopes and expectations, which were followed by all the more severe disappointment. But even that was not enough. Ultimately, he did not shy away from destroying the best a human being can possess. For the question posed by Ludwig Feuerbach, son of the Court President Anselm von Feuerbach, still stands: 'Why did he go on persecuting him even in death?' In other words, why did even the memory of Kaspar Hauser have to be obliterated? The idea of Stanhope's great friendship with Kaspar Hauser, as described by Johanna, Countess Keyserlingk in her *Bilder und Studien* ('Pictures and Studies'), which appeared in 1986, is untenable in view of the known and newly discovered facts. Much more convincing appears the view regarding Stanhope expressed by Eduard Feuerbach in a confidential letter to his brother Anselm: 'I suspect in fact, that he...was an instrument in the hands of the enemies of Hauser and knowingly worked for them.'

*

A life path that zigzags through the multi-layered and complicated politics and cultural histories of England, France, Austria, Bavaria and Baden is not easy to follow, especially when it moves along such intertwined and sometimes curious paths as that of Philip Henry Stanhope. For the connoisseur therefore, much in what follows may not seem detailed enough, too selective, too much abstracted from the larger historical picture; other parts may seem too general. However, the often widely juxtaposed viewpoints result from the facts of Stanhope's life as they emerge from his biography. The reader may note the absence of numerous extremely important facts and even whole sections of Kaspar Hauser's life and times. It would be impossible and superfluous to repeat them here. They have been dealt with in detail in the works of the great Kaspar Hauser researchers and writers. The reader is referred for instance to the books of Hermann Pies, and the study presented by Peter Tradowsky and myself, published in 1984 under the title *Kaspar Hauser—Das Kind von Europa, dargestellt in Wort und Bild* ('Kaspar Hauser—The Child of Europe, in Words and Pictures'). In these works can be found comprehensive documentation which will also be referred to throughout the present volume.

This book could not have been completed without assistance from many quarters, especially in Great Britain. My thanks go in the first place to 'The Administrative Trustees of the Chevening Estate', and especially to Major General J.D.C. Graham, Captain J.D.W. Husband and B.E. Duncan in Chevening, the County Archivist W. Nigel Yates, and W.G. Hopkin of the Kent Archive in Maidstone, John P. Fuller, librarian in London, and Rev. Maurice Hewett in Sevenoaks. I also have to thank Prof. Dr. Renate Riemeck, Inge Thöns, Prof. Dr. Hermann Hummel-Liljegren, Dr. Hans-Peter van Manen, Dr. Peter Mayet and Dr. Wolfgang Veit for their knowledgeable advice on the manuscript, numerous indications and suggestions.

Finally, special thanks go to Roswitha von dem Borne, who, as interpreter in the archives, as translator of over a thousand texts and as editor, made such a substantial contribution to the production of this book.

Johannes Mayer
Stuttgart, November 1987

1. The Parental Home

Childhood and Youth, 1781 — 1800

Philip Henry's father Charles, the 3rd Earl Stanhope (1753–1816), was born in London on 3rd August 1753. At the age of eight the highly gifted child was sent to Eton. An unwritten law decreed that a schooling there was a prerequisite to future status and an elevated social position.

At the age of nine, following the early death of his elder brother Philip (1746–63), he inherited the title Viscount Mahon, which had been awarded in 1717 to the first Earl, James Stanhope (1673–1721), Commander-in-Chief of British forces in the War of the Spanish Succession, in recognition of his successful conquest of the island of Minorca (1708). Mahon was the name of the capital and harbour of the island, and from that time on, the title Viscount Mahon was bestowed on the firstborn son of the family.

In July 1764 Charles travelled with his parents to Geneva, where he received his further education. Still affected by the early death of their eldest son, his parents had a memorial plaque erected on the north wall of the old church of St Gervais:

> Philip Stanhope,
> Viscount Mahon,
> Eldest son of Philip
> Earl Stanhope
> and of
> Griselda Hamilton,
> his wife
> Born 5th July 1746
> Died 6th July 1763

Through the presence of a sizeable colony of British expatriates in Geneva, and through Griselda (1719–1811) who, as stated on the plaque, was born a Hamilton, the family had ready-made contacts in the region. The cradle of Swiss Freemasonry, the city of Rousseau's birth and the place where, from his Castle Fernay, Voltaire had sent out his impulses for the European Enlightenment, Geneva had first been visited by provincial Grand Master George Hamilton in 1737, '...who had been sent from England and had founded many lodges'. Philip Stanhope, 2nd

Earl Stanhope (1714–1786), soon began his lodge work in the city in the 'true' Templar system—a system of Freemasonry strongly promoted by Johann Christian Schubart (1734–1787) and Diethelm Lavater (the brother of the physiognomist), which had spread especially in Switzerland and America. 'It took a lot of patience and a lot of money to be admitted into the Order's inner circle...' [1]; both appeared to be available. In the middle of the nineteenth century (1854) there was still a lodge on the Route du Lac that had been established with financial aid from Stanhope. A caretaker showed to Stanhope's descendant, Philip Henry the 5th Earl (1805–75), the Stanhope coat of arms hanging in the lodge chapter house and nearby, a portrait of his great-grandfather wearing the surcoat of a Templar knight with a drawn sword, which means that he was the 'army commander' of the prefecture of Geneva, who was responsible for conferring knighthoods in the fourth and last grade of the Order. 'This knightly grade was the actual Order, which ruled the whole as its head and which commanded absolute obedience from the lower grades, without having to justify its actions to them.'[2]

It was from here that the 'Strict Observance' promoted by Schubart took its start, a form of Freemasonry which lay at the root of the lodge system widely dominated by Karl Gotthelf Hund (1722–1776) in his day. Despite borrowing their name, this variant of Freemasonry had nothing in common with the historical Templar knights and their last Grand Master, Jacques de Molay, but through the association conveyed by the name, it was endowed—perhaps intentionally—with a certain aura.

In the Geneva lodge a gold medallion presented by the 2nd Earl Stanhope was still on display in the nineteenth century, which, aside from the motto devised by him, related to a timeless symbol of Freemasonry—the 'Arch', also called the 'Keystone'. Based on the archetype of the keystone which supports the tension in a vaulted arch, a special higher grade had been founded in Ireland, called the Royal Arch, or Arch of Solomon. This gift from Stanhope was for a long time worn by the Grand Masters of the Order on festive occasions.

In the environment of this still small city and in this freemasonic 'enlightened' family culture, Charles spent the formative years of his youth. Parental conviction also determined the choice of his teachers and educators. Among others the, 11-year old was taught by G.J. Le Sage, who instructed him in the first rudiments of an 'exact science'. Already around 1770 the youngster was busying himself with the writings of Rousseau, for which his teacher had planted an enthusiasm in him. The influence of this certainly premature preoccupation with the philosophers of the Enlightenment was later to show both in the course of his own life and especially in the education of his children.

Precocious and gifted with a brilliant intelligence, Charles gained much ready acknowledgement and admiration. Lady Mary Coke, who visited the family in Geneva in October 1769, wrote of the boy's 'amazing gifts'. 'His paintings would astonish you, and he cuts out people from paper as others can do only by drawing. He has invented a mathematical instrument that suits his purposes far better than any other of such kind. And yet he is not even 17 years old !' At 18 Charles solved a prize-winning question on the laws of pendulums set by the Academy of Stockholm.[3]

After 10 years in Geneva the Stanhopes travelled back to their family seat at Chevening in 1774; in the same year, the 21-year-old was presented at court. His father, who was more than frugal in his private affairs, did not approve of his son having his hair powdered for the occasion 'because wheat is too expensive'. This led to his son, whose black hair was adorned with a white feather, becoming an object of mockery in jokebooks which reported with glee that he had appeared at court 'tarred and feathered'.

Nevertheless, the new beginning in his homeland cannot have been completely lacking in good fortune. The mutual friendship which quickly sprang up between himself and the 24-year-old future Prime Minister William Pitt (1759–1806) led to a favourable meeting with, and the subsequent affection of, Pitt's sister, Lady Hester Pitt (1755–1780), whom Charles married in the year of his return from Switzerland, on 19th December 1774.

The first child born of the marriage was a daughter, Hester (1776–1839), the future 'Queen of the Desert', the legendary mistress of the Lebanon, also known as the Queen of Tadmor, who was to play a role at least for a short period in the life of her stepbrother Philip Henry, later the foster father of Kaspar Hauser. Two more daughters were born from this reportedly happy but brief marriage—Griselda (1778–1851) and Lucy (1780–1840).

At that time, it fell to Charles Stanhope to accompany Pitt the Younger to the House of Lords, a duty which he carried out with enthusiasm. On 7th July 1778, when William Pitt the Elder (the Earl of Chatham) collapsed with exhaustion during his last speech on the freedoms of the American colonies, his son William and Charles rushed to his side to support the aged politician. The dramatic moment was

2. The Death of the Earl of Chatham *by John Singleton Copley (1738–1815) actually depicts not Chatham's death (11th May 1778) but his collapse in the House of Lords, 7th April 1778. At his feet is the 3rd Earl Stanhope.*

captured in a painting by John Singleton Copley (1738–1815). The anxious son-in-law kneels at the feet of the old man. (Fig.2). After Chatham's death, the happy years were to be overshadowed again, for on 18th July 1780 Charles' wife Hester died at the age of 25 after just six years of marriage.

The family's sorrow over the early loss of the young wife and mother of three infant daughters was deep, so the general amazement in 'society' was great when just eight months later, on 12th March 1781, Charles wed Louisa Grenville (1758–1829), his dead wife's cousin and the daughter of Henry Grenville. When Lord Holland recalled that Charles had been 'a bad husband, an unkind and perhaps even unjust father', that had to do with this second marriage, which, as the family knew, could not have been exactly a love match. There is a portrait of Louisa Grenville by Pompeo Batoni (1708–1787) which shows the 12-year-old Louisa in Rome as a coquettish precocious little person (Fig. 3). Something of the 'stiff, cold, icily conventional' Lady Louisa entered her husband's soul, revealing a side of his character that had hitherto remained hidden. Drollery, obstinacy, a domineering tendency and extremely odd behaviour towards the children now came to the fore.

In one point, however, the marriage brought evident fulfilment: sons and thus the much-desired heir that would ensure the family name and estate. First came Philip Henry (1781–1855), the subject of this book, then in 1784 his brother Banks, who died in the year of his birth; he was followed by Charles Banks (1785–1809) and James Hamilton (1788–1825).

As godfather for his firstborn, the father turned to a more than peculiar member of the Chesterfield line of the family—Philip Stanhope, 5th Earl of Chesterfield (1755–1815), a distant cousin of the Freemason and founder of various lodges, Philip Dormer Chesterfield (1694–1773). To the 5th Earl of Chesterfield, who would later be the main heir and successor in the peerage, Philip Dormer sent as a kind of legacy a total of 281 letters, similar to the ones he had sent to his own son of the same name who had died an early death (1733–1768). Gebhard Wendehorn, the minister of the German congregation in London, contributed something to the story that grew up around the birth of this son, namely, that Philip Dormer had only imagined that he was the father; a ship's captain apparently proved to have been the real father. This ill fortune—according to Wendehorn—occurred in racy fashion when Petronella Melusine von Schulenburg (1693–1778), illegitimate daughter of George I, took ship from Holland to England at the request of her future husband (Philip Dormer) and 'straightway threw herself into the arms of the ship's captain'. In the years 1738–1763 Dormer wrote well over 300 letters to his growing son Philip, which, a year after his death, appeared under the title 'Letters to his Son'[4] and immediately assumed a leading position in British chronicles of scandal. What the father communicated to his son led to Voltaire's comment that 'one [would] never be allowed to sell the book in France'. Friedrich Christian Schlosser called the collection 'excellently written, polished in form and style—but the morality of a scoundrel'.

The intentions of his cousin did not leave our Philip Henry's godfather unscathed. His character impenetrable, his life listless, the constantly ailing Philip Stanhope died in 1815 after a not very active life. The letters—'a perfect example of impudence and immorality' (H. Hettner)—had lamed and poisoned his soul. It was he who, at the age of 26, had stood at the cradle of Philip Henry and accompanied his first years of life.

Philip Henry Lord Mahon, later the 4th Earl Stanhope, was born on Friday the 7th December 1781 at Chevening House (Fig. 4) and among other astrological difficulties in his horoscope, Mars was square to

3. *Louisa Grenville (1758–1829), later Countess Stanhope, second wife of Charles, 3rd Earl Stanhope, mother of 4th Earl, Philip Henry Stanhope. Painted by Pompeo Batoni (1708–1787).*

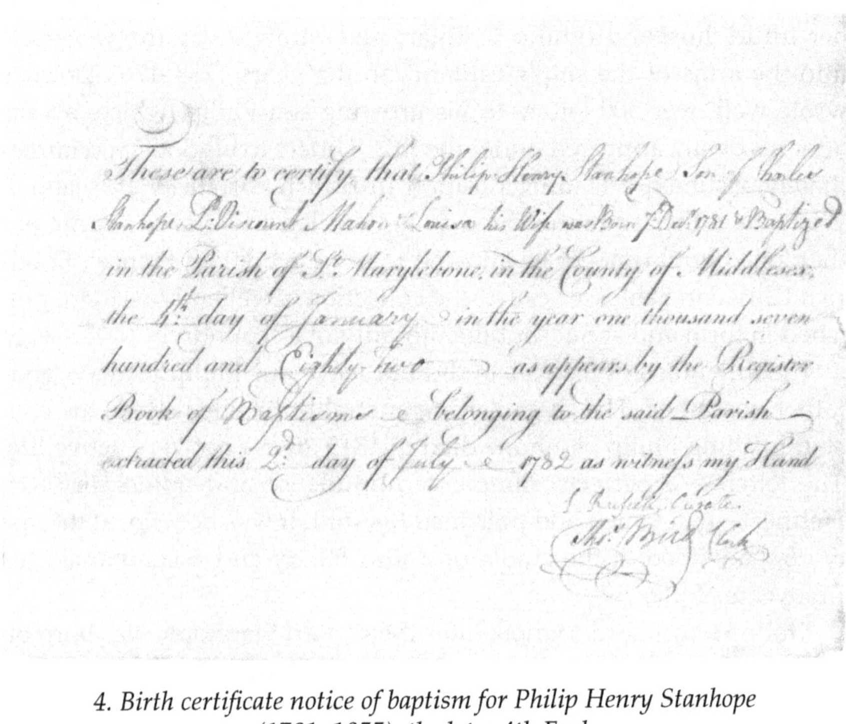

These are to certify that Philip Henry Stanhope Son of Charles Stanhope Ld. Viscount Mahon & Louisa his Wife was Born 7 Decr. 1781 & Baptized in the Parish of St. Marylebone, in the County of Middlesex, the 4th day of January in the year one thousand seven hundred and Eighty two as appears by the Register Book of Baptisms belonging to the said Parish extracted this 2d day of July 1782 as witness my Hand

J. Russell Curate

Thos. Bird Clerk

4. *Birth certificate notice of baptism for Philip Henry Stanhope (1781–1855), the later 4th Earl.*

Jupiter, which is viewed with some concern by astrologers.[4a] The first years of his childhood did not turn out as they should have done. He lacked a sense of security and motherly affection; most of the time only his father was present. His society-loving mother did indeed host numerous parties at Chevening but spent almost as much time at balls and other entertainments in London. She would 'rise after ten in the morning', reported her stepdaughter Hester,

> go for a drive and come home to have herself dressed and have her hair done, and there were only two London hairdressers who could do it to her satisfaction; both were French. Once dressed, she would drive somewhere for lunch and from there she would go to the Opera, and then to soirees and only rarely would she come home before daybreak. Lord Stanhope, meanwhile, was busy with philosophical undertakings and political projects, so that we children rarely got to see either of them. Lucy once said that she would scarcely recognise her stepmother were she to meet her on the street.

Chevening seemed a depressing place, as Lady Chatham, mother of William Pitt the Younger, wrote: 'I dined at Lord Stanhope's yesterday: we had a most magnificent dinner, perfectly well-served in all respects, eight in livery and four at least outside; a fine and very convenient house, but a sad situation…' In view of her many social engagements, Lady Louisa had little time for her children. The children of the first marriage, on the verge of neglect, were looked after by their grandmother whenever possible. The father, who was now, since the death of the old Stanhope in 1786, the 3rd Earl (Fig. 5) and therefore a member of the House of Lords, was extremely active in politics and for whatever reason, permanently found himself in hopeless opposition to everything and everybody. First, in Parliament he challenged his former brother-in-law, the Prime Minister, in hefty debates over Pitt's plans to repay the national debt, which he attacked in a polemical pamphlet 'Considerations on Pitt's Plan for the Reduction of the National Debt'.

Charles' pamphlet was only taken seriously by satirical caricaturists who portrayed him to a jeering public as a cane-wielding schoolmaster. More damaging, however, was the fact that he fell out with Pitt over their respective assessments of the French Revolution and became president of the 'Revolution Society', founded in 1788, which, on the occasion of the centenary of England's 'Glorious Revolution' of 1688, sent an exuberant salutation to Paris which he soon followed with one of his own, celebrating the fall of the Bastille. Hester, Philip

5. Charles, 3rd Earl Stanhope (1753–1816)

Henry's stepsister, was later to tell her physician: 'Father was enthusiastic about the confused ideas which filled the heads of the *Philosophes* and Economists in those days and which found expression in illuminated freemasonry'. Such a view of things accorded with his membership of the 'Philadelphia Philosophical Society', a 'disguised Freemasonic lodge'[5]. The name Stanhope features in the very earliest records relating to the founding of British masonic lodges. On St. John's Day, 24th June 1721, a meeting took place that was presided over by the second Grand Master of the Grand Lodge of England, George Payne (d. 1757), in which he presented the important Cooke Manuscript, one of the earliest constitutions of operative masons, stemming from the 15th century. According to the diary of one of the participants, Dr. Stukely: 'The Masons took lunch in Booksellers' Hall. Present were: Duke Montague, Lord Herbert, Lord Stanhope etc. Dr. Désaguliers gave an address. Grand Master Payne displayed a 500-year-old manuscript of constitutions, which he obtained in the west of England. He read out a number of articles which merit attention.'

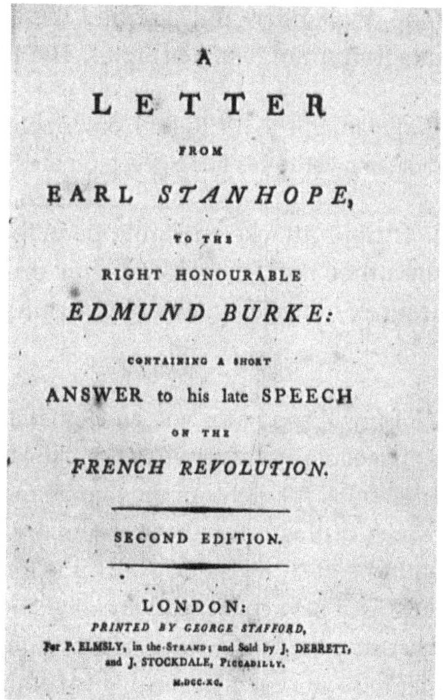
A
LETTER
FROM
EARL STANHOPE,
TO THE
RIGHT HONOURABLE
EDMUND BURKE:
CONTAINING A SHORT
ANSWER to his late SPEECH
ON THE
FRENCH REVOLUTION.

SECOND EDITION.

LONDON:
PRINTED BY GEORGE STAFFORD,
For P. ELMSLY, in the STRAND; and Sold by J. DEBRETT,
and J. STOCKDALE, PICCADILLY.
M.DCC.XC.

6. Title page of Charles Stanhope's 'A Letter from Earl Stanhope to the Right Honourable Edmund Burke' (1790).

From these basic activities had developed the plans which were to carry Freemasonry far beyond its own political and linguistic borders. In 1731 the name Stanhope appears again. In the more intimate collegium of those who were sent out to found lodges abroad, there were two Stanhopes, John and Philip Dormer; the latter set up the lodge in The Hague, and there in the same year, Lord Philip Dormer Stanhope Chesterfield, a member of a deputation in the legation of the British chargé d'affaires which had been sent over from London, admitted Emperor Franz of Austria as a companion of the 'Royal Art'. But to return to Charles Stanhope…

In January 1790 the book *Reflections on the Revolution in France* by Edmund Burke (1730–1797) appeared, in which the famous statesman protested against the popular uprising in France which had set aside the principles of civilised statehood and had replaced monarchy by the tyranny of the mob. For Friedrich von Gentz, the publication of this work was opportune. It appeared three years later, translated by him, in a two-volume edition in Berlin. Charles Stanhope, however, had tackled Burke's work earlier than Gentz. Just a month later, in a

36-page pamphlet, he welcomed and justified the Revolution as one of the greatest events in human history (Fig.6). The title was:

> A Letter from Earl Stanhope to the Right Honourable Edmund Burke Containing a short answer to his late Speech on the French Revolution

This response led to furious attacks on Stanhope in the House of Lords. From France, on the other hand, the country against which Pitt had sworn the most bitter resistance, came effusive approval. A Mr. Navier from Dijon wrote:

> This work, my lord, will secure for you an everlasting title of gratitude from all friends of freedom and especially from those of the French nation.
>
> You have represented the rights of the human race with an elegance of expression which distinguishes those spirits who are filled through and through with the great truths on which the fortune of the people rests. These truths win new converts every day; and we need have no doubt whatsoever that England will soon rectify the errors of its government, in order to secure complete enjoyment of the freedom which it has defended against the excesses of arbitrary power with such courage and clarity...We shall give to the whole world the best model of government. Most certainly, there will be fewer wars when the peoples no longer allow themselves to be suppressed by the caprices of kings and no longer have to shed their blood for the private quarrels of those who call themselves their masters.[6]

This was quite to the taste of the author of the tract, who did not hesitate to point out to his government the errors of its ways. On 14th June 1790 'Citizen Stanhope', as he had become mockingly known, sent his congratulations to Count La Rochefoucauld expressing his heartfelt enthusiasm for the revolutionary freedoms achieved in France. The two aristocratic cheerleaders of the Revolution knew each other personally and held each other in the highest esteem. 'With great joy,' wrote La Rochefoucauld, 'I nurture the hope you give me of seeing you again this year in Paris. My family share this feeling and have asked me to thank you for your gift.'[7]

La Rochefoucauld, the most prominent member of the 'Nine Sisters' lodge founded in 1769, the 'leading workshop of freemasonic thinking'[8], considered Stanhope's letter of support so important that he read it out at the next lodge meeting and afterwards made it known to all French Freemasons through a circular. On the 21st July the same letter was read out in the 'Crown and Anchor' tavern, one of the oldest Masonic meeting places in London.[9]

La Rochefoucauld quickly recognised this opportunity of taking revolutionary politics directly into the centre of political opinion-making in London with the help of a member of the House of Lords. He regarded his contact with Stanhope as so promising that he was even able to persuade Talleyrand to convey the answer of the National Assembly to his old friend personally. La Rochefoucauld's proposal of Talleyrand for this task was natural in that Talleyrand, more than any other politician, was an advocate of close cooperation between the two nations. 'He' (Talleyrand), wrote La Rochefoucauld, 'would wish to have the honour of being able to get to know you, and I am quite sure that this wish corresponds to your own. He is one of the men whose insights were among the most helpful for the Revolution.'[10]

La Rochefoucauld proposed to link the interests of Britain and France; an alliance which, he believed, would certainly have the power to 'provide bread for the world'. Then he went on: 'Talleyrand would be very disposed to be the organ for such an arrangement, if your foreign ministry were disposed to receive him.' The proposal was based on a false impression both of the political situation and of Stanhope's reputation in the House of Lords. In order to add weight to Talleyrand's mission but also to strengthen Stanhope's political position, on the same day the famous Louis Marie de Nouilles, President of the Society of the Friends of the Constitution and member of the National Assembly, wrote a long, handwritten letter to Stanhope in which he drew the Englishman's attention again to the significance of his political position and at the same time expressed the hope that both nations might join in a common world political mission for humanity and for civilisation.

> The Society of the Friends of the Constitution has requested me to communicate to you what hopes it holds in regard to the manner and way in which the friends of the English constitution celebrated the day on which the French won their freedom.
>
> If we had doubts as to the noble feelings with which they were endowed, then your company would give us an excellent example of such feelings. We are deeply impressed with such intentions and wishes.
>
> Doctor Price, so commendable for his great wisdom and so worthy of our recognition for his philosophy, long ago won our respect and our affection. Nothing surprised us in the lecture which he gave on the occasion of your memorable celebrations and which was so full of sensitivity, reason, and power.

But may we be permitted to express an even greater satisfaction with yourself, Sir, in whom we see one of the most outstanding Englishmen, and with Mr. Sheridan, who is one of the most famous speakers and is equally notable for his way of thinking. We recognise in you both not only friends, who are worthy of being heard among the lawgivers of Great Britain, but we also see you resolved to prepare the most noble union, the most meaningful and the most powerful that has ever been since human beings began to seek the advantages of civilisation.

Indeed, Sir, the friends whose feelings I express to you agree wholeheartedly with the vows that your company has made known. Freed—and free from any fear, we hope with you that a happy union may bring to an end all petty jealousies between France and Great Britain, so that these two great powers will rather vie with each other to ensure that all other nations of the earth will share in the blessings of peace, virtue, and freedom, and that an alliance between France and Great Britain will guarantee the happiness of the whole world.

This holy union can only be consummated in a spirit of the noblest loyalty and deepest respect; it can only be maintained through relationships which are in the fullest accord with the free principles which would bring both nations closer to each other. We conceive of this brotherly pact as a great moral rebirth of human society; as the most beautiful triumph of freedom over the hateful and barbaric politics which until now has been able to do nothing but draw up treaties only to break them and conclude peace only to create new instruments of criminality and destruction. Oh, what would our two united nations have to fear for their freedom and their real interests if they were but to honour and respect each other? Once they become enlightened, peoples feel that the human being is in no sense a natural enemy of other human beings; that this sad prejudice is a work of despotism, that wealth only makes men suspicious; that peoples who have been led into error through their exuberant wishes first approve the growing debt and then end up groaning under the burden of taxation.

Your government, Sir, can no longer regard us as a people of slaves. It can no longer mistrust the plans of a power which from now on is subject to the will of a legally proclaimed nation. It has chosen justice as its guiding principle and as its government one that alone provides strength and power. But when it chose these, it hastened to declare that it would make use of this strength and this power only to defend itself and never to harm the freedom of any other people.

> The far reaches of the Kingdom of France, which are guided by the same principles of freedom and governed in the same manner only need to vote for their permanent assembly. In which other system would they have more advantages? What better protection could there be for them? Where would they find it?
>
> We do not think that a people which is a friend of freedom would molest another people which had achieved such things and now sought to secure them on the basis of justice and reason. No, Sir, your government, which has distinguished itself by its enlightened attitude and its intelligence, can only harbour supportive feelings towards your Society, and there appears to be every indication that the whole nation shares this feeling.
>
> May we soon see the day when such happy predictions are fulfilled, when mankind, happy at the precious fruits of freedom, will praise Englishmen for having preserved their beneficent legal system, our brothers in the United States of America for having so clearly formulated the rights of Man, and our nation for having put aside destructive differences, affirming and ensuring their renunciation for all time.[11]

Charles Stanhope, convinced of his ability to establish an Anglo-French alliance, set to work with renewed energy, but his efforts only drew scorn and mockery (Figs. 7,8,9). The culmination of his political blunders was his motion of 22nd January 1794 aimed at a recognition of the French Republic which, after all preceding debates, was only experienced as a provocation by the members of the House of Lords and earned him the epithet 'Minority of One'[12]. The Lords were as infuriated as they were amused and they had a medal struck at their own expense (Fig.10) illustrating Stanhope's political standpoint. The face of the medal showed the unfortunate Stanhope in profile with the above-mentioned epithet over his head, and on the reverse side the sarcastic words:

> Stanhope
> The friend of
> Trial by jury
> Liberty of the press
> Parliamentary reform
> Annual parliaments
> Habeas corpus act
> Abolition of sinecures
> And of an early peace
> With the French republic.

7. Caricature of Charles, 3rd Earl Stanhope, appeared in March 1794: 'John Bull's Sacrifice to Janus—a Design for a Peace Offering to the Convention'.

8. Caricature of Charles, 3rd Earl Stanhope, appeared in March 1794: 'Citizen Don Quixotte becomes the Champion of French Principles'.

9. Caricature of Charles, 3rd Earl Stanhope, appeared on 14th April 1794: 'The ST.....E Republican Gunboat, constructed to sail against Wind and Tide'.

10. Scornful medallions aimed at Charles, 3rd Earl Stanhope—'The Minority of One—1795'.

On the reverse side: 'Stanhope, the friend of trial by jury, liberty of the Press, parliamentary reform, annual parliaments, Habeas Corpus Act, abolition of sinecures, and of a speedy peace with the French Republic.'

11. Chevening House. After the removal of the roof and of the decoration of the façade.

The anti-Stanhope mood developed into an explosive situation, which finally culminated in the trashing and burning of his London home. On the night of the 11th to the 12th June 1794, a 'paid mob', as Stanhope publicly insisted, tried to set fire to his house in Mansfield Street, but despite several attempts did not succeed completely. Branded as a Jacobin and a republican, lampooned by cartoonists as the 'Don Quixote of the Nation' who kept 'his own windmill going by gesticulating with his arms', the Earl moved inexorably towards his political demise. At the same time, the first signs of a mental breakdown were already beginning to show themselves. Hester later wrote of this period: 'If people think of contradicting him or of disapproving his conduct, he immediately suspects them. Was a man in the Duke of Bedford's situation & politics to resist his arguments & blame his conduct, he would fancy they must be bought over by Ministers, & have lost all principle. How then is it possible to act towards such a character?'[13] In 1795 Charles left Parliament and only in 1800 did the idiosyncratic politician succeed in making a modest new start.

Strange things were also going on at Chevening. The children experienced how their father, who after coming into his inheritance had been called the wealthiest peer of Kent, had the roof of the house (Fig. 11) taken down as well as the window architrave from the facades and

12. Caricature by James Gilray of the wedding of Lucy Stanhope and Thomas Taylor on 4 March 1796. 'Democratic Leveling—Alliance a la Françoise;—or—The Union of the Coronet & Clyster-pipe'.

the stucco from the rooms, considering these to be superfluous luxuries. He had the wall hangings, a present from Frederick the Great, removed, and finally the horse and carriage disappeared, because he wanted the family to go on foot. 14-year-old Hester had to raise turkeys, and with reference to the unhappy fate of the French Dauphin, the children were sent to learn from the village blacksmith so that they could at least become good artisans. All smart clothes were disposed of and instead, the family, probably uniquely in aristocratic circles at the time, were only allowed plain linen clothes. The father slept with his window open in summer as well as in winter, without a nightcap but wrapped up in twelve blankets. 'When he got out of bed, he would put on a fine coat, kept on the silk trousers he had been wearing in bed and wore slippers but no socks. He would sit there like this in an uncarpeted part of the room, drink his tea and eat a little brown bread.'

The strangest of his peculiarities was that in the window of his room stood a telescope with which he would survey the house grounds and did not fail to notice whether his wife and children or the servants were keeping themselves busy or not.

On the other hand, the father was a gifted researcher, scientifically trained and engaged throughout his life in constructions and experiments. When at the age of 16, his youngest daughter married Thomas Taylor, a surgeon from Sevenoaks, whom the cartoonist James Gilray evidently was only willing to acknowledge as an apothecary—'An alliance à la française or the union of the coronet and the clyster-pipe [enema tube]' (Fig. 12)—the old republican wrote to his friend William Smith on 25.1.1796:

> Dear Citizen, From the friendship which you have often shown me (and which I so cordially return), I am induced to inform you of a thing which gives me pleasure. My youngest daughter Lucy is soon going to be married to a most worthy young man of her own choosing. Her Mind is liberal, and she despises Rank and Aristocracy as much as I do … The Person she has chosen is young Thomas Taylor, the surgeon at Sevenoaks. Dear Mahon is better. In a few days I go to make my grand experiment with the Ambi-Navigator ship[14]…

Charles had worked devotedly for many years on the construction of this ship, and for the same period the children had not been allowed to go too near to the small lake in the park. The Admiralty had found the experiments with the steamboat so promising that a 200-ton copy was built under the direction and supervision of the inventor. Another invention was less successful. A new method of propulsion developed by Charles—duckfeet paddles at the stern—had been abandoned by the admirals after it only proved capable of a maximum speed of three knots.

Especially exciting for the children were the fire experiments, in which their father had been engaged since 1777. For a realistic demonstration he had a 50-feet-long, two-storey wooden house built in the park. Downstairs, bundles of twigs, straw, and pitch were piled up 'from floor to ceiling', as reported by the *Morning Chronicle* of 3.7.1777; upstairs sat the guests, who were specially selected to participate. As soon as they had taken their seats, the Earl set the building alight in order to demonstrate that a fire without an oxygen supply would extinguish itself. 'To the great astonishment of all those present, who saw the flames blazing out of all the doors and windows and from all sides of the lower floor, all the material therein burnt up without causing the slightest damage; the house remained standing even though it was made of wood. Throughout this time those on the upper floor directly above this enormous sea of flames did not notice the slightest heat or anything else of the powerful fire below.' (*Public Advertiser*, 3.7.1777.) While the fire raged beneath them, the guests, members of the Royal Society, the Lord Mayor of London, some councillors and foreign envoys sat upstairs eating ice cream.

Charles went on to construct chair scales on which his guests were obliged to weigh themselves before and after meals (Fig. 13). But his inventive spirit also brought forth several practical devices: a very effective printing press, the so-called Stanhope Press, two calculating machines, a microscope named after him and a binding material for cement. In 1806 he published his 'Principles of the Science of Instruments with Fixed Tones'. Despite these occasional attractions, however, life at Chevening was dull and dreary. When in 1787 Count d'Adhémar, the French chargé d'affaires in London (from 1783–1787) paid a visit, the vibrant, elegant courtier, adorned with a plumed hat, seemed to the children like a being from another world. No record remains of what the French ambassador communicated to Stanhope so shortly before the Revolution. The envoy's wife was that 'lady of the palace' at Marie Antoinette's court who had received the visits of the Comte de St. Germain at Versailles; he had predicted the Revolution with all its consequences long before the event.

13. Seat scale, constructed by Charles, 3rd Earl Stanhope.

Hester later recalled that

> the brilliant livery of his servants, with white feathers in their hats, the count's bows and all the French courtly manners made such a deep impression on me that I developed an irresistible desire to see France. When, soon after, I was sent to Hastings with a governess, I found an opportunity to get unnoticed into a boat that was lying on the beach and succeeded in untying it and pushing off. It was my firm intention to sail across the Channel to France and to look around over there.

She was prevented from continuing her adventure by some fishermen, who brought her back and thus saved her life.

These circumstances did not bode well for the children's education and upbringing. 'Mahon'—who was very tall for his age—'could not be taught at the age of seven or eight, that two and two make four.

Efforts were made with money and beans to get him to understand this, but to no avail. When the beans were taken away, he replied that two and two made five, or that they made beans.'[15]

Only to his favourite daughter from his first marriage, the wild and impetuous Hester, did the father try to introduce the principles of logic, but only after having ordered the other siblings to leave the room. And when his teaching did not produce results as quickly as he had hoped, it could even happen that he would reinforce his lesson by holding a naked blade to his dear Hester's throat. Beyond that, the tyrannical father was of the opinion that a sound and comprehensive cultural education was damaging and therefore unnecessary.

This was evident in the choice of tutors for the children. They were required to demonstrate their suitability not so much in terms of pedagogy or scientific knowledge but rather in terms of their political and ideological orientation. One of young Mahon's tutors was Charles Stanhope's private secretary, the revolutionary writer Jeremiah Joyce (1763–1816) (Fig. 14), who deviated from all conventional views and who, on 4th May 1794, was arrested before the astonished eyes of the family at Chevening, arraigned before the Privy Council and charged with high treason. At the Stanhopes', the stubborn rumour persisted that brother-in-law Pitt was behind the arrest of this glorifier of the Revolution and that for this purpose the Prime Minister had even temporarily suspended Habeas Corpus, which expressly prohibits arrest without a judicial arrest warrant.

Joyce's release from the Tower of London after a 23-week imprisonment was celebrated by Charles Stanhope's masonic lodge at the 'Crown and Anchor' with a festive speech by the Earl, which appeared in print shortly afterwards. Another honour was bestowed on this occasion: Stanhope was made President of the lodge. In reply to his address in the lodge, Walter Savage Landor wrote a twenty-page-long poem, 'Moral Epistle to Lord Stanhope', which did not portray Charles very favourably.

But Joyce did not remain silent either. Shortly after his release, he published 'A Reprimand' (23.2.1795), in which he defended his views. It included an Appendix with a report on his arrest and trial, in which he went into details about the charges, calling them: 'treacherous practices!' The teachings of a rebel like Joyce may well have awakened in Philip Henry his first inclinations towards secret political affairs.

14. Jeremiah Joyce (1763–1816)

Equally dubious was the influence of his second tutor, Dr. Crauford. Philip Henry, who eventually fled from the sinister man, may have received from him instruction of quite another kind. He once wrote to his sister (29.7.1800): 'He has the habit of cursing in the blackest manner during lessons.'[16] And his grandmother, Grizelda Hamilton, who had been expelled by Philip Henry's father from the 115-room house to a garden house at the end of the park, wrote: 'I am sure he has been a Packman [a pedlar] from the way he walks. You may depend upon it.'[17]—a sarcastic remark, which probably does not contain any serious indication as to his earlier history. The cursing Crauford, who was afflicted with a peculiar gait, was also nicknamed the old 'Crystal Pate' by which the pupil was doubtless referring to some strange peculiarity of the teacher. Since, remarkably, Crauford was also often referred to by the Stanhopes as 'the Scot', the question arises as to whether something else was meant than just his country of origin, about which otherwise nothing is known. 'Scot' was also a masonic term; there were 'Scottish' degrees, which had nothing to do with the Scots as members of a nation or with their ancestry. In cases where both coincided, which happened not infrequently, one would refer to a Scottish Scot; consequently, there were also Prussian Scots or the Scot from Paris, referring to the grade of Scottish Master. The Freemason A. Mellor justifiably comments: 'The geographical differences of all these Scots allow for only one interpretation: It is a matter of relationships between local groups within a political organisation that has innumerable branches.'

Scottish Freemasonry as a lodge system is also, strangely enough, not Scottish in origin, but first arrived in England in 1740—from France. Its predominant characteristic was its striving after 'a latent occultism'. These 'Scottish masons' are not to be confused with the workmen's lodges of the same name which belong to the oldest in the world. Edinburgh Lodge No. 1 lists the name Crauford for the year 1732, who later served there as Grand Master. Whether this man was related to the same Crauford as Phillip Henry's tutor has not been established, but the similarity of the name makes a family relationship conceivable.

Hester later always described this man as the 'scoundrel', who 'had every conceivable power' over her half-brother. Crauford craved and possessed this power. Besides Philip Henry's highly eccentric father Charles and his peculiar godfather Philip Chesterfield, he had, then, two most unusual men as teachers—Joyce the revolutionary and Crauford the Scot, the scoundrel and the 'Chrystalpate': such were the men who formed the boy's early education, and one can have an inkling as to the foundations he received for his path in life. But it was not only this miserable and oppressive education that marred young Philip Henry's days. If he wanted to go out, he had in accordance to his father's dictate to be accompanied by one of the family lackeys, 'who had formerly been a base, arrogant, and wily man, who spied regularly on [Mahon's] activities'. Mahon, who was embarrassed at having to go around with this constant overseer, preferred to stay at home, 'looking out of the window watching other young people amuse themselves'.

Hester (Fig. 15) was the first to put the demeaning conditions at Chevening behind her when, in Spring 1800, her Chatham grandmother invited her to the family seat at Burton Pynsent. She had experienced her uncle, the Lord Chancellor William Pitt (Fig.16), in the exalted atmosphere of the Court and also in his own environment as a politician and she had developed a strong affection for that

15. Lady Hester Stanhope (1776–1839), daughter of Charles, 3rd Earl Stanhope and his first wife, Lady Hester Pitt. Half-sister of Philip Henry, 4th Earl.

16. William Pitt the Younger (1759–1806)

self-assured man of the world. King George III had taken notice of her and had requested that this relative of the Pitts be introduced to him. She had since made friends and acquaintances of such men as the extremely wealthy parliamentarian Sir Francis Burdett (1770–1844) (Fig.17) and particularly, the young diplomat Francis Jackson (1770–1814) (Fig. 18) and his brother George (1785–1861). Now she felt strong and influential enough to be in a position to help her beloved brother, who was being 'very ill used by Dr. Crauford', and she intended to place him 'on the protection of Mr. P.' [Pitt]. Meanwhile, from Chevening, Philip Henry wrote desperate letters to his sister: 'I desire more anxiously and even more ardently than ever to be *freed* from this bondage with an ever greater yearning to be freed from this bondage under which I have so long groaned.'[18] First Pitt made an attempt to get the father to change his outlook and to suggest to him other, better ideas, and then Burdett tried his luck. He wrote 'an extremely bold letter' to the old Stanhope, who showed not the slightest intention of reading it, believing that 'everything that the letter could possibly contain, was probably lies'. At any rate, it was now clear to the father that, with the aid of his daughter, his son was seeking outside help in order to escape from his situation, which only enraged the Earl further. 'Mahon,' wrote Lady Hester to Francis Jackson, 'during this time was treated like a dog with promises that his life should be made ten times worse if he did not *repent*'. All his contacts with other people were cut off. The teacher Crauford watched over every minute detail of his daily routine, to the extent that Philip Henry 'had the Scotchman at his elbow till he went to bed'. What was the purpose behind the teacher's constant presence and what did he actually achieve?

Slowly the relationships at Chevening developed into a scandal. Lord Lansdowne reported to Hester a meeting with the old Stanhope, whose 'comments about his children had shocked him more than he could express'. Another family acquaintance, Lord Glastonbury, after a visit to Chevening, drew the painful but, as we know, probably the only right conclusion that, for the sake of the children, their father should be certified ! Measures had to be taken, at least to save the property, 'in that it was said that he [the father] was no longer mindful of the proper conduct of his affairs and therefore must actually be placed under public guardianship'.[19]

But nothing changed. Uninfluenced by any attempts at assistance, the old Earl did not move an inch from the course he had set himself. Everything remained as it was, and Mahon's situation grew more

17. Francis Burdett (1770–1844). Portrait by Sir Thomas Lawrence (1793).

18. Francis James Jackson (1770–1814)

unbearable with each passing day. The last recourse was to arrange for an escape from the family home, which Hester, with the help of Pitt, Burdett and Jackson, now took in hand. Mahon's journey was to take him to Germany and end in Erlangen. The reasons why the choice fell on the former Margravate of Ansbach-Bayreuth will be explained in the next chapter.

2. Flight and Return

Studies in Erlangen, 1801–1802

In 1791 Karl Alexander, Margrave of Ansbach-Bayreuth (1736–1806), renounced his title in order to settle in England. The choice of time and place were determined by his Hohenzollern family's legal arrangements and by his second marriage. From Karl Alexander's mother, Frederike Luise, the art-loving sister of Frederick the Great, to whom Bayreuth owed its castle, its theatre and its incomparable Eremitage park, stemmed the political and legal connection to Berlin, which counted for so much in the circumstances that the territories of Bayreuth and Ansbach would fall to Prussia if the Bayreuth marriage were to remain childless—an agreement reaffirmed by the Peace Treaty of Teschen.

The clever decision of Karl Alexander to give up the rulership of his country earlier than foreseen by the contracts may have been suggested to him by a study of the French Revolution; or the suggestion may have come from his close acquaintance with the Comte de St. Germain, who had been his guest at Triesdorf Castle in 1774–1776. St. Germain had already very early on (1743) spoken words of warning, which he repeated to Marie Antoinette in Versailles shortly before the outbreak of the Revolution, the course of which he predicted: 'He who sows the wind will reap the whirlwind'. But also the prospect of spending carefree years abroad after 30 years of 'numerous and continuous obstacles, chicanery and litigation' was enticing; for an annuity of 300,000 talers, Karl Alexander renounced his rights in favour of Prussia in a secret contract of 16.1.1791, and the government passed into the hands of Karl August von Hardenberg (1750–1822).

Karl Alexander's second wife, the sparkling Lady Elizabeth Craven (1750–1828), daughter of Augustus, 4th Earl of Berkeley, had long been known to the Ansbachers as the victorious rival of the famous French actress Mademoiselle Clairon (1723–1803)—whose real name was Clair Josèphe Hippolyte Leris—and as the writer of several comedies which had been performed at Triesdorf Castle. Allowed to take part in these was Lady Elizabeth's seven-year-old son Keppel, whose paternity was denied by her first husband, Lord William Craven; Elizabeth had left him in 1780.

With Lady Craven the Margrave travelled 'throughout his country unabashed, just as though she had no husband and he no wife....'

However, the Margrave was forced to abandon his plans for marriage temporarily after Lord Craven himself had resisted a divorce settlement of £30,000. However, when Alexander's wife and Lady Elizabeth's husband both unexpectedly died in the same year (1791), the two lovers resolved to marry and settle in England. Emperor Franz II raised the countess to the rank of Princess Berkeley. The bewildered people of Ansbach, who had been unaware of the existence of any state treaty, learned of their sovereign's decision to abdicate from the newspaper. *The Intelligence* of 8.2.1792 carried a final farewell and the explanation: '...that on our own initiative and after careful consideration and for the most important motives, we have finally resolved to completely lay aside the business of government and the cares and hardships associated therewith, in order to spend our remaining days far removed from them in peace, in a place of our own choosing.'

The place was London. In Hammersmith on the Thames the couple bought a stately home, which they named 'Brandenburg House' and where they began their quiet life among exalted circles.

It was in their immediate neighbourhood that there came together, from the summer of 1800 onwards, the circle of conspirators who had taken on to free Mahon from the power of his father. In the correspondence now necessary between them, Prime Minister Pitt figured under the pseudonym 'great man'; Burdett was 'the beard', his younger brother 'the brother', while 'R' signified Philip Henry's intended companion-in-flight, Mr. Rice.

The plan took shape in the autumn. It was now no longer only a matter of obtaining money and travel documents, but also of letters of recommendation and above all, of Philip Henry's eventual destination, which, especially in accordance with Hester's wishes, was to be somewhere in Germany, and at a university where her brother would be able to make up for the completely inadequate education he had thus far received.[20] A name and a place were soon arrived at that met the requisite criteria: the Margrave from Bayreuth, his wife and their connection to Erlangen. Pitt knew Karl Alexander, now resident in London, while Francis Jackson had been friendly with Karl Alexander's sister since his own stay in Erlangen. At Schloss Elisabethenburg (Fig. 29), the designated residence of the widows of the Margraves of Bayreuth, lived the old Dowager Margravine Sophie Karoline (1737–1817)(Fig. 28), much revered throughout the town and country, 'whose court had always lent to the town the character of a capital city, even if a modest one'. Since his earlier stay in Erlangen, Jackson had been a protégé and confidant of the Margravine, who had at the time recommended him most warmly for the diplomatic service; this resulted in his being appointed secretary to the ambassador in Berlin. Sophie Karoline's mother was the sister of Frederick II of Prussia. The Margravine shared with Jackson the most private matters. When her elderly brother, Margrave Alexander, fell in love with Lady Craven, she wrote to Jackson (2.11.1789): 'I do not fear that the Margrave will lose his life, but I do fear that he will lose his head.'

It was hoped that with the help of Margrave Alexander, and above all through the recommendation of Jackson, Mahon would have a friendly reception from Sophie Karoline, who was well-known for her warm-heartedness and kindness. Even when her modest finances were scarcely sufficient to pay for her small court, this did not stop her showing generosity towards the poor.

During his rule, Margrave Alexander had always done a lot for Erlangen despite his considerable debts because, as a well-read and always highly cultured man, his country's sole university was close to his heart (Fig.21). He succeeded in securing a number of significant appointments, so that the university made a favourable impression on Friedrich Gedike, who visited it in the summer of 1789 in the service of Frederick the Great: 'There are some excellent teachers in all faculties.'[21]

In addition, the university, which at that time had hardly more than 200 students, was attended by many of the sons of Frankish noble families—a sure guarantee that it would provide a suitable environment for Mahon. Names such as Tucher, Binder, Klüber, von Fahnenberg and von Dobeneck, which would later play a role in the events around Kaspar Hauser can be found in the matriculation lists of the time.

After Hester and her friends had decided on the destination, a family had to be found, which would host the future student. Most probably it was through the Dowager Margravine that they were introduced to Professor and Court Counsellor, Dr. Johann Friedrich Breyer (1738–1826) (Fig. 25), then 63 years old. 'A man,' according to Hester, 'of great ability and most extensive knowledge', he had taught Logic and Metaphysics at Erlangen since 1770 and also, after the death of his colleague Ludwig Müller in 1776, German literature and Humanities and he was prepared to provide lodgings for the noble guest.

Now the time had come when the escape and its preconditions had to be determined and a date fixed. Before the accompaniment of

Mr. 'R' was decided, however, there was another well-meant recommendation which was based on complete ignorance of the true state of affairs in Chevening and which drew a typical reaction from Pitt. It was for Philip Henry to be accompanied on his escape into freedom by, of all people, the 'scoundrel' Crauford. '*By no means!*', declared the outraged Prime Minister, 'with one of those looks which must imprint it upon one's mind till the day of one's death.'[22] What predisposed Pitt to give such a look? Did he know or did he guess who Crauford, the 'Scot' really was and what he had already been up to in his sinister practices with Philip Henry? Mr. M. Rice was thus decided upon. Sir Francis Burdett was then approached for the appropriate financial assistance. The peer, who had achieved extraordinary wealth through his marriage into the Coutts banking house, showed himself only too willing to help. He made available generous letters of credit, which he was careful to hand over to Jackson, 'since he [Burdett] did not want to know anything of the plot'. Finally, Jackson procured a pass for the young Mahon which was made out in the innocuous name of Mackwell, and wrote not only a letter of recommendation to his old friend the Margravine, 'but also to the most distinguished people in the town' of Erlangen.

By the evening of 10th February 1801 all was ready. The first phase of the escape organised so brilliantly by Jackson went off as expected. After dark, Mahon slipped out of the mansion and climbed into the waiting carriage, which Mr. Rice, dressed as a servant, drove to the nearest stagecoach station. They then travelled on to the small town of Romford, some 36 miles distant, where the two arrived late at night and secured accommodation. On the way, outside London, the fugitives were recognised by a maid of Hester's who, through lack of accurate knowledge, later spread the rumour that old Stanhope's son had left Chevening in the direction of Scotland. 'When he [Mahon] saw her, he covered his face with a handkerchief and shouted something to the coachmen, who speeded up and were soon out of her sight.'[23]

The following morning Mahon and Rice took the first coach to Harwich (Fig. 19), which they reached on the evening of the 11th February. Ships belonging to companies that plied between England and the German ports, especially Hamburg, were docked there. The pair did not immediately press on with their journey, whether due to rough seas caused by spring storms or to some other reason is not known, but the fact is that Philip Henry and Mr. Rice did not board ship until 19th February.

19. *Harwich harbour*

By the time the enraged old Stanhope learned of his son's escape, the decisive first phase of the enterprise had already been accomplished; those sent in pursuit could not hope to track the travellers. Hester wrote to Lord Glastonbury: '...with Mr. J's directions, he has got on wonderfully well. M[ahon] has a man with him, in capacity of a servant, whose fidelity I can rely on: this man, with directions from me accomplished M's escape from Chevening most astonishingly, for tho' he was pursued in a few hours, no tidings could be had, & till this moment, they have never been able to trace him one step.' After the couriers returned without the runaway, the furious Charles tried to get Pitt to take measures to ensure the return of his son, but it was the Prime Minister himself, unbeknown to the father, who had been the planner and accomplice of the escape, and so all the father's resentful attacks met with no response from Pitt. The enterprise had worse consequences for those left behind. The deceived tyrant threatened to beat those responsible to death and wanted to have Hester, whose participation he suspected—not without reason—whipped if he could get hold of her. She had been clever enough, however, not to inform her brother and sister of the details of the escape plan so that their innocence was soon apparent. Hester kept herself at a safe distance from her father's campaign of revenge by staying at the home of the Lord Chancellor's mother in Burton Pynsent.

On the 12th February Mahon sat down to write a short farewell letter to his father by way of clarification. Without specifying his location other than 'at the port', he stated that he could no longer stand living at Chevening and that in future he would take no more orders from his father. We know more about the contents of the letter indirectly from a writer whose identity is unknown, who turned to Hester with the request to find out: 'To whom in Scotland can [Philip Henry] think of going? His relations there are not I think likely to countenance the step he has taken; nor can I think that he has a female companion with him'. The Scotland story, perhaps encouraged by Hester, had spread rapidly, and now the elder Stanhope—through the above-mentioned unknown writer—tried to find out more details, in the certain knowledge that his son, who was still legally a minor, would immediately be returned to him from any territory under British jurisdiction.

At the end of the letter some further addresses are mentioned, in the hope that Hester would confirm or deny one or the other. 'We thought he might have gone to Sir Francis Burdett, but he declared to Mr. Scott last night his ignorance. I sent to Mr. Taylor's who was also ignorant.' Hester saw what was happening and tried on her part to counter her father's intentions. 'I have just received a long letter from a lawyer ... but I clearly perceive it was *dictated* by 'a Logician' [i.e. Mahon's father, Earl Stanhope] desiring to know that if I knew anything I would instantly communicate it...'. After she had learned that Mahon had safely landed at Hamburg, she told her father's lawyer that her brother was not to be found in Scotland, but had 'gone abroad, was in good hands and that no further news of him was to be expected from her in the future'. However, should her father wish to write to his son, she was prepared to pass the letter on to Mahon's current place of residence.

The response from Chevening to this offer was, as expected, complete silence. '*Fear* keeps them quiet,' wrote Hester to Lord Glastonbury, 'now they see it is a dead thing, & that there is no chance of recovering him in a common way, extremities which might irritate him they dare not venture upon, lest he should betray facts not unimportant, perhaps, to them...They do not dare take the matter further, because it might bring certain things to light which would not be very congenial for them.' Hester continued to explain the real background of the affair to her circle of acquaintances and thereby succeeded in her aim of preventing her father from pursuing her brother further. She wrote to Lord Haddington on the 9th April 1801:

> It was impossible to do anything legal for Mahon while he was still a minor, although it would have been of the greatest importance for him to enjoy a liberal education before he matured to the point where he was equipped for life in society. If he had been sent to college, he would probably have been removed by his father. But once he was abroad, it was easier to prevent any kind of investigation into his whereabouts than to fend off the claims that would have been made against him had he been discovered in this country. But cowardice is generally a characteristic of those who would oppress helpless individuals, so a serious pursuit is not to be feared. A foreign university was therefore the only means of providing Mahon with a good education.

*

After their arrival in Hamburg on the 2nd March, a letter supplied by Jackson announcing this was posted to Professor Breyer. Philip Henry then acquired a coach, 'very strong and convenient'. The unfamiliar freedom, the free air never before enjoyed, the foreign country, the wealth of new impressions had such an overwhelming effect on Philip Henry that everything that happened from then on has to be seen in the light of his former privations. For the first time, the young man was beyond the narrow bounds of his homeland, the master of his own decisions, which, unsurprisingly, was to have repercussions for the forthcoming journey to Erlangen. Although the original intention had been to proceed with the journey without further delay, he now decided, having saved £30 by not hiring an extra servant who 'was to have been taken on in Hamburg', to use the money thus saved to enjoy his new freedom.

In ice and snow and on reasonably good roads—'the roads in this region are considerably better'—they headed at three miles an hour in the direction of Hanover. The town was en route and was a tempting if not obligatory place to visit as, since the death of Queen Anne, 'the last Stuart', and the thwarting of James III's accession to the throne, the Kings of Great Britain had all been of the House of Hanover and ruled England and Hanover in personal union until 1837. Neither the first of the line, protestant Elector George of Hanover— King George I of England— nor his successor George II, were proficient in English and had to deal with their Ministers in Latin. Then came the third George, with whom Hester had become acquainted in London at court, and finally, [after the ten-year reign of George IV 1820–30—*transl.*], the last of the Hanoverians, William IV, who could no longer understand a word of German and ruled for only seven years (1830–7) before the accession of Queen

Victoria. George III was connected with the events surrounding Philip Henry only insofar as Hester was acquainted with him through the Prime Minister William Pitt and managed to derive from this fact some assistance for Philip Henry's escape. William IV, on the other hand, later took a direct interest in the question of Kaspar Hauser.

*

A stop was made at Celle, where they visited the Residenz (palace) of the Dukes of Brunswick and Lüneburg, which, however, made a poor impression: 'The palace, as it is called, is actually a very miserable building.' Also, the apartments of Queen Mathilda of Denmark who had lived there in exile until 1775 were found to be of no distinction: '...many of the rooms being nothing but bare plaster & the others hung with hideous paper or tawdry tapestry. We saw the Bed where Mathilda Queen of Denmark died & a hall where the French & Hanoverian troops fought with swords so desperately that they not only hacked each other to peices [*sic*] but the floor also.'

At the end of his diary entry Philip Henry commented on the town's church and the tomb of the Celle line of the ducal house, which contained one of the most significant works of Renaissance art of its kind in North Germany— the memorial plaque with the splendid epitaph to

20. Hotel Strelitz, Hannover.

Duke Ernst the Confessor: 'There is nothing to be seen here worth looking at, & we have just been to see the Church, which contains nothing remarkable. They led us into a vault and showed us the coffins of all the former Dukes & Duchesses of Brunswick & a picture 800 years old.'

On the following day, the young men travelled on from Celle to Hanover, their actual destination. They took rooms at the 'Strelitz', 'a very good hotel'. Then they went to the Leine Castle on the gables of which the coat of arms of Great Britain and Hanover were everywhere to be seen. In the arsenal the young lord noticed a 'three-hundred-year-old iron boot', which looked to him just like 'the ones with the pointed toes which the Bond St. dandies wear'. He recommended Hester to visit the stables on account of their cleanliness and beautiful horses. There followed an excursion to the castle and gardens at Herrenhausen, which failed to make much impression. The following day, they visited the Lutheran church of St. John in Neustadt, where they spent some time in front of the stone bearing the inscription '*Ossa Leibnitii*' (the bones of Leibniz). The philosopher and mathematician Gottfried Wilhelm Leibniz had died in Hanover in 1716.

On their journey the two prospective students endeavoured to learn a little German. 'I have not had much time until now to study German, but if you are desirous of speaking it, I can give you an infallible Recipe,' wrote Philip Henry to Hester. 'Take a few hard words that sound rather gritty, snuffle one half of them through yr. nose & speak the others in yr. throat, as if you were almost choked, intermingle a few hems & hawks & give every now & then a good loud snort. This short description will enable you to form an idea of the German language & of its harsh & guttural sound.'

Philip Henry found German security measures in Celle and Hanover tiresome: 'We were stopped by a sentinel at one end, who insisted on our entring [*sic*] our names in his book. We afterwards wrote them at the Inn, from whence they are sent to the English Commissary, a third time at the other end of the town, & again a fourth time on entring [*sic*] Hanover, all in the course of one day.'

The journey via Halberstadt to Halle proved equally unpleasant:

> We were much plagued on our route by a number of German sentinels who insisted on our writing down our names & etc every ten yards. They worry us to death with all sorts of absurd questions; as for instance, going through Halle where we did not stay an hour. We were stopped by an old fogram [an old fogey—*Ed.*], who asked us what nation we were

> of. I said we were Englishmen. He asked me whether I was a Merchant or a Servant. I said I happened to be neither, but an English Gentleman. He then said Are you a Courier? No Sir, I am not. Where do you come from? From London. What towns have you been through? What is your name? Who is that in the Carriage with you? How many trunks have you? Where are you going? To what Inn are you going? Do you stay there all night? What is your name ? & etc & etc.

The travellers fared no better in Leipzig, which they reached on 10th March:

> We had not gone on half a dozen yards before a soldier …asks me…all the same questions over again. After going about the length of half a street … another soldier hollows out: 'Halt! *Was ist seiner Name?* (*What is his name?*) [the first sentence in German written by Philip Henry], and after repeating a few more of these same questions suffered us to proceed to the Inn, where we had no sooner sat down than the old Inn Keeper brought us a large folio volume, where we were forced to write down our names again.

Philip Henry's report from Leipzig included the expectant words: 'I hope to be at Erlang [*sic*] next Sunday.'

*

On the 16th March, after a lengthy trip lasting two weeks, the pair arrived in Erlangen, a town that had been organised on functional lines by Huguenots. After the fire of 1706, the streets had been newly laid out on the basis of the old Carrée system so that this 'ideal town' might still have retained its air of purposeful rational sobriety. After being greeted by Professor Breyer and rooms having been made ready for 'Mylord Mahon', a further week went by before he ventured to the university. On the 22nd March the name of 'Philip Henry Lord Viscount Mahon Earl Stanhope' was entered in the 'Album Sacri Romani Imperii Comitum in Academia Regia Friderico Alexandrina Erlangensi'. This looks like an impressive beginning but it does seem like the oversized title of a book that has yet to be written. At the beginning of April, the student was still full of the prospects for this new phase of his life. On 18.4.1801 he wrote to Lord Lansdowne, the former friend of his father:

> My Lord, having so cruelly wasted the former part of my life in a situation of all others the most odious and oppressive, it is, my Lord, essentially necessary for me to profit by those advantages of Education which I now

> enjoy & to endeavour by a close application, by an unremitting assiduity & by an ardour for the acquirement of knowledge which nothing can abate, to store my mind not only with useful information, but also with much refined & elegant accomplishments.

He wrote to his sister in a similar vein: 'As this place is dedicated to study and to the improvement of existing capabilities, I hold it to be an

21. The University of Erlangen around 1800.

22. Philip Henry, 4th Earl Stanhope. Miniature. (1781–1855)

advantage that there are so few opportunities for distraction or anything that could draw me away from attention to my literary studies.' This would soon prove to be a premature assertion.

In Erlangen, gentlemen playing at studying, especially students from noble families, were nothing out of the ordinary. Leopold Maximilian Julius von Braunschweig-Lüneburg spent only a few days at his alma mater, while others stayed somewhat longer. Whether Philip Henry actually did any studying is not at all certain, and definitely not mathematics, as his family had been led to believe. His correspondence relating to a difficult problem of geometry had perhaps given rise to this notion. The hard nut to crack in this case actually was conceived by his grandfather Philip, and even his mathematically highly gifted father had later been unable to solve it. Philip Henry shared the problem with four known authorities in Germany, who all tried to tackle it. He spoke about it to Professor Langsdorf in Erlangen and corresponded with the mathematicians Pleiderer in Tübingen, Mayer in Göttingen and Georg Simon Klügel (1739–1812) in Halle. Mayer and Klügel replied, the latter with a long Latin tract on this 'Theorema geometrium'. Philip Henry thanked Klügel courteously for his complex, lengthy treatise, which only a doctor of Mathematics could understand, and with this, his slight excursion into this science came to an end.

Of another professor, however, Philip Henry maintained grateful memories well into old age and sent many gifts from England to the university town. This was Ernst Wilhelm Martius (1756–1849), one of the leading specialists in pharmacology. Here was an interest in studies of which no mention was later made.

Evidence of academic work from Philip Henry's period of studies in Erlangen has not come to light. Certainly, of his initial good intentions— 'I shall take care to improve by those valuable means of instruction which I shall find at Erlangen, & shall endeavour, I hope successfully, to merit the approbation of Mr Jackson and my other friends.'—little was to remain.

At first, Mahon lived, as arranged, in the modest home of Professor Breyer, who since 1782 had lived at No. 108 on the grid system devised by Christian Erlang—today 4, Innere-Brucker-Strasse. Philip Henry was initially 'quite enthusiastic and very taken with the old gentleman,' as Hester reported to Jackson. 'He speaks in high terms of the Professor's attention & civility & says he [Breyer] has politely lodged him in his own house with the two other English students.' But when

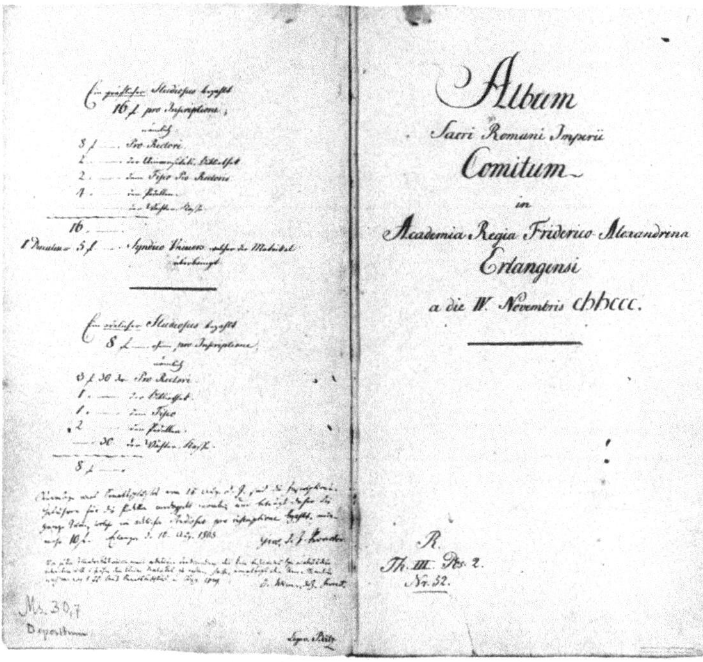

23. *Title page of the Matriculation List of 1801 at Erlangen University.*

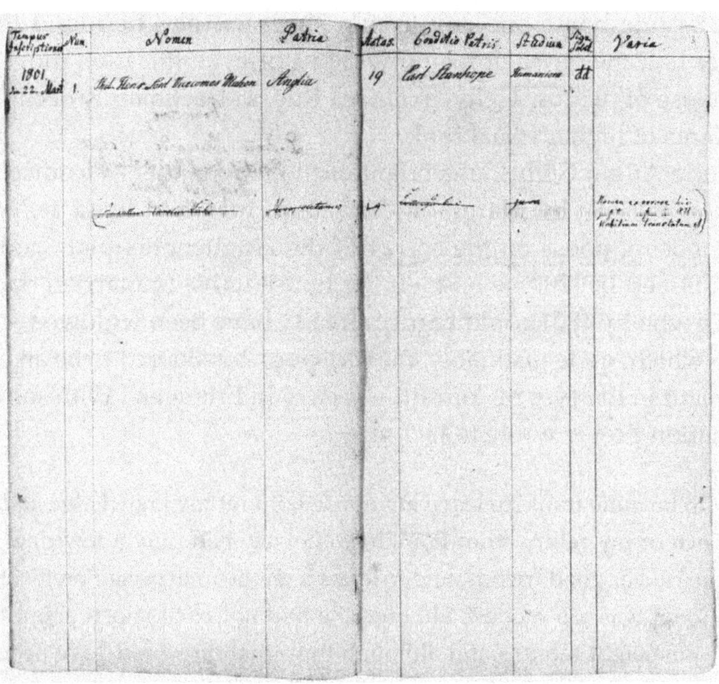

24. *Matriculation List at Erlangen University, entry of 22 March 1801.*

25. *Johann Friedrich Breyer (1738–1826)*

Breyer came home one day from a short journey, he found that his lodger had the day before and without prior notification moved into the house of 'widow Gelly' in Grand Rue, a street mainly occupied by residents of higher social rank.

Pierre Anton Gelly, descendant of the Huguenots welcomed to the country in 1686 by Margrave Christian Ernst, had lived at No. 172, an imposing house on the corner of the Huguenottenplatz, today 21, High Street. In 1799 he had left the house to his unmarried daughter Judith who by 1801 could hardly already have been widowed—a situation which, quite justifiably, the professor considered to be an embarrassment in the eyes of 'our little society in Erlangen'. With some consternation Breyer wrote to Jackson:

> To be quite frank, to leave my house without my knowledge and on the eve of my return from Frankfurt after we had only a few days before parted as good friends, and to leave it on the unexpected pretext that his room was too modest, although he had not complained about this for some eight months and although the situation would have been easily remedied either by moving the bed a little further away from the wall or else simply by installing a few wooden planks above it—I must confess

26. Residence of Prof. Breyer in Erlangen 1801. From the middle of the picture, the third house on the left. Today, Innere-Brucker-Strasse 4.

27. Residence of widow Gelly in Erlangen 127 on the Hugenottenplatz, first house on the right, today Hauptstrasse 21.

> to you, my best of friends, that his lordship's conduct appeared to me at first most peculiar and, moreover, embarrassing in view of our small society here in Erlangen, so that I could not refrain from reproaching him in a serious and decided manner for the impropriety of his behaviour and insisting that he tell me the real reasons, in the name of the friendship which he has for you. But the only result of my sustained requests was merely his admission that his conduct had been thoughtless.

It was not long before Stanhope's finances too were in dire straits. Mahon travelled around the locality, making purchases and incurring debts which had not been agreed with his teacher, who was meant to be responsible. 'It was therefore necessary to present to him a clear picture of his financial affairs.' Breyer did all he could to consolidate the situation: '...but it was quite a task for me... to bring order into his accounts, which for the most part had become confused...through the carelessness of the young gentleman...' His friends, 'all impetuous aristocrats', included a Duke of Württemberg, the Prince of Essenbourg, the Prussian, Buynisch, and the gentlemen Messrs Kerrl and Warre. It suited him well that now and again a case of port from home would arrive in Erlangen, although most of the bottles were broken in transit. In short, life in the little capital, where the 'distractions' were certainly more attractive than the effort of studying, proved to be more expensive and time-consuming than expected. Studies and amusements were incompatible, and the latter invariably prevailed. Only once do we hear of an interest in study. Mahon wanted a copy of the book *The History of English Revolutions*, which Breyer was unable to obtain in Erlangen. 'In our library there are no books on the various revolutions in England. If you think it is important for him, he will have to send for one from his homeland.'

The life of a *gallant* appears to have taken up more and more of Mahon's time, and soon Breyer felt himself no longer able to cope with the situation. On 9th Feb. 1802 he wrote to Francis Jackson:

> Consider his expenditure on gratuitous purchases in Frankfurt, which he made without telling me and which he has charged to my account without troubling to enquire whether it was capable of sustaining such costs—after he had deposited a draft for £1500 sterling in gold in Erlangen. Sir, was this draft entrusted to him or to me, and was I not led to believe that I could rely on it as part of my own resources, given his inexperience, of which I am just as much convinced as yourself? When I

> accompanied him to Nuremberg to cash in on the said draft, it emerged that he had already presented it to the bank two months earlier, when the rate of exchange had been to his advantage, while on the day we went it was rather low, resulting in a loss of 72 florins. Being informed of this, I reiterated to him: 'My Lord, *from now on please place either no more trust in me or else your full trust.*' It was therefore not I who gave him a free rein but rather those who arranged for him to be the custodian of his money.[24]

When the 'illustrious scholar my lord Mahon' included the fee for Prof. Breyer in the financing of his undertakings, the professor severed the relationship:

> Young people and—allow me to say—above all your English young people, believe themselves entitled to withhold from their professors the 40–50 pounds sterling determined upon as an honorarium for their appointed lessons, for they consider the sum contributes to a perceptible reduction of their state and is not at their disposal for their own needs and amusements. I have too high a regard for your nation to believe that parents in your country think in this way... I shall do something for the occupation of the gentleman, but you will understand if my efforts are not especially obliging.[25]

This seems to have been the end of Mahon's 'studies' in Erlangen.

*

While Mahon was beginning to find his feet abroad, at home Hester was wondering about her brother's future. It was premature for him to wait to come into his inheritance, which was not likely to amount to much. The days of the wealthiest lord of Kent were over; the Stanhopes were practically bankrupt. Hester's agitation over her father and his way of administering the family's fortune was not unfounded.

> Not until the age of 21 did he [Mahon] first think of helping himself by turning to his friends because there were things he wished to learn. He would never have been able to get on in the world, he would have been at a great disadvantage, which *now* no longer obtains...As to the question of agreeing to his father's proposals with regard to the inheritance, no-one could imagine that he would do anything about it. It is so mad, really I must say, crazy of him, to ruin himself by allowing his

> father unrestricted control over his own future property, which has most certainly been squandered in the most absurd ways. I have often heard him say that if it had been in his power, he would have liked to transfer his assets abroad. As hard as the duty may be to set my father's conduct in the right light, it is nevertheless a duty in relation to the persons most directly affected.[26]

Seeking advice, she wrote to another friend: 'Do you not believe that it would be better to make a drastic cutback at once than to lead the lonely and unhappy life that my father does? Is it a greater disgrace to admit to the world that one is in financial difficulties than being ostracised by all respectable members of society ?'[27]

No hopes could be entertained of property, wealth, or return on capital either then or in the near future. A career would have to be found for Mahon, which was both congenial to him and feasible. The delicate youth seemed just as little suited to an officer's career as to the diplomatic service or even work in finance or commerce. Besides Hester, it was the two friends Pitt and Jackson who now set about devising for Mahon a suitable professional career.

Already in April 1801 Hester wrote to Francis Jackson that Pitt had taken up the issue. 'After the Council this week, I hope the G Man [William Pitt, the Prime Minister—*Ed.*] will have time to consider over M[ahon]'s business a little, he has spent a good deal of his time with my Scotch cousin at W[almer Castle] lately, and I dare say their wise heads have been consulting upon the subject.'[28] Jackson soon learned of the results of the meeting, and in view of what Mahon continued to receive by way of advice and help from this confidant of Pitt's, one must conclude that Jackson was privy to the details of these considerations about Mahon's future.

Already in 1801 there existed the outline of a plan to prepare Philip Henry gradually for the occupation of a political secret agent. A solution in this direction seemed obvious, since it was clear that a respectable position in society could not be established in the short run on the basis of a ruined family inheritance. Travelling as a secret agent would achieve two purposes: his occasional absence from the country would prevent revelation of the family's dire economic situation—a clear advantage in terms of social standing—and above all, such an occupation could guarantee an income commensurable with its success. It was agreed that certain capacities for such work, which Mahon seemed to possess, would continue to be monitored and that, above all, opportunities would be created which would make it possible for

28. Sophie Karoline, Margravine of Ansbach-Bayreuth (1737–1817)

29. Schloss Elisabethenburg. Dowager's Residence of the Margraves of Ansbach-Bayreuth.

him to learn all that was necessary for the role. First thoughts in the direction of Vienna belong to this period as well as ideas about the trip to Sicily, later undertaken in 1812, and culminating in his taking up the post in Dresden in 1814.

In this sense Jackson seemed taken with Mahon's reports from Germany. He wrote to Hester: 'His letter from Leipsic [Leipzig—*Ed.*] is an exact delineation of the character of that Class of Germans he had seen, & a very accurate Description of the Mode of travelling through the country. If he can profit so much in so little time, and indeed, with so few means, what may we not expect when he comes to exercise his judgement & his Talents in a higher and more extensive Sphere?'[29]

Not long after this first small indication of his ability, the question of the above-mentioned trip to Vienna was discussed. But Jackson did not want to send Mahon off on his travels too early. '…if he should obtain a Dispensation from this & Leave to remain at Vienna,' he tells Hester, 'that place is six Days Journey from Erlang[en], & it will of course be desirable that Mahon should some time prosecute his studies uninterruptedly. *When he does travel* [to Vienna], *it shall be my Business to procure him Introductions….* [emphasis—Mayer]'. The intended occupation required training, which also included the development of real ability in expressing himself in writing. It was therefore deemed instructive for Mahon to send all his letters, still unsealed, to Jackson, who would read them, seal them and then send them on to Mahon's correspondents. The diplomat soon expressed satisfaction with Mahon's progress: 'From the experience we have of M's epistolary Talents & Discretion', he wrote again to Hester, 'there is every hope that he will write nothing but what is extermely proper...'[30]

It is unlikely that, at this time, Philip Henry himself had been fully informed as to the plans for his future. This conclusion is borne out by his ill-considered actions and his student life far from the lecture halls. There were also Breyer's reports back to England, and what Hester read between the lines of her brother's letters gave her cause for concern: 'Mahon's letter', she wrote to Jackson, 'was not very full of business... [it] was of a nature though in the end to give me satisfaction, yet it tended to make me rather dull [morose—*Ed.*] for the moment.'[31] That Philip Henry participated in life at the court of the Margravine during his time at Erlangen or that he even received some kind of education there was a cleverly circulated rumour. The fact is that immediately after his arrival, Philip Henry was received by the Margravine and invited to supper at Elisabethenburg Castle. She afterwards wrote a very motherly letter to Jackson in which she assured her old friend that she had 'saved a young plant [Mahon] from the inhuman principles of Jacobinism', expressing herself delighted with the 'informality and manliness of his behaviour' and concluded: 'Now, I promise you, we shall make of him a useful and honourable person.' Philip Henry too was delighted by this first meeting, as he was with most other things, and wrote somewhat precociously to Hester that he found the Margravine very pleasant and that she must certainly have been 'a handsome woman' and appeared determined 'to remain so as long as possible'. After that, no further meetings or attempts at conversion took place between the two. Philip Henry felt himself drawn to other adventures, and the Margravine would also soon have realised that she had nothing to offer that would satisfy this young man hungry for experience who was rapidly gaining in self-confidence. Sophie Karoline was poor and lived modestly with a small number of her loyal retainers. She had to ask Baron von Haller to sell a chest of drawers with six gaming tables for her. Apart from a few servants who worked in the kitchens, stables and gardens, her only court attendants were her lady-in-waiting, the elderly Luise von Dobeneck and her Court Chamberlain Baron von Reitzenstein. Her lifestyle completely lacked what a princely court of the period required to give it sparkle, namely, a sufficient number of court officials. In Philip Henry's time the Margravine had to argue with the Prussian administration over the supply of wood for the few ovens that were still in use. Seven fireplaces were listed for the whole castle. 'I am shut up within my four walls,' wrote the 65-year-old to her brother. 'I read, write, play clavier a little, work a little. I have no company and I organise my own reading matter myself. I only feel comfortable in my pretty suite.'

*

At the beginning of 1802 Hester prepared for a stay in Baden-Baden. She was able to travel, most likely through the good offices of Pitt, in the entourage of the Duke of York (1763–1827)[32], a brother of the King. Wanting to take the opportunity to see for herself what had become of Philip Henry, she spent February there in the meeting place of the high society of Europe's nobility; Philip Henry hastened there to see his sister again.

As she wrote to Lord Haddington on 23.10.1803 after her return from the Continent, Hester was, with a few reservations, 'more than satisfied with the progress he has made in his studies'. 'I am sorry to find him inclined to be too old for his age and approaching a quiz in manner and dress. But as far as these details are concerned, I still have the hope that he will improve himself.'

In Baden-Baden, 'the salon of Europe', there was talk not only of the benefits of the spa's healing waters but of Europe and politics, especially when the brother of the King of England was the centre of attention. Since Bonaparte had taken over the government by *coup d'état* in November 1799, Paris had become the centre of European politics on the grand scale. By the Treaty of Luneville (1802) the Holy Roman Empire had had to surrender to France all territory on the left bank of the Rhine. This included the loss of the Palatinate [Pfalz], and the part of the Palatinate which lay to the east of the Rhine was handed to the Duchy of Baden-Durlach, which at a stroke (1803) increased its population from 190,000 to 450,000 inhabitants. Subsequently, Margrave Karl Friedrich was raised to the rank of Grand Duke. The meeting place of Europe's high society where such questions were considered and discussed was therefore the land of Baden, which had recently seen such a remarkable expansion of its territory. Bonaparte gave as his reason for this generous concession the excellent qualities of the then sovereign prince of Baden, Karl Friedrich—qualities which had been particularly commented on with favour by Frederick the Great of Prussia.[33] Napoleon's real motives, however, lay elsewhere. Through such a political manoeuvre, not only did he come a step closer to achieving his goal of creating a central German state—the later Confederation of the Rhine—but he had at the same time provided for a *'fédération germanique'* on his eastern frontier, which would be dependent on France and which could be used politically and militarily against Austria and Prussia at short order.

Such a policy and its potential consequences were topics of anxious conversation in Baden-Baden, and here in this circle of knowledgeable and politically active individuals, Philip Henry, with his growing sense for political relationships, may for the first time have sensed something of the dynamism and the destiny-forming power of the Corsican—and also, of the fear and aversion, the scorn and hatred against him and all his family.

With this new development that would come to affect his own career, the future secret agent found himself, without recognising it, within a course of events that would occupy him for decades. The imminent elevation of Baden to the status of a Grand Duchy was the result of a geostrategic design by Bonaparte which, while creating new relationships, would also demand sacrifices. For Stanhope's destiny, it would prove decisive.

Napoleon's Policy of Dynastic Marriages and the House of Baden

Elucidation of Bonaparte's dynastic policies at this point will prove useful for the development of our theme. A study of the connections between the families forced into alliances by Napoleon yields insights which illuminate both the biography of Stanhope and the Kaspar Hauser question.

In 1803 the new 'First Consul of France' instituted a new order among the German states, which would later become the Confederation of the Rhine. For the purposes of the present study, only the thrones of Baden, Württemberg and Bavaria are of interest; Napoleon wished to bind these to himself permanently. They were insignificant as military opponents, and he could have overwhelmed them by force without the slightest concern. However, it was more farsighted of him in this case to seek to bind the princes of southern Germany to France through dynastic politics, thus providing a more solid foundation for his own empire which he established on 8th December 1804. This called for relationships to be entered into with the princes and princesses of the emerging empire, forging links with legitimate dynasties. The Houses of Zähringen, Wittelsbach and Württemberg were thus to be united with the Bonaparte family. The French ambassador in Stuttgart had already experienced the kind of ancestral pride and class consciousness such intentions were likely to come up against and had reported to the Emperor: 'What do you want of me?' the Elector Friedrich [of Württemberg] had shouted: 'Your troops are flooding my country and violating my neutrality. This is a betrayal! What does your Bonaparte want here? A freshly baked prince, a parvenu sovereign, threatens violence against me— I who am descended from a race of princes! But I am master here! And that I shall show him: I utterly reject such blackmail!'

That was the one objection and reservation which would permeate politics and diplomacy even after the Congress of Vienna: at all costs the Napoleonids must be kept out of the European power structure. The 'anointed upstart', the parvenu must not be allowed to insinuate himself into families of princely blood. But Napoleon's dynastic policies were an integral part of his imperial rule which he was determined to carry through at virtually any cost.

The imperial chamberlain, Auxonne Marie Théodore de Thiard, Count de Bissy (1772–1852) was entrusted with the delicate mission of sounding out the situation and of establishing initial contacts, which would then be consolidated by the planned double marriage

30. Amalie, Margravine of Baden (1754–1832)

with Baden and Bavaria. Accordingly, Princess Auguste Amalie (1788–1851), daughter of Elector Max Joseph of Bavaria was to be married to Napoleon's stepson, Eugène de Beauharnais, vice-regent of Italy, which immediately presented the greatest difficulties, as Amalie of Baden, the widow of Crown prince Karl Ludwig of Baden, had long had her own quite different marriage plans for the Princess. Nor was the Elector inclined to agree to the match: firstly, because the Princess had long been engaged to Amalie of Baden's son, Crown prince Karl of Baden, and secondly, because Eugène was not of equal rank. Napoleon let it be known that, if his wishes were not instantly complied with, he would 'take an Austrian lady for my stepson'. That had an immediate effect; the wedding took place in Munich on 26th December 1805 in the presence of the Emperor and Empress.

Insufficient attention has been paid to the connection between Napoleon's decisive interference in the marriage plans of the power- and class-conscious Margravine Amalie of Baden and the story of Kaspar Hauser. Amalie felt the deepest hatred for Napoleon and all his family. She not only firmly upheld the old princely rights that Napoleon was threatening to overturn; she could never forgive the fact that Napoleon had sent French soldiers onto Baden's territory to arrest and execute the Duc d'Enghien, who had been highly regarded at the court in Karlsruhe. In protest against Napoleon's action, she had ignored the invitation to Paris to attend the coronation of the 'usurper' under the pretext of the imminent confinement of her fifth daughter, the Duchess von Braunschweig-Öls, to avoid having to meet the 'parvenu'. She categorically forbade[34] her son Karl, the father of Kaspar Hauser, from taking part in the short campaign waged by the Corsican upstart against Austria,[35] which incidentally cost Grand Duke Karl Friedrich the crown of Baden; Napoleon had rewarded the rulers of Bavaria and Württemberg by raising their duchies to the status of kingdoms. She simply refused to welcome the Emperor outside the gates of Karlsruhe when he stopped in Baden on 1st October 1805 during his advance on the fortress of Ulm in Ettlingen. Baron Sigismund von Reitzenstein,

31. Stéphanie de Beauharnais (1789–1860). Charcoal drawing by her cousin, Hortense, Queen of Holland.

32. Karl, Prince-Elector of Baden (1786–1818)

33. Luise Karoline, Imperial Countess of Hochberg (1768–1820)

34. Karl Friedrich, Grand Duke of Baden (1728–1811)

Baden's ambassador, was extremely apprehensive about the imprudent and provocative attitude of the Margravine and feared the wrath of Napoleon all the more after his victory on the Danube.

When the forced marriage of Princess Auguste Amalie of Bavaria and Prince Eugène de Beauharnais eventually took place despite Amalie von Baden's energetic resistance, and the Empress Joséphine went to Munich for her son's wedding festivities, the Bonapartes received a further insult. Empress Joséphine broke her journey in Karlsruhe and was received by Amalie—after bitter family quarrels—with an offensive arrogance on the highest step of the terrace to the rear of the vestibule. The Empress's reception could hardly have been more insulting. Bitterness and hatred grew still further when the Margravine realised that Napoleon, through his stepson Beauharnais, had not only thwarted her own plans for a marriage union with the House of Bavaria but had devised a similar fate for Baden.

What had worked in Munich in 1805 was repeated in Karlsruhe in 1806. The old Grand Duke Karl Friedrich and his eldest son Karl were informed that instead of Amalie of Bavaria, a wedding to Stéphanie de Beauharnais (Fig. 31), Empress Joséphine's niece, was planned. Napoleon had already shared with Elector Max Joseph his own view of the matter: 'Are Princesses permitted to love at all? The fact is, they are merely political commodities.' Nor was Karlsruhe in any position to stand against the will of Napoleon. When Amalie of Baden, 'the Mother-in-Law of Europe', heard of the wedding plans, she again adamantly refused her consent owing to the couple's inequality of rank. This 'person', declared the Margravine haughtily, this daughter of a poor French squire, was to be betrothed to her son Karl (Fig.32) without so much as a 'by-your-leave'? The negotiations in this matter, that is, Napoleon's wishes, were expedited officially by Grand Duke Karl Friedrich (Fig. 34) and his morganatic wife the Countess von Hochberg (Fig. 33), who was held in but slight regard by Amalie, and who, to Amalie's annoyance, had already expressed her own approval of such a union. This was a calculated move on the part of the Countess, undertaken in the hope of furthering, through Stéphanie, her own wishes, namely, the raising of her own descendants to the rank of princes[36], something Amalie had always strenuously resisted. She had already asked her daughter Luise Elisabeth (1779–1826), the wife of Czar Alexander I of Russia, for diplomatic assistance. The Czarina reassured her mother; in 1803 (15th March) she had written from St. Petersburg: 'It would be an outrage if the little Hochbergs were to be granted the right to succeed to the throne. The Emperor has promised me that, if asked, he will deal with the matter in accordance with your wishes.'

Meanwhile, interest in the notion of a Hochberg succession appeared to have faded substantially in Paris, where only Stéphanie and Karl were now seen as the bearers of Baden's future. From this moment on, Karl Friedrich's second wife knew that the only obstacle to her ambitions would be princes who might result from the planned marriage.

When Napoleon was expected in Karlsruhe en route from Munich on 15th January 1806 to receive Karl's definitive consent to the marriage, Grand Duke Karl Friedrich decided that his grandson should ride to meet the Emperor in Augsburg. Outraged, Amalie objected to this honour—which Napoleon regarded as correct form and no more than his due— in the hope that the offence would induce the Emperor to abandon his intentions. When Karl, nevertheless, expressed his wish to go, the Margravine, beside herself, screamed 'that she would curse him for this'. Only Karl's threat to renounce his right of succession in favour of the Hochbergs moved Amalie to agree begrudgingly to his ride to Augsburg.[37] The hour-long conversations between Amalie and Napoleon the following day focused exclusively on the marriage between her son and Stéphanie de Beauharnais. The Emperor, who tried his best to flatter the Margravine, received only brusque replies in return. 'These few tokens of favour,' replied Amalie, 'are no reason for me to agree to the wedding proposed by your Majesty. I wish my son to marry a German princess of his own rank.' To Amalie's challenging remark 'If the young lady were at least of your own family…', Napoleon reacted with the rash and unexpected reply: 'Eh bien, je l'adopte' [Well then, I'll adopt her]. Even Amalie had to accept an imperial Princess, *'une fille de France'*. She wrote to her daughter Wilhelmine (1788–1836), Duchess presumptive of Hesse:

> I am not ill, but my head is troubling me; it's my nerves. It's hardly surprising, for God knows the worries and cares I've been plagued with these last four months. It has now been decided that my son will marry Mademoiselle de Beauharnais, who will be made a Princess of France; he [Karl] has agreed to this without demur and his grandfather also. I have fought against it for four weeks on my own.[38]

The forced marriage between Karl von Baden and Stéphanie de Beauharnais duly took place on 8th April 1806 in the Tuileries in Paris.

Soon afterwards an imperial decree bestowed on Stéphanie a courtly rank which placed her, as Her Imperial Highness, above the Margravine. This amounted to an actual and very visible rebuff for Amalie, who had to hand over the Crown jewels, which she herself had worn for twenty years, to her daughter-in-law, who would wear them on ceremonial occasions. When Amalie visited the palace, instead of greeting her at her carriage door, Stéphanie received her at the top of the staircase—exactly where Amalie had greeted Joséphine barely a year before.

Furious, Amalie withdrew to her widow's residence at Bruchsal, where she proceeded to gather round herself an anti-French faction. Amalie never forgot this —in her eyes—humiliating defeat and more than once she tried in later years to bring about a divorce between Karl and Stéphanie. This history should be kept in mind when evaluating Amalie's actions at the time of the birth of Stéphanie's first son (Kaspar Hauser). In view of such disputes, Stéphanie's delivery was not likely to have been accompanied by the heartfelt sympathy which Amalie claimed to show. The credibility of her letters to her daughter Karoline, the Queen of Bavaria, in this regard may well be doubted.

Also unclear in this connection is the role of the physician and Privy Councillor, Dr. Schrickel, who delivered the baby. It is known that he was closer to the Hochbergs than anyone else and he was from that time on (1812), a very strange man. As the 'Cagliostro' of Karlsruhe, he engaged in all kinds of alchemical experiments, which consumed a great deal of money but showed not the slightest result. Particularly during evening gatherings, the doctor would tell the weirdest of ghost stories. Margrave Wilhelm described the atmosphere among Schrickel's listeners when the doctor told them of ghostly apparitions. He claimed to have frequently seen 'the woman in white...which often made his listeners shudder'.[39] It was little wonder that such apparitions would play a role on other occasions.

Of great interest is the fact that on 18th August 1807 Baron Nicolas Marssias, the French chargé d'affaires in Karlsruhe, reported to the new Foreign Minister in Paris, Jean Baptiste, Comte de Champagny, a significant observation: 'Margrave Ludwig and the Countess Hochberg...are united in their determination to rule in place of the Grand Duke...' If this was true, then the two would well have appreciated what the birth of a son to Karl and Stéphanie would mean for their plans.

In Napoleon's dynastic policy, only Württemberg remained to be dealt with. He had decided on his brother Jerome as the bridegroom for Princess Katharina, but Jerome had declined and had instead married Elizabeth Patterson, daughter of an immigrant Scots merchant, in 1805. Napoleon was able to enforce a legal separation of the couple, but not an ecclesiastical dissolution of the marriage, which Pius VI initially refused.

Having later reconciled himself to his imperial brother's wishes and obeying Napoleon's summons to return, Jerome was rewarded with the captaincy of a frigate and in 1806 was appointed Rear-Admiral. Finally, in 1807, he was made King of Westphalia, a condition that Elector Friedrich of Württemberg had insisted upon for the marriage to his daughter Princess Katharina. Meanwhile, the Curia had relented on the dissolution of Jerome's marriage to Elizabeth Patterson, so that nothing now stood in the way of Bonaparte's dynastic union with Württemberg, which had first been promised in 1806. The wedding of Jerome and Katharina was held in Paris on 23rd August 1807.

Thus within three years—1805–1807—the three southern German ruling Houses were linked with Napoleon's family, which was very much to their own advantage. Karl Friedrich of Baden became Grand Duke with the rank of king, while the Electors Friedrich of Württemberg and Max Joseph of Bavaria were now entitled to call themselves Kings of Württemberg and Bavaria respectively. Baden received the Ortenau, a part of the Breisgau region as well as a few towns on Lake Constance, which increased the size of the Grand Duchy to 249 sq. miles from the 30 sq. miles it had been at the accession of Karl Friedrich, while the number of inhabitants grew from 90,000 to more than 911,000. Württemberg received the remaining part of the Breisgau and a considerable slice of Swabia, while Bavaria was given the whole of the Voralberg region, the bishoprics of Eichstädt and Passau, and Austrian territories in Swabia, as well as the city and bishopric of Augsburg.

Military strategists held that Southern Germany was, alongside Northern Italy, the best possible corridor for French military campaigns against Austria and for that, Napoleon was prepared to pay.

Meanwhile, Friedrich von Gentz saw the whole disaster developing and wrote pleading letters to his old friend Pitt and to Francis Jackson, who by then had become British Ambassador in Berlin: 'You are going to unleash a continental war without first having brought about a change of government in Austria and without having won round the King of Prussia. You will soon have cause to rue these two errors—

this war will have no happy outcome; its conception is fundamentally flawed; God the Almighty Himself will not be able to save us!'

However, let us return to Baden-Baden in the year 1802.

*

In this fashionable spa town on the Oos Philip Henry had his first encounter with Europe's high society. The political perspectives here with all their associated minor and complicated relationships, the power interests, all the many obvious but preferably secret intrigues which were the stuff of everyday life, the stimulating company of the powerful and their potential gratitude for discreet service—all this fascinated the young man and found a resonance in his soul. In Baden-Baden, a place he was to visit again many times in the future in similar circumstances, he received the first practical confirmation that he belonged to this circle in some way; it was an experience of crucial importance for his whole life. After the weeks in Baden-Baden the Stanhope siblings decided on further recreation for the late summer—a cultural trip to Italy, part of the Grand Tour of every cultured Briton, in order to familiarise themselves with its most important cultural and historical sites. At the end of September [1802], Hester Stanhope, accompanied by the married couple Mr. and Mrs Egerton, travelled through France as far as Lyons, there to meet up with her brother on 16th October who was to make his way there from Erlangen. From Lyons they passed into the French Alps, the mountainous world of the four-thousand-metre-high peaks of the Grand-Rousses and Vanoise, as far as the Italian border. In the mountain pass near the heights of Mont Cenis (22nd October), which Hannibal and Napoleon had used for their crossings of the Alps, the siblings secretly left the rest of the company, who proceeded by coach, and rode on alone on rented mules through the wild rocky landscape of the high mountains. In a mountain hut there was fresh trout for lunch. This first experience of such powerful mountain ranges, of gorges and peaks made a deep impression on Hester and Philip Henry.

In Turin (2nd November) there was still a reasonable harmony between brother and sister. Via Parma and Bologna their journey went on to Florence, where they stayed over the weekend of 13th–14th November. By this time, however, they were arguing constantly. Hester, more interested in landscape and people, did not want to spend a long time trailing after her brother through museums and churches, while he reproached her for her lack of culture. Hester was also increasingly perturbed by her brother's precocious and arrogant discourses on European politics, his vanity and his conspicuous way of showing off his newly acquired knowledge. When she had received from Erlangen the first unsavoury news about Philip Henry, she had been unwilling to entertain any suspicions: 'He does not conduct himself as though he were speaking as his own master.' From a distance she did not want to acknowledge the changes in her brother. Now that she was travelling with him, she experienced the reality daily. His foppish clothes, his overly rapid speech—'he converses not pleasantly, too much like a Frenchman, apparently out of humour'—his black poodle, which had recently become his constant companion, all this irritated her and moved her to scorn and teasing, which the sensitive young man found all the more intolerable when she compared him to her uncle, the Lord Chancellor. That was the limit; the earlier harmony between them was gone. They had become strangers who no longer understood each other; their paths diverged.

Hester travelled on to Naples with the Egertons and spent the winter in Italy. In the spring, travelling to Paris via Stuttgart, Hester, as a relative of the great Pitt, was received by Elector Friedrich II (later King Friedrich I) of Württemberg. Philip Henry meanwhile, had decided to return to England before the year (1802) was out, which did not seem so simple given his spectacular flight the year before. On 30th December he reached Calais, made the crossing and set foot once more in the old homeland just a few hours before the New Year began. But where was he to go now? Not to Chevening, as his father had completely disowned him, and so once again he had to turn to Pitt, who, amongst other things, from 1792–1805 was Lord Warden of the Cinque Port of Dover and its powerful fortress, 'the key to England'. His uncle Pitt made it possible for the returnee to lodge at Dover Castle, with the prospect of eventually becoming vice-governor there; at least it was a beginning and ensured a modest livelihood and accommodation.

*

Immediately after Philip Henry's premature return, the Prime Minister seems to have considered the further promotion of his career as an agent, which he had originally conceived with Jackson and others. While the short stay in Erlangen had not turned out to be a full course of study, it had nevertheless served its purpose. Now it was a question of how to proceed with the appropriate development of the young man. It is not improbable that Pitt intended to train his relative to be able to serve on the staff of foreign agents who were responsible to him personally. Several years earlier, two such agents in Paris were the diplomats Hugh Elliott and William Augustus Miles, who were entrusted with the task of encouraging revolutionary activities, which could even entail the need to join a Jacobin club. Miles belonged to such a club until its closure in 1795; until then he had been able to render the greatest service to Pitt. Was Pitt thinking of similar work for Philip Henry in Switzerland, albeit with a different aim? Stanhope's language abilities in the meantime had become really excellent. As he wrote to his mother at this time: 'I read and speak German as fluently as English.'

Among other documents of a conspiratorial nature among Philip Henry's papers is a letter of 18th October 1802, addressed not to him but to Pitt. Assuming that he did not acquire this letter by dishonest means, the only possible explanation is that Pitt himself—who had been entreated by the writer to destroy the letter 'under all circumstances' immediately—had passed it on with a particular aim in view. But what was it about and who was the writer, who not without some justification, suspected that 'preservation [of the letter] could be dangerous for me in the future'?

It was a case of conspiracy at the highest level, proposed to Pitt by Louis Philippe, Duke of Orléans (1770–1850). The Duke—'I am a natural enemy of Bonaparte'—was the son of Louis Philippe Joseph, Duke of Orléans and cousin of Louis XVI who had played a multifaceted role in the early phase of the French Revolution. The intentions of the father explain those of the son. Under the cover of the popular unrest with which the actual Revolution had begun, the ambitious father had wanted to seize power himself. His not exactly noble plan had aimed at the overthrow of the Bourbons with the help of the masses and his being called to assume the crown to empower a new royal order based on rights grounded this time on the will of the people. It was therefore only logical to set 'the will of the people' against the principle of kingship by the grace of God, as a result of which, the Duke became one of the most active promoters and preparers of the Revolution. His closest allies in the struggle for power were the French Freemasons, whose Grand Master he had been since 1772. The most important connections to the Paris lodges were maintained by the Duke's private secretary, the writer and officer Pierre Choderlos de Laclos, Master of the soldiers' lodge 'Henri IV', who himself was to play a decisive role in connection with the outbreak of the Revolution. Laclos hid his identity as a key director of the revolts, and was described by the French historian Octave Aubry as an unrecognised genius.

The Duke, who had meanwhile taken the name of Philippe Égalité and who spent more time in England than in France, was a close friend of the Prince Regent (1762–1830), later King George IV, who himself held the office of Grand Master of all English freemasonic lodges [but only those known as 'Modern'; his brother, the Duke of York, controlled those known as 'Ancient'; Freemasonry in Britain was split between these two systems from 1755–1813—*Ed.*]—the overarching common interest is therefore clear. The deliberately planned process of confrontation of the Orléanists with the court culminated in the demand for the king's abdication, which they were prepared to carry through by force if necessary. When in 1793 the Duke went as far as to vote for the execution of Louis XVI, it became obvious—and was generally assumed—that he wanted to take power himself. Under this charge he was arrested, found guilty and guillotined in Paris the same year. His son—the writer of this letter to Pitt—emigrated to England where, at least at the beginning, he plotted, just as his father had done, to gain the throne of the Bourbons, which he believed was still possible. In this connection, the proposal laid out in the young Duke's letter to Pitt is of far-reaching significance. At the head of armed forces financed by England he wishes to defend neutral Switzerland against Napoleon's armies.

Twickenham, 18th October 1802

Sir,

Through an erroneous report that you would be in town today, I visited your residence at York Place to ask for a conversation with you. I wished to share with you some ideas which seem to me advisable in view of current conditions in Europe and above all in Switzerland. It is clear to me that I could be charged with presumptuousness in seeking to address you on this subject, but the opportunity spurs me on and absolves me of the charge. Allow me to add that in writing to you I must place myself in your honourable trust and ask you to treat all that I am about to write in confidence, hoping under all circumstances that you will destroy this letter since its preservation could be dangerous for me in the future. I can give you no greater token of the high esteem in which I hold you. It is superfluous to go into the necessity for Switzerland to be saved from the claws of the current French regime. Its significance as a military base is now recognised by all. In fact, it determines military operations in Germany, France and Italy, and in my opinion, its occupation by the French was one of the main reasons for the battle of Marengo and the disaster that followed. If it is worth your while, I should like to explain to you what advantages I would see in an occupation [of Switzerland] by the Allies for continuing the war wherever they wish, and especially in France, which lies open on this side, because neither Louis XIV nor Vauban ever thought of defending this part of the border since they never believed that Switzerland would ever infringe its neutrality. My concern at the moment is only to lay out before your keen perception some possibilities of how Switzerland could be effectively defended and to offer you my services for this purpose.

The Swiss need money, weapons, munitions and c....[*sic*!] But above all they need a firm *guarantee* that their country will not fall prey to those who wish to support them against the French, and they would like *a kind of commitment* to be able to hold their assemblies and to be able to maintain the strength of their resistance through the preservation of unanimity. I fear that they will not be convinced by proclamations that Austria does not intend to seize their country. A good independent Swiss army, led by a man working in the interests of England and Austria and approved of by them appears to me the best *guarantee* and *commitment* and at the same time the strongest assistance against France that the Swiss can receive. It seems difficult for its leader to be a Swiss. They have neither princes nor any other men of high rank who could assert a supremacy over his fellow citizens necessary to enable them to hold together against the common enemy, so to suppress disunity in their own country and to ensure respect abroad. In earlier times the Dutch were defended by Prince Maurice of Nassau against their lawful ruler and his representative, the Duke of Alba, and if it had not been for the Prince, they would in all likelihood have been overwhelmed. This, Sir, is the role I would wish to take on for Switzerland against her tyrants and for Europe against its oppressors. I offer myself to you in full trust because I believe that my situation and my connections are *uniquely suited* to this noble cause. The honour of my descent from those kings who were the protectors of the Swiss and who protected them for so long and so faithfully would make me popular among them. I can speak their languages and I have lived among them for two years, part of which I spent wandering in their mountains without fixed abode. I am therefore no complete stranger to their land and customs. As for my family's circumstances, I find myself in that particular situation which I do not need to describe to you, Sir, but which has brought me to the point where I feel duty-bound to serve the interests of Europe since I am minded to make my career elsewhere than in France, where I see too many shallows in order to be able to steer a strong course and to continue that line of honour and integrity from which I hope never to deviate. I am neither English nor Austrian. I am a natural enemy of Bonaparte and of all similar governments, to which I shall never be able to reconcile myself, therefore I cannot be unpopular amongst the Swiss and must be above any suspicion. Nevertheless, through my unusual situation, England and Austria could find in me all the advantages of a French Prince without the unacceptable elements which would normally follow from such an identity, so that I will be an honourable and upright friend to them without having to speak of gratitude, respect, similarity of views, ideas, wishes etc.

This, Sir, was what I wished to communicate to you in the private conversation which I believed you would grant me. I could trust none other than yourself, whose character, noble sensibility, and rare gifts sufficed to inspire me to entrust you with a communication such as this. I assure you that the fact that I have written this letter to you is the greatest proof I can give you of the sincerity of my wishes: that the affairs in which this country is engaged may be successful; proof also of the deeply felt gratitude for the generous support and hospitality which your country has extended to me and of my deep respect for you, Sir, who as Minister have made this available and have made it possible for me to be thus received as was the case both by the government as well as by *all others.* I am well aware of the testimonials you have given of me. Therefore, you need not be surprised if, for my part, I now beg to offer to render some service in return for this generous support insofar as it lies within my capabilities. It is not that I crave glory and honour. I would not consider myself worthy of respect and support if these feelings did not inflame my heart or if I were to be content to be a burden on the generosity of this country. Remember, Sir, that I have nothing to lose but much to gain. If you hold this to be an idle dream, throw this letter into the fire and let its contents slip into oblivion until better times come, and do not even reply. But if, on the other hand, you think that a good result could come from it or from another plan in which I could be of use, I am at your disposal, Sir. Show me the way and I shall follow it.

I have the honour to be, Sir, with the greatest respect,

Yours, the Duke of Orléans.[40]

What conclusions did Pitt draw from the proposal? Apart from the fact that Switzerland itself would probably not be in a situation to muster a serious defence against the French, did he conclude perhaps that the

Duke had another agenda? Was he planning a march on Paris with an army entrusted to him? We do not know how the Prime Minister gauged the talents and realism of the Duke and whether on reading the letter, quite other thoughts crossed his mind. It is conceivable that he handed the document over to Stanhope and gave him the task of preparing an analysis of background factors, possible ambitions, an assessment of success and of the risks involved. This could have been a chance for Philip Henry to show his inventiveness—to demonstrate on the basis of a concrete example whether he possessed a sense for strategy and tactics, cunning and political instinct. That Orléans had to be handled with caution Pitt knew from a series of events which played itself out openly before his own eyes.

Friedrich von Gentz had arrived in London accompanied by the same envoy, Hugh Elliott, who had helped stir up the unrest in Paris and had announced his intention to call on the Duke of Orléans amongst others. In Parliament the two listened quietly to a fiery speech by Pitt's rival, Windham, who inveighed against Bonaparte and Britain's [i.e. Pitt's] weak defensive measures and saw in England the only bulwark against French plans for world domination. 'Seems bad' (for Bonaparte) declared the Duke gleefully to Gentz. Before England's new friend left for home he spent his last evening at Twickenham Castle. From there Gentz wrote to Adam Müller: 'You will be surprised to hear that of all the people I know here, this Prince [Orléans] is the one most thoroughly in tune with my political ideas……'

Pitt knew that Gentz, Elliott and the Duke of Orléans had been seen side by side in London—and shortly afterwards, he was in possession of Orléans' letter, the implications of which were not easy to assess. Gentz, who regarded Switzerland as a mere vassal, 'a province of the French Empire', did not attach the slightest significance to the country's claimed neutrality. On the contrary! 'A declaration of neutrality springing up from *this* soil loses all legal claim to the name with which it adorns itself!' In the worst case scenario, this would mean that a guaranteed neutrality would be disregarded and a universally acknowledged international law would be infringed—a plan of attack with a very uncertain outcome, which Russia would certainly never support. Pitt could not avoid the suspicion that he, Windham's rival, was to be drawn into a political adventure which could have brought his controversial second period in office to a premature end. Philip Henry might possess the necessary connections and possibilities to enable him to bring to light the real intentions of the letter's author.

Other correspondence, possibly from the same suspicious source—not addressed to Stanhope but in his possession—also involves conspiracy. General Charles François Dumouriez (1739–1823) was the victorious commander of the French forces at the Battle of Valmy (1792); his opponent was the Duke of Brunswick. Shortly after Valmy, Dumouriez found himself up against the Austrians once again at Neerwinden in Belgium and this time suffered a disastrous defeat. The National Convention sought to bring the General to trial on this and other grounds. He was accused of having planned to march on Paris with the rest of his army in order to enthrone the Dauphin—in other words, to restore the constitutional monarchy. Emissaries were sent by the Convention to arrest him and bring him to France. Knowing what that would lead to, Dumouriez crossed over to the enemy. His flight cost France its possession of Belgium, just recently conquered, not to mention the ensuing military debacle. By fleeing, Dumouriez saved his life, but lost his reputation and his career. He eventually finally found refuge in London, where thanks to his old connections, he was able to provide the English with valuable espionage services. Among those connections was the son of Friedrich II, Landgrave of Hesse-Kassel, whose first wife was Princess Mary of Great Britain, which made the King of England his father-in-law. His son Karl[41] also later Landgrave of Hesse-Kassel (1744–1836), was, amongst other things, Stadtholder (Governor) of the Duchies of Schleswig and Holstein, which meant that he had access to information about Napoleon's ship-building activity in Boulogne. It had long been known that Napoleon was planning an invasion of Britain from the Continent, and since Pitt's second appointment to the premiership in 1804, he had given much attention to the expansion of the Royal Navy and had seen to the improvement of coastal defences.

The anxious and overriding question for Pitt and Lord Charles Camden, Secretary of War, was obviously: *when* would Napoleon launch the invasion? The letters in question deal with precisely this question. Dumouriez believed that he could reveal the date of the attack and supported plans which envisaged the destruction of the French invasion fleet in their base at Boulogne.

First, the General committed the indiscretion of showing the revealing letters of his friend Karl von Hesse-Kassel to Pitt and Camden. The information, if accurate, had come not a day too soon; evidently, the invasion plans were already well underway, which made the timing of its discovery all the more essential. Such insights into the enemy's cards could be decisive for the outcome of the war. The General forecast that an attack on the English coast would take place in July. 'My Lord,' wrote Dumouriez to Camden,

> I have the honour of sending you the extract of a letter from Paris, which I beg you to forward to Mr. Pitt if you judge it necessary. All my correspondence from the Continent forecasts the attack for July, but I believe that this will be preceded by the Holstein attack, perhaps to unite the Danish navy with the flotilla at Texel, either by force or by agreement. I drew the attention of my close friend Prince Karl of Hesse to this danger a long time ago. I have included one of his letters which contains some thoughts worth consideration. I shall call on you on Wednesday at two o'clock to collect the Prince's letter....[42]

Then follows the Prince's letter to Dumouriez, which, among other things, first reads:

> ...The return of Mr. Pitt is a great event. You will remember, I am sure, that he has long been my hero. His outstanding genius, his wisdom and his energy will save England even were the invasion to succeed, which I consider almost *impossible*. In the meantime, be prepared for the attempt to be made at any moment. Bonaparte must do something very big if he wants to become a real Emperor. At the moment he has to appear very peace-loving to the Continent if he wishes to be recognised by the Powers. He will therefore stage the invasion in order to silence those who are envious and dissatisfied, and there are many of them. You can count on the fact that he will be completely in the trap by July at the latest. And then come what may! He will certainly be there, and that will be the great moment that will determine everything. One could wager a thousand to one at the moment that he will lose then, but the *one* thing could happen and the invasion could take place. However, since some of the disaffected in the country will not be wholly behind him, which I cannot imagine will be the case in England, he and his army will be lost...[43]

Written nine days later on 31st April 1804, the Prince's second letter also deals with Napoleon and his intentions.

> Since the declaration of the Emperor of Russia in Paris there has been a change of theatre, which displeases me. Bernadotte has just taken over

command of the army of Hannover. That is certainly only for show, but war on the Continent may follow.

The sudden proclamation of Napoleon I as Emperor is truly remarkable. It will have great consequences. No unhappy ones for the King, who I believe, will thereby be reinstated in all his rights and for whom the situation will perhaps be easier than it might have been otherwise. We anticipate major events, above all in Italy. Do you remember what I told you about Rome? Great things are being prepared there, and will come blow by blow. To be recognised, Bonaparte needs peace above all, and this is therefore the first act in his play. May God grant that England, and above all London, does not sleep through it and that it will be considered right to conclude a peace, but without disarmament and without all this farrago of nonsense!

Do you know anyone in the new Ministry? Farewell, dear general. I embrace you. Charles.[44]

Included in this correspondence was a letter from Paris that reported on a command of the Emperor's that the embarkation of the ships of the invasion fleet be accelerated.

Paris, 1st June,
Orders have gone out from the rg. [?] to accelerate the embarkation. He will soon betake himself there, and Bernadotte will soon attack Holstein. An attack from the rear will now be able to destroy him more easily. Talleyrand receives his orders through the Abbé Sièyes, who prompts the place he is to occupy. I doubt that the laggard Talleyrand will die in his bed. Réal is of the opinion that he should be put on trial. Captain Wright has had his money taken away which is being returned to him louis for louis. It would be possible to render him some assistance. I cannot describe to you the consternation, fear and dissatisfaction of the French. Morgan will be employed for the army against Denmark...[45]

Then Dumouriez turns again to the Secretary for War personally to assure him that the destruction of the invasion fleet in Boulogne would definitely be possible. On 30th July 1804 he writes to Camden:

Captain Congreve had enough confidence in my experience to ask me for my opinion with regard to the important memorandum that he has to submit to the Minister concerning the destruction of the fleet at Boulogne. I believed that I needed to represent my opinion to him and I dare

> to say that I do not doubt the outcome, provided that all the conditions listed in the memorandum, which is a credit to his genius as well as to his patriotism, are fulfilled. He consulted with us on more than one point, and I would ask you to name the day when I might have the honour of meeting you.[46]

What were these papers that were potentially of decisive importance for the outcome of the war doing in Stanhope's hands? To what end were they entrusted to him? It is not unthinkable that Pitt, in the last phase of his second ministry and faced with a direct threat to his country, entrusted the brother of his beloved niece with a mission for which the possession of the letters was imperative. The fact that they had been handed over to him, the Prime Minister's personal agent, must have been connected with the expected invasion, which would have to be countered with all available means, including counter-espionage. Did they serve Philip Henry as evidence in black and white to convince others that the hour had struck and that counter-measures would now have to be devised?

3. Founding a Family

Mission to Sicily, 1803–1813

After his return home, the 22-year-old Lord Mahon decided to marry. His choice fell on Catherine Lucy, the fourth daughter of Robert Smith, first Baron Carrington, whom he took as his wife on 18th November 1803.

After only a few months, it became clear that affection alone would not suffice to guarantee the continuance of the marriage. The Vice-Governorship of Dover Castle, which Pitt had made available, provided no adequate foundation for the family's future, and it therefore seemed advisable to seek a reconciliation with his father. Also, Dover Castle, frequently battered by sea storms, was by no means ideal for a prolonged stay, so as soon as possible a move was made to the coastal fortress of Walmer Castle (Fig. 35, 36), further along the coast to the East and much more homely. There lived Pitt, who, amongst his other responsibilities, was Warden of the Cinque Ports, and Philip Henry's half-sister, Hester.

Philip Henry wrote to his father: 'I should indeed feel doubly happy if that event [Philip Henry's marriage—*Ed.*] were to procure me an opportunity of being restored to your paternal regards, of which it has always been a matter of the deepest regret to me that any circumstances should have deprived me and which it is the earnest wish of my heart to regain. I shall ever continue, my dear father, your very dutiful and affectionate son.'[47]

That was something the elder Stanhope, due to his own very different experience, could not believe. Reconciliation of the kind proposed by his son would have required soul qualities which the father simply did not possess, and it was not surprising that his answer was courteous but unbending. The situation was not helped by the fact that his son's protector was the odious Pitt.

'My dear son,' he replied,

> Your happiness and real welfare have ever been objects too near to my heart for me not to feel a lively interest in the coming event. I most cordially wish that it may in every respect contribute, as I hope it will, to your felicity ... That you may ever respectively promote each other's happiness is my sincere prayer to that infinite Being, on Whom all events

35. Walmer Castle on the Channel coast, with a view to the sea.

36. The view from the coast at Walmer Castle.

> depend. You know me; and you must be certain that my views are and ever have been uniformly directed towards the happiness of my fellow-men. I shall be frank. Your close connection with Mr Pitt and certain other persons of his acquaintance will certainly prevent our being reconciled. But be assured that I shall never cease to have towards you the love and warm feelings of an affectionate parent.[48]

Despite its fine words, this amounted to a refusal, and did not get Philip Henry, who was looking to provide financial security for his family, any step further. He was counting on a sum of £1200 and a yearly allowance of £800, but all efforts to deal with his unrelenting father came to nothing. After this failure, Philip Henry tried to involve Pitt, who had even less chance of breaking the stubbornness of the old man. 'I am very much grieved and rather surprised (after what had passed),' wrote Pitt to Mahon, then still in Dover, 'at the strange letter from Lord Stanhope. It certainly puts an end to all reasonable ground of hope from that quarter, and is in the manner of it very provoking. But as no good can arise from any answer you can return to it, I think it clearly best for you to take no notice of it, and to let the business drop in silence.'[49]

Mahon also shared his vain efforts to convince his father with George Jackson, brother of his sister Hester's helpful friend:

> I had no sooner arrived in this country than I made first overtures to my Father for a reconciliation and a second time in informing him about my intended marriage to which he gave his consent and of which he expressed his perfect approbation. I renewed the offer a third time in a personal interview with him but still without success. He has permitted me however to see and correspond with my mother, and I am truly happy to see that I have found in her a tender and affectionate parent.... He expressed however a readiness to conclude with me some pecuniary agreement for our mutual benefit as two indifferent persons who had a common interest in a certain estate. These negotiations began many months ago, soon after my return, and notwithstanding the real and kind interest of his solicitor who has acted through the whole business like a very sincere friend, they have been drawn out to a most extraordinary length and reams of paper have been consumed on either side in writing 'Controversial polemical papers', as Mr. Pitt calls them.[50]

Pitt finally found two minor posts for Philip Henry, which did not require any work but brought in £1000 a year. For example, he had to act as an intermediary in Dublin for the collection of money from the Irish Treasury and for its transference to England. It would later emerge that the accounts for these revenues were kept very carelessly.

Philip Henry and Catherine had three children. Philip Henry, the later 5th Earl (d. 1875), was born on 30th January 1805, while they were still at Walmer Castle; he would become a famous historian. The other two children were George Joseph, born in 1806 (d. 1828) and a few years later, Catherine Lucy Wilhelmina (1819–1901), later the Duchess of Cleveland.

As his father remained hard-hearted and unrelenting even after the birth of his first grandson (1805), Philip Henry finally began legal proceedings against him. In March 1806 the case of 'Mahon versus Stanhope' was opened at the Chancery Court—a drama for the family and for 'society' which was to last six years. In defending his case, his father did not omit even the slightest detail of the actual or imagined offences he had suffered over the years. For example, Mahon had had a few trees cut down at Chevening without his father's knowledge, which caused the Earl to lament in court that if the son were to die before the end of the case, then it would be with the dastardly burden of having robbed the estate of £80,000 through the depletion of its woods. It is doubtful that this sum was even approximately realistic. Then the magistrates were told in great detail that Earl Stanhope was the most persecuted of men, his life having already been threatened four times, including an attempted poisoning. Although he did not consider his son a suspect on account of his age, he nevertheless felt that the good-for-nothing had demonstrated his base character; Charles even thought his son capable of patricide. If there had remained even a vestige of goodwill between father and son after Mahon's flight to Germany, the court case completely destroyed it; the last bridge between the two was broken.

Later, after Earl Stanhope's death, it emerged that already in 1805, the year of his first grandchild's birth, he had altered the effect of his will, disinheriting his children to the fullest degree legally permitted and had instead made over the remainder of his goods and property to the ten executors named in the will. After the complete rupture with his father, Philip Henry was now more than ever dependent on the helpful ideas of Pitt and on the support of his father-in-law, Lord Carrington, who began by getting him a seat in the House of Commons. Being politically of the same mind, the son-in-law tried, without much success, to support Carrington's programme in the election campaign.

It soon became evident that he was not exactly cut out for a life in the public eye. Words from a satirical song by his political opponents hit the nail on the head: 'What else can be expected of Lord Mahon than that he follows the orders of his father-in-law?' Hester had already guessed where all this would lead: 'He goes his way, but as I see it, he will never be suited to public life'—a judgement that was borne out at the first test. After these experiences, his short venture into the House of Commons was over for the time being.

But politics remained Philip Henry's passion, if not of the public kind, then of the more conspiratorial, for which he seemed to possess better talents. Conservative to the core in his thinking, he described himself as an 'old Tory of Mr. Pitt's school', though his own pessimistic outlook differed markedly from that of his great model.

In Mahon's eyes, the future was always gloomy and fateful; revolution and misfortune were always to be expected. His political confession of faith—'a Tory of Mr. Pitt's school'—is not without significance in the story of Kaspar Hauser. Insofar as Pitt had pursued and conceived of his European policy and the struggle with Napoleon, his easily influenced admirer was, in his political thinking, the exact counterpart and mouthpiece of the Prime Minister. The question of what *political* interest Stanhope could have had in the case of Kaspar Hauser is to be looked for and found in this direction.

Already in 1805, he knew that he had to make contact with Philip, Count of Artois (1757–1836), whose plans he had known of since 1802. Artois, who was to reign as King Charles X of France from 1824 was the brother of Louis XVI and of Stanislaus Xavier (1755–1824), later King Louis XVIII (1814–24). As the most prominent member of the Court party and thereby enemy of the Duke of Orléans, he had been the most vociferous and fanatical defender of the royal rights of Louis XVI, but the first to leave the King in the lurch after the fall of the Bastille. His all-too-rapid flight to England set off such a powerful wave of imitation among the leading aristocratic families that this very betrayal itself largely led to the collapse of the monarchy through inner debilitation. At the crucial moment Louis XVI was abandoned by most of his trusted confidants, and the leader of this stampede of aristocratic exiles was Artois. After the execution of the King, Stanislaus had claimed for himself the regency in the name of the seven-year-old boy he now called king—Louis XVII—who was held prisoner in the Temple in Paris. He then followed his brother into exile in England (1807) in order to claim the throne for himself as King Louis XVIII after the Dauphin had been declared dead. He named his brother Artois, Marshal of the Kingdom. In this capacity Artois took part in many fruitless invasions of France, which he obviously was not able to finance solely from his English pension of £15,000 per annum. Stanhope was in correspondence with him at Walmer Castle from 1805. He expressed his regret for the brothers' destiny and asked 'to speak about how I [Stanhope] could be of service'.[51] It was primarily the brothers' task to lead the fight against Napoleon, and Stanhope wanted to be there when Napoleon's head would roll.

After the establishment of Philip Henry's family, the death of Pitt in 1806 came as the second interruption in his formation as a diplomatic agent. How long this condition continued exactly is not yet possible to ascertain, but already by 1808, his connections with Francis Jackson were increasing again. With the planned occupation of Hanover by Prussia, Jackson had been ordered back to London from Berlin in 1806 and in 1809 received a new appointment, this time to Washington.

But Philip Henry was still not yet in a position to be able to undertake tasks himself in the area of activity originally intended for him. He and Jackson remained in touch, however, and waited for possibilities, which would most likely result from the all-consuming, never-ending conflict with France and Napoleon.

England and Austria—Allies against France

For Pitt, Stanhope, and as will be shown later, Friedrich von Gentz, Bonaparte (Fig. 37) was the figure 'in whose hands destiny now' lay (Goethe). He was the very apotheosis of a frightening, even demonic counter-principle that sought with the unscrupulousness of genius to destroy almost everything, especially the hierarchical social structures that had grown up over the centuries. With an irresistible energy, he had set himself to thoroughly revolutionise Europe, to force it away from old rotten forms and into his own new mould. As Goethe expressed it to Eckermann, 'To create new epochs in the world, two things are known to be necessary. First, that one should have a good head, and second, a good inheritance. Napoleon inherited the French Revolution.' This inheritance and the genius of the Emperor were the constant concerns of England and Austria, to name but the two states that will figure most prominently in what follows. For an old Tory—and what was Friedrich von Gentz but an old 'Austrian Tory'—the maintenance of absolute monarchy was both a fundamental fact of life and the standard of his own political actions.

37. Napoleon I (1769–1821). Copperplate engraving by Noël François Bertrand. Detail from a whole body portrait by Jacques-Louis David (1808).

How then must those two youngsters have been regarded—Kaspar Hauser and the Duke of Reichstadt, Napoleon's son from his second marriage, to Archduchess Marie-Louise of Austria, the boy who was later held under Metternich's oppressive supervision? Both were 'Napoleonids' and as such, were seen by the opponents of the House of Bonaparte as possible inheritors of the unhealthy principle of the reordering of Europe.

The fact that it was England that first stirred up, and then fought the Revolution is only an apparent contradiction, because all along, the intention was to regain control of European affairs after various complex operations had been carried out. The Revolution had many roots and reasons, and it would be an altogether one-sided interpretation to ascribe the arrangement of the whole affair entirely to England and to secret societies; such a multi-faceted, far-reaching event cannot be so simply planned and executed. The Revolution was also an inevitable part of the evolution of humanity and as such was certainly independent of the wishes and designs behind England's continental politics. Nevertheless, there did come from England *one* of the driving forces that was mixed up in this event—and not the weakest.[52]

Since the end of the 18th century England had specifically dealt with Europe in the context of imperial designs and actions. As Napoleon put it to Las Cases on St. Helena:

> Pitt had command of European politics. He had the moral destiny of the nations in his hands, and he made a bad business of it…Future generations will realise this and will see him as a scourge. This man who was so highly prized in his time will one day come to be seen as an evil genius. I do not consider him cruel, I do not even doubt that in his innermost being he was convinced that he was acting rightly. Many believed they were behaving honourably on St Bartholomew's Eve! [the St. Bartholomew's Eve Massacre of the Huguenots in Paris, 1572—*transl.*] The Pope and the cardinals ordered a Te Deum to be sung and among them were many who believed in their honourable intentions.

Napoleon had little reason indeed to entertain friendly memories of English secret diplomacy. 'It is of little account,' the British chargé d'affaires Drake had revealed in Munich, 'who brings the animal [Bonaparte] to ground; you must only all be prepared to hunt him.' There were consequences. 'The situation became ever more tragic. About 40 conspirators, murderers, and others were arrested who had been supplied with plans, armed with daggers and paid with English gold.'[53] There had already been a conspiracy against Napoleon in 1800. Suspicion fell first on Abbé Godart, in whose house documents were discovered, 'which made it clear that the assassins were in the pay of the English government'. In 1804, Napoleon had the Duke of Enghien arrested in neutral Baden and shot in Vincennes Castle; he was accused of 'stockpiling arms for use against the Republic and of being in the pay of England'. And so on. 'On the basis of official evidence I can point to more than thirty conspirators who sought my life,' said Napoleon to Las Cases, 'quite apart from the many who have certainly remained unknown.' The Emperor reckoned most of them were instigated by the British.

It may be objected that Napoleon's suspicions in this connection were unjustified or that Pitt had no personal involvement in these conspiracies, which is most likely, but that England's agents, the so-called 'Hanoverian envoys',[54] did carry out such operations stands as proven. In relation to our theme, there is also the need to consider the role of Austria and the two statesmen Prince Clemens von Metternich (1773–1859) and Friedrich von Gentz (1764–1832) (Fig.54)

When, after the end of the failed peace congress in Rastatt in 1799, two of the three French envoys Roberjot, Bonnier and Debry, were killed by Szekler Hussars—troops under Austrian command—because it was hoped that important papers detrimental to Prussia would be found on them, Friedrich von Gentz of the Prussian War Ministry, in a widely noted article, 'On the Murder of the French Envoys to the Congress', took the side of Austria and also England, which first brought him to the attention of London, and a golden snuffbox from Emperor Franz I of Austria. His assertion of Austria's innocence could later not be sustained. 'Fifteen years later,' wrote Gentz to Prokesch, 'I discovered the opposite was true.'

London was delighted with Gentz's essay; such unexpected support deserved a reward. At that time, 'it was in the Spring of 1800 that Gentz first received money from the English: £500 from the Foreign Secretary, Lord Grenville'.[55] For his first visit to Gentz in Vienna

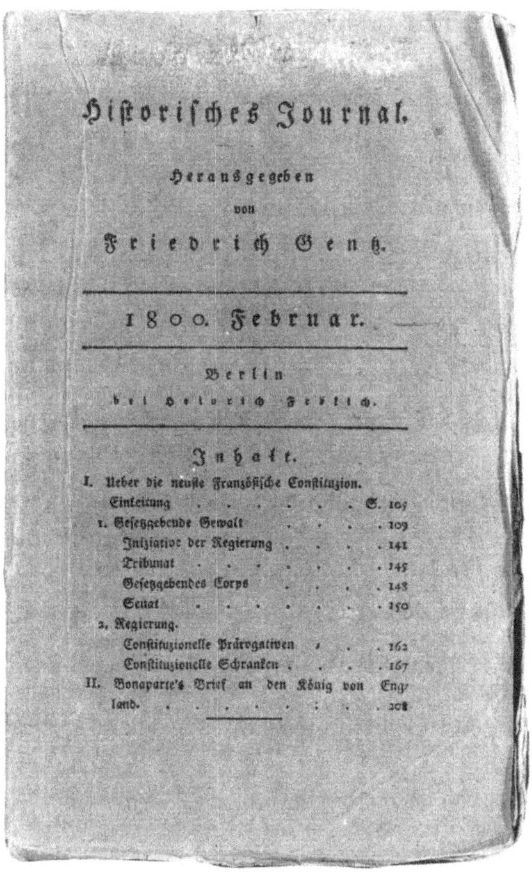
Historisches Journal.

Herausgegeben

von

Friedrich Gentz.

1800. Februar.

Berlin

bei Heinrich Frölich.

Inhalt.

I. Ueber die neuste Französische Constituzion.
Einleitung . . . . . . S. 105
1. Gesetzgebende Gewalt 109
Iniziative der Regierung 141
Tribunat 145
Gesetzgebendes Corps 148
Senat 150
2. Regierung.
Constituzionelle Prärogativen . . . 162
Constituzionelle Schranken 167
II. Bonaparte's Brief an den König von England. 208

38. Title page of the 'Historical Journal' published by Friedrich Gentz.

in 1816, Philip Henry's mother, Louisa Grenville, may have referred her son to the good old family connections which had been so helpful to the young Prussian military counsellor at the beginning of his political career. When, for example, Gentz fell into financial difficulties over his self-published *Historical Journal* (Fig. 38), Lord Grenville who, like Gentz, was a passionate supporter of Pitt's war policy against France, came to his assistance. Gentz wrote to the Foreign Secretary through the British ambassador in Berlin, Lord Carysford: 'that the diabolically clever French propaganda would definitely have to be confronted, [and] that he could no longer maintain his journal and needed money'.[56]

Grenville accepted his proposal. 'After that, money came irregularly whenever London saw fit to send it—£100, £1000. Gentz, who ten years earlier had begun to write as a young defender of philosophical virtue about rights and freedom, was now an international agent, secretly highly-paid—a dangerous position of the kind no-one before him had ever had in Germany.'[57]

From this time on, Gentz saw himself as an active defender and interpreter of English interests, and even Pitt had his well-informed writings translated. In Gentz there had unexpectedly appeared a brilliant writer with a keen political mind who fought unreservedly for British interests, and with notable success; this was something unique and sensational. It was thus inevitable that 'Pitt's agent' would receive an invitation to London, which came in 1802. His reception was unprecedented. According to an article in the *Morning Post*:

> Mr Gentz has just left the service of Prussia for that of Austria, and the reception extended to him by the whole of London was certainly more friendly than any foreign private visitor to this capital has ever received. But precisely the universality of the favour shown to him is sufficient proof that it is based on personal achievement and well-deserved fame, without any admixture of secret political intentions. It was in no wise restricted to a particular [political] party. Mr. Addington and Lord Hawkesbury competed with one another before the famous writer. No secret reasoning is required to explain why Englishmen of all parties show their gratitude to this most capable defender of England...[58]

Grenville was greatly impressed by Gentz and later spoke of him enthusiastically: 'When he came to England, he visited me immediately and asked to make the acquaintance of Fox, of my brother, and of the other great men of the day. I invited them to luncheon with Gentz and myself. They came and were so delighted with the Prussian statesman that they declared that they wished to dine with us the following day also.'

Gentz then took up his post at the Viennese court for which he received 4000 guilders a year from the Emperor and another £1000 from England. 'For this he was expected to influence Austrian politics in a British direction and to provide periodic reports, advice and propaganda.'[59] Pitt and Gentz corresponded personally from that time on, which may also have facilitated the beginnings of Philip Henry's later activities in Vienna. To have the Grenvilles and Chathams [Pitts] as relatives was a first-class recommendation for any diplomatic venture.

'My hatred of France,' wrote Gentz, early in the new century,

> of this faithless, vain, small-minded, arrogant, blasphemous, villainous usurper who through the infamy of his contemporaries has screwed his way, first to greatness and then to the insanity of greatness, has now become a passion, the only one which consumes my innermost being. If today someone were to prophesy with certainty that I would never contribute to the downfall of this monster, then life would be for me from this day onwards a loathsome burden.

State Counsellor Gentz gave vent to countless other such statements. But how could this mind, which in its way knew with certainty what a genius nevertheless resided in the 'blasphemous, villainous usurper', have come to such astonishing judgements? Goethe, who did not feel compelled to observe life from the viewpoint of the [Vienna] Hofburg, came to a comparable but completely different conclusion:

> Napoleon was quite a fellow! Always inspired, always clear and decisive, and at every hour endowed with sufficient energy to set to work immediately on that which he had recognised to be advantageous and necessary. His life was the progress of a demigod from battle to battle and from victory to victory. One could very well say of him that he found himself in a condition of constant inspiration, which is why his destiny was so brilliant that the world before him did not see it and perhaps will not see it after him either.—Yes, Yes, my dear friend, he was quite a fellow, the like of whom we shall certainly not see again!

Gentz and Metternich must have been disturbed, even panicked by the appearance of this epochal figure—others could hardly comprehend the attacks made against 'this compendium of the world' (Goethe) or the vituperativeness of the scorn and revengeful feelings directed against him after his downfall.

The scale of the threat determined the choice of allies. The strongest partner was England, with whose most important head Gentz remained in contact. Between 1806 and 1809, after the death of Pitt, he received from London '£4,500—more than an under-secretary gets.'[60] He obtained the services of the Krauss brothers, who he employed as secret couriers. They were available at any time to take information secretly to England.

Then happened the incomprehensible event, the catastrophe, when Gentz almost lost his reason: in 1810, out of pure calculation, Metternich arranged the alliance between Napoleon and the House of Habsburg on the assumption that the future son-in-law would keep his distance from the Emperor Franz and Austria. Napoleon was prepared to enter into such a deal with one of the Great Powers, because he perhaps thought like Metternich that his wife's father would never become his enemy; in this he was to be disappointed. Apart from Russia and Austria, there were no other parties of equal standing, and to the master of Europe there did not seem any point from dynastic considerations in extending his hand to a *second-rate power*—that is what his not exactly small family was there for. When on 6th February the news came from St. Petersburg that the Princess Anna, who had just turned 15, wished to stay true to her faith and wanted to have her own Russian chapel in the Tuileries as well as a number of Russian priests, Napoleon decided in favour of Austria.

Metternich wrote to his wife, who was then in Paris:

> All Vienna is speaking only of the marriage. One can hardly believe how all circles are going on about it, how popular it has become. If I were the saviour of the world, I could not have been showered with more good wishes and honours for my part in this, which in the opinion of everyone have been well deserved. With my next preferral, I shall receive the [Order of the] Golden Fleece, and it can indeed be said that I did not steal it.

On the 11th March the solemn wedding of the Emperor Napoleon and the 18-year-old Archduchess Marie Louise took place in the Augustiner Church, with Marshall Berthier standing in for the Emperor. Vienna had transformed itself into a sea of flowers; garlands, wreaths and illuminated pictures decorated the houses, and in the Kärtnerstrasse it was written:

> The two Emperors are friends, so we light up the houses!

The sentiments expressed by this naïve verse drove Gentz to fury. Not wishing even to watch the evening firework displays from a distance, let alone leave his house, he threw himself on his bed weeping, no longer able to understand the world.

*

On the 19th March 1811 Napoleon held his son, 'the King of Rome', in his arms and felt deeply moved. His happiness over the arrival of Napoleon II, the paternal care and gentleness he showed the infant, were something special in the life of the great commander, who could apparently, quite untouched, lose hundreds of thousands of his soldiers—his 'children', as he called them—and sacrifice the armies of his allies when necessary. He later said to Metternich in Dresden: 'On my campaign to Moscow I lost 300,000 men', and with a certain satisfaction, he added: 'There were not more than 30,000 Frenchmen amongst them.' But faced with this one child, his son, 'he wept emotionally…fat tears streamed from his eyes……the mere happiness of being a father had softened this soul, which had hardly seemed to be touched by the most glorious victories and the most sincere displays of public enthusiasm' (Constant Wairy). 'He never let the little one go,' recalled Méneval, 'sometimes he would simply switch off the great thoughts which unceasingly moved his mind, and would lie down on the floor with his beloved son and play with him with the informality of a big child, whose sole concern was to amuse the infant or spare him any disappointment.'

The campaign against Russia began the following year. The Emperor travelled to Dresden to assure himself once more of the loyalty of his allies, the German princes. On the 29th May he moved East. After the great fire of Moscow, when returning via Smolensk, a courier brought news from Karlsruhe. The chamberlain von Hainau brought the happy news that on the 29th September, Napoleon's adopted daughter Stéphanie, the Grand Duchess of Baden, had given birth to a healthy son. Following the birth of the King of Rome, this was the Emperor's second heir, who would one day inherit a throne that was both strategically and politically significant; the Emperor himself wished to become the godfather of this prince of Baden.

But on the 17th October, the prince 'died' under mysterious circumstances without having been given a name and after a merely perfunctory emergency baptism; his confused mother at first accepted the death. The disturbing news was brought to Napoleon at his headquarters at Vyazma by Major Hennenhofer. The unhappy Stéphanie wrote to her adopted father on 20th December 1812:

> I was so happy, Sire, to be able to tell you that I had a son and to ask you to cherish him and protect him. A son allowed me to forget many troubles and was indeed very necessary for my position, the duties of which often weigh heavily upon me. I have had to abandon all my hopes; only the certain knowledge of Your Majesty's sympathy gives me the courage to bear this misfortune....[61]

Mission to Sicily

Philip Henry was at this time a young man of 31, concerned for the support of his growing family. His sons, Philip and George, had been born in 1805 and the following year, and his expenses well exceeded his income of £1200. The situation could not go on. A look back over the past few years must have made clear to him that it had been a mistake to have interrupted the political career begun with Pitt's help. The death of the Prime Minister and his own marriage had occurred at almost the same time so that the newlyweds were at first understandably obliged to stay at home. But now external problems pressed one after the other, and it became necessary to reconnect with the ideas of Pitt and Jackson. It may have been the latter who was on the lookout for suitable missions, and the candidate did not have long to wait.

The destination was Sicily. There were tensions and dissatisfactions in the relationship between England and the King of the Two Sicilies, Ferdinand IV (1751–1825) (Fig. 39), whose rump state of Sicily England had committed to protect. Ferdinand's arch-conservative court was known for its lavish, incomparable corruption. As the Kingdom of Naples had been under the rule of the Spanish Bourbons since 1735, Ferdinand's entry into the alliance against France in 1793 had been inevitable. Bonaparte's victories in northern Italy, however, had forced the court to agree to a ceasefire with France, which was not even disturbed by the anchoring of Admiral Nelson's fleet in Naples during his pursuit of the French to Egypt.

39. *Ferdinand IV, King of the Two Sicilies (1715–1825).*

40. *Maria Carolina, Archduchess of Austria, Queen of the Two Sicilies (1752–1814)*

At the side of the weak and incapable Ferdinand was the actual ruler of the kingdom, Queen Maria Carolina (1752–1814) (Fig. 40), daughter of Empress Maria Theresa and sister to Marie Antoinette, who had been executed in the name of the Revolution. Maria Carolina encouraged and organised the struggle against Napoleon with the help of her father Emperor Franz I of Austria, who sent the ageing and unlucky Field Marshal Karl Mack, Baron von Leiberich (1752–1828) to Italy to reorganise the defeated Neapolitan army.

Once again, three years later in 1798, Ferdinand marched his army against Rome, and the city was taken at the end of November after a fearful bloodbath. The occupation lasted for just a month. Putting up little resistance to the oncoming French forces, Ferdinand's ill-equipped troops retreated back to the coast, and Bonaparte reoccupied Naples.

The King and Queen fled to Sicily on Nelson's flagship, and in January 1799 Field Marshal Mack agreed to a second ceasefire with France. After the French had quit Naples in May, only three months passed before Ferdinand and Carolina returned. Peace did not last long. In 1805 the War of the Third Coalition against France broke out, and in contravention of the terms of the ceasefire of 1799, Carolina opened the port of Naples to the British fleet. Napoleon replied with a terse but definitive decree: 'The Bourbon dynasty in Naples has ceased to exist.' The Emperor's forces drove Ferdinand and Carolina from their thrones a second time, and Naples received as its new ruler Napoleon's brother Joseph, and from 1808, his brother-in-law, Joachim Murat.

Under the protection of the British fleet, Ferdinand and Carolina established their court in Palermo and had to allow themselves to be governed by the British envoy and commander-in-chief of the British forces stationed there, Lord William Henry Bentinck (1774–1839). In constant conflict with Carolina, Bentinck was the de facto ruler of the island and he gave the state a constitution on a British model. The consequence was an unceasing opposition between hostile factions and parties which coalesced at different times around Ferdinand, Carolina or Bentinck. Two groups in particular fought each other for years: the 'peace party' of the Marchese di Gallos and the 'war party' of Queen Carolina, which was supported by Sir John Acton. The 'war party' gained its first success when Nelson destroyed the French fleet at Aboukir on the 22nd September 1798 and again after Trafalgar. But such victories at sea were countered by defeats on land, for three times Bonaparte had forced the court to flee from Naples to Palermo, which gave an impetus to the 'peace party'. It was into this unpredictable situation of the Neapolitan court at Palermo that Stanhope now entered.

*

In Portsmouth on 10th March 1812, a clearly reluctant Philip Henry embarked, with his wife and children on the *Serapis* under Captain Lloyd, bound for Portland. 'I hate and detest long sea voyages more than I can say', but he could no longer decline the mission. 'Is it not offensive to be forced to stay in a place whether I will or no?.....But….' as he wrote elsewhere: 'I am but a humble servant of events.'[62] A most eventful voyage was about to begin. At the first destination, still on the English coast, the family transferred to the *Perlorus*, under Captain Rowly, who intended to head southwest to Plymouth but was already forced to seek safety in Torquay harbour. On the 20th, now again on the *Serapis*, with a still stronger wind and in a rough sea, the attempt was made once more to gain the open sea. After four hours of vain efforts the ship had to return to Torquay. In the morning after a stormy night, the *Serapis* broke its moorings, the anchor chain shattered, and the anchor sank to the bottom of the harbour. A second anchor, 4.700 kg in weight, was left on the ground but was also lost.

On the 21st, the ship was finally able to depart. But after a few hours, it was buffeted by powerful squalls which terrified the frightened passengers and crew. For the rest of his life, Philip Henry was to remember the tortures of the journey, the feared power of the equinoctial storms that by day or night gave him and the *Serapis* such distress. At seven knots an hour and in ever stormier seas the frigate struggled on by night from the 22nd to the 23rd past the island of Ushant—today the Ile d'Ouessant—and with a slight shudder, the passengers could make out in the distance lights shimmering peacefully on the enemy coast.

In view of the military situation, it was necessary to maintain a course well off the coast of France. On the 8th April a position of latitude 47°48'00' north and 47°55'00' west was reached, and a course was set for Cape Finisterre, which came into sight three days later. On the 13th in the Bay of Biscay the weather was clear, sunny and warm and at nighttime one could look all around at the mysterious lights of the sea. Before Captain Lloyd put in at Gibraltar on the 21st April at 10 a.m., passengers and crew, not without patriotic emotions, passed by Cape Trafalgar, where seven years before Lord Nelson in his last great sea battle had inflicted such a catastrophic defeat upon Bonaparte's fleet and had himself been killed by a musket-ball in his spine.

On the following two days, to port Philip Henry enjoyed views of the mountains of the Sierra Nevada surrounding Granada; their snow-capped peaks were clearly visible off the Spanish coast. To starboard lay the coast of Africa—modern Algeria—from where on the 1st May a cuckoo and a woodpigeon flew to the *Serapis* and remained for a while perched on the ship's rigging. From there the voyage did not go on directly to Palermo, which would have been nearer but, on the 17th March first stopped at Malta. The governor, General Oaks, and Generals Spencer and Campbell did the honours of showing Mahon around the fortress and of explaining its significance. Looking out from its parapets and down from its signal tower, the visitor from distant London gained a precise impression of the strategic importance of the island and its fortress. Accompanied by Col. Wright, he climbed St. George's Tower, which had been rebuilt after being struck by lightning, from where ships could be seen far out to sea, a matter of life-or-death significance to the defence of Malta. On one of his visits Philip Henry witnessed an escape attempt by a French prisoner of war who had sought to jump into the sea from the sheer rocks of the murderous cliff face. 'His fate deterred all the others. When I saw him, all his bones were broken…'

On the morning of the 28th March, his journey continued finally to Sicily on board the gunboat *Cephalus*, 'that frightful prison that is called a ship', under Captain Clifford. On the 30th Philip Henry reached the port of Messina and collapsed, completely exhausted, in 'upper apartments' of the palace of Princess Ceramis. From there he went on excursions into the neighbourhood, which sometimes entailed small adventures. He wrote to his mother:

> I shall now tell you about my last sea trip, which was very fine, which took us as far as the island of Lipari; but then we had strong winds which forced us to return to Milazzo. The Mediterranean is very often subject to these powerful, unpredictable and rainy winds, which are called squalls in England and Burrasce here. They start up at a moment's notice with a frightful violence and cease just as suddenly, not before one would wish but before one would expect. We ended up in Milazzo in a boat which was not very large, buffeted by the winds and enveloped by a frightful swarm of flies, bugs and midges. You can imagine how happy we were to get to land, but there was hardly any accommodation to be had, even though there were 9000 inhabitants and four battalions of soldiers in the town. A certain need, from which no-one is excepted and to which even the King must attend, enabled one of us to make the acquaintance of a Baroness of Milazzo who with great friendliness and hospitality offered us lodging for as long as the winds continued. We stayed with her for ten days, and I shall always remember this estimable family with the greatest gratitude.[63] [Translated from the French—*Ed.*]

After a few days the family travelled back to Palermo.

> We have found here a very pleasant house in a wonderful location with a view that every day provides us with new delights, the best air one can imagine and a really large garden with a fountain, orange trees, and a vine arbour. The house was, however, completely unfurnished and I was forced to buy a few tables and chairs. I had beds and a dinner service brought from Catania, for in a country like this one often travels with baggage the like of which one sees nowhere else.[64]

As for the land and people of Sicily, Philip Henry expresses generalised judgements of a kind which have long been quite conventional: 'The Sicilians do not appear to wish to cultivate any plants. They prefer to stroll along the streets and the seashore, to play cards and sit in coffee houses, instead of occupying themselves with plants.' With few exceptions, he encountered only 'idiots and scoundrels' who, as he wrote in letters home were richly blessed with other qualities:

> As people here are in general very lazy, they spend a great deal of time chatting with one another on the street or in cafés. This results not only in an awful noise but also in many calumnies. A further result is that those belonging to the nobility, who as a rule have not travelled widely, have but narrow horizons and do not concern themselves with reading. They therefore do not exactly shine in conversation... Everything here made of gold and silver is of appalling taste or is entirely lacking in taste and shows itself merely as ugliness...The town is dreadful. Robberies are numerous and there are murder attempts every night which often turn out fatally. Houses often carry the stamp of mistrust, for sometimes one no longer wishes to open the door even in the daytime without asking first: who is there? Or: what do you want?[65]

The well-travelled British governor, Lord Bentinck, was well acquainted with the situation. Sicily was the most barbaric land he had known. 'There is no law here' and he repeated to Mahon on a number of occasions: 'You have no idea of the savage murders which are committed here.' Bentinck several times mentioned that 'it had not even been possible to convict some Sicilians known to have committed five murders', because they had been protected by the locals.

In early July 1812, not far from Palermo, Philip Henry suffered a rare probable epileptic seizure which he wondered about for the rest of his life. With 'a still unsteady hand' he reported to his mother a 'rather strong shock' which, followed by a loss of consciousness, had torn him from his body for a short time. 'I shall always remember it for I experienced sensations which I had never had before on any other occasions: powerful cramps which caused me to scream with fright and finally, the presentiment of imminent death, which seemed to be borne out by the swoon which followed... But after a while I came back to myself again.'[66]

Two priests passing by—Diego Bonnelli and Antonio die Giacomo—were the first to assist him and managed to get the victim on to his feet again. Philip Henry emphasised in his letter several times how awful this experience had been. It was so extraordinary that he had 'never understood how these extremely remarkable symptoms were produced'. It is noteworthy that the fact that he could not understand the cause apparently disquieted Stanhope, as he had never experienced such a misfortune in the previous thirty years. (It was the summer of 1812. At this time, the Grand Duchess Stéphanie of Baden was looking forward to the birth of her second child, the Crown prince, who was born on the 29th September.) Such a seizure never recurred throughout Stanhope's life, and the unique event had no adverse consequences for his health. Immediately after regaining consciousness, it appeared that the attack had taken place with no negative effects, at least on the medical side. This seems borne out by the fact that soon afterwards, Philip Henry had his first reception at court.

His relationship with Queen Carolina developed more favourably than that with her husband Ferdinand, perhaps owing to the fact that showing marks of favour to this new envoy from London made it much easier to use him against the governor, with whom Carolina was at odds more than ever before. 'I conversed at length with the Queen this morning.' Such conversations could not be kept hidden from Bentinck.

Mahon was very satisfied by such a warm reception at court. He reported to his mother that:

> The court is brilliant, although there are not so many courtiers. Court is held but occasionally and always lasts only for a short time. Neither can I affirm that the Crown prince always takes sufficient care of his honour. When the Queen was last here, she was good enough to call me to the palace and spoke with me for an hour in her drawing room. When I was at Catania, she graciously sent me a message in which she expressed a wish to see me. I was delighted to have the opportunity to admire her prodigious talents in person and to experience the charm and amiability of her conversation. Since then, I have received some other communications from Her Majesty, and I am to spend a few days in the countryside with the King and Queen.

From these first meetings numerous others were to follow, and in the course of his stay of fifteen months in Sicily a relationship of trust developed between Stanhope and the royal couple which, in terms of his mission to the island, had the desired effect. From London's viewpoint, that could mean two things: firstly, that certain insights could be gained into the state of relationships at court, and secondly, that the 'war party'—that is, Queen Carolina—gained visible support against the high-handed Bentinck. What seemed to Mahon worthy of note, he wrote down and sent to England:

Pray tell L.C. [Lord Carrington — *Ed.*) that the Ministry is totally changed & and that a new one has been formed, like the Addington administration, without calling to Office the heads of the Opposition. Prince Belmonte, late Minister for Foreign Affairs, has been succeeded by Duke Lucchesi, an infirm old man who is a friend of the King, [p.110] with whom he plays at cards. Prince Villarmosa, the Minister of Finance, is replaced by the Marquis Ferreri, who is said to possess considerable talents & to be of the Court Party. He is very fond of Botany and Gardening. The Office of Minister of the Interior (or as it is called here, 'of Grace & Justice'), which was filled by Prince Carini, is now occupied by the Duke d'Averna (alias Duke di Gualtieri), and the Brigadier Naselli has become Minister for the Army and Marine instead of Ruggiero Selkino (brother to the Prince of Fitali). President of the House of Lords Prince Villa Franca has also resigned his situation under pretence of bad health. It is supposed that the late Ministers will continue to absent themselves from Parliament, in which case their party, as feeble in numbers as it is in talents, will gradually dissolve. It remains to be seen what course will be pursued by the Opposition in the House of Commons, or who will be found to conduct the affairs of Government in that House. The manner in which speeches are generally delivered there is extremely unnatural & absurd & very much resembles the tone in which 'last Dying Speeches' are cried about the Streets of London. I am surprised that no official situation should at the late change of Government have been offered to Prince Butera, who is the first Prince & greatest landed Proprietor in the island. His income, which however is much burthened with Debt, is said to be 80,000 pounds sterling & as he has always been a very kind and indulgent Landlord it is believed he could without difficulty draw fifty thousand of his Vassals into arms whenever he thought proper. His high rank, his vast possessions, his just popularity and his influence with the people would have given extraordinary weight to an Administration. He is Director-General of the Volunteers but at present lives at the Bagrasia & neither attends Parliament nor would he accept the situation which was offered to him of President of the House of Lords. He was formerly a zealous adherent of the Court and used to speak in a boasting style of the great feats which he could perform. That reached the ears of Ld.Wm.B. [Lord William Bentinck, Britain's plenipotentiary on the island—*Ed.*) who sent for him & told him that if he opposed the new order of things he should be sent into exile to a barren island near Sicily. To which Prince Butera, as he himself told me, made this reply: 'How can you suppose that I, who have so much to lose, can wish to promote a disturbance? So far from it, I have myself stopped several revolutions in this country!'[67]

Inevitable, but certainly also foreseen, was the first audience with Bentinck himself, on which Mahon commented with an interesting reserve: '....We were received in a most welcoming manner by my Lord and my Lady W. Bentinck, who seem to me to be in their private lives most estimable people.' Lord Bentinck held receptions twice a month, which Mahon always attended. His relationship with the Governor, however, hardly went beyond the limits of prescribed convention.

It was otherwise with the Queen, who showed him extraordinary kindness after he had been in Sicily only a short time, as is evident from a letter of thanks Philip Henry wrote to her on the 18th December 1812:

> Madame, I treasure the goodwill with which Your Majesty honours me and I am truly appreciative of the graciousness Your Majesty has bestowed on me in sending the wild boar, which was roasted for me this morning. I beg Your Majesty to do me the honour of accepting this expression of my humblest thanks and to believe in my deep and respectful feelings of devotion for You....[68]

Such marks of favour, which were repeated in the course of time, were not coincidental. Mahon's activities in Palermo were apparently so adroit that Carolina even felt obliged to acknowledge them in writing. For example, doubtless owing to his social position, it was not only possible for him to obtain 'medicines from the British headquarters' whenever the need arose but also a sea trip from Palermo to Catania, for which he put in 'a request for two gunboats' as he was forced to take the route from Messina that was within sight of the French-occupied mainland. 'Instead of which,' complained Stanhope, 'Brigadier Hall sent only one, the 'Mistika', which he said was the best in the flotilla under his command.' On another occasion an excursion was taken by gunboat to Milazzo, where the party inspected the citadel.

The details of all Mahon's activities in support of the royal House are not known, but out of a feeling of gratitude the Queen did not want to neglect 'to express how touched I have been by everything you have done for the King, my husband and for all our unfortunate family'.[69] The one so honoured must himself have been only too convinced of this. At an appropriate time he wrote to His Majesty of the 'services I have already rendered to Your Royal Crown', which must have referred to some prior concrete actions. Contrary to all convention, Philip Henry reminded Ferdinand of these services rendered and asked in an unashamed if nevertheless extremely decorous manner to be given the decoration of the 'Order of St. Januarius'.

On the 21st February 1813 he took up his pen and, after an unctuous introduction, wrote to Ferdinand that

> When I have had the fortune and great happiness to have rendered services to Your Majesty which express my enthusiasm then I would not fear so much to approach Your Royal Throne, indeed, then I could wholeheartedly and with full devotion dedicate myself to You in the most loyal of service. Since Your Majesty meanwhile had the goodness to judge me favourably, it would be the greatest joy for me to receive a sign of those feelings which Your Majesty has expressed to me. Allow me therefore to hope that Your Majesty will deign to decorate me with the sash of the Order of St. Januarius. I cannot say how great a joy it would be for me, which in every respect calls forth a true ambition and which is a real treasure. Humbly, I kiss Your Hand......[70]

In 1813 'the Order of St. Januarius' with its motto *In sanguine foedus* (in blood the covenant) was the highest decoration the King could bestow. In the name of the saint were united not only the religious but also especially the national feelings of his subjects, which were linked by the saint's name to the over-arching idea of the reunification of the kingdom. With the battle cry 'Long live St. Januarius!' the Neapolitans had thrown themselves against the French in the last battles on the mainland and Naples was lost. Established in 1738 with only one class, the Order was restricted to 60 knights

41. Decoration of the 'Order of St. Januarius', worn on a sash from the right shoulder to the left hip.

42. Star of the 'Order of St. Januarius'.

who had to be able to trace back their noble rank for at least four generations. The ponceau red sash was worn from the right shoulder to the left hip and bore the decoration itself, the Maltese Cross of the Order, which was worn on the left breast (Figs. 41,42). This highest of honours would be of significant usefulness after Mahon's return to England. In 'society' its mere visibility attested without the need for any self-advertisement to the fact that the wearer must have achieved something remarkable to deserve it.

Mahon's moment to put his request to the king was well-chosen. He had received news that called for his return to England, and that furthermore, his stay there would be short. Had his next posting to Dresden already been arranged? He wrote to his mother that the length of his stay after his return from Sicily would depend simply 'on circumstances', as a particular plan had been put to him which could result in a longer stay on the Continent, and that he did 'not see the prospect of being able to go to Vienna, since the news which I have recently received from there was not as I had expected'.

First, however, Queen Carolina travelled back to Vienna, her hometown, arriving there in January 1814. In anticipation of her approaching death, she had boarded ship with her own coffin and all the materials needed for the embalming. She took her leave of Mahon, who in fact she would never see again, with the words:

> My health is very bad and afflicted; in the last eighteen months pains, heartache and, I dare to say, undeservedly unspeakable troubles have ruined my health and cause me to fear that I shall not survive this long and arduous journey to which I have been forced against my will. What will my fate be between the rulers of states and allies? Sincerity and uprightness in my feelings and actions will never leave me and this certainty of my own conscience is what has given me and still gives me the courage to withstand all these pains and troubles.....I leave now and do not know whether I shall ever have the satisfaction of seeing you again, whether I shall survive this savage and unjustified persecution or whether I shall remain an innocent sacrifice, but whatever my fate, I shall always be a most lively, sincerely grateful and true admirer.....[71]

A few days after Carolina's departure, Mahon asked the King to obtain for him a villa on the coast. Such a request could only be positively complied with if there were grounds for gratitude on the monarch's part. Philip Henry indicated the house he had decided on unmistakably in such a way as to be sure of a positive response.

> The house of Prince Di Cuto on the coast would be perfect for me in every respect, and he will be kind enough to let me have use of it during the short period of my stay. But since the example of this courtesy could be misused by others, which could lead to inconvenience for him, he will do me this kindness with Your Majesty's permission. If Your Majesty would therefore grant that he might do me this favour then the Prince would not need to fear being seen to have compromised himself by those who might come with the same request, as this kindness would have been done to me through Your Majesty's good offices....[72]

Mahon's stay at Prince Di Cuto's villa could not have lasted long. News from London came sooner than expected, so unexpected was it in fact that it was not even possible for him to bid a personal farewell to Ferdinand IV. In 'great haste' Philip Henry left Sicily on 17th August 1813.

> My heart is filled with deepest gratitude at the honour Your Majesty has shown me. With complete devotion to Your Sacred Person and to the Interests of Your Crown I humbly beseech Your Majesty to accept my good wishes and not to cease to bestow Your Graciousness upon me. It was my duty to give expression to Your Majesty personally of my most loyal service, but since a health problem prevents me from paying Your Majesty that honour, I must depart from Sicily in great haste and so I take this first opportunity to express it in writing. Your Majesty's kindness has instilled me with a deep feeling of gratitude and the wish to be of further service.[73]

Ferdinand regretted Mahon's sudden departure 'because I would have liked to see you again at lunch', but as he himself writes, he entertained 'no suspicions', putting it down to the health problem his guest had indicted. Mahon, however, quite apart from his recall to London, evidently saw the matter very differently: 'I am not very happy with Palermo and I shall leave it without regret.'

The next day already Philip Henry was on board the *Brune*, commanded by Captain W.S. Badcock, on the open sea with a course set for Minorca, to which, correctly supposing he would never again visit this part of the world, he thought of paying a visit that would be historically significant in the annals of his family. Both the capital and the port of the Spanish island bore the same name, Mahon, as did all firstborn males of his own family until they inherited the actual family title.

After a short landing there on the 29th August which probably lasted no longer than was necessary for the crew to take on fresh water and provisions, the ship put to sea again on 31st August, heading for the Spanish coast. In peacetime, the fastest way home from there would have been to take the land route to Bordeaux. Two or three days would have sufficed for this stretch and for a moment his impatience to get back to England gained the upper hand, but the impossibility of such a route was already obvious; it clearly would have been to tempt Providence. Instead, the *Brune* spent a week ploughing through the waves back through the Straits of Gibraltar, along the coast of Portugal and this time in the middle of autumn storm season which Philip Henry had only a few months before earnestly sworn to avoid. 'I have no intention,' he brooded at the time, 'of exposing myself once again to the equinoctial storms and I hope that my journey will be on a warship. If you knew how much I fear and loathe the sea!'

This time everything went surprisingly quickly and otherwise than expected. On the 31st October—the Battle of the Nations at Leipzig had decided Napoleon's fate only a few days before—the ship's position was 45° latitude and 9° longitude, well west of the coast of France. Continuous storm squalls from the middle of October and a waterspout on the 12th November slowed the return voyage. It was almost a whole month before the *Brune* was able to drop anchor in Portsmouth on the 24th November. There must have been a pressing reason for such a hasty return under the worst of conditions. While still in Palermo, Philip Henry had written, 'I am not without hope that the time for a general peace is not far off and that a plan that has been put to me will enable me to go to the continent.'[74] The time had obviously come.

On the 28th November 1813 Philip Henry was sitting once more in Walmer Castle and looking no doubt often from the fortress to the southeast in the direction of the new tasks that would follow on from his Sicilian mission. On the continent, however, things had not developed so rapidly from the standpoint of British diplomacy, and he had to wait. Only in the following year did the French also withdraw from Italy and Napoleon finally abdicated.

As the year 1813 came to an end, it found Mahon with no money left, and although new sources of income were in the offing, they were not yet available. Philip Henry saw himself forced to place notices in various magazines asking for the loan of promissory notes totalling £5,500, repayable on the death of his father.

But the time did not go unused. Numerous letters passed between him and Ferdinand IV. The news all focused more or less on the regaining of the throne of Naples. For this correspondence, both men made use of their own couriers, who did not always display the hoped-for reliability.

> My Lord, my courier has arrived with your letter of the 16th February together with the copy of your letter of the 27th November in which you told me from Castelcicala that you had sent to me from there via Maddalene, but which I never received, which is the reason for my present advice to you no longer to make use of the said Maddalene, who is not a trustworthy subject.[75]

Mahon took heed of Ferdinand's advice as far as he could and tried to have his correspondence sent through diplomatic channels. 'Feeling uncertain as to whether Your Majesty would receive the letter which I had the honour of writing induced me to give a copy to the Prince of Castelcicala, who would be certain to place the letter in Your Hands.'[76]

In those days important correspondence also went missing in other ways. Five months earlier, when Mahon was still in Sicily, a British post vessel with 'important reports...and a very consequential letter for Lord W.' fell into the hands of 'an American privateer' near Cape St. Vincent. Mahon and many others were 'greatly disturbed by this mishap'. Such ill luck was now repeated. 'My Lord,' wrote Ferdinand,

> On the 23rd May I sent you a courier from Castelcicala with a reply to your letters of the 27th November 1813 and of the 16th February this year. The misfortune that beset us is that an American pirate ship stole the British post which included your letters, which I fear must have been thrown in the sea. I recently received this lamentable news and it pains me that owing to this situation, you will not yet have been able to read my reply.[77]

However, the contents of the lost or mislaid correspondence can, apart from a few gaps, be reconstructed. There was only one issue that concerned the two men and in which Philip Henry had invested the effort that would earn Ferdinand's certain gratitude: the reconquest of Naples!

'That would be the happiest event for Your Majesty', gushed Philip Henry, with all due wishes for its accomplishment. 'War has been declared against the usurper of Naples, and success cannot for a moment be doubted….' Ferdinand also shared such sentiments and, indulging himself in anticipation of coming events, imagined how he might thank his admirer and helper. 'In the lovely climate of Naples I would be happy to receive you as the representative of your Court.'[78]

Stanhope sent similar letters to Queen Carolina in Vienna:

> If I could take some comfort in this respect, it would be the hope instilled in me by political events of seeing the Kingdom of Naples restored to Your Majesty and Your illustrious husband, so that the injustices of which some have made themselves guilty will be brought to an end, and of seeing the rights of sovereigns once more established in their full integrity and equally, the independence of nations.[79]

From Schloss Hetzendorf, where she lived during the Congress of Vienna, Marie Carolina thanked Mahon for this 'great interest', which had already been recognised through his decoration with the Order of St. Januarius. It was the last letter she was to write to him. On the morning of the 8th September [1814] she was found lying on the floor of her bedroom, her arm outstretched reaching for the bell cord, 'the lips half opened as if in a cry for help'. The burdens of the last months had been too much for her heart and had brought her stressful life to an end just before she reached her longed-for goal. Everything had become too much for her. 'At one time,' she had written to Philip Henry,

> injustices were weighing upon me from all sides, and it was quite the usual thing for me to be burdened and overwhelmed by pain…I am now in the land of my birth and I find myself in the middle of all the great and brilliant events and successes which border on the miraculous and which move one to contemplation. I thank you from my heart for the good wishes you have sent to my dear and most beloved family and to the King, my dear and honourable husband, the eldest of the rulers of Europe, who still has the loyalty of his century. I accept your happy predictions. May heaven grant our wishes and that we shall have the satisfaction of meeting again so that I shall be able to express to you what I feel with great gratitude and esteem.[80]

It was a letter of farewell.

On the 10th September her body was transported to the Hofburg. She lies now in the main rotunda of the imperial crypt, next to her parents—'consort of Ferdinand IV, King of Sicily', not yet once again 'the Two Sicilies'. Mahon, sensing how things would turn out, addressed his reply to Marie Carolina as Queen of the Two Sicilies already before the event became fact. She was holding this last letter from Mahon in her hand when she died. In it, amongst other things, he indicated his connection to the political situation, especially that of Sicily:

> At the present time, when everything must presumably be subject to further developments, the presence of Your Majesty in Vienna—and I doubt not that it is so—will have the most important influence on the interests of Europe….I dare to state that You will have the same success in Naples as elsewhere. I cannot express to Your Majesty enough *how very important for me is the destiny of this land, for political reasons* [emphasis—Mayer] but above all because of the affection which, in all sincerity, I feel for its rulers.[81]

The 'great events' referred to in the letter included the French withdrawal from Italy, the first Paris Peace Treaty, the enthronement of Louis XVIII and of the Bourbons in France and in consequence of all these events, the restoration of the Kingdoms of Sardinia and Sicily. Good wishes, which could not yet be sent to Naples, Stanhope still had to address to Palermo, since Joachim Murat—torn between the allied camp, to which the traitor offered his services, and a new victorious enthusiasm for Napoleon during the 100 Days—was in no way prepared to give up the throne of Naples in 1816. Afterwards, the King no longer designated himself Ferdinand IV, but as Ferdinand I, King of the Two Sicilies. 'The restoration of the reins of government to Your Majesty', wrote Philip Henry on the 3rd August 1814

> is the most illustrious and happiest event for Your subjects, to whom Your Majesty has always been a most devoted father….For me, who has had the honour to be one of Your most faithful servants, it is impossible to express in the most exalted words the human satisfaction that I have felt….I should very much like to take part in the re-enthronement of Your Majesty, for as a spectator, the expression of feelings of the general happiness can be felt by no-one as enthusiastically as myself….In truth my prayers have not yet been fully heeded as they always consist in wishing to see the reinstatement of Your Majesty in Your Kingdom in

> Naples.....The burning enthusiasm which I feel for Your Majesty's interests makes my heart long that I may soon be allowed to experience with inexpressible satisfaction that Your Majesty and Your just cause will be regarded together with the current situation in Europe.[82]

The description of the trip to Sicily and Philip Henry's relationship with the royal couple in the years 1812–14 should be considered together and as of far-reaching significance. A preview of the course of events could not therefore be avoided. The following chapter will deal with the events of 1814–15 that are significant in the biography of Mahon.

4. Mission to Dresden

Meeting with Gentz in Vienna, 1814–1816

The year 1813 was, despite a few rays of hope, the harbinger of dramatic events. In May near Lützen in Germany, Napoleon, victor of more than fifteen battles, had won another great victory; but a victory with an 'army of children'. The 'greybeards' of the 'Grand Army' had been lost in the snows between Moscow and the crossing of the Berezina. The Emperor brooded: 'I can fight against men, but not against the elements; the winter cold brought me low. In one night I lost 30,000 horses.'

Now fifteen-year-olds had to be called up. It was their first experience of war, but despite heavy losses, they achieved a victory over the Prussian cavalry. Napoleon then struck the Russian army in the Battle of Bautzen and moved into Silesia. Despite the family connection [Napoleon's Austrian wife—*transl.*], Austria did not remain neutral as Napoleon had hoped, so he decided on an armistice. 'I decided on it for two reasons: my lack of cavalry ... and the hostile position taken by Austria.'

In June Napoleon travelled to Dresden for peace talks with the Austrians during the armistice. He sought a meeting with Metternich which he opened with the provocative question:

> You want war? Very well. You shall have it. I annihilated the Prussian army at Lützen; I defeated the Russians at Bautzen; now you want your turn. Let it be, then! We shall meet again in Vienna! People are incorrigible; they just will not learn from experience. I have already restored Emperor Franz to his throne three times. I promised to live in peace with him my life long; I married his daughter. Then I said to myself, it is all foolishness, but it is now over; today I regret it.

In the course of the almost eight-hour-long, evermore tense debate Napoleon committed the error of expressing to Metternich a deeply wounding truth, which gave the diplomat his *casus belli*. In his *Memoirs*, written down by Las Casas, Napoleon appeared beset with difficulties on all sides; Metternich gave ground on all points after Napoleon had declared that the cession of Illyria would not be his last word as far as Austria was concerned. The Emperor believed he had won Metternich round, when in his excitement he let slip the words: "'I have given you 20 million. Do you want another 20? I shall give them to you. How much has England offered you?" These words cut like a knife. Metternich became deathly pale, and Napoleon knew immediately that he had made a terrible error and had created an irreconcilable enemy. There was a deep silence between the two men.'

At the end of this dramatic confrontation which led to no unity, the Prince—in von Gentz's stylistically elaborated *Memoirs*—declared loudly that: 'You are lost, Sire. I had a premonition of it at my arrival. Now at my departure, I am certain of it.' The prophecy was a true one. Napoleon's star was in irreversible decline. In the campaign against Prussia, General Rapp found the Emperor, who took him by the arm, sunk in his thoughts: 'Do you not see it? …That is my star. Here before us, shining… it has never left me; I see it before all important events. It beckons me to press onwards and that is for me a sign of good fortune.'

This time there were gloomier signs of what was to come. The campaign in Saxony began. At Delitz, the Austrian General, Count Merveldt, was taken prisoner; Napoleon sent him back to his father-in-law, Emperor Franz, with another peace offering. The offer was refused 'as Austria could no longer make peace alone but only together with the other allies. Above all, an agreement had to be reached with England, which was financing the war.'

A decisive battle could no longer be avoided. It began on 16th October at Leipzig—'We are approaching the great day of world justice' exclaimed Metternich happily—and Napoleon, who was no longer in a position to determine the course of events, found himself continually on the defensive. Three days later, on the 19th, the dice had been cast, and Napoleon took his defeated army back across the Rhine. His Confederation of the Rhine, which only a victory at Leipzig could have sustained, fell to pieces. On the 20th November, his most loyal ally, the Grand Duchy of Baden, withdrew from the Confederation and joined the victors. With deep resignation the Emperor commented: 'There you see what men are. There you see how dependable they are!'

On New Year's Day 1814, Blücher crossed the Rhine at Kaub and forced the French troops back. In the victorious army which marched into Paris was the Count of Artois, with whom Philip Henry was in friendly correspondence. The Count took over the government in the name of his still absent brother Louis XVIII. Four months later, on 6th April Napoleon abdicated unconditionally.

Now an Englishman could once again travel unhindered on the Continent and around the German states. At the end of April Stanislaus Xavier, the brother of the Count of Artois, left London and on 26th April arrived on French soil once more at Calais. On 3rd May he became King Louis XVIII and as such entered Paris. In June Czar Alexander and King Frederick William of Prussia travelled to London to discuss the consequences of the fall of France with the British government. On the 26th they left for Vienna by way of Dover. The farsighted von Gentz had already in 1809 drawn up the main lines of the programme of the Congress that was now to begin on the 25th September 1814.

*

On the 14th October Philip Henry and his family also boarded ship at Dover for Calais. His situation had until shortly before been so dire that he had had to write IOUs to be paid on the death of his father. How then did his sudden affluence materialise? The story becomes more mysterious when his travel plans are considered. The stay in Germany (Dresden) was projected to last 27 months, and all members of the family were to accompany him. How was this considerable enterprise to be financed, given that Philip Henry had access to 'no expenses or provision from my paternal inheritance', as he acknowledged before a committee of the House of Commons. How could one live for a year and a half in Dresden as an English lord without an income or official mission? On what would a hopelessly indebted English lord live, who could not access the dubious inheritance of his equally indebted father and who otherwise had no known occupation? 'There are many important reasons why I have to spend much time abroad,' he wrote before his departure to his mother-in-law Lady Carrington in a statement that disguised more than it explained.

Before leaving England, on the 22nd September Philip Henry sealed up a packet of 120 letters of remarkable historical value which would remain unopened for a hundred years. These were important papers of a French émigré nobleman. Travel passes, War Minister's correspondence, news about the Count Artois, Louis Joseph Bourbon—of the Prince Condé, a copy of Louis XVI's Will, dispatches of the Prince of Saxe-Coburg and of the Duke d'Enghien as well as news about Duke Karl Wilhelm of Brunswick who had commanded the forces opposing General Dumouriez, the defender of the Revolution, at the Battle of Valmy. The packet also included a report of former Empress Catherine (the Great) of Russia to Marshal Broglie and a proclamation by Prince Condé.

The papers relate to the period 1781–1801 and belonged to Count de Mornac. Philip Henry himself remarked that he had received them from the Count and had bequeathed them as a legacy to be handed over to authorised representatives of the de Mornac family. No such person appeared, and 100 years later it could no longer be established whether any members of the de Mornac family had survived the storms of the Revolution. But how had they come into Mahon's hands and why indeed into *his* hands ?

*

The family's first stay on the Continent was in Hanover, from 2–5 November: the Duke of Cambridge gave the family 'the kindest reception' and spoke with Philip Henry about the expected elevation of the status of Hanover to a Kingdom and gave him the address of a wine merchant who could provide excellent Hock. A few days later, Philip Henry had a second meeting with the Duke. 'We dined yesterday with him & and went afterwards out of town to Count Münster's sister [she would later appear in the Kaspar Hauser story] where, alas! there was a concert.' Stanhope's lifelong aversion to everything musical is of considerable psychological interest.

There he got to know the Russian General Levin, Count von Benningsen (1745–1826), a native of Braunschweig, who had played his part in history through his active involvement in the murder of Czar Paul in 1801. Czar Alexander I held him to be the man who actually murdered his father. However, since von Benningsen possessed indispensable military abilities, the Czar gave him the most important commands in the campaign against Napoleon from Moscow to Leipzig. When, after the Battle of Friedland, still allied to France, Alexander proposed von Benningsen for the Order of the Legion of Honour, Napoleon refused with the words: 'I shall give it with satisfaction to the soldier of your army whom you designate as the bravest in his company, but I refuse to give it to the General who laid his hand on his lord.'

The evening of that same day, the Stanhopes were again guests of the Duke: 'There is, sad to say, another concert this evening at the Duke of Cambridge's, but we mean to depart tomorrow the 6th for Brunswick.' On the 6th November Philip Henry arrived in Brunswick [Braunschweig] and sought an audience with the Duke of Brunswick only to learn that he had already left for the Congress at Vienna. The small palace town held him for only a day. On the 8th the trunks were packed again for the journey to Berlin 'to see there the Emperor [*sic*] of Russia and the King of

Denmark' and above all, Jackson, whom he had to thank for everything. He arrived in Berlin on 13th November. In expectation of the arrival of Emperor Alexander, however, all available accommodation had long been occupied. Even '...a Russian Princess and the French Ambassador ...have been here for a long while and are still at Inns from the total impossibility of finding a House, although the latter has been here for three months'.

The situation had its inevitable effect on Philip Henry's assessment of Berlin, which was 'a great disappointment!' It was otherwise with the meetings with George Jackson. But then, on 25th November, it was time once more to depart on account of 'the total impossibility finding a House'. The journey now finally made its way to Dresden, exactly according to that 'plan, which has been put to me'. There Mahon lived with his family from 28th November 1814 to 18th May 1816. This was no coincidence; there was a story behind it.

During the Battle of Leipzig, King Frederick Augustus of Saxony (1750–1827) was in the city on Napoleon's orders and had witnessed the course of the battle from the Sternwarte Tower. With the defeat on 18th October, Bonaparte gave the King the choice of continuing to follow him as an ally or not. Ultimately, he would have had the freedom to choose the best peace terms he could have expected. Despite the hopeless situation, Frederick Augustus chose to remain loyal to the alliance, which resulted in his becoming a state prisoner of the Russian-Prussian-Austrian coalition when Leipzig was occupied. On 23rd October the King was brought to Stettin via Berlin and placed under arrest. Saxony was administered by a provisional Central Administration Department under the control of Hardenberg, a 'restless person who understood nothing except how to shuffle cards' (Sophie Karoline von Brandenburg-Bayreuth), and Baron von Stein. Unlike the other states of the Confederation of the Rhine, Saxony had been too tardy in renouncing its alliance obligations to Napoleon, and for this reason Prussia demanded its annexation, which was opposed by Russia and Austria and most strenuously by the French representative, Talleyrand. He had in mind not only Saxony's loyalty at Leipzig but also feared above all an increase in Prussian strength. Despite previous disagreements with Prussia, England had at first no objections to the prospect of annexation. All the same, the Prussians' annexation of Hanover in 1806 had drawn the wrath of the British, who enforced sanctions against Berlin worth millions. However, England spoke up energetically on the Polish question, which led to the frustration of

Czar Alexander's expansionist plans and caused difficulties in the negotiations with William III. If Prussia were to have Saxony, then Russia would have to be allowed to take Poland, especially since Russian troops had played the largest part in the defeat of France. Prussia therefore objected to French participation at the Congress of Vienna. The head of the British delegation, Castlereagh, soon arrived at the insight that earlier agreements (e.g. the Treaty of Reichenbach, 1813) would have to be handled on the basis of new realities.

> It was impossible to deny that an agreement over Poland could not be reached, given the attitude of the King of Prussia, and that consequently, England and Austria could not support Prussia's demand as they had wanted and otherwise would have done. It was now a question of whether the King of Prussia would be able to get his way through the influence of Russia alone against the opinion of the rest of Europe.[83]

At the beginning of the Congress of Vienna the interests of the victorious Powers were already so contradictory and changeable that it was impossible to foresee how the negotiations would turn out. From the British viewpoint, it was natural in a political constellation of this kind to wish to set up an unobtrusive observation post. This explains the sudden recall of Philip Henry from Palermo. An arduous sea voyage from Sicily to England behind him and a situation ahead that was not yet completely penetrable, agent Stanhope was to be available as soon as he arrived in Dresden.

*

On 28th November, after his previous visits to Hanover, Braunschweig and Berlin, Philip Henry arrived in the Saxon capital and began to get his bearings. One can only note with amazement the exclusive lifestyle that the young lord embarked upon. Living in the capital with his whole family cannot have been exactly cheap and neither were visits from illustrious company. The children had lessons with Herr Faber, French lessons with Herr Schmidt, riding lessons with Herr Schober, dancing lessons with Herr Donato and German with Herr Zeiss. Even a music teacher was engaged. Each teacher received 15 Reichstaler and three talers a month were paid on the rent of a piano. The newborn ten-week-old poodle had to be looked after, and 'the keep and taxing' of the poodle incurred its own costs. Joseph Knoll was paid 60 Reichstaler to keep the apartment in the very best condition. It was located 'in the most pleasant street in Dresden', at 29 Schlossstrasse (Fig. 43) opposite the famous Hotel Poland. Philip Henry was a regular at the opera and the theatre, became a member of the Museum Association, 'subscribed to the Casino', engaged a chambermaid Birch and employed Mr. Norton as his servant and cook—an 'ugly Jewish-looking fellow'. A French priest, called by his friend Bottinger *'kinderfrau'* (the nanny) served the children as tutor but soon had to be dismissed. 'I shall immediately engage another,' decided the master of the house. In January 1815 Philip Henry asked his father-in-law for a year's rent, the amount of which could not have covered the family's running costs, let alone the expenses of this 'princely estate' if one considers that as a student in Erlangen, Philip Henry did not once manage to cover his costs over an appreciably shorter period of time for less than £1200 and that amount was already in 1801 somewhat less than the minimum needed to support himself. The desired amount was thought of rather as a subsidy on top of his running costs. The reason given for the request to his father-in-law is therefore not quite accurate. Certainly, the education of his two sons, eight and nine years old, was expensive, but it was definitely not the reason for the stay in Dresden.

> As to the amount of the Annuity, I am convinced, both by reflection & by experience, that £600 per annum, out of which the Income Tax is to be deducted for an indefinite period, out of which Mr. Keene's Salary & all the other expenses of my Children's education are to be defrayed is not more than adequate to my necessary wants, particularly as I ought to have the means of moving now & then from one place to another, as well as of going to England & of living there when my business or my inclinations may require it.[84]

It was, however, not just a matter of his own travel costs but also of those of Mr. Keen, for whose trips to London, from there to Cuxhaven and on to Hamburg, Philip Henry provided for on a regular basis. Another trip Keen made to Hamburg and Berlin and a few others between Dresden and Berlin. What services was Keen rendering to Stanhope and what kind of 'activities' were those to which Stanhope referred in his letter? What did they consist of? Whether his father-in-law agreed to his request is unknown. What *is* known, however, is that from the first day to the last of his stay in Germany, twice a month, punctually on the 4th and the 20th, Stanhope received 286 Reichstaler through the Dresden banking house of W.H. Bassenge

43. Schlossstrasse (Castle Street) in Dresden. The second building on the right side of the street, house no. 29, was Philip Henry's residence from 1814–1816.

& Co and that this amount was increased to 446 Reichstaler on 29th April 1815, a total of 893 Reichstaler a month. Before the family had left England therefore, someone or some institution must have undertaken the regular financing of the stay in Germany.

A modest amount of extra income came from Mahon's publication of a *Hymnal* he had written.[85] The title is misleading, as the little book contains neither notes nor song lyrics, merely some of his own poems Mahon had chosen somewhat coyly to publish under the ill-disguised pseudonym of Lord Mahre.

Whether the sentimental and bigoted verses enjoyed any success is indicated in the following:

Truth and Honesty

1. To him who rightly journeys,
   Who as a friend of truth,
   Sincere his deed and word is,
   Honest and ne'er uncouth,
   Who never lies nor flatters
   Nor plays the hypocrite
   Ne'er feigns a show of honesty
   But true and faithful sits.

2. Your goodness, God, will lead him
And always him surround !
An honest heart have You, Lord God
In such men loved to find.
To liars and traitors' falsehoods
Have you always shown your ire;
And appointed to evildoers
Their time that shall expire.

3. Let falsehood then and lies,
Lord God, always be far from me;
Ne'er let my lips them utter
But to my virtue see !
May my mind always remember
You hate dissembling so,
So might I always zealous be
In loyalty and truth to Thee.

4. O let me never promise
What I have not thought through;
Nor break my word once given
Because it troubles me so to do.
O let my soul be not bothered
By trivia and jokes
So that I never will regard as true
What viciousness evokes.

5. Give courage so I'll not falter
When duty presses me
To tell the truth whatever
The danger it may bring.
Give cleverness so I'll understand
When without any fear
I bravely forth must speak my mind
And when in silence bear.

6. O aid my battle to cast down
The one with dreadful guile,
The enemy who with evil will
Does lies against me rile;

And may I ever be ashamed
If I should refuge take
In lies as great as those of his
And not, Lord, in thy wake.

7. A heart that's full of truth and faith
That fears your eyes, O God
This shall no man e'er from me take
This gives me joy right good.
So freely may I upwards glance
And glory will on me descend
To cover my disgrace.

With Friedrich Daumer, one might say: 'How charming and worthy! Who could not doubt that all the wicked manifestations that have sprung from such contradictory behaviour, all the suspicion that has been raised against him [Stanhope—*transl.*] is groundless!' Let it be noted in passing that the words Christ or Christianity appear not once in this pious little book. It did, however, entirely express that freemasonic philosophy of an English persuasion which cultivated a Deism, the main focus of which no longer '[lay] in the struggles and polarities within the Christian church and its confessions, but rather in the struggle and opposition between philosophy and theology, between reason and revelation, between thought and faith'.[86]

In Dresden Philip Henry finally provided himself with a personal servant appropriate to his class who, on the return to England, was prepared to give up family, friends and country and, till the end of his life, served Stanhope with 'the most constant loyalty, honesty and conscientiousness'. He too had to be paid—£40 a month. Gentz had the Krauss brothers at his service, Stanhope the then 24-year-old Anton Heinrich (1792–1855).

Who Heinrich really was will most likely never be known. His origins remain mysterious, although he certainly was not of the 'lower classes'. The only extant piece of writing in his hand, written in the last month of his life, is something of a riddle and not easily interpreted. Dressed in Stanhope's family livery and armed with pistols, until the hour of his master's death Anton Heinrich was in continuous attendance upon him.

Excursions to Tetschen and Teplitz were not unusual during the period in Dresden. In Schandau, the environs of which 'very much exceeded our expectations in all points', Mahon rented in May 1815 a 'princely Mansion ... on the banks of the Elbe with a garden & a most superb view, before the windows, of the mountains & forests growing almost to the water's side, on the opposite bank'. The splendid estate, previously used by the Prince of Anhalt-Dessau, served Philip Henry and his family as a health resort, for 'it is very unpleasant as well as unhealthy to pass the summer in the middle of a town.' As for the beauty of the local environment, the 'Panorama of Nature', Stanhope's enthusiasm knew no bounds; it was somewhat more restricted, however, when it came to the Schandau locals themselves and their butter.

> Imprimis [Above all], the women are very ugly. Instead of complexions of lilies and rozes [*sic*], of that delicate and exquisitely beautiful texture of the skin which I admired at Dresden, the women here have coarse features & are quite sunburnt, which indeed is not surprising when it is considered that they till the fields & cultivate the gardens. Such to my astonishment and sorrow was, I found, the case. None of them, except a few who belong to the more genteel set, wear shoes or stockings & their dress is as unbecoming as it is quizzical. ...Alas! I cannot admire the fair sex of Schandau & all that I can say of them is that I would praise them if I could. Idiots are born here in a very great proportion, as is, you know, the case also in Switzerland. The next objection I find to the place is that the milk & butter are very bad. I am, however, not without hopes of finding in the neighbourhood some that are at least as good as what we had at Dresden & I might have expected to find them still better; I had expected that they would be better here. It must be the effect either of want of care or of want of intelligence for the pastures in the valleys are very fine...[87]

Philip Henry's inclination to remark on all that was disagreeable and to subject everything to immediate criticism led him to waste many a fine day. He would grumpily scold his driver for being 'a clumsy Clodhopper, a mere Bohemian ass', who ought to be driving 'a Hay Waggon or a Dung Cart' rather than Stanhope's coach. By contrast, Saxon horses came off better than British in his estimation, following an accident that passed off without serious consequences. Mahon had found himself in the dust of the street near the horse's rear hooves and later made light of the event: 'In England such an accident would probably have been fatal, but the distinctive character of German Horses is patience, docility, steadiness & humour. He remained as quiet as a lamb, as calm and composed as a Stoical Philosopher.' To such insights about animals were added others such as the claim that 'dirt and sloth' were more often to be found in Catholic countries than in Protestant ones.—And then Carlsbad! Who did not spend time in that famous place! There were 800 visitors when Mahon arrived in the resort. On his last visit there, a location not unimportant for *his* purposes, he spent three weeks unaccompanied, from 1st–26th September. This was where he developed his hypochondria and his idiosyncratic method of taking cold baths:

> I have lately adopted a very salutary custom, which I most deeply regret that I did not follow sooner, that of cold bathing. It has been of infinite service to me, but you must not suppose that I bathe in the preposterous manner which is practised in England, of jumping in over heads and ears. The violence of the shock is then very painful & may become very pernicious by driving the blood to the head or to the lungs & the breath is stopped very unnaturally. The mode of doing anything is, you know, often just as important as the thing itself, & I bathe according to what I consider philosophical principles. It is thus: after having undressed myself before the slipper bath, I sit some moments to cool & then I wash my head completely till it feels quite cold. I then wash my arms & legs & splash water over my body behind and before. Then & not sooner I enter the bath, but I content myself at first with letting the water rise above my hips. I then jump out & afterwards, when I stretch myself at length in the water which is perfectly cold, I feel no unpleasant shock nor does the water appear to me so chilly. When I leave the Bath, I feel revived, reanimated nay quite renovated. It was not from the advice of a physician that I have adopted this custom, but it was mentioned to me by a person of extraordinary judgment & who is at the same time a model of health & vigour. The mode of taking these cold baths was recommended to me by the same person, but I have a little improved it. I mention these circumstance [*sic*] because I think that they may be useful to others.[88]

*

At the beginning of 1814 Mahon's old friend Francis Jackson died in Brighton aged 44, 'after a lingering illness'. Jackson, who had had intimate knowledge of Prussian affairs, had been in constant contact with Gentz since 1804 until his early death. During his own time in Berlin, Gentz had had an affair with a Fräulein von Dorville; he lost her to Jackson, who married her. The two politicians remained close friends, however; their relationship was the prerequisite for Philip Henry's stay in Dresden, and Mahon had heeded a last recommendation from his mentor when he took up the important post. For Gentz, the new man was most welcome. In Vienna it was simply impossible to get to know Prussian intentions, but from Gentz's viewpoint, Philip Henry had already provided ample proof of his ability and had therefore recommended himself for the Dresden mission.

'When it comes to negotiations,' Gentz had declared with regard to the Saxon question, 'my main aim will be to keep Prussia in the dark', and this the intimate servant of Metternich did when the time came. But this strategy required above all a well-functioning intelligence service which had at its disposal secure sources of information, and which could penetrate deeply enough into Saxon circles. Mahon was the man who possessed the talents to arrange the necessary connections that could satisfy needs for information in both London and Vienna.

For Philip Henry this was, after Sicily, his second chance to test his mettle and at the same time, the fulfilment of the hopes he had nurtured since 1802. Pitt had not been the only one to have had his own personal agents; other significant members of the family surrounded themselves with informers. It was generally known that Secretary of State William Wyndham Grenville too maintained a number of diplomatic agents in France for his own purposes. Mahon was given a chance in this way to serve his country in a semi-political capacity.

Just at the beginning of his time in Dresden, in November 1814, Stanhope made the acquaintance which proved to be the most important and decisive for his mission. This was Karl August Böttiger (1760–1835) (Fig.44), a rather enigmatic but nonetheless well-known personality, an archaeologist by profession, half man-of-the-world, half figure of scandal, both feared and ridiculed as a brilliant reviewer, critic, and author, and known, befriended or scorned by almost all the great men of his day. After his death, Böttiger's son discovered his correspondence—over 20,000 letters containing more or less everything the period had had to offer in the way of scandals and stories: who had felt what towards whom, what this person had said or insinuated about that, for example, how Wieland had lost his gold-embossed walking stick while out on a stroll and how a merchant from Weimar had been suspected of finding it and unscrupulously keeping it for himself. This walking stick will figure again in Stanhope's experiences in Dresden.

44. Karl August Böttiger (1760–1835)

Böttiger's public reputation resulted from a countless number of energetic reviews of old and new works of art, literature and science and his own work *Sabina oder Morgenszenen im Putzzimmer einer reichen Römerin* ('Sabina, or Morning Scenes from the Dressing Room of a Rich Roman lady'). He published this between 1795 and 1803 in the *Journal des Luxus und der Moden.* He had repeatedly made disparaging remarks about Goethe's relationship with Christiane Vulpius and on account of these was regarded as a petit bourgeois in certain circles. When Böttiger, the literary 'harlequin', as Novalis called him, moved from Weimar to Dresden in 1804, Goethe and Schiller dedicated a characteristic verse to the 'Magister Ubique':

Give us what you have and we'll show ourselves thankful for it
But you give us yourself—spare us that, friend!
God sees only the heart, they say!
Yes indeed, God sees only the heart,
So take care that we too shall be able to bear the sight.

Schiller wrote to Korner: 'I congratulate you—and ourselves!—on your new acquisition, Böttiger. Thank God that we are now finally rid of this awful guest, and may he suit you all right well!' That was certainly not going to be the case. What he had begun in Weimar, Böttiger continued all the more productively in his new location. 'In Dresden,' as Treitschke described the situation,

> Friedrich Kind and Theodor Hell and a few other equally gentle poets gathered every week for tea and poetry readings and, with an unchanging politesse, professed mutual amazement at each other's listless novellas that were as weak as the Chinese tea they were drinking and which were published in the much-read *Abendzeitung* [Evening News]. Karl Böttiger, however, the most inexorable of reviewers, hastened to stamp the—as Goethe called it—lumpy mush produced by these bunglers and scribblers with the imprimatur of masterworks.

The satirist Heinrich Heine was also less than impressed; he left behind an exquisite poem about Böttiger's work at the *Abendzeitung* [Evening News]:

> In Dresden, that lovely town on the Elbe
> With its tobacco-, straw-, and poetry factories,
> A garland of songs and a vault of lyrics
> Has raised itself on high to bedeck the heads of all.
>
> With these are ladies and gents now occupied
> In reading aloud, their faces flushed with hot-blooded courage.
> Mr Kuhn and Miss Nostitz—O what delight!
> Ha! Sublime! Away critic, you dreary jaundiced one!
>
> The other day the newspaper declared
> Brightness [Hell] is swathed in brightness,
> The childlike child [Kind] is childish.
> Sycophantic between them the critical supplement creeps.
>
> Arnoldi cares for money and fame,
> Then comes Böttiger and creates a spectacle
> The Evening News is the world's oracle.

Böttiger's light-footed eulogies led the sarcastic Adolf Müllner (1774–1829) to coin the waspish word 'beböttigern' (i.e. to write like Böttiger, or to 'Böttigerise'), which was not, however, applicable to all his work. Wieland counted him among his closest friends and willingly gave his name in support of the *Teutschen Merkur*, which was produced by Böttiger almost single-handedly and highly regarded by many.

As a counsellor at the Saxon Court, Böttiger was until 1814 for more than ten years the Director of Studies of the prince's pageboys and then Director of the royal riding academy; as a result, he was well-known to and on good terms with the most important families in the kingdom. His former pupils, all of them from the Saxon nobility, had obtained important positions and had their eyes and ears in the country at large and in the *Residenz* (palace) in the very places where Mahon would have wished to have his own. The pedagogue had numerous contacts to the Freemasons' School on the Breiten Gasse [Broad Street] in the Friedrichstadt area of the city, where the children mainly of lodge brothers were taught. What else was there worth Mahon's seeking in this circle and in obtaining Böttiger's services as intermediary? Only by getting near to those formerly trusted by the King, who indeed had their own pressing interest in discovering Prussian plans and intentions, could Mahon fulfil his mission. Two paths lay open to him by which he could gain Böttiger's favour. The one went via Wieland, the other via the Golden Apple Lodge, the second oldest German freemasons' lodge, founded in 1738. A connection to the foundation of the lodge was not difficult to create, as the cousin of Mahon's godfather was the internationally renowned statesman and lodge founder Philip Dormer Stanhope, 4th Earl of Chesterfield (1694–1773), who was from 1764 the accredited British envoy at the Dresden Court and the Grand Master of the Lodge. This was probably the very reason for entrusting the mission to Mahon.

First, he turned to Wieland who, in 1809 at the advanced age of 76 and with the cooperation of Goethe, had still been a member of the Amalia Lodge in Weimar together with Goethe and had there met Böttiger, the welcome guest from Dresden in lodge circles, who had himself been Director of the Weimar Gymnasium [grammar school] for 13 years until 1804. As the close friend of Johann Joachim Christoph Bode (1730–1793) who, as Master of the Lodge, had initiated Goethe ('I heard it from Böttiger's own mouth,' said Friedrich Ludwig Wilhelm Meyer, 'that Böttiger had nothing less than his unlimited trust'), Böttiger assumed ever more honorary offices beyond Dresden. So, for example, in 1807 at the end of a lodge funeral in Weimar, it was Böttiger who spoke the [masonic] 'Call in the Chain'. Böttiger, initiated in 1781 in Dresden at the age of 21, and a prominent, well-known freemason throughout his life, was called on to give the annual St. John's Festival lecture at his Dresden lodge and elsewhere. Friedrich Ludwig Schröder (1744–1816), the Hamburg Theatre Director and Master of the 'Emmanuel zur Maienblume' lodge, author of *Materialen zur*

Geschichte der Freimaurerei sei ihrer Entstehung bis 1732 ('Materials on the History of Freemasonry from its Establishment until 1732') and founder of the irregular masonic lodge, 'Elise zum warmen Herzen' intended mainly for actors, had just as high an estimation of Böttiger as had the above-mentioned Friedrich Ludwig Wilhelm Meyer, Professor of Philosophy at Göttingen. When the need came to discover an anonymous reviewer who had written an article about Freemasonry in the Jena journal *Literaturzeitung*, Meyer wrote to Schröder: 'Böttiger, who knows everything, will certainly also know the reviewer.'

Schröder was linked to Böttiger at other high levels. When Schröder proposed new masonic rituals in 1800, he travelled to Weimar to consult with Goethe, Herder, Hufeland and Böttiger. 'We three (Herder, Schröder, Böttiger) were alone, and there followed two of the richest hours of my life,'[89] recalled Schröder.

Soon afterwards, Meyer also occupied himself with the rituals for Entered Apprentice, Fellow Craft and Master Mason and in that connection studied John Browne's 'The Master Key through all the degrees of a Freemason's Lodge' which he could not penetrate for lack of a secret reading key.[90] 'I confess,' he wrote to Schröder, 'that I am uncommonly interested in this book but it will be a sealed book for me unless you break its code with the number key found in Dresden. Brother Böttiger, who has advice about everything in the world, will also have advice for this. I ask again and as urgently as only I know how.'[91] The procurement of the secret key was entrusted to Böttiger and also the provision of Lessing's as yet unpublished 'Freemasons' conversations'. 'I cannot miss this opportunity to ask you to request Böttiger to obtain for us Lessing's unpublished "Epilogues to Ernst and Falck" which must be located in Berlin or Breslau.'[92]

It was the 'all-knowing' Böttiger that Mahon too now approached under a certain pretext. Not far from Mahon's own apartments in the pleasant Schlossstrasse was the Palais Cosel, once the residence of 'Countess Cosel, mistress of the gallant King of Poland'; this was where Böttiger now lived, 'many flights up'. Mahon appeared there one day and put to him his request. He asked for, and received, 'lessons' from Böttiger, who spoke good English. It should perhaps be added that Böttiger was known for his almost pathological need to be constantly creating new contacts and connections. 'He binds himself to every stranger like prickly burdock,' observed Jean Paul.

Two basically very similar characters thus sought and found each other. Böttiger's feelings for Philip Henry had developed so far by December 1814 already that he sent his keen student one of Wieland's letters of 1801, written in the master's own hand, which even then had a considerable value. Mahon then adroitly expressed his own enthusiasm for the works of the recently deceased Wieland, who had dedicated the poem 'An Mylord Chesterfield' ('To My Lord Chesterfield') to Mahon's godfather Philip Stanhope, 5th Earl of Chesterfield, during the latter's student days in Leipzig (1773–1776)—a fact which now ensured the desired connection to and trusted company of the best-informed man in Saxony and thereby to entry into the Dresden Lodge. Böttiger was perhaps from the beginning too easily inclined to initiate Philip Henry into the secrets of the Royal Art. What underlay the impetuosity of the 'Magister ubique' on this occasion can only be guessed at. Was it the complex German manner of the rituals, the occult background with its associated high expectations, the many symbols and ceremonies which first irritated Mahon? (Figs. 45, 46) All that may have caused the much-travelled Englishman to hold himself aloof from entering a world of mystery unconcerned with reason and intellect, in which he could find nothing of the Enlightenment philosophy of life with which he was so familiar.

The new pupil acquired the requisite garb for his initiation ceremony but then lost all courage. 'It was exactly two years ago, it was on this very day that the world was robbed of its greatest ornament of Wieland. I have been solicited here to follow his example in becoming a Free Mason, but having maturely considered the subject I have determined to decline entirely & for ever the proposal.'[93]

His resolution apparently did not last long. Böttiger—'my friend'—was able only three months later to win the waverer back to the lodge, which Mahon himself then more or less involuntarily attended. There he formed a connection with a man who had been friendly with Böttiger since his time in Weimar: Friedrich Justin Bertuch (1747–1822). Owner of the artificial flower workshop in which Goethe had first met Christiane Vulpius, secretary to Grand Duke Karl August of Weimar and since 1808 Master of 'Amalia' lodge, Bertuch was the publisher of the *Gesänge für Freimaurer zum Gebrauch aller teutschen Logen* ('Songs for Freemasons for Use in All German Lodges') and above all, the very man who had initiated Wieland. It is verifiable that until the year of Bertuch's death, Mahon counted this prominent freemason as belonging to the narrow circle of his most carefully nurtured friendships. Here again the theme of 'Wieland' in a particular way may have

45. 'Freemason's Pocketbook for the Year 1798'. Title of the illustration: 'Behold and revere the face of the Unseen.' On the table in the foreground a cup of poison, a dagger and a pistol and above them a plaque with the inscription 'In the hands of the wise, the last remedy for body and soul.'

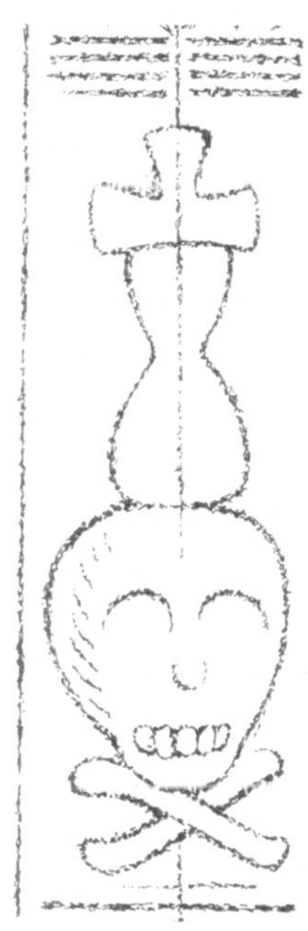

46. Initiation into the 33rd degree. Wall decoration with skull and crossbones (see also Fig. 45). In the foreground a dagger on the Bible. Below: Damascene design on the murder weapon with which Kaspar Hauser was killed.

secured him access. Philip Henry had a delicate feeling for such things. Perhaps it was from Bertuch that a new recommendation came to Böttiger finally to introduce the eager English admirer of Wieland to the lodge. A document from this period in Böttiger's hand provides clues that cannot be overlooked, which make Mahon's lodge membership more than probable. It is expressed in a typically colloquial manner, revealing a mood of intimacy which rarely occurred after such a short acquaintance with bourgeois life, especially in view of the differences in social rank.

One part of the content above all deserves closer consideration. From the poem 'My Mother Lodge' by the English freemason Rudyard Kipling—for many years the friend and correspondent of the 7th Lord Stanhope, we know how such colloquial terms were meant:

Outside: 'Sergeant! Sir! Salute! Salaam!'
Inside: 'Brother' an' it doesn't do no 'arm
We met upon the level an' we parted on the Square
An' I was Junior Deacon in my Mother-Lodge out there!

Böttiger, who was Mahon's older friend for two decades, wrote the following dedicatory verse for Mahon in a two-volume edition of Wieland's letters (Fig. 47) that appeared in 1815 and which Mahon had never read:

Honoured Lord,
To you I gladly send from Wieland's muse
This loveliest poem that greets the morning dews
But of what he here sings, you already own
For you are building it within your breast
With thirst for knowledge and a joy unpressed,
The recognition of the most beautiful throne.
So take his picture, which he with his own hand
Has made and sent to friends throughout the land,
Take his letters which of his youthful loves
And poetic joys to us glad tidings give.
With kindness and forebearance look thereon
And think as you do read within of one
Who with Father Wieland friendly was
And with him lived for fifteen years.

Dresden 3 May 1815 BÖTTIGER

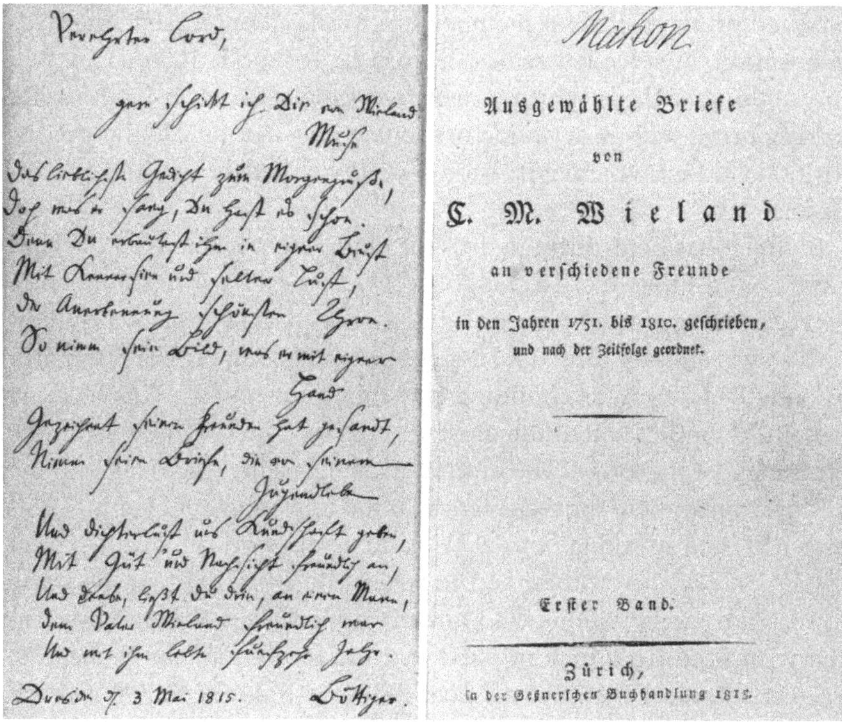
Verehrter Lord,

Dresden d. 3 Mai 1815. Böttiger.

Mahon

Ausgewählte Briefe

von

C. M. Wieland

an verschiedene Freunde

in den Jahren 1751. bis 1810. geschrieben,
und nach der Zeitfolge geordnet.

Erster Band.

Zürich,
in der Geßnerschen Buchhandlung 1815.

47. 'Selected Letters of C. M. Wieland'. Presented by Karl August Böttiger to Philip Henry together with a dedicatory poem in his own hand. On the title page is the notice of ownership: 'Mahon'.

Böttiger's personal 'morning gift' of this verse and dedication can probably be seen as his response to Stanhope's reception into the lodge.

The intimacy of the 'Du' form (You) even if here used poetically, is noteworthy in Stanhope's life, when seen in the context of his intimate correspondence. What Böttiger wishes to express to Stanhope by this verse and which needs to be more closely considered here is most evident in the third and sixth lines.

Wieland, one of the most gifted of Freemasons, was regarded by the brothers of the Weimar lodge as a noble model close to Goethe—a model figure who already incorporated the ideals of the group in that he had built the temple within himself—a representation of the World Creator's own Temple of Wisdom. A comparison with Mahon is a friendly eulogy, and it is doubtless an exaggeration when Böttiger says of his brother that: 'But of what he here sings, you already own.' What is referred to here is a certain inner quality, which in German lodges, unlike English ones, represented at least the beginnings of the expected prerequisites for membership. Wieland expressed what was meant here: 'A so-called seeker, even if he seeks for 1000 years, will find nothing with us which is worthy of the seeking, if he does not already bring with him on his first entry into the temple the predisposition for that which makes the essential character of the true freemason.'

Böttiger was here affirming that for Philip Henry. For what Wieland 'sang', or in other words, 'taught'—'*Du hast es schon*'! (You already own (it)). What should precede admission into the temple was in Böttiger's eyes already fulfilled. He goes on in the language of the brotherhood: '… For you are building it within your breast'. This formula contains an indication of the most central basic ideas drawn from the 'workings' of the lodge. The brother mason is called on to take up the craft practised there for the erection of the inner spiritual temple. Böttiger was here speaking both of Wieland's perfected achievement and of the goals of the brotherhood to which Philip Henry—in the sense of a friendly insinuation—had already approached through association with Böttiger, which implied that the receiver of the dedication was conscious of this highest goal. Böttiger thought that Wieland's far-reaching world of ideas—which in his later years Wieland believed, without contradiction, he could see in the lodges of his time as having achieved the 'spiritual building'—had now also been 'built' in Mahon in that he had understood the body of Wieland's teaching and accepted it.

Finally, Böttiger speaks to Mahon's 'thirst for knowledge'. What is meant by this? Knowledge and feeling for the powerful works of Wieland? Mahon, who when he read at all, preferred the sentimental Gothic novels of August Lafontaine? Evidently something else must be indicated by the thirst for knowledge referred to here. It may have to do with a common way of looking at things which was obvious to the dedicatee; the following lines contain an indication which is to be understood less philosophically than ideologically: 'Recognition' as the correct behaviour owed to the 'Master'—the picture of the throne, which points to the hierarchy of the lodge and represents the highest degree. Böttiger—this much is clear—employs for his eulogy a language of images that is at the same time concealing and revealing, as was often used for communication in the demi-monde in which he moved. Two months later, Philip Henry received from Bertuch 'an expensive jewel', a 'relic', which is not without significance in the present context. It was the 'most treasured little cap' that Wieland had worn. 'Oh! If only it were possible,' wrote Philip Henry from Carlsbad to Böttiger on 13th July 1815, 'that the head which now wears his little cap would also be ensouled somewhat by his spirit....' The January crisis seems to have passed.

*

A short while after Böttiger's suggestive dedication and Bertuch's gift, Stanhope spent some time in Weimar and sought out the merchant who had obtained for himself Wieland's gold-embossed walking stick. All Weimar knew of this and it had given rise to some unfriendly comment. On 28th August 1815, however, Philip Henry paid the 'finder' 25 Reichstaler cash in hand for 'Wieland's cane' and was able to call the costly object his own. The historic walking stick would make a final appearance in Stanhope's will. Whether Böttiger guessed what the noble lord was doing at all spending so long in Dresden is unknown, as is the question of what resulted from the news from Dresden finding its way to the Congress of Vienna. It is a fact that Gentz and Metternich had the greatest interest in a solution to the Saxon question that would be favourable to them and both were agreed in their assessment of Prussia's desire for annexation. George Jackson (1785–1861), brother of Stanhope's deceased patron Francis, who had meanwhile stepped into his brother's official position, travelled again from Berlin to acquaint himself with the situation on the ground in Dresden in order to be able to give further counsel. Metternich too, who had been Austria's ambassador in Dresden from 1801 to 1803, knew what to look out for and in which circles a judgement of the inner situation in Saxony could be obtained.

Men of the people, individuals on the fringes, such as Gottlob Seidel on the old market square, were among those from whom Stanhope drew his information, but more significant inside information was only available from those at the peak of 'society'. He gained access to them via Böttiger and the Dresden Lodge. In a letter to his mother-in-law Mahon wrote: 'Pray have the goodness to send it [his Court Dress] to me'; it would be needed for the coming receptions and 'society' gatherings. At these he could finally wear the decoration of the Order of St. Januarius, which he was not allowed to wear in England. It was, as he wrote to King Ferdinand, 'most unpleasant not to be granted permission to wear the Order in my homeland'. In Dresden, on the contrary, it was a minimum requirement in 'society' that one should be able to affirm one's standing and appearance with a decoration, even if with one as exotic as this.

48. Ludwig Siegfried, Count Vitzthum (c. 1800)

49. Detlev, Count of Einsiedel (1773–1861)

Soon Mahon could count the most significant personalities and influential families amongst his most familiar acquaintances and even circle of friends. The most prominent among them was Count von Loss, House Marshal of the King of Saxony, and the Counts of Vitzthum (Fig. 48), who for generations had played their not inconsiderable roles in the lower departments of state at the courts of Weimar and Dresden. At the Vitzthum Palace on Moritzstrasse Böttiger was a frequent guest.

Class and atmosphere impressed Mahon. One had to

> admire the composure and warmth of a German dinner, which is not interrupted as in England by the vulgar shouts with which people are urged to drink wine, offer to help others, or call to guests or waiters for food and drink. Here the conversation runs smoothly without interruption in a convivial manner. No words are wasted about the food, which, however good and plentiful it might be, is not deemed worthy of the thoughts or attention of one's company. As soon as the dessert has been taken, the company rises, bows politely to one another, and the gentlemen do not waste time in the most boring fashion with inane chatter….[94]

On the 10th April, for reasons unknown, Philip Henry presented Senior Chamberlain Ludwig Siegfried Count Vitzthum, who had 115 staff under his command, with the Complete Works of Wieland and shortly afterwards, Horaz's translation of the poet's works. It seemed important to Mahon to maintain his connections with such presents, and he did not neglect to make a careful record of such tasks.

Among his closest associates were the most influential family in Saxony, the Counts Einsiedel. They too served the King as ministers, chamberlains, ambassadors and ultimately, one of their family members stood at the summit of the state as prime minister.

Mahon's principal relationship interestingly was with Detlev, Count von Einsiedel (1773–1861) (Fig. 49) who, after the Battle of Leipzig, had accompanied the King into imprisonment and was later the Saxon plenipotentiary at the Congress of Vienna. He advised Frederick Augustus and led the negotiations which led to the King's restoration but which could not prevent the ultimate cession of the province of Saxony to Prussia. The most pleasant route to the Count's villa was upriver along the bends of the Elbe in the direction of Priessnitz past the small royal castle of Übigau. There on the left bank on a terraced estate, and surrounded by oleander bushes, stood the splendid building from the balcony of which one could enjoy a wonderful view in the direction of Dresden and Meissen.

Already in his first weeks in Dresden Philip Henry took up a relationship with another very influential and knowledgeable personage: Baron Joseph Friedrich von Racknitz (d.1818) First Court Marshal and Director of Entertainments. Under his leadership, Dresden enjoyed the most glittering period of its opera, though less so of its theatre, the director (Racknitz) of which, Schiller said, was 'timid of thought and limp in character'. Racknitz resided in a grand building in a well-known garden near the famous 'Japanese Palace'.

Not less profitable to Mahon was his close relationship with the Saxon Minister Gottlob Adolf Ernst Count Nostitz und Jänkendorf (1765–1836) (Fig. 50) from whom information of the greatest significance could be weaned. Nostitz was present at discussions pertaining to the new constitution and a trusted advisor to the king, with a position and voice on the Privy Council. In addition to his official duties, the Minister published poetical ballads and epics under the pseudonym Arthur von Nordstern, a name that became known through the founding of the literary circle 'Dresden Poets' Tea Party' but later in 1815 was renamed the 'Song Circle' (*Liederkreis*). Gerhard von Kügelgen

50. Gottlob Adolf Ernst von Nostitz und Jänkendorf (1765–1836)

51. Christoph Friedrich von Ammon (1766–1850)

attended it, as did Ludwig Tieck, and also Schopenhauer, who mocked the gatherings mercilessly.

> This circle, through its colourful mix of noblemen and bourgeois, of small talents and many dilettantes, was a highly characteristic mirror image of Dresden society at that time. In the admittedly relaxed but still strongly box-like character of the palace, the circle formed, so to say, a free enclave and raised aspirations towards a certain independence of thought and even universality. No stranger to the deeper meanings of life neglected to ask for an introduction into this circle. Throughout the north of Germany people pricked up their ears in surprise when they heard that in Dresden there was a literary society that was led by a Minister of State. So it was hardly surprising that the influence of this society went far beyond Dresden, so that the society came to represent a lively forum of public opinion, and that its organ, the 'Evening News' (*Abendzeitung*) was soon elevated to the position of a leading news and entertainment paper.[95]

Nearby there was a social circle that was no less interesting, held by Frau von Krock. Philip Henry was frequently in and out of both houses. At Frau von Krock's he met the politically not insignificant Rudolf Count von Bünau, formerly the Elector of Saxony's ambassador

52. Joseph Fouché, Duke of Otranto (1759–1820)

in Paris, and above all, the still very important Friedrich Count von Luxburg, the Bavarian ambassador in Dresden and later in Paris and Kassel. His brother was the Director of the Mannheim Court Theatre, Karl August von Luxburg (1782–1849) whom Stanhope met on every one of his visits to Mannheim and who would play a role in the Kaspar Hauser affair in the years 1831–33.

In this circle he also met the Hanoverian ambassador von Hammerstein and the Court Chaplain Friedrich von Ammon (1766–1850) (Fig.51), a rationalist and bitter opponent of Schleiermacher. Ammon was 'a clever man who sought to affirm the interests of the greatest Lutheran established church' in that he insisted on a strict union of Church and State, whereas Schleiermacher was striving in precisely the opposite direction. Ammon enjoyed a certain notoriety among the citizens of Dresden due to his unpleasant pronunciation and the poor acoustics in the Sophia Church. He too soon belonged to Stanhope's circle. The spectrum that resulted from this overall picture of the inner social situation in Saxony was fairly complete. Whether Baron Oelssen, the Prussian ambassador accredited in Dresden after the division of Saxony, was ever present in the circle is questionable. Due to the political constellation of the time, he belonged to the 'opposition', but nevertheless also to Philip Henry's circle of friends, which would be only understandable given the nature of the agent's task. Communicating news of Mahon's activity was the responsibility of Mr. Keen, who was connected to the British chargé d'affaires in Prussia. The existence of this courier service is evidenced by a further connection that Stanhope made in Dresden.

One of the worst characters that appeared during the French Revolution was Joseph Fouché (1759–1820) (Fig.52), Minister of Police during the Year of the Terror and the guillotine, and later, Duke of Otranto. He had been one of the first to vote for the execution of King Louis XVI. Fouché's dreadful bloody tribunals in Lyon, where, amongst other things, he personally took part in mass shootings, were too much even for Robespierre, who even tried to eject him from the Jacobin Club on account of his cruelty. That Robespierre instead was overthrown by Fouché only underscores the penetrating intelligence of this cynical despiser of men. Only Napoleon was able to thwart Fouché's intrigues in short order when the latter was found to have been conducting secret negotiations with England in 1810. The bloodthirsty Police Minister was exiled. However, Napoleon during his government of the Hundred Days was unable to manage without offering this singular expert his job back, which Fouché immediately accepted. In this position, after the second Peace of Paris, the ever-flexible power seeker simply continued working for the government of Louis XVIII, which also thought it could not do without his knowledge and talent. This man, said Barras later, always betrayed everything just at the right time: the Revolution, the Directory, two Empires and the Bourbons. It was not long before some royalists in the King's circle, acting on evidence of Fouché's gruesome role during the Revolution, called for and obtained his dismissal. On 15th September 1815 he was sacked as Minister and sent as ambassador to Dresden, where he arrived at the end of the month.

It is not clear whether Stanhope got to know Fouché immediately, but their relationship must have developed quite soon because a letter was exchanged between them during the last three months of that same year. Fouché himself was clear that Dresden would be the last stop for him before his arrest and that now only Prussia, Austria or England could save him; he had been in secret negotiations with the latter already in 1810. But why did Fouché turn to Stanhope? Was the former Police Minister better informed than others as to the reason why Stanhope was in Dresden and about the connections that were available to this English agent—including those to Vienna? The tone and style of the letters on both sides is already in 1815 very familiar and leaves one to conclude that some earlier meetings must have taken place between them. 'I would like to know,' writes Fouché to Mahon, 'in which spirit the articles in the German gazettes are being edited, especially those in Berlin, in relation to that which concerns myself... In matters of this kind I place more value on the manner and style in which things are done rather than on the content, which appears to me to be improving on the whole.'[96]

From a further short note in January 1816 can be gleaned that Mahon had a connection to Wellington in what was for Fouché a matter of survival and was also instructed as to the mission of the Duke of Richelieu. 'I have learned from a letter from the Duke of Richelieu that Mr. de Fabry is entrusted with the representation of French affairs at the Court of Saxony until there is a new ambassador. My letter to Lord Wellington is ready and I beg you to convey it. If you would like to be acquainted with its contents, I will read it to you tomorrow morning at 11 o'clock...'[97]

This letter to Wellington played a not inestimable role, as Fouché sought by it to maintain his political and moral integrity without which he could not reckon on obtaining any pardon even from the Allies. His real aim, however, was to have the privately written letter published (Fig. 53) so as to have it distributed in leading political circles. In this document Fouché demonstrates to the victor of Waterloo his innocence in all relevant points and thereby takes the wind out of the sails of any damaging indictment. Such was the plan, and Mahon seemed to be the man to make Fouché's wishes known. From this period there is another extant letter which testifies to the connection with Wellington but also to the Prussian ambassador. In this letter Fouché invites Lord Mahon to dinner together with the Prussian chargé d'affaires Baron Oelssen and the Napoleonic Marshal Emanuel de Grouchy (1766–1847). Napoleon had put almost all the blame for the defeat at Waterloo on the shoulders of Grouchy, who had first been raised to the rank of Marshal of the Empire during the Hundred Days, as he had brought his troops too late to join the main force. The former Marshal had since 24th July 1815 been on List 1 of the Bourbon Decree of Arrests and found himself a fugitive. He had lain low for a while in a farmer's house in Calvados until he turned up at Fouché's in Dresden, seeking help for escape to North America.

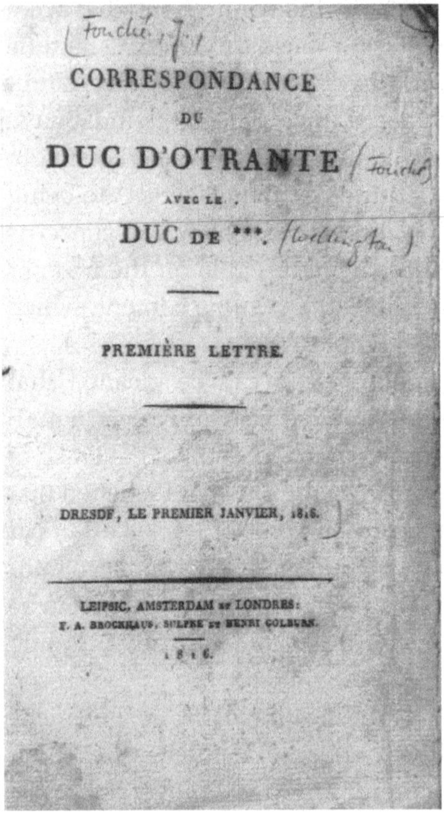

CORRESPONDANCE
DU
DUC D'OTRANTE
AVEC LE
DUC DE ***.

PREMIÈRE LETTRE.

DRESDE, LE PREMIER JANVIER, 1816.

LEIPSIC, AMSTERDAM ET LONDRES:
F. A. BROCKHAUS, SULPKE ET HENRI COLBURN.
1816.

*53. Title page of Fouché's book: 'Correspondence of the Duke of Otranto [Fouché] with the Duke of *** [Wellington].*

Interestingly, the letter of invitation to the meal bears the date 25th January 1816. Two different things emerge from this which further illumine both the person of Fouché and the assistance expected from Mahon. On 4th January 1816 the Amnesty Law in France outlawed all 'regicides' and removed them from their offices with immediate effect, which as far as one could see, applied only to the former Minister of Police. Fouché, knowing only too well what this meant for him, first remained silent about his dismissal and only handed the notice of it to the Saxon government on the 23rd January. The invitation to the Prussian ambassador however, carried not the slightest trace of this event. In view of the seriousness of the accusation and the fact that Fouché was no longer the French ambassador, the Prussian could scarcely be expected to turn up for a jolly meal at his house. 'I am having a dinner,' wrote Fouché to Mahon, 'on Sunday for the Prussian ambassador and General Grouchy and would like to invite you also. My letter to Lord Wellington is ready and copied. We are thinking of a way of getting it to him. It is a little different from the original which you know, and I shall give you knowledge of this.' It is significant that this letter contains the first indication of the intelligence contact that Philip Henry must have had with Metternich: '…I owe Prince Metternich an answer. Do you think that Count Spiegel will undertake to convey it ?'[98]

This must mean that at the latest by 1816 a firm connection to Vienna existed to which Fouché sought to appeal directly. Count Spiegel would later become very active in the Kaspar Hauser Affair (see p. 265). Another note confirms the early Vienna relationship and makes clear which position was here filled by or entrusted to Stanhope:

> I have received a letter from Prince Metternich and I wanted to answer him. Could you arrange for my letter to reach him via the English ambassador in Vienna? I will also give you a letter for Lord Castlereagh and a second for Lord Wellington. They are ready, but I am waiting for my courier before I seal them. My respects to General Grouchy, to whom you will certainly share the news I gave you. P.S. It appears that you have no news from Berlin ?[99]

This rather anxious question at the end relates to a final desperate request of Fouché's to Stanhope to secure Prussian protection in Berlin through Jackson, since the situation in Paris had become extremely dangerous for him: either the death penalty or life imprisonment with hard labour in a Siberian mine were apparently being demanded for Fouché. On 1st February 1816 the former Police Minister, who had also unscrupulously betrayed Bonaparte in the end, wrote to Stanhope in the best conspiratorial manner and without any form of address or greeting the anxiety-ridden words: 'the only thing that can save us all now is the death of the Emperor... In the case that the events in France would no longer allow the Duke D'Otranto to remain ambassador at Court, could he then find security and peace of mind in Prussia? Can he rest assured that he will not be handed over to his enemies?'[100] George Jackson could or would not act as intermediary; Metternich and especially Wellington also declined. Fouché therefore had to become an exile a second time, this time in Trieste, where he died in 1820. The whole episode again throws a distinctive light on Stanhope's position in Dresden and draws attention to the impressive intensity and variety of his relationships. The circle of people who appeared in the foreground accords in an ideal fashion with the demands of his mission, which provided other, more powerful figures with a basis for their judgements.

For Metternich and Gentz, Prussia's advance into Saxony was and remained a difficult challenge, in which England—here represented by Stanhope—was one of their most reliable collaborators.

'...The conquest of Saxony,' according to Gentz's later report,

> monstrous as it was, signified for them [Prussians] merely the beginning of a series of operations through which they hope, sooner or later, to bring over the greatest part of north Germany to themselves, put Austria out of action and gain pre-eminence throughout Germany. Counting on the assistance of Russia in carrying out this *long range plan,* they wanted at least to bring home from the Congress the foundation stone of their building; and even if Austria did not succeed completely in frustrating their intentions, then at least there was the slight merit that, thanks to our efforts, they did not achieve everything they had imagined.

Such results were, amongst other things, possible in that the existing situation was transparent to Vienna through early intelligence of the opposition's intentions. Stanhope wrote at the time quite in the sense of a friend from Dresden: 'The hard fate which Saxony (I say nothing of its King) has suffered by the dismemberment, all these causes have excited here much ill humour, much ill will against the Prussians & party spirit is now more virulent than ever. In that many Saxons refuse to go into any company where they may meet Prussians.'[101] From Berlin, George Jackson wrote to Lord Castlereagh:

> Those who have deeper insight into what goes on charge Prince Hardenberg with having neglected Prussia's interests the previous year at Kalisch and in the negotiations with Austria and Bavaria. To the departure from the basis which Russia at first endorsed, and which, as Your Lordship will recall, the strong recovery of Prussia from its situation in 1806, with the sole exception of Bialystock, affirmed, and to the confirmation at Paris of the cession of Ansbach and Bayreuth to Bavaria is being ascribed the humiliating alternatives with which Prussia is now allegedly faced, either to commit an act of flagrant injustice with regard to Saxony, or else, after so many sacrifices, to be forced into a worse situation than existed in 1806 ....There is already talk again, however, of provisional measures, and Prince Wilhelm of Prussia is regarded as the most likely Regent. This, my Lord is, I believe, a true picture of the present state of things; but there is unlikely to be any change due to the King's aversion to state affairs and the weaknesses of the political opponents of Chancellor Hardenberg.[102]

To the insights which determined such practical politics, Philip Henry also made his contribution, and if one recalls that he was later very much in a position to suggest to the British secret service that certain monies be paid to Gentz, then contours of that 'activity' indicated in Stanhope's letter to Carrington become only too visible.

Stanhope becomes still clearer in another letter, and indeed to George Jackson, of 31st May 1815. At the beginning of June, when the Final Acts of the Congress were signed in Vienna and the Saxon question was also clarified, Philip Henry's presence in Dresden was no longer necessary, and the question arose as to how the career on which he had successfully embarked was to be continued. From where and from whom did Stanhope always receive such timely instruction? 'The hopes which I expressed in my last letter'—a question which Stanhope must have concerned himself with earlier—

> on the diplomatic arrangements that might be made on the rewards that might be offered for past services receive, I think, new strength by the intelligence which has just reached me... & by the consideration that no appointment appears to have yet taken place for Cassel, where in former times there was always an English Minister. There are therefore two Courts, which may be regarded as vacant, and one of them would certainly be very agreable [*sic*].[103]

The question about Kassel came from Stanhope's awareness that George Jackson, another talented diplomat like his brother Francis, had served for a time in Hesse-Kassel. Philip Henry may also have recalled the letter of Prince Karl von Hesse-Kassel which, together with the writings of General Dumouriez, he had received years before from Pitt, and in which the Prince had effusively described the Prime Minister as his hero. He, Philip Henry, had been actually related to the great man and befriended by him! He wanted to link onto his first and, as it seemed, successful mission and press for further use of his services. It is noteworthy therefore that Jackson anticipated or arranged a return home via Vienna. Philip Henry, however, had known for some time that a stay in Vienna would certainly take place, as is clear from a letter of Ferdinand IV, which that king, albeit prematurely, had addressed to Vienna on 20th April 1814. Most probably, Philip Henry carried with him a letter of recommendation from Böttiger, which would open the door to Gentz. Böttiger was an old friend of the man who had in the meantime become such a famous statesman. Back in 1806 Gentz had spent the most oppressive days of his life in Dresden. His sponsor William Pitt had died precisely during those weeks, when Napoleon, 'the sabre of France', had struck down Prussia and Russia with devastating force; 16 German states had banded together under his Protectorate in the Confederation of the Rhine on 12th July 1806 and abandoned the union of the Reich; Emperor Franz II had laid down the imperial crown, which meant the end of the Holy Roman Empire; and Gentz himself had had to flee for his life, helpless and confused. There seemed at the time to be nowhere he could hold up. In neutral Saxony he found an exception, and Böttiger, who himself had only been in Dresden for two years, had taken the refugee in and looked after him. Ever since, the two men had stayed in contact and had maintained a warm friendship.

Philip Henry could thus embark on his first visit to Vienna well prepared. It can well be regarded as equivalent to the hour of birth as regards his involvement with the story of Kaspar Hauser.

On 18th May 1816 the Stanhopes left Dresden but did not set a course for a return journey to England, which was postponed for later. Lord Carrington had kept them constantly informed of the fact that old Earl

54. Friedrich von Gentz (1764–1832)

Stanhope was nearing his end in Chevening, but instead they headed for the appointments which now had to be kept in Vienna. There was no question of altering the travel plans. Philip Henry could have gone to meet his father while he was still alive but something more important was now in front of him. It was only after his later return to England that Philip Henry learned that Charles, 3rd Earl Stanhope, had died of dropsy on the 15th December at the age of 63, and had been buried in the family tomb on the 24th December; he had died unreconciled with his children. His son evidently felt no sadness; on the contrary: 'My feelings are such as I should in vain attempt to describe. From the bottom of my heart, I thank the Almighty for being allowed to see this thrice happy day.'

*

The 'homeward' journey from Dresden in early 1816 was a leisurely affair and passed not without a number of curiosities. The route to Vienna was taken along the border between Bohemia and Moravia. On the 31st the company together with their servant Anton Heinrich reached Salzburg, where they took quarters for a full five weeks. From there until the 2nd October, they travelled back and forth between Salzburg—which was close to the border—and Munich, staying for varying periods of time. Stanhope most likely established his first connections to the Bavarian Court at this time. He had corresponded with the King of Bavaria from Dresden, and it is more than probable that their first meetings took place in the autumn of 1816. These would have been easily arranged with the help of Count Luxburg, the Bavarian chargé d'affaires in Dresden, an old friend from their student days in Erlangen. Philip Henry had shown himself still 'surprised' a few weeks before in Dresden by 'the arrival of one of my friends from Erlangen, who is now adjutant to the King of Bavaria'. He may have been the most necessary connection.

When Stanhope later met Maximilian I in 1822 in Baden-Baden, he spoke of the 'warm reception' he received, which certainly would not have been so intimate if a cordial relationship had not previously been established. For the discussions he had ahead of him in Vienna, it was also certainly an advantage to be able to refer to the contacts he had already made with the House of Wittelsbach, with whom the Court at Vienna traditionally had a tense relationship. But Maximilian for his part may have seen advantages in acquaintance with an Englishman who apparently had the protection of both London and Vienna. Did this early initial approach to Munich stem from an idea of Stanhope's friend Jackson? On the 7th October finally came the arrival in Vienna. The family's stay in the Austrian capital would again be long, lasting almost two months, until on the 25th November they finally set out for Calais.

Stanhope spoke many times of the old friendship that bound him and Gentz. There is no reason to suspect that the links which had been variously built up through Pitt the Younger, the Grenvilles, the Jackson brothers, Böttiger and others did not lead to a meeting with Gentz during Stanhope's stay in Vienna. In view of the Vienna contacts which had been made and which had especially been arranged by letters from Dresden, it would have been incomprehensible to spend eight weeks in the city incognito without making this obvious visit. That it did in fact take place during this time has not yet actually been verified, unlike later meetings between the two men,[104] but those meetings do indicate that Stanhope's acquaintance with Gentz (Fig. 54) cannot have been new.[105]

During the months of October and November 1816, it may be assumed, a plan took shape which none of those involved in devising it at the time could have foreseen what it would cost and how long it would take to realise, but for this plan the capable man from Dresden was seen as the one most suited. Stanhope had acquired noticeable linguistic skills in both speech and writing—'he speaks German with a remarkable fluency' (Gentz later to Metternich)— and had a good feeling for regions and people together with a lust for travel and political affairs. He had brilliant relations to both England and Austria, was politically an 'old Tory of Mr. Pitt's school' and was therefore not only a declared enemy of the old France and all descendants of Napoleon, but, as his maiden speech in the House of Lords would later show, also an enemy of the new France; it was an enmity which even his close acquaintance with Count Artois, later such a master of fortune, could not prevent. All this made the intelligent, socially experienced, elegant 35-year-old ideal for the role of professional secret agent. (Fig.55) This seemingly independent English lord who, with a German servant and his own carriage with his family crest on the doors, travelled about apparently for nothing more than his own amusement, belonged to another category altogether in comparison with those little people who did not know how to make contacts with those of high rank. For the moment, there remains only the interesting question: in whose service was Stanhope acting? Was he a British agent who was at liberty to get closer to a newly befriended Austria? Was he, from that time on, active on a double mis-

55. Philip Henry, 4th Earl Stanhope (1781–1855)

sion or did he take on his coming task on his own account alongside his other duties? None of these explanations can be excluded.

But what occurred in those months of October and November in Vienna? After his time in Saxony, did he take up a task which, instead of the wished-for post in Kassel or Dresden, necessitated more travelling—travels which could only achieve their goal by maintaining a cover of the greatest discretion and caution?

Josephine, Alexander I and the Death of Baden's Heir Apparent

After the abdication of Napoleon in 1814 but before the beginning of the Congress of Vienna, a conversation took place between Joséphine, Napoleon's first wife, and a French peer who, for understandable reasons—his own 'downfall' was imminent—did not reveal his name. In the Tucher family archive, there was a handwritten note (Fig.56) with the title:

> 'Extract from the Memoirs of a Peer of France', Vol. III p.418
>
> The first of the two points we spoke about was of such an importance and was bound to produce such strange results that I recoiled

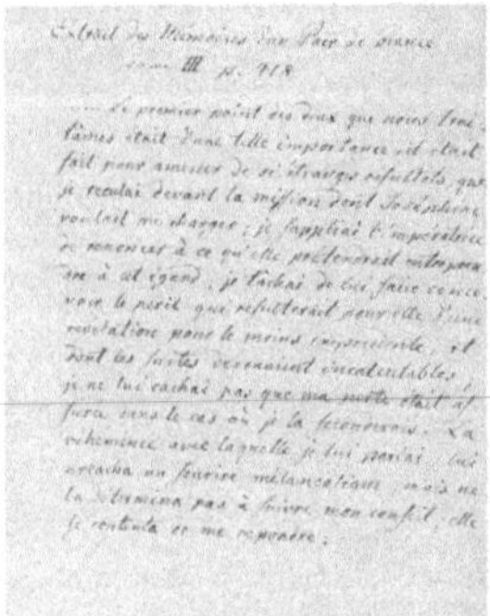

Extrait des Mémoires d'un Pair de France
tome III p. 918

.... Le premier point des deux que nous traitâmes était d'une telle importance et était fait pour amener de si étranges résultats, que je reculai devant la mission dont Joséphine voulait me charger ; je suppliai l'impératrice de renoncer à ce qu'elle prétendait entreprendre à cet égard, je tâchai de lui faire concevoir le péril qui résulterait pour elle d'une révélation pour le moins imprudente, et dont les suites devenaient incalculables. je ne lui cachai pas que ma perte était assurée dans le cas où je la seconderais. La véhémence avec laquelle je lui parlai lui arracha un sourire mélancolique mais ne la détermina pas à suivre mon conseil, elle se contenta de me répondre :

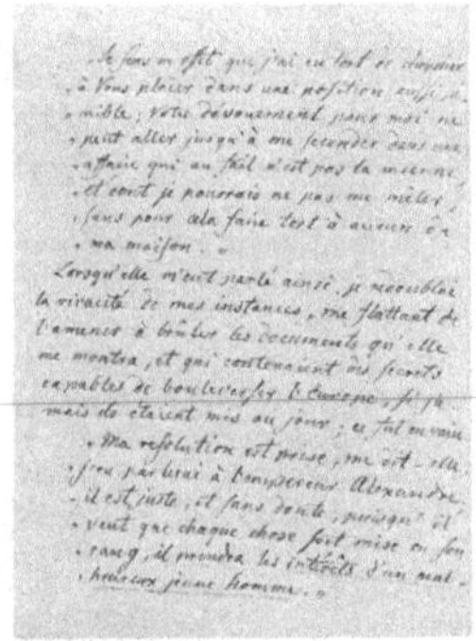

« Je sens en effet que j'ai eu tort de chercher à vous placer dans une position aussi pénible ; votre dévouement pour moi ne peut aller jusqu'à me seconder dans une affaire qui au fait n'est pas la mienne et dont je pourrais ne pas me mêler sans pour cela faire tort à aucun de ma maison. »

Lorsqu'elle m'eut parlé ainsi, je redoublai la vivacité de mes instances, me flattant de l'amener à brûler les documents qu'elle me montra, et qui contenaient des secrets capables de bouleverser l'Europe, si jamais ils étaient mis au jour ; ce fut en vain.

« Ma résolution est prise, me dit-elle, j'en parlerai à l'empereur Alexandre, il est juste, et sans doute, puisqu'il veut que chaque chose soit mise en son rang, il prendra les intérêts d'un malheureux jeune homme. »

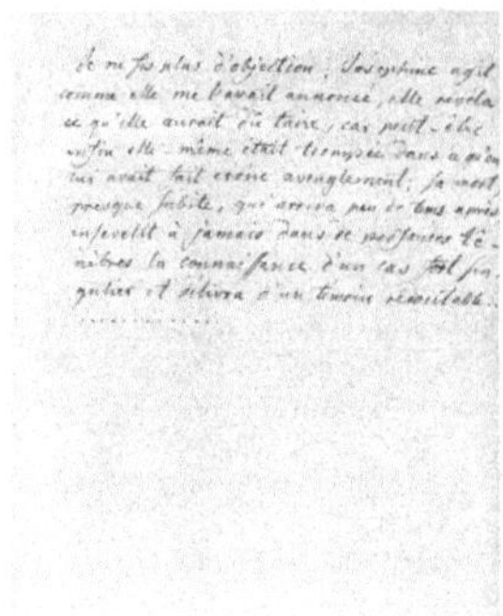

Je ne fis plus d'objection ; Joséphine agit comme elle me l'avait annoncé, elle révéla ce qu'elle aurait dû taire, car peut-être enfin elle-même était trompée dans ce qu'on lui avait fait croire aveuglément ; sa mort, presque subite, qui arriva peu de temps après ensevelit à jamais dans de profondes ténèbres la connaissance d'un cas fort singulier et sèvrera d'un témoin irrécusable..
. . . .

56. Joséphine de Beauharnais and the Kaspar Hauser Question. Memoirs of an unknown 'Peer of France'.

from accepting the mission with which Josephine wished to charge me. I asked the Empress to abandon what she was minded to undertake in this respect; I tried to apprise her of the danger that would result for her from an imprudent revelation, the consequences of which could not be foreseen; I did not hide from her the fact that my downfall would be assured were I to undertake this mission. The earnestness with which I spoke to her only drew from her a melancholy smile, but did not persuade her to follow my advice; she was content to reply: 'I feel that in fact I was wrong to try to put you in such a difficult situation. Your devotion to me cannot go so far as to support me in an affair which actually is not my own and in which I could not involve myself without doing wrong to a member of my house' [she was referring to Stéphanie Beauharnais]. When she had spoken thus to me, I redoubled my earnest entreaties to convince her, in the hope of getting her to burn the documents which she had shown me and which contained secrets capable of turning Europe upside down if they were ever to come to light: it was in vain. 'My mind is made up,' she told me. 'I shall speak to Emperor Alexander about it. He is a just man and because he wishes that everything be given its rightful place, he

> will without doubt take up the interests of an unfortunate young man.' I raised no more objections. Josephine did as she had told me; she revealed that about which she should have remained silent, for perhaps in the end she herself was mistaken in that which she had blindly been made to believe. Her death, quite sudden, which occurred a short while later, shrouded for ever in deep darkness the knowledge of an extraordinary affair unveiled by a courageous witness...

That this conversation took place is affirmed by the historian Prince Friedrich Ernst of Saxe-Altenburg who writes in an unpublished work that Empress Joséphine '...shortly before her death in 1814 entrusted Emperor Alexander of Russia with the secret of the pretender to the throne of Baden (Kaspar Hauser)'.

For Joséphine, the affair which had been mentioned to her was only too conceivable. Something similar had occurred in Paris during the Republic in 1795 at the time of the peace negotiations with Spain. The King of Spain, a descendant of Louis XIV, demanded the release of the two children of Louis XVI who had been imprisoned in the Temple by the Committee of Public Safety after the execution of their parents. The issue of the release at least of the son was a matter of the greatest significance, for Louis XVII was the legitimate head of the French monarchy.[106] But suddenly the child was said to have died, and his release was rendered hopeless. In 1812 Jean-Marie Hervagault, the probable Dauphin, died in questionable circumstances. On his deathbed he 'asserted the truth of his statement with a striking power of conviction'.

That was in the most recent past for Joséphine. But who was now in possession of the documents which were capable of astonishing all of Europe? Stéphanie would seem just as unlikely a candidate as any of those from the circle of the Hochbergs. At this time it would have occurred to no-one —at least in Karlsruhe—to discuss the future destiny of a Napoleonid. The one who gave the papers to Joséphine could certainly not have foreseen that the former Empress would be sure to meet Czar Alexander and that her appeal would have met with such an unexpectedly warm reception, as it had been the Czar's wish to get to know the first of Napoleon's wives.

Passing on the information to Joséphine had at first apparently not been intended with the nonsensical aim of claiming a Napoleonid's right to the throne at the worst conceivable time. But Joséphine was then the only person of any 'weight'—after Napoleon's second wife had eventually obtained a full divorce from the Emperor—to whom a family question could be addressed in both senses of the word. Joséphine was a Beauharnais like Stéphanie and just as much linked as her with the fate of the Emperor. They were almost certainly French documents which had been prepared in 1812 and afterwards and which had been passed to her immediately after Napoleon's abdication. Count Nicolay, the French chargé d'affaires accredited in Karlsruhe in place of Bignon, was a sharp observer of relationships and had special instructions from Napoleon for Stéphanie, with whose protection he had been expressly charged.

On 1st April 1812 Grand Duke Karl had a long conversation with Nicolay about the elevation of the Hochbergs, in which it was also made clear to the diplomat what this key change could mean for the House of Baden. After the surprising 'death' of the heir apparent, it was therefore Nicolay, immediately suspicious, who called for the post mortem. The resulting cause of death given was not seen by Nicolay as the actual one. On 16th October 1812 he wrote to Hugues Bernard Maret (1763–1839), Duke of Bassano since 1809. The Duke was a close confidant of Napoleon and his Foreign Minister from 1811–1813: 'The sudden death caused me to do my utmost to ensure that the corpse was examined to discover the cause of death.'[107]

Without sufficient evidence however, the chargé d'affaires of a foreign power, even if, as in this case, that of France, was hardly in a position to make demands of a German princely house. The doctors, who incidentally, were not sure whether they had examined the corpse of the baby prince or that of another infant, diagnosed 'gout and suffocating catarrh'; Nicolay 'appeared to have been satisfied'. Or perhaps not, for he continued to occupy himself with the process.

With perceptible emotion he reports on the next day (17th October) again to Foreign Minister Maret how Grand Duchess Stéphanie had taken the news. She had 'cried out: "Oh don't tell me that my child is dead...."'[108] Did these moments of suspicion together with many statements from other informers' statements produce the Paris dossier which as a whole led to the conclusion that with *this* 'death', as with that of the Dauphin, not everything had been in order? At any rate, the interests of France had been directly and very materially damaged when a Crown prince sponsored by Napoleon himself and whose godfather he personally wished to be had lost his life in such an unusual manner. After the wedding of Karl and Stéphanie, as a clear token of his feelings, the Emperor had sent to Karlsruhe a beautifully

57. Alexander I (1777–1825). Engraving by G. von Kügelgen.

58. Joséphine de Beauharnais (1763–1814) First wife of Napoleon I. Painting by P.P. Prud'hon c. 1805.

crafted cradle in which he wished to see princes. That the very first of these had spent only a few days in the cradle would not have been seen in Paris as a normal event after Princess Luise had been born the year before and was in the best of health. And now in April 1814 there was, notwithstanding all the dynastic dimensions, an extraordinarily gripping human problem if the documents were to be given credence. Meanwhile, Princess Josephine of Baden had been born in 1813 and was also in good health.

The opportunity to discuss the subject came when Czar Alexander I (Fig. 57) was staying in Paris before the opening of the Congress of Vienna. On 14th April Prince Leopold of Saxe-Coburg, who was in the service of Russia, wrote to Joséphine that it be the Czar's 'heart's wish' to make her acquaintance. The meeting took place two days later in Malmaison. For Joséphine (Fig. 58) this was a fateful day in several respects. On the cool evening of 16th April Joséphine, too lightly dressed, went for a long walk with the Czar in the palace park at Malmaison and caught a very heavy cold, of which she died on 29th May. That memorable day, however, was at the same time the beginning of an inner friendship which, after Joséphine's unexpected and sudden passing, was carried over to her children. Her meeting with the Czar was blessed by a remarkable magic that would last for just another 43 days. But in the weeks before the sad event brilliant festivities were held under the Czar's protection at which almost all the leading figures among the victorious Allies were present. Only a short time after the collapse of France, this was a most unusual constellation between members of the hated Bonaparte family and their former enemies. Hortense Beauharnais, former Queen of Holland, sang at the piano; Eugène, Napoleon's adopted son and previously Vice-regent of Italy, did the honours together with Napoleon's brother Joseph, formerly King of Spain. After that event there was no doubt that the Beauharnais enjoyed Alexander's special protection. After Joséphine's sudden death, the Czar took on the responsibility for the Beauharnais family she had left behind, regarding it like a legacy, and said about the unexpected and intense meeting between himself and Joséphine: 'An enemy has become your complete protector.' The loneliest of the Beauharnais but the one closest to Joséphine's heart and the one for whom she had lovingly taken on the role of mother was Stéphanie, Grand Duchess of Baden (Fig. 59). The Czar remembered Stéphanie from his first meeting with the 18-year-old during the Erfurt Congress of Princes in 1809.[109] Since then, he had felt a warm connection also to her and to the House of Baden; his wife was, after all, Princess Luise von Baden (1779–1826), a sister of Kaspar Hauser's father, Karl von Baden, who was now spending time in Paris and attended the festivities at Malmaison. When Joséphine died, Alexander wanted at first to take part in the funeral procession but in the end allowed himself to be represented by General von Osten-Sacken. Grand Duke Karl, however, did take part in the procession and was the only reigning prince to accompany the procession from Malmaison to Ruel, where Napoleon's first wife was laid to rest.

It is clear from the background to these events that Alexander felt strongly motivated and obliged to take care of the interests of the House of Baden. That the territories of Baden remained untouched after 1815 was due solely to his intervention.

But to return to the question posed above, what could have been the contents of the papers which Joséphine handed over between 16th April and 29th May? What could have been seen at this point in time as so dangerous that even the one who brought such news believed he had to fear for his life? There was only one worry, if not to say fear, which was shared far and wide, and that was Napoleon, and everything connected with the name. The only conceivable thing, moreover, that could have shocked all Europe at this time would have been that

59. Stéphanie Grand Duchess of Baden (1789–1860)

one day in the not-too-distant future an offspring of Napoleon would take the throne of one of the Allies and even quite legitimately. A baseless rumour going round at the time, and assiduously spread from the circle of Prince Metternich, sought to insinuate the idea that the father of Stéphanie's first son was not Karl von Baden, but Napoleon himself.

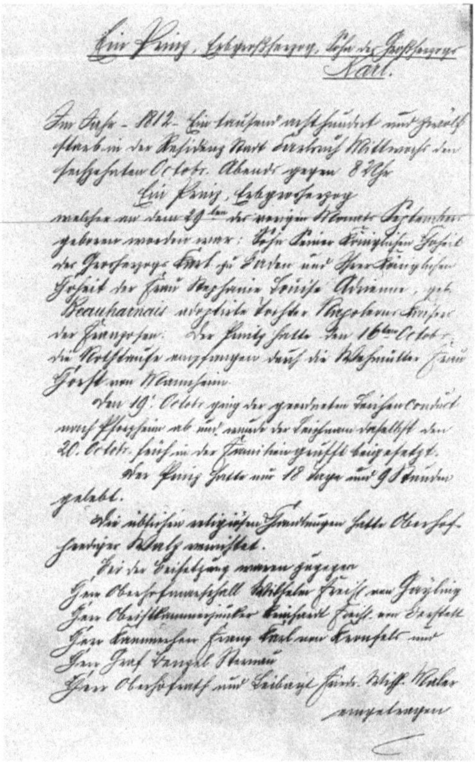

60. Death Certificate: 'A Prince, Grand Ducal Heir-Apparent, Son of Grand Duke Karl.'

In Vienna, it may be assumed, Czar Alexander brought the matter up in the most intimate possible circle and under every conceivable obligation of confidentiality. What diplomatic possibilities and what kind of measures could have been used? Officially, the nameless Crown prince of Baden died on 16th October 1812 and was buried in the Zähringer family tomb in Pforzheim (Figs. 60, 61, 62). A death certificate, post mortem report and 'eye witnesses'—all were available. Could it be doubted? How would the child's father, the ruling Grand Duke, who sought to represent Baden's interests, be treated in Vienna? Above all, where was the exchanged prince being held in concealment? As far as this question was able to be seriously debated at the time, from official documents and political statements, there was only one answer: this chapter of the history of Baden is in no way to be opened up. But the Czarina, the Grand Duke's sister, wrote a strange letter to Karlsruhe: 'One can well say that there was an all-out struggle over this matter. The emperor strongly protected Karl, perhaps for secondary reasons, but it was good for Karl.'[110] What other motives can be

61. Castle and Collegiate Church of St. Michael, Pforzheim. Child's sarcophagus (wood) (length: 0.99m, width: 0.44m, height: 0.45m) of the nameless Crown prince of Baden. Its present condition.

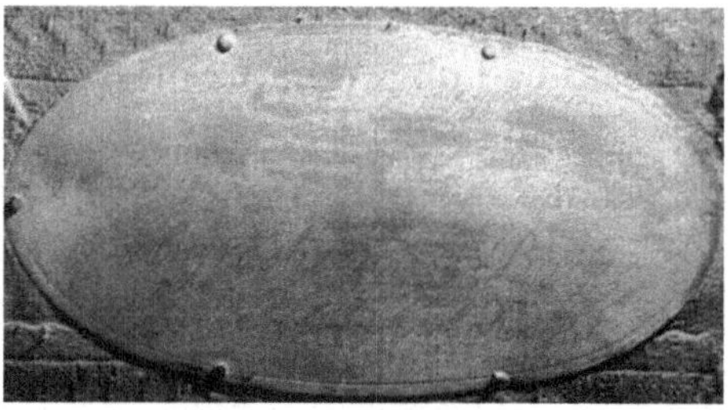

62. Illegible text of the silver-plated inscription plate: 'The Grand Ducal Heir-Apparent of Baden / Son of H.R.H Grand Duke Carl' born 29 Sept. 1812 / and deceased 16th October 1812 after receiving emergency baptism.

imagined in the circumstances and why were they not indicated? It is conceivable that with his well-known sense of justice, which Joséphine so highly esteemed, Alexander wished to see the Grand Duchy left untouched in the interests of the absent Crown prince until, at a later date, everything should become clear.

The Congress of Vienna ended suddenly and unexpectedly following Napoleon's return from Elba, which gave further proof of the danger represented by the parvenu. Louis XVIII together with his coterie fled from Paris and betook themselves to Ghent. 'There are things,' wrote Görres,

> to be heard which are so legendary and unbelievable that you could fool the devil himself by the telling of them. To such belongs the story the French have provided us with, in which, against the will of 24 million people, expressed in clear, strong words, a kingdom has been lost within 20 days and without a single sword stroke to a beast cursed and damned by all who, with only a thousand men, succeeded in escaping from exile. It is impossible to exaggerate the virtuosity of this wickedness, and though we Germans have provided examples of similar fine work in other areas, all such acts are overtaken and put in the shade by this so that we are washed entirely clean of all blemish...

Despite the truly fearful situation which would require another powerful effort by the Allies, Metternich allowed himself to make a very typical joke at the expense of his friend Gentz which was all the more effective as it would have hit Gentz in the very centre of his being, namely, his paranoid fear of Napoleon. With horror, the secretary of the Congress of Vienna read the notice which Metternich had had placed in the morning newspaper, 'that Napoleon had offered a substantial reward for the head of the Court Counsellor von Gentz'. Neither Gentz nor others found this at all funny. Archduke Ernst let it be known that 'This annoyed me, for I found no amusement in it but much seriousness [*Ernsthaftes*].' [The author is making a joke here with the word *Ernsthaftes*, which means 'seriousness' in German—*transl.*]

After the Battle of Waterloo, however, 'the beast' was incontrovertibly and finally brought down, the second Peace of Paris concluded and the much feared Napoleon sent away to the lonely island of St. Helena in the Atlantic Ocean, thousands of miles from France. Such, in short, were the key events of 1815.

In November 1816 when Stanhope was in Vienna a remarkable report appeared in the French state newspaper *Moniteur* on 5th November (Fig. 63) and similarly in the *Vossische Zeitung* in Berlin on 16th November (Fig. 64), which without question must have come to the attention of Gentz, as he, who was informed about everything, could hardly wait for the arrival of the daily newspapers from England,

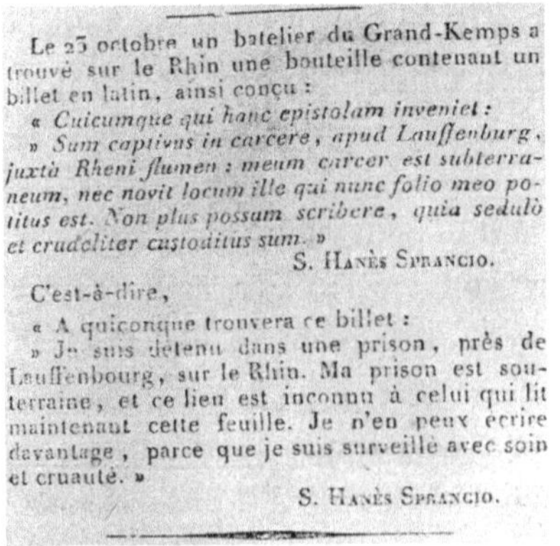

Le 23 octobre un batelier du Grand-Kemps a trouvé sur le Rhin une bouteille contenant un billet en latin, ainsi conçu :

« *Cuicumque qui hanc epistolam inveniet :*

» *Sum captivus in carcere, apud Lauffenburg, juxtà Rheni flumen : meum carcer est subterraneum, nec novit locum ille qui nunc folio meo potitus est. Non plus possum scribere, quia sedulò et crudeliter custoditus sum.* »

S. Hanès Sprancio.

C'est-à-dire,

« A quiconque trouvera ce billet :

» Je suis détenu dans une prison, près de Lauffenbourg, sur le Rhin. Ma prison est souterraine, et ce lieu est inconnu à celui qui lit maintenant cette feuille. Je n'en peux écrire davantage, parce que je suis surveillé avec soin et cruauté. »

S. Hanès Sprancio.

63. Moniteur, *5th November 1816 with the Latin and French text of the bottle message.*

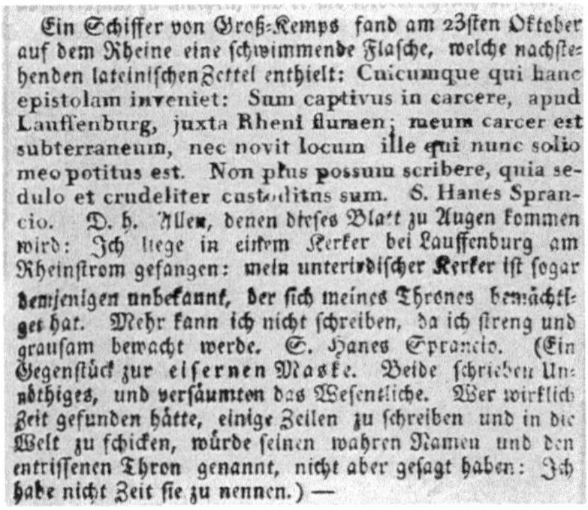

Ein Schiffer von Groß-Kemps fand am 23sten Oktober auf dem Rheine eine schwimmende Flasche, welche nachstehenden lateinischen Zettel enthielt: Cuicumque qui hanc epistolam inveniet: Sum captivus in carcere, apud Lauffenburg, juxta Rheni flumen; meum carcer est subterraneum, nec novit locum ille qui nunc solio meo potitus est. Non plus possum scribere, quia sedulo et crudeliter custoditus sum. S. Hanes Sprancio. D. h. Allen, denen dieses Blatt zu Augen kommen wird: Ich liege in einem Kerker bei Lauffenburg am Rheinstrom gefangen: mein unterirdischer Kerker ist sogar demjenigen unbekannt, der sich meines Thrones bemächtiget hat. Mehr kann ich nicht schreiben, da ich streng und grausam bewacht werde. S. Hanes Sprancio. (Ein Gegenstück zur eisernen Maske. Beide schrieben Unnöthiges, und versäumten das Wesentliche. Wer wirklich Zeit gefunden hätte, einige Zeilen zu schreiben und in die Welt zu schicken, würde seinen wahren Namen und den entrissenen Thron genannt, nicht aber gesagt haben: Ich habe nicht Zeit sie zu nennen.) —

64. Vossische Zeitung *of 16th November 1816 with the German text of the bottle message and the suggestion of a 'similarity to the story of the man in the iron mask'.*

Austria, France and Germany. That Gentz was a regular reader of the *Moniteur* was confirmed many times by the man himself. The sensational text read:

> On 23rd October a boatman from Gross-Kemps found a bottle floating in the Rhine. It contained a scrap of paper on which was written in Latin: 'To all who come across this letter: I am lying imprisoned in a cell near Lauffenburg on the Rhine: my underground cell is even unknown to the one who has usurped my throne. I cannot write more, as I am kept under a careful and cruel surveillance. S.Hanes Sprancio.'

Even if one were not at the time able to make out the secret anagram—which deciphered, reads *Sein Sohn Caspar* (His son Caspar), the message four years after the birth of Stéphanie's first son still gives the clear indication that the prisoner was one with right of succession to a throne and who, as would be disclosed much later, was also in fact named Kaspar, whose inheritance had been stolen by someone who did not himself know of the prisoner's lot—something which from everything in the papers of Joséphine could only mean the House of Zähringen. On that November day, Gentz, the secretary to the Congress of Vienna, must have recalled the Czar's concern for and very engaged awareness of all Baden's interests and he must have suddenly put two and two together. This issue, which the year before allowed of no discussion had now become a case that deserved the greatest attention. 'It is only too obvious,' wrote Prince Friedrich Ernst of Saxe-Altenburg in his historical writings referred to earlier

> that in the German dynasties there was no inclination to mix their bloodlines with one of inferior status that had been forcibly produced by Napoleon. Above all, after the fall of Napoleon, they utterly recoiled from the prospect of allowing a Napoleonid on a German throne. But this danger seemed to be present in the case of Baden. Metternich in any case did not wish to tolerate an offspring of Napoleon, whether legitimate or illegitimate on a German throne. To Metternich, the living symbol of Reaction in post-Napoleonic Europe, it must naturally have been a matter of the greatest concern to prevent the penetration of the revolutionary blood of the Corsican anywhere in the leading circles of old Europe. After the fall of Napoleon and even later after the emperor's death, Metternich consciously pursued the Napoleonids wherever he could and sought everywhere to restrict their influence as much as possible.....If we keep before our eyes this central train of thought, the idea of the Napoleonic world

> empire, the attempt to realise which had shaken all of Europe only a short time before, we can well imagine why Metternich above all staked everything on preventing an heir of Napoleon's (Kaspar Hauser) from getting into the centuries-old structure of the pre-Napoleonic Age on a European princely throne. He knew that once the Napoleonic blood had found its way in, it would soon spread everywhere through the widely ramified relationships of the old dynasties....

That summarises and characterises the situation of which the two newspaper reports had made people in Vienna only too aware. Stanhope must have perceived such concerns. When Bonaparte had left Elba the year before to intervene once again in the destiny of France, Stanhope, the admirer and defender of Christian virtues, had noticed a turmoil within himself, which had created the preconditions for the conversation he was about to have in Vienna. The reappearance of Napoleon 'haunts me perpetually', he had written at the time, 'The progress of Bonaparte ...preys so much upon me that it is the first thought which wakes with me in the morning & the last which disturbs me when I go to sleep. ...If he is not assassinated...God alone knows what the consequences may be.'[111]

Now, alongside the Duke of Reichstadt [Napoleon's legitimate son by Marie Louise of Austria, born 1811—*Ed.*] the dreaded hydra had grown another head in 'S. Hanes Sprancio'. For it could not be overlooked that Stéphanie was the hope of all the Napoleonids who were still alive, and that she was the only member of the Bonaparte family at the side of a reigning Grand Duke who had survived the political collapse of 1814 untouched. The House of Baden would therefore have been the only one possible that was legally able to continue what for Metternich should be ended once and for all.

But did the situation (in October 1816) essentially seem any more promising than in the autumn of 1814? From an intensive investigation of the location, it must have been clear that the Napoleonid held in captivity far from his throne was certainly no longer to be found at Lauffenburg since the approximate location was there to read in two international newspapers. Added to which, for Metternich, Gentz and Stanhope, there was nothing to confirm whether the paper in the bottle was not a deliberate decoy intended only to lead away from the actual facts. From the view of things possible at the time, it must have seemed simply absurd to keep a pretender to the throne locked up and let him rot if he was later intended to take over the government. Was it not much more likely that a prince was being educated in secret? The message in the bottle was therefore a ruse, a feint. First investigations appeared to bear out this view.

Official documents at Colmar show in fact that long before the news appeared in the *Moniteur*, which pointed to the Upper Rhine region, the French Minister of Police Décazes had had the relevant banks of the Rhine searched on 30th October—without success, as was to be expected. But in fact, there were circles in which the real situation was known, and which for reasons not at first evident, pointed to the fate of an ousted Crown prince.[112]

The only thing to be done was to keep one's eyes on the case in the near future and to conduct an intensive search throughout Germany, especially in the south, to see whether the new location of the hidden prince was not to be found there. That meant building up relationships and contacts and waiting for the moment when something would again become noticeable in this awkward affair. Who was better suited for this task, even predestined for it, than the man who was at that very moment staying with Gentz in Vienna—Philip Henry Stanhope?

From that autumn on, Stanhope made another 24 journeys to Germany where, apart from Vienna, his interest mainly in the south German states or the Courts at Munich, Stuttgart and Karlsruhe never flagged. It is most unlikely that his family or his servant Anton Heinrich knew the real reason for these journeys. The need for absolute silence in this affair was paramount. In none of the letters addressed to his family or close acquaintances in the following years—until (and including December 1833) after the murder of Kaspar Hauser—did Philip Henry mention the slightest detail about the background to his almost annual visits to Germany.

In the late autumn of 1816 Stanhope headed back to England. Too much significance need not be attached to the fact that on the way home (4th December) he already paid a visit to Mannheim for the first time. But to the total picture of his stay in Vienna it adds a piece to the mosaic and therefore is not without a certain meaning. There was no need for hurry in the circumstances as the hidden prince was at this time only four years old; there was no immediate danger of his accession. From the only perspective then possible in Vienna, one would have said to oneself that those who were planning to bring forth the pretender from his current oblivion at a later date would now be doing all they could to cover their tracks. It would therefore be cleverer to wait for a while in the certainty that the secret could not be hidden for ever, which would in any case be nonsensical if the intention were to put the boy on the throne in the not-too-distant future. How the drama would actually play out, no-one in Vienna at the time could even guess.

With his servant Anton Heinrich, Stanhope went via Paris (10th to 21st December), reached Calais on Christmas Eve and was back in his homeland on 28th December. With the death of his father, Philip Henry was now master of Chevening and had been awaited accordingly. 'We arrived close on 11 o'clock and were received with such an expression of joy and warmth that I was deeply grateful. I had never before experienced the like in this place. The village was beautifully decorated. Flower arches with inscriptions and garlands had been erected and we were escorted by a large crowd of people and bands.'

5. Family Life in Chevening

Parliamentary Activity, 1817–1820

The New Year began with the renovation of the family residence. Craftsmen and particularly painters set to work, and as soon as the smell of the paint was gone, the family moved into the castle which, after the late Earl's furious and frequent spasms of rebuilding, had looked much the worse for wear.

With his father's death, Philip Henry relinquished the title Mahon, which now passed to his son and was, from this point on, the 4th Earl Stanhope, Peer of the Realm, with his due seat in the House of Lords. He had the event commemorated with a fine etching by S.W. Reynolds. With his calmly reflective gaze directed into an uncertain future, his serious posture, his right hand placed masterfully on the hip, and his free leg self-consciously placed forward, he presents himself in his robe of ennoblement, with its ermine-lined mantle, his peer's crown in his left hand and in the distance the towers of Westminster Abbey. An imposing picture! (Fig. 65)

This sudden new episode in his life immediately opened with a new beginning in a field where he had already years before experienced some painful defeats. There was the memory of his exit from the political stage, accompanied by scornful commentary, when he had been parliamentary assistant to his father-in-law. In contrast to those days when he had been a clueless youth in political terms, he was now the 4th Earl Stanhope, a man to be taken seriously. This changed certain relationships and enhanced his status.

On the 11th February 1817, he acknowledged receipt of news sent by Ferdinand I—previously Ferdinand IV when Murat had occupied the throne of Naples. The news was conveyed by Leopold, Prince of Salerno (1790–1851), acting on instructions from the King of Two Sicilies. Leopold was a son of Ferdinand and Marie Carolina, and married the same year to Princess Anna of Saxony. Such a development, news of which soon got around, enhanced Stanhope's prestige. He also formally took up his seat in the House of Lords at this time. The new-baked Peer opened his maiden speech with some dashing statements. He began by declaring that 'he was not enrolled under the banners of the executive, and did not receive or adopt with implicit faith every statement that ministers might choose to make.'[113] He followed

65. *Philip Henry, 4th Earl Stanhope. Mezzotint sheet by S.W. Reynolds of Bayswater. Based on the portrait by Haines.*

this with strenuous attacks on France which were keenly taken note of. There was only one way to have real peace in Europe: 'the dismemberment of France'.[114] Quite apart from a flood of angry opposition from Paris, his brother James, who was then staying there, was immediately forced to hire a bodyguard, and Lady Stanhope, who was also spending some time in the French capital, was so concerned about the possibility of attempts on her life that she promptly decided to return to England. Not bad for starters: it was indeed a speech by 'an old Tory of Mr. Pitt's school'.

On the 16th May followed his first debate in the House of Lords 'on the Catholic Petition'. Stanhope the Ultra-Tory inveighed against the call for Catholics to have equal civil rights with Anglicans. It would lead too far to enumerate all the results and curiosities he brought forward in the course of his zealous speeches in the course of the debate. Old Carrington, his father-in-law, had once very elegantly pointed out to him that the denial of equal rights to Catholics could not last much longer and that he had the same view of the issue as Stanhope's father: 'I am old enough to remember in your father's time the minorities of one, and unless I forget myself, you were not insensible to the unpopularity of eccentric sentiment.'[115]

But what changes has the wisdom of age ever effected? In the slavery debate, in which Stanhope repeatedly expressed contradictory views, Lord Brougham finally taught him a scornful lesson: 'I am perfectly well aware that the noble Earl will always stand for that which he has once laid down; and that even after it has been proved to be absurd, —after everyone else has admitted the the absurdity of it—the noble Earl will still stand up for it, aye stand up and speak for it as often as your Lordships like.'[116]

Stanhope then proposed that a commission be sent to the West Indies to study the question. But the new member was not really taken seriously. 'Allow me to ask the noble Earl,' said the scornful Brougham,

> whether he will go with me, and if he will, whether I may calculate upon the pleasure of hearing seven or eight speeches from him upon the same subject—they must be upon the same subject—in the space of four and twenty hours; and whether the noble Earl will promise that they shall all of them be as entertaining and instructive as three or four speeches made upon the presentation of a petition but having no connexion whatever with the subject of that petition?[117]

66. Caricature of members of the House of Lords; upper row, centre: Philip Henry Stanhope. Washed pen and ink drawing, attributed to Isaac Robert Cruikshank.

Lord Greville noted in his diary that this was 'the most beautiful piece of sarcasm and complete cutting up (though with very good humour) that ever was heard, and an exhibition to the like of which the Lords have not been accustomed'.

Philip Henry's questions and answers only seemed to provoke amusement and real bursts of laughter in the Upper House and at some point, he must have noticed that his sister Hester's prophecy—that 'he will never be suited for public life'—also seemed to be valid for this new period of political activity. It became painfully clear to him that his contributions to debates not only had no effect but merely served the general amusement as well as the caricaturists (Figs. 66, 67, 68) and so he came later to the self-justifying decision: 'The House of Lords cannot now be considered, as a deliberative body in this debate, as anything else than a mere meeting place to deliver opinions, and therefore I do not think that I shall after tomorrow attend any of its meetings.'[118]

He did not actually carry out this resolution as he continued to make speeches in the House, but the statement reflects a certain emotion. His step back from public life, which was in no way a selfless act,

67. Caricature of Philip Henry's activity in Parliament
'Evidently NOT CONTENT'.

I fear that we have made
A rather bad business of it…. To be sure
There is a melancholy satisfaction
In reflecting that we have pulled down the Duke.

An Attorney General too!
Who won't let one do what
One wishes with one's own.

Aye! But who have we set up?
See them, there laughing in their sleeves
At us! and worse than all, look at the woolsack!!!
Melancholy satisfaction indeed!—I think we
Are much in the condition (to use an elegant simile)
Of the Man who cut his nose to vex his face.

created unintended space for his love of travelling. It is hard to decide whether a successful parliamentary career would have compensated for this tendency, but as he was not successful, his urge to travel was strengthened. At the end of the first period of his new parliamentary career which had promised much, he was thus forced to accept that he had no other choice but to set out once again on his long journeys with Anton Heinrich. The attempt to establish himself in other areas of life having failed, the lack of alternative possibilities meant that the only course open to him was the career of secret political agent recommended by Pitt and Jackson.

68. Caricature of Philip Henry's activity as a parliamentarian.

'A Pair of VERY RIOTOUS FELLOWS alias RADICALS of the NEW SCHOOL'.

I say, my worthies, can't you go on quietly & not make such a confounded noise? Why, you will frighten all the old women out of their wits—

That's a pretty thing to say to people in our desperate condition! ***Go on quietly & don't make a noise!***

I can tell you my fine fellow! that you must submit to hear ***more noise*** *unless something be done for the people—I know the law as well as you or any man in England—and D---- me! I'll make as much noise as I like.*

Close observers of biographical development have noticed the presence of a rhythm that occurs approximately every 18 years and 7 months, sometimes slightly earlier or later, and which as a rule leads to uncomfortable turning points which are not seldom experienced as something that thrusts one out of accustomed connections.[119] In 1800, at the age of a little over 18, Philip Henry fled from his parental home and now in his 37th year, again due to a certain gentle pressure, he embarked on activities in a new phase of his life for which he seemed predestined and which he first took up with great enthusiasm. His stepping back from parliamentary activity signified at the same time his real entry into that phase of his life which consisted of discreet travels, and which notably continued without any significant interruption until his 55th year.

*

He set out once more for Germany already in October 1817. After landing at Calais on the 10th his route went via Dunkirk in the direction of Bonn, as he wanted to see the Rhine Valley. 'I cannot tell you how much I was delighted with the banks of the Rhine. Much as I had often heard of their beauty they surpassed my expectations, & they afford the most magnificent as well as the most pleasing scenery which the mind can possibly conceive.' In Cologne he was interested in the new perfume by the Farina brothers which all of society was after, and therefore also his mother. 'I enquired very particularly at Cologne about the Cologne Water which is so justly celebrated, and I heard that there are above thirty Manufactories of it, only two of which are genuine, those of Jean Farina and Jean Marie Farina, but as it may be vended under their names tho' not made by them, I have learned the real seal which distinguishes it, & I will bring you a bottle as a Specimen.'[120]

From Frankfurt the journey continued via Weimar to Lützen, where Stanhope viewed the battlefield and the monument erected to Gustavus Adolphus who had fallen in the battle of Lützen [1632]. Napoleon had once met Eugène Beauharnais here. Sometime during these days the news reached Philip Henry that on the 18th October the Wartburg Festival had taken place, which for Goethe, had been a 'source of unpleasant conflict'. Student delegations from almost all German universities had appeared at the invitation of the Jena *Burschenschaften* [fraternities] for the parallel celebration of two events—the Battle of Leipzig and the 300th anniversary of the Reformation—liberations from political and papal domination. As it had been declared dangerous to the State, the event began on the evening of the day of commemoration, when symbols of the still prevailing limits on freedom—pigtails, stays, and a corporal's staff—were publicly burned on a pyre along with books by twenty-eight authors. Metternich feared the worst and immediately after the day of protest sent spies to report on the students' groups in Leipzig, Eisenach, Weimar, and Jena. Stanhope too was at the centre of events at this time, in Weimar on the 22nd October and in Leipzig on the 12th November. Then, on the 14th he also visited the centre of the turmoil in Eisenach and gained a clear picture for himself of the gathering that Metternich had considered a conspiracy against the holiest of principles.

His journey proceeded next to Dresden. The city had not only been the place where with his family he had been happy to live for almost two years and where he had had numerous encounters with more or less important people of the day, it had also seen the beginning of his career, and could therefore be described as a place of destiny for Stanhope.

But now apparently—or at least, so it seemed, the city of his period of apprenticeship as an agent could no longer hold him. 'I shall leave this place without regret.' That sounds rather cold and scornful, and probably relates to an unpleasant affair which had prevented him from returning to the city of his own accord. Not so long before he had sounded quite different:

> On seeing Dresden I thanked God that He had granted that I should see this beloved and splendid city again, for which I feel the greatest inclination and a sense of belonging as if I had been born there and had spent my life there. There is no place as far as my experience has extended, which is so desirable a residence as this for a person of small fortune.[121]

Now, however, he thought that 'it appears very improbable that I should ever visit it again' but only of leaving 'as soon as the business which brought me here is terminated'. Whether the work in which he was engaged was related to a Marquess Moratalla is not known, but a man whose real name was Drowlow was living in Dresden under the name Moratalla, and Stanhope met him repeatedly. More is not known.

For the next three years at least, Philip Henry's whole heart now belonged to his wonderful home in Chevening with its great park and small lake with fountains and swans. 'Dresden,' he wrote to his mother, 'does not please me as much as it did formerly...My affections are now centred in my dear Chevening, a spot which I love inexpressibly, & my happiness is now found in the station which the blessing of God allows me to enjoy….'

On the 12th November, the journey continued via Naumburg, Fulda, and as mentioned above, via Eisenach to Paris where they arrived on the 23rd. He stayed in the French capital for three weeks and had already had only the worst to report to his mother in an earlier letter from Frankfurt: 'I am persuaded that you would be disgusted with

France as it is now & would find in it nothing that could remind you of the charms that inspired you with regret on leaving it. There is no longer any degree, I will not say of politeness, but even of civility, everything is bad in quality and dear in price; roguery is excessive & the nation seems transformed into a set of blackguards and of ruffians.'[122]

But what then kept him so long in Paris? It could hardly have been the healthy living, as he wrote home: 'I am in perfect health & nothing can be more regular than my mode of life. I rise at five in the morning, set out at six & travel until about seven, dining at two or three. I go to bed about nine, but the whole day is passed in moderate exercise in the open air, so that I have an excellent appetite & a good digestion.'[123] That Philip Henry would spend three weeks in a city where 'roguery' was the norm, where commodities were expensive and relationships bad, surrounded by 'blackguards and ruffians'—all on account of the fresh air, is hardly plausible. One gets closer to the real reason for his stay when one knows that there were a number of men living in Paris whom he knew and who were awaiting his visit. La Rochefoucauld, the canny politician of 1789, an old friend and brother mason of his father's, was a gentleman of 70 years old but was still full of life. Influential and knowledgeable, he could open doors and set up connections which would otherwise have been beyond the reach of the newcomer. That the threads of 'his case' were also bound in Paris must have been clear to him from the beginning. Seen from this viewpoint, a stay in Paris was essential, despite being both undesirable and also not without danger. The man who had caused unbelievable offence by his ludicrous call in the House of Lords for the dismemberment of France as the only solution to the French Question was certainly not forgotten in Paris. The fact that Philip Henry had remained in friendly correspondence with the King's brother, Count Artois, could only be helpful in such a situation.[124] Did this relationship guarantee a peaceful stay in Paris? That is certainly plausible, as the King was doubtless stalked by the same concerns as the gentlemen in Vienna. Both governments could, indeed must have welcomed the success of an undertaking such as had been conceived. For Louis XVIII, any offspring of Napoleon's was just as uncomfortable and dangerous a prospect as for Metternich and Gentz, who had quite other considerations to keep in mind.

After three weeks, on the 20th December Stanhope had concluded his affairs, and his carriage set off for the coast which, after a few short stops, was reached on the 23rd in order to make an immediate crossing.

Christmas Eve in Calais or Dover was nothing unusual on Stanhope's itineraries. This time he arrived in Dover on the 24th December.

*

Stanhope spent the next two years in England occupied with the development and embellishment of his estate and for the first time, if only for a short period, felt himself quite at home. In the first minutes (12.15 a.m.) of 31st May 1819, his wife Catherine gave birth to their third and last child, Catherine Lucy Wilhelmina.

Meanwhile, Philip Henry headed a well-tended household at a not immodest level of expenditure—the complete opposite of what his father Charles had considered necessary. Following an old design which probably stemmed from his grandfather, he had an extensive labyrinth laid out in the gardens, which is still worth seeing today. One who called at Chevening and praised its opulence and its lifestyle was the world traveller Prince Hermann von Pückler-Muskau, who later also sought out Lady Hester Stanhope in her rock palace in the wilderness of Lebanon, where the talk was often of Freemasonry in general and of Lady Hester's connections to it in particular, and where they spoke of the Duke of Reichstadt and of the one (Kaspar Hauser) Hester was expecting after the Duke's death.

> As one can find everything in England, I met an Englishman of rank who had endeavoured to introduce into his house German customs, German household ways and a German social tone. This was Lord Stanhope, who lived in our fatherland for a lengthy period in rather restricted conditions and suddenly became very rich. The only English element was the red livery of his servants with their bright yellow breeches and stockings; everything else was German. Even mealtimes were similar to ours. The length of the meals I found most tiring. I sat there as if on coals, especially because I was expected elsewhere.[125]

The German way of living must have made an impression on the young Mahon, and most recently, the Viennese milieu provided him with outlooks and views on life which he no longer wished to miss. How literally Pückler-Muskau's words about the Stanhopes' *richesse* are to be taken must remain open to question.

Stanhope himself emphatically denied it a few years later in another connection and even complained and expressed himself amazed as to how such a nonsensical rumour could have developed. Since the estate, as we know, had been substantially degraded by his father, the remark that his present wealth had been 'suddenly' acquired is not insignificant. At this time Philip Henry had access to income which could scarcely have come from his inheritance yet which nevertheless enabled him to go on lavish trips which lasted for months. To return to the country 'in which I have experienced countless blessings' may have been an honourable reason for his next trip to Germany, which was planned for the autumn of 1821, but it was only *one* reason. The key factors will become clear in the following chapter's consideration of the personalities, incidents and locations visited in the years 1821–1825.

6. The Three Journeys to Mannheim and Karlsruhe

The First Meeting with Grand Duchess Stéphanie, 1821–1823

At the beginning of 1821 the Crown prince of Baden was in his ninth year. Normally, this age was regarded as the ideal time to begin instruction, education and preparation for one's later life tasks. Nervousness and helplessness on the part of those who were concerned about the whereabouts of the prince led them to surmise that this might be the time when the Napoleonid would gradually begin to make his presence felt again. Was there nowhere in Baden a boy being educated who was identical with the S. Hanes Sprancio of the Lauffenburg message in a bottle?

In the midst of this tense situation came the news that on the 5th May Napoleon had breathed his last in exile on the island of St. Helena. It took a British ship nearly eight weeks to bring the news to Europe and another few days for a courier of the Rothschild Bank to reach Vienna with it. At first, one could hardly believe that Napoleon, who had been in the best of health had died at the age of only 52. Stéphanie learned of the Emperor's death on the 25th July and wrote in her diary:

> He before whom the world trembled, whom the Kings of the earth flattered and then betrayed, is no more. He is no more!...He died on a rock more than a thousand miles from his own and from his fatherland. But a few friends at least remained loyal to him, comforted him in his final days and lightened his last moments. You whose devotion serves as a model but rarely finds an echo, accept the homage of a heart that understands you! But thou who incorporated the geniuses of centuries, incomprehensible Being who conquered the world, thou diest in chains! Thy life belongs to history yet thy last years are shrouded in a realm of dark happenings where one can hardly uncover the truth! Console thyself that death has set thee again upon thy throne; thy failures—or should I say thy errors ?—are now overshadowed by the fullness of thy great achievements, thy astonishing success. As the blinding rays of the sun prevent one from seeing its spots, so will it be easier for those who read about thee in the annals of the ages to come to admire thee than to pronounce judgement![126]

69. Eugène de Beauharnais, Duke of Leuchtenberg (1781–1824). Copperplate engraving by Paolo Caronni (1810). From a drawing by Giuseppe Longi.

Many felt similarly who had been touched by the Emperor's hand of destiny and whose thoughts in this moment went involuntarily to Napoleon's son, the Duke of Reichstadt. His father's last words at his second abdication were not forgotten: 'My political life is over, and I proclaim my son under the name Napoleon II to be Emperor of the French.' Might not the death of Bonaparte unleash an incalculable movement among the people who, as was known only too well, despised the flabby Bourbon regime and yearned for the days of the Empire?

What did the Emperor's sudden death, which no-one had reckoned would come so soon, mean to Gentz, Metternich and Stanhope? Since the Duke of Reichstadt was frittering his life away in the security of Schönbrunn Palace, would someone now at least try to bring Stéphanie's son into play? For Vienna the possibility could in no way be excluded, so it could well have been a motive to engage more intensively with the Baden question. Stanhope's activities, which got underway with surprising speed, and were focused directly on Stéphanie's environment, provide unavoidable confirmation for such a supposition. Added to this were other developments which strengthened suspicions that there was movement in the old Napoleonic circles. Only a short time before, Eugène de Beauharnais, Duke of Leuchtenberg had spent time in the summer capital Baden-Baden, and from 'beyond the Rhine', Varnhagen tells us,

> came many Frenchmen from Switzerland who paid homage to the stepson of their former Emperor; much was spoken of and arranged which could not be kept from the Badeners....Numerous diplomats from Karlsruhe, Stuttgart, Munich, Frankfurt and elsewhere availed themselves of the spa waters or went back and forth to them. The famous Las Casas had turned up after he had had to leave St Helena.... A Countess Lagorce, who had earlier been a trusted friend of Empress Josephine and was now close to the Duke of Leuchtenberg made common cause with the Liberals for similar reasons.[127]

It had not remained unnoticed that not such a long time previously the Duke had met Stéphanie several times in the small spa resort of Hüb. The south German Napoleonists had gathered there.

> The Duke of Leuchtenberg [Fig. 69] cared much for the welfare of Grand Duchess Stéphanie and showed a lively sympathy for her and her husband. Such motivations were shared by most of the Frenchmen and women who came to Baden, who included Lavalette, Felix Desportes, General Rapp and especially Bignon, who in earlier times had been Napoleon's ambassador in Karlsruhe and now gave important support to Baden's cause in his writing.

Such support for example was evident in 'On the Dispute between the Courts of Bavaria and Baden' (Fig. 70) in which Bignon took Baden's part on the basis of his intimate knowledge of the facts. Interestingly, the work also appeared in German in the year of Grand Duke Karl's death and must certainly have been known to Stanhope. Here in Baden-Baden a conversation took place, the content of which Ludwig I's brother, the Duke of Leuchtenberg, who died in 1824, shared with the Bavarian Minister Friedrich August Giese, namely that Stéphanie had firmly maintained that her eldest son whom she had not seen dead, had not died but had been taken away. King Ludwig I later committed this to his diary: 'Giese also told me ...that Kaspar Hauser was the same (boy).'[128]

August von Leuchtenberg, Duke Eugène's son, who later visited the foundling in Ansbach, told Dowager Queen Carolina of Bavaria years later that Stéphanie had 'asked much about Kaspar Hauser'.

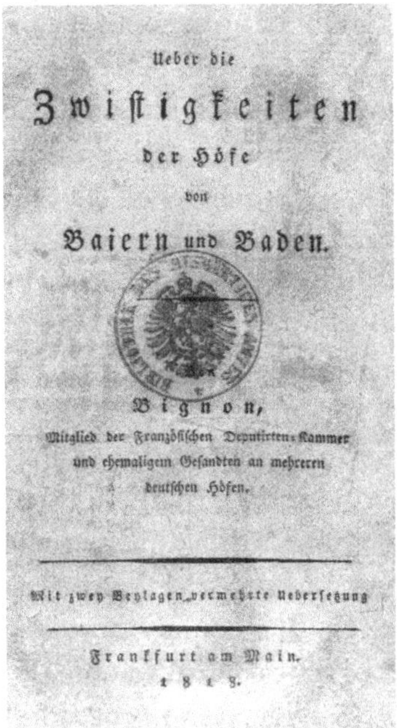
Ueber die
Zwistigkeiten
der Höfe
von
Baiern und Baden.
Von
Bignon,
Mitglied der Französischen Deputirten-Kammer
und ehemaligem Gesandten an mehreren
deutschen Höfen.

Mit zwey Beylagen vermehrte Uebersetzung

Frankfurt am Main.
1818.

70. Cover title of the German edition of 'On the Quarrels between the Courts of Bavaria and Baden' by Louis Pierre Eduard de Bignon.

*

Just three years before, in 1818, Grand Duke Karl, the father of Kaspar Hauser, had died, and Marquis Ludwig had come to power as 'the last Zähringer'. The misdeeds and intrigues of this ruler would fill a book in themselves, and the same would apply to the machinations between him and the Imperial Countess Hochberg, who died in 1820. Both, for different reasons, had an interest in seeing that the sons of Karl and Stéphanie would not head the government. The manipulations around the succession, which culminated in the exchange of the infant Crown prince (Kaspar Hauser) for a child of the same age (Blochmann) who was killed the same day, have been incontrovertibly addressed by Fritz Klee and Hermann Pies.[129]

Here only so much will be brought forward as bears upon the question of where the sought-for prince would again appear. From the papers of Joséphine and the evidence of the Lauffenberg bottle message, the prince was still alive in a secret location, and clearly the identity of that location was not likely to be Karlsruhe, Baden-Baden or Mannheim. But first harbingers of a possible return or careless pointers to the secret location might result in conversation through indications or intrigues, and so Stanhope prepared himself in the autumn of 1821 for a first 'reconnaissance' visit to the modest estate of the widowed Grand Duchess. Travelling by day with only short stops in

Brussels and Frankfurt the journey pressed on to Mannheim, to where Stéphanie had first moved in the middle of 1820.

Stanhope arrived on the 20th October and stayed for four days. On the 24th he took his leave and arrived back in Chevening on the 12th November. What took place at Stéphanie's residence at that time can be reconstructed to a degree. Stanhope first unobtrusively approached a number of significant individuals in the Grand Duchess's household, well aware that he needed to sound out the circle of people around her before he could get close to her. Through this circle Philip Henry hoped by means of recommendations and conversations to gain access to the mother of the missing Crown prince either then or later. That his calculation succeeded is shown by the following two journeys to Mannheim. Of interest here are the individuals whom Stanhope marked out as those who would serve his purposes. With some amazement one discovers a circle of people who, after Stanhope's short but very direct visit, are by no means accidentally able to enjoy the Lord's friendship. Naturally everything proceeded harmlessly at first—eccentrically philanthropical and not least political. After his return, Stanhope sent a thank you greeting to his newly gained friends: one of his speeches in the House of Lords, recently

71. Karl Christian, Baron von Berckheim (1774–1849)

printed.[130] On the list of intended recipients appear some highly noteworthy names. Closer consideration reveals all those named to be personalities who have a direct connection to the question of the missing prince.

First there was Karl Christian, Freiherr (Baron) von Berckheim (1774–1849), Senior Court Chamberlain to Margravine Amalie in 1806, State Counsellor in 1812. In 1814 he had accompanied Grand Duke Karl to the Congress of Vienna and was named by his sovereign envoy to the Bundestag in 1817. From 1813–1817 he was also Minister of the Interior in which office Grand Duke Ludwig had just newly confirmed him in 1821. The autopsy on the corpse of the dead 'Prince' had been carried out by nine doctors in Berckheim's presence in 1812; under his eyes the court ceremonial of the lying-in-state, the dressing and embalming of the 'Crown prince' all took place. The autopsy report bears the signature of the Minister, who was present at all important phases of the 'Crown prince's end'.

Also on Stanhope's list was the name of the Chamberlain and later Minister of State[131]—in 1821 an ambassador of Baden—Friedrich Karl, Freiherr von Blittersdorf (1792–1861), born in Schloss Mahlberg, later the seat of the notorious Major Hennenhofer. The Permanent Chamberlain, ear-and eyewitness to the demise of the 'Crown prince', supervised the wake during the lying-in-state in Karlsruhe.[132]

72/73. Maximilian Roth von Schreckenstein (1794–1862). Seal of the Court Marshal.

Then appears the name of Baron Maximilian von Schreckenstein (1794–1862) (Figs. 72, 73, 74) who from 1819 was Stéphanie's Chamberlain and from 1832 Court Marshal. He was the only one then as before to enjoy the Grand Duchess's intimate trust; in 1821 she still lived under the suspicious watch of Baron Wöllwarth and later of Joseph von Roggenbach. Schreckenstein stood closest to Stéphanie; to gain his trust meant to be particularly close to her thoughts and feelings. Significantly, the name of the spy Roggenbach is also on the thank you list, which throws a great light on Stanhope's true intentions. From Roggenbach could certainly be gained very different and possibly decisive infomation.

A copy of Stanhope's speech was also sent to Franz Oliver, Count von Jenison zu Walworth (1787–1867), who had been accredited as Bavarian chargé d'affaires in Berlin, Petersburg, Paris and London. At this time often called away to his post in The Hague, he was often to be seen at the Court in Mannheim. 'The Grand Duchess,' reports Count Sternberg

> who was always constantly watched, was not able to receive everyone. She had further to distinguish between those whom she accepted. Nothing was more onerous to the intelligent lively woman than this pressure.

74. Red chalk drawing (1822) by Grand Duchess Stéphanie. A present for her Court Marshal Maximilian Roth von Schreckenstein (see also Fig. 85).

> She never felt herself better than when sitting at her round dinner table with trusted acquaintances. Count Jenison was among these, a man of the world and a man with a fine sense of form and of rare conversational gifts.[133]

Jenison also possessed Stéphanie's trust in every circumstance and belonged therefore to that narrow circle which was the focus of Stanhope's interest.

Next was the Grand Duchy of Baden's Chamberlain Carl Heinrich, Freiherr (Baron) von Fahnenberg (1779–1840). After his studies in Erlangen, Fahnenberg began his career in 1810 as Ministerial Counsellor in the Ministry of the Interior and advanced in 1819 to the position of Director of the Postal Service, in which position he got to know Stanhope. As head of the postal service information and insights were available to the much courted von Fahnenberg that would have been gold dust to a man like Stanhope. Furthermore, von Fahnenberg turned out to know something that was very relevant to Stanhope's theme. In 1818 he had made a name for himself with the publication of his essay *A Study of the Baden Territorial Question*

In the year after he made Stanhope's acquaintance Fahnenberg was first provisionally and then from 1826 formally appointed to the important post of head of the Grand Duchy's office of the State Debt. When Fahnenberg's only son Albrecht was born, Stanhope was named godfather. Clearly, such intimate honours showed that he was 'well received at the court of the Grand Duchess' [134] and were a testimony of how far he had managed to develop his connections.

This favourable reception at court doubtless went back to his new godson's mother, who had formerly been a trusted lady-in-waiting to Grand Duchess Stéphanie—then under her maiden name of Wilhelmine von Freystedt—and to her father, who was an illegitimate son of the old Grand Duke Karl Friedrich. Wilhelmine's sister, Karoline Sophie von Freystedt, was lady-in-waiting to Margravine Amalie from 1801 until her death in 1832. Amalie, the mother of Grand Duke Karl, was the figure around whom the conservative group at the Karlsruhe court coalesced.

A no less significant figure was the Bavarian ambassador Count von Reigersberg, whose father was Minister of Justice and Minister President of Bavaria from 1817 1825 under Maximilian, Count Montgelas. The next name on Stanhope's list was Johann Philipp von Wessenberg (1773–1858) (Fig. 75). He spent his whole life in the service of

75. Johann Philipp von Wessenberg (1773–1858)

Austria and was a close friend of Gentz and Metternich. As diplomat and ambassador in Paris, London, Berlin, Kassel, Frankfurt, Munich, Milan, and St. Petersburg, he had had a personal relationship with Napoleon and Joséphine and was then an advisor and participant at the Congress of Vienna. Later, he would be prominent as the chairman of the Military Commission of the Frankfurt Parliament which, among other things, had the task of settling the territorial dispute between Baden and Bavaria. With his decisive input, the dispute was resolved in almost all particulars in Baden's favour, including the matter of the succession of the Hochberg line, which had been an open question until then but which was thenceforward regarded as settled. In 1820, at his own request and, so it seemed, for the purposes of recuperation, Wessenberg retired to his Feldkirch Castle estate in Breisgau from where he travelled many times to Karlsruhe and Mannheim.

Another name on the list was that of Konrad, Freiherr von Schäffer, General, Commander-in-Chief of the armed forces of Baden and Minister of War. After Napoleon's return from Elba, Baden mobilised a contingent of troops which was not, as was generally expected, placed under the command of Margrave Wilhelm von Hochberg but under that of General von Schäffer. That was a noticeable manoeuvre against Hochberg, who was both popular and successful.

Schäffer also accompanied important diplomatic missions during the reign of Grand Duke Karl, in whose service he travelled to St. Petersburg in 1817 to represent Baden's interests to Czar Alexander. Finally, he was sent to Stuttgart in 1818 to further Baden's interests by strengthening the influence of the Queen on her brother the Czar.[135]

Finally, a name appears on Stanhope's list, which looks more interesting than it is and to which Stanhope had therefore perhaps attached too much significance, for he also dedicated his brochure to the Privy Councillor Freiherr von Baden.

With the exception of the last-named personage then, all those who received Stanhope's thank you gift were, remarkably, high-ranking witnesses to the tragedy of the infant prince or else were courtiers in the Grand Duchess's immediate circle or such officials who could have had access to information that would be useful.

Stanhope's procedure was vital from a conspiratorial viewpoint: to discover what information the other side possesses or does not possess is the first precondition for the achievement of an undertaking such as his, in which the key is that the agent appears as a true friend. The same play-acting can be seen again a few years later when Stanhope sought to gain information about the investigations Feuerbach was conducting into Kaspar Hauser's origins. The all-important thing for Stanhope was that he had got his foot in the door at Karlsruhe, and from then on the English Peer was a welcome guest in Stéphanie's court circle.

On the way home Stanhope stopped off at Herrnsheim near Worms. Here Emmerich Joseph Duke of Dalberg (1753–1833) (Fig. 76) owned a respectable castle in the middle of a magnificent extensive park to which he would escape as often as his affairs in Paris would allow. The monumental Empire style building—the centrepiece of the Dalberg estate—had been erected by the Duke in 1810 on the foundations of the family's mediaeval home destroyed during the French Revolution and he had it expensively furnished and decorated with the help of his wealthy wife, the Marquessa von Brignole Sale.

How did Stanhope make the acquaintance of this central figure in the history of Baden? Had it been Gentz, who had known Dalberg well since the Congress of Vienna and had already been Dalberg's guest at his palace in Paris, who had given Stanhope this excellent indication? When it came to knowledge of the histories and tragedies of the Zähringer and Hochberg families, Dalberg was, along with State Councillor Klüber, the man who knew most about the secrets of Baden. Certainly, for Stanhope, his acquaintance with the Duke, who was in a position to give him vital information, was of great significance. On the 20th October Philip Henry arrived at Herrnsheim and stayed as a guest of the politician for four days.

After his studies in, amongst other places, Ingolstadt, where he had been in close contact with Adam Weishaupt and his Order of the Illuminati, Dalberg had entered the service of Baden and was from 1804 ambassador in Paris. In 1810 he received from Napoleon's own hand both French citizenship and ducal rank and thereafter was regarded 'among all Germans as a disreputable turncoat'.[136]

In Paris, due to his friendship with Talleyrand, Dalberg worked more in the interests of France than of Baden, so that in 1808 Napoleon arranged for him to be appointed Finance Minister and in 1809 Foreign Minister of Baden. In Karlsruhe the malice and ambition of Talleyrand and Dalberg were often compared. It was Dalberg who arranged Napoleon's marriage to the daughter of Austrian Emperor Franz I.

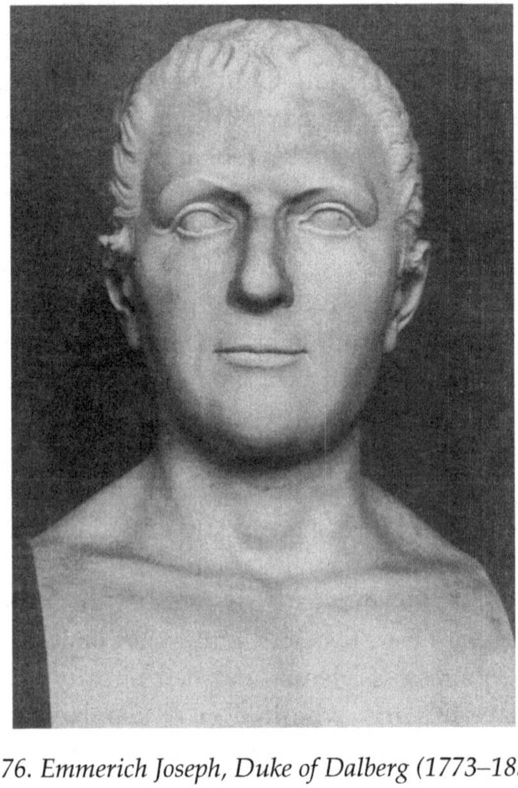

76. Emmerich Joseph, Duke of Dalberg (1773–1833)

After the fall of Napoleon, Dalberg was a member of the five-man provisional government of France headed by Talleyrand, in which he now worked hard for the Restoration, that is, for the Duke of Provence, the later Louis XVIII. In this role he also acted as French plenipotentiary at the Congress of Vienna. After that he served the new government as Minister of State, was raised to the rank of Peer of France and was accredited as occasional ambassador in Sardinia.

Dalberg was linked in numerous and subtle ways with the history of Baden and the Duke was certainly in a position to make an important contribution to the details of Stanhope's case. He knew the individual who was the most deeply embroiled in the question, the Imperial Countess Hochberg, as well as he did Karl and Stéphanie. Already in 1803 he was occupying himself with the question of whether it would make more sense to create a new territory for the Hochbergs. His memorandum '*Coup d'oeil jeté sur l'Europe de l'observatoire de Petersbourg 1803*' contains the idea that a new principality could be created for the Hochbergs 'from the land lying between the Jura, the Biel and Neuenburg mountains and Lake Geneva'.[137] He was involved with the whole process of the fateful marriage of Elector Karl and Stéphanie de Beauharnais right from the beginning in Paris in 1806. He was actually supposed to sign the marriage contract on 8th April. But the Emperor decided otherwise, which angered Dalberg greatly. When the first news of disagreements between the married couple soon reached Napoleon's ears, it was Dalberg—perhaps because of old insults—who spread the rumours to Stéphanie's disadvantage.

When he was staying in Karlsruhe, this influential man would ride out to hunt with Count Wilhelm von Hochberg, whose chamberlain he was and more or less confidante, also in private matters, which included the debts of Wilhelm's mother. The morganatic wife of the aged Grand Duke, Luise Karoline, Imperial Countess Hochberg, born Geyer von Geyersberg, had constantly been the cause of the greatest problems to the small state because of her enormous debts. We know from a pleading letter of hers to Minister Reitzenstein that she owed money to over 200 families, which she was unable to repay. Karl Friedrich had already once paid nearly a million in part repayment of her debts, but now the State Treasury was required again to provide a sum almost as large. In her desperation she decided on a coup against the ruling Grand Duke, which would also clear her debts by means of a new constitution. Dalberg, then the Finance Minister, received his notice of dismissal from her hand without the knowledge of the Grand Duke. Dalberg immediately turned to Crown prince Karl, who was just as ignorant of events and his energetic protests succeeded in securing the arrest of the plotter. At Dalberg's insistence all further State proclamations by the ruling Grand Duke were to be co-signed by his son Karl.

From that time onward, the animus of the Countess Hochberg against Dalberg was extreme and only worsened when he then demanded a complete statement of her financial situation. All the essential events of the following years, the births and deaths of Stéphanie's children, and the speculations and rumours surrounding them—Dalberg knew the details of them all. He read and inwardly digested the weekly bulletins of the French ambassador in Karlsruhe, Louis Pierre Eduard, Baron de Bignon (1771–1841) and of his successor from 1812, Count de Nicolay. And what did the two men not write, week after week! They and their agents missed nothing that disturbed the feelings of the court, whether it be courtly gossip or serious problems. The news was in Paris within eight days. The reports from Bignon and Nicolay were only one source, however. The other was Charles Maurice de Talleyrand (1754–1838), a close friend of Bignon and from whom the latter held nothing back, including matters that should only have been for the ear of Baden's chargé d'affaires. The Countess Hochberg therefore accused him of treason. Certainly, Dalberg was both an avowed opponent of the Hochbergs and of Grand Duke Ludwig [reigned 1818–1830], which must have been of crucial importance to Stanhope and his concerns. In addition, Dalberg had been involved with the issue of the promotion of the rank of the Hochbergs and therefore here too informed as to all the particulars of the process. As for Stéphanie, Dalberg had at his disposal an especially excellent source of information. His sister was the leading lady-in-waiting Frau von Venningen—the wife of the Senior Cupbearer at the Court at Mannheim, whose task it was to attend on the Grand Duchess especially during her illnesses. Frau von Venningen was just as sly as her brother. Amongst other things, she advised Stéphanie to take a lover if Grand Duke Karl did not pay her sufficient attention. Although Stéphanie did not do so, rumours circulated that insisted to the contrary.

We know that Stanhope bade Dalberg a friendly farewell after his four-day visit and arranged to see him in Paris the following year.

*

The journeys of the previous months had been of crucial significance for Stanhope. For the first time he had succeeded in acquainting himself with important personalities in the Grand Duchess's circle and in weaving a net of connections which would, sooner or later enable him to open the doors of Stéphanie's salon. After he had maintained a proper distance for a good six months, his confidence would permit a further visit.

An earlier appointment was in any case not possible for another reason. There was a great commotion in Chevening when at 2 a.m. on the 4th April 1822 a fire broke out. It spread from the so-called 'Red Room' but was fortunately able to be brought under control. It took Philip Henry several weeks to interrogate the servants and take statements from them all. But even this event, which required clearing up and refurbishing work, could not hold up the next trip to Mannheim. This time Philip Henry must have deemed it appropriate to take his wife Lady Catherine Lucy and the children along with him again. It probably seemed necessary to counter the rather disadvantageous impression of a constantly travelling paterfamilias. The visit this time was on a more extensive scale with a clear focus on Karlsruhe and Baden-Baden and culminating—between the 8th and 10th September—with a day in Griesbach!

On the 30th May the travellers arrived in Calais and retrieved their old carriage from the shed in which it had been parked since the previous year. They then set off in the direction of Brussels, stopping on the 2nd June to visit the site of the Battle of Waterloo. To encounter the *genius loci* where the ultimate fate of Napoleon could be so impressively imagined better than anywhere else was a long-cherished wish of Stanhope's. A feeling of satisfaction comes naturally to every Briton in that place. The party then pressed on with few interruptions, apart from another four-day stop in Frankfurt, towards southern Germany.

Stanhope first spent eight days in Mannheim (21–29 June) then a day in Karlsruhe, travelling on for two days to Baden-Baden and then via Rastatt (4–5 July) back to Karlsruhe. Here finally there took place on the 22nd July the meeting with Grand Duchess Stéphanie that he had prepared for the year before. We know this from a letter he wrote to a relative, Emily, congratulating her on her marriage. 'We came to Karlsruhe to see the King of Bavaria, who extended us a warm reception. And we were introduced to the Grand Duchess of Baden, who was related to the Empress Josephine...'[138]

It is noteworthy that Stanhope remarks casually on the relation to the Bonaparte and that the King of Bavaria, Maximilian I, extended him a 'warm reception', which is only conceivable assuming previous

77. Town house of Grand Duchess Stéphanie in Baden-Baden; the later Palais Hamilton.

acquaintance. That is accounted for by the fact that on the previously mentioned name list from Stanhope's time in Dresden the King of Bavaria appears as a recipient of a written report. Did Crown prince Ludwig also meet Stanhope for the first time on this occasion? Stéphanie travelled to Baden-Baden in the days afterwards, and Stanhope followed her there with the intention of following up on their initial meeting. At first, he had no success.

On the 24th July Philip Henry returned to Karlsruhe for eight days to prepare his things for the journey home. But already on the 3rd August he appeared again in Baden-Baden, where since the death of Grand Duke Karl [1818] Stéphanie had been in residence during the summer, and he stayed for the first part of the month at the 'Dragon' hotel. On the so-called Rettig hill in Baden-Baden Stéphanie had a pavilion in an extensive park that bordered directly on the River Oos and also a town house, the later Palais Hamilton (Fig. 77). She was also free to make use of accommodation in the new castle above Baden-Baden. Whoever wished an audience with her had to present himself to her chamberlain von Schreckenstein in the morning who would then decide who was to receive an invitation to Stéphanie's company in the evening. This presented no problem for Stanhope, as the chamberlain had for months been among his closer acquaintances. One who was equally able to pass Schreckenstein's testing gaze was General Baron Gaspard Gourgaud (1783–1852). On the 8th August he too together with his servants had lodged at the 'Dragon' and had requested an audience with Stéphanie. He had been one of Napoleon's most fervent admirers and had voluntarily accompanied the Emperor on the journey to St. Helena. Napoleon's path had always been his own—already at Ulm, the artillery officer had fought at Austerlitz, Jena, Friedland, Ostrolenka, Eggmühl, and Wagram and had become Napoleon's Officer of Ordnance. He had been one of the first to enter the Kremlin in Moscow, a fact which was the source of the greatest satisfaction to him till the end of his life. Evidently, what moved the General most deeply was the fact that it had been granted to him to save the Emperor's life on the 29th July 1814 when at Brienne he had cut down a Cossack cavalryman who had sought to lance Napoleon. Later, in 1840, Gourgaud was one of the few who took it upon himself to make the long voyage to St. Helena to bring Napoleon's body home to Paris. On St. Helena, Napoleon had until 1818 dictated his memoirs to Las Casa but also especially to Gourgaud, who had handed the manuscript '*Mémoires pour servir à l'histoire de la France sous Napoléon*' to the publisher immediately before setting out for Baden-Baden. We know the honour in which Grand Duchess Stéphanie held her adopted father and how deep was her consternation at the news of his death. For Stéphanie that painful event lay exactly a year behind her and she was waiting impatiently for Gourgaud who would tell her of his last years with Bonaparte.

The long audiences with the General must have struck Stanhope, and he must have been interested in the man himself who had spent his life at the Emperor's side and was now playing a privileged role at Stéphanie's summer residence. Stanhope even succeeded in engaging the old warhorse in conversation a few times, as they were staying at the same hotel. But who knows whether Gourgaud somehow hesitated to trust the Englishman who so conspicuously and assiduously sought the company of the Grand Duchess? Was it due to the distaste of an old former enemy in war, or was it a personal aversion? The conversations were not of the sort that Stanhope enjoyed. Perhaps Gourgaud too wanted to do some investigating of his own, which may be why Stanhope noted: 'He did not appear distinguished in his manners or conversation.' Clearly, that was not Gourgaud's intention. Stanhope took offence and 'together with Herr Söhne and his servants' moved to the 'Sun' Hotel.

He had more success in his conversations with Stéphanie. At first, she focused on the tragic moments of the past few years, the death of her husband Grand Duke Karl, who had been convinced that he had been poisoned like his sons and who had more than once declared that 'he was lost', as the biographer Varnhagen von Ense had put it. 'There had been too much concern about him; he had been hit too hard; his princes had not been allowed to live and he too had become a target; his inheritance was to be torn away from him by the hands of strangers.'[139]

These last emotional months Grand Duke Karl had spent in the humid, tiny Black Forest resort of Bad Griesbach, shut away from the world. On his deathbed he had on the 22nd August 1818 issued the constitutional charter on the indivisibility of Baden, which took account of the fact that his 'sons had been taken' from him. In line to succeed there was only the unmarried and therefore childless Ludwig, with whom the ancient Zähringer line of the ruling House of Baden was threatened with extinction. The famous Hufeland, called to the Grand Duke's deathbed from Berlin in order to save at the last minute what could no longer be saved, showed himself appalled at the narrow dark valley location and recommended an immediate transfer to Montpellier.

Sometime during the course of the seven o'clock audience with Stéphanie, Stanhope steered the conversation to the marriage, the children and their destiny. At one point the talk even touched on the question of all questions. But it was still too soon, too improper to press upon. Most of what was said was already known to him through Dalberg and others, but that was not the point. The important fact is that the theme was touched on at all. In a letter of the 23rd August 1822 Stanhope informed his mother of the meeting. The old lady in Chevening learned that the marriage had not been contracted with Karl's agreement but that before his death it had developed into one of great affection. Then the letter spoke of 'an illness of many months' and finally of the children. 'He has left three very pretty girls but as there was no Son who survived, he has been succeeded by his Uncle.'[140] A noteworthy phrase, which is not exactly correct. Did it come from Stéphanie, who in her not quite perfect German wanted to indicate that she meant her second son Alexander was the child who died in 1817 but not her nameless firstborn, whom she had demanded in vain to be allowed to see and of whose death she was by no means convinced? Why did Stanhope not write to England that which was common knowledge in Baden—that there had been two sons who had lost their lives one soon after the other? Did Stéphanie want to give the impression that for her the death of the *first* remained unclear? It is certain that Stanhope approached this point in the conversation and that the Grand Duchess did not openly speak of two sons. At some point the conversation must have turned to Sophie, wife of Margrave Leopold, later [from 1830] the Grand Duke of Baden. Philip Henry made a point of reporting that Stéphanie had doubts about Sophie's mental state.

After a stay of 28 days in Baden-Baden, Stanhope had made quite some progress. But it seemed necessary to him also to visit the place where Grand Duke Karl had spent the last days of his life. On the 8th September he arrived in the spa resort some 50 km distant, stayed a day and returned on the 10th. What did he want in Griesbach? (Fig. 78) Did he want to re-experience through witnesses the death of the father of the one he was seeking? Was he hoping for information that could lead him further?

In the summer of 1818 the Grand Duke, as already mentioned, was moved for reasons 'of an unusual nature', as Varnhagen puts it, from

78. Bad Griesbach c. 1800

Bad Rippoldsau to the lonely Bad Griesbach, and accommodated in the so-called 'Red House', an annexe of the then existing spa building, in the 'musty lounge of a farmer's house' and in those pitiful lodgings he remained.

> Those around him were miserable.....one could not tell the sick man how badly things stood with him, but he himself often repeated, wailing pitifully, that he had not long to live and that he had been poisoned.... He sat all day long bowed and bored...it was obvious to see that such a life in this place and such influences could bring no improvement and could not continue for any length of time without the most harmful consequences. Such a realisation added to the sad present only the prospect of a most gloomy future.[141]

The Grand Duke complained bitterly about the hostility of the House of Bavaria. His early death had been counted on, which unfortunately would follow only too soon.

A last chance made possible by the visit of Hufeland on the 8th September 1818 was not grasped by Karl, whose willpower by now had completely atrophied. He told those around him that 'not only he [the Grand Duke] did not want it enough, but also that others did not want it because it did not suit their purposes and advantage'.[142] What was Varnhagen thinking when he wrote that? Whose interest would Karl's early death have served? His end was near. Crown prince Ludwig of Bavaria had already 'prepared for the day'. To provide him with the relevant exact information he had sent Count Pappenheim who located himself in the same neighbourhood specifically to be able to observe the process of the Grand Duke's illness and report back to Munich.

'It would be difficult,' wrote Metternich on the 21st November 1818 to Karl Theodor Ritter von Hruby,

> to imagine the level of irritation in the three cabinets against the Bavarian government. The causes of the situation make themselves only too obvious through the presumptuousness in which the Court at Munich has indulged for years and especially through the emotional and maladroit behaviour of the Crown prince in the territorial question. So, for example, at the time when the Baden affair was being discussed, news arrived here that the Crown prince had quartered his adjutant Count Pappenheim in the area of the (terminally ill) Duke's favourite country spot where he was living with the intention of informing him the min-

> ute the man departed this life. This circumstance led quite naturally to words which the King on his last visit to Baden himself expressed to respected officials of the government of Baden and which went so far as to assure them that in the hour of the Grand Duke's passing, he would occupy the Baden Rhenish Palatinate and the Main and Tauber region with troops, to which end he had positioned in Rhenish Bavaria the army corps returning from France.[143]

Prince Wrede, it had been decided, would order Bavarian troops into the Palatinate as soon as the news came in. 'Privy Councillor Friedrich reported from Switzerland that a Bavarian State Councillor had told him the same thing, as he regarded Friedrich, a man born in the Palatinate, as already half Bavarian. Then came news from Speyer and Würzburg that in both places preparations for troop movements were being made in stealth.'

Finally, his death imminent, the Grand Duke was brought in November to Bruchsal and then to Rastatt where at least suitable rooms were available where he could die in peace and with dignity. Shortly before his death, Emperor Alexander of Russia urged Karl's sister, who was married to the hostile King of Bavaria, to bid him a farewell visit: 'he would disapprove of political propriety being carried so far; it is not only advisable but necessary that the Queen should come'.

At the beginning of November brother and sister met for the last time and here again there was talk of the family's distress: the loss of both sons which, as Karl asserted, was due to poisoning, went back to the coercion that resulted from the political changes around his wife Stéphanie the Napoleonid, who since 1814 was no longer the 'daughter of France' but once again 'the little young French mademoiselle Beauharnais', the extinction of the old Zähringer line, the indivisibility of the country and the irreconcilable dispute with Bavaria because of the Palatinate. Karl had believed that 'he would feel better in that he would have not to show the whole misery of his situation; but his effort failed; the emotions which the visit stirred in him gripped him so powerfully that he sank into a great weakness and when he saw the Queen weeping, moved to tears himself, he grasped her hand and let his tears flow freely.'[144]

While this sad scene was taking place around his sickbed, in the antechamber a conversation was going on that cast an even more chilling light on that gloomy picture. According to Varnhagen:

> the Countess von Taxis, the Queen's secretary was waiting there for her mistress's return and was conversing with some Baden courtiers. She raised the question of the rumours of poisoning, which had spread throughout the country and wanted to know what the courtiers thought of them. They remained silent with embarrassed looks, but Baron von Ende boldly spoke out that the rumours were everywhere and indeed well-founded for there was no doubt that the Grand Duke had been poisoned. Shocked, the Countess asked who could have been responsible for such a wicked deed? 'That is what everyone is thinking' came the answer, 'but no-one says it'. 'You surely don't believe that...?' she retorted, not finishing her sentence. As if to leave her in no doubt as to what they thought, Ende exclaimed: 'Oh yes, we all believe it!' After a moment's reflection, the Countess said indignantly: 'I would put my hand in the fire for the King and Queen! As for the others, I have no idea!'

At almost 9 a.m. on the 8th December 1818 the 33-year-old Grand Duke Karl's life came to a close. Interestingly, a witness, Karoline von Freystadt, a confidante of Margravine Amalie, wrote in her memoirs: 'The new regent, Margrave Ludwig, the late Grand Duke's uncle, arrived at Rastatt an hour after his nephew had breathed his last. The just widowed Grand Duchess was in no state to receive him; the sisters of the deceased Grand Duke turned their backs on him as if he were an illegitimate successor—behaviour that could scarcely be justified by the pain of their bereavement.'

*

What was Stanhope after on the 9th September 1822 in the lonely vale of Griesbach, almost four years after Grand Duke Karl's death? (Fig. 78) He must have had another reason for his visit of one day and two nights than sampling in such hurry the beneficial qualities of the mineral water that had been well-known since the 16th century. He stayed at the 'Kaiser' inn. The owner, Friedrich Dollmätsch was a Karlsruhe citizen just like the Privy Councillor Kölreuter. The Councillor lived in Bad Griesbach as a spa doctor paid by the government of Baden; the new owner of the spa baths since 1817 was Anton Montsch.

What were the dignitaries of Griesbach and of Karl's small court doing there in the autumn of 1818, at that time of year when darkness came to the valley earlier than to the plains of the Rhine below? People sat together in the inn and told each other, just as Baron von Ende had spoken of his master to Countess von Taxis about the slow death of the Grand Duke.

Grand Duchess Stéphanie and Varnhagen too, who had arranged for Hufeland's visit, could do nothing else, lacking other possibilities, than to spend evenings in the 'room of the lonely farmhouse'. There too, Karl's small court must have given free vent over glasses of wine to their 'complaints about the cursed visit...where they must have died of boredom'. But not only that—all the latest news of gossip and intrigue here and in Karlsruhe was discussed. Life at court was not held in high regard.

> There were waylayers everywhere, nets and traps, little ruses and acts of spitefulness. It was virtually impossible to escape them all and clearly also scarcely worth the effort....He [Grand Duke Karl] preferred to be alone and if the local people were allowed to speak to him, it was mostly to tell crude stories and anecdotes which drew from him a sad smile, and the Grand Duchess, the only woman present, had to endure such embarrassing company, though she must have been grateful that at least the effort was made to speak to the patient.[145]

Though she may have been able to bear such soul torture, there were other anxiety-inducing and dangerous circumstances for the Grand Duchess as she faced her husband's imminent demise; there had been more than one call for the couple to divorce after the fall of Napoleon. In Griesbach she was surrounded by 'hostile opponents, and by those who sought to embarrass her and report on her; nobody could be trusted completely. She had to mind every word, control her every expression in order not to give rise to misunderstandings and intrigues which were constantly lay in wait.'

When they did not manage to join the company of the Grand Duke, these connivers and opponents would sit in the inn and the witnesses to their conversations were Dolmätsch, Kölreuter and Montsch. Before he finally left Griesbach, the Grand Duke personally assured Montsch that 'My sons and I have been done to death.' If he had said this to Montsch, then perhaps he had said other things, more significant things, which would be of interest to Stanhope and which would make the journey to Griesbach more than worthwhile.

Who were 'the others' of whom Varnhagen reported that they 'did not want a cure because that would not suit their purposes'? They too were guests of Dolmätsch. Not that the master of the 'Kaiser', Dolmätsch or Kölreuter could have had the slightest to do with Karl's infirmity, but Stanhope could gain from their firsthand experience of the situation; he could find out from them who had been at Griesbach at that time, what they believed, thought and hoped for.

The agent only needed a single day to obtain the information he sought in Griesbach, where little ever happened and where those events of four years before were still fresh in the memory as if they'd occurred only days earlier. Perhaps, as on other such occasions, the information was more forthcoming with the help of a few guilders. The following day Stanhope was back on the road to Baden-Baden.

There in the meantime a whole row of guests had arrived to join Stéphanie who was already there; it was a constellation of a singular kind. Never before or afterwards were so many people who played a part in the destiny of Kaspar Hauser gathered together in that place at the same time. Not all knew each other, and neither had Stanhope already been in contact with all of them, such as, for example State Councillor Anselm von Feuerbach, who arrived in Baden-Baden on the same day as General Gourgaud and took up modest lodgings with the master weaver Ignaz Weiss. Others, however, were old friends: Berstett, Blittersdorf, Berckheim, and Jenison. On the 23rd August Nostitz von Jenkersdorf arrived at the posh hotel *Zum Salmen* from Dresden and Fahnenberg from Karslruhe checked in at the *Sonne* on the same day. Also staying at the *Salmen* were Rüdt von Collenberg (see pp. 281–289) and the banker Haber from Karlsruhe.

An especially noteworthy group that day was the presence of Herr 'Garnier' from Rastatt where Joseph Zeder lived, Herr 'Hennenhofer from Gernsbach', who put up at the *Hirschen* and the 'Pastor Enggesser from Freiburg'.

That these three should be in that place at the same time is indeed worthy of notice. Hennenhofer's role in the Kaspar Hauser story is known. To see Joseph Heinrich Garnier (1800–1862) there and then is most unexpected, but not incomprehensible. We find his name in the case files relating to the murder of the student Lessing (1835) (see also Fig. 110) in the course of which investigation letters of Hennenhofer's unexpectedly turned up. In these he offered a co-defendant (Ferdinand Sailer) money to distance himself from a pamphlet published by Garnier. At this point we shall simply identify Garnier as a French spy. He would later become Hennenhofer's most dangerous enemy who was familiar with the most intimate details of the Kaspar Hauser affair and who strongly accused Hennenhofer in his book *Contributions to the Story of Kaspar Hauser* (see Fig. 174). That the Baden government banned the pamphlet, which is still hard to obtain today, and bought it up and that Hennenhofer finally sought to buy Garnier's silence says something about the author. In the book Garnier not only gave very accurate and previously unknown information about Hennenhofer but also about Enggesser.

> This Enggesser was a simple village priest when he made himself known to Ludwig, who was then already on the Grand Ducal throne. In a little more than a year he had risen to become Director of a Ministry, a man before whom all bowed and scraped. In addition, the Grand Duke, normally a miserly man, rewarded Enggesser richly with houses and money...The priest is still alive; he has become a rich man.

And a few pages later: 'How large is the sum Ludwig paid to Enggesser; and what does the gift signify?' There are some additional very telling indications about Enggesser. We find him and Hennenhofer not only jointly accused of being the actual string-pullers in the Kaspar Hauser case in Garnier's Foreword to his pamphlet, but also as accessories in Rüdt von Collenberg's commemorative protocol in regard to the session of the Council of State in 1830 (see p. 281–289).

When Kaspar Hauser had to be hurriedly removed from Beuggen after the appearance of the bottle message in the Rhine, he was not immediately taken to Pilsach. Stops en route were Hochsal near Beuggen, Mundelfingen, and probably Gernsbach. Even these days it is still related how Kaspar Hauser was kept captive for a time at the house belonging to Hennenhofer at Amtsstrasse 1. In Mundelfingen the priest from 1814–23 was the Revd. Enggesser. In December 1823 he was called to the Catholic Church Section in Karlsruhe where he stayed till 1832. The clergyman then returned to his parish where he was able to live more or less peacefully until 1848. In that year of revolutions Enggesser evidently had to seek safety in view of the anger of his fellow citizens and had to flee Mundelfingen after incensed inhabitants threatened him and shouted 'Kaspar Hauser murderer!' after him on the street. That he certainly was not, but contemporaries for their part were quite convinced that Enggesser had not only been an accessory but had been directly involved in the affair. Through the fact that he and Hennenhofer met in Baden-Baden, these far from unreasonable suspicions receive a certain confirmation. And Garnier—had he at first, for whatever reasons, also been a fellow conspirator and was thus later so well informed? (See pp. 271–493.)

Stanhope stayed two more weeks in the vicinity of the Grand Duchess Stéphanie. Whether the two had further conversations after his excursion to Griesbach is not known. Then, the period for Baden-Baden for this season at an end, Anton Heinrich was ordered to pack the luggage. But the travellers were not yet bound for home.

On the 24th September they went back to Karlsruhe and from there in day-long stretches along the bank of the Rhine, stopping at Bingen, St.Goar, Andernach and finally Bonn which was reached on 3rd October. From there they headed for Paris, where they arrived on the 14th October and settled in for a month. Since the time when Stanhope had been in a position to help the then King of France and his brother, the Count of Artois, when they were exiles in London, the relationship had continued. For them too the still living spirit of Napoleon and his progeny must have seemed a serious danger. As Stanhope had the task of finding one of the Napoleonids, he could call on the memory of services rendered to obtain conversation partners in Paris. What couldn't he tell about Stéphanie, the Duke of Leuchtenberg, General Gourgaud and the emigrés who had gathered in southern Germany and were conspiring down there to resurrect the old Bonapartist connections. Information from such a good source was only too welcome in Paris. Is it impossible that from here too financial assistance came for Stanhope's costly lifestyle? Stanhope's adaptability with regard to France and some of its citizens is interesting. He wrote only a short time before to Böttiger about his children's former German teacher in Dresden who had gone to France and abandoned the 'blooming pastures of his homeland' to lead a 'small town life among the French'. On this point the 'taste and way of thinking [of the teacher] are quite opposed to mine'.

It was mainly Dalberg, and sometimes 'my old friend' [Artois] with whom Philip Henry spent his time in Paris. In the Duke's palace on the Rue Anjou the evenings were long and the two could tell each other about the months past, exchange old and new information about the case of the princeling and build up a common picture which might yield answers to the riddle. Owing to the importance which the case could have for France and the firm friendship between Dalberg and Talleyrand, it would have figured prominently in the conversation between Dalberg and Stanhope. The weeks in Paris after Stanhope's reconnaissance mission in south Germany show themselves to be a consequence of the political situation. If a son of Stéphanie's still lived, that would have been of concern not only to Metternich and Gentz but also to the Count of Artois and the Duke of Orléans.

On the 15th November Anton Heinrich and Stanhope left the city and made for Calais. With their arrival in Chevening on the 19th the second journey was over; it had been a great success. Stanhope and Stéphanie had met several times. Now it would be a matter of building on this first personal acquaintance in the coming years.

*

According to plan and in line with the increasing amount of available information, the third trip, in 1823, also made directly for Mannheim. It is clear that Stanhope's constant area of operations was southern Germany and that almost all his reconnaissance missions, including the later ones, took place within an area 8–14°E and 48–50°N. In the decisive 21 years between 1814 and 1835 he was simply not interested in any other region. His seventeen trips in this area always returned to the same towns and parts of the country; only the routes there and back varied.

In 1823 the trip got underway on the 21st May. Philip Henry stopped for a longer period three times in Frankfurt and twice in Heidelberg before arriving in Mannheim on the 17th June. He had stayed a long time in Frankfurt on his two previous trips. This time during his three visits to the city in June, July and August, he stayed a total of 33 days in the former Free Imperial City, in which, since 1815, the Federal Assembly had met continually under the presidency of Austria, and where all member states were represented through plenipotentiaries with the rank of ambassador. Here too Stanhope built up a network of political and social contacts as he had done in Dresden.

Soon it included some of the most important diplomats and dignitaries of the city, such as the Dresden-born Prussian delegate to the assembly (1816–1824) August Friedrich Ferdinand, Count von der Goltz (1765–1832) who had been Prussian Foreign Minister from 1807 to 1813 and then Prussian Court Marshal. Then there was the above-mentioned Friedrich Landolin Karl, Baron von Blittersdorf (1792–1861), the Federal Assembly delegate from Baden from 1821 and later Foreign Minister of Baden. Also, the Württemberg representative Karl August, Baron von Wangenheim (1773–1850), whose master King Wilhelm I, as Crown prince, had already in 1803 come close to treason by wishing to stand with Napoleon. Wangenheim was one of the King's most intimate confidantes, and in Frankfurt made a special point of keeping his eye on his Prussian colleague Count von der Goltz, which could only suit Stanhope, who had his eye on them both.

> The Assemby delegates were all slavering over a letter which the liberal Minister from Württemberg, Wangenheim, had written to his King recommending his own proposal for a constitution and which he had had published. In it Prussia was described as a state completely ruined by secret societies, and the Stuttgart despot was presented with the temptation: 'If a revolution were to break out in Prussia and at the same time a German state with a free constitution existed in the south, a transformation of things would be possible such as the boldest phantasy could scarcely imagine!'[146]

Such activities were a source of amusement in Frankfurt but criticism in Vienna. Metternich and Gentz, who were extremely suspicious of the liberal noises emanating from Württemberg, saw Wangenheim as the actual guiding spirit who was giving the King such advice. Already in 1814 Gentz was noting not without concern that the relationship between Crown prince Friedrich Wilhelm and the Czar's sister, Princess Katherina Paulovna, spelled danger for Vienna. Gentz confirmed the Crown prince's talents, but

> it is just these qualities that make him all the more dangerous, because at the same time he possesses a character that is uncommonly ambitious, fickle, devious, and vindictive, and which invites little trust. Neither can one say that the Princess is of a gentler or calmer disposition. These two high-ranking individuals could therefore, through the exercise of their influence upon the Emperor [Alexander I of Russia], one day undertake a great deal and contribute to many upheavals.[147]

After Wangenheim's letter, this prognosis seemed ever more apposite, and so it is only logical to see Stanhope's friendly relations with Goltz, Blittersdorf and Wangenheim in the light of Vienna's need for information.

No less instructive is his connection to the Hanoverian representative at the Assembly, Hans Detlev, Baron von Hammerstein, who on account of his unruliness particularly with regard to British interests, had to be repeatedly reprimanded by his superior Count

Münster. Such contacts were primarily of interest to [Stanhope's] 'friend', George Jackson. A marginal figure, though not without influence on internal German developments, was the Dutch envoy Johann Maria Karloman, Count Grünne. He too was counted among Stanhope's inner circle of acquaintances.

Finally, mention must be made of one of the most influential bankers of his time, Simon Moritz von Bethmann (1768–1826), whose Frankfurt banking house lent considerable sums to Austria and Denmark, and whose father enabled the King of Württemberg to defend Mömpelgard with another 72,000 guilders. Bethmann had specialised in the business of political finance, which allowed him—he had also been Russian Consul since 1802—to play a not insignificant role as a diplomat. Interestingly, Johann Philipp von Wessenberg's son had been instructed by the Vienna State Chancellery to develop 'a congenial relationship' with Bethmann, when Wessenberg, like Stanhope in Dresden, had been given an 'observation post' in Frankfurt at the beginning of his career in 1803. Stanhope maintained his contacts with all these men, including the British colony and the British ambassador Cartwright; there was plenty of information to be obtained from them that would be useful for his own mission.

His interest was especially focused this time upon a new citizen of Frankfurt, Johann Ludwig Klüber (1762–1837) (Fig.79) State Councillor of Baden and member of the Privy Council from 1808–1817—'the

79. Johann Ludwig von Klüber (1762–1837)

Der

Sponheimische

Surrogat- und Successionsstreit

zwischen

Baiern und Baden.

Mit einem Anhang,

betreffend

die Baierische Territorial-Frage.

Gießen,

bei Georg Friedrich Heyer, Vater.

1828.

80. Cover page of Klüber's book 'The Sponheim Surrogate and Succession Dispute between Bavaria and Baden'.

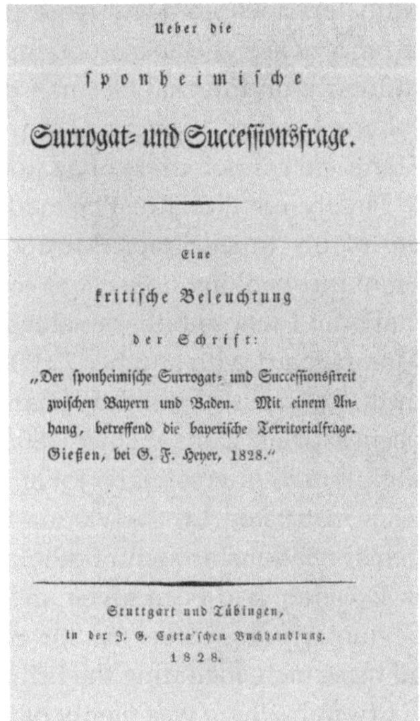

Ueber die

sponheimische

Surrogat- und Successionsfrage.

Eine

kritische Beleuchtung

der Schrift:

„Der sponheimische Surrogat- und Successionsstreit zwischen Bayern und Baden. Mit einem Anhang, betreffend die bayerische Territorialfrage. Gießen, bei G. F. Heyer, 1828."

Stuttgart und Tübingen,

in der J. G. Cotta'schen Buchhandlung.

1828.

81. Cover page of the Bavarian counter-argument text which sought to refute Klüber's expert opinion.

one who knows all of Baden's secrets',[148] former advisor to the Countess Hochberg and publisher of the Acts of the Congress of Vienna. From 1817–1823 he was a Prussian State Councillor and had been obliged to retire in 1823 at the age of 62.

At this point we need to jump forward a little to the events of the coming years in order to present the appropriate background to the personality of the State Councillor. Stanhope could not then have known what was yet to develop through Klüber in relation to the Crown prince of Baden, but from all the information he had at his disposal, he could well have regarded Klüber as a central figure. Klüber, to whom Feuerbach addressed his last questions about Kaspar Hauser before he met his own mysterious death, became Kaspar Hauser's guardian after Feuerbach's death. As Klüber himself remarked, he had had contact with Stanhope from very early on. That he did not at all behave in Stanhope's sense as a real man of honour raises the question why this man 'who knows all Baden's secrets', the advisor to the Hochbergs, should later be a firm upholder of the credibility of Kaspar Hauser. The official line of argument taken by the Baden authorities would rather have inclined to the version of events that saw Kaspar Hauser as a swindler and a suicide. Did Klüber know from his time in Vienna as the representative of Baden's interests of those papers that Czar Alexander had received from Empress Joséphine and did they appear credible to him, the knower of secrets? When Stanhope in 1832, but especially after Feuerbach's death in 1833, wanted to drop Kaspar Hauser, he came to perceive Klüber's position. Was it that the State Councillor in a quite personal capacity as 'one in the know' did not wish to bear any blame at least for this part of the drama? From the later correspondence between Stanhope and Feuerbach we know that Court President Feuerbach considered Klüber to be a 'weak authority' in the Kaspar Hauser affair. In support of this view, Feuerbach referred to the fact that Klüber was 'always active in the interests of that family [the Hochbergs] which could profit and really has profited from Kaspar's murder or else abduction'.[149]

Feuerbach certainly knew of the tract anonymously written by Klüber 'The Sponheim Succession Dispute between Bavaria and Baden' (Fig. 80) in which Klüber had spent 174 pages researching the rights of the Hochberg Line and had come to the conclusion that 'These documents declare the right of succession to the government of all the states of Baden to be indisputably in favour of the sons of the second marriage [to the Countess Hochberg] and their male descendants.'

A review in *Hesperus* magazine of 27th September 1830 shows how Klüber's assessment was favourably received: 'Without doubt Klüber's tract is the best for Baden in the Sponheim affair, because it steps into the ring calmly and armed with convincing arguments. Baden has much to thank this man for—I say Baden—the dynasty and the country....'. The success which the tract had among the politically engaged public was based on previous consultations of a quite singular nature, as the Bavarian ambassador in Karlsruhe reported to Munich on the 14th August 1827: 'Klüber, who is known to be devoted to Mother Hochberg, has recently been here in Baden, where Margraves Leopold and Wilhelm were very preoccupied with him.' Four months later, the result of that 'preoccupation' was seen in the form of the publication of Klüber's tract on the 25th January 1828. It was already available in bookshops everywhere by April.

Was the appearance of Kaspar Hauser in Unschlitt Square in Nuremberg on the 26th May an obvious answer, a visible countermove by unseen Bavarian operators?

Despite this, it remains a fact that that 'weak authority' already in 1832, thus while Feuerbach was still alive, both in letters to Stanhope and in legal contexts, had provided strong arguments, astute and humane, for the complete credibility of Kaspar Hauser. That Klüber contradicted his colleague Feuerbach in the Baden Succession debate in 1830/31 does not at all speak against the fact that he too was secretly convinced of the correctness of Feuerbach's arguments. It is too easily overlooked that the one who 'could profit' and whose family Klüber had served and still served, was the man actually sitting on the throne of Baden from 1830 and that furthermore, Klüber's son Friedrich Adolf (1791–1858), who had a clever head like his father, was the private secretary to the ruling Grand Duke Leopold. What responses other than those given could therefore be expected from Klüber senior?

*

On the 16th June 1823 Stanhope left Frankfurt and headed for Mannheim, which he reached the next day. This time he stayed ten days at the Court of the Grand Duchess (Figs. 82, 83) and renewed old friendships. As planned, he came a notable step closer to Stéphanie.

82. Stéphanie, Grand Duchess of Baden, contemporary copperplate engraving

83. Mannheim Palace, contemporary engraving.

Stanhope was possessed of an eloquence which only a few could see through. Gottlieb von Tucher and the two Daumers, mother and son, were among the few perceptive ones who soon recognised Philip Henry's character. But others, such as Feuerbach, Binder and Klüber either temporarily or until the end of the tragedy put their deepest trust in 'His Lordship'. At first, Stéphanie too apparently saw in Philip Henry an individual who could be granted access to her small court circle, whereby certainly the prevailing widespread cliché-ridden image of the English nobleman, who was supposed to be scurrilous, cranky and extravagant, worked in Stanhope's favour.

With hindsight, it can be seen how Stanhope had prepared his approach to Stéphanie step by step. His energy in pursuing for years the goals he had set himself is just as remarkable as the actual tactics with which he followed his course. The situation had taken on a certain urgency with Napoleon's death in 1821, as a result of Vienna's plans and the age of the young princeling, and Stanhope had asked himself how he could gain access to the mother.

First step: As a direct approach was out of the question, the Grand Duchess's immediate circle was targeted first. In 1821 came the visit to Mannheim and Karlsruhe with the aim of insinuating himself into the good graces of a number of the people in this circle. With ten of them the attempt was successful.

Second step: His new circle of friends prepared his reception by the Grand Duchess, which took place in Baden-Baden in 1822. He was able to spend 23 days in the area around Stéphanie with additional conversations and visits.

Third step: He gained access to Stéphanie's private circle. That Stanhope was accepted into this small group in 1823 was the result of a strategy followed step by step with patience and intelligence.

84. Music room in the Mannheim Palace. On the right, the 'round table'. Watercolour by P. F. Peters (1842)

85. Ink drawing by Grand Duchess Stéphanie (see also Fig. 74). A gift for Stanhope.

Karoline von Bergh wrote in her travel journal of her own reception by the Grand Duchess: 'She loves music above everything, and she makes music constantly, without practising, in that she sings anything desired from the score with a voice that reminds one of a harmony of youth and purity', and Alexander von Ungern-Sternberg wrote in his memoirs:

> The evenings at the Court, two or three times a week as a rule, were actually private gatherings, but private gatherings with an indescribable magic. The princess sat with her daughters and her lady-in-waiting at a round table [Fig. 84]—the old Senior Court Steward was seldom there—and the invited guests sat at the places she indicated for them without regard to difference of rank. There was reading, sketching and chatting. Paper, pencils and crayons were always available, and the princess herself sketched small landscape scenes with a remarkable ease. Whoever she especially favoured received such a sketch.

Stanhope too received one of these and proudly noted on the back of it: 'Drawing by Her Royal Highness the Grand Duchess Stéphanie of Baden. A gift to me at Baden 1823.' (Fig. 85) He therefore also sat at the round table and painted and sketched with the other guests, chatted with them and produced such pleasant pages that the Grand Duchess considered it appropriate to show him her 'special favour'. In his ten days at the Court, Philip Henry may have taken part in three of Stéphanie's private gatherings and had received the small landscape sketch as a memento. Never did he later reveal that his relations and contacts with the Grand Duchess went back to a much earlier time, namely to 1822, and how close he had been to the princeling's mother since that time. When in 1832, he was asked to take Feuerbach's book *Example of a Crime against Human Soul* to the Grand Duchess in Mannheim, the author and those in Ansbach and Nuremberg who were aware of the enterprise believed that Stanhope was going to have the honour of being received at the Court for the first time, whereas in fact, he had been involved in a very close relationship with the Grand Duchess's Court for a decade.

After a three-month trip Stanhope arrived back in Chevening on the 29th August 1823, not only with a pledge of Stéphanie's friendliness in his luggage but also in the calm certitude that the pretender to the throne who had been held 'at Laufenburg on the Rhine' had not yet found his way into the world and that there were possibly good reasons for believing that he [Stanhope] might yet become the master of the situation.

That meant that in the future it would be necessary to maintain an overview of the situation, to remain on the social scene, to garner information and nurture relationships, to get to know the German states—especially those of southern Germany—ever better and more accurately. Almost monotonously, but always effectively, Stanhope therefore appeared on the Continent throughout the following years.

In 1824 his trip began on the 30th August. Via Kassel (14th Sept.), Eisenach, Erfurt (2nd Oct.) Anton Heinrich drove the carriage first once more to Dresden. There Stanhope learned that Louis XVIII had died and that his brother, the Count of Artois, now an elderly, dissipated gentleman of 67, had become King as Charles X. He had been crowned at Rheims in mediaeval splendour and later expressed the wish to see the historical site of Valmy where, years before, as he well knew, the destiny of France had been decided.

Philip Henry of course had had a close relationship with the new King for more than a decade since he had written to the royal brothers from Walmer Castle in 1805 to offer his services. Nothing had since changed in terms of his own goals, and perhaps the succession of the younger of the brothers, with whom he was more closely acquainted, only made him more clearly aware of the danger which still proceeded from the unclarified Baden question of Stéphanie's son, the Napoleonid.

86. Anton, Count Palffy (1793–1879)

From the 6th until the 26th October Philip Henry stayed in Dresden where he met up with his old circle of friends around Böttiger, the Vitzthums, Count Loss, Einsiedel and Nostitz and the Austrian envoy accredited since 1821, Count Anton Palffy (1793–1879) (Fig.86), the son of Prince Joseph Franz (1764–1827) from the princely branch of the older Nikolas main branch of the family. Kaspar Hauser's nurse at Beuggen was in Count Anton's service, and six years later, the police arrived to ask his wife Leopoldine, born Countess Kaunitz, questions about the foundling. Count Anton Karl and Wessenberg were very close friends, not least because Wessenberg had saved the Count's life on the evening of the 27th March 1814 at Saint-Thiébaud. 800 peasants, loyal to the Emperor, had attacked the wagon train that included his carriage because they suspected that one of those travelling in it was the hated Count of Artois, who was known to be returning to France.

The various connections between Stanhope, Palffy and Wessenberg in relation to Kaspar Hauser's Hungarian nurse will be discussed later. Interestingly, after Dresden Stanhope made a stop in Pressburg [today, Bratislava—*Ed.*] before heading on, as in previous years, to his familiar territory. This time, he visited Bayreuth, Bamberg, Würzburg, Heidelberg and Darmstadt.

Heidelberg was a place which Stanhope returned to again and again. There lived not only Count Jenison Walworth (see p. 170) from England, but also, since the death of Grand Duke Karl's death, his chamber servant Kemmler, who no doubt belonged to the circle of knowledgeable marginal figures. It is not known whether Stanhope sought him out on this occasion but it is not unlikely. On the return journey between the 13th and 18th November he stopped in Bockenheim and Königstein near Frankfurt. He must then have made a detour to Düsseldorf, according to his notes, but the exact date is unknown. There he sought out the old-established family of the Baron von Hompesch to which he had connections. The nephew of the famous Baron Ferdinand von Hompesch (1744–1805), Grand Master of the Order of the Knights of St. John of Malta, was General Karl von Hompesch (d.1812), who had served the British and with whom Stanhope had formed a relationship during his time in London. Ferdinand von Hompesch had served as envoy of his Order at the Court in Vienna for 25 years before he went to Malta, where he was forced to accept honourable defeat against Napoleon in the successful storming of the fortress in 1798. The French occupation did not last long; the island was soon reoccupied by the British in 1800.

Another nephew was the highly talented Bavarian Conference Minister Franz Karl von Hompesch (1761–1809), who died early after a brilliant career. During the absence of the King of Bavaria and his trusted Minister Montgelas, he was responsible for the affairs of the government and died a sudden death in 1809. Through Franz Karl von Hompesch came another connection for Stanhope, which Böttiger knew of: after a fierce row with Wieland, Friedrich Heinrich Jacobi (1743–1819), the co-publisher of the *Teutschen Merkur* and like Hompesch, a native of Düsseldorf, had been called to Munich by Hompesch.

None of these men were still alive in 1824. Did Stanhope have questions for those family and friends they left behind, which could be of use to his mission? Did he ask to see papers left by any of the men? When Stanhope himself had been in Malta in 1812 and spoke with various people, he could have come across something that still interested him; around the figure of the Grand Master there were secrets a-plenty.

After the loss of Malta Hompesch and his knights with all their archives had come under the protection of the Czar Alexander I, who following his father Paul I, was now the official Protector of the Order of the Knights of St. John. Between him, England and Napoleon, a bitter struggle broke out which went on for years as to which Power should become the protector of the Order on this strategically important island. Naples was involved, then again France, Great Britain, Austria, Spain, Russia and Prussia. But England occupied Malta in breach of the treaty and stubbornly refused to vacate the reconquered island, which led to an increasingly dangerous confrontation with France. The Malta question became the unforeseen symbol of a power political struggle which would show who was to possess the prime position in the world—France or England. The British defied all threats and after the Peace of Paris in 1814 received the island in perpetuity.

In the first years of the squabbles Hompesch still played a role. Did he welcome Napoleon's ambassador, who had demanded the reinstatement of the old Grand Master against the declared will of England? Both men met personally in 1798 during Bonaparte's expedition to Egypt. Did Hompesch stand in whatever sense closer to Napoleon than was suspected, considering the Emperor had sought with such emphasis to bring his recall into play?

After the days in Düsseldorf, Stanhope and Anton Heinrich finally travelled back to Calais, where the two took ship on the 27th November. The following day, the agent of Gentz was once more back home in Chevening.

7. Vienna

Gentz and Metternich, 1825–1827

The year 1825 brought Stanhope a brilliant event in his affairs. In Vienna he was to be introduced to Prince Metternich. This year he took ship on the 4th of July. The trip was planned for five months and as always, was intended to nurture old connections and create new ones.

After a tightly scheduled journey, Heinrich and his master first returned to Frankfurt on the 15th July. Through his new friends Wangenheim, Goltz, Blittersdorf, Hammerstein and Bethmann, and above all Klüber, the city had become for Stanhope a more important location than ever. The one 'who knows all of Baden's secrets', was certainly, next to Dalberg, the most productive conversation partner for Stanhope's purposes, and it is noticeable that Frankfurt figures prominently in the annual trips as a place to which he returned again and again. But it was just as impossible to overwhelm a man like Klüber as it was the Grand Duchess and the many others in the dense network of contacts that had been developed; consequently, a stay in Frankfurt became a must in Stanhope's planning of his trips, especially in relation to State Councillor Klüber.

After twelve days in the city, the journey proceeded directly on to Vienna (Fig.87) which Stanhope reached on the 5th August. With Gentz and his son Karl, Philip Henry went on a number of tours to mountain districts, which often took between twelve and fifteen hours to reach. These trips to take in panoramic views of the area probably exhausted the two men, whose delicate constitutions may have allowed little more than short strolls along the roadside.

Then came the great day. On the 20th August Stanhope received from Friedrich von Gentz the much-anticipated invitation (Fig. 88) which doubtless represented for him the high point of his career since the days of the first agreement with Gentz in November 1816.

> The undersigned takes the liberty of requesting that Mylord does him the honour of dining with him on Monday at 4.00 pm at the Weinhaus. Sir Henry Wetterley and his family and Prince Metternich will also be there.
>
> Vienna, 20th August 1825
>
> Le Chevalier Gentz[150]

87. City view of Vienna. The Elisabeth Bridge. Copperplate engraving from a painting by R. Alt.

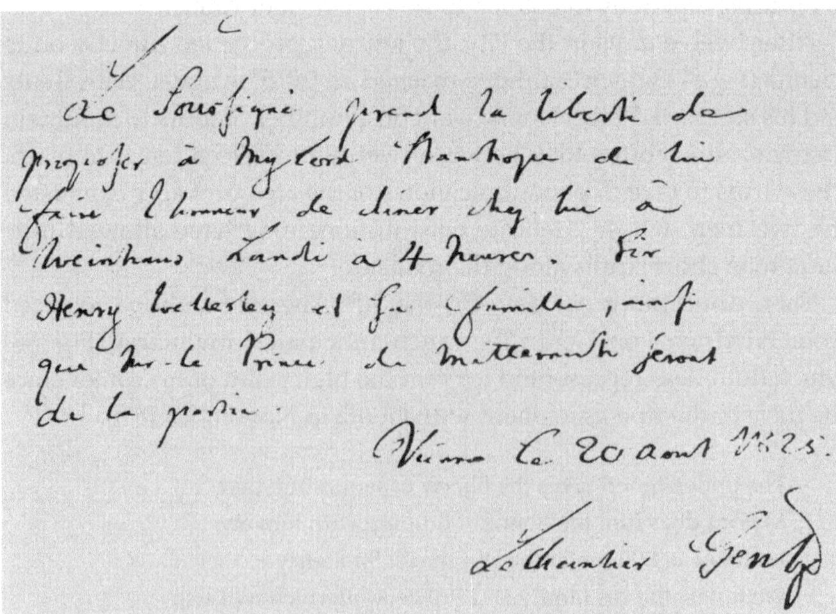

Le Soussigné prend la liberté de proposer à My Lord Stanhope de lui faire l'honneur de diner chez lui à Weinhaus Lundi à 4 heures. Sir Henry Wellesley et sa famille, ainsi que Mr le Prince de Metternich seront de la partie.

Vienne le 20 aout 1825.

Le Chevalier Gentz

88. Invitation to dinner from Friedrich von Gentz to Stanhope which also mentions that Metternich will also attend.

None of the participants at this first meeting or at subsequent ones have left any record as to the object of these meetings and conversations. But there is in Stanhope's own hand a fine report to his son, in which he invites him to make a visit to Vienna:

> ...If you should hereafter come to this place & if you will engage to follow all my good advice I would in that case give you a Letter to the first statesman in Europe, I need not say that I mean Prince Metternich & I flatter myself that it would be an excellent introduction. I feel most gratefully his kindness to me & at the conclusion of an Audience with which he favored me this morning [21st Oct. 1827—*Ed.*] he told me that he could not see me too often. He had the goodness to shew me at my request the unrivalled collection which he possesses of Foreign Orders & which he has honoured by accepting. The charm of his conversation & of that of my Friend, M. de Gentz would alone be a sufficient inducement to come to this place even if I did not feel for it the same local & personal affection & attachment.[151]

The stay in Vienna, the meeting with Metternich and the deepened relationship with Gentz called for a lifestyle which he certainly owed to his chosen profession but which also obviously was a reflection of rewards and honours for both past and future services. Philip Henry had considerable sums at his disposal and showed himself to be fastidious. He travelled these days in a carriage which, in its elegance and expensive outfitting, put all his previous ones in the shade. He described its refurbishment enthusiastically in letters home; apparently, such modifications were still unknown in England: 'I travel in an open carriage, but it can be closed at the front by means of a hood so that I am protected from the cold and wet. It is the smoothest and most comfortable that I have ever had.'[152] Neither did he lack anything in his accommodation. I have just engaged [a cook] who appears to be most excellent & who comes from the service of Prince Ferdinand of Saxe Cobourg [*sic*] where he has lived the last five years. He dressed yesterday a Dinner for me with which I was perfectly satisfied & understands throughly Confectionery, lces & etc...[153]

*

In mid-September Stanhope had his conversation with Count Palffy in Dresden (Fig.86) with the matter of Pressburg again in mind. On the 23rd of the month he took up the plan and visited the place which was not far distant. He wrote to his mother in Chevening: 'I went on a small trip to Hungary to see the procession on the occasion of the coronation of the Empress, which was very fine. But I did not at all try to see the coronation itself, as the church is very small & must have been very full for the occasion.'[154]

But as Philip Henry 'did not at all try' to make the effort to witness the actual event, there arises the suspicion that he needed the time to look into other questions. It may be that the coronation only represented a specific motive for the trip, about which he would be able to speak later without going into the real background. Just at this time—assuming the statements of the Cathedral preacher Johann Samuel Müller are correct[155]—the protestant minister Ludwig Wirth, who was from the Nuremberg region and would have been acquainted with Pilsach, travelled to Hungary to remind his Catholic colleague of something he had involuntarily overheard in 1816. Through Madame Dalbonne, the suspected former nurse of Kaspar Hauser at Beuggen, he told Müller that 'if I dared to reveal what I knew about the story of a child secretly being held captive in Bavaria, it would go badly with me, and my life would no longer be safe...'

At that time Müller is supposed to have heard by chance from a neighbouring room that Dalbonne had said to Wirth: 'For God's sake, what is then to become of this child ? He cannot be locked up forever.' In her fear, Dalbonne had probably not only told Müller later but perhaps also members of the Palffy family, who had constantly shielded her since then.

In his later denunciations Müller many times pointed to the masonic background of the affair and finally asserted that four of the main participants had actually been Freemasons. That would have very well applied to the Palffys in every sense. The Palffy brothers Joseph and Leopold—both of the middle branch of the older Nikolai main line of the family—were early members of the *Zur wahren Eintracht* (True Harmony) lodge, established in Budapest in 1781, and owing to their official positions in the government, they had available to them a far-reaching network of contacts, which extended to all Hungarian lodges and naturally also to the Pressburg lodges *Zur Sicherheit* (Security) and *Zur Verschwiegenheit* (Silence). In 1781 the twelve Hungarian and Austrian lodges banded together under their new provincial Grand Master in Vienna, and here again we come across the Palffys. This time it was Karl, Count Palffy, brother of the previous one, who now headed all the Austrian and Hungarian lodges.

The fact that the lodges were officially closed by Leopold II says little about what actually went on, as the occasional mention of the 'disbanding' of Masonic meetings in numerous police reports indicates. Even Provincial Grand Master Count Palffy 'also remained active after their cessation at the Viennese Court'.[156] That Dalbonne, Palffy, Wessenberg and Stanhope were all linked in a network of contacts is only too clear. But where did the unseen threads run on this puppet stage of destiny? What part in the Kaspar Hauser story, in which Prince von Dietrichstein, an acquaintance of Stanhope's, was also involved, was played out in Austria and Hungary?

It is clear that the probable guardian of Kaspar Hauser during his time at Beuggen stood under the protection of Count Palffy—the elder main branch of the family (cf. p. 264f.). Owing to its position and to a word from the Emperor, the family was able to fend off all researches in Austria and instead, with the help of Wessenberg, a friend of the family, to get Stanhope interested in the fiction of a middle-class Bavarian origin for Kaspar Hauser. According to this, the foundling was supposed to be the illegitimate child of an officer's wife from Munich. The remarkable fact that emerges from this is that Stanhope had more than one connection to the Palffys—or, rather should one say, more accurately, the Palffys had more than one connection to him?

In December of the year Kaspar Hauser appeared, 1828, the widow of Count Johann Palffy (1775–1821)—the cadet Johannine main branch of the family—had arrived from London and was staying at Chevening where there was clearly a mutual understanding: 'I hope,' wrote Stanhope to Vienna on the 20th December, 'that I shall have the pleasure of seeing you again here in the spring.'[157]

An invitation from the Palffys came first. Since Philip Henry had not left England in 1828, only the previous year 1827 needs to be considered in relation to what follows. On the 26th January 1829 Countess Palffy—born the Princess de Ligne—wrote to Chevening: 'The whole family remembers you very well. Will you be sure to come to us again?'[157] *The whole family!* This statement by the childless widow points to Stanhope's acquaintance with yet more members of the family, which must at least include Karl Anton, the envoy in Dresden whom he had known since 1824 and Franz Alois Meinrad Count Palffy (1780–1852), brother of Johann, who Stanhope visited in 1827. Was Madame Dalbonne, now in the service of the senior Nikolai main branch of the family, a key figure with whom so much could stand or fall?

Was it a well-laid plan by the Palffys to neutralise the possible danger of Stanhope's activities through family acquaintance and friendship? With this in mind, what is one to make of the 'Hungarian visitors' who Hauser received in Nuremberg? Moritz Saphir, born in Budapest, a personal agent of Metternich's (see p. 263), the Hungarian Dr. Manso, Ladislaus Count von Merey with his son and retinue, also from Budapest, who all merely wanted to know what and how much Kaspar Hauser could still remember? Was Count Merey in particular an envoy of Palffy's? If, as Stanhope later asserted, Merey had recognised in October 1831 that Kaspar Hauser no longer had any accurate memories, then one could have foregone the expense of the research visit to Hungary. It could just as well be that this reassurance about Kaspar Hauser's apparently weak memories of his nurse Dalbonne was the precondition for the enterprise of the trip to Hungary, which, as intended, had to end in fiasco. Looked at from this point of view, there was a significant remark made by the Nuremberg Mayor Binder to Feuerbach. On the 3rd June 1831, after a conversation with Stanhope, Binder wrote that Stanhope was asking to have sight of the documents of the investigation and indeed 'those which relate to the events in Hungary'[158] and referred to the 'extensive acquaintance with respect to Hungary' which Stanhope had professed to possess.

*

Shortly before Stanhope's departure from Vienna, the aged King Maximilian I of Bavaria died in Nymphenburg on the 13th October. From Philip Henry, who had met the monarch many times, this merely drew the astute comment that the period of a tensely maintained peace between Baden and Bavaria had run its course. He may have known only too well how relations had actually gone on between the two states and what the Grand Duke of Baden could expect from the new King Ludwig I. Given access to the diplomatic post by the secretary to the ambassador in Vienna, 'whom I have known well for many years', Stanhope wrote to England: 'The death of the King of Bavaria will not be a cause for enjoyable redress in Baden.' An accurate assessment. On the day after he received the news of his father's death, the new king Ludwig wrote in his diary: 'My first thought: construction of a plan to regain the Palatinate (the Palatinate on the right bank of the Rhine) ...'. How serious Ludwig was about this would soon become evident.

*

On the 19th October, after two and a half months in Vienna, Stanhope travelled to Nuremberg, where he stayed from the 24th to the 27th. From there, he was tempted to see Erlangen again after an absence of 23 years. The Margravine was no longer alive and Professor Breyer too had died in the meantime, but Philip Henry could still have met many others from his good old student days. However, he found everything very 'boring and dreary' and soon travelled on. The fact that the Margrave's palace had been damaged by fire and after its reconstruction was used by the university displeased him as did the newly built hospital at the end of the palace park. Nevertheless, 'a thousand memories' accompanied him on the journey back to Dover.

On the 20th November he was back in Chevening, which would see him again for a few months. While he had been travelling around Germany, at home his brother James (1788–1825) had committed suicide.

Philip Henry's 1826 travel schedule was still more lavish. He spent a good six months on the Continent. Earlier than the previous year, already on the 1st March, Anton Heinrich prepared himself for the Channel crossing. First, as they almost always did, the travellers made for Frankfurt, then to Darmstadt and Heidelberg. After a longer stay in Karlsruhe and Teplitz, Stanhope met Gentz again in Vienna on the 29th July. He remained his guest until the 5th September. At the end of the month the restless one was again in Baden-Baden, Karlsruhe and then once more in Frankfurt, Heidelberg and Darmstadt. Although this trip was certainly more opulent than those before it, outwardly it achieved little. Philip Henry established no new relationships and essentially visited only places he already knew, which suggests that mere courtesy visits were paid to his old acquaintances. He made himself visible but did not really know how the situation could be developed further. For weeks on end Stanhope and Gentz sat together and conversed. Certainly, they did not only discuss the matter of Stéphanie's son but they must have gone over the difficult hermetic nature of the problem, which they were as yet certainly far from being able to solve.

World problems and events in Stanhope's own homeland then played a role. In early autumn Philip Henry left Vienna and made for Calais. After his return, he wrote Gentz a letter on 20th October which is interesting from a number of viewpoints as it gives an insight here and there into what was motivating the two secret diplomats.

Gentz, ever fearful of revolution, asked for news from England on account of the widely noted disturbances which had resulted in connection with the debate over the Corn Laws. Stanhope wrote to Gentz:

89. Schloss Weiherburg near Innsbruck. Watercolour by J. von Jenner.

> Our Ministers have decided to effect a change in the Corn Laws and to put their plan before Parliament as soon as possible after the Christmas holidays, but they are disunited with regard to this issue...some Members of Parliament who nevertheless see the matter from the same angle as I do have said to me that one ought not to oppose public opinion too much. However, as long as one fears tumult, one could be led far astray, and if one is servile and timid; if on the contrary, one wishes to harness the mob and give satisfaction to its prejudices and its brotherhood, then one can expect a revolution. In fact, I see anxiety, worries, and unrest in feelings everywhere, and the more I observe the matter, the closer I look at it, the more plausible, the more certain seems to me the danger.[159]

Then Stanhope comes to speak of a plan conceived much earlier which had resulted from the frequent inconveniences of his annual trips. A residence of his own about halfway between Vienna and southern Germany would certainly serve as a favourable staging point for all necessary enterprises. On his numerous trips he had come across the ideal location. It seemed eminently realisable to own at least a 'piece of land' in Germany, and so he wrote to Gentz: 'I have seen one near Innsbruck, which I shall perhaps purchase...You will know Weiherburg Castle which was built by Emperor Maximilian I and which is known for its beautiful view, and I am very curious to know how you feel about it. I have been told that Prince Metternich visited it on his last trip through the area.'[160]

'Piece of land' is quite an understatement for the castle, which dates back to 1479 (Fig. 89). In 1827 the property, which was then owned by Philipp von Wörndel, was up for sale due to the extinction of the family line. Stanhope knew of this through his 'old friend, the governor of Salzburg'. Besides the castle complex itself (the *Meierhof*), the 'Weiherburg Estate' included a hunting lodge, 24,000 square *klafter* of meadows (I Klafter = 1.896m or 2.074 yards) and 12,000 square *klafter* of woods as well as the namesake 122 m^2 fish pond [Fischweiher] stocked by the Tuffbach brook and with a fountain in the centre. On the 20th September Stanhope had turned up at an auction at the castle. He got nothing out of it because Marie, the testator's daughter outbid her siblings at the last minute and kept the estate for herself.

But how much money must Philip Henry have had with him in order to be in a serious position to entertain such a purchase! Later—under the very unfavourable circumstances of a compulsory auction—Weiherburg was sold for over 200,000 crowns. Stanhope too must have had at least this amount at his disposal, which gives an illuminating insight into his financial circumstances at the time.

Or was the whole thing merely a confidence trick? Did he regard the adventurous plan to obtain such a possession as necessary to demonstrate the extraordinary possibilities which were available to a British Peer of the Realm? If one thinks of the years before and after this event, the suspicion grows that Stanhope only wished to make an impression on his 'friend, the governor' and also on Gentz, whom he had informed of his intention to purchase. A letter in which Gentz was told of such glad tidings, closed with the announcement that a scroll would soon arrive via the British ambassador in Vienna, 'which contains a copperplate engraving of Mr. Pitt, who felt a deep admiration for you'.[161]

*

In spring the following year Stanhope stayed at Chevening as usual, which he had to leave for a short time when the House of Lords met in London. There was a great deal for the couriers to do during these months. On the 24th March Gentz asked for news about imminent changes in the make-up of the government.

> The present moment is of great and decisive significance for England and for Europe, and the fact that another ministerial change has to take place just at this moment and in the face of so many difficult problems for the British Empire belongs to the most notable constellations of our time. If you have a free hour to send me in all confidentiality (and assured of my complete discretion) some of your views on what we have to hope or fear from this constellation, you would do me a splendid favour.[162]

The matter was evidently very pressing for Gentz. 'We are looking every hour for the arrival of a courier from London, who will illuminate much, eliminate much and—what is most important for me—bring me a letter from you.'[163]

His impatience grew. Something was not working out as he hoped. Gentz: 'The courier from London, whom we await every hour and who is to bring us the definitive composition of the new Cabinet, has not yet come in.'[164] Clearly, Stanhope was not only involved in the matter of the disappearance of the young Napoleonid.

Gentz for his part responded with firsthand information, which could be important for the British, and in addition threw in Stanhope's political assessment in the *Österreichischen Beobachter* which was published by his friend Joseph Anton Pilat. Some of Stanhope's thoughts can be read there under the rubric 'Great Britain and Ireland'.

*

In 1827 Stanhope prepared himself for his tenth trip to Germany. His single-minded lust for travel was noted in the House of Lords: 'Lord Stanhope is amusing, so seldom in his appearance, such an Ultra-Tory and anti-liberal in his politics, full of information, one part farce and one part extravagance, which he restrains here and only uncorks in Germany where he goes every year to amuse himself.' The diarist Lord Greville was mistaken in one point: Philip Henry did not take the long-term strain on himself for his amusement. Going to the same region year after year, without a noticeable break, and always to particular towns, constantly on the road for many months—this was not due to some special germanophile inclination, but was the consequence of the search for an answer to a question constantly held before him.

On the 1st August 1827 they set off for Dover. From Calais they travelled as usual towards southern Germany in daily stages, and the first main stop was again Frankfurt, then Heidelberg, Karlsruhe and Baden-Baden. On the 13th September they reached Vienna. Gentz and Stanhope this time came a step closer in their relationship, which was to have consequences in a very personal way. The necessary distance previously maintained between them was replaced by a familiarity that would have unforeseen consequences. It was towards the end of Stanhope's days in Vienna that Gentz 'out of modesty and delicacy' first spoke of the awkward subject, which had to do with the question of 'an advance payment'.

In October Stanhope first took up an invitation of Franz Alois Meinrad Count Palffy (Johannine branch), who probably knew from Gentz or other sources what Stanhope was actually interested in. Here too the evidence shows itself which in all of Stanhope's relationships sooner or later comes to the fore. But what was the Palffys' attitude? What defined their position in the question at hand? By protecting Dalbonne, they were blocking elucidation that would lead to the goal that Gentz and Stanhope sought. On the other hand, as feudatories of the Emperor of Austria, the Palffys could hardly be expected to go easy on a Napoleonid, who also disturbed the circles of Metternich and Gentz. Or did they have their own standpoint in this matter which took account of none of the known positions?[165]

*

On the 18th November Stanhope travelled via Altötting to Munich. After his 'warm reception' by King Maximilian I in Baden-Baden in 1822, he could assume this time too that a friend of Metternich and Gentz and a relative of Pitt and Grenville would be granted an audience. Stanhope must evidently have seen a difference in the fact that for the last two years, the former Crown prince Ludwig had been King; it was now a matter of seeking to draw forth the same warmth from the son as from the father. It is highly unlikely that Ludwig would have come into close connection with Stanhope in 1822 in Baden-Baden. At most the two might have known each other by sight; a new relationship would therefore have to be created with the ruling House of Wittelsbach. Ludwig did not receive Stanhope, and so in the attempt to create a new beginning a subtle disharmony was already perceptible which would never be absent from then on. With the exception of the late Maximilian, Stanhope never had it easy with the masters of Bavaria. In Stuttgart and Karlsruhe relationships were more liberal and much was more amenable to him, also in terms of the social and personal atmosphere. That he was able to sit so easily at the table of the Grand Duchess Stéphanie and paint with the other guests was possible in Mannheim, but never in Munich.

Nevertheless, his days there were not without some success. Between the 24th and 25th November he met Dalberg, who looked after the interests of France in Munich for a few months in a very adroit fashion. As Ludwig had turned to France for help over the Sponheim (Palatinate) question, Dalberg spent some time in Munich and had discussions with the King. The result of these were his warnings to the French Court not to underestimate the activities of Prussia in southern Germany. Dalberg was intimately familiar with the details of the Sponheim dispute between Bavaria and Baden, a fact which Stanhope (in 1827) perhaps did not yet interest himself too much until a few years later, when it became clear how much the Kaspar Hauser issue was linked with the dispute. For the few remaining days, as long as he did not have to be at the King's disposal, Stanhope's friend compensated him amply for the royal audience he had been unable to secure. Dalberg was after all a high-ranking diplomat who advised governments, possessed insights and had had a role in forming modern international politics for some decades. That their time together was restricted to just a few days had to do with Stanhope's schedule.

On the 29th November he travelled via Augsburg to Stuttgart where he stayed for exactly a week, from the 30th November to the 6th December. Here the 'noble Lord', obviously with letters of recommendation from Metternich and Gentz, was received by King Wilhelm I, whose country lay so clearly in the agent's field of operations; a personal acquaintance was therefore desirable, also from Vienna's point of view. Stanhope already had a connection to Prince Paul from many years back which he could call on. In Carlsbad in 1815 the two men had been immediate neighbours and had often met.

In Stuttgart Philip Henry decided to make a visit to Bruchsal. The relentless trip there and onwards, compressed between the 6th and 9th December, may have had a specific reason behind it, given that the day of departure from Stuttgart was the 6th December and the 8th already the arrival in Mannheim. Apart from the two overnight stays, there remained just one day, which was not used for the ongoing journey. But let us look a little closer at this day and the place where it was spent. The 7th December was Philip Henry's 46th birthday, and

Bruchsal was at that time the seat of the dowager margravine Amalie von Baden. 73 years old, she lived a cloistered existence almost alone in her castle, confronted with the eye problems that began that year and which would eventually lead to her blindness. A number of her once flourishing family had died long before her—her husband already in 1801, four of her promising married daughters, her only son Karl, and his son—all were dead. Only her daughters Karoline of Bavaria and Wilhelmine von Hessen were still alive and they did not often wend their way to the 'quiet, deserted Bruchsal'. The Margravine spent her days with her lady-in-waiting Karoline von Freystadt, which were increasingly marked by despair produced, as Freystadt often remarked, by the repercussions of a 'moral suffering'.

Did the much-travelled visitor now spend a quiet birthday at the silent widow's estate and did his visit afford a small diversion to the melancholy of daily life? Stanhope had come straight from Vienna and Munich via Stuttgart and had news to bring. For his part, did he perhaps ask Amalie about the events of 1812, which she had lived through as an eyewitness?

The next morning the journey went on to Mannheim. This time the Grand Duchess certainly did not see Stanhope. Stéphanie spent the autumn months in her small castle of Umkirch, which she had acquired in this year. She loved the rural seclusion of the place and the environment of Freiburg. 'I want to speak to myself, to my own self, and as I seek to discover the causes of my sorrow, I will perhaps better grasp what they mean.' Such were the thoughts she wrote down during these days in Umkirch.

The next day, Stanhope travelled on, which confirms Stéphanie's absence. Without any important stops he pushed on through some extremely bad weather towards the coast, which he reached on the 20th December. Winter storms prevented an immediate crossing, so they had to wait almost a week in dreary Calais. After their five-month long absence, Stanhope and Anton Heinrich were not back in Chevening until the 27th December.

In the last days of 1827 Philip Henry could let the adventure of his trip pass before him once again. A letter from Gentz, which had been put in his hands a day before leaving Vienna, may have represented a significant highpoint of their deepening relationship. On the 17th November, the famous man, who next to Metternich, was the circumspective co-shaper and guide of one of the Great Powers, had plucked up the courage to ask him, Stanhope the traveller, who provided information in the search for a pretender who threatened to disturb the politics of Europe, for a not inconsiderable sum of money.

Did Gentz not put himself completely into Stanhope's hands by doing this? Or did such a deal pose no danger to him because the creditor was dependent on him in other ways? The style of the letter is warm and at the same time plain. Gentz made no bones about the fact that he really needed the money. The time had not yet come when the ageing politician would give out riches with both hands to his beloved dancer Fanny Elssler. That was in 1829. Rather, according to Gentz:

> ...for the last few months there has been an almost fatal blockage in my financial affairs, and if a friendly hand were not to help me, I would find myself in a very serious situation by the end of the year. I therefore presume without further ado to ask you, my dear Count, if you would advance me a loan of £400 for about six months or until next summer, because in the intervening period the circumstances which currently make such a request necessary will with God's help be out of the way.[166]

The politeness with which Gentz broaches the matter cannot disguise the fact that he was hardly leaving Stanhope any room to decline the request. Reminding Stanhope to provide him with news of the first part of the trip and from Munich—by which he meant the Court—Gentz also told him, as if the deal were already agreed, how to forward the money in such a way that would expose him as little as possible:

> Out of a sense of modesty and delicacy I did not touch on this matter orally. As I have now written it down, I will regard it as a quite especial favour if, from Munich, after some news of the first part of your journey, you would mention in a general fashion and without going into the matter in question whether I can count upon the fulfilment of my wish. As for the payment itself, would you be so good as to effect it later from London by the simplest and most inconspicuous means. The best would be an instruction to the House of Rothschild, because *any other* could compromise me.[167]

Referring to 'the great and important questions...., which occupied us in our conversations here', Gentz closed the letter, to which Stanhope replied promptly and positively. On the day of his departure, the very same day he received the letter, the 18th November, he reassured Gentz: 'So that this business might suffer no delay, I am writing this letter with a request to enclose it with a note and send it off by the next Austrian courier.'

The note enclosed was the instruction to the Rothschild bank to pay £400 to Gentz:

> Gentlemen,
> I request that you will pay to M. de Rothschild of Vienna on the Account of M. le Chevalier de Gentz, the Sum of four hundred Pounds.
> I have the honour to be, Gentlemen, your most obedient, humble Servant
>
> Stanhope[168]

Stanhope was never to see his generous loan again. Once 'God's help' had failed to materialise, Gentz had never seriously contemplated a repayment.

On the 22nd December he sent off a letter so promptly that Stanhope found it waiting for him on arrival in Chevening. It included a consideration of the then current situation of Austria, England and France and shows impressively how intimate the unequal relationship between the two men had become. In the many-sided letter, from which only the beginning and a short extract from near the end will be cited, we read:

> I have had this letter written by a hand that is not my own but which is completely dependable, because I know that you like German letters the best and yet I worry that you might read my handwriting with more strain than an official document...The French government is the most loathsome and contemptible government in Europe today. Here all are agreed on this. How this miserable government which is gripped by a struggle to the death has handled the Greco-Turk question the historians of the future will scarcely believe. You will remember that on the 10th November at the first news of the destruction of the Turkish fleet the *Moniteur* began its article with the words: 'L'affaire de l'orient est terminée'. These words were considered the greatest possible combination of idiocy and boasting. They were wrong. Read the *Moniteur* of the 18th December! When the last hope for a peaceful outcome disappeared with the departure of the envoy from Constantinople, in that moment these idiotic ministers repeat the victory song of the 10th November and toast their *far-sighted wisdom!*
>
> And that is not all; next they seek to stimulate the vainglory and expansionist desires of the French nation by dropping hints about projects for conquest. The ministerial *Gazette de France* spoke recently of a

plan to drive the Turks out of Europe which Bonaparte and Czar Alexander were supposed to have drawn up together at Tilsit and in doing so regretted naively that this splendid plan had gone to the grave with its instigator. However, they added the following unambiguous words: 'At any rate, if Napoléon and Alexander are no longer here to accomplish their great plans, *France* and *Russia*, thanks be to God, are still here!'

God forbid that one could laugh about England's other allies as much as one can about the French cabinet! But when one casts a glance at *Russia*, one feels a serious shudder.

And all that sets England up for the most ludicrous of all fantasies, for the so-called liberation of the most unworthy rebels [i.e. the Greeks—*Ed.*] on whom the sun has ever shone. It cannot be! Fear of Russia and a hatred of the insatiable Power [i.e. France—*Ed.*] will and must in short become the general motto in England; and rest assured that the best part of all nations on the Continent will soon add their agreement in full voice!...[169]

*

The intimacy of this exchange of thoughts is instructive. Not so much the content of the otherwise interesting letter but more the familiarity of the tone enables one to conclude that the man who, after Metternich, was the most influential politician in Austria maintained a relationship with Stanhope that is not easy to interpret and which points to further mutual interests. Stanhope evidently played a role which allowed for such give and take. Gentz closed his letter with the words: 'I await your confidential communications with a real yearning!'

8. Kaspar Hauser Appears in Nuremberg

The Struggle for the Palatinate, 1828

Stanhope's series of trips to Germany was only broken in 1828. Almost as if the situation required such an exception, there stood Kaspar Hauser on Whit Monday on Unschlitt Square in Nuremberg and was taken in as a 'pledge of love'. Even to suspect that he was the one that had been searched for was impossible; the manner of his appearance could not have been more different from what was expected of the future Grand Duke of Baden.

It appears that Stanhope had very private reasons for remaining in Chevening in 1828. The purchase of Weiherburg Castle, for which he had had to put aside precious time for the journey there and back, had not worked out. In addition, he had had no notable success in his mission; the reappearance of the Napoleonid, who must then have been 16 years old, was long overdue yet there was still not the slightest indication of where he was.

Stanhope—now in his 47th year—after seven years of travelling in which he had spent many more months in Germany than at home and thousands of miles sitting in his carriage, may well have recognised the need for a break. Covering the distance between Kent and southern Germany had always taken more time than was spent in Baden itself. Then his family was overshadowed by the severe illness of his second son.

George Joseph had come home from Spain the year before with a case of advanced consumption, and the damp climate at Chevening aggravated the symptoms. The need for medical assistance was pressing; a warm dry climate was required for a cure. It was therefore decided to send him to join Lord Strangford's staff in South America. Strangford was a friend of the family and was about to be sent to Brazil on a special mission. It was hoped the sea voyage would ease the patient's suffering. But how advanced the illness already must have been is shown by the rapid course it took that led to George Joseph's death. The sad story is mentioned by his father only in note form:

20. August	sailed on the Galatea
5–6 October	crossed the equator
	very ill
16	arrival in Rio de Janeiro

25	disembarked
November	
19	a big improvement
25	fateful end

His son died that day and was buried in Rio de Janeiro. Catherine Lucy Wilhelmina, the nine-year-old sister of the deceased, wrote in her memoirs: '[1828] was calamitous, for it brought a life-long sorrow to my father and mother, in the death of my poor brother George… I don't think my mother ever mentioned George's name again so long as she lived… but my father though very rarely sometimes alluded to their great loss, always deeply with uncontrollable emotion...'.

*

Instead of anticipated conversations with Gentz in Vienna, a correspondence between the two men now began which did not continue through the whole period but which in its intermittent progress recognised the need to maintain a sharing of information. This not exactly equal relationship was accompanied by an undertone that does not fit into the normal sphere of an agent's activity. The two men's common interests showed no inner balance such as would obtain in the mere give and take of information. Gentz was always the taker who showed no reserve in presenting precisely delineated requests, which Philip Henry then fulfilled. As already mentioned, he had not received his 'loan' back from Gentz, and now more expensive gifts were sent to Vienna. Were the protections and numerous services which could only come from Vienna so indispensable that such expenditure came as matter of course, was even unconditional and therefore more or less had to be provided?

Thus over the course of the year a pound of snuff, exquisite porcelain, an expensive bowl, a wall clock, dark blue suit material, and books were sent to Vienna—all of them presents requested by Gentz. Some were also sent to Baron von Fahnenberg and Metternich. Stanhope noted a 'black clock for Prince Metternich' and a coffee service for Fahnenberg. As far as is known, Stanhope received no such presents.

Nineteen letters, some of them very long, and always by courier, went to England and perhaps just as many replies were received in Vienna, as Gentz had occasion quite rightly to ask for an answer. This correspondence will not be dealt with here, as it does not touch on the Kaspar Hauser question. The sometimes many-sided letters with their content relating to current political events do not so much represent the correspondence between two friends as the rapid exchange of news between two agents.[170]

One of those acting as courier was State Councillor Ludwig Count Lebzeltern (1774–1854), who was 'reckoned to be one of the most brilliant stars of Austrian diplomacy'. Lebzeltern, initially an envoy in Lisbon and Naples, gained the confidence of Czar Alexander on his last and most important post in St. Petersburg through his very anti-Napoleonic activities and was for Metternich and Gentz the most important man at the Russian Court. Lebzeltern was also a friend of Wessenberg's, so it is not surprising to see him on a visit to Stanhope. On the 18th December 1828 Vienna's trusted man stayed at Chevening, and it may be supposed that it was not a matter of a mere courtesy visit. Most likely, he was to hand over especially delicate papers that could not be entrusted to the usual courier service.

*

The surprising result of a look through the Stanhope-Gentz correspondence of the year 1828 is the fact that there is not a single mention of the Napoleonid.

That may well be because the speechless youth in Nuremberg could at first in no way be seen as the heir to the throne of Baden, but perhaps also because Stanhope and Gentz, as both agreed, had made sure to destroy any compromising material immediately. Perhaps they had also arranged not to put down particularly secret matters in writing, which is most likely, given the fact that even with couriers, correspondence was not completely secure.

Whatever these no longer ascertainable circumstances may have been, one thing is certain: Stanhope and Gentz could imagine all kinds of scenarios—the person they sought might have been in castles, fortresses, on estates and in aristocratic circles at home and abroad—but the reality of his situation they could surely not have imagined. They had pictured the appearance of the princely heir in a very different manner, and only gradually did the real picture become clearer from the given circumstances. There is something that Stanhope wrote to Gentz that year, without indication of day or month and without any salutation, the relevant passages of which will now be quoted without any further comment. It was most likely Lebzeltern who took the letter in Chevening and conveyed it directly to Vienna; its content is explosive:

...I would be concerned that your name might be guessed at, because it is known what attitude of mind I have devoted to you...
The question would be the following:

1. Is the matter held to be 'possible' ?
2. What would be the best and most appropriate means for its realisation? To which one can only add point 3:

Who is to convey the letter which you are thinking of writing to the Duke? The decision on question 1 appears to me to depend on another question, namely, what funds would be available for this purpose, without having to bring the matter before the knowledge of Parliament. This would without doubt be offensive to the Duke, and I believe that he would be wary of making such a step before the eyes of the Lower House which squanders large sums like many spendthrifts, but which is extremely mean and begrudging about spending small ones. For your part, in the obviously trusted position which you occupy and with a

clarum et venerabile nomen Gentebus

before the whole of Europe it would be unpleasant and therefore best avoided. However, I believe, and this is why I consider the matter to be 'possible', that apart from the so-called Secret Service money, the administration of which would never be betrayed and the amount of which would never be sufficient, the King possesses only the source under the name of the 4½ per Cent to date, which means with an outlay of 4½ p.C. on West Indian products, which depend solely on his own administration....One would not be able to prevent a Member of Parliament, who perhaps ought to report the matter, from making the matter public but just as little could Parliament prevent the matter or reasonably interfere in it.

By the expression 'gratification' I understand an annual pension and not only a single payment. In any case, would you please be advised to broach the matter in general terms in your letter to the Duke without mentioning a specific sum. Should the sum in his opinion exceed the boundaries which seem possible to him, he could refuse the application and hold it improper to offer you another one...[171]

This letter, which is not necessarily related to the Kaspar Hauser question, but may be, provides impressive confirmation that at this time the two agents were involved in some very shady affairs. Obviously, Count Lebzeltern was also in on 'the matter', which is why he was sent to Chevening just a few days before Christmas.

It is striking that Kaspar Hauser should have appeared at the time when the first signs of a declining zeal in the search for him became evident. In the very year that Stanhope for the first time in many years did not make the trip to Germany came the event that had been awaited so long. Were there circles that had noticed or indeed knew that Stanhope would not be coming to Germany in 1828? Was his 'inattention' perhaps a kind of 'precondition'? On the other hand, factors come into the balance which lead one to suspect certain intentions. Are those in the know, the stringpullers, to be sought in Bavaria? Were there reasons and a pretext for letting the heir to the throne of Baden free at this particular time—Whitsun 1828? Was a role played in this by the publication only a few months before of Klüber's tract 'The Sponheim Surrogate and Succession Dispute between Bavaria and Baden', which had affirmed the Hochbergs' permanent right of succession at a time when Ludwig, the last Zähringer, was still on the throne?

The date itself of Kaspar Hauser's appearance was from the beginning just as riddling as the intelligent management that had determined this point in time. However, the course of the event takes on a recognisable meaning in the context of the opposing standpoints of Bavaria and Baden: the appearance of the foundling at this moment could have led to a decision that would favour Bavaria.

*

What kind of human being was it, speechless and deathly pale, that tottered with his unsteady steps towards the people of Nuremberg? The well-known engraving by Johann Georg Laminit gives us only a very incomplete picture. Hauser later showed himself to be amused by it. From this early time only the pictures by Heinrich Adam and Konrad Hitz deserve serious consideration. In their way, they both enable one to feel something of the silent sorrow of this child who has stepped out of the darkness into the light. Unpublished for a long time, a miniature portrait (Fig. 90) by an unknown artist that was found in Ansbach showing Hauser not long after his appearance allows an enhanced impression that goes beyond the well-known pictures of him. The clothes in which he arrived have been transformed into those of a court exhibition room in that the blue gentleman's coat and the elegant cravat, which do not fit the rigid staring face under the straggly hair, can be understood as artistic licence. But that is of small concern. More important is : how did he actually appear and how accurate is our normal image of Kaspar Hauser as he appeared that day as portrayed by Laminit, Oertel and especially the Kreul portrait. (Fig. 127) The last mentioned, which has achieved a near canonical status due to its obvious artistic quality, shows Kaspar Hauser only at a very specific point in his life, something that Feuerbach also remarked upon. Already in 1828, he noted: 'Kaspar Hauser's face should have been painted by a skilled portrait artist, because it would certainly soon change. That wish remained unfulfilled, and the supposition was soon borne out.' However, Feuerbach's very reasonable suggestion, even if it remained unknown, was taken up by the private customer who commissioned the miniature. The physiognomy shown corresponds very exactly with first observations of Kaspar Hauser and differs markedly from the well-known portrayal by Laminit.

In his book *Example of a Crime against the Soul Life of a Human Being*, Feuerbach wrote:

> His face was then very common and when at peace almost without expression; its lower half protruded somewhat, which gave him an animal-like look. The vacant gaze of his bluish clear bright eyes gave the impression of a animal-like dullness. The form of his face changed completely within a few months. His gaze took on expression and life, the protruding lower half of the face withdrew, and the earlier physiognomy was scarcely to be recognised.

90. Kaspar Hauser. Ivory portrait miniature c. 1828/29

Tucher also noted down his earlier observations: 'His face looked rather like that of a silly peasant boy, the eyelids were somewhat sunken, the lower part of the face hung forward rather; shaggy hair hanging well down over his forehead.' This is indeed how one would look who had been kept for years in darkness like an animal.

All the available evidence speaks for the fact that after the appearance of the bottle message Kaspar was no longer held at Beuggen Castle on Baden territory but was brought to Pilsach Castle in Bavaria, and the question arises as to what reasons there could have been for bringing Hauser to here, of all places. Firstly, it should be clear that whoever was behind the bottle message, intentionally or otherwise, brought about Hauser's immediate removal from Baden-controlled territory. Whether the author of the message wanted to help the child or wanted to use him for political ends—by naming the approximate place of his imprisonment, the die was cast. Hauser had to be removed as soon as possible. Bavaria, according to the version of the story that is normally given most priority, was a neighbouring country quickly reached, and there did not necessarily have to be any pressing political reason to have fled there. Above all, it may be accepted that the choice of easily reachable and immediately accessible quarters for the hostage was limited and that Bavaria perhaps offered the only conceivable solution to which there was no alternative. It may have become clear to some only later what an undesirable course had been embarked upon and to what it would lead.

But what interest could there have been in this captive, and was there a relationship between this interest in the person and the timing of his later appearance? An answer to these questions requires an explanation of the relationship at the time between Bavaria and Baden, the nature of which almost inevitably created a grey zone in which intrigues of every kind could take root and flourish. An appalling mutual mistrust, territorial demands bitterly asserted and coveted that were bound up with the continuation or fall of the old Zähringer line, had created a climate in which the antagonists gradually came to feel themselves justified in resorting to any means of cutting through the Gordian knot. This conflict that went on for decades requires a thorough explanation so that its importance and Hauser's role in it can be properly assessed.

The Struggle for the Palatinate

That Queen Karoline (Fig. 91) and King Max Joseph of Bavaria (Fig. 92) would have arranged Hauser's transfer to Bavaria or would have known of it can be excluded. The same applies, at least in the first years, to Crown prince Ludwig (Fig. 93). The question is whether Ludwig's ignorance can also be accepted after the death of Max Joseph in 1825. For 'politics is a great double drama, and the game behind the curtain remains unknown to the general public. The Prince's own letters and the communications of contemporaries who were in the know, reveal that he exercised a decisive influence in many important questions already before his accession to the throne.' Such is the assessment of the historian Karl Theodor Weigel in his book on Ludwig I: *Plans to Regain the Baden Palatinate.*

After Kaspar Hauser had been brought to Bavaria in 1816/17 by those who at first perhaps did not realise the possible consequences of their actions, control over the captive passed forcibly into the hands of Bavarians who were no longer accountable to the consigners in the long-term. They would keep back their knowledge of the explosive nature of the case until the Bavarian Crown Prince acceded to the throne. It had long been known that since the Congress of Vienna he

91. Karoline, Queen of Bavaria (1776–1841)

92. Maximilian I, King of Bavaria (1756–1825)

93. Ludwig I, King of Bavaria (1786–1868)

had resented the cession of Bavarian territory to Baden more than his father and would leave no stone unturned to regain for Bavaria the former Wittelsbach family lands of the Palatinate on both the left and right banks of the Rhine.

As this was the case and was generally known, Grand Duke Karl of Baden on his deathbed in Griesbach had provided for the indivisibility of Baden through the proclamation of a law of the ruling house [in accordance with which, he would be succeeded by his uncle and then the Hochbergs—*Ed.*]. Varnhagen, who witnessed the last days of Karl's reign, wrote in his 'Memorabilia' of his firm suspicions about Crown prince Ludwig of Bavaria, who busied himself with the Palatinate Question, and also wrote further on the attitude of Karl:

> His early death had been reckoned with, which unfortunately would occur only too soon, but not so early, he hoped and wished, as to prevent him from strengthening and securing the undiminished state of the country and the succession of the Hochbergs to the entirety of the state through the ruling of the Great Powers. He declared that he would by no means agree to give way; earlier, he had indeed entertained such thoughts because he had given up hope and had believed all resistance to be impossible but now, he thought otherwise; Tettenborn [Baden's chargé d'affaires in Vienna] had opened his eyes; they could do violence to him and rob him and he would have to let it happen despite at least trying to defend himself against it; but he would never go along willingly! He did not believe the King of Bavaria [Max Joseph] to be so bad; the King even showed himself ashamed, embarrassed and uneasy when the awkward issue was mentioned in relation to himself, but the Crown prince [Ludwig] was full of spiteful ambition; any means seemed justified to *him* and to gain Mannheim and Heidelberg was for him a constant obsession; he always proclaimed that the Palatinate was the land of his childhood which he must have back![172]

However, the 'awkward matter' which caused King Max Joseph 'embarrassment' and 'unease' revealed, quite contrary to Varnhagen's memories of it, that not only Crown prince Ludwig cast covetous eyes on the Palatinate but that in fact his father had also: 'As the Grand Duke's condition worsened by the day, the impatience of the Munich Court could hardly be contained,' wrote Treitschke.

> Max Joseph and his Minister Rechberg both declared to the Prussian ambassador that they were prepared to compromise but that if

> the Grand Duke were to die before a deal was done, Bavaria would regard the Palatinate as having reverted to Bavaria and would assert its rights. Soon after, warnings poured into Karlsruhe from all sides: Bavaria was arming and massing its troops on the frontier of the Palatinate. The Grand Duke now ordered all those on leave to return to their duties.

Wilhelm I of Württemberg, who also felt himself threatened, had his envoy in Munich, von Gremp, ask in writing whether it was true that on the death of Grand Duke Karl, the Palatinate would be retaken by force, in which case, he added in warning 'it would lead to the certain expulsion of Bavaria from the German Confederation'. The King certainly hurried to deny such plans, but there was no longer any real will to guide Bavarian diplomacy away from its fatal path. The unfortunate plan for a military intervention ultimately stems not least from the fact that Vienna, which had originally taken Bavaria's side in the Palatinate issue, had meanwhile changed its view to favour the claims of Baden. We shall now briefly recapitulate the process that had preceded this sudden crisis.

The Palatinate territory on the *left* bank of the Rhine had already been lost to France in 1796. Six years later, Napoleon ordered the *right* bank Palatinate territory to be ceded to Baden; it had belonged to the Dukes of Bavaria since 1214. Bavaria received Ansbach as compensation in 1805, but Napoleon also then took Berg from the Duchy. The Wittelsbachs then claimed and received Trient, Brixen, Tyrol and Vorarlberg, Salzburg, Berchtesgaden, the Inn region and parts of the Hausruck region. After the fall of Napoleon, Bavaria again lost its possessions on the border with Austria and received back in turn the desired *left* bank of the Rhineland Palatinate near Schweinfurt and Würzburg. The county of Sponheim which had been taken by France in 1796 was overlooked. It had been held in common by Baden and Bavaria and had been given to Baden only by the French as a substitute in the form of a few *right* bank territories, while the claims of Bavaria to it had remained unconsidered.

The loss of the Palatinate, especially of that part of it on the *right* bank of the Rhine, which was finally determined after the Congress of Vienna, had never ceased to astonish Crown prince Ludwig, who had spent a part of his youth (1789–99) in the old ancestral Palatinate lands. In 1809 the pining prince wrote in a poem: 'The Palatinate exists no more, the Wittelsbachs no longer hold sway on the Rhine where they flourished for 600 years....'. Twenty years later, in 1829, his thoughts were equally melancholic:

> ... and on the Rhine all alone
> Returns the Palatinate Count
> With tearful gaze;
> The town where once he lived
> As child and boy is now a grave.
> He never will go back.

The reconfiguration of the disputed territory that was conceived at the Treaty of Ried in 1813 should the Zähringer Line become extinct, was successfully countered by Grand Duke Karl following the deaths of his two sons by his declaration of the indivisibility of Baden (Law of the Ruling House 4.10.1817) and of the Hochbergs' right of succession to the throne (Constitution of 22.2.1818); both had been solemnly guaranteed by the Great Powers. No protest by Bavaria could move the principals of the Congresses of Vienna, Aachen (1818) and

Verfassungsurkunde

für das

Großherzogthum Baden.

Konstanz,
gedruckt und im Verlag bey J. M. Bannhard.
1819.

94. Cover page 'Constitutional Charter for the Grand Duchy of Baden

Frankfurt (1819) to agree to any territorial compensation, as it was feared that this would give Bavaria a clearly pre-eminent position in southern Germany. The Aachen Congress in particular, which was chaired by Gentz, had once again confirmed Baden's claims at the expense of Bavaria's. In Munich on his return to Austria Gentz had written to Metternich: 'in response to these results Crown prince Ludwig moaned and cried out in horror'. In his book on Ludwig I, M. Dirrigl cites the King as being in no way satisfied with the situation: 'My fervent wish and my fixed thought remains the achievement of the possession of the Palatinate.'

Undeterred, on the 7th October 1818 Ludwig wrote to Alois Count of Rechberg (1766–1849): 'The Palatinate! In the Holy Scriptures it is written: He who has a hundred sheep and loses one, leaves the 99 and goes in search of the one until he has found it.'[173] There were, however the views of the Great Powers, which also determined the course and result of the territorial commission in Frankfurt, where the Great Powers sought to settle the Baden-Bavaria territorial dispute once and for all. England, above all, was not prepared to depart from the decisions of the Congress of Aachen, whereas Austria showed itself quite willing, at least at the outset of the negotiations, to accept Bavaria's wishes. King Ludwig's rigid position, however, prevented any accommodation. On the 9th March 1819 Emperor Franz wrote to Metternich with concern: 'In addition I also wish to know when and how Bavaria will renounce the reversibility of the Palatinate after the extinction of the grand ducal house and equally, when and how far we ourselves shall be freed from our obligations which we entered into through the Agreements at Munich and Ried.' In his biographical study,[174] A. V. Arneth writes: 'We do not know Metternich's answer to the Emperor's question, nor do we know whether he succeeded in calming such thoughts...Unfortunately, the stubbornness [of the Bavarian government], he later wrote to Metternich, had only increased because Pfeffel's moderate advice had only inflamed Crown prince Ludwig's wrath.' His ultimatum was to accept the money offered and at the same time to reserve all rights for himself. 'It is impossible,' Wessenberg said later, 'for a government like that of Bavaria to make itself useful...'

That the influence of Crown prince Ludwig was greater at the Munich Court than that of any other also showed itself in the fact that despite the restraining counsel of Pfeffel, Bavaria now carried out its threat and protested against the decisions of the Great Powers both in

Frankfurt as well as in Aachen. Wessenberg expressed the view that no intrigue should be allowed which aimed to introduce any kind of tension between Austria and the Great Powers allied to it.

> I confirm that I no longer believe that the Munich Cabinet has any such intention, as I have factual evidence here at hand that no such definite plan exists. Suffering from many inner embarrassments, disunited in itself, in dispute with the heir to the throne, who dreams of nothing but the conquest of the Palatinate, the Bavarian Ministry ekes out its existence from day to day and only dares to make hesitant steps forward...

About two weeks later, Prince Metternich repeated to Baron von Wessenberg his approval of his behaviour...Hruby was given the task of getting the Bavarian government to realise the fruitlessness of their efforts and of insisting that they pursue their course no further. But despite the firmness of the tone which Metternich adopted, it produced no persuasive effect on the position of the Munich Court. There the decision lay as ever in the hands of the Crown prince who had made his views clear a short while before in the words he had directed at Pfeffel after the latter's recall from Frankfurt: 'It is preferable to me to see you come home empty-handed rather than with a shred of territory which would have necessitated us to make a complete renunciation without guaranteeing us satisfactory compensation.'

With things in this situation at Munich, where the Russian envoy Count Pahlen also noted that 'the single-mindedness of the Crown prince' appeared to have become 'the actual driving wheel of the governmental machine', no pliability whatsoever was to be hoped for any longer from the Bavarian government, and little remained but for the Frankfurt territorial commission, which consisted of the representatives of the Great Powers, to end its work without the agreement of Bavaria.

'Immediately on his accession to the throne (1825),' wrote Dirrigl,

> he [Ludwig] considered the time had come to renew Bavaria's claims to the Rhenish Palatinate with all the means at its disposal. In a letter of the 2nd October 1826 he assured Metternich that he went to bed and woke up with the thought of the Palatinate...and that were he not to pursue this thought with the greatest steadfastness and exertion, he would not be able to achieve his aims even temporarily. Karl Theodor Baron von Hallberg-Broich (1768–1862), the 'hermit of Gauting' and a personal acquaintance of Field Marshal Wrede, wrote to Ludwig on the 25th April 1827 that the Palatinate could only be won by military occupation (*coup d'éclat*). The

> rather passive attitude of the leading Ministers in the territorial question had made a not insignificant contribution to the fall of Montgelas. It had been the last difficulty for all his opponents. In fact, the leading members of the Opposition were men of the Palatinate, and their leader was Field Marshal Wrede, the declared protector of all Palatinaters in Munich.[175]

The Kaspar Hauser researcher Fritz Klee described the situation similarly and came to the noteworthy observation that it was in just *this* context that Kaspar Hauser suddenly appeared in Nuremberg. 'The military circles in Bavaria were inclined to move against Baden aggressively, so Heidelberg in the autumn of 1827 had reason to fear an attack from neighbouring territory. Diplomacy had not succeeded in achieving the cession of the region in question. During this political turmoil Kaspar Hauser now appeared in the picture in 1828.' Klee believes that Hauser was brought forward not for any vague reason but intentionally, with a specific function in view at a definite political moment. The precondition for the use of such an instrument was that the desired effect would somehow be imaginable, which in this case meant that the strategists in the background would have known who Kaspar Hauser was and what could be achieved with him in the existing situation.

On the 16th February 1828—three months before Hauser's appearance in Nuremberg—the King had drawn up some quite concrete but risky plans for intervention, which are of interest from the psychological viewpoint. On the one hand, his determination to regain the Palatinate by military force is unbroken, but on the other hand, he concerned himself with the question of how a military campaign might look that would spare Bavaria from firing the first shot. The whole concept proceeded from pure speculation. Ludwig expected that the resulting situation would force the Great Powers to agree to the new circumstances. How unrealistic such fantasies were had later to be made clear to the King by his ministers.

Ludwig's plan bore the title: 'Plan of events observed from Bavaria if the Grand Duke of Baden were to die without agreement having been reached between the two Courts with regard to Sponheim'. The King then laid out his ideas:

> A Bavarian corps is to prepare to move immediately into Baden (where? this must be decided by the circumstances) and occupy two districts [*Kreise*]... Not a shot must be fired from the Bavarian side, even if the Badeners attack and then not more than necessary, in order to save Bavaria's honour. Should Baden troops be positioned in places in the territory

> thus occupied, they would be requested to withdraw. Should they refuse—in all probability they would not—the location is to be encircled with such a superiority of forces that they could start nothing....Without an invasion Bavaria will not gain its rights....But once this energetic step on Bavaria's part has been taken successfully, then Prince Metternich, who wants no war, will seek a settlement and that such would not be possible without Bavaria's agreement, he would certainly feel; alongside others, such a consideration will also have an effect on the Empress—the King of Bavaria will count on her at the decisive moment. Seeing Bavaria's earnestness expressed in its deeds, the other Powers will also not allow the situation to come to a war in order to create a somewhat larger territory for the Hochbergs....Then when the matter of Sponheim itself has been concluded, will the matter of the Palatinate be taken up, which is much more difficult, but which may be alleviated through the above-mentioned method.

Heinz Gollwitzer[176] accepts that the Justice Minister Georg Friedrich Baron von Zentner (1752–1835) persuaded Ludwig to shelve such hopeless ideas. In the spring of 1828 the King therefore realised that the situation could not be altered *directly* either by military or diplomatic means. He then could have brought to fruition a plan which other advisors thought had a better chance of success: the introduction of the young man from Pilsach. That the King was also thinking in such a direction is evidenced, in retrospect, by entries in his diary from the 27th April and 5th May 1836. The Foreign Minister Friedrich August Koch, Imperial Baron von Giese (1783–1860) had told him that he had heard in Switzerland that people were seriously convinced there that Hauser was the son of the late Grand Duke Karl of Baden. In his diary, Ludwig writes: '...whose murder had happened without the knowledge of the Grand Duchess. He [Giese] however had learned of it at the time, in order to use that knowledge for the Sponheim inheritance, as I'm sure I said to Giese...'[177] In other words the King admits to have known 'at the time' where Kaspar Hauser's birthplace was, as well as—and this is especially important—wanting *to use* this knowledge for the Sponheim inheritance, which was only possible with Kaspar Hauser *alive*. It follows from this that these ideas come from a time when Ludwig was still brazenly wanting to get his hands on Baden, in other words, before 1830! But what does this 'wanting to use' actually mean if one were to bring the imagined possibilities of using Kaspar Hauser—from the viewpoint of the desired successful outcome—into relation with the facts of the situation?

The secret strategic link between Hauser and the Palatinate question is further revealed in a remark of Giese's, which the King noted on the 5th May 1836:

> To bring in the same idea through a revelation....with regard to the so-called Kaspar Hauser; that one would not dare to declare oneself for Baden against Bavaria: if it were to go that far that it could happen

95. Karl von Griesenbeck (1787–1863)

96. Schloss Pilsach near Neumarkt in the Upper Palatinate. Historical photo.

> without a dispute in the [German] confederation,....then it wouldn't be questioned by the other Powers—the cause would be lost—, unless [we] move into the Palatinate and then negotiate...[178]

Such was the Bavarians' risky military strategy, accompanied by a no less peculiar political strategy. A year before the death of the 'last' Zähringer in 1829 the King dwelt on the long-term consequences which would result for the Palatinate from the accession to the throne of the second line of the House of Baden. In order to regain the Palatinate, he was even seriously prepared—this was the peak of his irrational inspirations—to sacrifice his beloved kingdom of the Hellenes, '...if the whole House of Hochberg were to be moved to Greece'.[179] [Ludwig I of Bavaria was a passionate Hellenophile; his second son Otto was elected king of Greece in 1832—*transl.*]

To those, therefore, who knew how difficult, impossible even, a retrocession of the Palatinate on the basis of existing treaties was, the use of an entitled pretender to the throne of Baden may well have seemed the most suitable means of applying pressure. With this as security, Grand Duke Ludwig of Baden could perhaps be forced to give way if he wanted to avoid a scandal. King Ludwig himself would hardly have been cognisant of all the details of Kaspar Hauser's imprisonment. But Wrede, who was born in the Palatinate, might certainly have been involved, together with other fellow officers, in putting the plan into operation while the King half-knowingly looked on.

> Furthermore, the King later let no opportunity go by of recalling the Palatinate negotiations of 1826: in view of the unrest and growing resistance to authority in the Palatinate in 1832, Prince Wrede wrote to the Russian Chancellor Count Nesselrode and used the opportunity to emphasise to him that the lack of a territorial connection made it very difficult for Bavaria to uphold peace and order : because Russia also regarded this as so important, the Field Marshal (16th Nov. 1832) declared himself for the idea of raising once again the issue of Bavaria's claims to the Palatinate, for which he was 'embraced' in a letter from his King.[180]

Since 1808 a member of the Bavarian officer corps, Baron Karl von Griesenbeck (1787–1863) (Fig.95), had been the owner of Pilsach Castle (Fig. 96) where Kaspar Hauser's cell was later discovered. As an officer with various commands, Griesenbeck was as a rule at Pilsach only two or three times a year in order to see to his legal and administrative duties as owner of the property. Otherwise, the small moat-ringed castle was uninhabited. At first appointed to ceremonial duties in Munich, Griesenbeck became a lieutenant at seventeen (1804) and a major in 1810. After a short break, this knight of the Max-Joseph Order became squadron chief in Passau. Until then there is nothing unusual about Griesenbeck's career. Things took on a miraculous turn, however, in the period when Kaspar Hauser must have been brought to Pilsach. On the 31st May 1817 already Griesenbeck was appointed a royal Bavarian chamberlain and his second son Max Joseph was given the honour of having the King himself as his godfather. Called to Munich in 1821 as a member of the King's Life Guards, Karl von Griesenbeck was appointed Commander of the Officer Cadet Corps and finally promoted to major general. The gentleman's shirt which Kaspar Hauser wore on his arrival in Nuremberg was embroidered with the giveaway initial 'G'.

*

Now there is no lack of ideas and comments which pour scorn on suspicion of the King for conspiracy and the choice of just this method on political and logical grounds, since a recognition of Kaspar Hauser as heir to the throne of Baden must necessarily have ruined any hopes of regaining the Palatinate, thus paradoxically making Bavaria the cause of this nonsensical result. Such a view was expressed most strongly by the Baden parliamentarian and publicist Georg Friedrich Kolb (1808–1884), who was otherwise an intelligent and tireless champion of the cause of Kaspar Hauser and who not least because of his advocacy, finally had to leave his homeland. He emigrated to Bavaria and settled in Munich. 'What role,' writes Kolb,

> is King Ludwig I seen to play here in order to achieve his goals? He actually believes to have a claim to possess the Baden Palatinate (Mannheim, Heidelberg etc.) and seeks to justify this claim by arguing that the main branch of the old Zähringer line has died out and that the children from the morganatic marriage with the Countess Hochberg have no rights of succession. To support this argument, he King Ludwig himself, is supposed to have 'spread it about' that the legitimate son of Grand Duke Karl is still alive in Kaspar Hauser. To King Ludwig I therefore is ascribed the nonsense that, in trying to make good his claim, he has himself 'peddled' the evidence which, at least at the time, he could not possibly possess; for if a legitimate son of the Grand Duke Karl were alive, King Ludwig could make no claim to the throne! This is what people are trying to ascribe to this monarch. This is how stupid the readers are considered to be![181]

Kolb's question only needs to be put once more in a new and more precise fashion and not under the assumption that Ludwig was stupid, but rather that he was intelligent, for in any case, a conclusion has to be based on what the King actually thought, said and did and what he did not.

Here it first needs to be noted that Kolb had no knowledge of any of Ludwig's diary entries already cited or of the memoirs of those who had conversations with the King in this context, to which we have access today, and which, taken together, tell another story. Here also belong the words of the Justice Minister Baron von Zentner who already on the 30th June 1827 regretted that 'His Royal Majesty, in the lively feeling of the righteousness of Your claims...should have given a gracious hearing to various insinuations about the way in which means of persuasion can be used in Karlsruhe and the secretive methods to be employed in connection with them.'[182] What were these insinuations and secretive methods to which the King had lent a gracious ear? Obviously, they were such as could not be openly discussed. When his close friend Baron Heinrich von der Tann told Ludwig about the rumours in Baden, the King was on his guard, and added 'that he too believed in Kaspar Hauser's origins in Baden'. Later, Ludwig was to insist 'that he had said nothing about his opinion that Grand Duke Karl was Kaspar Hauser's father to anyone except his wife Therese',[183] What facts was the King silent about? To whom was he silent? What sense did his silence make and why?

But it was noticeable already at that time that Ludwig was careful to show a marked reservation as soon as it was clear that Kaspar Hauser was *officially* known to the authorities. That much is obvious from the very reserved tone of the exchange of letters with Stanhope, in which it is clear that long before the appearance of Feuerbach's writings, Ludwig knew that Hauser was no mere newly-arrived hobo. He wrote to Stanhope on the 8th December 1831 that Kaspar Hauser 'was certainly not born in that darkness in which he was held by his enemies'.[184] One might almost think that Ludwig made a tactical calculation deliberately to avoid a confrontation with Hauser. Prince Adalbert of Bavaria (1886–1970) was right when he stated that the King would certainly have had the possibility of having the foundling presented to him—for example on the 20th August 1828 in Nuremberg, and also later. The prince merely concludes from this that Ludwig did not wish to know about Hauser. 'Official reports, however, add something to his [Adalbert's] picture and compelled the view that the King knew more than is revealed in his private writings.'[185]

Between Ludwig's secret diplomacy and his official stance there was therefore in fact a contradiction. The key to his behaviour is not to be found in the realm of conventional logic but solely in the categories of thought which Machiavelli ascribed to those in positions of power. 'Soon after Ludwig's accession to the throne,' wrote Friedrich Walter, the biographer of Stéphanie of Baden, 'the Baden envoy in Munich warned of the tireless scheming and the unpredictable nature of the King of Bavaria, who would make use of every favourable opportunity to achieve his goals.' Grand Duke Karl too, as mentioned earlier, had believed Ludwig capable of every wickedness. Full of zealous spite, he had disputed Karl's rights to the Palatinate and in that struggle 'any method [seemed] justified' to Ludwig. One of these methods was to take no official cognisance of Hauser whilst at the same time allowing the question of his origins to be discussed ever more openly. Naturally, Karlsruhe was aware of how the game was being played. And was it only in Munich that one was supposed to be so naive as to believe, after Hauser's death, in his Hungarian or other origins? King Ludwig did not once take up an *official* position with regard to the Kaspar Hauser issue with the exception of the statements necessitated by the law which had to be made on account of the murder attempts. The King made a clear distinction between on the one hand, the Palatinate question and state affairs, and on the other hand, political calculation and private opinion. If Ludwig had ever conceived of pursuing his territorial claims *legally* with Kaspar Hauser's help, Kolb would have been right in his assertions, but such was not the case. The only imaginable effect would come from the conscious revelation of Hauser's identity, and pressure could only be put on Baden by holding out the possibility of an official recognition of his claim to the throne. Grand Duke Ludwig could certainly conclude that Bavaria would in fact lose its as yet unstated claim to the Palatinate—and not for all time—if Munich were seriously to present the legitimate heir to the throne of Baden. But he must have realised just as keenly that in that same moment his own rule could come to an end in humiliating circumstances. So in the context of the conflict, there could only be a worse outcome for Baden, however the issue was tackled, than for Bavaria. What struck Kolb about the affair was also obvious to Ludwig : namely, why the lever had been applied not to the territorial issue but crucially, to the question of legitimacy, in consequence of which the matter of the old ancestral lands would come into the discussion. That was the intended means of persuasion to which the King had extended his gracious ear.

The calculation went like this: if the ever-increasing talk of a 'prince of Baden' were to lead to an 'offer' [from Karlsruhe] in the Palatinate question, it would be met with the understanding that from then on, the Nuremberg foundling and Bavarian subject would no longer be supported in any legal claim, which would be held possible by the people and not a few European ruling houses. For '...experience teaches,' wrote Count Colloredo to Metternich on the 1st March 1838, 'that the character of His Majesty [Ludwig I] reveals itself in sharp polarities and his imagination allows him to be guided into the most divergent channels.'[186]

Grand Duke Ludwig, who could feel himself secure in the territorial question through first class guarantees from the Great Powers, was actually vulnerable only in the matter of legitimacy and put to the question of a choice between losing power or renouncing the Palatinate, he would in any case have to decide in favour of remaining in power. The Wittelsbachs' strategy was thus a decisive one, which Karlsruhe recognised only too well.

But Grand Duke Ludwig (Fig.98) also had his advisor in the affair. His aide-de-camp Johann Heinrich David von Hennenhofer (1793–1850) (Fig.97) was a reliable man who had been in on the very beginnings of the Kaspar Hauser drama when the infant prince had been

97. Heinrich David von Hennenhofer (1793–1850)

98. Ludwig, Grand Duke of Baden (1763–1830)

abducted and set aside. From that time on, his advice and actions had always been at Ludwig's disposal, and he was recognised in Nuremberg and Ansbach as present prior to both murder attempts on Kaspar Hauser's life. Later, he was to declare to posterity only too clearly what he had done 'for the blessed Grand Duke' as he had been forced by 'his conscience to reveal dreadful things'. His blackmail letters to the Grand Duke's lover, Countess Katharina von Langenstein in Dresden contain the illuminating passages which relate to participation in the substitution of the babies, and the later abduction and murder of Kaspar Hauser. On the 26th June 1837 he wrote to Dresden: 'In full consciousness of what I did for the blessed lord and what I have suffered because of him, I feel myself able to turn to his descendants without embarrassment. And yet I am embarrassed. I have two manuscripts prepared, the sale of which would bring me more than that sum, but I cannot now decide on a price for them. Now is not the time.'[187]

There was a real background to the threats with the 'manuscripts', as is shown by Fritz Klee, who quotes a remark of Napoleon III: 'Hauser's princely status was spoken of and Napoleon, who was well-informed about it, explained: "Major Ennendorf (Hennenhofer) sold me the most important documents (about Kaspar Hauser). I have read them, sealed them and preserved them. They are not to be used against Baden."'[188] From which it follows that they could indeed have been used against Baden, and with what devastating success or with what evidence that would have been possible is revealed to us by Louise Baroness Belli di Pino, a social companion of the Dowager Grand Duchess Stéphanie in October 1853 on the trip to Compiègne and Paris which followed their invitation to the wedding of Emperor Napoleon III and Countess Teba: 'Louise, can you imagine, that one had the cruelty to tell me that C.H. [Caspar Hauser] was my son! Now, that he is dead, that he has been assassinated!'[189]

Hennenhofer had therefore provided Napoleon III with such convincing evidence that the Emperor considered it proven that Kaspar Hauser was Stéphanie's son. Given this situation, is it then a mere coincidence that Major Hennenhofer, Grand Duke Ludwig's trusted aide, 'the man who was in on all the horrible secrets' was appointed Director of the diplomatic section of the Ministry of Foreign Affairs precisely in 1828, the year of Kaspar Hauser's appearance—a position which would enable him to carry out all the operations which were now lined up and waiting?

His first was the murder attempt of the 17th October 1829. This was the only move that promised success in answer to the almost casual introduction of this Bavarian 'possibility' which could cost Grand Duke Ludwig the throne. The fact that, due to Hauser's survival, the calculation did not succeed, is another question.

Grand Duke Ludwig, however, was just as seriously threatened by the keeping open of the 'possibility' as his successor Leopold without the Palatinate ever having been the main issue for them. If Ludwig's legitimacy was put in doubt by Hauser, it was no less the case for Leopold who also sat on a shaky throne as a result of the one-sided disposition of Grand Duke Karl Friedrich. Without the agreement of his nobles, the old prince had promulgated the House Law which recognised as eligible to the succession the children of his morganatic marriage to his second wife, who did not belong to the imperial nobility. Ludwig I of Bavaria was within his rights as a German monarch to challenge that ruling.[190]

The price of the renunciation of such easily realisable possibilities would have brought the political point envisaged by Bavaria to the fore; for Baden, unlike Bavaria, had a fundamental dynastic problem, from which Grand Duke Ludwig and later Leopold could have bought their way out through coming to an agreement on a secondary issue. This made sense in terms of realpolitik and for just this reason, it would have been a mistake for Bavaria to support the Kaspar Hauser prince theory *officially*. But Karlsruhe had to be kept thinking that Munich held Hauser's noble origins to be a possibility. That alone rendered the threat effective, which was why its subject, Kaspar Hauser, had to be put *visibly* into play. Before the eyes of Baden, he made clear that *if* a claim were to be made openly on his behalf, then even a throne—namely that of Baden—might begin to topple. Only twenty years later did the Palatinate question lose its significance for Ludwig. 'Since this method of regaining the right bank Palatinate had also proved to be unfruitful and the King had abdicated,' wrote Prince Adalbert of Bavaria in the work already mentioned (see n.128), 'he lost interest in the Hauser case.'

In the long unpublished second volume of his memoirs, Margrave Wilhelm concludes that the whole Kaspar Hauser episode was a conscious Bavarian plot against Baden. 'The Bavarians had discovered him in order to damage us in the eyes of the public....'[191]

From the Hochberg viewpoint this was an understandable argument, but a weak one. Against it, in a letter to King Ludwig eight days after Grand Duke Leopold's accession to the throne (8.4.1830) Anselm von Feuerbach shared his view, which corresponded fairly well with the facts, namely that 'our mysterious foundling [is] a son of Karl and

Stéphanie's side [of the family] who has been exchanged and abducted and consequently, is no less a person than the present *real* Grand Duke of Baden'.[192] Given that this early piece of information contradicted all the later tactical professions of uncertainty by Ludwig I, he could have recognised, if the situation required it, that there was no difference between the old and the new constellation.

King Ludwig would therefore have been rather cleverer than Kolb and others credited, and so indeed he was right to the end! For who could have provided the 10,000 guilders that were made available for information in the Kaspar Hauser case? A subject of the Grand Duchy of Baden?

The tragedy of this excellent plan lay in the end result. That Hauser would succumb to a second murder attempt had essentially been assumed by this indirect approach. Ever stronger grew the assertions that he was the rightful heir. More and more crowned heads were prepared to agree with this view—whether for good or ill—and ever more helpless and dangerous did the position of Baden become. Since there must be a certain degree of probability in every threat, in whatever form, the question arose as what the power of the 'Bavarian discovery'—if it was such—could be based on. For how was it possible to put Baden in a state of anxiety and fear if there was no real basis to the affair? Is it conceivable that all Baden's defensiveness was based on pure fiction? It is understandable that the Hochbergs, and especially again Leopold's brother Margrave Wilhelm found it *incomprehensible* that 'various Bavarian writers'—by which is meant amongst others Feuerbach, Daumer, and Tucher—took the matter so seriously. It is also very understandable why the Margrave could only consign the Kaspar Hauser affair to the realm of fantasy:

> That such a fable should be taken up with satisfaction by various Bavarian writers in order to be used against us in the dispute then obtaining between Baden and Bavaria over the surrogacy of the county of Sponheim is in itself easy to grasp; even the King of Bavaria had not been shy of employing even more reprehensible methods against us. But how this shameful calumny could have put down such roots to the point where so-called German scholars posited it as historical fact and could write such nonsense is beyond all reason.[193]

But that is and has until today remained the question: how was the case of Kaspar Hauser able to put down such 'roots'?

9. The First Murder Attempt

Stanhope in Nuremberg, 1829

Three months after the death of George Stanhope, Philip Henry's mother also died, aged 70, in Charles Street, Piccadilly. Under these circumstances, it would have been understandable for his eleventh trip to Germany—as in the previous year—at least to have been put back. But despite all considerations in view of these two fateful blows, his departure this time was even characterised by a perceptible sense of urgency. From Baden the rumour had first gone out that the Nuremberg foundling might possibly be the son of Karl and Stéphanie and such news could not be kept from Philip Henry. This would explain the noticeable pressure to test the viability of such suspicions.

Already on Monday, the 8th June Philip Henry and Anton Heinrich had boarded ship at Dover and, despite a stormy sea, attempted to cross the Channel the same day. But the predictable happened: all day long the ship was tossed up and down in the roadsteads off Calais and could not make port. As Calais at that time still had no quay, passengers had to be put ashore in small rowing boats, which was only possible with a fairly calm sea. They were not able to land until the 12th June.

In daily stages of unusual length—travelling the whole weekend with no stop in Brussels this time—their journey went directly to Mannheim. News of mayor Binder's announcement of Kaspar Hauser had meanwhile spread far beyond southern Germany and had found a resonance. Throughout Europe and even in New York, Boston and Philadelphia the newspapers were reporting on the events in Nuremberg. The *General Theatre Newspaper for Art, Literature and Society* [*Allgemeine Theaterzeitung für Kunst, Literatur und gesellschaftliches Leben*] in Vienna, then in its 23rd year, and a widely known paper in the German-speaking world, reported on Kaspar Hauser more than 25 times in 1829.

The first rumours, which had already become quite loud, were that Kaspar Hauser was Stéphanie's son. Graffiti to this effect is supposed to have been found on the castle walls in Karlsruhe. Binder (Fig.113) had already in July 1828 received an anonymous letter from Baden which wanted to know: 'Isn't Kaspar Hauser a son of Grand Duchess Stéphanie?' Feuerbach knew of a similar letter of the 13th December 1829. So the assertion had been on the record since 1828. Stanhope's stay at Stéphanie's residence was short. On the 19th June they were again on their way—to Vienna. Stanhope apparently only wanted to know how the matter was regarded in Mannheim and how much credence was given to the rumours.

On the 3rd July the coach arrived at 73 Teinfaltstrasse, Gentz's address in Vienna. Now the object of their long search was suddenly within grasp, and the situation was completely different from on previous occasions. Gentz and Stanhope had to confer immediately and extensively about the new situation: already the next day, the 4th July, and again twice after that; on the 5th July the Baden chargé d'affaires General Friedrich Karl Baron von Tettenborn (1778–1845) (Fig. 99) was also present. After a brilliant career, Tettenborn had been appointed Russian envoy to the Congress of Vienna, where he had got to know the Grand Duke Karl, who was then already very shy of company. What moved the general to leave the prestigious service of Russia for that of the tiny Grand Duchy of Baden is not clear, but from then on, he fought decisively for Baden's interests, and his greatest success was at the Congress of Aachen in 1818. He was born in the County of Sponheim, which was at the centre of the dispute with Bavaria, and the fact of his birthplace may have played a role in the struggle. After the death of Grand Duke Karl in 1818, he became Baden's envoy in Vienna for Grand Duke Ludwig, and one who could possibly pose a danger to his present sovereign was that foundling in Nuremberg, Kaspar Hauser.

It is noteworthy that later, after Tettenborn's death, the Grand Duchy of Baden was prepared to settle his debts of 1.5 million guilders. The Grand Duke was certainly not able to do so much for all his State servants, which only leads one to conclude that extraordinary services must have been rendered. In his view of the power struggles and territorial claims, Tettenborn could not have been indifferent to the possibility of a deliberately prepared pretender to the throne as a possible lever of Bavarian politics, so it is understandable that he should have been present at the meetings planned in Vienna: two on the 6th July and more on the 7th, 8th, 9th, 10th and 11th of the month. On this last day of his conversations with Gentz and Tettenborn, Stanhope wrote an interesting letter to the 'honourable Charles Arbuthnot' in London:

> Dear Sir,
> I avail myself of the opportunity which is offered by a Courier being sent to England to renew and earnest request that you would have the goodness to recommend to the favourable consideration of Lord Aberdeen

99. Friedrich, Baron von Tettenborn (1778–1845)

the case of our Friend [the name 'Gentz' is crossed out here in Stanhope's own copy of the letter—*Ed.*] & I ardently hope that the result may realize our wishes. The kind interest which you manifested in this business & the zeal with which you endeavoured to forward his application convince me that the delay which has taken place has not originated with yourself, & I flatter myself that Lord Aberdeen did not feel any objections to a measure in which, as I understood, the Duke [of Wellington, the Prime Minister at the time—*Ed.*] had expressed his acquiescence. I know not however what view the former may have taken of the subject nor whether the sum of Secret Service Money which may have been voted by Parliament was fixed with reference to this object, but in case that any difficulties should have arisen with respect to the amount of that Fund I would suggest that a portion of the Sum required, such for instance as £1,000 should be paid for immediate relief till the remainder can be supplied. As soon as Lord Aberdeen notifies his approbation, for which I have waited with the utmost anxiety, an application may forthwith be made through Lord Cowley whose recommendation will no doubt have the weight to which it is justly entitled from his public & private character & from his official situation. I need not on this occasion repeat the various grounds upon which, when I had the pleasure of seeing you, I pressed this application in behalf of a Friend to whom I am most warmly

attached and to whom both England and Europe owe obligations which it would be difficult to requite. His long and eminent services, the intrepidity, energy, and talent with which he defended the good cause & the interests of England under circumstances of great danger & alarm are indeed superior to all praise, & the situation in which he is now placed gives him the means and opportunity which he is always willing to employ of rendering invaluable assistance. Those services have been well-known & acknowledged by the Duke, & I fervently trust that they will now receive the consideration which is due to them. Allow me again to assure you that a compliance with this request will contribute as much to my satisfaction as it can to his own, & will confer the greatest obligation on one who is with great regard and esteem,
most faithfully yours,
Stanhope

P.S. Since I wrote the above, I have conversed upon the subject with our Friend, who feels very strongly the extreme importance, of which you will, I am persuaded, be fully aware, that the business should be conducted in such a manner as would not commit him, but would be strictly private and confidential, & might not require the intervention of Lord Cowley which for several reasons he is very anxious to avoid & which appears superfluous if the Duke [crossed out—*Ed.*] Lord Aberdeen approves of the proposition. If I can be of any service in this business during my residence here which will, I expect, extend to the middle of September I shall be happy to render myself useful. Our Friend is so much impressed with the necessity of secrecy in a case of this nature that rather than adopt any course of a different nature he would relinquish altogether the hope and expectations which he has formed. I entreat you to send to me as soon as possible an answer upon the subject.[194]

It must remain an open question as to whether this letter relates to the Kaspar Hauser question, but it is quite clear that Stanhope and Gentz were dealing with issues which required handling in secrecy. However this document may be evaluated, its timing is noteworthy.

On the 12th, another meeting took place. Gentz informed Stanhope by letter:

I have every reason to believe that the English courier will leave *this evening*. I will write my letter now and take it with me into town, where I am to be at 12 o'clock. My lord, would you do me the favour of coming to me between two and three o'clock so that we could discuss matters further? This is all the more necessary because I fear that I shall not be at the

> *Weinhaus* this afternoon as I am dining with Prince Metternich—I shall certainly be here again this evening between seven and eight o'clock.[195]

On the 13th there were two more meetings, which were continued on the 14th and 16th. 'Prince Metternich told me today that it would be *most pleasant* to see you in Königswart, and that with the greatest satisfaction he will provide you with accommodation at his castle for however long you would like. He will confirm this to you himself when next you meet.'

Gentz, Metternich and Stanhope had thirty meetings during this period. Tetterborn, the Baden chargé d'affaires, was present at nine of them. During this timeframe there was a noticeable need to send and receive news. The courier post to England, which was to remain hidden from the curious gaze of unauthorised persons, had to be secure, and 'official assistance' was part of the process. 'Would you be so good My Lord as to take the letter in question to London to Lord Crowley for me. I have a *more secure* means of getting it through.' Similar things were contained in many of the notes received.

Alongside the political business were the social engagements. Soirées in the *Alpengasse* at the home of the lovely Flora Countess Wrbna who

100. Entrance to the villa of Friedrich von Gentz in Weinhaus near Vienna.

since the days of the Congress of Vienna had been the undisputed mistress of the arrangement of 'living tableaux'; Metternich also attended. Then a dinner with Prince Dietrichstein, 'about whose name one may not speak', which most likely had to do with the fact that the Prince did not wish to give up the Freemasonry that under Emperor Francis II, was still prohibited in Austria. That would have led to social disgrace in the prevailing circumstances at Court. It had not been so long since the Grand Master of the Grand Lodge of Austria had been arrested when one of the secret lodges under his leadership in the City Hall area had been closed by the police. Dietrichstein was also one of the unloved teachers of the Duke of Reichstadt [Napoleon's son, who had been effectively held a prisoner in Vienna]. Dietrichstein wrote letters to the duke's mother, Marie Louise, in which he wrote things which would also be written later of Kaspar Hauser: 'I was surprised at the beginning [about]...the inclination to wickedness, the desire to tell lies...' The two destinies resembled each other even in the manner in which they were slandered.

Joseph A. Edler von Pilat, Gentz's friend and secretary and publisher of the *Österreichischer Beobachter* [Austrian Observer] took part 'in the frugal lunches' at Gentz's idyllic property. This villa in the Viennese suburb of Weinhaus at 169 and 171 Währingerstrasse (Fig.100) surrounded by a large garden was a well-known and already very fashionable meeting place for Viennese high society—a place that excited passions. The grimly sarcastic memoirs of Gentz's political opponent, the liberal Franz Grillparzer have left us a picture of the place that half resembles the 1001 Nights.

> I still recall the contradictory impression which the man's residence made on me. The floor of the antechamber was covered with carpets so thick that every step was like sinking into a swamp and gave one a kind of seasickness. On all the tables and chests of drawers there were glass balls full of fruit preserves for the sybaritic master of the house to nibble on whenever he took a fancy; finally, he would lie down in the bedroom on a snow-white bed in a grey silk dressing gown. All around him inventions and conveniences. There were moving arms which brought ink and pen at request, a writing desk that moved itself here and there; I believe that even the chamber pot, when a spring was pressed, presented itself for use.

But even more well-meaning observers gave effusive descriptions of Gentz's lifestyle. 'Invitations to his dinners', writes Victor von Fritsche in his miniatures,

> which he put on at his villa in Weinhaus and his apartment on the Kornmarkt, both decorated with great elegance and refined luxury, were the most sought after, where beautiful cultured ladies in the days of the Congress would gather and numbered among his friends. In his country villa in Weinhaus Gentz had combined the most expensive furniture, pictures, souvenirs and knick-knacks with great taste in an elegant, visually appealing interior. In the garden there was a temple-like pavilion and in the glasshouses in summer there bloomed the loveliest and rarest flowers with which he would delight his female friends.

To Philip Henry, who had been subjected to a spartan education and whose father had banned all luxury from Chevening, the pompous ambience of Gentz's lifestyle was a compensation for the dreary years of his youth. In his eyes, Gentz was a *bon vivant* of the kind he himself would like to be, and so it was with a great relish that he spent time as the guest of the great man.

They would send each other brief notes on their movements: 'I have the honour to notify you that I shall be eating at four o'clock in town, from two till four o'clock at home and returning home again to Weinhaus towards evening.'—'I shall await you My Lord at half past one. I cannot come home earlier, as I am here *stuck* here in the Prince's Cabinet.'—'Unfortunately, I am engaged with the Russian ambassador in Grünberg today; but tomorrow I shall have the whole afternoon and evening *for you* at home.'—'Yesterday I had to lunch with the Duc de Laval at Grünberg, returned to town in the evening, and had a distant hope of seeing you. But this could not be; yet I had no cause to be dissatisfied with the evening, because I spent it in an important conversation with General Nugent, who is travelling to London today.'—'Today offers a favourable prospect: I am invited to dine with Tatischeff and shall return to town from there with Prince Metternich. The morning is as good as exhausted.' A dozen such notes have survived.

According to a contemporary,

> Viennese society is quite particular; houses of the first rank (Schwarzenberg, Auersperg, Liechtenstein, Saxe-Coburg etc) entertain very often, but have formed a coterie of about 300 persons who have lived together for centuries and no-one who is not born among them can gain entry. If someone succeeds in doing so, he is treated just like the others but under the condition that from thenceforward he will live with no-one but among this coterie. It is a kind of freemasonry that begins at high school and continues at university and throughout life.

It appears that for the first time Stanhope too succeeded in this year through the protection of his influential friend Gentz in gaining the coveted access to 'the families'.

As befitted his rank, Stanhope was always accompanied by his servant, which was unavoidable under the circumstances. Anton Heinrich was newly fitted out. On the 11th September he received a splendid cloak and on the 4th October two new liveries, the decoration of which Philip Henry had determined on precisely: lapis lazuli blue 'which looked very pleasant', with gold braid tresses, both matching the peer's coat of arms on the carriage doors and the gilded harness.

In those days Ferdinand Raimund, the sometime rival of Nestroy, was all the rage. After he had become the director of the Leopoldstädter theatre the year before—1828—his own plays were also featured on the programme. On the 6th September, Stanhope saw and experienced with Gentz the 66th performance of *'Der Alpenkönig und der Menschenfeind'* ['The King of the Alps and the Enemy of Humanity']. On the 30th September they saw *'Der Bauer als Millionär'* ['The Farmer as Millionaire'], on the 11th October once again the *Alpenkönig* with Raimund himself in the lead role as Master von Rappelkopf. Stanhope was much impressed by both plays. Gentz, by contrast, who was quite the aesthete and man of the world, found the elements of magic and local farce quite impossible in parts, but tended to express this contrary opinion politely to Stanhope: 'Although I found much that was offensive in yesterday's play,' he wrote to Philip Henry, 'I can now imagine much better than before how and why you found the play at the Leopold Theatre so satisfying.' Perhaps it was the melancholy undertones of Raimund's magical fairy tale, which found a response in Stanhope's soul, so much so that he later even translated parts of it into English. Stanhope's translation of *'Der Alpenkönig und der Menschenfeind'* was put on at London's Adelphi Theatre as an original production.[196] It filled both 'the house and the cashier's box' for many months.

Another cultural interest the two men shared shows up only very modestly on the margins of their activities in one sentence but throws an illuminating light on the situation, as it makes visible for a moment at least a part of the content of the discussions of those thirty meetings and conferences during Stanhope's days in Vienna. Before the Earl left the city on the 16th October to travel via Pressburg straight to Nuremberg where the first attempt on Kaspar Hauser's life was made on the 17th, Gentz wrote the following note to him on the 10th: 'I have the honour of reporting to you, my dear Count, that today I shall be lunching with General Tettenborn in Hütteldorf, but this evening I shall go to Weinhaus and spend the following day there....I am sending to you with this the pages of *Hesperus,* of which we spoke yesterday and before you leave Vienna, I shall go with you again to the *Kasperl*.'[197] Gentz underlined the words *Hesperus* and *Kasperl*.

Not only are the further meeting with the Baden envoy and the reference to '*Kasperl*' of note, but also the reference to the meeting of the day before. Significant here is the context of the imminent trip to Nuremberg for which the 'pages from *Hesperus*',[198] an encyclopaedic magazine for cultured readers, had provided the backdrop. The sophisticated weekly, published by Christian Carl André at Haus Cotta, reported mainly on European events and for German affairs had the column 'Bavaria' in which again Nuremberg correspondents provided running commentary on all kinds of events. Numbers 16,17, and 19 with which Gentz, Tettenborn and Stanhope concerned themselves, carried the latest reports about Kaspar Hauser on everything Daumer had discovered about the foundling's progress in his mental development and naturally, the question of all questions: where did this most unusual human being come from?

These new reports were of the greatest interest, so it was hardly surprising that it was this magazine, which gave a general impression of Kaspar Hauser, that was the subject of the Vienna group's discussions. The information explains the course of action and the resolution which determined events from this time on.

On the 19th September Stanhope had left Vienna and travelled first to Pressburg with Anton Heinrich. The Cathedral preacher Müller (see p. 204) had been at his post for the last two years. He had in his time received an unmistakable warning from Pastor Wirth from Bavaria. Müller had of course long been aware of the Nuremberg sensation and had soon drawn the obvious conclusions from it, for it was precisely the case to which his knowledge related. Stanhope's stay in Pressburg this time lasted for three weeks, for which he must have had his reasons besides the attractions of the town that was not far distant from Vienna. In the Kaspar Hauser affair Müller was a figure who would soon set ministers of two governments in motion and as Stanhope spent so long in Pressburg before travelling on to Nuremberg, the suspicion of a connection can hardly be avoided. On the 16th October his journey continued into southern Germany in daily stages at a far from leisurely pace. On the 21st he had arrived already in Nuremberg where he checked in at the *Wilden Mann* hotel [Wild Man]. The previous suspicion that Stanhope was in the city on the day of the attempted murder, 17th October, is therefore not borne out; this is not to exonerate him, since the deed was never seriously attributed to the Englishman. It is also true that, as he often later professed, he had to have repairs done to his carriage, which supported the assertion that his presence in Nuremberg was only accidental. For the 22nd October, one finds the note: 'Repairs to the carriage'. But since the same entry had been made for the 20th, and then the 26th and the 30th without any indication that the journey had been interrupted, it was a case, as in Nuremberg, not so much of a broken axle, broken shaft or some similar major problem but rather of a small detail. A wheel had been damaged at Burgfarrenbach; but one could always have gone on. The cost of the repairs in Nuremberg was three Bavarian guilders [*gulden*] and 26 *Kreuzer.* That this should have required a day's stay in Nuremberg does not convince. The visit seems much more to have been in order to conduct an on-the-spot inspection of the situation as it had developed after the attack had been carried out. Most likely, the later foster father travelled on from Nuremberg in the knowledge that an attack was to have been made on Hauser sometime between the 10th and the 20th and indeed from Baden. As opportunities for the attack had first had to be reconnoitred, the exact day could not be fixed.

It can be surmised from the good relations they had with Tettenborn that Gentz and Stanhope had been informed that Baden would no longer stand for a 'son of Stéphanie' walking around openly and the danger that inevitably represented. Hennenhofer, as we know, had made some suggestions as to how to deal with the situation. But the circle of those behind the curtain is not yet complete. Wessenberg and Hennenhofer were also acquainted with each other. We know this from an undated letter of Hennenhofer's to an unknown addressee, which strangely found its way into Stanhope's possession but which certainly was not meant for him.[199] Gentz, Tettenborn, Hennenhofer, Wessenberg and Stanhope had so much mutual information and experience at their disposal that a plan of this significance could certainly succeed.

The most important element was evidently Hennenhofer himself. The enterprise stood and fell with him; they all knew that. Cold-blooded, sly, tenacious, bold—he had already given plenty of evidence of his skills. Documentary evidence exists for the fact that this most disreputable man was made use of several times in this affair. An otherwise trivial criminal case in Zurich later unearthed incidental evidence of this. A few days before Stanhope's arrival in Nuremberg, a stranger answering to Hennenhofer's description was seen by a number of eyewitnesses and was also described well by Kaspar Hauser himself. His indications of the criminal point clearly in Hennenhofer's direction. A similar exact description of the attack in 1833 points unmistakeably in Hennenhofer's direction.[200]

Those in the background also included the Baden Minister Karl Theodor Baron von Hacke (1755–1834) who was also connected to Tettenborn. As can be read in Varnhagen, Hacke had played an unhealthy role at Court around Grand Duke Karl and had a number of wicked intrigues on his conscience. In later reports from the year 1834 Tettenborn and Hacke were identified as accessories 'who could give information about Kaspar Hauser as the son of the Prince of Baden'. In his envoy's report from Hanover on the 10th November 1834, Baron von Hormayr stated that

> The Hanoverian nobility has many connections with circles north and south of the [River] Main through the Wallmoden, Rottenhan, Münster, Wangenheim, Giech, and Kielmansegg families. Through such connections came the firm conviction that no-one had had a livelier and visibly more anxious interest in everything to do with Kaspar Hauser than the Baden Minister von Hacke. Among the first in Nuremberg after the attempt on Kaspar Hauser's life, he spent many days in a most noticeable state of excitement. The news that the attack had only half-succeeded affected him so powerfully that one did not know whether it was out of joy or horror. I have heard this by chance countless times as something that in Hanover no-one any longer doubts.[201]

Now Stanhope was in Nuremberg and sounding out the situation with the greatest alertness. This is not without significance in that according to his own assurances Kaspar Hauser had been of no special interest for him on the 22nd October. In fact, after taking note of the failure of the assassination, Stanhope travelled back to England with a burning interest and, according to the account of his daughter, the Duchess of Cleveland (in her book *The True Story about Caspar Hauser*) already in 1829 developed a plan for his further activities. Who would have thought that on the same day—the 22nd October 1829—Stanhope would have requested the Nuremberg banker Merkel in writing to send on to him in England the most accurate news about the attack including a picture of Kaspar Hauser as well as information about what the police and the authorities had found out up to that point! This fact deserves attention because it throws light on what would happen in 1831. Stanhope was only able to gain access to inquiry documents relating to the incident when he succeeded in establishing an officially sanctioned relationship to Hauser. Once he had done that, within a few weeks he had achieved his goal. Why did Stanhope not concern himself with the documents in 1829? Was it to be known that an English lord had demanded a picture of Kaspar Hauser or wanted information about the victim of the attack? Was he perhaps the only Englishman in the city during those days, and his name would therefore too easily have been noted? Why was a connection between him and this news to be avoided? At any rate, Stanhope had a reason to avail himself of the silence of his banker—the son of the founding member of the *Zu den drei Pfeilen* ['Three Columns'] masonic lodge and himself a Freemason—in order to avoid any recognition. A clerk at the bank made a handwritten copy of the letter of 18th January to Stanhope.

> Sir, we were honoured by your letter of the 22nd October. We enclose herewith copies of the reports which were published on the 7th July 1828 in relation to our foundling Kaspar Hauser. The printed version is difficult to obtain. We have also provided a picture of Kaspar Hauser. The attempt to murder him was made by a man who was dressed like a gentleman but left no tracks. On the 17th October the poor foundling was sitting in the outside toilet when the murderer emerged from a wooden shed opposite and cut him on his forehead with a broad-bladed knife. If the murderer had had enough space to strike vertically instead of horizontally, then the poor foundling would not have come away alive. The man also said at the time: 'You will never leave this town alive.' Hauser fell down as if dead—now he is alright again and is guarded day and night. Perhaps he will not give up his lessons. He is in good shape again. The researches into his origins have been taken up again earnestly, but kept secret by court order.
> With the greatest satisfaction we stand at your disposal and we are
>
> Your most obedient servants,
> Loedel and Merkel[202]

Stanhope was therefore raising the question of origins already this early, and the news about the court's insistence on secrecy could only have confirmed his suspicions that the one who had been kept prisoner at Laufenburg and the foundling of Nuremberg were one and the same person. No such powerful defences would have been thrown up around a runaway farmer's boy from the Palatinate. The interest that he and Gentz had shown in the *Hesperus* show the two had grasped this and how they had tried to reconstruct the story on the basis of the facts already known to them. How intensively Gentz applied himself to this may remain an open question—most likely he did not, but that Stanhope did there can be no doubt. He also took what hints he could from the literature that was current at the time such as *The Man in the Iron Mask* or Kotzebue's historical drama *Der Taubstumme* ['The Deaf-Mute'] (Fig. 101). The Man in the Iron Mask was thought to be a son of Louis XIV who had been deprived of his rights to the throne, while the story of *Der Taubstumme* referred to a case which had actually taken place in Paris. The relevant short extract of the drama will be quoted here in full because the context and above all the theme in general is rich in analogies which must have given Stanhope much food for thought.

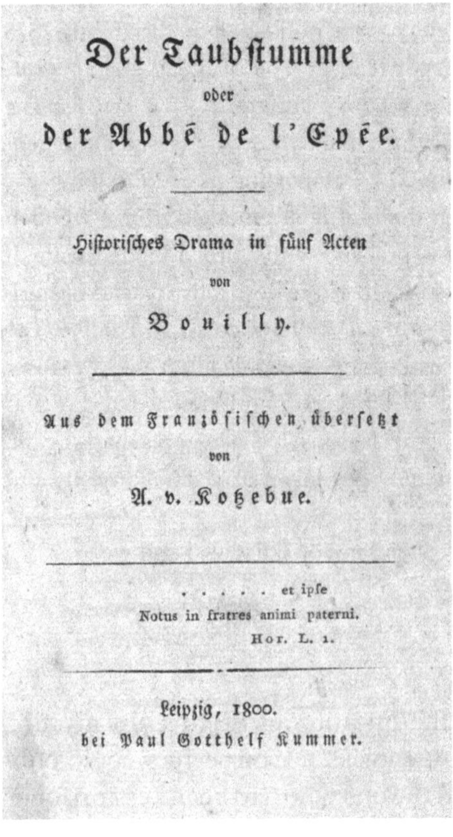

101. Cover page of Kotzebue's 'The Deaf-Mute or the Abbé de l'Epée'.

A child was brought one day to the Abbé de l' Epée, the director of an institution for deaf-mutes. His story is told by the main character of Kotzebue's drama: 'It is eight years since a policeman one autumn day brought me a young deaf-mute to me in Paris. The watchman had recently found him late at night on the bridge. The child seemed about eight or nine years old and was a likeable lad. The coarse rags that covered him led me to think at first that he belonged to a poor family and I promised to look after him. The other morning when I looked at him more closely, I soon noticed a certain dignity in his looks; he seemed surprised to see himself in rags and I surmised that the poor child had been deliberately dressed in such clothes and put out on the road. Straightaway I made his case known through the newspapers; I gave an exact description of him, but in vain! No-one hastened over to enquire when it was a case of the return of an unfortunate. When I saw that my researches were fruitless and convinced that that this child had been the victim of some kind of secret intrigue, I now tried to gain some enlightenment from the boy himself. I named him Theodor and made him one of my pupils. He soon excelled himself and fulfilled my hopes so greatly that after three years had gone by, his soul opened and appeared like a new creation. I spoke with him through signs which were as fast as thoughts; he answered me likewise.

'One day, when we were going past the Court of Justice in Paris, he saw a magistrate get into a carriage and was unusually excited. I asked the cause, and he gave me to understand that a man, dressed just like that in purple and ermine, had often pressed him in his arms and wept tears over him. I concluded that he must be the son or the close relative of a magistrate who, because of his costume, could only be one of the highest judges, and that consequently, my pupil's birthplace was probably to be found in a capital city.

'Another time, when we were passing through the suburb of St. Germain, we came across the funeral procession of a person of rank. I immediately noticed in my Theodor a movement which became ever stronger as the procession approached. The moment the coffin had passed by, he trembled and threw himself around my neck. "What's the matter?" I asked him. "I remember," he answered in sign language, "that just before I was brought to Paris, I had to follow the coffin of a man who had been so good to me; I was wearing a black cloak and my hair was dishevelled. Everyone was crying and I was crying too."

'I concluded from this that he was an orphan, the heir to a great fortune, which doubtless greedy relations had stolen from him, taking advantage of his helpless condition to remove him for ever from his homeland in order to help themselves to his property.

'These important discoveries strengthened my zeal and my courage. Day by day Theodor became more interesting to me and the intention grew in me to restore him to his own condition. But how was I to go about it? He had never heard his father's name; he did not know where he had been born nor to which family he belonged. I asked him whether he still remembered the scene when he saw Paris for the first time. He said yes and assured me that he could still see the barrier in front of him, through which he passed. The next morning, we began to check the Paris barriers. As we got near to one which is called *de l'Enfer* [Hell], he signed to me that he recognised it, that someone had come there with a carriage and he had got out with the two people who had accompanied him and that he could recall how they looked. These new indications showed me that he had come from the south of France. He added that he had been on the road for many days. The horses had been changed every hour. I calculated the time and distance and was no longer in doubt that my Theodor must be from one of the big cities of southern France. After a thousand useless searches, I finally decided to journey through southern France myself with Theodor. The memories that filled his soul led me to hope that he would easily recognise his birthplace. The undertaking was ambitious and difficult. To be able to hope for success we would have to travel on foot; I am old, but heaven gave me strength!—Despite my age and infirmity, I left Paris on a journey of 66 days. I went through the barrier *de l'Enfer* which he recognised. When we were in open country we embraced each other, called on God for assistance and ventured forth full of courage. We visited every town one after the other; Theodor, filled with the urge to find his hometown again, often led me to places which later proved to be unknown to him. My strength began to ebb and already my consoling hope was slipping from me when on that morning we stood before the gates of Toulouse.

'We entered the town; Theodor urgently gripped my hand and signed to me that he knew the place. We stepped forwards; with every step he became more lively and tears filled his eyes. We crossed the market square and suddenly he threw himself down, raised his hands to heaven, jumped up again and announced that he had found his homeland again. Drunk with joy, like him I forgot all the hardships of the journey. We crossed many districts of the town and finally came to this one in which he saw the palace opposite your residence; he let out a loud cry, threw himself breathlessly into my arms and showed me that this was the house of his fathers! I enquired and I learned that this hotel had previously belonged to the family of Count Solar whose last offspring my

> pupil is, and that all the property of the same, including this hotel, is in the hands of a certain M. Darlemont, the child's guardian and maternal uncle who is in possession of it all as a consequence of a false death certificate. I immediately sought out the most famous lawyer in Toulouse to whom I could entrust this important case. I was given your name Sir, and here I am, come to lay upon your heart that which has meant the most in the world to me, the fruit of eight years of work! The destiny of my Theodor! God gave him to me in order to complete his creation. Receive him from my hands in order to restore to him the most precious thing a human being can possess, a legitimate worthy name and the inalienable rights which nature and law acknowledge him.'

Stanhope's reason for occupying himself with such material lay in the fact that to his mind, the content of the bottle message of 1816 had, against all logic and suspicion, shown itself to be true and now an answer was to be found to the question of why the heir was actually to be eliminated. Then he must have had a misleading thought, namely, that Stéphanie's son apparently ought really, for reasons of another kind, to be given his rights. The climax of Kotzebue's drama might then have seemed to Stanhope like a vision of the future:

> Crushed by what Dupré had told me—I hurried away—my father had shut himself in—I forced the doors of his room—Dupré followed me and told him that he confessed everything—that he would now go away and give himself up—'I shared in your crime', he added, 'You will share my punishment!'—This threat shattered my father—I seized the moment—I placed the point of the dagger against my breast 'if I am to be dishonoured so young,' I cried, ' I would rather die now before your eyes! Die here on this spot! If you do not immediately recognise Julius de Solar in writing!'—The sudden outbreak of doubt, the possible disgrace and the certainty of my death finally had their effect on him—nature won the victory—my father was moved—and with a shaking hand he wrote down these lines—'I acknowledge the pupil of the Abbé de l'Epée, named Theodor to be the Count Julius de Solar and am prepared to reinstate him in all his rights. Darlemont.'

We do not know with what feelings Stanhope finished reading this, but one can imagine that he could visualise a similar ending to the story of Kaspar Hauser.

*

At the end of 1829 a noteworthy meeting took place in Nuremberg. On the 18th and 19th December at 5 p.m. in the *Zur blauen Glocke* ['The Blue Bell'] inn on the Kornmarkt, the jurist Gottlieb von Tucher (1798–1877)—he was not then Kaspar Hauser's guardian—Georg Friedrich Daumer (1800–1877), the foundling's teacher, district councillor von Roeder and the mayor Binder met with a lecturer Dr. Hentzler who had travelled from Würzburg with a medium in order to try to study what they could about the background of the 'Child of Europe'.

Kaspar Hauser—who incidentally made no good impression on the lady—was presented to the 'somnambulist' in his waking state before her doctor proceeded to put her into a deep hypnotic sleep. Gottlieb von Tucher's protocol accounts (Fig. 102) of the two meetings, which cover 42 sheets of paper, contain not only very surprising but also in part some very pertinent statements, which, however, the criminologist Feuerbach appeared to think unreliable at the time. Above all, the jurist found fault with their lack of any value in court.

> There is no doubt that they provide the judge with no clues at all. A somnambulist as such has not the slightest credibility, at least before the law. Her statements might only have some indirect judicial value if she did not allude to facts which were shown to proceed from other methods or which were made to seem probable by them and served to justify judicial procedures...Of that which we do not know, but which we need to know, she tells us nothing. Not even a single instance which we could follow up.

Nevertheless, the woman from Würzburg with her tentative, unsure manner of description, did get rather close to the complex phenomenon and it is just the complexity that marks the content of her statements: they are contradictory where it is a matter of the whole, and in certain important particulars, they are accurate.

Binder was so impressed by the gatherings that despite an agreement to maintain silence about them '...he told the whole town that same night' which drew Tucher's scorn: 'What a wuss!' For us only a part of the protocol is of interest. After a short break in the first sitting—Daumer had already left—the medium herself spoke up without having been asked any questions:

> It seems to me as if devilish art has already been
> worked upon the boy. It is as if there is a haze around
> him that I am not to see [through].

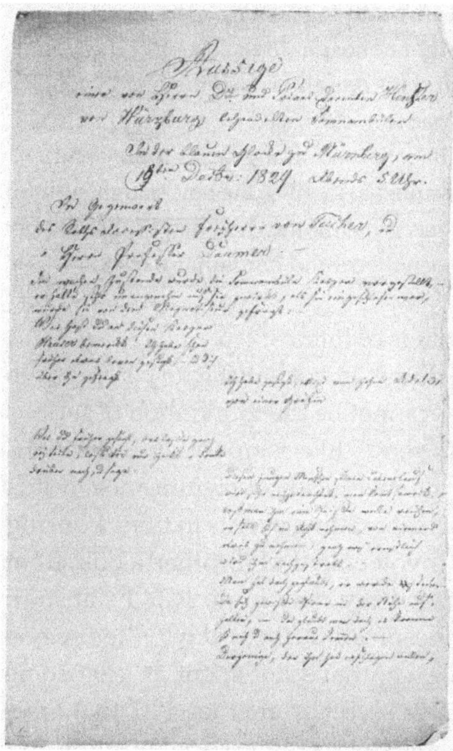

102. The first page of the protocol manuscript by Gottlieb von Tucher on the session of 18th and 19th December 1829.

Dr. Hentzler: What kind of devilish art is that?

Something appeared to me like from a certain masonic group. The boy's father... there is something...they don't say that they are behind it... and when their time is up, then they die such a death that one doesn't know where they've ended up...it is such a hard group, it appears to me as if it had been like this before, that something like a dagger had been stuck in his portrait, you know, like when you magnetise me and I fall asleep. It is like they support each other when they are down and then, when he appears again, then they go after his life...

Dr. Hentzler: What do you think the intention of the groups is?

... 'pause' ... I don't know, people in Würzburg were talking about it once that many were locked up... There are several of them there. Several of them are actually after the boy's life.

Dr. Hentzler: Can the group arrange it so that you confuse us?	I am confusing nothing ...'pause' ... my right to hospitality ....no—but the Count and his daughter, as if they had even.... 'pause' ...sacrificed [something] … that ...it is so strange.... as if they had wanted to sacrifice the boy, slaughter [him] ... as if the mother had had him put away secretly behind her father's back.

So much for the relevant extract that is of interest.

Even today, information from mediums is not satisfactory because in fact information from such sources cannot be the foundation of serious research, but it can in Feuerbach's sense, like many other indications from seances nevertheless 'have indirect juridical significance' if it is understood to be the expression of real existing events in time. Looking at the 18th and 19th centuries, the involvement of 'brotherhoods' from the beginning of the Kaspar Hauser story may in no way be absurd. The facts are that lodges were widespread in those days—'today one will meet few people of any rank who have not spent at least some period of time as a member of such a secret brotherhood',[203] that Freemasonry was in its heyday and possessed a unique social position and rank, and that some of its members, with more or less success, followed particular cultural, political, geographical but also occult aims.

10. The 'Last' Zähringer—the First Hochberg

Aspects of the Transfer of Power, 1830

Stanhope's story will be continued in the next chapter. An understanding of specific motives and reactions will first require a closer examination of the situation prior to the transfer of power at Karlsruhe in 1830. This event brought up essential questions of motive for all those involved in the main question, including Stanhope; a more exact understanding of the relationships existing at the time would therefore seem necessary at this juncture.

*

For months there had been unrest again in France, which culminated in the July Revolution, forcing the abdication of the Count of Artois who had reigned as Charles X since 1824. He was replaced by his cousin, Duke Louis Philippe Orléans (1773–1850) as King Louis Philippe I.

'Like a stroke of lightning,' wrote the historian Treitschke, 'the news struck the Court at Vienna. Prince Metternich had often warned blind governments against the machinations of Freemasonic Orders, and now Emperor Franz hurried to strengthen the prohibitions against the Orders which had long been in force in Habsburg Crown territories and extend them to the Lombard-Venetian kingdom.' These developments must have startled the 'old Tory' Stanhope, who had been in friendly correspondence with the Count of Artois since 1805 and who knew only too well how to judge the direction of the new political wind. All the more remarkable to him must have seemed the accession to the throne of the Duke of Orléans, who had described himself in that letter, which Philip Henry had obtained from Pitt and still possessed, as a 'natural enemy of Bonaparte'. On the other hand, the Duke's father had presented himself to the public mind as an unyielding opponent of the Bourbons, so at least that side of the change of scene made sense. In Paris Delacroix's painting of the revolution was being celebrated which showed the tricolour in the fist of a female revolutionary. The July Revolution of 1830—a frightening event for monarchists—impressively affirmed the victory of 1789, or, in other words—the sovereignty of the people.

After the death of Napoleon, the secret society of the so-called 'French Carbonari' had formed itself underground. It gathered much support from the army lodges of their former master and had as its single goal the overthrow of the contemptible *ancien régime* of the Bourbon brothers. Away from the eyes of the secret police of Louis XVIII and Charles X, they had planned their coup for a decade and had struck at a decisive moment. Treitschke again: 'The most sinister aspect of this revolution was the power of the secret associations, which showed itself so strongly. They had the power to compel enthronement as well as abdication, both of which the Duke of Orléans was to experience.'[204]

The victory of the revolution was ultimately a victory over the monarchy and a triumph over the treaties of 1814 and 1815, and as the symbol of the revolution and of the old rulership of Bonaparte the tricolour was once again solemnly raised in place of the fleur-de-lys. It was no longer a disgrace to be a Napoleonid; on the contrary. 'Down with the Bourbons!' cried the revolutionaries between the barricades and the slaughter in the streets. 'Long live freedom and the republic! Long live Napoleon II!'

Sixteen years after the Emperor was exiled, Paris resounded to the cry for his son, the Duke of Reichstadt, who had had to spend his days as an unwilling neighbour of Metternich's at the palace of Schönbrunn. The phase of the Restoration 1814–1830, formed by the diplomacy of Austria, was over.

Metternich was concerned about these developments; Gentz for once was not. He had taken the Chancellor's order to move to the Bohemian Königswart Castle badly. In these months he only had eyes and ears for Fanny Elssler; all his thoughts and attention went exclusively to her in this period. The way was thus clear for new unexpected developments in France to occur somewhat beyond his political awareness—and also in Baden!

Metternich, however, with Article 2 of the Confederation Treaty in mind, applied himself to 'the upholding of the external and internal security of Germany'. He therefore cast a sharp eye on Baden and Bavaria in the Kaspar Hauser question. A possible government crisis in one of the German princely houses could, in view of the events which had led to revolution in France in July, cause a spark which might spread to the other members of the Confederation and finally to the Austrian Empire itself. For Metternich, the system of European order was at risk; monarchy as a form of government was under threat. The Chancellor knew very well that one trips over molehills not mountains. Vienna's reaction to the Kaspar Hauser question, which was influenced by events in France during the build-up to the July

Revolution, had a marked effect in Munich and Karlsruhe. Ludwig I of Bavaria and Ludwig of Baden—and after the 30th March Leopold—had to draw their own conclusions.

Metternich first had to address the tricky question of how to steer the problem away from Austria, which seemed to be necessary, as on the basis of information provided by the Cathedral preacher Müller (see p. 204 ff.), Madame Dalbonne, as a subject of the Emperor, was under strong suspicion as an accessory and participant according to the information available to von Sedlnitzky's secret police.

On the 27th March 1830, three days before Leopold's enthronement, Tucher wrote to Feuerbach:

> ...This same person is now supposed to be in Pest (Budapest) with a Countess Palffy. A man came to this Countess Palffy when she was alone and said he was from the police and asked after a Madame *Bonneval*. She assured him that she knew everyone in the house but there was definitely no-one of that name among them. He excused himself and left, saying that he was following a man whom he had been told about *in order to find out something about Kaspar Hauser*. When the governess and the Countess's steward gathered for lunch with the Countess, she told them what had happened in the morning when the children had been out. When the Countess had finished her story, the governess blanched and fell to the floor unconscious. Since that time she has been insane. It is not known whether the madness is faked or real. This governess entered the Countess's service under the name of Madame Dalbonne.

This information was of course also known in Vienna. The fact that there everything relating to the Palffys was later denied would seem to bear it out rather than contradict it. Two days later, Gottlieb von Tucher reported on an article in the journal *Der Bazar*, published by Moritz Gottlieb Saphir (1795–1858). No. 26 stated that Dalbonne had been arrested, but 'the embassy of .... [*....sche Gesandschaft*] had succeeded in effecting the person's release'. The letters represented by the dots can be completed by '*badische*' [of Baden] —Saphir left that as a question, but he must have known. The banker Salomon Rothschild had personally introduced Saphir to Metternich. 'Your Highness can make of this man whatever you wish.' Metternich and Saphir were soon working together. The agent wrote to Rothschild in his curriculum vitae that he wished to serve the 'keen observer of the times and of life, the illustrious lord, [Metternich] in whose name you speak to me' and that in return for a regular fee, he was 'prepared to devote himself to the good cause with all my strength and with the zeal of a man of honour...'[205] Saphir's efforts with regard to Kaspar Hauser appear in a new light.

A Budapest police report of March 1830 states: 'Generally it is believed that Dalbonne is an accessory to the crime committed against Kaspar Hauser. The House of Palffy indicated something of that sort in the beginning when the story first caused a stir, but now almost all associated with the House of Palffy defend Dalbonne and appear to want to know nothing.'

In view of the prevailing situation, this latest reaction of the Palffys makes one wonder. What would have happened, how would the Emperor and Metternich have reacted, if further investigations had established a connection? Instead, a clear sign went out that things were to be left as they were.

Anton Karl Count Palffy—already before the new posture of denial—had been asked about Dalbonne by the Bavarian authorities, as the Count told the Hungarian Court Chancellor Count Reviczky. Madame Dalbonne was living in the Count's castle. His father bore the title *Magister Tavernicorum regalium* and thereby was a member of the third highest rank in the Hungarian aristocracy. An intimate friend of the Count, as has already been mentioned, was the diplomat and opponent of Kaspar Hauser, Johann Baron von Wessenberg, who as an intimate of Stanhope, we shall have reason to discuss later.

On the 22nd February the Court Chancellor reported to the Emperor on the Kaspar Hauser affair. On the 26th two documents from the Emperor had already left the Hofburg: 'The content of this presentation has served to inform me, and I await the prompt presentation of the disposition you have made together with a preliminary opinion as to what further measures should be taken.'

The Emperor directed the President of Police Count Sedlnitzky to occupy himself more thoroughly with the affair:

> From this report of my Hungarian Court Chancellor you will gather what problems he has had to deal with on account of the information obtained by him in Ofen [Budapest] on the occasion of a so-called requisition by the Nuremberg Magistrate because of the incidents that have happened to C.H. As I now need to establish, also through the sources known to you, more accurate and dependable information as to the actual facts in relation to the reliability, credibility, morality, character, and financial affairs of the Cathedral preacher Müller, the woman from Majthényi and the dal Bon [*sic*], you will concern yourself with providing me with this together with anything new pertaining to this matter as soon as possible.

A day earlier, on the 25th Metternich had already written to the Austrian chargé d'affaires Kaspar Count Spiegel. At the end of the letter, which emphasises the fact that the Emperor was taking a lively interest in the whole matter, Metternich wrote: 'The Bavarian government should therefore either address us through E.E. or the Cabinet should communicate its wishes to me in quite direct ways. The inquiries which can certainly be carried out in the first period of the business more along police than strictly legal lines would then be controlled and guided and every damaging report avoided.'

The Austrian chargé d'affaires passed this on to the Bavarian Minister of the Interior Joseph Ludwig von Armansperg (1787–1853), who for his part ordered the Bavarian envoy in Vienna, Count Bray, to give Metternich an immediate reply. Bray wrote: 'The communications will only take place between the Justice Ministry and myself, quite in secret, and will be passed to the Imperial Minister via diplomatic channels. In this way, it will be guaranteed that nothing will leak out.' After a considerable amount of investigation, the confused interim results of which does not need to be repeated here, Metternich, at the Emperor's behest, arrived at the noteworthy dictum that Vienna wished to regard the Kaspar Hauser affair as an exclusively Bavarian matter; the Bavarian courts were asked for a correspondingly positive response to this position and duly obliged. The Chancellor insisted: 'be so good as to ensure that the legal authorities of the Bavarian Crown will, as soon as possible and in an official manner, explain the investigations that have been going on in Hungary on account of the Kaspar Hauser affair and how the resulting data may be presumed to express the nullity of the information given by the Cathedral preacher Müller'. That was a demand that bordered on a perversion of the course of justice.

If it be supposed that the investigations had been allowed to run their course and it had been revealed that Müller's information contained a kernel of truth and that Dalbonne had been an accomplice—the imaginable consequences would have been civil unrest, at least in Baden. In view of this possible scenario, Metternich had no other choice but to suppress the matter at its source. But are activities of this sort organised at the highest level because of 'a mere swindler'? All this diplomatic activity shows that basically, Kaspar Hauser's true royal identity was certainly believed to be possible.

*

103. *Johann Friedrich Cotta von Cottendorf (1764–1832)*

National-Kalender
für
die deutschen Bundesstaaten
auf
das Jahr 1830.
für
Katholiken, Protestanten, Griechen, Russen,
(nach dem Stuttgarter Meridian)
zum
Unterricht und Vergnügen
für
Geistliche und Weltliche, Lehrer, Beamte, Bürger und Landleute
(eßlich eingerichtet
von
Christian Carl André,

Achter Jahrgang.
(Mit 5 Abbildungen und 2 Musikblättern.)

Stuttgart und Tübingen,
in der J. G. Cotta'schen Buchhandlung.
1830.

— 165 —

LXIX. Kaspar Hauser.
(Man sehe das Titelkupfer.)

104/105 The 'National Calendar' published by Cotta with the opening article about Kaspar Hauser.

Irrespective of all this, the year 1830 began with a notable publication, at the root of which may have lain a very specific idea. The story of the foundling was then, after two years, generally known and as a result of countless newspaper reports, talked about everywhere. Hardly a single page had avoided the sensation. And how then did this year 1830 begin?

Published by Johann Friedrich Cotta (1764–1832) (Fig.103) in Stuttgart, the high-circulation *Nationalkalendar* (Figs.104,105) for the German Confederation was on the desks and in the hands of all 'cultured and civilised teachers, officials, citizens, country people'...'Catholics, Protestants, Greek and Russian Orthodox'. This issue of 1830 contained, next to a picture of Kaspar Hauser, another highly detailed account of the story that was already known. What may have moved Cotta,[206] who is known to have wanted to win Schiller and others to his side for a political daily newspaper and who, incidentally, knew his Hennenhofer and how to evaluate him, to focus on this of all themes—which appeared to have nothing more sensational to offer—at such an historically pregnant moment in a publication which was read by almost all culturally active and politically responsible contemporaries and which guaranteed long-term exposure of the issue for a whole year? It had been known for months that Grand Duke Ludwig would not be reigning for much longer, and the deliberate publication once again of all the known facts relating to Kaspar Hauser appears not to have been serendipitous. This *Kalendar*, as the stamp on the copy illustrated shows, came into the hands of rulers as well as members of parliament—also in Baden. This too was the intention of the publisher. That Cotta was a decided supporter of revolution may be taken as proved. It was not only that his contemporaries spoke of him respectfully as 'the Napoleon of the booksellers'. When the revolutionary armies had occupied his country in 1796, he had proudly celebrated the birth of his son Johann George (1796–1863) with the words: 'A healthy republican has been born to me!'

But beyond such personal demonstrations, it is generally not known that he was also extremely politically active in that he sought to bring the spirit of revolution into deeds, that is, into the formation of opinion. Secretly, he fully financed, including the salaries of the co-workers, the much-read *Strassburgische politische Journal* of his brother Christoph Friedrich Cotta (1758–1838), an 'honorary citizen of France', which, according to its founding maxim, would always carry 'the latest political curiosities'. Now Johann Friedrich himself provided a 'curiosity' which under certain circumstances had what it took to bring down the ramshackle establishment in Karlsruhe. Before a change in government which would inevitably bring the Hochbergs to power, the Kaspar Hauser issue was once again to be clearly put before those involved. How clearly his colleagues in the publishing world in Karlsruhe understood the signal from Stuttgart is shown by the fact that with the appearance of the No.1 issue of 1830 of the *Karlsruhe Unterhaltungsblatt*—a Sunday newspaper—a series of articles on Kaspar Hauser began extending over four issues, which for a month repeated all the known facts. Nos. 1–3 literally reproduced text from Cotta's *Nationalkalendar*, while the fourth and last in the series included an editorial comment that closed with the words: 'It is now clear that more is involved in the life of Kaspar Hauser than had somehow been believed, and that he has been the victim of a monstrous crime, probably a crime of acquisitiveness.' For which group of people in Baden was this last sentence intended?

One of those who must have felt himself directly addressed by it was Klüber, who had always decided in favour of the Hochbergs and yet held Hauser to be credible. As long as Ludwig, the last Zähringer, lived, there would be no practical consequences from Klüber's convictions, and he did not need to prove how serious the Kaspar Hauser affair was or whether Kaspar could represent a danger for the second line of the House of Baden. And as long as Ludwig ruled, the Baden Privy Council could scarcely undertake anything officially to investigate this. But how did the situation look if the often-imagined scenario were now to become reality? The inevitable and expected event then occurred. In March of that year came the dramatic situation when the one who de facto had stolen the throne from Duke Karl's firstborn son faced his end. At the beginning of this decisive year, however, the Prussian police chief Merker, later a friend of Stanhope, published his tract 'Kaspar Hauser—not unlikely a fraud', which was immediately answered by the Bavarian Rudolf Giehrl's booklet *Kaspar Hauser, the Honourable Foundling*. Through Cotta's entry into the fray, the pros and contras between Baden, Bavaria, Württemberg and Prussia unexpectedly became a topic of renewed discussion among the widest public, but for the representatives from Baden, partisanship for or against the foundling took on existential significance. The struggle around the question of Hauser's credibility was now in full swing, similar to the later question: suicide or murder?—whereby the latter would almost assume the status of fact. This time the conflict, just as significant, was centred on the question: honest or not? There was no need to speak about the swindler but of what should one speak in the opposite case? Pointedly, but in Kaspar Hauser's favour, a correspondent styling himself 'Freymütige' (Frank) noted: 'If what Kaspar Hauser says of himself is true, then no-one will deny him the most justified claim to support from the police and at least from the general public. But what will he deserve if he were to be a fraud? To be looked after and raised by the State and by humanity in the most careful fashion, for he would be an extraordinary genius.'

In view of the debate that had broken out, Klüber, who accepted Kaspar's story, must have been certain of the probability of a possible danger posed by the 'foundling'. At the end of July, he travelled to Munich to meet his brother, who worked there as an archive official. On the way, he broke his journey at Ansbach (1–7 August) to speak to Feuerbach. From 8–28 August he was in Munich, where his brother—so much may be concluded—gave him insights which strengthened rather than weakened his suspicions. In addition, it may also have been true that, as the magazine *Hesperus*, another Cotta publication, reported on the 27th September, that Klüber had made his trip because he was '...commissioned to do so by Baden'. On his return journey, Klüber once again checked in at the 'Stern' hotel in Ansbach (28th Aug.—4th Sept.), where he again met Feuerbach and this time also with Gottlieb von Tucher, who came over from Nuremberg. If after all this, Klüber's convictions and attitude remained positive with regard to Hauser, which certainly did not correspond to his brief, the conversations in Munich and Ansbach must have been so firm in their evidential value that Klüber, without violating his conscience, could do nothing other than defend Kaspar Hauser's credibility, even after his death.

*

Grand Duke Ludwig died at the time when preparations for the annual trip to Germany would have been underway in Chevening. Stanhope, however, who would have liked to have been on the road, was under irresistible pressure to stay at home. William IV, 'the Sailor King', as he was popularly known and 'a narrow-minded gentleman', had only recently become King of England, and new elections were set for the summer. By law every member of the House of Lords was obliged to be present at Parliament. In the middle of the election campaign came the news of the July Revolution; it was now unsafe to travel through

France. The forced interruption was more than inconvenient, as it prevented Stanhope from following the inevitable conflict in Karlsruhe at first hand. The question of the Hochberg succession was now posed de facto for the first time. The decision had to be made whether the second line of the House of Baden would take power or whether the right to the throne would be held open for another possible legitimate heir—not by Hauser himself, but perhaps by a number of Baden parliamentarians who for reasons of conscience would deny Leopold the right to succeed because of the absence of the suspected pretender. Cotta's *Nationalkalendar* and the following reactions of Karlsruhe editors for or against Kaspar Hauser—all this was known and could not be ignored.

That Ludwig's reign especially in its last years had been overshadowed, especially by the failures of Hennenhofer, who was forced to resign by Grand Duke Leopold because of them, was a fact that was felt throughout the population of Baden. On the occasion of Grand Duke Leopold's birthday in August 1831, the town vicar of Lörrach, Friedrich Koch, declared in his sermon: 'Let me pass over the last decade in silence—we still stand perhaps too close to the recent past to be able to pass judgement over it—but with hand on heart, and before the eyes of God! Not in every heart did today's full festive joy blossom!'

Everyone remembered that in this last period, scarcely two years before, Kaspar Hauser had appeared, and then the first attempt had been made on his life, and soon the rumours sprang up that would not be stilled: that his birthplace was not somewhere beyond the Bavarian border, but in the palace at Karlsruhe. How serious, how real this suspicion had become showed itself as Leopold's succession was about to take place.

Georg Friedrich Kolb, a Baden parliamentarian reports a conversation in Zurich with his 'old friend, Privy Councillor Welcker, the experienced and influential member of parliament' in which the day had been spoken of which was now before them.

> Our conversation turned to the Kaspar Hauser affair, and I did not fail to ask Welcker to share with me his honest opinion. Since Welcker was among close friends (present were Dr. Wilhelm Schulz, his wife and myself), he did not hold back from sharing with us those partly startling things which I recorded the same day (30th August) and have since published. Naturally, as long as Welcker was alive, I observed great discretion. Some of his remarks, namely the fact that Grand

Duchess Stéphanie had not been permitted to see her son, either sick or dead, agreed exactly with what my friend G. Fein had heard from the words of Countess Benzel-Sternau, who had been at the Court (as a lady-in-waiting?) at the critical time and had already told me. The facts which Welcker gave about the case were incontestably of a crucial nature. I only need to recall a few facts in this connection that have nowhere been contradicted. The eldest prince's wet-nurse herself told Welcker that she (like his mother the Grand Duchess!) had not been allowed to see the child either when he was sick or when he was dead. When Grand Duke Ludwig died, some Baden parliamentarians took the opportunity to discuss among themselves as to whether their consciences would allow them to affirm Prince Leopold since in all probability, a son of Grand Duke Karl still lived in the person of Kaspar Hauser. When Garnier, who wrote the pamphlet that was condemned allowed himself to be arrested on Baden territory, he was thrown in jail but not put on trial; they wanted to keep him locked up without having been tried, and only when Welcker, together with his liberal colleague, the Minister Winter, threatened to make the matter public in the chamber did the Minister, who had at first stubbornly resisted, agree to free the prisoner rather than letting it come to a public trial. When Welcker later visited England (after the parliamentary session of 1835) the exile Garnier showed him there a letter written in Hennenhofer's hand in which he [Hennenhofer] offered Garnier, who had accused Hennenhofer of the murder, a not insubstantial amount of money if he would agree to certain conditions; whereupon Garnier then actually stopped work on the publication he had already begun. [See also p. 284 & 493f.]

Welcker went on: when the few indications which Feuerbach had before him led his keen senses to the conclusion that Hauser was Stéphanie's son, you will understand on what numerous and weightier facts my opinion is based. He added: when the Hauser affair became known, besides himself, various Baden parliamentarians, some of them strong monarchists, felt themselves deeply disturbed in their consciences as to whether they could acknowledge Grand Duke Leopold when everything was indicating that Grand Duke Karl's son still lived as Kaspar Hauser. He himself had been in great doubt as to what he was obliged to do. Rotteck's view had prevailed, namely that one ought not to concern oneself with the private relationships of princes.[207]

Similar thoughts were expressed by other members of parliament. 'This is how it is with the "crown council". My grandfather Frommel,' wrote his descendant,

> died when I was twelve years old, my grandfather Bähr, when I was a student, so I knew him better. My father told me that there had been a meeting called by Grand Duke Leopold which my grandfather Frommel attended, where the Kaspar Hauser affair was discussed, since Leopold, convinced of the rightfulness of Hauser's origins, wanted to abdicate, but all those present advised him that Hauser was too little developed. My grandfather Bähr, who was then a ministerial councillor, told me this. Fr. von Göler, the former President of the First Chamber who died several years ago and was a close friend of Leopold, told me the same thing. Shortly after Grand Duke Leopold's (expression of) his intentions to abdicate—which incidentally had brought Baden into a difficult situation because of Bavaria which had continually sought to gain the part of the Palatinate around Heidelberg—Kaspar Hauser was murdered in Ansbach.[208]

Welcker, Frommel and indirectly, Bähr and von Göler, therefore confirmed that in March 1830 the question of Leopold's legitimacy was actually discussed and that there was a delegation which had addressed itself immediately to Grand Duke Leopold. Gottlieb von Tucher noted in the 1870s, after a conversation with the diplomat Xaver, Baron von Andlaw, a connoisseur of Baden politics and chamberlain to the Duchess of Hamilton (born Princess Marie of Baden, and thus Kaspar Hauser's sister), that he too (Andlaw) considered it 'completely true that [such] a Council of Ministers had taken place following the death of Grand Duke Ludwig at Grand Duke Leopold's orders prior to his succession.[209]

*

Since the question of a State or Crown Council meeting or a delegation of parliamentarians is of considerable significance, it is worth looking further into this affair which was credibly attested to on the one side but vehemently denied on the other. For decades it was impossible to discover the official position of the Baden authorities on the matter, and only in 1887 came the first extremely sketchy yet polemical revelation to which can be attributed a semi-official character, in that its author, Professor Dr. Antonius van der Linde (1833–1897), maintained a relationship that can be described as personal to Grand Duke Friedrich I, Leopold's son. Evidence of this will be given in what follows in a few quotations from letters.

It is not unimportant to understand the motives and circumstances of life that brought a man like van der Linde to produce one of the most unobjective contributions to Kaspar Hauser research.[209a] Before examining in more detail the controversial matter of the State Council meeting, some statements by van der Linde will therefore be cited which have a direct bearing on the theme and throw a sharp light on the later situation. Because things were still unclear in 1830, it was necessary to deal with the consequences of what had happened.

'He [Grand Duke Friedrich] *himself* reads aloud what I write to his wife,' boasts van der Linde in recently discovered and long unpublished correspondence with royal Privy Councillor Gustav Adelbert Seyler in Berlin.[210] In these letters great pains are taken to establish that Kaspar Hauser's mother was somewhere else, which can only mean that even with the excellent contacts van der Linde had with the Grand Duke and thus with the archives of the grand ducal house, the assertions on which everything either stood or fell, about Kaspar being Stéphanie's son, could not be contradicted. One must first familiarise oneself with Linde's letter-writing style and his compulsive attempts to use Bavarian dialect with which he, as in his other writings, shows almost a manic desire to mock Kaspar Hauser. That the nature of his connection to von Seyler is not known is immaterial—rather, it is significant that van der Linde urgently needed this evidence.

> Owing to frightful insomnia as a consequence of mental stress I had six months' leave and wanted to search for the mother (on foot). But the 'border' was too 'bohemian' for me! Through *your certainly very correct restrictions comes* light. 'Here the sword of the Lord from Gideon!' Decorations, pine forests, professorial chairs, 'everything's available' if I could succeed in that. I shall come to you as soon as you call me from Bavaria....For *me*, finding his mother would be a *life question* and I have devoted myself to it...The Grand Duke is getting old and infirm. Oh, if only we could find in *this* the conclusion to an issue that for us is already interesting enough *in itself*. A revelation such as the one you suspect, thus a *negative* one, would be as *positive* as it gets...

In another letter:

> Dear Friend, I have just read, or rather, devoured with real relish your quite excellent news! The Grand Duke wrote me a very satisfactory

> letter...What you wrote in your letter about the 'writing names' makes my forehead damp with anxiety. *I* hold that to be a moment of hide-and-seek (interruption, not reported etc.); if *you* are right—and that *could* be—then the threads will break asunder, oh alas! What if in the village you surmise (O, why so silent! You need not fear an *atom* of rashness on my part, or that I will *somehow* stick my meddling nose in there. I shall just sleep *even* less)—the 'little Kaspars' were not seldom there?! It's a 'right good farmer's name'. I have searched for 'Kaspars' in the relevant *regiment* at that time, but I was told that in Bavaria *those* lists had all long been destroyed. It's just as well, for what to do 'with all those documents'; they wouldn't have helped much. But now there are possibly many copies of the Number C[aspar] paper, for *which* it would be a sin to spare a few marks. I'm a veritable recluse and *happy* to say so.

It was then, a matter of finding a village 'on the Bohemian frontier' where someone named Kaspar had been born in 1812 and who, according to this scanty speculation, had deserted from his regiment in order 'to act the fool' in Nuremberg. But the fact that those born in 1812 could not have been recruited until 1833 at the earliest would have to have been noticed. Von Linde's envisaged line of proof is one that is still often followed today but has long been in vain, and success in that direction would be no mean achievement. The question would have to be answered: 'When, where and by whom was the child that was supposed to be Kaspar Hauser born?' (A.A. Lieb). The corresponding answers are only to be found in Baden. Several things were at stake for van der Linde. The works written by him were intended to destroy the 'Kaspar Hauser Mythos' once and for all and at the same time liberate him from severe financial straits which were the result of the 'swindler's debts' of his second wife, who had run away from him. If one asks the cause of so much unrelenting literary bile, one comes across a very dubious point of departure for this research topic. The would-be Kaspar Hauser interpreter van der Linde closes his letter of 24.12.1882 to the well-known Freiburg Professor Franz Xaver Kraus[211] with the words: 'dripping with hatred of Germans' and an additional insult in the postscript: 'You don't need to put yourself out: I have the right to murder.'

How van der Linde wanted his prodigious efforts on the Kaspar Hauser theme to be understood he indicated in another letter to the same correspondent on 18.2.1882, namely, as '...my literary testament for the boorish German Michel [a figure symbolising the German people that originated in the Middle Ages and is analogous to John Bull—*Ed.*] and then I'm on my way to England.'

The story behind this book, which opponents of Kaspar Hauser have often liked to cite and make use of, is just as instructive. On the 11th May 1885, van der Linde wrote to Kraus:

> In the dreadful winter of 82/83 when I stayed in the library until midnight for lack of fire and light, I sought to numb myself by studying the Kaspar Hauser Question. I got deeper and deeper into it, brought together the most complete literature, and wrote a critical account which (finally) grew into a large book.
>
> Is there something to be done with this *liberation* of the dynasty of Baden from the dogged Kaspar Hauser Mythos? From a little book ever more Hydra heads follow. The prospects for my big book are *poor*, so I will have to pay out another hundred marks, which I absolutely cannot manage. A Court Councillor, Wagner (I think) once handled my situation with your Culture Minister (Nikk?). It's only a thought, because it's for Baden. Obviously, I could get nothing started with the 'Zähringer decoration'.

The idea then was that van der Linde would free Grand Duke Friedrich from his problem and in return, the latter would free van der Linde from his immense burden of debts. Eight days later, on the 20th May 1885, in another letter to Kraus: '...longing to be out of this foul mood ...a nine-year-long bitterness strikes deep roots. I am miserable.' In this 'foul mood', in 'bitterness' and 'dripping with hatred of Germans', van der Linde went on with his work on Kaspar Hauser. Things took an unexpected turn, however, with its favourable reception by the Grand Duke. On the 18th February 1882, the author wrote to Kraus: 'I would rather tell you about Karlsruhe. In confidence, only that I had and knew *much more* than the K.H. Court Commission. But my reception by the Grand Duke was as kind as it was unexpected. Now, however, comes the limping messenger: *Beware of Bavaria*'. [*For the Kaspar Hauser Commission, formed by Friedrich I, see n.221].

What can have been the cause of this anxiety? Had the author got together so much material that could be used against Bavaria too that the Grand Duke and his advisors had demanded deletions be made? Van der Linde's pamphlet against Kaspar Hauser, by far the most vicious ever published, appeared as mentioned in 1887 and Grand

Duke Friedrich bought 100 copies on his own account which apparently did nothing to ease the author's difficulties. The provisional end to this chapter is a letter of 8.1.1892 in which we meet once again the Baden envoy Jagemann already encountered in other Kaspar Hauser connections:

> ...At the beginning of April 88 I sent a long letter to the Grand Duke [then in Berlin] so that my final considerations might be commended in *higher* places...The Grand Duke answered through Herr von Babo that 'he had taken steps for me and was *certain* that my wish would be granted'... With financial troubles on all sides, in October I finally had to turn to the Grand Duke with the request that he be so good as to give *me* some support for certain (earlier) printing costs related to Kaspar Hauser. That also happened fortunately at the lecture by Herr von Jagemann. With this, however, the *mentally* unbearable situation here has become unbearable. I *cannot* return to Holland....Go over to England perhaps? I have spoken about that basically with von Heydebrand and Lasa. I go to the Culture Minister and from there to Althoff: *circulus vitiosus*... my last hope would be the following: *Could the the Grand Duke not ask the Emperor that I be pardoned* and pensioned off on my salary? I beg you, 'from the bottom [of my heart]' to consider this and if even something is possible, to seek to expedite it. I would then go back to the southern Black Forest, to the country, where medical certificates are available for me...

The background and speculation associated with this book throw a sharp light on the position of Baden when one considers what kind of company Grand Duke Friedrich I had to keep in order to get on top of the Kaspar Hauser Question. That critical questions could find no place in a work of this kind is equally indicative of what an inconceivable mistake Karlsruhe had made in first fostering and then continuing to tolerate an 'academic' of this nature as their interpreter. His hatred of anything German—'Kaiserreich beer mania'—'miserable cultural backwater'—'stuffy bigotry'—'half-Asiatic hinterland'—and the people 'tight, boozy, screwed'—culminated in the threat : 'I cannot say anything yet; but after my death there will be an ethnological-ethical study of the German national vice (characterlessness and moral cowardice) brought out abroad, and the rest will then be revealed.'

Was this the only upright man who was to deal conclusively with the Kaspar Hauser Question, of all things? In passing, the friends and quoters of van der Linde can be recommended to study essential information on the character and capabilities of the Kaspar Hauser specialist that can be read in the publication of the historical Commission for Nassau, Vol. XXV (1963). The former pastor of a reformed sect in Amsterdam who was married several times is here confirmed as suffering from a total breakdown, 'psychopathic traits', 'self-adulation' and 'delusions of grandeur', so that inevitably, 'his private life was as catastrophic as his professional career'. The library director tried to embellish some of his works by cutting out pictures and engravings from old valuable books from the library for which he was responsible, behaviour which was interpreted as larceny and abuse of office. So much for the main pillar of Baden's defence against Kaspar Hauser.

*

Let us now return to the question: Did a meeting of the State Council take place on the 30th March and what was its object?

Dr. Otto Mittelstädt, the Imperial Public Prosecutor commissioned by the House of Baden who then, as he himself writes, enjoyed the full support of the grand ducal archival authorities, was not in the deputation nor did he address the State or Crown Council. The same applied to van der Linde, who merely allowed himself a short polemical remark about it. It can therefore be surmised that in fact the decisive question was put to the Grand Duke, either during a regular formal meeting of the State Council or Council of Ministers or at the fringes of such a meeting, or during a meeting with a delegation of concerned parliamentarians. That a meeting at first denied many times really did take place was first admitted very late, only in 1926, by the Director of the Baden Archives and Privy Councillor Karl Obser:

> The only meeting of the State Council which took place on that day, *as I additionally confirm* [emphasis, Obser] concerned itself solely with measures that had to do most directly with the succession: the notification of letters patent, the recall of those on leave, the renewing of the army's oath of allegiance, and the dispatch of dragoons to the Tauber district, the last of which was then dispensed with.

From this it can be stated once and for all that a meeting *did in fact* take place, which the extremely competent Obser calls a *State Council meeting*.

However, the year before—1925—in his 'Memoirs', Baden envoy Eugen von Jagemann, referring to excellent sources, describes this very meeting as an audacious fabrication, and quite unnecessary as 'the transition [occurred] calmly and promptly'. According to Obser, the denial of the meeting would be an audacious fabrication and the partial mobilisation of the military the opposite of a calm transition.[212] Van der Linde goes into this in more detail on p.142 of his 'Book 3': 'Seiler does not once mention Seybold's State Council meeting that was hardly sufficient for a theatrical farce.' He is here referring to this chapter of Baden's history that has yet to be completely clarified.

Now we first need to be clear that the sorry effort of Friedrich Seybold referred to here —*Kaspar Hauser, oder der Findling* ['Kaspar Hauser or the Foundling'] (Fig. 106) was published in Stuttgart in 1834 as a novel, and its subtitle—*A Romantic representation by* * * * indicates that the author preferred, or was forced, to remain anonymous. Having just served a prison sentence, Seybold could certainly have reckoned on re-arrest. The style of the little book is unappealing. It is also correct that the State Council meeting described here for the first time was mentioned again in 1840 in modified form by F. Sebastian Seiler under the pseudonym N.E. Meesis [= Nemesis!—*Ed*.], in his book *Kaspar Hauser, der Thronerbe von Baden* ['Kaspar Hauser, the Heir to the Throne of Baden'] (republished 1845, 1847) and that Fischer von Karlsruhe took up the story again in a different form in 1883 in his *Kaspar Hauser—seine Lebensgeschichte und der Nachweis seiner fürstlichen Herkunft* ['Kaspar Hauser—the Story of his Life and the Evidence for his Princely Origins']. Finally, Alexander von Artin (who was actually Fischer) offered a further variation in his 1892 pamphlet *Kaspar Hauser—des Rätsel Lösung* [Kaspar Hauser—The Solution to the Riddle]. All these writings were republished several times and were always confiscated or their publishers punished with fines. (Figs.108, 109.)

For the sake of those connoisseurs of the story who like completion, it can be added that a friend of Friedrich Seybold in his youth, so not the author himself, had an affidavit written on the 22nd May 1883 to the effect that everything, especially the State Council meeting of 1830, had been pure fabrication on the part of Seybold, who had merely wished to indulge himself in a hoax.

Now despite numerous deficiencies, the writing of precisely this piece of text by Seybold presupposes knowledge that can hardly have been pure fabrication. It is likely that in writing the chapter which features the State Council, he had to hand a description of it by someone else, which Seybold put entirely into his own words and made the centrepiece of his novel. The person who revealed this statute-barred

Kaspar Hauser

oder

der Findling.

Romantisch dargestellt von ***.

Stuttgart

P. Balz'sche Buchhandlung.

1834.

Kaspar Hauser

der

Thronerbe von Baden.

L'édifice social du passé reposait sur trois colonnes : le prêtre, le roi, le bourreau !

Victor Hugo.

Paris.

1840.

106. *Cover page 'Kaspar Huser or the Foundling', romantically presented by *** [Friedrich Seybold].*

107. *Cover page 'Kaspar Hauser or the Heir to the Throne of Baden' by F. Sebastian Seiler.*

Coblenzer Anzeiger.

für

das Jahr 1840.

Hundert und achtzehnter Jahrgang.

Coblenz.

Redigirt und verlegt von C. Doetsch, Besitzer der Krabben'schen Buchdruckerei.

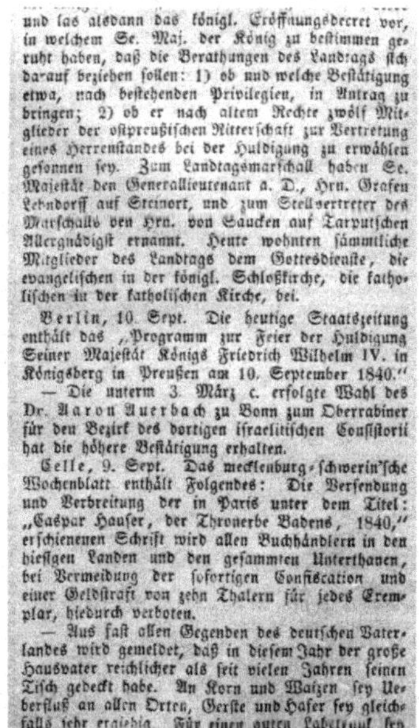

und las alsdann das königl. Eröffnungsdecret vor, in welchem Se. Maj. der König zu bestimmen ge- ruht haben, daß die Berathungen des Landtags sich darauf beziehen sollen: 1) ob und welche Bestätigung etwa, nach bestehenden Privilegien, in Antrag zu bringen; 2) ob er nach altem Rechte zwölf Mit- glieder der ostpreußischen Ritterschaft zur Vertretung eines Herrenstandes bei der Huldigung zu erwählen gesonnen sey. Zum Landtagsmarschall haben Se. Majestät den Generallieutenant a. D., Hrn. Grafen Lehndorff auf Steinort, und zum Stellvertreter des Marschalls den Hrn. von Saucken auf Tarputschen Allergnädigst ernannt. Heute wohnten sämmtliche Mitglieder des Landtags dem Gottesdienste, die evangelischen in der königl. Schloßkirche, die katho- lischen in der katholischen Kirche, bei.

Berlin, 10. Sept. Die heutige Staatszeitung enthält das „Programm zur Feier der Huldigung Seiner Majestät Königs Friedrich Wilhelm IV. in Königsberg in Preußen am 10. September 1840."

— Die unterm 3. März c. erfolgte Wahl des Dr. Aaron Auerbach zu Bonn zum Oberrabiner für den Bezirk des dortigen israelitischen Consistorii hat die höhere Bestätigung erhalten.

Celle, 9. Sept. Das mecklenburg-schwerin'sche Wochenblatt enthält Folgendes: Die Versendung und Verbreitung der in Paris unter dem Titel: „Caspar Hauser, der Thronerbe Badens, 1840," erschienenen Schrift wird allen Buchhändlern in den hiesigen Landen und den gesammten Unterthanen, bei Vermeidung der sofortigen Confiscation und einer Geldstraft von zehn Thalern für jedes Exem- plar, hiedurch verboten.

— Aus fast allen Gegenden des deutschen Vater- landes wird gemeldet, daß in diesem Jahr der große Hausvater reichlicher als seit vielen Jahren seinen Tisch gedeckt habe. An Korn und Waizen sey Ue- berfluß an allen Orten, Gerste und Hafer sey gleich- falls sehr ergiebig. Für einen guten Labetrunk sey am Rhein und Main auch gesorgt und am Nach-

108/109. Coblenzer Anzeiger *for the year 1840 with the prohibition banning booksellers from selling the book 'Kaspar Hauser or the Heir to the Throne of Baden'.*

offence was Seybold's friend at the time and later a lawyer, J.F. Widmann in Stuttgart.[213]

Once aware of this, it is obvious that Widmann's later so-called remorseful confession can be seen in a different light. When for example in 1883 the dispute between Dr. Julius Meyer —the son of Kaspar Hauser's Ansbach teacher—and the publisher Coppenrath over Fischer von Karlsruhe's writing which was based on Seybold came before Regensburg county court, Eugen von Jagemann, who was already versed in the Kaspar Hauser Question, obtained this witnessed legal interpretation at the instigation of the government of Baden and with it was able to show that Fischer's text was an absurdity. In his statement, documented by Herr Bauer, the judicial representative of the Kingdom of Württemberg, Widmann declared variously not less than four times that Seybold had quite definitely possessed no *actual* sources and that it had all been the result of his creative imagination.[214] So that was what it was all about!

Instead of already overdue research in the archives and the publication of resulting documentation, this requested, if not to say conjured up, explanation was seen to be necessary. This remained, as in the case of van der Linde, a very weak point in the plaintiff's case, which nevertheless enjoyed the highest levels of protection through the support of the Ministry in Karlsruhe, as the employment of the Baden envoy von Jagemann shows. But this was not enough—in an atmosphere of tense public expectation, the *Strassburger Post* stated on 17.4.1883 that 'as reported, the government of the Grand Duchy of Baden, at the request of the plaintiff, has put at the disposal of the court the relevant documents in the Kaspar Hauser story'. When the court case was over, Grand Duke Friedrich I sent the lawyer Hänle a superbly framed large photograph of himself, together with some 'extremely obliging written comments'. Hänle, who had not been able to give an incisive clarification on a single point of the Kaspar Hauser Question, had represented Meyer in a libel case, not the Grand Duke. The question arises as to what could have moved Friedrich I to show his thanks in this manner and what was the reason for this gesture from his side?

A clear analysis of the factual substance of the Baden defence shows the whole event to have been a rare and very insubstantial farce. Not a single sheet of paper appeared of the Kaspar Hauser documents during the trial, only Jagemann's transparent action to procure them. At a time when the case could have been clarified by an independent court, Karlsruhe missed an opportunity to achieve ultimate victory that was unlikely to be repeated! Or was it impossible to enter into a serious examination of the actual heart of the matter, and was there consequently no presentable evidence that could exonerate the grand ducal house? An alternative conclusion is scarcely imaginable. This is substantiated by a contemporary who a few years before had already tried to bring some light into an affair that was hard to penetrate. Fully ten years before the awkward legal battle, the Berlin scholar and known historian Professor Dr. William Pierson tried to grapple with the subject. In March 1872, he wrote to Gottlieb von Tucher,

> I too am of the opinion that the position of the government of Baden is suspicious. In its archives at Karlsruhe there are whole stacks of documents about the Hauser case; it has also until very recently been receiving threatening and blackmail letters; at the same time, it does not want to satisfy the requests of a scholar for documentary material with a view to solving the riddle, but rather rejects such an attempt with the comment: why bother to rake up this irrelevant and silly old story? This at least was what I was told by the Baden ambassador here (von Türckheim) when last spring I put that request to him verbally after he had failed to reply to my letter.[215]

What motive was there in Karlsruhe for rejecting the requests of a historian, if everything was in order and the whole affair was a 'fairy tale' ?

*

Common to all the named texts is the fact that they had their actual midpoint and high points in the meeting of the 'State Council' in order to play out similar scenes. In accordance with their literary claims and abilities, the authors appear here in pseudo-historical or, as in the previous case, in a purely novelesque mode without any recognisably scientific pretensions. But in one place, they all share almost identical passages: in the so-called 'Meeting Report' of the State Council. This raises the question: did Seybold possess a model for his description of the meeting? If one looks at the rest of the background story in its simple diction, the relatively weighty section about the meeting stands out, and is stylistically and especially in terms of its content distinct from the characteristic naivety of the rest.[216]

If the content of the State Council meeting could for a long time only be handled speculatively, there is now a basis on which it can be discussed, because a text was discovered which serves as a model. It even suggests that a copy of the 'draft of the memorandum' which, through an indiscretion, came into the hands of the former officer Seybold, who belonged to the liberal Opposition, was the single point of departure for the entire novel. Seybold, dismissed from military service on account of his convictions was forced to sit out a few months in the Fortress of Asperg, where he may have put to use the documents that had been passed onto him.

The copy of the account of the meeting, which will now be quoted, was originally in the possession of one of the participants in the State Council meeting, Baron Franz Karl Julius Rüdt-von Collenberg (1789–1860), grand ducal chamberlain, State Councillor,[217] second vice-President of the Upper Chamber of the Assembly of the Estates and former President of the Ministry of the Interior. Through inheritance it belongs to the present owner to whom Golo Mann wrote, amongst other things, about the document: 'It is indeed of great interest. Its origin also lends it the weight of probability.'

Rüdt-von Collenberg's great-granddaughter made a copy of the original which was written by her ancestor and added at the second paragraph a significant sentence to the accompanying lines: 'My great grandfather von Rüdt was also present.' Further, the memorandum was first written down after the death of Kaspar Hauser, probably under the impression of his having been murdered, and thus three years after the State Council meeting. The original text, reproduced here for the first time, and which, incidentally, appears in none of the variations in the works mentioned earlier in a complete or syntactically comparable form, reads as follows:

> On the 30th March 1830 at 3.45 a.m. Grand Duke Ludwig died in his 68th year. With him, the old line of the Zähringers came to an end. The consternation felt by all those who had to do with the affair was great.
>
> The Privy Council assembled that same night in Karlsruhe to discuss the question of the succession. The secret State documents relating to the Hauser affair were still extant and disappeared only after the death of Kaspar Hauser. A secretary, Hacker [see p. 293], removed them, made indiscreet use of them and concealed them abroad. The Foreign Minister, Baron von Berstett chaired the meeting. All the Ministers (also my great-grandfather von Rüdt) were present (except for Herr von Berckheim). Grand Duke Leopold also took part in this meeting. Privy Councillor Enggesser and Major Hennenhofer had been ordered to wait in the adjoining room; they were regarded as under arrest by Minister von Böckh and Lieutenant-General von Schäffer.

Before the heir to the throne appeared, Minister von Berstett opened the meeting and said: 'You know, gentlemen, that a legitimate heir lives, who in a criminal manner has been robbed of his succession in the Grand Duchy. The most convincing evidence exists that participants in and accessories to this crime are still alive, whose statements will add amply to what is missing. The reigning Grand Duke has departed this life and it is now a question of who is to succeed him. The legitimate heir is not here. He is a youth ruined in mind and body. An interruption in the succession would be damaging to the ruling family and to the country. It is a pressing situation and must be handled with all the wisdom at the disposal of the State.'

The assembled were sitting there in silent consternation when the door opened and Grand Duke Leopold came in. The Privy Council stood, and the Prince walked to the upper end of the table and spoke the following words: 'The President will have presented you with the state of things as they are. It would be superfluous for me to express to you my pain over the distressing facts. I vouch to you for my character that I have firmly decided never ever to take away from my relative the rights which are his due by birth. The question now is how that could happen without disadvantageous consequences for the country in the short-term. This will be the object of your deliberations.'

[Note by Rüdt-von Collenberg: from the legal point of view, it would have been right in a constitutional state like Baden, to inform the people's representatives of the crime, and leave it to them to establish a guardian's regency.]

The hearing began of the two persons under arrest. The President first had Privy Councillor Enggesser come in and put to him the following question:

—'Did you know about the crime committed against the legitimate heir to the Grand Duchy?'

'Yes, but only after it had begun and could no longer be stopped!'

—'Why did you not inform the legal authorities?'

'The Privy State Council? How could I? The Grand Duke was the chairman. What evidence would I have had, if I had dared to challenge the most powerful man in the State, and in what conceivable situation would I have put the grand ducal family and the country? My considered duty required me to stay silent. My conscience told me that I had nothing for which to reproach myself and I confidently await your judgement!'

The President wished Enggesser well and expressed his satisfaction that he had cleared himself of strong suspicion.

[Note by Rüdt-von Collenberg: It must be said further in Enggesser's defence that he had found himself in a very precarious position and if he had informed, he would have had to fear for his life. Nevertheless, he ought not to have enabled the crime to continue for twelve years. The State Council—(and Leopold)—this addition was made by my mother!—did nothing after this hearing to improve the situation of the unfortunate Kaspar Hauser and thereby condoned the crime!]

The hearing continued. Hennenhofer was allowed in and stepped forward quietly, casting a scornful look on those assembled.

The President addressed the following question to him:

—'Do you know of an individual who has recently appeared in Nuremberg by the name of Kaspar Hauser?

'Of course, I know of this person, and you also appear to know of him. This individual is, to put it in other words, your legitimate sovereign, who was robbed of his throne and is the son of the widowed Grand Duchess Stéphanie. What else do you wish to know?'

—'You speak with such certainty about a great crime committed against this person. You must surely know more about this crime?'

'Certainly, no-one is better acquainted with the details than me.'

—'Did you then also take part in the crime?'

'You call it a crime? That is a peculiar term for what was merely a coup d'état of the kind that has occurred thousands of times before. That is what our Grand Duke of blessed memory did; it is quite natural that he required assistance to do it, and I had the honour of possessing my prince's trust. That was not a crime, but a well-justified coup d'état. Would you care to know more?'

—'If you are seeking to improve your invidious position by impudence, you would be making a big mistake!'

'Herr Minister, my position is not so bad, but actually good. If you believe that I am afraid, then you will be disappointed. If the Privy Council were as little embarrassed as I am in seeking to extricate itself from this bad business, then it could congratulate itself!'

—'A citizen who knows his duty and stands on the side of justice cannot be in doubt as to what he should do!'

'If that is the case, then let justice take its course! Put the Grand Duke's corpse on trial and bury it under the gallows instead of in the State church. Declare to the Grand Duke here present that his throne is forfeit and send a deputation to Nuremberg so you can put on the throne the legitimate heir, who is crippled in mind and body. Suspend the oath of allegiance, at the risk of giving it to foreigners—then and then only can you put me on trial!'

—'These steps are not needed to punish you for this crime. You have been arrested and have confessed, and that is enough to apply legal sanction against you!'

'Herr Minister, you cannot hope to frighten me with empty words. You will not be able to advance things so far. Excellency, I know better how they stand. The reputation of the deceased Grand Duke, the dignity of the grand ducal family, the future of the country, will not be put at risk merely in order to punish me. Do you believe that I would spare anyone if I were put on trial?'

Silence from the President and general embarrassment. After this short silence, the Grand Duke moved toward Hennenhofer and said to him in a contemptuous tone:

'You are a wretched person. You are right that the memory of the blessed Grand Duke, who unfortunately was weak and in bad hands, will not be besmirched, and still less will the future of the grand ducal family and of the country be put in danger because of you. None of this is necessary to give you the punishment you deserve. In such a case, where it is a matter of the welfare of the country, it will be for the State Council, with my assent, to take upon itself to depart from the normal process of the law. In order to bring you under control, you will be taken from here to a prison where your mouth will be shut for the rest of your life.'

Without hesitation Hennenhofer retorted:

'Do you think so, gracious Prince? We shall see! Obviously, princes are easily led astray, the victims of their environment. They are simply weak, and all their sins are loaded onto the shoulders of their instruments. But that does not disturb me. I know that one must oneself be depraved in order to seek out and find instruments and collaborators for one's depravity. I do not want to make myself seem better than I am, but who reaped the fruits of his coup? I should pay so that the name of the family is not branded? I am not so stupid. I am to be thrown into a lonely cell and my mouth shut for an eternity—without a trial, I am to be locked up like Kaspar Hauser? Which of these gentlemen will put out his hand to commit such a crime? You would in any case be powerfully mistaken, for I have been intelligent enough to plan for all eventualities. Secure arrangements have been made to publish the whole sordid story if I am subjected even to the slightest harm. Now bury me in a prison cell if you wish. I have nothing more to say.'

The Council President took the Grand Duke and Lt. Gen. von Schäffer to one side. The latter ordered Hennenhofer to leave the room and for the time being to return home under house arrest; the sword which he had had to surrender on entering the room was handed back to him. He left with a scornful and triumphant look around the room and before he returned home, he had nothing better to do than to go to the Margrave's palace and make a report to Margrave Wilhelm on the whole proceedings.

That meeting of the State Council went on for half the night, and the result was that in the morning the following proclamation was issued:

'I, Leopold, by the Grace of God, Duke of Zähringen etc. herewith do declare: Almighty God has seen fit to recall to His bosom the Most Excellent Prince and Lord, Ludwig, Grand Duke of Baden and Duke of Zähringen, Our most profoundly honoured brother and gracious Royal Highness, early this morning at 3.42 and thereby to bring Us, Our House and the whole country into a state of the greatest sorrow. Through this unforeseen event, the government is, by the power of the Basic Laws of Our House and of the country, transferred to Us and We have already embarked thereupon. We declare this to Our Subjects of every rank and at the same time command them, in accordance with the duties of allegiance which they have already assumed, and which now are owed to Us, to be just as well-disposed and prepared to be as obedient to the existing and future laws and ordinances as they were to Our Lord Brother and gracious Royal Highness and His legal ordinances. We hereby confirm Our strong Will to hold sacred the Constitution of the Land, to promote its welfare with all possible means, to give powerful protection to each and all in their dignities and offices, and We expressly acknowledge this especially to Our Servants in the areas of activity entrusted to them. Given under Our Signature and under the Seal of State in Our Capital and Resident City of Karlsruhe the 30th March 1830 Leopold.

Signed: Baron von Berstett by Command of His Royal Highness
Signed: Eichrot'

*

How reliable is this written memorandum, which may certainly not be termed, as is occasionally the case, a protocol (see also n. 212), but which describes a process that happened essentially as portrayed? It must definitely have been written in the spring of 1834, because it mentions the death of Kaspar Hauser, and also Seybold's book appeared in the same year. In this fact lies the strongest evidence for the participation of Rüdt-von Collenberg because at the beginning of 1834 hardly a single contemporary would have such a remarkable knowledge of

Hacker, Enggesser and Hennenhofer as the author of this document. No-one else in the spring of 1834 would have known of Hacker's misappropriation of documents, Enggesser's complex role and the name of Hennenhofer, all in this special connection to Kaspar Hauser. Certainly, later in the same year Garnier's tract appeared that has already been referred to, in which the very names Enggesser and Hennenhofer were mentioned, but which did not present such detailed remarks as Seybold's extract. More generally held suspicions could be deduced from the known bad reputation of Ludwig's adjutant [Hennenhofer] and from the essays in *Hochwächter* of 8th and 9th June 1831, which had led to Hennenhofer's dismissal a few years before but which had shown no direct link to the Kaspar Hauser Question. More accurate information about Hennenhofer, which can confirm the meeting of the 30th March 1830 retrospectively, all comes from later periods. The publication of documents by Dr. Joseph Schauberg (Fig. 110) in the case of the murder of the student Ludwig Lessing in 1837; the blackmail letters to Countess Langenstein were first published by Karl Birner in 1927; Baron von Varnbühler's eyewitness report on the day of the murder in Ansbach in relation to Hennenhofer in the 'Memoirs' of Prince Philip

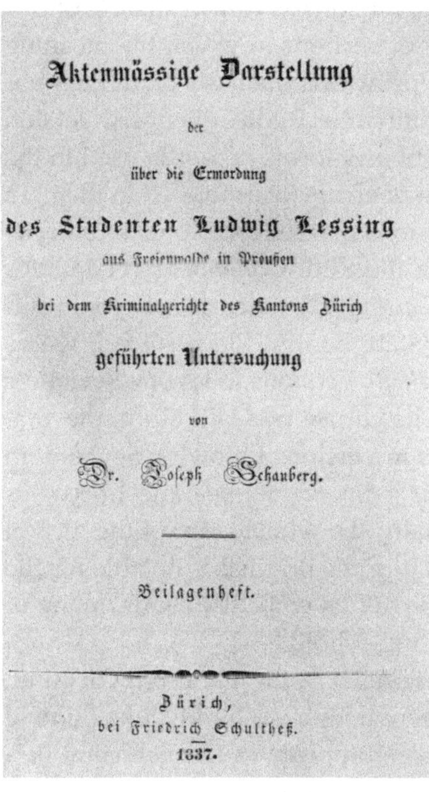

Aktenmässige Darstellung

der

über die Ermordung

des Studenten Ludwig Lessing

aus Freienwalde in Preußen

bei dem Kriminalgerichte des Kantons Zürich

geführten Untersuchung

von

Dr. Joseph Schauberg.

Beilagenheft.

Zürich,
bei Friedrich Schultheß.
1837.

110. Cover page 'Presentation with Documents of …the Investigation conducted into the Murder of the Student Ludwig Lessing'.

zu Eulenburg-Hertefeld appeared only in 1934. All the detailed knowledge about Hennenhofer's function and participation, which was necessary for an accurate assessment at the time, could hardly have been fabricated so well, but has only been available in recent times.

The possible objection that the text presented here may have been written later and based on the books that had been published, in other words plagiarised, can be answered by pointing out that apart from the provenance that has been secured, none of those pieces of text that could have betrayed the author Rüdt-Collenberg have turned up in any of the later versions. Before the unauthorised passing on of a copy of the original, they were apparently eliminated just like the mention of the secretary Hacker who had removed the documents and whose role has for a long time been insufficiently investigated.

The fact that Hacker's name appears in this and *only* this account is evidence once more of insights that only a highly placed and knowledgeable individual could have had. And the fact that he actually possessed the documents and had later offered them for sale to Duke Ernst of Sake-Colourg and Gotha, among others, was not even known in high aristocratic circles in 1834. On the other hand, errors that cropped up in copying and appeared in later versions as well as the use of certain sentences and whole passages or sections in which the meaning was distorted can show that a blueprint was the basis of all the published versions. In terms of credibility, the Rüdt-Collenberg version must take priority due to the content and forms of words used in the other versions as well as the system of errors incorporated in them. In Seybold and all the plagiarised versions that followed one finds copying errors absent in the original. In the Rüdt-Collenberg version, for example, there is: 'A citizen' [*Ein Staatsbürger]*, whereas in Seybold and all following versions one reads: 'State bodies' [*Staatskörper]*; where the text should read 'legally' [*gesetzlich*], versions following Seybold's superficiality have 'legitimately'. The corpse was laid out in the 'Staatskirche' [*State church*] and not, as in versions following Seybold, in the 'main town church' [*Stadtkirche*]; *Ansehen* [appearance] becomes *Andenken* [memory] and so on. Finally, the whole tenor of the diction is characteristic of the record, which in the original is notable for the absence of any exaggerations or garrulous embellishments, many of which, by contrast, are to be found in Seybold.[218]

Lastly, and obviously with the originator of the manuscript in mind, Seybold gave all the characters different names. Grand Duke Ludwig is Prince Ludwig Anton; Hennenhofer appears as Dangelmann. Berstett is given the name Burnitz; Grand Duke Leopold is Prince Franz, and Grand Duchess Stéphanie becomes the widowed Princess Eugenie. The others figure only as anonymous speakers, and they and their comments are represented only by 'the first', 'the second', or 'a fourth'.

One final detail may be mentioned which gives rise to a suggestive idea about the Rüdt-Collenberg record. The sharpest critics of publications, as we learn from the Forward to the second edition of Seiler's book, included members of the Rüdt-Collenberg family. Was there a connection between that extant record and the zeal to ensure that it did not become better-known?

When Grand Duke Leopold died in 1852, 'on his deathbed, he did not want to be separated from the picture [of Kaspar Hauser]'. This was later reported by Marie von Hamilton, sister of the nameless prince who had been born in Karlsruhe in 1812. In a long conversation in Baden-Baden in 1874 with Gottlieb von Tucher the Duchess explained further that Grand Duke Leopold 'had had Kaspar Hauser very much on his mind'. After this conversation—'the conversations in my three long visits to the Lady Duchess, which lasted nearly an hour each and revolved almost entirely around Kaspar Hauser'—Gottlieb von Tucher sent the Duchess a picture of Kaspar Hauser on the 23rd May 1875, receipt of which she confirmed two days later.

Soon afterwards, in the summer of the same year, she had a visit from Count Bogdan von Hutten-Czapski (1851–1936) during which, pointing to the garlanded picture of Kaspar Hauser, she said: 'That is Kaspar Hauser, my unhappy brother. My mother [Grand Duchess Stéphanie] and I were always convinced that he was my brother.'[219] On the 19th April 1875 Baroness Louise Belli di Pino—former companion of Stéphanie—visited the Duchess in Meidling near Vienna. From there she wrote to Gottlieb von Tucher on the 8th May: 'I said to Her Grace that I was convinced that he [Kaspar Hauser] had been the son of the Grand Duchess. She replied: "Mother died in that conviction! And I believe that he was my brother."'[220]

We know from other sources too that the Duchess took this statement very seriously. In 1926 Count Franz Folliot de Creneville-Poutet wrote to the Kaspar Hauser researcher Dr. Ludwig Wagler, who was at the time Commissioner of Police in Leipzig that the Duchess had shown 'the picture of "her brother" (Kaspar Hauser) that was on her desk' to his brother, the Legation Secretary of the Austrian Embassy in Stuttgart, which also handled affairs with Baden. It may have been more of a need on the part of the Duchess than a request of the diplomat.

Let us recall what has been said that described the actual position of a direct participant in that State Council meeting and let us cast our mind back to Leopold's hour of death, the picture of Kaspar Hauser in his hands. This event has been verified and there is no possibility of doubting it, so the question arises as to what caused Leopold's statement and his moving behaviour? Kaspar Hauser had been dead for 19 years yet only this picture of someone who had died through murder in the third year of Leopold's reign, meant anything to Leopold as he faced his own death. Did the Grand Duke feel that this deed was directly related to the State Council meeting of 30th March 1830 and with those questions of doubt which were also brought to him on that day by a particular member of the Baden parliament?

In Leopold's hour of death, when Kaspar Hauser once more appeared powerfully before the soul of the dying Prince, his family were present and they could not have failed to have asked the father what he wanted to see before he died—a last request. His firstborn son, Ludwig II, who turned out to be incapable of governing, later implored the Duchess of Hamilton that 'the story of Kaspar Hauser should be removed from his mind. Then he will be healthy.'

Five years after Leopold's death, his youngest daughter, Princess Cecilie, also a witness of his final hour, married Grand Prince Michael of Russia. Her only son from that marriage, Grand Prince Nikolai later fulfilled a bequest of his mother's and wrote a manuscript based on two excellent sources available to him at the time: the papers which Joséphine had passed to Czar Alexander I in 1814 and those which Grand Duke Friedrich I of Baden had put together on Kaspar Hauser.[221]

Baroness Luise von Reibnitz-Maltzahn, close friend of Grand Princess Anastasia, the sister of Grand Prince Nikolai, read the results of his research. In her 'Memoirs' she writes:

> He [Grand Prince Nikolai] was President of the Imperial Russian Society for History and a Member of the Institute of France, an honour which was given to him for the many historical and geographical works which he had published in French. The University of Berlin also recognised his scientific achievements and made him Dr. Phil. *honoris causa*.
>
> Mostly, he occupied himself with historical studies and memoirs ...As a sincere friendship bound the Grand Prince and myself, I was frequently able to hear him read from his works. At that time, at the end of the '90s, he was mainly interested in the story of Kaspar Hauser. In an incisive

> presentation, unfortunately unpublished, he showed that Kaspar Hauser was the Crown prince of Baden, that is, the eldest son and heir of Grand Duchess Stéphanie of Baden, born Beauharnais, the beautiful and cultured adopted daughter of Napoleon I. As the Grand Prince's mother was a princess of Baden, he certainly had at his disposal sources which were unavailable to other historians. I only knew of the manuscript...

This communication is supported in a similar way, though quite independently of Reibnitz-Maltzahn's memoirs, by Princess Cecilie of Prussia, daughter of Crown prince Wilhelm. Also with the House of Baden in mind, in her 'Memoirs', she tells of the 'unnatural deaths' of both of Stéphanie's sons:

> Uncle Nikolai was a .... great connoisseur of history. He could relate things from his studies in a most stimulating manner and in doing so, he awakened in me a great interest in history in general and in family history in particular. He also had a firm belief in Kaspar Hauser's princely origins about which he wrote a book (unpublished). Because of his close relationships to the House of Baden, he had access to the family archive.

One of the last surviving witnesses who knew the Grand Prince personally and who heard the story of Kaspar Hauser from his mouth is the Berlin doctor Wladimir Lindenberg (born Vladimir Alexandrovič Čelisčev, 1902), a scion of the legendary House of Rurik, which until the 16th century provided Russia with all its Grand Princes and Czars. Lindenberg knew the Czar's family and numerous members of the Russian aristocracy personally and at the beginning of the 20th century was frequently a guest at Court in St. Petersburg. 'We often spoke of Kaspar Hauser,' he assured the author in conversations in Berlin in 1986 and 1987, 'and we all knew that he was the Crown prince of Baden. No-one at Court had the slightest doubt that Kaspar Hauser was the legitimate heir to the throne of Baden.'

The evidence compiled by Grand Prince Nikolai was so convincing that Prince Max of Baden promised Nikolai in 1913 that 'he would make sure that right after his accession, Kaspar Hauser's remains would be brought to Pforzheim'. This plan was clearly related to a certainty that was felt widely among the people of Baden and was mentioned by the Kaspar Hauser researcher and jurist A. Bartning:

> I grew up in Karlsruhe, went to elementary school and high school there and heard an endless amount about Kaspar Hauser. As already men-

> tioned, the people of Baden, up to the highest levels of society, were convinced of Hauser's princely rank but harboured no ill-will against the ruling family. Grand Dukes Friedrich I and Friedrich II were so excellent and such generally popular princes that no hostility was ever directed against them. There was only a kind of theoretical opinion that things were like that once. I also know from the best sources of gentlemen whose profession made it necessary for them to appear frequently at Court that even a man as upright and irreproachable as Grand Duke Friedrich I would until his death become surprisingly nervous by mention of the Hauser question.[222]

Already a long time before—in 1889—Otto von Bismarck treated the tragedy of Kaspar Hauser as part of the dynastic history of Baden when he came to discuss the nationality issue in his *Gedanken und Erinnerungen* ['Reflections and Memories']. Finally, in this connection, Empress Elisabeth of Austria (1837–1898), through her mother Ludovika of Bavaria (1808–1892), most certainly had access to special knowledge of the Kaspar Hauser Question. When she received the news of the death of Prince Ludwig of Baden (1824–58) she said the following about his premature passing: '...the House of Baden will die out because it came to power through the crime against Kaspar Hauser...' She could not have made such a remark without knowledge of what had happened, knowledge shared no less by Queen Victoria of England: 'When Grand Duke Friedrich of Baden married Princess Luise of Prussia, Queen Victoria of England spoke to King Wilhelm, the later Kaiser, of her displeasure that he should link his daughter with a family which all held accountable for the murder of one of their number.' (Friedrich Wencker-Wildberg)

After the death of Grand Duke Leopold, the Austrian ambassador at the Karlsruhe Court, Baron von Philippsburg wrote in a report to his superior, Minister Count Karl Ferdinand Buol-Schauenstein (1797–1865) on the 7th December 1853:

> ...Already a number of times before and again quite recently, a well-known person came to speak to me about certain secret papers that Grand Duke Leopold had handed to this man, his confidant, in a metal box shortly before his death with the command to give them [to]* someone in his family; these papers concerned the life and death of Kaspar Hauser and were for the most part taken from the papers of Major Hennenhofer. Notably they included very compromising letters from an

> apothecary's apprentice named Sauler [should read Seyler—*Mayer*], who lived near Major Hennenhofer's residence, but on the left bank of the Rhine, in Alsace. The letters make clear that eight days before the murder, Herr Sauler went to Ansbach, and after the catastrophe they speak constantly of pangs of conscience and of his father's curse. The point is then always blackmail demands for money or rather, demands to keep to stipulated conditions under threat of publication of the whole affair, since Herr Hennenhofer's finances were ruined in his last years.
>
> [*Nb. the German has : '...dieselben *an* irgend jemand in seiner Familie zu geben.' Johannes Mayer notes: This *'an'* should be read *'nie'* (never), which would mean that it was precisely the Grand Duke's family who should *not* receive the papers. This is cited erroneously in Pies and Sittenberger etc.].
>
> Grand Duke Leopold must often have spoken with horror to this confidant about a crime which had probably occurred in his family and must have averred that no blame attached to him so that he could accede to the throne with a clean conscience. The explanation that one would be inclined to give is that a crime was committed against the sons of Grand Duke Carl [*sic*], which was arranged by the Countess Hochberg and in collaboration with Grand Duke Ludwig and Major Hennenhofer. The murders of a bodyguard in Vienna and of a Court chamberlain's servant in Karlsruhe are connected with this crime.
>
> Until the spring of this year, only the Duke of Coburg, brother-in-law of the Regent, seems to have learned of the existence of the papers in the metal box by some means or other, at least he swore to get hold of them.[223]

This he evidently did not manage to do; nevertheless, the existence of the metal box, though sometimes doubted, is confirmed by a first class witness. Duchess Alexandrine herself (1820–1904) speaks of the papers. She was the eldest sister of Grand Duke Friedrich of Baden, and from 1842 the wife of Duke Ernst II (1818–1893) of Saxe-Coburg-Gotha. Her father had told his confidant about the box in the way it is described in the ambassador's report.

'The duchess,' writes Walther P. Fuchs in his informative researches on Friedrich I,[223a]

> said namely that a secretary, Hacker [see pp. 282 & 287], who had died long before, had in 1852 when her father, Grand Duke Leopold, was 'on the verge of death', offered her husband Duke Ernst papers relating

to Hauser—as she had first learned much later—which were kept in a metal box in the Grand Duke's bedchamber. The offer was of course refused. She had never seen the papers themselves nor did she know what had become of them. The duchess wrote to her brother [Grand Duke Friedrich I]: 'Why should he who brought K[aspar] H[auser] such a sad fate [i.e. Leopold] not have entrusted his secret to the House of a Regent so that it could be passed on from one Grand Duke to another; for we cannot possibly believe that K[aspar] H[auser] was a fraud; but he must have behaved out of character from time to time. There must have been a secret about his person and his life which made him dangerous for someone or other; why else would the defenceless foundling have been murdered when he began to become a human being? I really do not understand why it has never occurred to all of us to discuss this subject.'

Such a discussion would have been instructive. Although posterity was not entrusted with any papers, so much information has already become available through family traditions, and that would have been possible especially through the House of Coburg. Prince Leopold of Saxe-Coburg (1790–1865), the later King Leopold I of Belgium had, as already mentioned, been the confidant and relative of Czar Alexander and as such, in 1814 he arranged the Czar's first meeting with Joséphine in Malmaison. He knew the Empress, had met Napoleon in 1808 at Erfurt and had there got to know Stéphanie, who was present at the congress of princes. From the prince's special position, it may be assumed that he heard from the Czar about the careworn conversations [with Joséphine] relating to the House of Baden and especially the unusual 'death' of the infant Crown prince.

Due to hopeless state indebtedness, the House of Coburg with its many children lived in circumstances of near poverty in those days, and especially in view of its many princesses, had to be on the lookout for parties who could help. Victoire, the youngest of the four daughters, married Duke Edward of Kent and thereby became the mother of Queen Victoria who married her Coburg cousin Albert in 1840. Against this background, the Queen's statements and judgements in the Kaspar Hauser Question (p. 292) are of extra significance, as they were doubtless based on Coburg sources. Princess Juliane, after her marriage Anna Feodorova, married Grand Prince Konstantin (1779–1831) in 1795, the brother of Czar Alexander I. The Czar thus became brother-in-law to the Coburg princes Ernst, Leopold and Ferdinand, and as a result, Ernst was accepted into the Russian officer corps. At 17, he was named General of the Guards. Leopold, only five, could only become a Guards cadet at first, and Ferdinand had not yet been born. In later years, Leopold especially achieved great success as an officer and rose to the pinnacle of the Russian army at the battles of Lützen, Bautzen and above all at Leipzig, where he was in charge of covering the entire central section. In 1814 he was with the allied troops when they entered Paris, and shortly afterwards, the Czar entrusted the prince with the mission of making contact with Joséphine.

Then Alexander travelled with Leopold to London, where the prince married soon afterwards the heir to the British throne, Charlotte Augusta. Alexander returned to Vienna without him and at the beginning of the Congress of Vienna met up with the brothers Leopold and Ferdinand, who, together with the Czar and the King of Prussia, made a splendid entrance at the Congress. After a successful command in the Austrian army, Ferdinand became a respected and widely regarded personality in Vienna. There in 1816 he married Antonie von Kohary, daughter and heiress of the wealthy Hungarian Prince Joseph von Kohary. Is it only a harmless coincidence or a helpful indicator that a few years later—in 1822—Stanhope took the young couple's personal chef into his service? Such servants usually knew more about their masters than the latter suspected.

But to return to the Congress of Vienna, Duke Ernst I (1784–1844), who at one point in the territorial negotiations was also offered the Rhenish left-bank region claimed by Baden, may have taken a special interest in Joséphine's suspicions reported by Alexander and Ernst's brother Leopold, who was heavily involved in those negotiations. The Czar guaranteed the Palatinate for Grand Duke Karl of Baden, but also gave decisive assistance to Ernst, from which it is clear that Alexander had two dynastic protegés: Baden and Coburg. This explains the continuous interest of the two Houses in the Kaspar Hauser case.

This background also explains why it was the wish of Duke Ernst I of Saxe-Coburg (Gotha from 1826) to ask Kaspar Hauser for a conversation when, with Lieutenant Hickel, Hauser travelled through Gotha during the Königsheim case. We do not know the details of their conversation on the 20th January 1833, but we do know to what judgement it led. The duchess expressed it when she wrote: 'we cannot possibly believe that Kaspar Hauser was a fraud'. In the *Fränkischen Zeitung* (No. 278) of 1.10.1924, Dr. O. Beyer shows that this perception was shared by following generations of Coburgs. He refers there to a conversation with a 'prominent member of the House of Coburg' in which he was literally assured that 'Kaspar Hauser's origins were no legend, and the Countess Hochberg had achieved her goal'.

As already mentioned, the Secretary Hacker is also named in Rüdt-Collenberg's record as the one who had caused 'the secret State documents in the Kaspar Hauser affair' to disappear in order to use them for the purposes of 'indiscretions'. These papers and those in Grand Duke Leopold's box cannot have been identical. It is also hardly necessary to ask whether Hacker had abused the trust placed in him in that, instead of handing the papers over to the Duke of Coburg as he was supposed to, he offered them for sale. Whether parts or the whole of that bundle made up the writings which Napoleon III later acquired from Hennenhofer must remain open to question. Hennenhofer may certainly also have supplied his own materials. Duke Ernst II described himself several times as a personal friend of Napoleon III. Did he himself decline the purchase and direct Hennenhofer to Paris?

At any rate, it is clear from these family traditions there were papers which could have clarified Kaspar Hauser's origins.

A look ahead at the *last* days of Leopold of Baden and the period thereafter appears necessary at this point, because they stand in an illuminating relationship to the *first* days of his reign. But the basic problem was the existence of Kaspar Hauser as the possible prince of Baden and a Napoleonid and in 1830 that problem was still there; the apparently unchallenged accession of Leopold had brought no clarification on that score—on the contrary. Because those responsible had officially suppressed the admonitory facts and questions and perhaps could have done nothing else, it became established in a risky fashion that the old Zähringer line had finally died out. With an inevitability and an increasing urgency the new situation in 1830 provoked action, for at least in the view of Stanhope, Vienna and Baden—especially Grand Duchess Sophie—nothing had basically changed. The old question remained the same and was still unresolved. This insight would be kept in mind by Stanhope and his circle in the following year of 1831.

11. Negotiating Adoption

Stanhope becomes the foster father, 1831

In February 1831 the Cabinets in Vienna and Berlin received some correspondence which actually dated back ten years earlier but which was deliberately brought into play just at this point. It was known to Duchess Auguste von Leuchtenberg, who referred to a letter she had received from Rome on 27.1.1831 from Hortense Bonaparte. In it, Hortense mentioned a secret agreement that Louis Philippe, the reigning King of France, had proposed to Eugène Beauharnais in 1821. Through this secret treaty, Duke Philip of Orléans, then living in exile in London, wanted to secure his political future. Should fortune favour either of the two parties in a new revolution (which took place in 1830), in other words, should either of them become ruler of France, he would leave the door of return to France open for the other. It is significant that Duke Eugène, who was well-regarded in his homeland and certainly considered capable of ruling, did not go along with the deal. If a new situation were to be created in a revolution which helped him—Eugène Beauharnais—to power, then the crown should by rights go solely to Napoleon's son, the Duke of Reichstadt, and Beauharnais would acknowledge only him as Napoleon II.

The correspondence went back ten years, as mentioned, and meanwhile, not Reichstadt but the Duke of Orléans now sat on the throne of France. As sovereign, he was little respected either by the French people or by friendly governments, so the communication from Hortense Bonaparte, put forward just at this time, must have given food for thought. The serious possibility of bringing about a favourable change in the situation could hardly have pressed itself more strongly on Metternich, Gentz and therefore also Stanhope.

The detailed conclusions Metternich drew from this information are well-known. The Duke of Reichstadt died within the year. The main cause of his death was not so much the often-cited chill he caught, which was only the final symptom of an inner crisis, but rather the circumstances of his life, which were prescribed by Metternich and which robbed him first of his psychological and finally of his physical health. Contingency plans would also have to be developed for Stéphanie's son in view of the possible failure of existing arrangements. Stanhope now turned his attention to just such a task.

111. Philip Henry, 4th Earl Stanhope (1781–1855)

When he (Fig. 111) again set out for Germany, this time already on the 29th April, it was with the intention of taking control of particular matters in the case of the foundling. After an eight-day stopover—once more again in Frankfurt from the 14th–22nd May, he arrived in Nuremberg on the 26th of the month, exactly three years after Hauser's appearance in the city, and got straight on the case. With reference to his servant Anton Heinrich, Stanhope's diary for the 17th May has the entry: 'repairing pistols'. First, he bought some 'Pamphlets relating to Kaspar Hauser' for 2 guilders 6 kreuzer and wrote a letter to the banker Merkel, whose prompt reply of the 27th, with its reference to the coming meeting with Kaspar Hauser on the 28th and its lack of any surprise over Stanhope's sudden appearance, gives an indication of what was being planned.

'I have the honour of informing Your Excellency that Mayor Binder will be awaiting your visit at two o'clock tomorrow afternoon, and I shall collect you for this purpose at your lodgings. You will find Kaspar Hauser with Mayor Binder, so further applications to Baron Tucher will be unnecessary. I have the honour respectfully to remain Your Excellency's most obedient servant Merkel 27 May 1831.'[224]

Within 24 hours the course had been set by means of a well thought-through plan without raising a single suspicion. The whole thing could hardly have been the result of a sudden insight Stanhope had first had there on the spot. Merkel's letter therefore needs to be read carefully to see what the writer and the one making the request (Stanhope) were up to. It was generally known that Tucher (Fig.112) went so far to protect Hauser as to keep all disturbing visitors away from him for pedagogical and health reasons. It was therefore impossible to get to Kaspar, who since the attempt on his life had been constantly guarded by two armed policemen. Merkel got round this obstacle in a most cunning manner by arranging a harmless meeting at the Mayor's luncheon table, which Tucher, who had no idea of Stanhope's presence, would otherwise have had to regard with the utmost seriousness. Any concern by the very alert Tucher was thus avoided by this splendid manoeuvre, so that from the very first day, Stanhope could make the most of this unhappy moment. Further 'applications' to Baron Tucher were from then on unnecessary.

112. Gottlieb, Baron von Tucher (1798–1877)

113. Jakob Friedrich Binder (1787–1856). Lithograph by A. Weber from a portrait by F. Hahn.

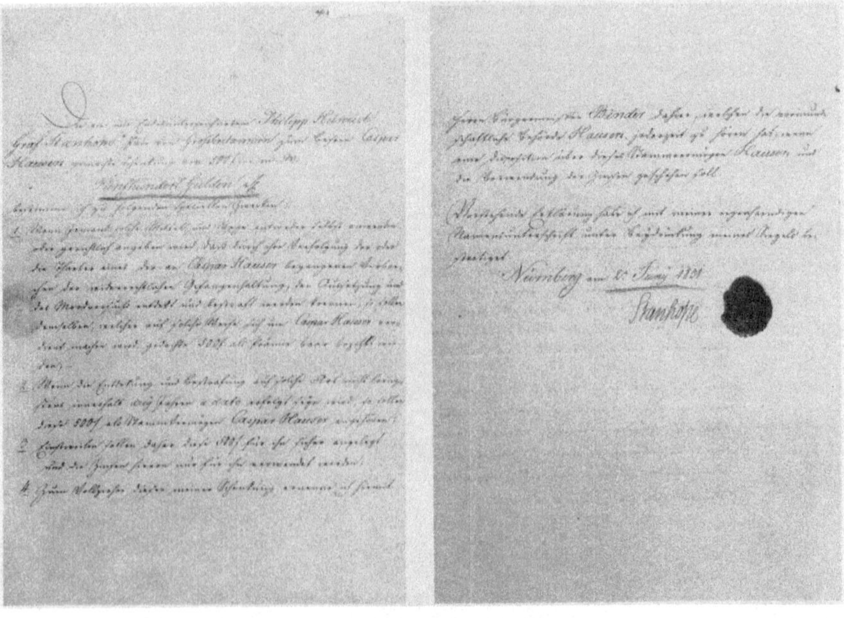

114. Deed of gift of 500 guilders 'for the welfare of Kaspar Hauser', drawn up on 2 June 1831 by Lord Stanhope.

For successfully arranging the meeting, Stanhope thanked Merkel the same day with the present of a book. It seems that from now on, not a moment was lost in progressing towards the final goal. The question now was, how could it be brought about, practically under the noses of the public, that the foundling would be handed over to the travelling Englishman who just 'happened' to be passing through Nuremberg, and indeed handed over more or less unconditionally and permanently?

After Binder (Fig.113) had announced to the world that '...the community [of Nuremberg], which has taken him to their bosom, loves him and regards him as a pledge of love sent to them by Providence, which they will not step back from without full evidence of the claims made on him by others'. The chances of substantiating such claims or at least something similar must have been ranked very slim, especially for a foreigner. To do so required the appearance of a personality who possessed the essential qualities necessary for the task. Stanhope thus first had to show himself very moved by the fate of the boy and then to establish a relationship that would seem out of the ordinary, even destined so as to be able to recommend himself convincingly and credibly as the only possible foster father, who above all would spare no expense to clear up the matter of the crime—and finally, he would have to give evidence that he possessed the means to sustain such an undertaking.

With skill and energy Stanhope represented himself as just what was required—an exemplary man of the rarest humanity and at the same time one of the greatest earthly wealth and thereby, he won the first and most decisive round of the negotiations. Binder, the good and homely man, was no match for him. On the same day the first magnanimous deed was decided on and carried out the day after.

> Dear Messrs. Lödel and Merkel
> Be so good as to pay against this order 500 guilders to Mayor Binder, which he will use for Kaspar Hauser.
> Nuremberg, 29th May 1831 Stanhope.

Three days later on the 2nd June, Stanhope signed the deed of gift 'for the welfare of Caspar Hauser' (Fig. 114). To make a good impression on Kaspar himself, the wealthy Peer thought of something special. For 16 guilders he bought a 'musical box' for the foundling, which he presented to him personally on the 1st June.

Binder was impressed by all this, reporting it to Anselm von Feuerbach on the 3rd June in an effusive letter, in which he also passed on a prompt request from the new benefactor to be allowed to see documents pertaining to the criminal investigation. Stanhope thus expressed this wish right from the beginning. He had read Feuerbach's publication 'Some important documents relating to the unfortunate foundling Kaspar Hauser' (Fig. 115) some time before and quite rightly guessed that the documents that interested him were certainly not included in that publication.

'....The fate of our Kaspar Hauser,' wrote Binder to Feuerbach,

> with which so many hearts both near and far are concerned, has also made such an impression on a respected Englishman that he decided to avail himself of the opportunity of his present journey through Germany and other parts to become acquainted with him and his situation....During his eight-day stay here which he devoted almost exclusively to Hauser and his friends, and which he arranged through an introduction to me via Market Chairman Merkel, this noble man Count

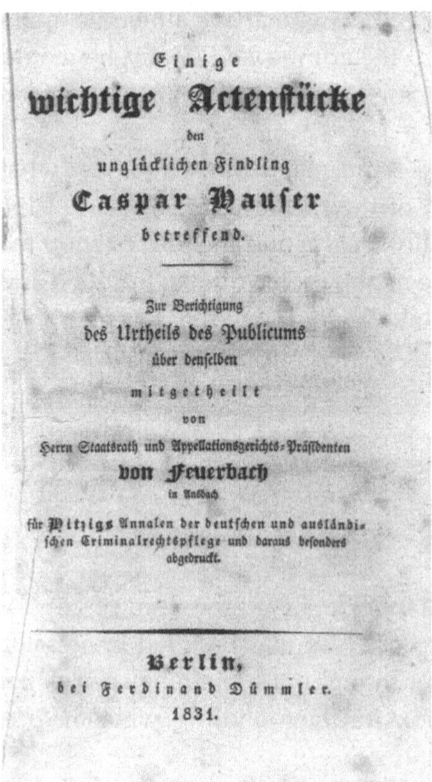

Einige
wichtige Actenstücke
den
unglücklichen Findling
Caspar Hauser
betreffend.

Zur Berichtigung
des Urtheils des Publicums
über denselben
mitgetheilt
von
Herrn Staatsrath und Appellationsgerichts-Präsidenten
von Feuerbach
in Ansbach
für Hitzigs Annalen der deutschen und ausländischen Criminalrechtspflege und daraus besonders abgedruckt.

Berlin,
bei Ferdinand Dümmler.
1831.

115. Title page of Feuerbach's first book about Kaspar Hauser 'Some important documents relating to the unfortunate foundling Kaspar Hauser'.

> [*sic*] Stanhope from London, a Peer of the Realm, warmed so much [to Kaspar] as he got to know him that not only did he present the round sum of 500f as a reward for the discoverer of the identity of the man who committed the crime against Hauser, but he even determined immediately on a regular income for him and also decided to embark on a collection for Hauser in England so as to put [Hauser] in possession of such an income as would correspond to his simple lifestyle and enable him to be independent. But as his idea will only be possible if the more refined members of the public in England can be made familiar with an accurate, concise, comprehensive description of Hauser's story that as far as the circumstances of the investigation allow, is based on the relevant documents. He has therefore decided to call on Your Excellency in person to discuss with you the ways and means this could be done and to ask for your help and participation in drawing up such a description. The further purpose of his conversation with Your Excellency would then be to ask you to give him, insofar as it does not adversely affect the case, *notes relating to those documents that will put him in a position to present the relevant items of evidence, namely those relating to the events in Hungary* [emphasis—Mayer] personally and at the disposal of his widespread acquaintances in Germany, Austria and partly in Hungary, who are convinced that perhaps only a Briton would be able to pursue such a philanthropic aim with such energy and prudence....[225]

Binder's letter could only have been in Ansbach a few hours when on the 4th June Stanhope was already standing before Feuerbach's door (Fig.116). Here too Philip Henry was immediately presenting himself as the generous patron who had the plan that Tucher, Lieutenant Hickel and Kaspar Hauser should—all naturally at his expense—travel to Hungary to discover the foundling's origins. The whole affair of the Hungarian trip, which of course could have led nowhere, has long been familiar and does not need to be reiterated here. In relation to it, however, it is noteworthy that at a decisive moment Stanhope already gave himself away. He gave Tucher a letter for Count Joseph Sedlnitzky (1778–1855), President of the Austrian Police and Censor's Office, which, among things, said: 'Kaspar Hauser, with whose most mysterious story you will surely be well-acquainted, especially because Prince Metternich received a letter about him from the Bavarian courts last year and most graciously recommended the execution of the investigations he desired...'[226]

116. Anselm von Feuerbach (1775–1833). Pastel portrait by Joh. Lorenz Kreul.

Stanhope, who was not in Germany in 1830 and who also had not visited Vienna on this 1831 trip, therefore knew that Metternich had been active in the Kaspar Hauser affair the year before. The letter was sealed, so Tucher remained unaware of its contents. Otherwise, the game would have been up for Stanhope. Stanhope put up another 2000 guilders for the trip to Hungary; he had thus spent 2500 guilders on Kaspar Hauser within a week. That does not include the extravagant pocket money of 100 guilders and the presents, all for the month of June only.

After this short but sensational first appearance, which lasted eight days in all in Nuremberg and Ansbach, Stanhope took his leave and arrived in Munich on the 13th June. As Hauser was supposed to journey to Vienna and Pressburg with his companions, Philip Henry's presence was for the time being no longer necessary. After his previous success, he could regard the further course of developments in a more relaxed frame of mind, since he saw himself well on the way to the critical point that would decide everything—the handing over of responsibility for Hauser. The Nurembergers had pricked up their ears at his bluffing offer to provide for the foundling until his death should Hauser be entrusted to him, which, as we know, left behind quite an impression and led to Feuerbach giving him the desired sight of the investigation files.[227] These showed that three months previously, on the 25th March the economy councillor Cuno from Ratibor had, with regard to Kaspar Hauser, sent the 'bottle message' article from the *Moniteur* of 5th November 1816 (see p. 148f., Fig. 63) to Feuerbach, who had added it to the investigation files. Whether Cuno did this as a result of wide reading of his own is questionable. Prince Hohenlohe-Schillingfürst, who was not prepared to regard Kaspar as a tramp, and who probably had knowledge others lacked, came from Ratibor and was living at that time in Nuremberg. Was he responsible for sending the article? It is possible that this knowledge was significant at this point in time and affected the following steps in Feuerbach's further handling of the case. For it must have been clear to Stanhope that the President was beginning to see a connection or at least was on the verge of doing so.

*

On the 3rd July Kaspar left Feuerbach, after spending a while at his home in Ansbach, to start off on the 'journey of discovery' to Hungary paid for by Stanhope. Feuerbach stopped his departure. On the same day he wrote a long letter to Stanhope, which he sent to Munich.

> I feel myself obliged to inform Your Lordship that our dear angelic Kaspar left here early this morning at 5 o'clock for Nuremberg accompanied by Lieutenant Hickel. He will meet Mr. von Tucher in Nuremberg and then tomorrow will probably set out on his first great trip, on which may God protect him and lead him to the right goal.
>
> The three weeks which I spent with this pure, quite unsullied child's soul will be eternally memorable for me and of great benefit for my literary work. He is so suprahumanly good, so loving, so faithful, open and true like a child, so grateful even for the smallest thing and also so generous and sociable with those who do him ill, even with those evildoers who so cruelly took from him the paradise of his childhood, that I would not know what he would lack to deserve the name of the best and most virtuous of men. All the members of my family were so sad to see him leave and accompanied his departure with tears. His leaving was heart-rending for us all. Weeping, he went round the circle of my family, offered his hand to each one, thanked them and asked each one in a

melancholy voice for forgiveness if he had done them any harm. No-one had any reason to forgive him; all had reason only to thank him for the pure human joy his purely human nature had given to each of us, for the rare, quickening example of a really good and pure soul he had left in all hearts. His last words at his leave-taking were to express to me the request to write to Lord Stanhope to tell him how dear he was to him and to inform him that he had now set off. I shall not burden Your Lordship by relating all the details which had to be set aside or overcome before we could arrive at the point where we now are.

But one point is too noteworthy to pass over; it is a real source for various considerations. In order to enable Hickel to travel with us, I addressed myself, as was necessary, in an official letter to the General Officer Commanding of the Gendarmerie in Munich. I explained not only the causes and purposes of the trip but also—because I know my people—the important point at issue, which was that the trip would not cost either the State or His Majesty *anything*, as it would be underwritten by the generosity of Lord Stanhope. The General Officer Commanding of the Gendarmerie could not make a decision himself, but had to report to the Ministry of War; even the War Ministry was unable to deal with the dispatch of an officer of the Gendarmerie and had to seek a gracious decision from His Majesty. The reply received (literally) read as follows:

'His Majesty permits the dispatch of Sub-lieutenant Hickel of the Gendarmerie for the purpose of the Kaspar Hauser investigation, but exclusively at the cost of Earl Stanhope and commands that in order that the purpose of the trip be unobstructed, strict secrecy is to be observed until it is ended.'

Your Lordship will not only recognise the great personal interest with which His Royal Majesty has commended and impressed upon us the cautionary measures enjoined in the final sentence of this rescript, but will feel deeply grateful for the great honour and graciousness which has been shown you by the magnanimity of His Royal Majesty. For can there be a more splendid token of honour for you, noble and worthy man, than that a German King, in a sacred affair of humanity, has expressly declared his royal prerogative to act in an honourable manner in order, by means of a formal rescript no less, to entrust that which belongs to him exclusively to a private individual, a noble Briton? One experiences much when one becomes old!

Please be assured of the deeply felt esteem in which I shall remain until my last breath as Your Lordship's obedient servant,

Sir Anselm von Feuerbach,
State Counsellor and President,
Ansbach, dated 3 July 1831.[227]

Ludwig I's diplomatic behaviour is again of note here, which Feuerbach can do nothing but describe as magnanimous. The fact that the King did not wish to pay for the expedition either out of the State Treasury or his own pocket did not raise any questions for Feuerbach. He could not guess that in Bavaria such activities could be discussed just as little as the possibility, which could only be hinted at, that Hauser was a Hungarian magnate. Such origins would certainly not serve in the struggle with Baden. The trip to Austria carried the additional danger that it might bring about undesirable diplomatic developments, because the Kaiser and the Chancellor [Metternich] were agreed that the Kaspar Hauser case should remain a matter for the Bavarian authorities.

This is to say nothing of the continually smouldering dispute about the Bavarian territorial claims, in which Austria had declared itself clearly in favour of Baden. On the other hand, keeping the trip secret, Hauser and Tucher assuming false names with the King's permission and having Stanhope pay for it all, and the whole enterprise nevertheless enjoying the royal blessing, must be regarded as a diplomatic achievement.

*

Besides its inevitable pleasures, Stanhope had a reason for his forthcoming trip, which was connected with one of the most sensitive points in the whole Kaspar Hauser affair, and which is of decisive significance for the last two and half years of the foundling's life, but which has nevertheless remained impenetrable until today. At the end of August [1831], when Tucher and Hauser would have returned from Hungary, Stanhope—the future foster father—wanted to visit Nuremberg. Beyond a few surmises, it has not yet been possible for Kaspar Hauser researchers [in 1988—*Ed.*] to clarify more exactly what was going on between the 13th June and the 5th September.

With regard to concern for Hauser's future and his unconditional handover to Stanhope, in Nuremberg, despite the Earl's very generous conduct, the question of creditworthiness had arisen; it must have been mentioned at the latest by the time of his return to Nuremberg, in other words, before arrangements could have been made for a legal hearing. People did not want to hand Hauser over to a hitherto unknown travelling lord who had only spent a week in the city, merely on the basis of a few presents and other assurances.

After this feeling had become clear, Stanhope realised what had to happen. His dealings with the authorities had begun well; it was now a matter of concluding them so as to ensure that Hauser would actually be handed over to him, and that depended on the financial situation remaining solid.

Early on the 13th June Stanhope had left Nuremberg in the company of a recently acquired young friend, the enterprising Count Alexander von Ungern-Sternberg (1806–1869) (Fig. 117), [228] and made his way to Munich. Sternberg, 'an eccentric', as another of Stanhope's friends, Baron von Fahnenberg assured him, was 'a cold, introverted man, difficult to make out'. But with Stanhope he was soon the best of friends. Sternberg had early on made a name for himself as a literary figure and unlike Stanhope, was a very cultivated and well-educated man, which, at least in these years, had created for him quite a readership. But a conspicuous feature of this relationship too was the essential connection to Freemasonry, which may have been a precondition that eased the way for this new friendship. Sternberg's masonic novellas *Lessing*, *Voltaire in Fernay*, *The Pupils of the Jesuits*, the novel *The Missionary* which featured a secret society, and *Marcaran or the Philosophy of the 18th century* all clearly testify to his interests and influences.

117. Alexander von Ungern-Sternberg (1806–1868)

In the weeks that followed, Sternberg apparently played the role of a social intermediary that is not to be underestimated, especially in the Stuttgart days that were to be decisive in the further course of Kaspar Hauser's destiny. The two travellers also met up for a number of other joint enterprises later on.

During his visit to the royal palace in Munich Stanhope was not yet aware of King Ludwig's graciously and distantly professed concern for Kaspar Hauser. He received Feuerbach's letter towards the end of his stay in Munich so that with regard to the real reason for his visit it may be assumed that the future foster parent thought to enlighten himself as to the interests that obtained at the Court in Munich which—as he knew the Baden Court well—could not be a matter of indifference for him. He himself mentioned in a letter to Feuerbach on the 9th July, the day before he left Munich, that he had tried, unsuccessfully, for four weeks to gain an audience with the King: '...but I was not presented to the King'. He played down his failure, attributing it to the absence of the British ambassador. But it is more likely that even had he been present, Ludwig would have avoided a conversation with Stanhope. That had to remain a conundrum for Feuerbach and Stanhope for, as Feuerbach had written to Stanhope effusively on the 3rd July: '...can there be a more splendid token of honour for you, noble and worthy man, than that a German King, in a sacred affair of humanity, has expressly declared his royal prerogative to act in an honourable manner in order, by means of a formal rescript no less, to entrust that which belongs to him exclusively to a private individual, a noble Briton?' Now such a man of honour was standing before the King's door and was not once granted the grace of an audience.

But this was always Ludwig's posture in the Kaspar Hauser affair: to keep the affair going without compromising himself. It is not unlikely that Ludwig had been apprised of Stanhope's arrival in Nuremberg and that he suspected, not without reason, that a number of consequences would develop as a result of the appearance of the 'noble Briton'.

Whatever happened, Stanhope was not received at Court. He spent the time of waiting on excursions with Sternberg into the area around the city. On the 7th July he visited Schleissheim Castle, which was already in those days regarded as a picture gallery. The following day saw the publication in Saphir's Munich newspaper *The Bazaar* (see pp. 206 & 263) of Police Commissioner Merker's vicious pamphlet on Kaspar Hauser. Stanhope, who possessed almost all publications relating to Kaspar Hauser, added it to his collection. Merker's comments about the 'fraud' Kaspar Hauser could hardly be overlooked in Munich, and the fact that Stanhope finally had to leave Munich without achieving anything also certainly had to do with the content and timing of the publication, which was domestically most inopportune for Ludwig.

The King, who was not in the least inclined towards Metternich, had been put under great pressure by the civil unrest in Munich in December 1830. The crisis dominated the whole of the following year. Troops had to be called out to deal with rebellious students. The closure of the university, the prosecution of agitators, the censorship of the Press went on and on and was very stressful. Under such circumstances, it is understandable that Ludwig did not wish to know about any 'royal privilege' magnanimously granted to Stanhope.

The stay in Munich was on the whole anything but a success, and time slipped by. The useless waiting in antechambers, the impossibility of gaining access to higher Court circles only now, it may be surmised, suggested a second-best solution, namely to visit the residence of the Dowager Queen at Tegernsee. Stanhope must have decided on this in the meantime; whatever else would happen around Kaspar Hauser, the situation was not without its dangers for a man like himself risking manoeuvres between different fronts. Baden and Bavaria had very dissimilar interests, and Stanhope and his future foster son could easily get caught up in the field of tension between these polar interests. Bavaria, whose subject Kaspar Hauser now was, could have no interest in his leaving the country; the case was quite otherwise with Baden, and Stanhope could only act rightly in Vienna's view when he acted with the interests of Karlsruhe in mind. Since the scene of events was Bavaria, the grounds for any possible conflict were only too evident.

Before Stanhope's next move is considered, Stanhope's first letter to Kaspar Hauser (16.6.1831) which he wrote from Munich, should be examined; Hauser would find it waiting for him on his return from Hungary.

> My dear friend!
> I enclose for you a collection of various sealing waxes which are made here and of which some are fragrant and others not. I would also like to find a seal for you with a symbol on it, such as for example the symbol of *hope. Trust in God and hope that His favour will lead you to the goal at the right time* should always be in your heart and will encourage you when

you might otherwise feel troubled. His ways are unknown to us, and we cannot conceive why you had such a hard destiny in earlier times although you are good and innocent, but we know that His goodness and His power are infinite and therefore we can confidently expect that He will conduct everything as it should be.

You soon will be making a journey for which you have longed, and which, as I hope and believe, will be of very great importance, and I pray to our heavenly Father that it may help you to reach your goal, which would be for me an unending happiness. Be calm and relaxed on the journey and let neither joy nor anxiety nor hope disturb your normal composure; otherwise, it would be disadvantageous for your health and you would perhaps not be in a condition to carry out your plan. I do not need to tell you that you should promptly and faithfully abide by the wishes of our excellent friend, Baron von Tucher; for I am convinced that you will always do this out of the love, gratitude and respect which you must have for him. I shall with longing await news of you and shall heartily enjoy receiving letters from you. That God give you all good fortune and blessing and that your hopes may very soon be fulfilled, is the most zealous wish of your faithful friend,

Earl Stanhope.[229]

118. Impression (enlarged) of Kaspar Hauser's seal with the symbols of heart, anchor and cross surrounded by a serpent biting its tail.

Stanhope later purchased the seal in Frankfurt. The only extant copy of it shows a heart, a cross and an anchor bounded by a snake that is biting its own tail (Fig. 118). It may be the snake was a coincidence and expressed no deeper intention. On the other hand, it is a remarkable fact that it was just the symbol of a snake which Stanhope chose for Kaspar Hauser.[230]

But back to Stanhope and Count Ungern-Sternberg who passed the time in 'society' and at the theatre until they left for Tegernsee on the 10th July. The Dowager Queen Karoline of Bavaria (Fig.119), Kaspar Hauser's aunt, had lived there since spring 1828 after the death of her husband King Maximilian in October 1825. The Cabinet preacher von Schmidt wrote in his memoirs:

> The Bavarian Court was actually at Tegernsee [Fig.120]. Everyone that counted for anything in the world gathered there. Numerous guests populated the extensive palace. The diplomatic corps frequently held meetings there....All eminent travellers from all over the world would spend a few days or often weeks at Tegernsee when they came to Munich... Tegernsee had become a famous royal seat to which people made their way from very distant locations, and Queen Karoline was honoured by all and received oaths of loyalty from all those who spent time in the area!

119. Karoline, Queen of Bavaria (1776–1841), Princess of Baden, sister of Grand Duke Karl of Baden.

120. Royal pleasure castle Tegernsee.

Now Stanhope too was spending time at the beautiful Tegernsee. Did he try to confer with Karoline about Kaspar Hauser, as he also later did when the clever woman saw right through him? Did he want to discover how Karoline would regard his becoming Kaspar Hauser's foster father? If not, then if everything went well as he now planned, he might manage to ease himself into the confidence of the royal family—which Karoline could not then have known, but would become clear to her—as the 'protector' of a not yet but perhaps later legitimate member of 'her family'. Is it completely unthinkable that Stanhope, who was now in a tight squeeze financially due to his outlays in Nuremberg, after receiving indications of the possibility of such a connection, should first seek here the means to achieve the transfer deal he would seek in Nuremberg in September, a deal which would go far beyond the obligations that might be expected from the charity of a private individual? Kaspar was not only a possible relative of Karoline's, but as things stood, he was a Bavarian subject. And in the sense of Stanhope's commission, was there not a tactical need to seek help first here in order to avoid the accusation that the whole enterprise had been financed in advance by another interested party? His behaviour in any case had to seem so inconspicuously normal so that the approaching act of the transfer of guardianship would not be endangered by a misperception of roles. The fact that a short while later, however, he received from Karlsruhe what he required was evidence of the real situation.

Stanhope was not received by Karoline either, which removed the possibility of further speculation as to conceivable motives and consequences, which an audience would have caused. Most probably,

Ludwig, whose behaviour towards the queen—according to Cabinet preacher von Schmidt—was 'not the friendliest', had forbidden all communication with Stanhope in order not to endanger his own plans.

After eleven days of fruitless hoping and waiting, the two had to travel on for a second time with nothing to show for their efforts and in the sobering knowledge that neither at Munich nor Tegernsee was there a readiness to regard the Hauser question as anything other than a criminal investigation. In the struggle against Baden, the Bavarians could only achieve their aims by clarifying all questions of Kaspar's origins and the claims about him. Stanhope had perhaps not realised that.

Then on the 21st July the two men travelled on in daily stages through Weilheim, Kaufbeuren, Lindau, and Friedrichshafen to Tübingen, where they arrived on the 29th. There, or already en route, Philip Henry decided to visit Ludwig Uhland. One could almost detect a rumbling of thunder signifying that such a visit was unlikely to meet with a pleasant outcome. Could two cultural attitudes have been further apart? Can one imagine the presumption with which our enlightened rationalist Stanhope arrived in Tübingen intending to put to Uhland the archetypal Swabian, the most German of all Romantics, the comrade-in-arms of Jacob Grimm, ideas that promised would bring him more success as a writer?

Such a misjudgement of the task and mission of the poet and scholar who later could not bring himself to accept two of the highest decorations for Science and Culture—almost simultaneously awarded —for the power of his poetry and scholarship, the 'Pour le mérite' of the Peace Class, proposed by Alexander von Humboldt and the Bavarian Maximilian Order: to make the contemptible suggestion to such a man that he should copy the style of a current pulp fiction writer in order to enjoy greater public success—that was doomed to failure!

Does the wish to make such a suggestion not perhaps reflect something of Stanhope's tragic misjudgement in regard to his future foster son? One can immediately grasp that he was basically incapable of perceiving Hauser's 'angelic being' and that had he been able to do so, it would have drawn him to make different decisions.

But back to Uhland and the reason for the visit. Philip Henry had read one of the over 160 trivial sentimental family stories of Lafontaine, not the famous French fable writer but the German canon August Heinrich Julius Lafontaine, who haunted the cathedral chapter in Magdeburg. Philip Henry had literally shed tears over his *Quinctius*

Heymeran von Flaming. (Fig. 121). Lafontaine was certainly one of the most popular contemporary writers of romances. Even Humboldt had to read to King Friedrich Wilhelm III on his travels from the works of the King's favourite writer for whom the king had provided the canonry in Magdeburg so that Lafontaine could continue producing his stories unencumbered by other duties. But for cultivated people Lafontaine was always an abomination. The novel Stanhope read, for example, included this passage:

> 'O my Ovid!' he said softly and crept closer to the bed. Käthe must have been having a sweet dream; for her breast rose and her cheeks were glistening. Quinctius stepped softly right to her bed and trembling, lifted one of her lovely blond locks from her shoulder, laid them between the scissors and cut and—Käthe did not awaken despite the noise of the scissors. 'O my Ovid!' said Quinctius softly and gazed on the face of the lovely maiden lying there, her eyes still closed and her bosom rising and falling. He brushed his lips at first softly and then more firmly on the rose of her mouth; and she did not wake. Now (as Ovid called it, the quintessence of love) he pressed the lasting mark of his teeth so firmly into the waxen shoulder of the lovely sleeper that she gave a start; but still she did not wake. He was amazed that Ovid had been so right and could not understand why his cousin did not wake. 'O my Ovid!' he said again softly and with his booty, stole from thence.

And so it babbles dully on through the fifteen hundred pages of the four volume work. The tears actually shed by Philip Henry show not only his own sentimentality but more incisively, a mental horizon which could not stop him from committing a quintessential literary sin.[231] His advice to 'Master Uhland' was to emulate Lafontaine if he wished to be famous.

Accompanied by Count Ungern-Sternberg, the dandy knocked on the scholar's door on the 29th July; Uhland was then living in Gardenstrasse in Tübingen (Figs. 122, 123). His companion tried in vain to dissuade him from the enterprise, since 'the celebrated poet would never understand why he should need to emulate this long forgotten, sentimental spinner of love stories'. 'But why not?' asked the Earl, surprised. 'Isn't Lafontaine an excellent major writer?....If Master Uhland really wants to have a great effect on his countrymen and on his era, what better can he do than copy Lafontaine?' The same unembarrassed and tactless disregard for all cultural facts and principles is seen again

Quinctius Heymeran von Flaming.

Von

August Lafontaine.

Turpe est difficiles habere nugas
Et stultus labor est ineptiarum.
Martial.

Erster Theil.

Neue, verbesserte Auflage.

Berlin,
in der Vossischen Buchhandlung.
1798.

121. *Cover page of 'Quinctius Heymeran von Flaming' by August Lafontaine.*

122. *Ludwig Uhland (1787–1862)*

123. *Uhland's house in Tübingen, Gartenstrasse.*

with a similarly revealing directness when Stanhope visited Daumer for the first time in 1834 after Kaspar Hauser's death. Daumer could not endure Stanhope's criticisms and untruths about the dead Kaspar, to which Stanhope responded: 'It no longer hurts him!'

Uhland, who had just begun his readings on the history of the sagas of the Germanic and Romance peoples, was not willing even to exchange a few words with Stanhope. The poet must have experienced Stanhope's naive prescription for success as an insult. Here, where in not a few villages and towns 'Uhland limes' had been planted for the man of the people, where his wonderful songs, not least the deeply felt '*Ich hatt' einen Kameraden*' (I had a comrade...) could be heard from many voices, in just those years of his studies in mythology, Uhland was pressing on toward an imagination of a rare depth:

> The old masters walk with a noble proud stride
> Like giant spirits with strange wondrous songs.
> In the slumbering valleys awakens the joy of singing.
> Whoever feels a spark of youth arise within his breast
> Rejoices, moved to the depths, thanks to this following dawn
> Which leads us back to you, *German poesy*!

For Uhland, Stanhope's advice to become famous by emulating Lafontaine must have been utterly incomprehensible. The garrulous assault of the vain agent must have seemed like a case of madness to the friend of Justinus Kerner, to the poet who was loved and honoured as no other apart perhaps from Schiller and who, according to Peter Lahnstein, was 'the epitome of honesty and uprightness; a man who did nothing, absolutely nothing to curry favour with anyone or to make himself loved, to put himself in the spotlight or bang his own drum'. Ungern-Sternberg recorded the memorable meeting:

> Like all Swabians, Uhland is not very approachable; he is even less so than the rest of his countrymen. In all social relationships there is no more secluded nature than his. He is not only not communicative, but he understands the special way in which it is possible essentially to stifle the communications of others in his presence. There is an art of listening which extinguishes anyone's desire to relate anything, and Uhland practises this art to perfection. He was therefore always silent; he said nothing, and through his silence prevented others from speaking. The talkative Earl found such a Trappist atmosphere very oppressive, so he

> went on talking by himself and in doing so delivered his gospel of Lafontaine. Uhland said neither yes nor no. Frau Uhland, however—heaven knows what led to it—began to speak about fashions in wigs and of the lengths to which people would go, especially in Paris, to get hold of such ornaments for bald heads. At this, Lord Stanhope pricked up his ears and listened with growing attention, as he himself was wearing a splendid chestnut brown wig with curls. He could not but think that Mistress Uhland was taking the liberty of mocking him and this, together with her husband's continuing silence, put the Earl in a rather bitter mood and provoked him to take an early leave. On the return journey, he gave full vent to his anger. These German scholars are loathsome! he cried; not only do they accept no instruction, they train their wives to mock strangers who come to them. Did the lady not speak in the most suggestive manner about wigs when she saw that I was wearing one? That did not occur to her, I replied; she only spoke about wigs to amuse you! (Stanhope:) Rather, to remind me that I no longer have any hair! In England it would be called a 'gross impertinence'. From that time on, the Lord abandoned his efforts to convert German scholars.[232]

Stanhope must have taken this perhaps completely intentional mockery of his wig very badly. He paid special attention to his wig, which was certainly not of the cheapest variety. Every day he would apply a few drops of rose oil to it from a bottle he constantly had with him so that it would give off a pleasant fragrance, which could not have failed to have an effect on the Uhlands—here evidently with an unexpected result.

After this fiasco the pair left Tübingen and took themselves to Stuttgart. Here the die was probably cast for Stanhope's next move, for here the lacking financial resources were somehow magically produced which would enable him to move into the decisive phase—gaining control over Kaspar Hauser.

Stanhope spent 22 days—30th July to 22nd August—in the Württemberg capital. A letter has survived, despite all precautions, that casts a certain light on the scenario. With no salutation at either beginning or end, no sender's name indicated, and full of unclear abbreviations, it has the flavour of a conspiratorial text. Written in December, it applies to Stanhope's stay in Stuttgart.

> Milan, Dec. 31, Dearest S[tanhope], I am very disappointed to have nothing from you since you left S[tuttgart]. Perhaps I will find a letter

> in Geneva where I shall stay a night tomorrow on my trip. I hope you will write to me soon and give me any details about C[aspar] Hauser—don't get mixed up in that yourself, I am afraid you too may be attacked, I would like to hear soon that you are safe. I enclose a letter which I received yesterday from Lord R....Mrs R has not yet received her wages nor anything of the most urgently needed content since they left Egl., I have not used up all my expenses, so you would have to have a large amount of cash in hand, but I assume that they will count their money in Paris. I still have my 200 at Coutts, which P. gave me. Farewell, I wished I could have heard something of you if need be, I could have met you when I travel via…? …to Geneva, also on the way from Baden to Frankfurt—an excellent road.[233]

'Don't get mixed up in that yourself...' In all direct actions related to Kaspar Hauser Stanhope had taken care to avoid doing just that. Whenever something happened, he was in the background or in the area—a director!

But who was it who wrote to him that he had not used up all his expenses and who apparently indicated a meagre contribution of £200 intended as a bridging amount? A traveller like himself? Who is 'P'? No answers suggest themselves to any of these questions, but the tenor of the letter throws a sharp light on the situation in Stuttgart in that the writer, who apparently has no knowledge of Stanhope's tasks in Nuremberg, assumes that actually a larger amount of cash must still be available. One can imagine that from here couriers went over to Karlsruhe. Or was Stanhope himself in a remote location for the decisive conversation in order to achieve a solution to the problem facing him?

It almost seems as if his last reserves would have to be drawn on. Countess von Albersdorf, who was born Lady Graham and was on Stanhope's trail already during his lifetime, writes about him turning up again in Nuremberg a short time afterwards:

> One wonders that a wealthy Englishman in possession of such large letters of credit would hand them over to a merchant for safekeeping; he would have to have received from the latter only money for his day-to-day expenses. When Herr Merkel was asked what letters of credit he actually was given, from English or German banking houses, he replied that he had had nothing to do with England and neither had he seen any English letters of credit from Stanhope. The letters which he had in his

> hands from Stanhope were from *German* banks, upon which he advanced him the money. The whole cost of Stanhope's journeys at that time as well as his maintenance of Kaspar Hauser until the latter's last hour was defrayed by Herr Merkel with his *advances* and then only when all was balanced out were the letters given back by [Herr Merkel]; whether directly into Stanhope's hands or straight to the Houses in question, I do not know...The large letters of credit were *not* his own but were entrusted to him by those into whose hands he was supposed to deliver Kaspar.[234]

That may be essentially correct, including the point that Stanhope certainly did not have at his disposal any wealth of his own. Somewhat later—in 1835, after Kaspar's murder—he had even complained to his son 'about the great inconvenience & disadvantage of being supposed to be very rich & also very credulous & of becoming more exposed than I was or to attempts at imposition or extortion'. Such suspicions, however, resulted from Stanhope's munificent behaviour. He had spoiled Hauser immeasurably with money that was not his own and in order to reach his goal, he declared in the protocol given on his application for wardship to the royal district and municipal court that God had so richly blessed him with earthly goods that he could easily take on the duties of care required.

Fritz Klee comes a step closer to the matter in a side comment in relation to his Kaspar Hauser research when he writes: 'In the past September (1928) the Hauser question was touched on at the congress of judicial recorders in Heidelberg, where mention was made of the fact that Lord Stanhope had paid in *Baden* government-issued notes during his time in Nuremberg.' This statement can be definitively amplified today with the knowledge that these were certificates from the Haber Bank in Karlsruhe. This fact is highly significant, and the reason why it was precisely this bank that supplied an impecunious Englishman with letters of credit on such a scale is not difficult to understand, when the background for Haber's liberality is considered.

*

With the beginning of Grand Duke Leopold's control of the government [1830] a personality stepped to the fore who had previously played no significant role: Grand Duchess Sophie, Leopold's wife. Her link to Stanhope and to the Kaspar Hauser affair has to do with the banker Baron Moritz von Haber (1798–1874) who, it can be demonstrated, had a very close connection to Stanhope. His father Salomon von Haber

(1760–1839) (Fig.124), who had become rich during the Napoleonic wars through military supplies, served the House of Baden from 1810 under Karl Friedrich and later under Grand Duke Karl, whose successor Ludwig raised the financier to noble rank in 1829. From that time onwards, his son Moritz, then a banker in Paris, called himself Maurice de Haber. According to the 'Memoirs' of Margrave Wilhelm, public funds borrowed from Haber had to be repaid at 9% interest. 'At that time,' wrote the Margrave, 'the banker Haber put together his huge fortune, in that he handled foreign exchange for the Treasury which, when the market fell, always had to be prolonged with many extra costs as they could not be redeemed. In this manner he must have drawn 15% of his funds.' 'The Baden Rothschilds' [as the Habers were called—*Ed.*] owned the largest private house on the main street of the capital Karlsruhe, the Langen Strasse, a palatial building, the broad many-windowed frontage of which gave out onto the promenade.

After great loss-making speculative business that led to the bankruptcy of the Paris Haber Bank, Moritz returned to Karlsruhe as the Court Banker in his father's business. With Leopold's accession, he became the financial adviser mainly to the Grand Duchess, her confidant

124. Salomon von Haber (1760–1839)

and counsellor, also in political questions. He had easy access to the royal palace and enjoyed the right to a royal audience without prior application. Through his agents in the financial capitals of Paris, London, Vienna and Frankfurt, he had insights not only into the international money markets but also into the politics of those countries, which soon led to his becoming a counsellor to the Grand Duke also. To the annoyance of the Baden aristocracy, this parvenu, who was one of the richest men in the Grand Duchy, took charge of foundations and patronages which had traditionally been at the disposal only of the oldest nobility in the land. The ambitious and unscrupulous Sophie (Fig.126) recognised very early on the danger that could emerge from the Kaspar Hauser affair for her husband's government. This awareness occurred at a time when the Grand Duchess entered into a liaison with the banker that very much incurred the displeasure of the people of Baden. His unrestricted visiting rights at the palace were therefore soon interpreted as relating not only to the financial affairs of the Grand Duchess but also to affairs of a different and very private nature. Compromising boasts by Haber only stimulated such suspicions; he occasionally pulled out of his pocket evidence of his intimate relationships in the form of little written messages, commenting, 'These are from Sophie.'

When he made and won the tasteless bet that he could tell in advance what the Princess's evening wear would be, it was not only Karlsruhe that was convinced that the rumours about Sophie and Haber were based on fact. The Baden nobility viewed the growing influence of Haber with increasing distaste. When Sophie went so far as to entrust the banker with a kind of supervision of the princes' education, her brother-in-law Margrave Wilhelm protested, and this was followed by concerns raised in 'society'. Haber was denied entry to a ball for the nobility, which he took as an insult since, as the 'Jew Baron', he was not accorded the right of satisfaction. He was widely regarded by the public as the father of the Grand Duchess's two daughters, who were born in 1834 and 1839.[235]

These connections make Sophie's role in the Kaspar Hauser affair in 1831 clear. They also point to the concrete beginnings of the actions on which she embarked in 1833. Sophie had doubtless always known more than those around her suspected. In 1819 she had married Leopold, the eldest son of the Imperial Countess Hochberg, old Karl Friedrich's morganatic wife, who had lived another two years. There was then in 1820 only a single person left who must have been fully initi-

125. *Leopold, Grand Duke of Baden (1790–1852)*

126. *Sophie, Grand Duchess of Baden (1801–1865)*

ated into the crime of the exchange of the children: Sophie! She admitted as much to Archduchess Hildegard, daughter of Ludwig, King of Bavaria, with the words: 'There is a crime in the House of Baden.' The Archduchess expanded on this confession of Sophie's with the comment: '...She must have been thinking of Hauser.'[236]

She had to take charge because the accession of the Hochberg line depended solely on whether the change of dynasties would succeed with Leopold. At the same time, after the death of the Countess Hochberg there must have been a co-conspirator who, besides the Countess herself, had a vital interest in the same goal and who could consequently prevent Grand Duke Ludwig from entering into a marriage that might possibly be blessed with princes by holding over him the knowledge of an existing legitimate Zähringer heir. Until Hauser's appearance, Sophie's role may not have been significant. She must also have known that the little stone building in Beuggen Castle grounds, hard by the Rhine, had stood empty since 1816. And when Ludwig died in 1830, her calculation had worked out. But she must have realised with a shock straightaway that the threat to Ludwig had immediately become a threat to herself, because there was no longer anyone in the government of Baden who could serve as a helper; how secure would her husband's throne then be? This is why, in these circumstances and also in relation to the Stuttgart situation, the connections which Stanhope had to Haber and which Haber in turn had to Grand Duchess Sophie were so important.

*

Within two weeks—from the 26th May to the 12th June—Stanhope had already spent about 3000 guilders on Kaspar Hauser, and as the Stuttgart letter shows, he was at the end of his financial resources. If, as planned, it was to come to a legal recognition in September of his position as foster father, then that would be possible on the basis of evidence of a corresponding outlay, which would have to be provided by letters of credit. In view of the situation, which German banking house would have provided them, and why did Stanhope have no English letters of credit with him? The Haber Bank, however, was prepared to give immediate and discreet guarantees. Stanhope had been either in 1830 or 1831 in Karlsruhe or Mannheim—but at any rate since the month of August 1831—in possession of letters of credit from Haber. They must therefore have been handed to him most likely in Stuttgart in the period from the 30th July to the 22nd

August, which makes clear that his visible presence in Karlsruhe just at that time, and furthermore at the Haber Palais, would have been a unpardonable error on his part; Grand Duchess Stéphanie at least would certainly have learned of it.

But why was the banker prepared to enter into this business at all? This is explained by Grand Duchess Sophie's insights into dynastic and family politics and her special relationship with Haber. For the credit was not provided to Stanhope but rather, one can say, to the Grand Duchess. She vouched for it; Stanhope only had to pay it out properly. Sophie was faced with a problem of State politics, for the solution of which a few thousand guilders more or less might not be sufficient. Stanhope therefore had to be provided with enough money, at least when he left Stuttgart, so that on the one hand, nothing more would stand in the way of a legal recognition of his guardianship and on the other, the spendthrift nobleman, who had already so successfully begun to play his part, could continue to do so.

Via Schwäbisch Hall, Mergentheim and Würzburg he first headed for Erlangen (29th August) where old friendships were refreshed and remembered with gifts. Frau Bärbel and Miss Sophie were among those whose first names only are known. On the 5th September Stanhope appeared on stage once more in Nuremberg. Events now followed in quick succession. With breathtaking speed Hauser was wrested from the authorities and from his guardian, Tucher. The latter had to be achieved first if the agreement of the authorities was to be obtained, for it had to be Hauser's *own will,* he had to agree to the transfer to Stanhope; indeed, he had to request it.

Stanhope's plan was simple and effective. What no-one had been able to do until then, he did and succeeded the second time. On the 8th September the assault on the still introverted, simple child began with an appeal to his vanity. Stanhope took Kaspar Hauser on a trip to Ansbach where he commissioned the well-known and widely regarded portrait painter J.F.C. Kreul to paint a pastel portrait of the foundling for 20 guilders (Fig. 127). 'To Professor Creul of Ansbach for a pastille-portrait of Kaspar Hauser = 20 fl.' On the same day—it may well have been a rainy period—the youngster received an umbrella costing 10 guilders, on the 9th a puzzle, on the 13th watercolour paints, on the 15th tickets for a firework display and on the 20th a golden pocket-watch, for which Stanhope paid 68 guilders (Fig. 128).

127. *Kaspar Hauser. Pastel portrait by Johann Friedrich Karl Kreul (1831).*

128. *Kaspar Hauser's gold watch, a present from Stanhope.*

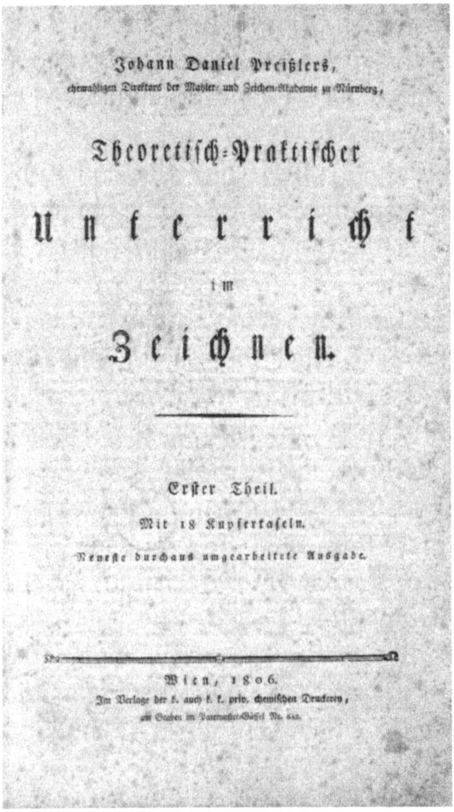

Johann Daniel Preißlers,
ehemahligen Direktors der Mahler- und Zeichen-Akademie zu Nürnberg,

Theoretisch-Praktischer

Unterricht

im

Zeichnen.

Erster Theil.

Mit 18 Kupfertafeln.

Neueste durchaus umgearbeitete Ausgabe.

Wien, 1806.

Im Verlage der k. auch k. k. priv. chemischen Druckerey,
am Graben im Paternoster-Gässel No. 612.

129. *Cover page 'Theoretical and Practical Instruction in Drawing' by Johann Daniel Preissler.*

On the 21st Kaspar was enrolled for drawing lessons and provided with the necessary implements. He was taught using Johann David Preissler's *Theoretical and Practical Instruction in Drawing* (Fig. 129).[237] The pupil soon showed himself a keen observer who could accurately reproduce the forms given to him (Figs. 130, 131). The fee for a month's instruction was 20 guilders and was paid immediately. On the 24th brushes, new colours and paper were bought, a fine sketchbook followed on the 27th. The 28th was a big shopping day. First, drawing lessons were paid in advance for the month of October—20 guilders—then more colours, a pair of gloves and a silk cravat.

Meanwhile, on their excursions together, Kaspar learned from his new friend that he was probably a Hungarian magnate and the heir to a large fortune, but he was not to abuse his unexpected good luck and should treat his future subordinates with care and love. Can the unhealthy effect of such a vision of the future so earnestly presented to a child be overestimated?

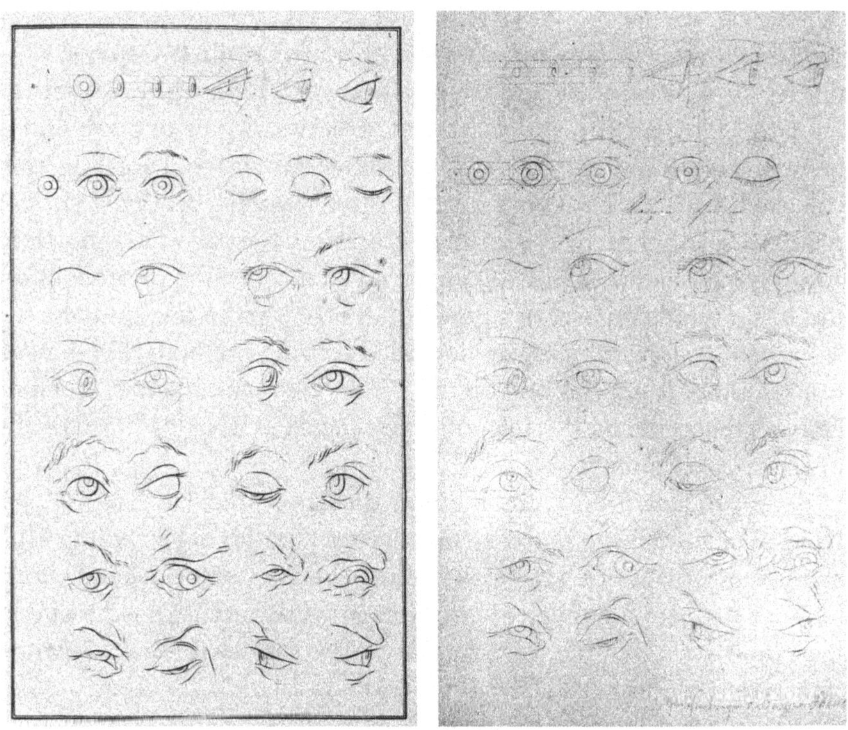

130. Studies of eyes. Left: examples from Preissler's instruction book; right: Hauser's copies.

131. Composition studies. Left: examples from Preissler's instruction book; right: Hauser's copies.

The following month began no less liberally. On the 1st October, Kaspar received a splendid jacket, a waistcoat, and long white trousers of the latest Parisian cut, and more watercolours. A pair of boots and a boot-jack were bought on the 4th. A songbook ordered for him was collected from the bookbinder's. On the 7th varnish and new special paper were purchased, and another portrait of Kaspar was completed, although it was not a success. He received a collection of brushes on the 10th, a whole box-set of colours on the 14th, and a few guilders for 'sundries', among which were included coloured ribbons. On the 19th came another songbook and on the 27th another pair of boots. November was the same: on the 1st another waistcoat and on the 5th 100 guilders as pocket money.

Baron Tucher found this method disconcerting. He had Hauser hand over to him the more than generous sum for safekeeping. This showed that Stanhope's tactics had already achieved the desired effect, because Kaspar had already become so inwardly accustomed to life in the grand style that he caused a scene. The confused letter which he then wrote to Stanhope states (Fig. 132):

> I am no longer to be trusted! Oh, I am all alone without you! Today was another sad day for me. My dear, dear friend; I have had to give up the

> 100 florins which you gave to me on the 7th of the month (November) at the parting which was so heart-rending for me. Herr von Tucher came today at six o'clock this evening and asked me if I had received money from the Earl? I said yes. I shall keep that for you, said Herr von Tucher. I responded quite well and said that if the Herr Baron would be so kind, I would keep it myself and if he wished to know on what I spent the money, I would always show him the bill for what I needed to buy. No, he said, I shall keep it for you and when you want something, you can tell me; I gave it to him with many tears as you can see here on the letter...[238]

The next day, the 8th November Tucher received from Ansbach a letter from Stanhope, which closed with the words: '...He [Kaspar] heeds my advice very well, which is always directed to his welfare, and I have the happy expectation that we shall experience much joy from him.' Kaspar's guardian would slowly realise what was afoot.

Sure of his success and of the tactics he was applying, Stanhope bought more presents for Kaspar: silk shirts, coloured ribbons, drawing crayons, theatre tickets to a performance of Scribe's *Fra Diavolo* (Brother Devil) (Fig. 133) on the 14th November at the Interim Theatre which included a character named 'Lord Cockborne, an English traveller'. Then came galoshes and on the occasion of his benefactor's 50th birthday on the 7th December different pyjamas with matching belts, hats, a purse with a lock and another only for

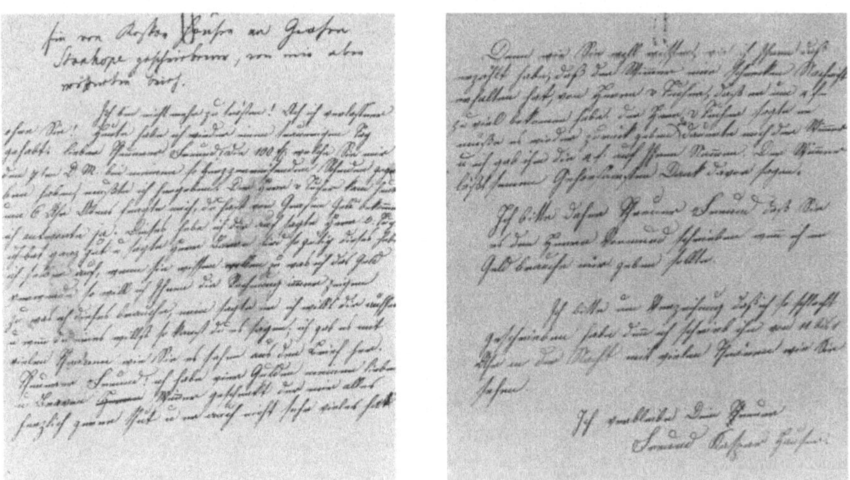

132. Letter of Kaspar Hauser to Lord Stanhope, from which the intended alienation from Gottlieb von Tucher proceeded.

items of clothing. In these weeks Hauser received 49 presents and 100 florins of pocket money, for which Stanhope had to lay out 370 guilders.

Strangely, during these early days the Earl also sought through gift-giving to make the acquaintance of a man who has until now

Nürnberg.

Interims-Theater auf der Schütt.

Mit gänzlich aufgehobenem Abonnement.

Montag, den 14. November 1831.

Zum Vortheile des Musik-Direktors Anton Dittmaier:

Fra Diavolo,

oder:

Das Gasthaus zu Terracina.

Große Oper in 3 Akten, von Scribe, übersetzt von Ritter, Musik von Auber.

Personen:

Fra Diavolo, Anführer einer Räuberbande unter dem Namen Marquis San Marco — — — — Geißler.
Lord Kokburn, ein reisender Engländer — — — Herr Ball.
Pamela, seine Gattin — — — — Dem. Trautmann.
Lorenzo, Brigadier eines Corps Carabiniers — — Herr Eike.
Mattheo, Gastwirth — — — — Herr Hosel.
Zerline, seine Tochter — — — — Dem. Germer.
Giacomo, Beppo, Räuber-Gefährten des Marquis — — Herr Frank d. j., Herr Huber.
Franzesko, Zerlinens Bräutigam — — — — — — —
Ein Bauer — — — — — Herr Wagner.
Ein Carabinier — — — — — Herr Kleining.
Carabiniers, Bewohner von Terracina, Diener des Milords, Aufwärter, Räuber.
Der Ort der Handlung ist ein Dorf in der Gegend von Terracina.

Die schon gemachte Einladung wiederholend, und einem zahlreichen Besuche entgegensehend, zeichnet mit vollkommenster Hochachtung eines verehrungswürdigen Publikums

ergebenster
Anton Dittmaier.

Eintrittspreise.

Reservelogen 1 fl. 12 kr. Logen des Balkons 48 kr. Logengallerie 30 kr. Parterre 24 kr. Amphitheater 12 kr.

Eintrittskarten auf alle Plätze sind von Morgens 9 bis 12 Uhr und Nachmittags von 2 bis 4 Uhr in der Theaterkanzlei, Nro. 38 bei Herrn Chirurg Fischer dem alten Theater gegenüber, und später an der Kassa zu haben.

Das Textbuch dieser Oper ist in der Theaterkanzlei, so wie an der Kassa für sechs Kreuzer zu haben.

Die verehrten Logen-Abonnenten werden höflichst ersucht, bis Mittags 12 Uhr gefälligst anzeigen zu lassen, ob sie ihre Plätze zu behalten gesonnen sind.

Die Kassa wird um 4 Uhr geöffnet.

Anfang 6 Uhr. Ende halb 9 Uhr.

133. Theatre ticket. Interim theatre in Nuremberg.

134. Friedrich Wilhelm von Hoven (1759–1838)

135. Karl Heinrich, Ritter (Knight) von Lang (1764–1835)

played no part in Kaspar Hauser researches. This was the Nuremberg doctor Friedrich Wilhelm von Hoven (1759–1838) (Fig. 134), who had studied medicine with Schiller at Duke Karl's 'Military Plant School' near Stuttgart. A sharp opponent of his homeopathic colleagues, to whose work he attributed a not insignificant number of avoidable deaths in Nuremberg, he was a keen student of the philosophy of Kant. For him it was solely a matter of demonstrating 'the groundlessness of all metaphysics'. Hoven wrote: 'Convinced that man cannot possibly know anything positive of the supersensory world, I held that what Fichte, Schelling, Hegel and all other speculative philosophers had said about it were but empty dreams.' That must necessarily have led to a cognitive blindness with regard to the phenomenon of Kaspar Hauser and a rejection of Daumer's views of the case. Hoven thus naturally counted among the first of those who energetically doubted the veracity of the murder attempt on Kaspar Hauser, the 'wonder boy', in Daumer's house. 'I believed,' wrote the doctor,

> that he had wounded himself and did it in order to draw to himself the attention of the public, and what seemed to confirm the rightness of my opinion, apart from the wound itself, which from the place where it occurred could not be understood as a wounding by another's hand, was that it appeared to me incredible that the hired assassin, instead of dealing him the intended deadly blow, would have satisfied himself with a mere wounding.[239]

The two doctors Preu and Heidenreich who also lived in Nuremberg and who acted as positive witnesses for Kaspar Hauser were not consulted by Stanhope either in 1831 or in the years 1833 or 1834, let alone given presents. Von Hoven, whose closest friend was Ritter (knight) Karl Heinrich von Lang (1764–1835) (Fig.135), the author of the *Hammelburger Reisen* [Hammelburger Journeys], promptly had his assessment ready for this harshest of critics of Kaspar Hauser just as he did after the second assault, namely that

> the vain, spoilt, even pampered person sought to save himself by a second futile attempt on his life from the memories which threatened him. He decided on another self-wounding in the hope that the outcome would be as fortunate for him as it was the first time in Nuremberg. But this time he did not get off so lightly. He stabbed wrongly, the knife went in deeper than he had wanted, the wound was fatal and he died a suicide, not as the victim of wounding by another's hand.[240]

Naturally no-one knew at the time of this earlier connection with Hoven, who was only the first of a whole row of sceptics and critics of Kaspar Hauser who Stanhope gathered round himself in the course of time. In these days Philip Henry now urged Mayor Binder to push forward the handing over of Hauser and deliberately fell out with Tucher.

How impertinently Binder was put under pressure is clear from hitherto unpublished correspondence between him and Stanhope which will be quoted later. After all Stanhope's initiatives, Tucher was concerned for the psychological health of his ward and on the 11th November wrote a clear and at the same time imploring letter to Stanhope:

> Nuremberg, 11th Nov. 1831
>
> Most Respected Sir and Friend!
>
> With the warmest and most intimate gratitude, I have to recognise the many favours, the many indications of your goodwill with which, in the few months you have been here, you have truly overwhelmed me; from the bottom of my heart I must lay before you my most genuine and true respect to which I am pressed by the acknowledgement of the great and unending goodness of your heart and by the rareness of your nobility of spirit.
>
> From this feeling of gratitude and respect springs to mind a third duty, that of trust—a duty which you so often and repeatedly impressed upon me and for the fulfilment of which quite certainly also from your side the same, or at least a confidence, is created, that I truly and honestly think that nothing in the world can take away my firm conviction of this, other than a sense of a wrong done against me.
>
> In such a mood I shall now put before you, honourable Sir, in a direct and open manner and in the certain confidence that you will grant my words a gracious hearing.
>
> Kaspar is not as you appear to regard him. Kaspar is a child, who in his entire being, in the moral aspect as in his spiritual development, is at the level of a 10/12-year-old. If nevertheless, in many things and in certain directions he shows a development of his character which one is accustomed to seeing only in adults, I mean for example his cleverness and craftiness in his relations with others, his quick sense for what is to his advantage in dealings and his great ambition, the determination and firmness of his will, his stubbornness—he is nonetheless a child, and the above-mentioned qualities still belong to the many unknown factors, the

many riddles that are associated with his whole being—and yet he is still quite a child whose special being deserves the greatest attention, the highest care in dealing with it, if this wonderful creature is not to lose the ground under his feet and become inevitably corrupted.

The great and rare goodness of your heart must have felt itself drawn by the expression of his childlike nature and the above-mentioned special qualities of his made him seem worthy of your complete trust.

Without wishing to credit the manner in which I have been predisposed to deal with him, which has been more through an indirect feeling than by anything rationally consistent, only through this can I feel myself entitled in good conscience to declare that this way of handling him is the only correct one in that, aside from that dire story of lies which I told you about, during these 1½ years I have had scarcely a single occasion to be indignant with him, whereas earlier, when he was with Daumer and Biberbach, there were the worst examples of lying, wicked falseness and hypocrisy of all kinds and he was, so to speak, chased out of the homes of these two certainly highly estimable men—and whereas he, I say this with a heavy heart and in all modesty, has since your last visit seemed as one changed and transformed.

I am very far from wishing to give you any kind of reproach hereby and I beseech you not to seek to find any such in what I have written—you are quite without blame in this matter: How could you even get to know this wonderful hermaphroditic creature who is neither wholly man nor child since indeed his whole manner of dealing with people and also his intercourse with you, for which he is grateful for so much, indeed for everything which his heart craved and desired even to the point of a certain hope of security in his future destiny—since all this led him inexorably in your eyes to appear only in the best possible light? And how excusable is that not also on his side? Just as I would not wish to charge you with even the slightest blame, so can I not bring even the gentlest reproach against Kaspar.

A reproach, a properly signal reproach would I see, however, as being justifiably raised against myself were I to avoid sharing with you further my experience and my knowledge of the boy. To do this now is the purpose of this letter. I am his guardian, and legally obliged to do the best for him. I and only I am responsible if I remain silent; I must therefore speak.

You will now first ask me what it is that has turned him round and changed him so? The answer to this question also contains the answer to the question as to the nature of this change. It is just through those special qualities of his that you have been tempted to make him your friend and to make a man of him. You have shown him a trust that one can only give to an intellectually cultivated and developed man. Without any kind of reserve about his relations with regard to the development of his destiny—what should be undertaken in this regard—in a word, you have placed the child, in his own self-image naturally, on the level of an adult.

Into the boundless vanity, which good nature has laid in his soul to such a rich extent, and which the insensitive and unreasonable behaviour of simple-minded people here has nurtured and cultivated, you have quite blamelessly brought into his already sick being a poison, which no psychologist, not even the best, will ever again be able to remove.

What now follows from this? The boy now feels himself endlessly unhappy, oppressed, persecuted, misunderstood. How could the way of dealing with him which I reasonably provided, namely that of treating him as a child, now appear to him, in his position as a man of understanding, as anything other than an outrageous injustice? The Lord Earl has satisfied each and every gentle wish of his heart in such a liberal and magnanimous manner that he now believes that since this cannot be expected of me, the cause is to be found only in a lack of real love, or, what is worse, from the intention, for God knows what reasons, not to satisfy his justified desires. The Lord Earl has made him a present of 100 guilders, a sum which a child cannot hold in his hands. I took it from him albeit with the definite assurance it would be used for those of his wishes which were useful and expedient. He wept the whole night long and now feels himself totally abandoned and without friends apart from yourself. The whole recent period, for a long time now, before you departed from here, he has been, despite all the friendliness and love shown to him, cold, loveless, and unfriendly, almost every third word a lie—how can he now any more trust people who misjudge him so much, who pay so little attention to his worth, which he has found the Lord Earl understands so well? My mother, a very experienced, intelligent and certainly a most loving woman has through his behaviour now lost all the trust and goodwill which she gave to him earlier to such a rich extent, for she has become convinced in all certitude that in this manner the kind of relationship that obtained formerly could no longer be maintained. His faithful memory will not let him forget anything; his vanity makes him paint all his experiences in the loveliest colours. Recognising this basic evil and foreseeing the forms it will take in the future, she has declared firmly that she does not wish to have Kaspar in her house at any price next winter, so I would really be put in a most awkward situation in such a case, since my winter accommodation is too small to have him with me.

I myself—who have shown him only love and the most well-meaning concern have had to tell him off repeatedly recently and this all the more since I have noticed the change in him and therefore did all I could to reduce or stop it—have lost his trust completely, which shows itself, to give but one example, in the fact that he never tells me so much as a word about what you and he have spoken of together e.g. the portraits and similar commissions. Naturally! In his own mind he is now quite another person from the one who was under my guidance and care! The most careful and considered reflection now leads me to put to you the following proposals:

Either, you have the goodness to assume responsibility for the boy and relieve me of my duty of guardianship and therefore the responsibilities incumbent upon me or you have the goodness to provide a year's funds which would put me in a position to help him exclusively through education and cultivation to become an intelligent, cultivated man—though where I could accomplish this, I now own I do not yet know, especially in view of his necessary police guard—or finally, you have the goodness for the course of at least a few years to abjure all and every communication, written and oral, in which case I will oblige myself to provide you with constant uninterrupted reports on Kaspar's state, his deeds and activities.

Only in these ways will I be able to find tranquillity and believe that I will be able to meet the requirements which are made of me and which Kaspar himself will make of me when he has grown up.

I have here quite openly and in the fullest confidence addressed myself to your great goodness of heart, to your superior insight, to your nobility of spirit. Please give me now also confidence from your side that I have expressed myself according to my best conviction, and after a mature consideration of all the circumstances from which I cannot depart unless I can be provided with evidence that I am in the wrong, from which conviction even the thought that what I have said has astonished your honourable heart cannot dissuade me.

I repeat once more that my whole heart, my reason declares you to be free of all blame; you followed only the impulse of a noble and excellent feeling, for which a gracious Providence will reward you richly. Above all, I beseech you, for the sake of your love for the boy, not to let what I have said diminish your goodwill and your favour towards him but to remain for him no less than heretofore a true and loving father of a now misguided child.

Finally, please extend also to me your gracious affection and your confidence and please rest assured that I shall never cease to remain, with the deepest and warmest respect,

Your most obedient servant G. Baron von Tucher.[241]

Such suggestions of pedagogical dillettantism were too much for Stanhope. He complained to Feuerbach about Tucher's proposals. Feuerbach was forced to pass his complaints on to Tucher.

'I must admit,' replied Tucher to Feuerbach on the 18th November,

that I had not imagined that Lord Stanhope could behave with such unreasonableness. I do not feel myself predisposed in the slightest to withdraw what I wrote after mature consideration in a calm and rational frame of mind. If the tenor of my letter seems too hard and brusque to you and to Appeal Court Counsellor Schumann, I would ask you most politely to bear in mind that *everything* I wrote to Lord Stanhope I had already expressed to him verbally on repeated occasions. But admittedly, it would have been quite different had I written in the same tone as that in which I spoke. How little my verbal representations to him made any impression is shown by his astonishment that the reason for my letter should have emerged in the first days after his departure...In the letter the expression: Kaspar had been chased out of Daumer's and Biberbach's homes has caused offence...with the approach of summer Biberbach begged me countless times most urgently to do whatever I could to get Kaspar out of his house, he could no longer put up with him. Insofar as that expression was overstated do I feel myself moved to retract something in my letter, but otherwise not one iota!

To my great satisfaction, yesterday the Chairman of the Chamber of Commerce Herr Merkel and not he alone completely agreed with me in finding Lord Stanhope's conduct most unusual...It would be equally unconscionable of me, since the Lord does not wish to have Kaspar with him, to push him away from me now because I know of no-one, here at least, who could take him on with a good conscience. It would be unconscionable in the highest degree to hand him over to the Mayor. I would prefer to bear everything patiently and try to settle what can be settled. The loving and caring treatment which on the whole he still receives will hopefully contribute at least to prevent him from making any hypocritical accusations against me, and so I would therefore like to hope for more good from the future than my view of the matter would lead me to expect. Appeal Court Counsellor Schumann has required Kaspar to speak about me. The clever smart lad had already long since left; why then would he wish to come here, it would at least affect him and his relationship to me, but one does not need much knowledge of his character to imagine what he would say and what he also had no external cause to deny. It is quite obvious that what he said to me does not express his real views. I abhor nothing more than self-opinionatedness, therefore I am happy to take a different view when it serves others best, as far as my honour allows. I do, however, hold my honour sacred and it is worth more to me than Kaspar. This is why I want to try once more to see whether it is possible with him, even by means of communication with his Lordship. If only further disadvantages show themselves, however, then whatever it may cost, I shall no longer hesitate to terminate the relationship.

It will be valid, however, only until next winter, so through this winter and next summer; time will then tell what my mother will then find acceptable. Now therefore comes my urgent request to Your Excellency: could you please pass it on as a request to Lord Stanhope—no further conversations or written communications with Kaspar that relate to his origins and to the precautions that are taken because of him, nothing whatsoever which raises him beyond his position as a child. The extraordinary honour in which His Lordship holds Your Excellency will make it easier for His Lordship to hear Your words. Time mellows all and here too we want to hope for the best from it.

With my constant and inextinguishable respect, Your GT.

A further letter from Tucher to Feuerbach followed on the 18th, in which he once again spoke of Stanhope's negative influences:

> Appeal Court Counsellor Schumann required of me a categorical statement that he could take with him back to Ansbach as the result of his mission. I could give him none other than the following. If His Lordship will not desist from his corrupting influences upon Kaspar, so I for my part wished to keep Kaspar with me since in the present circumstances hold it to be unconscionable to cut off communication or to push Kaspar away from me in that the former would lead to a complete break with His Lordship whom one cannot do without and the latter would have an even worse disadvantage in that I know of no-one to whom I could with a good conscience entrust Kaspar...[242]

The following day, the 19th, Tucher tried again to put his views to Stanhope in the mistaken notion that something could still be arranged that would be to Kaspar's advantage. In fact, the matter had already progressed further than Tucher imagined; by this point His Lordship no longer needed to hear anything of the guardian's ideas. He was sitting at the Hotel 'Zum wilden Mann' [The Wild Man] putting the finishing touches to his formal proposal for the handover of the 'unfortunate youth', while Tucher was still hoping for very different proposals from him. In this vein, he wrote to Stanhope in an almost placatory tone:

> I have heard from Legation Counsellor Schumann how much grief and offence my letter of the 11th instant has caused you. I am sorry for this from the bottom of my heart, and God knows how far it was from my intentions that this should occur and how much I feel obliged to show to you only my fullest confidence.
>
> If Your Lordship would be pleased to remember that everything I wrote to you in my letter I had put before you repeatedly by word of mouth, despite which, it did not seem to me that I had been able to convince you, so I considered it my duty to put my views before you once again and with greater firmness, in the hope that counterarguments would help me to see if I was at all in error. On this account I did nothing in the sense of making proposals; it was not my intention to set conditions, and I am very much prepared to listen to counterproposals which, I assure you, I shall consider in the calmest spirit of moderation, but above all I repeat that I can easily be drawn from my conviction by evidence that I am in error and out of love for the poor youth whose moral welfare seemed to me endangered, will accept this handover with the greatest pleasure…[243]

Stanhope saw no need for a reply. Two days later, without further communication with Tucher, he applied to him formally for the handover of Hauser with the help of a sophistic interpretation of the relationship which had since developed between the foster child and Tucher—something that the court could not suspect was exclusively a result of Stanhope's own activities. One will not be surprised when, after recounting everything that he wished to provide for Kaspar, Stanhope wrote: '…all of this, however, under the assumption and on condition that Kaspar Hauser is transferred to me myself for his direct care'. In view of this far-reaching desire and the lifelong duty incurred, one must be clear that the man who was the cause of such a disturbance of feeling, the man who had led the foundling to believe in a golden future, from that day onwards played a visible role in the life of Kaspar Hauser for only another 59 days. After Stanhope's departure on the 19th January 1832 Kaspar was never to see his new foster father again.

Stanhope's application to the Royal District and Municipal Court (Fig.136) read:

> Ansbach 21st November 1831
> The most obedient Undersigned, who has heretofore taken a human interest in the person and in the fate of the unfortunate youth Kaspar Hauser, has herewith come to the distressing conviction that on the one hand, the upkeep of the latter has become an unwelcome burden for the city of Nuremberg, and that on the other hand, his entire existence and indeed his whole future are endangered in that the approval or withdrawal of the 300 fl., which had until now been approved from the city's budget for his education and upkeep, are dependent merely on the changeable views of those who are responsible for authorising or cancelling the city's undertakings. Here too the Undersigned has had to realise how inappropriate the education and instruction of that extraordinary human being have been for the individuality of the same or, in the case that his origins should not be discovered, how little forethought has been given to the possibility of his being able to create for himself a necessary livelihood. For the above reasons, the Undersigned, whom God has blessed with such favours that enable him to be so fortunate as to be able to carry out duties of benevolence towards his contemporaries, feels in his heart all the more the call to assume a fatherly role for the unfortunate Kaspar Hauser, as he [Stanhope] has through various experiences in long contact with him [Hauser] gained the paternally benevolent conviction of how devoted this childlike mind was to him in loving devotion and gratitude.
>
> I have therefore after mature consideration decided to take upon myself the duty of care for Kaspar Hauser's existence and to provide for his education and maintenance not only during the course of my life but also to ensure for its continuity in case of my death, all of this, however, under the assumption and on condition that Kaspar Hauser is transferred to me myself for his direct care. I obediently request the Royal District and Municipal Court to regard this my statement as a legally binding document and, since my stay in Germany may only be of short duration, to expedite the matter speedily and with resolution and to proceed with all further matters swiftly. Since in this matter

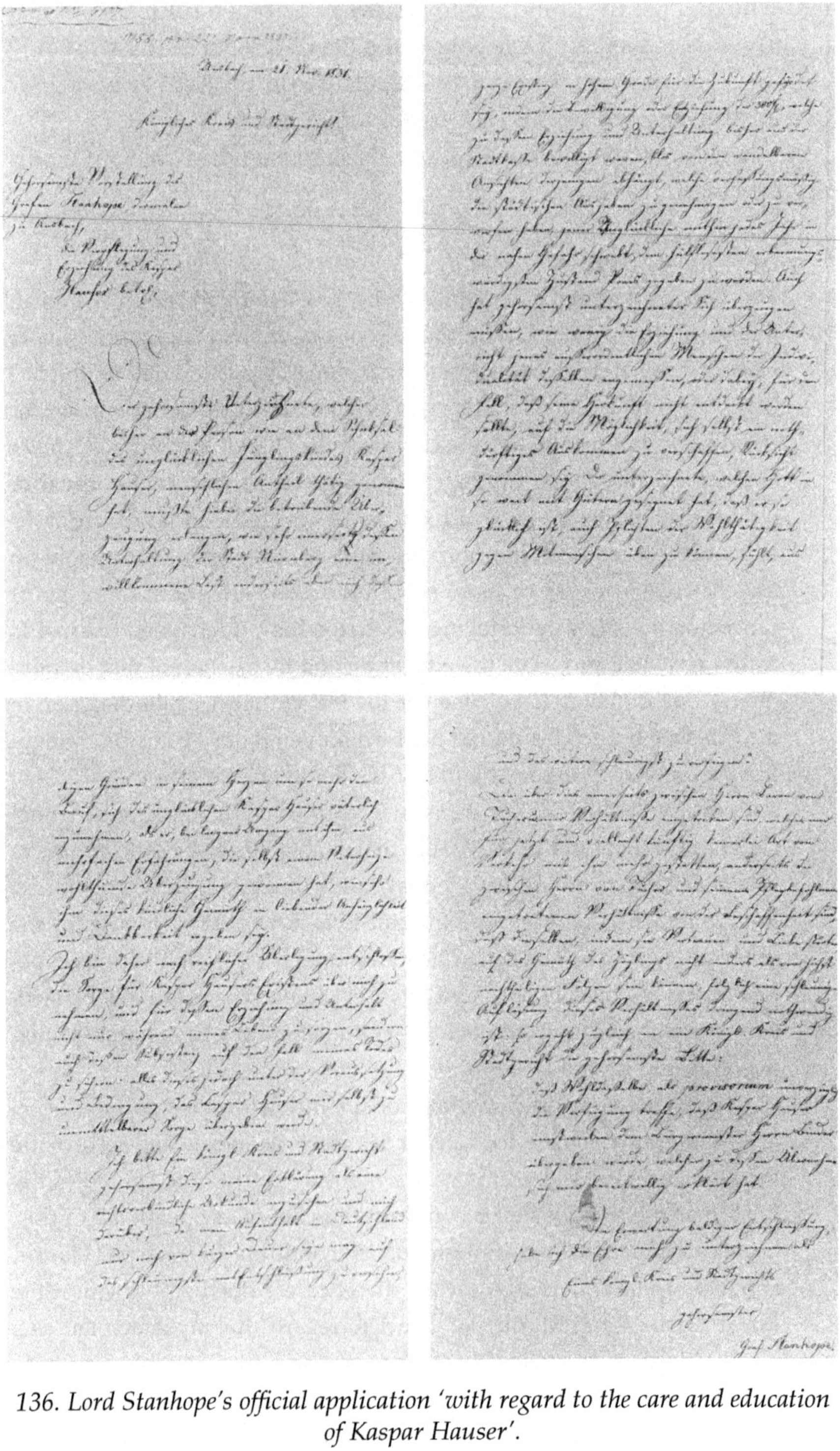

136. Lord Stanhope's official application 'with regard to the care and education of Kaspar Hauser'.

relations between myself and Baron von Tucher have taken on such a character as to permit no further intercourse with him for now or perhaps in the future, and on the other hand, those between Herr von Tucher and his ward are of such a nature that insofar as they disturb trust and affection, cannot but have the most disadvantageous consequences for the feelings of the pupil; as a result, a rapid cessation of this relationship is urgently necessary. Hence the following request is most obediently made to the Royal District and Municipal Court: that as an immediate provisional measure, Kaspar Hauser should for the time being be handed over to Mayor Binder, who has declared himself prepared to transfer him to me.

In the expectation of a prompt decision, I have the honour to sign myself as the Royal District and Municipal Court's most obedient

Earl Stanhope.[244]

On the same day Stanhope began to apply pressure for Hauser's handover:

...I submit herewith a copy of the statement which I have today given to the Royal District and Municipal Court and I beg that my wishes with regard to the R. District and Municipal Court be expedited *swiftly*. It is a real comfort to me that the willingness you have expressed to me through our friend Schumann for the temporary handover of Kaspar gives me hope that my wishes will be satisfied *without delay*.

Allow me to point out to you that under the *present* circumstances and after what has recently occurred, it would be *highly recommended* that Wimmer should *always* have loaded pistols with him.[245]

The 24th November was the date of Kaspar Hauser's hearing at the Municipal Court. Once again it was clear that the investment of 49 presents, some of them on a grand scale, the prospect of moving into a castle in England, all the flattery and promises of his own wealth and authority had had real effects on Kaspar. Tucher, by contrast, was helpless; on the basis of his correct and necessary pedagogical insights, he simply could not compete. Stanhope's conquest of Hauser's feelings was complete. Ignoring all the necessary requirements of a child's age, he had prematurely stimulated the youngster's desires and had set them seductively in motion so that by contrast with the sober and—in the best sense—firm Tucher, Stanhope was in an easier position. For Hauser, the noble lord meant the big wide world,

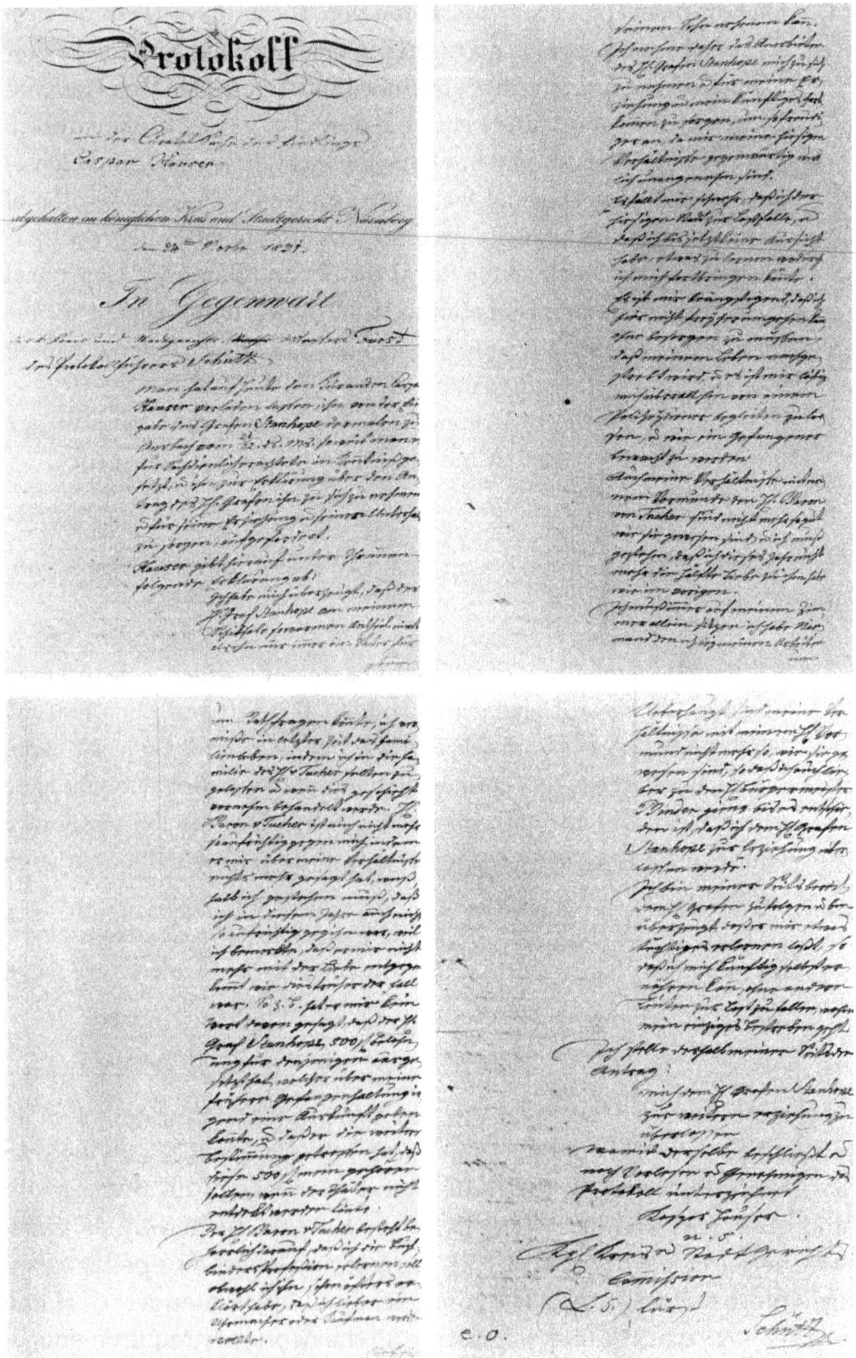
Protokoll

In Gegenwart

137. Protocol in the Wardship of the Foundling Kaspar Hauser, 24 November 1831.

while Tucher represented the narrow society of Nuremberg. That was intentional and was bound to show corresponding results. On the 24th November Hauser himself was now to declare how he stood in regard to Stanhope's intentions and wishes. Whether the expenditure of the last few weeks would bring the desired results was about to be revealed. (Fig. 137)

Protocol on the guardianship of the foundling Kaspar Hauser, held at the Royal District and Municipal Court of Nuremberg, 24th November 1831.

In the presence of: R. District and Municipal Court Assessor Fürst and Protocol Secretary Schütz.

The ward Kaspar Hauser was today summoned, cognised of the petition of Lord Stanhope, at Ansbach, on the 21st/22nd instant as far as could be usefully ascertained, and called upon to declare himself as to the proposal of Lord Stanhope to take responsibility for him and for his education and maintenance.

Hauser, weeping, made the following statement:

I am convinced that Lord Stanhope has taken a warm interest in my fate such as only a father can for his son. I therefore happily accept the offer of Lord Stanhope to take care of me and for my education and future development, all the more so since at present the relations I formerly enjoyed have become really too unpleasant. It pains me that I have become a burden to this city and that until now I have had no prospect of learning something through which I could advance myself. It troubles me that I cannot go about freely here without having to worry that my life is in danger and it is burdensome to have to be accompanied everywhere by a police officer and to be watched like a prisoner.

Also, my relations with my guardian Baron v. Tucher are not as good as they were, and I must confess that this year that I do not feel half the affection for him that I did last year. I always have to sit alone in my room; I have no-one from whom I can ask for advice about my work; recently, I have missed a family life in that I have seldom felt able to do as I pleased in the family of Herr von Tucher, and when this has occurred, I have not often been treated in a dignified manner. Herr Baron von Tucher is also no longer so sincere with me, in that he has said nothing more to me about my relationships, so that I must confess that this year I have also not been so honest with him, because I noticed that he no longer showed me affection as was previously the case. So, for example, he said nothing to me about the fact that Lord Stanhope had offered a 500 fl. reward to anyone who could provide information about my former imprisonment and that he had decided further that this 500 fl. should be mine if the criminal could not be discovered. Herr von Tucher insists that I should learn the profession of bookbinding although I have told him many times that I do not care for it and that I would prefer to become a watchmaker or a merchant.

My relations with my guardian are no longer at all what they were, so I would prefer to go to Mayor Binder until it is decided that I am to be handed over to Lord Stanhope for my education. For my part, I am ready to follow the Count ['Earl' is not a title used in German; Kaspar here said '*dem Herrn Graf*'. Stanhope was referred to in Germany as der *(Herr) Graf Stanhope—trans.*] and I am convinced that he will have me learn competently so that I shall be able to support myself in the future without becoming a burden to other people, which is my sole aim.

I therefore for my part request that I be placed under the guardianship of Lord Stanhope for my further education.

Whereby he concluded, and following a reading out of the protocol and having given his assent to it, signed it.

Kaspar Hauser
R. District and Municipal Court Commission
Fürst Schütz.[246]

This eventful day had not yet ended when Binder already had in his hands the next urgent letter from Stanhope.

My dear Mr. Mayor,

I have just seen my friend Hickel, who will soon have to go away on official business, but who is willing to leave *this coming Sunday evening* in order to arrive in Nuremberg between eight and nine o'clock that evening and at ten o'clock the following morning to pick up Kaspar and bring him here, and he will be accompanied to ensure the greatest security by my personal servant who will have pistols with him. Although this was not settled at the time by the Court, I hope that no-one will object to Kaspar being entrusted to me temporarily on a visit. In this case, all his possessions should be ready and packed by seven o'clock on Sunday so as to be ready for departure *without delay,* and I have the *ardent* wish, which you will certainly share, to have him brought to a happier place the sooner the better. I therefore beg you to be so good as to let me know as soon as you can whether the matter can be thus expedited so that I may make the necessary arrangements. Please be assured that in true respect and friendship I remain your faithful and devoted Count [*Graf—Ed.*] Stanhope

P.S. I enclose herewith a few sentences for Kaspar with the request that they be transmitted to him *personally*.[247]

This note to Hauser renewed the old promises and included the key sentence: 'I hope that we shall see each other sooner than you now think and under happier circumstances than the present.'

Hauser's ability to speak for himself was bound to Stanhope's intentions with presents, words and promises. His only wish and desire now was: away from Nuremberg, off to England and Chevening, to his new friend's castle, to freedom and a life without cares.

Dearest best friend! I received last night from Lieutenant Hickel your last letter and your first from Appeal Court Counsellor Schumann.

The content of these two letters has, as you can well imagine, distressed me deeply, and I could tell you much about that; I shall leave it for the present 1. because I have the happy expectation to see you again before my departure and 2. because I have indeed begun with what I wish to do for you though I have not yet set it right. Since I came here and I have constantly and zealously sought to promote your welfare and I have received the closest cooperation in this from my esteemed friend President Feuerbach, with whom I have here daily the opportunity to converse about it. You will well remember what I said to you on the 7th November when I had to depart: 'I hope that we shall see each other sooner than you now think and under happier circumstances than the present.' If I am not mistaken, this hope will soon be fulfilled, and when all is set right you will learn of it from your first protector, Mayor Binder, who will hand you this letter. Then I shall write to you about it in detail; until then I cannot do so and can only ask you to be calm and confident and to look forward to a happy future, which hopefully is not now far off. I always found from long experience and that after undeserved misfortune, Providence brings us circumstances through which we can gain confidence and relief. The counsels of Providence are for us unfathomable and lead us sometimes along dark and thorny paths but under no circumstances should we lose our trust in its goodness or neglect to make ourselves as worthy as possible of this benevolence. Until we meet again, always your warmly loving friend, Count Stanhope![248]

Binder answered Stanhope's letter of the 24th promptly the next day and appeased Stanhope's renewed pressure:

> ...I therefore beg you kindly to calm yourself until I am provided with a written decision by the R. District and Municipal Court but also to rest assured meanwhile that on the same day on which I receive it if there is still time before noon, I shall inform you of it through the post, in fact by express and I shall leave to your discretion by which means he is to visit you in Ansbach in all security.[249]

Finally, on the 26th Stanhope repeated his demand for an immediate handover:

> ...I beg you urgently to be so good, as soon as you are authorised and he has been transferred to you by the R. District and Municipal Court, to send Kaspar to me here accompanied by Wimmer and by another police officer and with all his belongings, in a rented carriage in which Wimmer and the policeman will return, and if he departs at seven in the morning, he will get here in good time. By this you will save much time and trouble instead of, as you propose, writing to me in advance...[250]

Three days later came another reminder to hand Kaspar Hauser 'definitively':

> I beg you to be so good as to hand this document in my name to the Municipal Court *without delay* and as soon as you have been informed by the Court as a consequence of this document that Kaspar is to be handed over to me definitively, that he be brought here to me in the manner I have already indicated, which hopefully will be possible as early as the day after tomorrow....I hope that the District and Municipal Court will send me an official letter as soon as Kaspar *is definitively handed over and entrusted* to me.[251]

Like Kaspar Hauser, Gottlieb von Tucher as his guardian was now summoned to be heard by the Court. But Tucher did not wish to make a direct oral statement in view of the nature of the case: 'The case is too important to me to be able to express myself in testimony on the spot. I therefore petition that I may be allowed to make my statement in writing by tomorrow.'

> The complete text of Tucher's letter in the Kaspar Hauser wardship case read as follows:

In accordance with the order given to me today to express myself with regard to the proposal of Count Stanhope of the 21st instant, I hereby comply by respectfully submitting the following:

Before, however, I proceed to the fulfilment of my obligation, I consider it my duty, as much to myself as to the respected guardianship authorities before me to justify myself on account of several accusations contained in the petition that has been made. Count Stanhope shows himself by this statement as an excellent man, worthy in his convictions, from whose mouth however, comes the declaration that between him and me relations have developed that allow of no further kind of intercourse with me and which must put my previous actions in the worst possible light. Through unfavourable relations of all kinds, to which I shall take the liberty of not referring, it so happened that after a year of living with us, Kaspar's moral development took a direction which justified one in a concern for his future: a high degree of vanity had already appeared, an unreasonable tendency to lying, falsity and hypocrisy embittered people against him in a most alarming way who had been responsible for his direct education and care, so that in the end, after I had meanwhile been made guardian, I saw myself obliged to try to take him into my house and to care for his moral and spiritual upbringing myself. Through careful monitoring, a precise setting of boundaries to his actions and impulses, through loving and friendly dealings with him within these limits and through firm and consistent strictures when such boundaries were crossed, I could now hope to lead this boy, who was not wicked in himself or by nature but had only fallen into bad ways and foolishness, onto the path of order through habituation to the good.

Without therefore wishing to confer upon myself any merit, as all this occurred on my part more out of spontaneous feelings than out of reasoned knowledge, I had the joy of seeing my goal attained. I can certify that in the 1½ years that he spent with my mother and me, there was not a single occasion which was the cause of displeasure or censure.

Then Lord Stanhope arrived, and all at once, especially since his last stay here in September and October, it was as if all the good influence upon the boy disappeared and as if his [Stanhope's] very well intended treatment of the boy which was nevertheless extremely harmful for his individuality called forth once more in a most decisive manner the wrongfulness that had lain within him earlier. I shall cite just a couple of examples. He told the boy that it was most probable that he, Hauser, was a Hungarian magnate and that one expected that, as his destiny would soon be decided in this connection, he was not to misuse his unsought-for good fortune but rather, was to treat his subordinates with mercy and love. Then he told him everything that had recently happened with a view to the discovery of his origins—it can well be imagined that in view of his [Hauser's] vanity, this was sheer poison.

Naturally, I could not long put up with this harmful influence, and as I had realised the source of it, I represented to His Lordship freely and openly my view of Hauser's character and asked him, unfortunately in vain, to conform to the reasonable and purposeful manner in which I was behaving towards Hauser. Since all my repeatedly expressed and, as it seemed to me, friendly representations remained fruitless, but rather, on the contrary, new manifestations of a wilful blind love appeared which treated the boy as a friend and grown man rather than as a child, I saw myself obliged to write to His Lordship the attached letter in order to tell him thereby clearly and truly but also most decidedly what had caused me to ask him to alter his highly damaging behaviour towards the child. This letter is the reason for the 'relations that have taken on such a character as to permit no further intercourse' with me. I did nothing more than what my position as guardian justified but which my heavy responsibility also obliged me to do.

A second no less painful accusation against me lies in the fact that Lord Stanhope believes that he has noticed 'how inappropriate the education and instruction of that extraordinary human being have been for the individuality of the same or, in the case that his origins should not be discovered, how little forethought has been given to the possibility of his being able to create for himself a necessary livelihood'.

While this judgement against me from the mouth of a man who was so incapable of being able to assess the individuality of the child can in itself be passed over in all quietude, I note merely that in initiating the whole process of his instruction, I, who am a stranger to the specialist field of education, have solely and expressly followed the advice of two extremely sensible men who have been no less concerned for Hauser's fate.

I had no other thought than to decide on some trade for him, but it seemed to me to be still too early to give him a particular regular occupation. The doctors' reports on him held him to be in December of last year a child of from ten to twelve years of age, an age at which one cannot think of giving a young person an occupation which one could hope would be successfully pursued. In addition, his eyes, his musculature, his nerves are of a nature that I did not think it possible to find him a job that would be suitable. He has therefore until now enjoyed a simple schooling and if, as part of this, Latin has been regarded as the necessary foundation of oral instruction and His Lordship does not approve of this, I note that neither I nor His Lordship will decide the well-known struggle between the humanists and the realists. The circumstances mentioned in the protocol today by Kaspar Hauser are all untrue. The truth is that since His Lordship's recent arrival, he [Hauser] has incurred numerous rebukes and reprimands through his refractory, wilful, obstinate and mendacious behaviour. A naughty child always considers the reprimands of his educator as a lack of love and sympathy. After His Lordship's departure, he fell ill and indeed, a child and a brother could not have been more lovingly cared for than the way in which my mother and my sister cared for the ingrate.

As a man of honour, I can declare, and my conduct of life heretofore will hopefully bear out my words: if the municipal authorities had revoked the 300 fl. provided, wholly or in part, I would have seen to it that Hauser would in no wise have suffered and I would certainly have put forward the means necessary for his further education. I submit this justification of my actions to the evaluation and judgement of the wardship authorities, but also as a protest *ad acta* in case unpleasant results should appear in consequence of later action by His Lordship.

I now believe myself also able to answer the questions put to me in the report. In his attitude and his heart, I have got to know His Lordship as a quite excellent noble man of a rare good nature. Equally so does public opinion describe him as a—by our standards—extremely affluent man in that he is said to enjoy a substantial annual income of £20,000, about 300,000 fl., an income which incidentally in no wise puts him as Earl and hereditary Peer of England among the richest. On condition that the esteemed wardship authorities succeed in providing for the requisite security in the case of an unexpected decease or other events conceivable as arising from the political situation in England, from the financial point of view, as guardian I have nothing at all against the transfer of Hauser to Lord Stanhope.

What advantages could accrue for the ward from a moral point of view, however, is quite another question, and in that sense I regarded it as my duty as guardian most determinedly to refuse my assent in that His Lordship has amply shown that he does not at all know how to cope with the individuality of the boy and on this account would only exercise the most harmful influence upon him if my relations with him were not to oblige me to deny my assent to the handover.

1. as His Lordship has expressly set the conditions for an exclusive handover,

2. no other accommodation whatsoever is conceivable from which the influence of the Count could be removed without causing his disengagement,
3. it can yet be hoped that he will follow the counsel of insightful friends and perhaps also take note of unpopular experiences and will hand the boy on only to sensible, cultured men.

Now that Hauser too has finally been acquainted with what has already occurred, it will surely happen that his hostile attitude towards me and my family will lead to all kinds of unpleasantness. I therefore request that, as soon as possible, he be removed from my house and that the aforementioned provisional measures be put into effect. In conclusion, I note that a number of weeks ago I submitted to the City Treasury my account of expenses for 1830/31 on the 300 fl. provided for Kaspar Hauser and my outlays for October and November 1831 will be added to that directly.

In addition, I still have 88 fl. in cash of the 100 fl. which Lord Stanhope presented to Kaspar as pocket money. I hereby hand over this money and therewith request that I be kindly granted a discharge from a guardianship which has brought me only cares, troubles, burdens of all sorts, and now also ingratitude and misunderstanding of my honest goodwill.

With the greatest respect,

From the most obedient servant of the R. District and Municipal Court

G. Baron von Tucher[252]

*

After all these events Kaspar Hauser found himself on a path with no return. Who would have thought that everything would happen so rapidly and smoothly! 'The pledge of love sent by Providence' was to be handed over only to the one entitled to receive him, assigned only to 'the one who would furnish full proof of a claim'. Where, when and in what form had Stanhope brought or submitted such proof? Not without fascination does the observer perceive the means employed by the agent who worked secretly and effectively to achieve such an astounding and unexpected result. Was it not realised how everything would proceed, and in fact was bound to proceed? Who, apart from Tucher, made any protest, recognised the danger or even described it accurately: that 'His Lordship has amply shown that he does not at all know how to cope with the individuality of the boy'? At this point in time, only his former guardian, no-one else. In these days and weeks, a kind of clouding of the public consciousness must have occurred in Nuremberg. It was as if a curtain had been lowered between formerly firm intentions and present actions, a curtain that formed a barrier which could no longer be penetrated by an impartial power of judgement. On the 2nd December, after not even half a year of personal acquaintance with his protégé, Stanhope had achieved his goal: the Royal Bavarian District and Municipal Court formally handed Kaspar Hauser over to the energetic applicant:

> After Lord Stanhope has furnished the requisite legal documents in which he obliges himself to care for the purposive education and upkeep of the foundling Kaspar Hauser, to ensure for the adequate subsistence of the same even in the case of his own decease, and to take all the measures which are required for Hauser's personal safety, the foundling Kaspar Hauser will be handed over to him for his education and he will be informed that Hauser can be handed over to him from Mayor Binder here to whose care he has been provisionally transferred. In addition, since Hauser was resident here for so long until he obtained another domicile and since the wardship entered into here will have to continue for some time yet, Lord Stanhope is also called upon to submit from time to time, and at least once a year a report on Hauser's education. Mayor Binder and the guardian Baron von Tucher have been apprised of this arrangement and Mayor Binder is called upon to report when the handover has been completed.[253]

The fuss was soon over, but as for the decisive phase, it had been a brilliant and surprising success for Philip Henry. Beyond Nuremberg there was strong criticism of the unusual course of events. In his second paper on Kaspar Hauser, the royal Danish Counsellor of Justice Schmidt-von Lübeck wrote: 'The city of Nuremberg, which apparently declared him [Kaspar Hauser] to be its adopted son, adding that it would never hand him over to anyone who did not provide the fullest proof of a legitimate claim to him, has nevertheless seen fit to hand its adopted son over to the British Lord Stanhope to be his foster son.' And after making some critical observations about Hauser's education, he went on: 'We must leave open the question of whether this is the only reason why the lord has taken him on, or whether there are other grounds which have moved him to it.' The author does not credit mere generosity alone. What other grounds could he have meant? Did Schmidt-von Lübeck too suspect that Stanhope was not acting of his own accord? He goes on: 'Just as little has it been made clear to us yet whether the city of Nuremberg has really bidden farewell to its adopted son in this manner or whether its connection with him will remain stronger and how it would react if someone with legitimate claims to the foundling were actually to appear.'

The Nurembergers had given no further thought to this admittedly unexpected possibility and unfortunately, the situation was exactly as the *Sachsenzeitung* (No. 29) of 3rd February 1832 communicated to its readers:

> The Child of Europe
> Mr Kaspar Hauser
> has been assigned
> by the Nuremberg Council
> to a British eccentric
> who a few years ago
> published a new German song book
> in Dresden!

*

Life-changing years are years of destiny. 1831 was such a year for Kaspar Hauser. Lord Stanhope appeared just over halfway—36 months—through Hauser's public existence, and thereafter, the youngster had only 31 months left to live. The turning point marks the beginning of a tragic phase, the rapid end of which was a given. From which perspective this fact is viewed is immaterial. It is clear that the arrival of Stanhope was a decisive signature. It is also evident that Stanhope's intentions led to an unambiguous result. And just this result, which solved completely to Metternich's advantage both the agonising questions of the Zähringer-Hochberg succession as well as the accession to the throne feared by Vienna, leads to the question of whether this story that was so full of 'coincidences' was the end of the affair or something else.

*

Bonaparte's son Napoleon François Joseph Charles, Duke of Reichstadt (1811–1832) was also granted only a short life, in Vienna under Metternich's oppressive close supervision. At about the same age as Kaspar Hauser, he was to die an equally early and tragic death. He was not murdered but died under circumstances which allowed him no inner space—circumstances which robbed him of his life in a subtle fashion. The Duke was not supposed, was not allowed, to experience what was going on in the world. Metternich's worries were not groundless. Among the people, there was still sympathy, even respect for Napoleon Bonaparte, and these feelings increasingly flowed towards his son, who at his birth had received the title King of Rome. In children's playrooms mothers sang the rhyme:

Der König von Rom
Napoleons Sohn
Ist noch zu klein,
Kaiser zu sein.

[The King of Rome
Napoleon's son
Is still too small,
An emperor to become.]

Harmless certainly, and yet it was evidence enough for the imperial eavesdroppers. 'Prince Metternich's aversion to the Duke of Reichstadt,' wrote Count Prokesch von Osten, 'has greatly increased.....The boy is a major problem for the Prince's system. Now, 20 years old, he suddenly appears before the Prince, who hates in him everything that he blames on the boy; the fact that he has to trouble himself over him alone suffices to make the Prince behave unpleasantly towards him.'

The destiny signatures of the Duke of Reichstadt and Kaspar Hauser not only show surprisingly similar traits in their origins and ages of life which point to common characteristics between them but also conspicuously to that constricting withdrawal from life which led both of them to a premature death. These parallels raise questions.

*

Stanhope's activities between 1816 and 1836—including his last blows against the dead Kaspar Hauser, from 1833 to 1836—relate to a larger question. From this perspective, of particular significance is the correspondence of the months of November and December 1831, which is cited below and which has until now for the most part remained unpublished. This period occupies a special place in the biographies of Hauser and Stanhope.

For Hauser, it was the break with those in Nuremberg who had regarded him as one of their own, and his consequent entry into the second, darker period of his life, in Ansbach. For Stanhope, it was the hour of satisfaction after a goal fully achieved. It was also the only and final short period of their lives that was spent together. This fact takes on a cynical character, in view of the ample protestations of love made by the new foster father. Thereafter, Stanhope simply abandoned Kaspar Hauser. Stanhope must therefore have read the letters of these days in full consciousness of the imminent end of the relationship.

After the official handover of Hauser, from Ansbach Stanhope first wrote to Daumer, with whom until then he had not been personally acquainted. It was a letter of self-justification, which in its key sentences, as so often with Stanhope, avoided the truth. That an opportunity for a meeting with Daumer during the months in Nuremberg should not have been possible is incomprehensible, given his importance in the Kaspar Hauser affair. There had been no such difficulties in meeting the doctor, von Hoven, to name only one. Rather, it is more likely that Philip Henry, following his infallible sense for delicate situations, avoided a meeting with the scholar. Direct perception of the putative foster father by Daumer would possibly have resulted in a disapproval of his activities that might have been supported by the municipal authorities.

The letter—previously unknown—which he wrote to Daumer underlines such suspicions. Stanhope's conflict with Tucher—the most important point of the affair—is here represented in a manner that in no way accords with the truth.

Daumer was able to perceive the veiled tone of the letter from a certain characteristic style in the text, the obsequious undertone of which, mixed with artificial expressions of effusive joy, was designed to represent the scheming procedure of the arrangements with the authorities—in effect the aggressive appropriation of Hauser—as something which it actually was not. This unfailing recipe was also later evident on similar occasions when Stanhope professed selfless motives for aims that were in his own interest. His equally effusive assessment of Feuerbach's book should also be indicated here—a judgement which would soon be revised as fundamentally as his apparent affection for the 'splendid youngster who loves and honours me as a father'.

'Most esteemed Herr Professor', begins Stanhope's flattering letter,

> although I have not had the satisfaction of making your acquaintance personally, your famous name has long been known to me through

the great and unforgettable services which you rendered to my young friend Kaspar Hauser. You were his first foster father and also gave him his first forming as a human being, and the deep gratitude which he owes you and which he feels will only cease to exist when he does himself. It would have been desirable and advantageous if the state of your health had allowed you to continue your supervision of him longer, for then he would have enjoyed quite another education than the wrongheaded and inappropriate one he has received of late. I have often regretted this and often sought to alter it, but in vain. Yet now I have the unexpected good fortune of being able to direct his education according to my own devices, and I have asked my friend, Mayor Binder, to give you sight of the letter which I wrote to him recently about Kaspar's current studies and affairs. It is most gratifying to me and accords with my keenest wishes that I have now become the foster father of a most splendid youngster who loves and honours me as a father and who shows me such trust, gratitude and obedience so that I am in a position to able to guide him as a father. But I did not seek to end his relations with his previous guardian; the cause of that was a letter which I received from him here to my indescribable astonishment. Four days after my departure, his previous guardian wrote me a long letter in which he declared that everything that I had said to or done for Kaspar had worked on him like '*poison*' and in which he put to me the following alternatives, of which previously he had made no mention whatsoever:

either I should take on Kaspar completely myself and provide for his care and education or I should give him an annual allowance, with which the guardian would seek out another teacher for Kaspar, or that 'at least for a few years I should desist from all and any *written* or *oral* communication with Kaspar'.

I shall never under any circumstances accept this last proposal, which I find highly offensive. Of the two options I naturally chose the first, which course of action has, to my great satisfaction and peace of mind, now been carried out.

You will be pleased to hear that my esteemed friend, President von Feuerbach, has written a comprehensive, thorough and highly interesting work about Kaspar Hauser, which is now finished and hopefully will soon appear in print.

He was good enough to let me have sight of it, and I cannot esteem it highly enough, not only on account of its excellent individual style but also because of the handling of the content and a ceaseless array of most noteworthy facts which confirm the truth of the story and are of inestimable value for psychologists. He has made grateful use of the numerous notes which you collected and has in many places praised you and your family most respectfully. This work, which will certainly accord with your wishes spares you from a great effort which in your present unfortunate (!) situation of ill health would be much better avoided in that it would place a great strain upon you to publish a book about Kaspar. For the sake of the cause itself, which is so dear to all of us, it seems to me desirable that there should not be two such works, which might divide the attention of the public.

Please be so good as to commend me to your mother and kindly be assured that I remain your faithful and most obedient servant,

Count Stanhope

Kaspar is now healthy and happy and greets most warmly 'the professor, his mother and sister'. (Ansbach, 9.12.1831)[254]

After the false description of the handover arrangements, Stanhope makes a proposal to Daumer that reads more like a threat than a well-meaning recommendation. Daumer, who at this time, as Stanhope notes, was already a very sick man, is given the unusual advice not to go ahead with a book about Kaspar which he had intended to write. Was not he, Daumer, Hauser's first teacher and most attentive observer, the very man to write such a work? Yet Stanhope seems to want to prevent its publication. Such attempts at interference makes it understandable why, to his last years, Daumer felt himself the victim of persecution.

But how might Daumer have understood this letter? At this early stage of the new state of affairs, besides himself only Tucher noted that Hauser had indeed been thrown into a frenzy of joy by the haste with which everything had been carried out and which had been necessitated by no outer circumstances, and that the city fathers had fulfilled their obligations with relief—yet apart from that, a much deeper question that had to do with the nature of the phenomenon remained unanswered: namely, how firm could the show of friendship, love even, which Stanhope professed for Hauser possibly be after such a short period of time? In December 1831 for Hauser and the authorities all still seemed for the best—of that there was no doubt. The new foster father was fulfilling his promises very correctly. During this period, he received from the bankers Lödel and Merkel confirmation of an arrangement entered into on the 5th December, whereby 60 gulden a month were to be paid to Lieutenant Hickel of the Gendarmerie. This was also an obligation which the new foster father had taken on.

But the appearance was deceptive. There was another side to it. Most instructive in this connection is a letter, published here for the first time, that Stanhope wrote to Grand Duchess Stéphanie. Before citing details from this letter, which is of great significance for an assessment of how she stood in relation to Kaspar Hauser, it should be recalled that in December 1831 Grand Duke Leopold was in the second year of his reign and that it was clear both to him and to his wife Grand Duchess Sophie what the Nuremberg boy could mean for the continuance of their rule. That under such circumstances there was no deep friendship between Sophie and Stéphanie is just as obvious as the fact that under these same circumstances it seems at first incomprehensible why Stanhope should at this point write a letter to Stéphanie that could almost be described as personal.[255] Were Grand Duchess Sophie and Moritz von Haber partners in an arrangement that aimed to render Hauser harmless for the Hochbergs? Was Stanhope planning on luring the mother of the heir so far into the net that she might recognise Hauser as her son, which would then have the inevitable consequence of a countermove by Metternich? Seen in this way, Stéphanie's careful reactions in which, with great inner assurance, she held back from taking the dangerous outward step, were a greater, indeed the actual, protection for Hauser. From this perspective, all the over-emphasis on her later, very reserved comments in the Kaspar Hauser affair loses its argumentative force. The Dowager Grand Duchess—'the only metaphysical head among the women' (as the contemporary social commentator Rahel Varnhagen von Ense had noted)—could at no point in time officially recognise her son without exposing him and herself to the greatest danger. Since the death of her husband Grand Duke Karl in 1818, she was no longer in possession of a single lever of power, either in Karlsruhe or in Paris. But within the confines of behaviour that was not deemed a danger to the State, she did indeed concern herself very much with the destiny of Kaspar Hauser.

We know this from the testimony of her daughter Marie—'My mother and I were always convinced that he was my brother'[219]—and from the examination of Viktor Bohrer in the Lessing murder trial in Zurich: '...the Grand Duchess, widow of the late Grand Duke Karl, had in the region of Landau and Weissenburg plied him with questions and promises, as she knew that he was well-acquainted with matters relating to Kaspar Hauser, and she offered to pay him whatever he wanted....'. We also know it from the following letter that Stanhope wrote to Stéphanie on the 22nd December 1831:

> The lively interest that Your Royal Highness has taken in the fate of my friend Kaspar Hauser allows me to believe that you would find it pleasing to have some recent news of him and perhaps have the opportunity to see him. The devotion and gratitude which he has shown me, the excellent qualities which he possesses and which have filled me with friendship and respect, the desire to improve his lot, which was most unfortunate in Nuremberg and only based on a very modest and insecure allowance, all this has moved me to take on the task of fostering him, and since with great joy and ardent enthusiasm and in full agreement with his former guardian, I have undertaken to care for his upkeep and education, the city authorities have entrusted him to me. At present he is here, pursuing his studies but in the coming New Year he will travel with me to England, accompanied by my friend Lieutenant Hickel, who is in the service of His Majesty, the King of Bavaria. This officer, an extraordinarily conscientious man of the most estimable personal qualities, has concerned himself very much with research, which is still being carried out, in order to clarify the mysterious story of Kaspar, which gives one reason to believe that he is probably the offspring of an illustrious family and certainly of a considerable fortune. I do not doubt that with the blessing of Heaven, all will soon be revealed and that he will be restored to his rights, of which he was robbed with such cruelty and injustice. If Your Royal Highness saw fit to grant an audience to the Lieutenant, who has been entrusted with this letter, he could have the honour of explaining some of the circumstances which could be of interest to You, and at the same time, he could respond to your commands with regard to Kaspar, who would, as far as possible, travel incognito in order to avoid pursuit by his enemies who have already once before sought to murder him, and also to shield him from trouble with which he would be faced, whether it be through curiosity or through the interest that people have in him, but he could have the honour of being presented to Your Royal Highness in a way that would not arouse public attention and have irksome consequences. I am, with the deepest respect, Madame, Your Royal Highness's most humble, faithful and devoted servant, Count Stanhope.[256]

It is therefore certain that Stéphanie had already shown a 'lively interest' before December 1831 and that, unsurprisingly, given their old acquaintance, she had had connections with Stanhope over the affair for some time. In 1830 Philip Henry was not in Germany, so beforehand perhaps? And what does Stanhope mean when he writes that Hickel could describe circumstances which 'could be of interest' for her? Still more usual is the offer that the Lieutenant could 'respond to your commands with regard to Kaspar'. If Stanhope took all this for granted, then it was also clear to him what ultimately lay at the basis of the Grand Duchess's 'lively interest'. What was still being mentioned with a hand over the mouth, as it were, in February 1832 between Feuerbach and Karoline of Bavaria was already obviously being discussed between Stanhope and Stéphanie.

Also noteworthy is Stanhope's offer to introduce Kaspar Hauser to the Grand Duchess, an offer he repeated a few weeks later when he visited Mannheim. And finally, could Stéphanie's interest be kept hidden from Grand Duchess Sophie, who regarded Kaspar Hauser as a dangerous rival? The month of December brought more significant correspondence, this time from Munich. On the 23rd the President of the Government of Bavaria, Arnold von Mieg wrote:

> Highly Honoured and Most respected Count! I have just left your residence, to which I wanted to hasten in order to hand to Your Lordship a letter received from my King this evening. His Majesty has not remained unacquainted with your beneficent work for the welfare of the once so unfortunate foundling Hauser. From his own high sensibility and depth of feeling, the King himself is best able to appreciate activities which proceed from similar convictions. He recognises in you a Briton, a man—a friend of humanity. It gives me the liveliest pleasure to be the bearer of a letter in which this recognition is expressed. Kindly accept, dear Count, once again my expression of the greatest respect with which I have the honour to be your Lordship's most obedient servant, Mieg.[257]

Included with this note was a letter from the King, already dated the 8th of the month, in which, this one single time, Ludwig lets slip half officially that for him too, Hauser is in no sense a runaway peasant boy, but rather '...certainly not born in that darkness in which he was held by his enemies...' and that accordingly, due to such elevated origins, he was entitled to the best care:

> My lord, my ministers have reported to me on the humanitarian interest that Your Lordship has shown in the mysterious foundling Kaspar Hauser in Nuremberg. This generous deed on behalf of an individual

> notable for his singular destiny, who was certainly not born in that darkness in which he was held by his enemies. This beneficence towards someone who is probably one of my subjects earns my satisfaction and acknowledgement, which I cannot fail to express to Your Lordship in these lines, and it is a real pleasure for me to have the opportunity to assure you, Mylord, of the feelings of real respect with which I am Your Lordship's very affectionate Ludwig.[258]

Stanhope replied on Christmas Eve. This important letter—also published for the first time here—does not appear in the work of the often-cited critic of Kaspar Hauser, Ivo Striedinger; rather, Striedinger cites four other, insignificant letters from Stanhope to Ludwig, which he [Striedinger] published and which were with justification sharply critiqued by Hermann Pies in the *Zeitschrift für bayerische Landesgeschichte* ('Journal of the History of Bavaria'). The archivist succinctly notes: 'The "address" in which Stanhope expresses his thanks for the [royal] recognition printed in No. 1 is evidently lacking.' Does the discernible unanimity on the question of Kaspar's origins appear to Striedinger inconvenient for his theory? It is at least noteworthy that precisely this letter is not supposed to have existed in the Privy Archives of the Kingdom of Bavaria. The text is as follows:

> Sire, the letter which Your Majesty was gracious enough to send me on the 8th of this month and which arrived yesterday evening, does me an honour of which I feel justly proud and which I most respectfully and gratefully beg to be allowed to acknowledge. The approval which Your Majesty has deigned to express is the highest reward for the modest services which I have had the great good fortune to provide for Kaspar Hauser, whose unique fate and undeserved misfortune has stirred worldwide interest and whose kind and excellent qualities have filled me with real friendship and respect. The protection which he has received from Your Majesty's subjects in Nuremberg, and especially from Mayor Binder, has filled his heart with gratitude, which he would be most keen to manifest to them, were Providence to restore to him the high position of which he was robbed through no fault of his own and with such cruelty and injustice. All the circumstances of the case indicate with absolute clarity that, as Your Majesty noted, he was certainly not born in that darkness in which he was held by his enemies. It seems impossible to doubt that he spent his earliest childhood in a foreign land, that he is of very high descent, and that he is heir to a great fortune and perhaps even one greater than that of a subject.

> The humanitarian sentiments with which Your Majesty is so extraordinarily endowed would find their highest satisfaction in a restoration of his rights and I trust that with the blessing of the Almighty this can be expected in the not-too-distant future. It could in many respects be of advantage and perhaps of significance for a State which had adopted him until then and with which he is connected through so many bonds of gratitude and devotion. I can claim no credit if I follow the call of my heart and show my friendship for one who shows me the love, respect and obedience of a son, but it is for me the greatest honour as well as the best good fortune that Your Majesty has been pleased to remark in so favourable a manner on my conduct with regard to him [Kaspar]. Your Majesty will perhaps allow me to mention that an authentic and most remarkable work on this theme is soon to be published by my friend President Feuerbach and that I intend to translate it into English for the education of my countrymen. I am with the greatest respect, Sir, Your Majesty's most humble, respectful and devoted servant, Stanhope.[259]

Everyone appeared to know that Kaspar Hauser could not possibly be the one whom popular opinion and the declaration of Binder had first made him out to be, but no-one, apart from Feuerbach, dared to say so. Stanhope, the only one who had access to the knowledge of almost all parties, the wishes, hopes and fears of the courts, especially of some of their principal members, stoked the looming conflict as he wished with information that turned this problem, unsolved on all sides, into a dangerous sliding weight that ran now this way, now that. Sooner or later, that would have to lead to consequences. These letters of December 1831 allow us a glimpse of the technique of the double agent, who knew better than anyone how to assess the state of relations between Baden and Bavaria and especially how they were affected by the Kaspar Hauser Question.

On the 22nd he had offered to take Kaspar Hauser to the Dowager Grand Duchess of Baden and two days later on the 24th, he asked the King of Bavaria to restore Kaspar to his rights—actions which laid explosive fuses in two directions, single as well as double, that could at any time lead to 'suitable' results. We know from Feuerbach's letter to Stanhope of the 4th February 1832 that Feuerbach had shared his 'prince theory' with Stanhope, so Philip Henry must have known that neither of his two royal addressees would seriously be able to think of doing anything of outward significance for the foundling. Ludwig's attitude was at this time more hesitant than ever, and with good reason. Since the Revolution of July 1830, the situation had markedly worsened: 'the liberal subversion, which threatened the thrones of Germany' was gaining strength, and a dispute of this kind between Baden and Bavaria could put the existing social order at risk. The Hauser Question would have to be reassessed. It was only logical that for his part, Ludwig should regard the preservation of the State to be a higher priority than the—from 1830 onward—secondary territorial issue, and in this sense, Kaspar Hauser was, from this moment on, no longer a prime instrument for gaining advantage in the game for the Palatinate.

It is doubtful that Stanhope was thinking on this level. Decisive for the question at hand was what he did, or what his ultimate intention was. First, the accepted role of the loving foster father was played out further in the style and the worthy thoughts expressed in the letters. But at the same time, the direction of decline which would gradually lead Kaspar Hauser into the dark side of life, was, at first carefully and then ever more openly, inscribed into his fate. We shall see how, within a few weeks, Kaspar's credibility and social reputation were taken away from him and how, at the same time, seeds of doubt in his origins and integrity were sown in the circle of his friends. The consequent inevitable isolation of the young Napoleonid was at this time evidently an accepted result on all sides, welcomed as much in Munich and Karlsruhe— even if for different reasons—as it was in Vienna and London. For 'the old Tory of Mr. Pitt's school' could in no way be expected to help a relative of the once feared principal enemy on the path to honour, esteem and enthronement. It is clear that Stanhope served more than one master, which had the inevitable consequence that what he said and did differed according to his place of operations and, when the situation required it, were even contradictory. He knew that such behaviour would have no ultimate consequences for him. Many followed suit, and England especially was to the fore in the utilisation of such unofficial manoeuvres.

> The activities of these diplomatic agents were not to be underestimated. They worked at the same time under the cover of official British policy. Unlike ambassadors, who were formally responsible for their actions, they could act, unhindered, all the more effectively in the interests of their governments. They were used when need arose, and could be disavowed at will. Their actions and impulses are hard to grasp in detail. Without doubt, they assiduously manipulated public opinion to suit

> their own purposes, and they certainly did not wish to know anything of a successful German policy...Their influence was especially strong in the smaller German states.[260]

What here applies to the army of British agents in general, accurately characterises Stanhope's activity in Bavaria and Baden right down into its details.

12. Separation

The Fraudster Theory, 1832

For Kaspar Hauser the first 18 days of the New Year passed like a dream. Just as in Nuremberg, his foster father continued to shower him with presents; more new clothes and whatever his heart desired. 'You would scarcely recognise him in his new blue tail-coat with its fashioned little buttons and his white neck scarves...' wrote Stanhope from Ansbach to Mayor Binder in Nuremberg. To the white scarves were added coloured ones, cravats, new breeches, a 'portfolio for Kaspar Hauser' and new spurs. Once again, Stanhope invested in about one present a day, 17 in all, before he finally and forever took his leave. On the 7th January the Ansbach publisher and printer Dollfuss brought out Feuerbach's long-awaited work: *Kaspar Hauser. An Example of a Crime Against the Soul Life of Man* (Fig. 138), and Stanhope was the first to purchase the sensational study, which also appeared in the United States the same year (Fig. 139). He paid 45 guilders for 25 *Copies of the President de Feuerbachs Work on Caspar Hauser*, one copy of which went the same day to the bookbinder with an order for a specially magnificent presentation copy 'for the King of Bavaria'. It was ready on the 14th January and sent off to Munich the following day, with an accompanying letter, which Ivo Striedinger also fails to cite:

> Sire, the graciousness with which Your Majesty deigned to remark on the services which I had the good fortune to be able to render Kaspar Hauser, allows me to dare to hope that in all modesty I may lay at Your Majesty's feet an excellent work about him that has been written by my honoured friend, President Feuerbach, and of which I have meanwhile made a translation into English, accompanied with notes. The friendly interest which Your Majesty has taken in the fate of this mysterious and extraordinary personality, who, as has been so faithfully and truly affirmed by the author, possesses 'an indescribable charm and goodness', will in itself be an ample recommendation for the work, which has been most beautifully written with the greatest refinement and deals with the theme in a most philosophic manner. I am, with the greatest respect, Sire, Your Majesty's most humble, reverent and devoted servant Stanhope.[261]

Kaspar Hauser.

Beispiel
eines
Verbrechens
am
Seelenleben des Menschen
von
Anselm Ritter von Feuerbach.

Herrn
Professor Abegg

138. Anselm von Feuerbach's 'Kaspar Hauser - An Example of a Crime Against the Soul Life of Man'. A copy presented by Feuerbach to his pupil Professor Abegg.

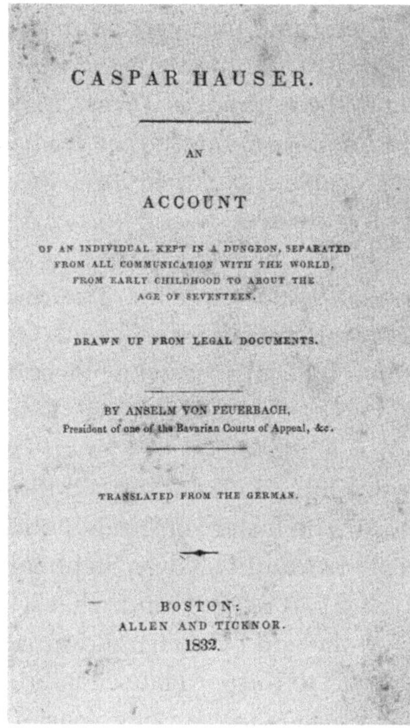

CASPAR HAUSER.

AN
ACCOUNT
OF AN INDIVIDUAL KEPT IN A DUNGEON, SEPARATED FROM ALL COMMUNICATION WITH THE WORLD, FROM EARLY CHILDHOOD TO ABOUT THE AGE OF SEVENTEEN.

DRAWN UP FROM LEGAL DOCUMENTS.

BY ANSELM VON FEUERBACH,
President of one of the Bavarian Courts of Appeal, &c.

TRANSLATED FROM THE GERMAN.

BOSTON:
ALLEN AND TICKNOR.
1832.

139. American (Boston) edition of 'Kaspar Hauser - An Example of a Crime Against the Soul Life of Man'.

Feuerbach was still the great criminologist and writer—but not for much longer. Just like Hauser he would be drawn step by step into Stanhope's ruinous campaign.

On the last day the foster father gave Kaspar another German-English dictionary, as it was supposed to be not long before they would meet again in Chevening. Until then he was to learn as much of the language as would enable him to make himself understood in faraway England. Was that not a final, very definite sign of how earnest the Earl was about bringing his foster son over as soon as possible? All the more astonishing is the fact that in all his extensive correspondence with his family in the years 1831 and 1832 there is not a single mention of Kaspar Hauser to his wife, children or relatives, let alone any indication that he would be bringing the foundling with him. That there is not the slightest reference to this possible intention shows only too well that there was never any truth to it.

Then came the heart-rending departure. Had Hauser guessed that the dream would so quickly come to an end? There was much embracing and weeping..... 'It was,' remembered Lieutenant Hickel, 'the separation of a loving father from his dearest child.' This day saw the irrevocable end of their time together; the curtain had already opened for the last act.

On the morning of the 19th January, Stanhope left Ansbach and headed for Mannheim. The distance was covered in two days via Schwäbisch Hall and Fürfeld. On the way, Philip Henry sent impressions of the journey, which despite a certain colourfulness in their trivial content, cannot deceive, when one contrasts them with what he was intending first in Mannheim with the Grand Duchess and later with Klüber in Frankfurt. Of those fateful conversations there is not a word. The foster son hears nothing about the fact that Stanhope had visited Grand Duchess Stéphanie on his account, how she and later Klüber had reacted, and what was moving Stanhope himself.

At the end of his truly dramatic visit to Mannheim, Stanhope sent a report to Kaspar Hauser as promised, but it contained only a collection of trivia instead of at least a few indications of the real reason for the visit to Stéphanie's palace.

> This town is almost as well-ordered as a chessboard and is very lovely and clean, but the surroundings are very flat and not at all attractive. The inns in this area are very good, though they are more expensive than in other more central parts of Germany, because so many Englishmen and other foreigners travel through these parts. The tables d'hôte contain a host of dishes which are all much better than the usual fare at the 'Star' or the 'Posthouse' [inns at Ansbach—*Ed.*] and one pays a florin for a large glass of wine or somewhat more. One can visit the grave of Kotzebue, whom I deeply respect as an author, and in the same cemetery lies his murderer, which is very unseemly, if not outrageous. His writings will continue to delight the public for a long time.[262]

And what was Stanhope actually doing in those days of 21–25 January? On the 21st he arrived in Mannheim, and already on the 22nd, was, as he reported to Feuerbach, 'very graciously' received by Grand Duchess Stéphanie, who asked him at table why he had stayed 'so long in Ansbach'. 'When I told her why I was there, she spoke to me for a very long time about the situation, but appeared to have only a superficial knowledge of it and no idea at all that the matter could involve her.'[263]

What Stanhope wrote here to Feuerbach is completely untrue. From Stanhope's own previous letters, we know that the Grand Duchess had long shown the greatest interest in the fate of Kaspar Hauser. On the 21st December 1831 Stanhope had written to her: '...the lively interest which Your Royal Highness has taken in the fate of my friend Kaspar Hauser...', so that it hardly accorded with the truth to inform Feuerbach in this inaccurate manner. It is in any case possible that being in the presence of others 'at table', Stéphanie could react in no other way. Stanhope could well have indicated this possibility but did not.

In the course of his letter to Feuerbach, Stanhope describes his conversation with Stéphanie in detail; as will be seen later, the astute criminologist would judge the conversation very differently:

> ...Amongst other things, she asked me, 'tell me honestly, who people think he is', and I [Stanhope] answered that it was not really known, but that it was certain and clear from the whole story that he must be from a very distinguished family and the heir to a great fortune. To which she replied: 'How would it then be possible that the mother could be an accomplice in such a crime?' I remarked that the mother could have known nothing of it, that the next heir in line had removed the child and locked him up in order to eradicate all his earlier memories and that the mother had presumably been told that the child was dead or abducted by robbers. She then asked sadly: 'How must the mother have felt?'[264]

After the meal, Stanhope presented the Grand Duchess with a copy of Feuerbach's *Example of a Crime against the Soul Life of Man* that included a dedication from the author, which Stéphanie kindly acknowledged, but which later, on leaving the table, she left lying there.

The following day, the 23rd January, Stanhope spoke to the Director of the Mannheim Court Theatre, Karl August, Count von Luxburg (1782–1849),[265] who hinted 'that the Grand Duchess was most curious to see Kaspar Hauser, to which I replied that if she were to express this wish to me herself, then I could have him come this way on his journey to England'. Stanhope spent the evening of the same day 'with the Grand Duchess, and as soon as I entered the room, she came to me and said "I read through the book most attentively and with great interest; I could not put it down".'

Stanhope next saw the Grand Duchess at luncheon, where she 'continued to go on talking about the case and in doing so, forgot about eating and drinking. She gave the book to one of her daughters to read, and her whole court now speaks of nothing else.' Stanhope also spent the evening of the 24th with the Grand Duchess (Fig. 140). Feuerbach then received the following report:

> I have just come from the palace, where the Grand Duchess and all those around her spoke continuously of your book and of the story. I was told that the Grand Duchess wept bitterly when reading the book and had red eyes for a long time afterwards. So great is the curiosity at the palace to read the book that the Chamberlain asked me to lend him a copy. The Grand Duchess asked 'if one could have the pleasure of seeing K[aspar] here?' to which I answered, 'that depends entirely upon Your Royal Highness's commands'. 'Yes,' she said, 'I would wish it very much.' I explained to her that it would be very necessary to avoid any sensation, and she remarked that it would be much better if he travelled under another name.

On the 25th, the last day in Mannheim, there were more significant conversations, which Stanhope also wrote down for Feuerbach. 'Count Jenison told me today "someone had been so shameless as to say that K[aspar] was a son of the Grand Duchess's and this opinion had even been expressed in the Press. Someone had even said so to the Grand Duchess herself. She had sighed deeply and said "I wish that I could believe it".'

How often was this exclamation of Stéphanie's later to be misinterpreted and turned into its opposite meaning! With few exceptions, everyone who spoke out against Hauser claimed that the Grand Duchess had hereby declared that she could not believe it, since she had only wished it as an expression of her doubt. However, her younger daughter, the later Duchess of Hamilton, reports: 'My mother and I were *always* [emphasis—Mayer] convinced that he was my brother.' The Grand Duchess remained in this conviction into her old age, as her granddaughter Countess Stéphanie Tascher de la Pagerie (1837–1859), who died young, also reports: 'that Grand Duchess Stéphanie as she got older [was] more and more ruled by the idea that her son had been taken from her and murdered'.[266] But let us return to Stanhope's letter to Feuerbach:

> I found it striking that afterwards, the Court Marshal [von Roggenbach] started the same conversation with me and said that K[aspar] H[auser] was a son of the Grand Duchess's...It was noteworthy that this evening too, which I spent in the company of the Grand Duchess, her Chamberlain

> [von Schreckenstein] began to speak of the same thing. He said 'one was everywhere of the opinion in Bavaria that K[aspar] has very much to do with us'... [i.e. with those in Baden—*Ed.*] The Court Marshal was delighted with your book, but also so shattered that he told me he had been unable to sleep and that his wife had read the book through twice. The Chamberlain was just as gripped by it and had to go out into the fresh air to cool down and calm himself. I spoke again with the Grand Duchess of the necessity for K[aspar] to travel undisturbed and without arousing attention; this made sense to her, and she promised to see to it accordingly. I told her that her entire Court, and other people, if she wished it, could see him, but that it should all be kept quiet and not be generally known, at least for a while after his departure. I said the same to the Court Marshal, and it was arranged that our friend H[ickel] should call on him and deliver the letter which I wrote in Ansbach for this purpose and that the Court Marshal should then ask the Grand Duchess when it would suit her to receive Lieutenant H[ickel] and K[aspar] and that she could in this manner see him without anyone knowing of it.

What may Stanhope have felt in writing the sentence about the many rumours from Bavaria, which said that 'Kaspar Hauser was a son of the Grand Duchess'?

140. Stéphanie, Grand Duchess of Baden (1789-1860)

This important letter is cited in its entirety in the book by Peter Tradowsky and the author [Johannes Mayer] in their book *Kaspar Hauser— Das Kind von Europa* ['Kaspar Hauser—The Child of Europe'], p.164ff. In connection with it, Tradowsky writes: 'Unfortunately, it is not known how Feuerbach reacted to Stanhope's report, which at least did not contradict his suspicions.' That corresponded to the state of research at the time [early 1980s—*Ed.*] The reply could indeed be imagined, because it seemed improbable that Feuerbach would not have commented on the rather more than merely confirmatory nature of the Grand Duchess's replies, but for a long time the existence of Feuerbach's letter was unknown. It is therefore a notable gain for Kaspar Hauser research that this important document has turned up and can now be presented. Feuerbach sees through the situation at the Mannheim Court completely; without letting himself be deflected by any conversational artifice and polite clichés, he sees how things really are behind all the etiquette.

> Ansbach, 4th February 1832.
>
> Your Lordship's esteemed letter from Mannheim, as you will readily imagine, has interested me endlessly, all the more so, since through the details provided, everything is so precisely and comprehensively represented as if I were seeing and hearing it myself. I often went hot and cold when I observed how the courtiers there see our cards or rather into our minds, for it is not in the least to be doubted that in that Court now it is known that we are looking for the seat of the crime in the related collateral line [of the family—*Ed.*] and even believe ourselves to have already found it there. When this transpires—all the more certainly to be expected, as the deeper the impression, the greater the stir caused by my little Kaspar book at the Court initially involved—it can lead to great difficulties or even new dangers for our Unfortunate, which is why the journey there must be undertaken with the greatest care, if it is to be made at all.[267] The most noteworthy thing in the matter is that, as I read it from Your Lordship's letter, from the publication of the Kaspar booklet and the oral comments which you have made in connection with it, they have really begun to believe in the possibility that things might not have been carried out so correctly with regard to the dead child. The great sensation which my Kaspar excites there, the disturbed nights, the tears etc., which it has caused seem to me explicable neither by a *general human* interest alone, nor by the effectiveness of my slight gifts of representation; apparently *personal* considerations and thoughts had the most

part in it alongside these other impressions. I am therefore not at all of Your Lordship's opinion that grounds for our earlier suspicion are now completely obviated, as you appear to consider. Also, the views which my esteemed friend Klüber expressed, have, far from weakening that suspicion, rather, have newly *strengthened* it—for, peculiarly! the firstborn, who was said to be weak, died (allegedly) in *October 1812* and, according to the letter Kaspar was carrying [when he first appeared in Nuremberg—*Ed.*] in October 1812 Kaspar was entrusted to the man, with whom [he said] he had always been! That the child was from his birth onwards sickly and weak—as the firstborn *usually* are or appear to be—made it all the easier to cover up and perpetrate the deception, as soon as the doctor was drawn into the affair. That many people saw the dead child proves nothing at all; any other dead child could have represented the child who was said to have died but who was actually abducted. Neither am I misled by *that* circumstance which at the time confused those much nearer the events. The mother[268] of those personages[269] who are currently in possession of the estates has the reputation of having been a most wicked intriguer, who bore a personal hatred against the mother S.[270] and who did everything for the sake of her own children. The crime, by which she got rid of all the male descendants, was in *every* way one for gain and brought nearer the hope of a future succession for the new, often questioned line [the Hochbergs—*Ed.*]. Where such great interests are involved, one is reckoning not merely with the present, but *in omnem eventum* also with the *more distant* future. Only from a woman are the most horrible deeds to be expected: the devil himself is certainly *in natura* not of the male sex but generis feminini.

Our brave Hickel, who unites an enthusiastic zeal for this case with his known insight and adroitness will soon apply for his passport to embark on the research trip for which Your Lordship has with such princely means equipped him. Between him and me the following arrangements have been made. On his return journey he will—if this does not make the discoveries in H[ungary] superfluous—travel to the castles in the area indicated by Klüber, and make a more precise investigation as far as [is] possible. For this purpose, however, Kaspar's presence will be useful. Then I myself would go there with Kaspar to meet up with Hickel and take part in the visits, which would at the same time be a pleasure and recuperation trip and for me of the kind I am accustomed to make every summer: naturally, at my own cost.

The good Kaspar is now my guest every Sunday and gives to me and all my family great joy. After meals he accompanies me to my study, where I try through conversation to contribute to his education and cultivation. He is a person in whom my interest never wanes and from whom I will eventually be parted only with the greatest pain. Only a non-human being could not love this pure innocent soul. He remains very healthy, has regained his glowing colour and makes good progress in learning.

As much as I am content with the real Kaspar, am I irritated by his image, the Kaspar born of my mind, which has already caused me so much frustration and horror that I would have to regret having written this booklet if I were not recompensed by the thought that I had for ever justified the unfortunate one against suspicion of fraud, supported Your Lordship's noble-mindedness, and done something in the way of fostering understanding and the sentiments of the heart in the few who have an appreciation for a genuine work of the mind or merely through their healthy reason are at least capable of some feeling. Here in Ansbach and in most places in Bavaria the booklet is, on account of its subject, merely food for casual curiosity and will neither be understood nor grasped rightly. Because I could not leave a few things unmentioned if I were not to appear before all the world as an *accessory* to his sins of omission and commission, Mayor B[inder], whom I generously allowed to retain the lawful punishment of the pillory, has become very ungracious towards me. I sent the work to him with a friendly inscription, and he had the impertinence not even to acknowledge receipt of the same. B[inder] should take care! I could still get back what has been missed and then he'll regret it!—Daumer's *finis* has now actually appeared; he himself sent it to me. What I feared has come to pass. Without any critical assessment, the whole pile of materials which Daumer collected has been laid *nude et crude* before the public. The most incredible things, partly even such as present an extremely suspicious side to the Merkers and others like them have been brought together. Daumer thus presents himself as a gullible enthusiast and through this, invites suspicion of the truth, which I have carefully presented in my booklet. He came to me, when I was leafing through his *opusculum*—for I did not like to read it—like that bear in the fable who in a show of affection smashes his friend's head with a rock. This too belongs to the events which have spoiled my happiness over my booklet. What pleases me greatly is the hope of seeing you here again soon, when we shall perhaps know more about Kaspar than [we do] now and will have received new material to discuss and puzzle over. Since I no longer have the pleasure of spending a good part of my evenings in your company, my life has become that of a recluse in

whose soul hatches almost nothing but gloom. Please be assured of my true respect and affection,
Yours, Feuerbach.[271]

In addition to his certainly realistic estimation of what Stéphanie and society at Court knew, suspected and considered possible with regard to Hauser or thought of pushing away from themselves what they deemed impossible, Feuerbach's letter also characterised State Councillor Klüber, who has already been discussed in this book. Klüber always adopted a helpful and positive attitude towards Kaspar Hauser and also after his death, but on one point, he remained impenetrable. After Stanhope's visit to Mannheim from 27th January to 5th February, he was Klüber's guest in Frankfurt, and every day Klüber had had 'on each occasion three to four hours' conversation with him' in which they had 'discussed various issues and [Klüber] tried partly to test the available data, partly to strengthen it and increase it'. Klüber then wrote to Feuerbach that his [Feuerbach's] theory with regard to the Karlsruhe Court was not tenable. Klüber, 'the knower of all Baden's secrets', chose a very diplomatic form for his answer to Feuerbach which makes clear how, as would be seen in the future, with regard to Stanhope he simply took the position that 'I fully convinced Stanhope that suspicion of Mannheim was completely groundless.'

Klüber, the adviser and agent of the Countess von Hochberg and her family, actually had every reason to deflect suspicion away from Mannheim, which is why he advised Stanhope pressingly under no circumstances to introduce Kaspar to the Grand Duchess—advice which, just this once, happened to coincide with that of Feuerbach, who had given Stanhope the same counsel, even though for very different reasons.

Feuerbach in fact saw through Klüber, but significantly, not through Stanhope, when he replied to Stanhope in the letter cited above that 'I am therefore not at all of Your Lordship's opinion that grounds for our earlier suspicion are now completely obviated, as you appear to consider. Also, the views which my esteemed friend Klüber expressed, have, far from weakening that suspicion, rather, have newly *strengthened* it.'

Klüber had spent a good twenty hours talking Stanhope out of his plan to introduce Kaspar Hauser in Mannheim. Why? Could it not have been all the same to him if the curiosity from Nuremberg had simply been there to gape at and then taken away again? Why spend so much time and why the allusion to intensifying investigations in Bavaria—in Marlofstein Castle for example—far from Karlsruhe? Klüber, it seems, knew a lot more, if not everything. But he never allowed himself to say that he regarded Kaspar Hauser as a fraud, which would have corresponded to the official Baden position, as he knew only too well whom he had before him, but also clearly recognised that an introduction of Kaspar Hauser, let alone an acknowledgement of him, would have unforeseeable consequences for the Grand Duchy.

This was the issue that Feuerbach wanted to clarify on his—in the double meaning of the phrase—'last journey', which took him to Frankfurt and to Klüber and then ended in his sudden death in the Ruhland Garden.

*

Stanhope left on the 5th February for Mainz, on the 6th for Bingen and in daily stages made his way via Bonn, Bergheim, Aachen and Brussels to Calais which, with Anton Heinrich, now familiarly known as Tony, he reached on the 17th. Every evening on his trip, he turned to his diary, and sent Kaspar six postings en route detailing stages of the journey in each letter. The harmless, droll reports, 25 in all, may have amused the abandoned Kaspar with its references to places which he would soon see on his own way over to England, and may perhaps have cheered him up. But he could not guess from reading these letters that the shadows which would soon turn into the darkness of night, had become longer and gloomier, and that Stanhope had long had other plans and thoughts in mind for him.

From a letter from Frankfurt Kaspar learned of a Mr. Albert who sold items connected with magic: '...He has a store of things which would surely excite your amazement and which at the same time would entertain and instruct you.' Then Stanhope writes of a large cake: '...I must also tell you of a remarkable cake which King August II of Poland had baked. It was 14 ells long, 6 ells wide and more than half an ell thick and to make it required more than 100 bushels of flour, 4800 eggs, 2 tons of milk, a ton of wheat and as much butter.'

In Frankfurt Stanhope visited a man who he mentions in no single letter but who played a role, albeit indirect, in the life of Kaspar Hauser. We only learn of his existence in a roundabout manner. Immediately after visiting this man, Philip Henry recommended his foster son to study 'oriental painting', an art which was making 'great progress' and especially an object of general amazement in London. He would try to find an instruction book in which Kaspar, as Philip Henry put it, would 'be able to study the colourings and forms which come from the East Indies or China'. The attempt to guide Kaspar towards cultures so completely different from his own also raises questions.

The young man mentioned had moved to Frankfurt in 1831. He claimed to be a painter by occupation and expressed the wish to give lessons in just this art of Chinese painting. He came directly from London where he returned in 1833 with his Frankfurt bride after their marriage. He was the 28-year-old legitimate son of George and Sarah Clark, and died five years later (1803–1836). His full name was James Abay Stanhope Clarke. What predisposed or justified him in adding Stanhope's name to his own and what was his connection to Philip Henry?

From Mainz, Stanhope's reports to Kaspar Hauser continued with a look back at his stay in Frankfurt. One might expect to hear something of the content of the more than twenty hours of conversation with Klüber, instead of which Stanhope reports:

> ...I shall not go again to the White Swan in Frankfurt, which is bad and expensive, nor shall I come again to the local White Horse, with which I am very dissatisfied, and now I am at the Roman Emperor. I have, as you know, travelled a great deal, but I have never met anything like what I have found here. The landlord, for example, is a coloured person or a half-negro and serving at table was another with woolly hair and very dark brown skin so that I found myself transported to the West Indian colonies.

From Bergheim Kaspar Hauser received a report about Cologne:

> The region between Bonn and Cologne is flat, bleak, and ugly. Cologne is a very large but very unfriendly city which is full of narrow, dark and dirty alleys...I ate there at the table d'hôte in an inn to which I shall never return and I looked in vain for a good one there. The road there from Bonn is bad and even worse here and a few years ago I told the King of Prussia that it was urgently necessary to have it improved.

Having arrived in Aachen, Stanhope told of his experiences at the Red House in Bergheim: 'The so-called "Red House", where I am lodging, is a very mediocre inn, which the landlord calls a "hotel", and it is so badly built that it shakes at every small movement, for example, when a door is closed, or when someone walks about etc and I even found that in bed, so that one expected that it would collapse.'

From Aachen, where he spent another day, Stanhope wrote another letter, this time about a ventriloquist: 'As I am staying here, I am thinking of seeing a ventriloquist this evening, who is very congenial, and also a wrestler, who comes from Frankfurt and is supposed to be so strong that here people say that he threw one man who wanted to wrestle with him up into the air with one hand and caught him with the other before he hit the ground.'

The only communication of any substance comes from Brussels, where on the 14th February he dined with Prince August von Schaumburg. Here too a bizarre light falls on the European aristocracy, which had its own particular store of knowledge about the relationships involved in the Kaspar Hauser case. 'I dined with the Prince..., who talked to me a lot about you...'

On the 18th February Stanhope and 'Tony' boarded ship in Calais for Dover, and this time were able to set foot on land within a few hours '...on the other side of the sea in beautiful Old England'. 'I had a very lucky and even pleasant voyage of 3½ hours,' wrote Philip Henry to Kaspar Hauser back in Ansbach, 'and the sea was very calm and the ship moved so little that you would certainly have no anxiety or unpleasant feelings of any kind.'

When, the next day, his arrival in Chevening was greeted as usual with peels of church bells, the longest yet of all his German trips was over. Behind him lay ten months of his last great effort to bind Kaspar Hauser to him. But immediately began, at first cautiously, and soon afterwards more strongly, his campaign of slander which would go on after Kaspar Hauser's death and would compare in its intensity only with his previous efforts to take possession of Hauser. Stanhope's first letter after his arrival went from London to Hickel, telling him that he was to search for Kaspar Hauser's diaries in order to 'see what was in them'.[272] What lies behind this request, if only with regard to the higher level of the whole affair, the whole course of events and the final result, which, however much the effort was made later to twist and turn everything around, was not accidental, but rather, completely intentional—and above all, convenient?

Lieutenant Hickel was travelling for a second time, at Stanhope's expense, to Hungary, and again without result. He had been asked by Feuerbach to stop on his way at Munich, where he was to hand the secret memorandum to the Dowager Queen Karoline of Bavaria, who as a princess of Baden was Hauser's aunt. It described the origin and fate of the foundling in a justification of his case that has yet to be refuted. The Court Chaplain Dr. Friedrich Ludwig von Schmidt (1764–1857) (Fig. 141) had arranged a private audience with 'Her Royal Majesty', and Hickel was thus allowed to travel. In his letter of thanks to Cabinet Chaplain Schmidt Feuerbach mentioned a detail that, due to all necessary caution, had not yet been discussed, which is all the more surprising, as it shows so clearly how daring Feuerbach's exposition was. 'It appears,' he wrote, 'that Kaspar had a younger brother, about whose life and death "the man, who was always with Kaspar" must have had some knowledge.'[273] This was Prince Alexander, who was born in 1816 and died the following year. Feuerbach thus disclosed the astonishing fact that Kaspar's captor knew of this, which means that the person in question must have known of the existing relationship but did not know how to keep his knowledge secret, since the criminologist had succeeded in discovering it. For Feuerbach, this 'knowledge' must have been convincing because through it, a vague suspicion became a tangible certainty.

The confidence with which Feuerbach disclosed such explosive information to the Court Chaplain has, remarkably, never led to questions as to what part Schmidt played in the Kaspar Hauser affair and how his activities are to be judged. If his name was ever rarely mentioned, it was only to the effect that he had arranged the audience with Karoline. Yet Schmidt was not only a very significant personality, but

141. Friedrich Ludwig von Schmidt (1764-1857)

a contemporary who was extremely well-acquainted with the whole question and with the issue of the Baden succession, and who, if the evidence is not wrong, was a silent defender of Kaspar Hauser.[274]

After the death of Elector Karl Theodor, his successor from the collateral line of Zweibrücken-Birkenfeld, the later first King of Bavaria, Max Joseph, had taken up residence at Munich in February 1799 with his second wife, that same Princess Karoline of Baden. She was Lutheran, and in the marriage contract her husband had agreed not only that she should be accompanied by a number of ladies-in-waiting of her confession, but also her own chaplain. Karoline chose Schmidt, who accompanied her on her entry into the Bavarian palace and remained there until her death and also his own.

With Schmidt, Protestantism entered into Bavaria, which, unlike all other German states, had managed to remain mono-confessional. With the name of this man was associated the foundation and the first activity of the Lutheran Church in Bavaria. In the early summer of 1799, under Schmidt, the first Lutheran service in Bavaria since the Counter-Reformation took place in a salon at the Nymphenburg Palace. Schmidt was not only an outstanding administrative expert, which gained him the friendship of the influential Minister Count Maximilian von Montgelas, but he was the man of the hour in a time that called for toleration to be translated into deeds, believing that 'in both confessions an honourable man could be a good Christian'. Educated both in the classics and in physics and mathematics, Schmidt was '...just the ideal partner at the time when toleration was bring introduced...pious of heart and of a well-rounded education, free from personal ambition and religious fanaticism, always discreet, legally trained, and a preacher of quality...'[275]

Such capabilities made Schmidt a central figure at the Bavarian Court and at the same time, the Queen's confidante. 48 years old at the time of the birth of the Baden Crown prince in 1812, he had, particularly as someone who was 'formerly' from the Baden town of Sponheim, consciously lived through and knew about the tragedy in Baden, and the yearnings of the people of Baden—and perhaps other things which were only spoken of in the circles of Baden clergy. Feuerbach trusted him completely, in that he expressed to him ideas which were no less dangerous than those in his memorandum to the Queen. As a result, Schmidt was well-informed and a collaborator of Feuerbach's. The Queen later wrote to her daughter Elise, Princess of Prussia: 'Many people are of the unanimous view that Hauser is one of the sons of my poor brother.'

Schmidt also carried on a lively correspondence with this daughter, Princess Elise, and into her hands came the testimonial, *The Memoirs of the Court Chaplain*, in which we find the ideas of the Dowager Queen referred to. Schmidt writes: 'The Queen never forgave the intrigues and equivocal role which the Grand Duke [Ludwig—*Ed.*] had played in these events. Yes, she blamed him for having sought systematically to bring down her brother [Kaspar Hauser's father] in order to gain the succession for the Hochbergs!.....' (*sic*!)[276]

Among those 'many people', one who held this view at the Bavarian Court was doubtless Friedrich Ludwig von Schmidt.[277]

*

On the 19th February Hickel handed over Feuerbach's secret *Memoire on Kaspar Hauser*, which is one of the fundamental documents of Kaspar Hauser research.[278]

Until now it was not known what Feuerbach said about the audience or what information he received about the conversations lasting several hours that took place on these two days. The Queen wrote to her daughter Elise in careful allusions on the 20th February that she had been

> ...receiving visitors until almost three o'clock, and today there were just two people, Herr Mortier, who has recovered from his severe illness, and before him an officer, whom I saw yesterday. He is stationed in Ansbach and is travelling to Hungary for research about Kaspar Hauser who has been under his protection for a long time and, as you know, has been adopted by Lord Stanhope, who will be taking him to England in June. I wish very much that the origins of this pitiful young man could be uncovered!—There is so much darkness in the story, and the two conversations yesterday and today have affected me very much.[279]

Elise then wrote about Feuerbach's memorandum from Berlin on the 11th March to her sister Amalie of Saxony:

> The author believes, without expressing it openly, that Kaspar Hauser is the son of our uncle Karl. *I know, you once spoke to me in this sense* [emphasis Mayer]. The portrait of this unfortunate youth looks really like our uncle...If that were possible! It torments and alarms me; I have been unable to sleep for two nights since I read it. Do get hold of this booklet. It is by a Mr. Feuerbach, I believe, in Ansbach...[280]

Amalie of Saxony must therefore have already expressed her own suspicions to Elise of Prussia at an earlier time! And on the 14th March 1832 Elise also wrote from Berlin: 'I had not the courage to write to Mama about the similarity of this unfortunate Hauser but I asked her to tell me who this Mr. Feuerbach thinks he [Hauser] is; for not long ago she wrote to me with great interest in this unfortunate youth and about investigations which an officer was to conduct in Hungary on the orders of the government...'[281]

Karoline answered her daughter's careful question about who Hauser was actually thought to be: 'Munich, Monday, 12th March 1832... Many people are of the unanimous view that Hauser is one of the sons of my poor brother. Although I am convinced that at least one of them did not die a natural death, I have unfortunately no doubt nevertheless that the crime was carried out to the full.'[282] Fortified by her mother's reply, Elise now asked whether Grand Duchess Stéphanie knew of the rumours. Karoline wrote back on the 26th March 1832 that Stéphanie knew of the suspicions about Kaspar Hauser. 'August Leuchtenberg, who saw him in Ansbach, told me that she had asked a lot about him.' (See pp. 165–167.) We also know that at this time Karoline spoke with many people in her circle about the destiny of the 'poor Kaspar Hauser', for example, from a letter of the wife of the British ambassador in Frankfurt, Lily Cartwright, who was born Countess Sandizell from Bavaria. How strongly the question moved Karoline and Stéphanie is shown by the fact that the Queen considered it essential to speak personally to the Grand Duchess about it. In May 1832 she spent two weeks in Karlsruhe, where she 'was together with Stéphanie almost daily'.[283] In view of the following references to Hickel, the subject of their daily conversations can hardly be in doubt. What Hickel reported about his audience can hardly be surpassed for clarity.

In another letter to Stanhope, published here for the first time, the whole extent of the tragedy is discernible. Prince Adalbert of Bavaria erred significantly when he wrote in his quoted essay that Karoline had probably shaken her head over Feuerbach's memorandum, which the Prince, without objectivity, called a 'concoction'. Karoline, on the contrary, must have gone very much further than this suspicion, further anyway than her daughter, since Feuerbach writes to Stanhope on the 12th May 1832:

> What I have heard from Munich and indeed from the mouth of the Queen Mother via H[ickel] will be of great interest to you. Before H[ickel] went

> on his trip, which was to lead him by way of Munich, I wrote a memorandum especially for the Queen in which I developed the reasoning and the facts underlying the supposition that K[aspar] may be none other than the eldest son of St[éphanie], who was said to have died. Through the Court Chaplain I arranged an audience with H.M. Hickel then actually had an audience with her lasting *several hours* and extending over *two days* in which facts came out which make me shudder when I think of them, and which explain St[éphanie]'s tears and sleepless nights which you told me about in your letter from Frankfurt. Before he went to Hungary, H[ickel] gave me a long report on that conversation. When I was still penning the previous pages of this letter I was thinking of inserting a copy of Hickel's report[284] into it; but when I took it out of my archive of documents about K[aspar] and read it again in order to copy it, I found that it would not be possible to entrust it to my letter without running into grave danger.[285] I must therefore here remain silent about the most interesting matter that has yet come up in the Hauser case and keep it from you until I either have the good fortune of meeting you again[286] or until I find a more secure opportunity of letting you have the document in question. It will astonish you and make you shudder. *Of all the horrors which I have come across as an experienced criminologist, the one that I have encountered in this case is the most horrific* [emphasis—Mayer].
>
> K[lüber] at Frankfurt is, I now realise and, if I had not been so forgetful since my illness, would have realised earlier, —a very weak authority vis-à-vis my supposition. K[lüber] was always acting in the interests of that family which was in a position to benefit from the murder or else the removal of Kaspar, and actually did benefit. He [Klüber] was and still is acting for them: but I fear that by this little I have already said too much.[287]

How concrete and confirming Feuerbach's report, which was unfortunately removed from his Hauser documents, must have been! Stéphanie's tears were no longer a riddle, and suspicion of a dynastic crime became a certainty. 'I must remain silent about the most interesting matter...It will... make you shudder. Of all the horrors which I have come across as an experienced criminologist...the most horrific....' Feuerbach's assertions leave no doubt or question that Queen Karoline had expressed herself clearly on the matter. '...But I fear that by this little I have already said too much.' Did Karoline at those two audiences, which had 'affected' her so much, say she thought it had been a case of an apparent normal death that had occurred twenty years ago, or had

Feuerbach's keen perception provided final confirmation of something she had always known? Everything speaks for the latter.

Feuerbach and Stanhope never met again, so Philip Henry never got to read the explosive document which the Court President dared not entrust to the postal service. But was Stanhope still interested in Feuerbach's conclusions? Had he not already long had very different ideas of his own?

Once again Feuerbach touches in his letter on the role of Klüber and again expresses his suspicion of the man. In his eyes Klüber was 'always acting in the interests of that family [Hochberg] which was in a position to benefit from ...murder'. That is clear and explains why Klüber for his part spent so many hours persuading Stanhope to abandon his plan of taking Kaspar to Mannheim.

*

What Karoline wrote to her daughter Elisa, (1801–1875), Princess Elisabeth of Prussia in Berlin, she also wrote to her third daughter Sophie (1805–1872), Archduchess of Austria, mother of the later Emperor Franz Joseph I. These letters were not without consequence as Sophie can hardly be thought to have kept such knowledge to herself. She would have told her husband and thereby caused a reaction, which was not to be considered an official expression of the view of the Austrian Foreign Ministry but would nevertheless achieve her purpose indirectly. The version of events represented by Feuerbach and Karoline, after it had become known in Vienna, would have to be countered.

It is very probable that the new account of Hauser's origins that now appeared stemmed from Sedlnitzky, the Chief of Police, who not only knew the rumours and the related police reports on the Palffys, but also the official instructions that expressly maintained that the Kaspar Hauser Question must remain a local Bavarian affair. However, not long after the exchange of letters between Karoline and Sophie, the story was spreading abroad from Vienna.

From March 1832, after Hickel's visit to Karoline, diplomatic channels were again used in Vienna to represent the affair as a purely Bavarian matter, this time as the indiscretion of an officer's wife. Such a story made the rounds in diplomatic circles in London in the spring of 1832. Stanhope, who was in a much better position to know how things stood, was able to make good use of this state of affairs for his change of course, which was just getting underway. The argument accepted and often repeated by some Kaspar Hauser researchers that members of his family apparently urged Stanhope to abandon Kaspar Hauser does not hold water; in fact, there were no such urgings. At the beginning of the year Stanhope was 'officially' still in line with Feuerbach, whose book he had had a splendid binding made 'for the Queen of England' while on a visit to Klüber in Frankfurt and which he had sent over to England to the Queen, who—as he wrote in a letter to Feuerbach on the 15th April—'has indicated to me through her chamberlain her acquaintance with it and the lively interest she has taken in the matter'.[288]

It was certainly not his family—who knew nothing of the matter—who were responsible for Stanhope's plans to withdraw from his foster son, but Philip Henry himself, with the significant assistance of the Austrian ambassador Baron Johann von Wessenberg (1773–1855) (Fig. 75) who, on Metternich's recommendation to Emperor Franz (Nov. 1830), was the second Austrian plenipotentiary at the 'London Conference' until his recall on the 15th February 1834.[289] Whether the diplomat knew what role Stanhope was actually playing remains to be an open question, but it is known that Stanhope learned of the new views in Vienna of Hauser's 'Bavarian origins' through Wessenberg. Whether the latter was only the intermediary, who wrote presentable, i.e. usable letters stemming 'from very secure sources', in which Bavarian cabals could be gleaned, is not known for certain, but it is very likely.

However, is it only one of the many 'coincidences' in the Kaspar Hauser affair that Wessenberg was a close friend of the Palffy family, some of whose members the Austrian authorities had interrogated because of Madame Dalbonne, which finally led to the Austrian reaction (see pp. 263–265)? In the eventful year of 1830 Wessenberg had been the only comforter of his friend Palffy at the latter's Malaczka Castle near Pressburg, when Palffy's younger brother Nikolaus was shot 'in a fateful accident' while out hunting in the area. That was in August. Soon afterwards, on the 28th November 1830, Wessenberg took ship for England. In any case, it was through him, knowingly or otherwise, that Stanhope was provided with some of the arguments he needed for a withdrawal from his foster son and it was through Wessenberg that these were then judiciously implanted. First, Stanhope succeeded in carefully distancing himself from Feuerbach. Hickel had—as was to be expected—returned from his second trip to Hungary without obtaining any results. One only needs to look at the map which Hickel took with him to Hungary to realise that 'the brave Frank' betook himself, all alone and without any ability in Hungarian, into that large country in order to seek for the infamous needle in the haystack. The enterprise amounted to a remarkable mix of dilettantism and naivety, above all, since Kaspar Hauser had never himself said that he came from the region. A couple of remembered words that probably surfaced from childhood memories of his nurse Dalbonne from the time in Beuggen—that was all. However, it had been Stanhope's idea all along, for whatever reason, to associate Hauser's origins with Hungary, although he had long known that Feuerbach was suspicious of this thesis almost to the point of certainty. Just a few weeks earlier, Stanhope had reported to Ansbach the views held in the circle of Grand Duchess Stéphanie and her circle that Kaspar Hauser might have 'much to do with "the House of Baden"', and now suddenly, after Hickel, as was to be expected, had returned with empty hands, he set to work, at first cautiously but then ever more insistently, to formulate the myth of Kaspar Hauser the fraud.

'I quite agree with you,' wrote Stanhope to Feuerbach on the 31st May 1832

> that there is nothing at all to look for or hope for in Hungary for him and that all the clues that we believed might be there were only will o' the wisps. Our friend H[ickel] has proved this to be the case *with complete certainty*, otherwise he would not have failed to make most important, if not decisive, discoveries, in that the localities appeared to be very definite, and he carried out his research with an amazing zeal, skill and accuracy which cannot be praised enough and which far surpassed my expectations. I know that you did not share my rash hopes, but if K[aspar] had spent the first years of his childhood in the region of Szalagusz, Nyitra etc. and had suddenly been lost or had disappeared there, someone in the area would have heard of it and could have some indications or at least anecdotes to tell. We must now confess, and this is what grieves me the most, that in this whole affair K[aspar] shows himself in a most unfavourable light. He appeared quite gripped, even deeply shocked when he heard the Hungarian words 'Istvan is going to Szalagusz', and we now know definitely that he was *never* there or anywhere nearby. When he heard the word 'Bartakovitch', he cried out 'that is my mother' and we now know that just as little as you or I did he have a B[artakovitch] as his mother. It can also be doubted that he even understands *a single word of Hungarian*, for as far as I know, he was unable to translate any, although he well professed to understand more and I find, on checking through the letter from Pirch again, that K[aspar] translated the Polish

> words for 'father', 'mother' and 'my dear' but not the Hungarian. Perhaps K[aspar] had picked up from the Mayor or from his wife something that was in the newspapers with regard to Hungary and *already* knew of it when he saw Pirch, so that the whole scene was a kind of theatrical, or dare I say, even a pretence? If his indications were so totally groundless in these cases and his feelings so feigned, how can we know whether they are completely true and certainly reliable in other situations? For example, it appears to me to be almost impossible that he is no longer able to tell anything of his journey and arrival in N[uremberg], although he describes everything so exactly and elaborately that happened only *a few hours later* at the captain's, at the police station, and at the tower, as is to be found in his own essay, which D[aumer] has had published. These points are of the greatest importance and should therefore be considered from every side and very precisely investigated, since the *first* people who K[aspar] saw in N[uremberg], the shoemaker W[eickmann], the captain's servant and another one testify against him, and the notes which D[aumer] collected can throw up many doubts, because he was not always possessed of a healthy understanding, appeared very exalted and credulous and had a strong feeling for wonders, which he shows in several places. The more I think about all these things and especially about those related to Hungary, the more dubious they appear to me, and it would be very worthwhile in all respects carefully to check the truth or untruth of [his] other indications.[290]

What had occurred to produce such mistrust? Stanhope had erred: one of his favourite and stubbornly-held hypotheses had been shown to be without substance. At the sound of the Hungarian words, Kaspar had remembered earlier experiences in Beuggen, and excited by this, had associated Dalbonne with his mother, which is hardly surprising, as he had never experienced a real mother. But how does that make Hauser a fraud? And who in the end had called for the trip to Hungary—Hauser or Stanhope? From all the knowledge available to us, can the possibility be discounted that Stanhope had foreseen the fruitlessness of Hickel's trip and included it in his calculations? The judgement that Stanhope from this point on expressed with regard to his foster son corresponded no longer to the facts as Hauser had himself related them, nor to the manner in which they were well understood by all those who otherwise had anything to do with him. Stanhope's break with Hauser, which was increasingly recognisable to others, took place between the 19th April and the 25th May 1832. That appears from the cause he sought and found to justify his decisive change of direction. 'The reason given by Stanhope for his doubts,' wrote Hermann Pies, 'Hickel's fruitless trip to Hungary, was, although negative in its results, no positive proof against Hauser that could account for the transformation of Stanhope's effusive and ardent show of trust in his "deeply beloved foster son" into precisely its opposite.' Pies too rightly suspected another reason.

Stanhope's ninth letter to Kaspar Hauser of the 19th April—fully a month earlier—had still been so packed full of overwhelming expressions of affection for his foster son, that it hardly allows for the conclusion that Hickel's fruitless journey could have produced such a reaction.

'My dearest Kaspar,' began Stanhope,

> I was so delighted to receive your dear letter... above all, I must, my dear foster son, reassure you and ask you not to have any fear about cholera... Your scroll contains a coloured and an uncoloured copperplate etching of your faithful, affectionate, loving foster father...you will be happy to learn, my dearest Kaspar, that I am now very healthy and have better appetite and digestion than before my departure....I miss you, my dear foster son, every day and almost every hour and I never see anything new, beautiful or interesting without ardently wishing that you were there with me. I never enjoy anything without regretting that you do not share it with me... I have bought a golden watch chain for you, my dearest Kaspar, which I find very beautiful. I hope it will meet your wishes and then I shall be very glad...The arts and crafts are making very great progress, and I have never found the shops in London so beautiful and amazing as they are just now. As often as I see them, I wish that my dear foster son were with me and could see them too...The feelings which you describe for me have gladdened me endlessly and I am so pleased that I have done something for your contentment and your wellbeing, my dear foster son. May divine Providence, in whose hands we are, deepen your happiness more and more and allow me further to serve as an instrument thereto and guide you at the right time and in safety toward the goal of all our ardent wishes! I am of the firm and happy conviction that you may see ahead of you a happy future and that your splendid heart, your noble, humanitarian convictions will remain unaltered. I am very certain that I shall always enjoy your love and friendship, which sweeten life for me so much, and that I shall never cease to deserve them, and your happiness will always increase mine, especially when I myself, as I so keenly desire, can be a witness thereof...I yearn to greet you again

personally and to embrace you once more. May God always give you, my dear foster son, happiness and blessings, which, affectionately and ardently, does also wish for you your faithful and deeply loving Earl Stanhope.[291]

The longing to hold his beloved foster son in his arms then completely disappears within a few days and not even a syllable mentions the previously often repeated relocation to England—instead, now everything is to be 'very carefully checked'.

The first witnesses, Stanhope suggests, should be questioned again, so for example, the shoemaker Weickmann, the first person Kaspar Hauser came across, to find out whether the cobbler could testify that Kaspar had already been able to speak complete sentences and had pretended to play a role. That would have been the beginning of the 'fraud'.

There were indeed local people in Nuremberg who asserted this. Stanhope himself questioned Weickmann in 1834, when, by a not insubstantial payment of money, he encouraged the production of the testimony he desired.

From April to June Stanhope occupied himself with Feuerbach's memorandum, which he had intended to translate into English in the first weeks after his return. On page 18 he came across the report of Dr. Osterhausen, in which the doctor referred to the anomalies in the joints in Kaspar Hauser's legs. On the 25th June Stanhope sent a letter to a doctor friend of his in London who —according to the way the question was put—was not so much to confirm this fact but to contradict it:

My dear Sir Henry

Allow me to beg your kind acceptance of the accompanying Pamphlet which is printed only for private distribution & and which may, I hope, interest & amuse you. I am very anxious to learn your opinion with respect to the peculiarities of the Sinews mentioned in page 18 whether they must not be supposed to be the original conformation, or whether they could have been superinduced by a long habit of sitting. & also whether a person who had constantly, day & night, & during years sat with his legs straightly extended would not have become so helpless that they must have sunk under him when an attempt was made to place him upon them, so that he would not without much time & practice have acquired the habit of walking, or even of standing upright, & whether

> the thighs & etc must not have been galled & excoriated. I trust to your friendship & indulgence which I have so long enjoyed to pardon this trouble, but the whole case is so very curious, physically, morally & psychologically, & both the King & Queen take a very great interest in the subject. Believe me to be with sincere esteem & friendship, my dear Sir Henry, most faithfully yours, Stanhope.[292]

It is thus clear that Stanhope is professing that he is no longer able to believe in Kaspar Hauser and considers that Hauser's appearance at Whitsun 1828 in Nuremberg was a pretence and his memories a constructed fairy tale. What accounts for this rapid reversal in Stanhope's attitude?

Just at this time appeared the previously mentioned four letters from Wessenberg, one after another, on the 9th, 22nd, and 27th June and then another on the 9th July, in which the Austrian diplomat refers to an 'important man', then a 'lady' and finally a 'person' who all give similar reports as to the identity of Kaspar Hauser's mother. Why does Wessenberg not name these informants? Is he not allowed to, or does he not know? Both questions are equally damning, and strengthen the impression that that the 'man' who enjoys his highest respect has just as little existence as the 'person' said to be befriended by Klüber. On the 9th June Wessenberg wrote to Stanhope:

> An important man has written to me that he believes himself to be certain that Kaspar Hauser is nothing other than the offspring of an illegitimate love between a Bavarian lady and an officer, and that the man who brought him up was tired of protecting him. My correspondent, who knows Feuerbach, avers that everything else is only mystification. I considered it my duty to acquaint you with this information. Perhaps the best would be to put the poor orphan into a cavalry regiment so that he might be assured of modest accommodation. I would not have ventured to tell you this if the man who wrote to me did not enjoy the highest respect. I assure you that I have mentioned it to no-one else.[293]

Thirteen days later, Wessenberg writes again: 'I have heard nothing further from my correspondent in Bavaria about Casparum H., but a lady has written to me from Munich, dated the 13th, that I can be sure that he is only the unrecognised son of some *loose-living Bavarian woman*, of the kind that exist here and there...'[294]

Five days after that, on the 27th June, came more news from Wessenberg about Kaspar Hauser:

> I wanted to tell you that yesterday, after I had seen you, I received a letter from a person who is friendly with Klüber, whom you know, and who told me that he is convinced of the mystification and that he would soon write more to me about it. I have lost no time in communicating this news to you, which will perhaps give you cause to wait a little with the publication[295] of which you told me yesterday. Klüber is a great authority for me. In any case, I am curious as to what Feuerbach was able to get out of the young man...[296]

Where do such decided judgements originate, and why did the Austrian ambassador suddenly get engaged in the Kaspar Hauser affair? For 'the young man', according to Wessenberg, 'knows more than is written about him in books, but he does not want to speak about it—therein lies the whole question. He would perhaps speak up if he were in Vienna.'[297]

*

On the 9th June Gentz died at his Weinhaus estate near Vienna. Stanhope was now without a partner. Metternich, one of the principals most involved, had never had much to do with Philip Henry personally—he had only received a few presents from the Englishman. His ideas had been communicated to Stanhope through Gentz. Yet the change in the direction of the Kaspar Hauser affair was in full swing, now more with the help of Wessenberg. The slogan 'Kaspar Hauser the fraud' had first been spread abroad by his accusers in the months after the failed assassination attempt of October 1829.

Stanhope's new attitude towards Kaspar Hauser, as evident in his letter to Klüber of the 22nd July, is to be seen against this background. The letter, fortified by Wessenberg's indication that Klüber too regarded the Kaspar Hauser story to be mystification, was intended to underpin doubts in the foundling's credibility. Stanhope wanted Klüber's 'authority' behind him and on the basis of Wessenberg's information, thought that he had already found an ally. The beginning of his letter to Klüber is similar in sense and phrasing to that he had written to Feuerbach on the 31st May. He continues:

> How is all this to be explained as anything other than a pretence? And if his indications on these points were so groundless and his feelings so feigned, how can one trust the rest? And would it not be possible, if he told everything truly and accurately, that the case would appear in

> another light? The doubts which now arise through this have moved me to reconsider all the real or apparent facts once more, and the more I look into them, the more many of the circumstances disturb me ...These doubts have prevented me from putting before the public my translation of the work by our friend Feuerbach, in that on mature reflection, it appears impossible to me that all the circumstances were as K[aspar] related them...Even if K[aspar] had spent many years away from Nature and from human contact, things could not, I am now convinced, have happened in the manner and under the circumstances which K[aspar] claims...[298]

Stanhope must have set too much store by Wessenberg's information; otherwise he would perhaps not have written this letter at all or else written it very differently. But in what light do Wessenberg and his dubious sources appear when one now reads Klüber's reply, in which there is no mention of mystification—quite the contrary! Wessenberg must have felt that by the passing on of his devious news, the veracity of which could easily have been checked, he had made a mistake that was far from easy to correct. On the 22nd August he therefore warned Stanhope already by discreetly hinting that he had learned of friction between Klüber and Feuerbach:

> My dear friend, I am sending you a letter from Herr Klüber which came my way yesterday from Frankfurt. My correspondent, whom I asked to send it me, says that Klüber appears to be somewhat shocked by your last letter and that he had concluded from it that you are no longer inclined to render your services to C.H. [Caspar Hauser], which would very much disappoint his friend Feuerbach, who seems to have shared his fears in this regard with Klüber. Fears which arose in him, Feuerbach, probably on account of the questions and doubts which you, for your part, raised about the matter regarding Kaspar Hauser.[299]

Klüber's letter of 2.8.1832, reproduced here for the first time, refers not at all to the opinions initially reported by Wessenberg, but rather, confirms once again the particular stance taken by the Baden State Councillor with respect to the way the whole Kaspar Hauser affair had developed, and which demanded of him, on the one hand, consideration of interests of state, and on the other, the exercise of his own moral judgement. Klüber therefore strongly refuted both 'the prince theory', which refutation he owed to the Hochbergs, the rulers of the state, but also the idea of fraud, on which he agreed, as ever, with Feuerbach. Klüber acted as he did towards Kaspar Hauser for reasons of state; as a human being, he was one of Hauser's strongest defenders.[300] Stanhope's hasty and confused withdrawal, his poorly thought-through conclusions, his now clearly emerging change of direction from its original pretence of ardent affection for Kaspar Hauser appear miserable in contrast to Klüber's honourable, clear thinking and powerful arguments. After Klüber suggestively cites Stanhope's motto *Vitam impendere vero* (Dedicate life to truth), he goes on:

> The key points at issue are the question of factual accuracy, conjectures, false conclusions and variations in the statements of those who have reported on this in public. Many of the facts could or should be clarified by reference to the documents held by the Nuremberg authorities. Conjectures sail on the broad seas of uncertainty, of possibility, and of the uninvestigable. They increase and decrease, and partly also weaken and contradict. The variations result from the differences which are grounded in the individual gifts of observation, objectivity and keenness of judgement of those who have made public statements. A discussion of every single question would have to be extremely detailed. It would be more suitable for a conversation than for a written communication. The conjectures of *Hungarian* origins appear to be based on simple error and now completely without force after the Hungarian language tests which I sent to our friend Feuerbach and which, according to his report, have been poorly received by Kaspar.
>
> Kaspar remains a great task for anthropologists, psychologists, and physiologists. As diverse and to some degree weighty the grounds for suspicion of *pretence* adduced by Your Lordship may be from the chronological or juridical side, be that pretence both single as well as in combination with others, in my modest opinion, two very weighty counter-indications remain unaffected by them. The one is of a mental, the other of a physical nature.
>
> Kaspar's consistently pure and unequivocally affirmed *childlikeness*—together with his common dialect, his awkwardness and gaucheness, his unmistakeable position on the lowest level of human cultivation when he first appeared in Nuremberg—is evidence of a natural child whose condition at that age is only explained by the story of a long incarceration since childhood. It is evidence of his intellectual incapacity for such a plan of pretence and its consistent execution; such a plan would have had to have been devised by others and taught to him. He could only have carried this out with the greatest and most persistent mischievous-

ness. The evidence for Kaspar's integrity is: his striking *modesty*, his constant insusceptibility for such physical enjoyments which people who had grown up in the greatest poverty and seclusion, although still in human company, such as a shepherd boy in the Swiss Alps, would give himself up to if the opportunity presented itself; his persistent holding himself from such things, his *dislike* for them, indeed partly his physical incapacity for them. Even [brought up] in the most miserable situations he would have discovered and maintained a liking and a capacity for other means of nourishment than bread and water; his *limbs* would have been significantly better formed for walking and jumping (locomotion) than was found to be the case in the first period of his time in Nuremberg, and he could hardly have succeeded, even with the greatest of skills at dissembling, to hide [the signs of] a better upbringing from the keen attention of open and secret observers.

Furthermore, suspicion of dissembling and fabrication is contradicted by: the [lack of] a rational goal; the indisputability of the long incarceration and seclusion; the murder attempt. The *goal* could only have been either to get rid of Kaspar or else to prepare a better destiny for him, or both. His very minimal needs in the miserable state of his body and mind in which he first appeared in Nuremberg were easy to satisfy throughout Germany, in extreme cases through charity or in welfare institutions. The abandonment of this most unemployable subject could hardly offer the prospect of a markedly better future. The best probable chance for him was to become a herdsman, day labourer or handworker of the lower classes. That would have been just as easily achieved in his homeland and without any danger of the heavy punishment threatened by the law for the crimes of personal incarceration, physical, moral and spiritual abuse and abandonment. If *the long incarceration* and the *enforced seclusion* had been a fabrication, it would ultimately have been exposed as such through the widespread publicity given to Kaspar's story even amongst the lowest classes of the people after his appearance in Nuremberg. The general sympathy for the foundling and the exact description of his personality provided by the authorities would have finally led to exposure. The *murder attempt* by a person unknown is essentially an incontestable fact, and while one may brood over minor details or take exception to statements made by Kaspar or others, the main point remains beyond doubt that the murder attempt was carried out by another, not Kaspar himself. What else could have decided someone to commit this great crime but the anxiety to avoid the discovery of the no less heavy crimes already committed against Kaspar? The long incarceration and abuse of an innocent boy, the sin committed against his body and soul, and finally, the callous abandonment. As for the riddle of Kaspar's journey to Nuremberg and his appearance in the city, could not the one who took him there have made use of *the drug* that was probably often employed during the incarceration, e.g. opium, in order to rob him of or weaken his senses for at least part of the journey? Under such conditions, he could have been transported in a barrow, a farmer's cart, a handcart or even in a carriage to *that* area of the city where he was found, without him being aware of it.

The error of the trail of *Hungarian* origins that emerged along the way appears to me to be less something that is to be laid to Kaspar's account than to that other error which let itself be carried away by a well-meant zeal to follow easy trails. Kaspar's mistake here seems to me to be as explicable as it is innocent. The frequent tests which were done on him, the constant experimenting and questions about his earlier situation stimulated his imagination, caused him to brood over the riddle of his story and awoke in him the idea of a superior heritage. It led to a striving to investigate his origins and solve the riddle of his history through mulling over and fretting about his memories. It even led to *dreams* from which images of people and deserted places that stimulate the senses such as castles, parks, and gardens (promenades) and the like may be lodged in his soul, which he later took for reality, for memories of the years of his infancy, which he later believed to be true, like Baron Münchhausen finally came to believe in the lies he had thought up in full consciousness. It is thus explicable according to psychological and physiological principles that in the periods of his education and development in Nuremberg, Kaspar was capable of and inclined towards illusions about his earlier personality. But it would be to do him a great wrong if one were to take this as proof of dissembling or to make him out to be a fraudster. In doubtful cases morality and justice, both natural and positive, rule this out. The cruelty of his fate would be greatly increased if an unwarranted suspicion of him served to take away the sympathy, benevolence and generosity which have been the only compensation for mistreatment of such unexampled barbarity.[301]

Was this reply from Klüber, who was for Stanhope 'a prime authority', enough to change his mind and restore his previous attitude of trust in his beloved foster son? There could hardly be a more convincing defence of Kaspar's innocence and credibility than Klüber's letter.

At first, it would appear that Stanhope was baffled by Klüber's unexpected rebuff. Had Wessenberg not assured him that Klüber had recently subscribed to the 'mystification' thesis and had even indicated that Feuerbach was inclining to the idea? The unusually long gap in correspondence—Stanhope wrote to Feuerbach first on the 5th and 6th October and then to Klüber—suggests that he did not find it easy to answer. Stanhope realised that he had advanced too soon and too far with his strategy. Nevertheless, he could not pull back from the discrimination he had embarked upon. His second letter to Klüber therefore continued in a similar vein; it carefully retreated on the main issue in order to renew the fraud theory all the more directly:

> You will have seen from my previous letter that I do not at all entertain doubts as to the main point at issue, which our honoured friend has so masterfully described and evidenced...I therefore never believed that the central issue was one of dissembling, only that it could not have happened 'in the manner and under all the circumstances' which K[aspar] claims. That he had been sitting for many years seems to be physically impossible.[302]
>
> I cannot believe that he did not look round when his hand was gripped [by the man who taught him to write at Pilsach—*Ed.*], that he heard no sound (not even thunder) from outside, although the noise of the rolling of his horse earned him a punishment,[303] that he could see on bright days after having been locked up in a dark hole for many years, that he can not remember anything from the beginning of his incarceration etc. Much can be suspected, especially all the circumstances relating to Hungary and not only after repeated efforts in that direction, of being attributable to self-delusion, created in him perhaps, as you believe, but in the first case with Lieutenant von Pirch. It should not be forgotten that two, if not three witnesses who appear to be objective and non-partisan, stated that he could speak at the beginning.[304]

Behaviour of Kaspar Hauser's mentioned by Feuerbach then provided Stanhope with a welcome opportunity to take up correspondence again with him and to continue in the same manner to put in doubt the credibility of his foster son.

'I read with regret in your last letter,' Philip Henry begins his hypocritical letter of the 5th October,

> that K[aspar] has behaved with arrogance and has therefore shown himself in a very disadvantageous light, and such a performance—that he

> had only to expect to become a distinguished gentleman—leaves very little to be desired if such should actually transpire. I never wished to nurture such an expectation in him, since it could be fraudulent [*betrügerisch—Ed.*] and very dangerous for him, on the contrary, I sought on many occasions to make him aware that one must rely upon the goodness of Providence but regard the future as quite uncertain, especially in these times, when we can lose everything that we already possess.[305]

Just a few months before, on the occasion of their departure together from Nuremberg, it had been the writer of this letter himself who had insinuated the notion of a noble heritage to the guileless Hauser and had warned him not to deprive his future subordinates of his good fortune but rather, to treat his people with mercy and affection. The seductive vision of that time, now half-conscious in Kaspar, was now honoured with the claim that it was 'fraudulent' [*betrügerisch*].

Meanwhile, there was no further mention of any imminent move to England, for which Hauser was still at this point longing. In expectation of his coming departure, he wrote on the 10th August 1832 in Ansbach in Frau von Bose's poetry album: 'Do not forget me when many, many miles separate us. When you then think of your friends, oh, so think again of me too. In memory of your dear friend Kaspar Hauser.'

But Stanhope did not touch on this. Feuerbach admonished him: 'Our poor Hauser has been utterly confused these days as to why for so long he has not seen a single sentence from his beloved and honoured foster father; and it will take much to calm him.'

In his desperation Kaspar Hauser wrote to the British chargé d'affaires in Frankfurt, Mr. Cartwright:

> Your Excellency will graciously forgive this unknown person, who in his great need, presumes to burden Your Excellency with the present matter. Since my foster father Count [*sic*] Stanhope wrote me his last letter on the day of his arrival in England from Chevening and as I have heard nothing from him since then, I am, as are his friends here, greatly concerned for him. Day and night I am tormented by all possible imaginings. I am especially perturbed by the thought that he may be ill. May God protect him from cholera! With such painful feelings, I dare to ask Your Excellency most humbly to be so good as to inform me of what you may know of the present whereabouts and situation of my dearest foster father and whether it might not be possible that his letters have been obstructed because of the cholera or on account of some other circumstances. Your

> Excellency would oblige me to eternal gratitude if you would be so good as to ease my concern as soon as possible.[306]

The months went by, and slowly it became clear even to Hauser that the travelling trunk would no longer have to be packed for Chevening. Disappointed by Stanhope's broken promise, the abandoned Kaspar pulled himself back: 'It can annoy me when someone promises something and does not keep his word.'

Yet still he went on sending melancholy letters to England. The condition in which the foster son found himself due to Philip Henry's behaviour is described by Feuerbach: 'Cares, sorrow and frustration have almost completely wiped away the meagre remains of a stunted youthfulness. There are lines on his forehead and around his eyes, his cheeks sag, his face has become pale.' Love betrayed.

But Stanhope turned the whole thing around and placed the blame for the fuss on his foster son. The noble lord wrote to Feuerbach:

> The letter which he wrote to me almost at the same time as yours shows that his melancholy stems from his misplaced hopes. He mentions you with the 'deepest sadness', calls himself 'an unfortunate', and 'pitiful' and speaks of his 'completely broken heart' which embitters everything, even his most pleasant conversations. The recent investigations would have turned out quite differently if his feelings and apparent memories had actually been what they appeared to be. This circumstance, as you know, has made a deep impression on me and has given rise to doubts in me, which I did not have earlier, as to his credibility. I therefore reconsidered his whole story and the more I looked into some of the key episodes, the more disturbing they appeared to me, and in order to present these doubts in a concise form, I have set out the 'questions', which our friend H[ickel] will share with you.[307]

Then at last, after six months of waiting, Kaspar Hauser received another letter. Stanhope, who after his departure from Ansbach still wrote to his beloved foster son daily for a while but thereafter only managed the letter of 19th April, could now for the first time of writing in months only bring himself to pen a rather cool and inconsequential letter, the opening of which put a very intentional dampener on Kaspar's hopes:

'Unfortunately no trail at all has been found,' he writes in his letter of the 15th October 1832, 'and one sees now with complete certainty that all the clues on which one was counting were quite unfounded and nothing but will o' the wisps. I would have very much to say about that and to investigate, [there is] much that I would wish clarified; much that would need correcting.'[308]

Why does Stanhope, who was himself the creator of these 'will o' the wisps' and untenable suggestions, write in such a way, with this only slightly moderated accusatory undertone, to Hauser, who had asserted nothing at all about himself? Stanhope *wanted* to make him into a fraud; the 'search for the truth' which he had previously urged on at so much expense had therefore now to be represented as untenable. He had provided his own false leads, and they had been shown to be groundless, which proved that the suspicions he had entertained about Hauser could not stand. What had been fabricated was itself now contradicted, and still stuck in this devious psychological trick was the guileless foundling, who had no idea of what was being done with him. But he sensed the change: 'I know that the Count thinks I am a fraud.' Daumer writes: 'This betrayal inevitably made the severest and most disturbing impression. As he realised it, he began to feel the deepest contempt for the Count, so that he could hardly any longer look at the letters which he still received from him.'[309]

While the consciously devised separation from Hauser was relatively easy, it was much more difficult to effect in the case of Klüber, Feuerbach, Binder, and Schumann. Stanhope had acted correctly throughout, signed binding contracts, undertaken lifelong obligations which no-one had talked him into and which had all been until a few months previously strenuously striven for, even fought for. Philip Henry noted the resistance he was coming up against and changed tactics.

As the loving foster father who he had been until recently, he could not criticise Kaspar Hauser so openly and did not wish to run the risk of angering Hauser's other main protectors; that might ruin the overall plan. It was for this reason apparently that he asked his friend Wessenberg to write to Klüber, which would make clear through the proposals it contained how Stanhope viewed the whole matter. Through adopting the position that he was no longer prominently connected to the affair, Stanhope wanted to create the impression that the 'young man' needed no special education at all, as he was but a 'subject' not a 'sovereign' and that accordingly, a course of public instruction would be good enough for him. 'I have the honour,' wrote Wessenberg to Klüber,

> of passing on to you a letter from Count [sic] Stanhope. The noble lord is constantly very occupied with the mysterious story of Kaspar Hauser. Everything that I have read about him until now is inconclusive, and it is without doubt that the young man knows far more about his story than is written in books about him. As an old friend of the family, I am very concerned that the generosity of the noble lord will not be abused and I therefore deem it most expedient to alter the situation so that the young Hauser should be withdrawn from a costly private education and transferred to a public educational establishment. In the interests of the members of Count Stanhope's family, I request that you write to the noble lord to the aforementioned effect insofar as you are able to concur with my opinion.[310]

But Klüber was not at all disposed to concur. The State Councillor answered the Austrian ambassador firmly on the 22nd December, clearly stating that 'it was a matter of *fulfilling* the obligations undertaken...'[311]

Stanhope remunerated Wessenberg for the service of friendship he had rendered in writing the letter. It is not very easy to gain an overall view of the apparent connection between Stanhope's letter to Wessenberg of the 10th November and the two gifts which the latter received from Philip Henry on the 16th and 26th of that month—first a seal and then an opera glass. Neither before nor afterwards did the Austrian ambassador appear on Stanhope's lists of 'Presents'.

Delayed by postal problems, Klüber's reply of the 22nd December to Stanhope's letter of the 6th October gave Stanhope a second, adroit lesson in morality and psychology. The letter—also published here for the first time—opens with a neat, flattering salutation, but from its very first sentence focuses on the main issue: the contract that had been signed and Stanhope's obligations entailed in it. The letter very politely but directly passes over the content of Stanhope's letter and instead, insists on how commendable it is that Stanhope wishes to stand by his obligations.

> Your Lordship's esteemed letter of the 6th October had a long journey; it got to me on the 16th December with a covering letter from Baron von Wessenberg of the 10th November, thus also of an old date.
>
> With real pleasure and great respect, I recognise in it your unaltered intention thoroughly to fulfil the obligations which you have nobly undertaken with regard to Kaspar Hauser, irrespective of the doubts about his complete truthfulness which have arisen in you since your

return to England. My firm belief in your generous and humanitarian convictions would not have led me to doubt that fulfilment even if it had not been made a matter of honour due to the publicity given to your agreement to it and a legal obligation due to the contract entered into.

Among the doubts now expressed to me by Your Lordship the most prominent seems to me to be that Kaspar is supposed to have *spoken* to two if not three witnesses at the beginning. I do not know of such a thing occurring. Assuming it to be correct, the first thing to take into consideration would be: what, how and how much did he speak in the presence of these witnesses?

That he does not remember having heard the rolling of *thunder* in his cell does not seem to me very pertinent. Underground, enclosed by thick walls, such sounds can only be heard dully, and within the dim limits of his ideas and experience in his long and total seclusion from the outer world, such a noise may have made little or no impression on him. On the contrary, focused as he was solely on playing with his little wooden horses, the only things dear to his heart and mind, what must have made a strong and consequently enduring impression on his feelings and memory was having to put up with physical beatings because of the noise made by the [horses'] rolling up and down. More important apparently, is that he did not want to see the *face* of the man [in the cell]. For Kaspar alone, who was ignorant of all human company and cut off from it, the *hand* of the man who served him must have seemed much more important than his face; and that hand he claims he knows exactly! That also makes perfect sense for him that he could distinguish people most surely by their hands.

That he could see in broad daylight after his release from his cell I would not see as valid grounds for suspicion. Nature did not give him the kind of eyes that distinguishes nocturnal creatures e.g. owls which only see by night. I also recall that when I remarked that seeing in daylight must have been hard on his sensitive eyes, Your Lordship pointed out that the cell had not been completely dark but that daylight had only penetrated slightly.

If Kaspar knew *more* of his earlier history than he claims, it would hardly be credible that he would not almost involuntarily have made the revelations and confessions that he did in the agitated state of his mind after the murder attempt.

In those first, most frightening moments, he must have felt released from all the promises to maintain secrecy that had been forced on him and from the fear of the consequences of the discovery of the secret with which he had been threatened. Yes, he said, 'if I had only seen his *hands* [the criminal's], I would have immediately known if it was the man [his jailer]'. That he suspected this man can be concluded from the fact that in his fever he often spoke fearfully of the 'man'.

I shall permit myself just *one* further question. Can it be assumed with any probability that, after the publicity given to Kaspar's most conspicuous appearance in Nuremberg, and his physical and psychological condition which was so often and so variously commented upon there; and [the publicity given] to the undeniable attempt on his life, all of which news has spread to the smallest corner of Germany, a fraud could have been perpetrated with and by him that has remained undiscovered these several years? However close the circle may have been in which Kaspar may have spent at least the last years before his release even without the kind of extremely harsh incarceration that he claims, his existence and his sudden disappearance from the location of his previous confinement could not have remained until today a secret of so few people that, especially with the publicly offered financial reward for the discovery of the assailant, it could have remained undiscovered for so long.

Furthermore, all observers agree that Kaspar has shown throughout only the purest childlike quality of feeling and the highest degree of moral goodness without the least trace of mischievousness or pretence.[312]

This letter shows that Stanhope had not been able to effect the slightest change in Klüber's former position, but on the other hand, it is indicative of how systematically the foster father continued to strive in these months to bring about a change in sentiment that would be to Kaspar's disadvantage.

It was not until recently at all easy to recognise how deliberately he was proceeding. His letter to Feuerbach of the 31st May was known but not the one to Klüber of the 22nd June, which was very similar in content. It is now known that Appeal Court Counsellor Friedrich Schumann, who was officially responsible for the Hauser case at the Court of Appeal, also received a similar letter defaming Kaspar Hauser. This was method at work!

The content of Stanhope's letter [to Schumann] can therefore be taken as read, but Schumann's answer will be quoted in its entirety, because it stands impressively among the series of documents in defence of Kaspar Hauser. Schumann implores Stanhope to abide by the fatherly duties he has undertaken, recounts the 'certainties' that these promises entitle Hauser to count on in his present life circumstances. Apparently in the hope of a return to the former situation, Schumann tries once again to stir the conscience of the foster father, who has already adopted a contrary position; Stanhope had left Germany fully eleven months earlier.

After a short introduction, Schumann begins his letter:

> With regard to your misgivings and doubts about Kaspar, I have quite another view of the matter. Already when Kaspar first appeared in Nuremberg I was of the opinion, which I still hold, that his earlier destiny was a riddle and that no human art or effort would succeed in getting to the truth of it but that rather, it would only be discovered *by means of accidents or divine providence.* With this conviction and in the leadership of the investigation that had passed to me, I assigned no exclusive value either to those circumstances that still seemed so important nor did I ignore facts which may have appeared insignificant or contradictory. The riddling aspect, which showed itself in the uncovering of particular traces, did not bewilder me in my investigations. Because the whole story is indeed a riddle, I did not find it surprising when single circumstances that related to it appeared to us as puzzling. *Without in the least wishing to approach Kaspar's character too closely, I placed no value at all on any of his earlier or later statements, whether they were partly true or partly perhaps only put in his mouth by others.* For it lies in the nature of the case that Kaspar, by dint of his physical and spiritual condition in which he found himself from the beginning, was completely incapable of telling me anything important about his fate that was reliable. At best, he was and is capable of giving small items of evidence and *even these perhaps not based on reality but on illusions of the senses.* This is indeed the main reason why his story is a riddle for the time being. For the investigation would have taken a different form a long time ago if it had been possible for Kaspar to share even a little more certain information about his earlier circumstances. Herein also lies the reason—and I ask for your consideration of this—why all the brooding over this case can lead to no results, for it is absolutely impossible satisfactorily to answer the questions that force themselves on investigators. But this is not even necessary, as we could not reach the goal on this path. Much that now appears unbelievable or contradictory is merely so because we do not know how the circumstances are related. At present, this connection is not clear to us, and the whole story of Kaspar's early life is still shrouded in an impenetrable darkness. Single circumstances which show themselves later are indeed partly mysterious and must be all the more so when the requisite basis is

lacking that would enable a judgement to be made as to whether they are at all related to each other or to the main events. *It is not therefore justified to draw conclusions from a distance about the existence of an intentional deception; rather, such conclusions are to be excluded. The case itself is and remains very curious, and the single circumstances relating to it may be arranged in the ways we have put them together until now from what Kaspar has told us, or in other ways.*

The area of possibilities in this story is too large for us to be able to comprehend through actual reason or even through probability. Instead of satisfying ourselves with useless and partly unjustified doubts, we wish to do our duty. And this is a double duty, namely, we have to continue our investigative efforts energetically as often as opportunity presents itself. This is being done in all honesty. This very day an investigative report has arrived from a police director in Saxony which requested that a true likeness of Kaspar Hauser and a lock of his hair be sent to him. This was immediately complied with; this relates to a communication about which Herr von Feuerbach, earlier but only very generally kept under the seal of the strictest confidentiality. Your Lordship will see from this that investigations are still in train. Our second duty—until the time comes when the riddle has been solved—would consist of merely holding to the certainties of the case.

It is certain that Kaspar had to endure a cruel fate, the reason for which it is impossible for him to uncover.

It is certain that Providence guided the noble heart of a magnanimous Peer from Great Britain to Kaspar Hauser at a time when his life was once again endangered.

It is certain that this noble Lord, with a truly royal magnanimity made significant sacrifices in order that the amazing story of Kaspar Hauser be revealed as much as possible.

It is certain that this distinguished humanitarian, by taking over responsibility for the care and education of Kaspar Hauser from the hands of the authorities charged with his wardship, made himself Kaspar's greatest benefactor and second father and gave him the moral certainty of being able to see an end to his unparalleled sufferings.

It is certain that the withdrawal of the love and confidence of his second father would be a most undeserved and still crueller fate for Kaspar, even more than his earlier mistreatment was. Better than that would be for him still to be languishing in his cell!

Therefore it is also certain in all honesty that it is impossible for Kaspar's second father to prepare his foster son for this bitter fate, and that rather,

> the noble work already commenced, which Feuerbach through his writing has made known to the whole civilised world, who have taken the greatest interest in Kaspar's destiny, should now be completed, to guarantee Kaspar's future against the vicissitudes of this world and in this manner to prevent a time from occurring when the otherwise beloved foster son should be more unfortunate than he was in his imprisonment, in which, apart from the bread and water given him, he knew of no other needs.
>
> These certainties, Your Lordship, are what completely reassure me as to the future destiny of Kaspar Hauser who has shed many bitter tears over your long silence. *Should Kaspar's first lineage not be discovered, although, as mentioned above, hopes in that direction have in no sense been abandoned as yet, he has for a long time now ceased to be the poor foundling Kaspar Hauser. For in the eyes of all Europe he has now gained a second lineage and a second father, who, though even more riddling questions may arise in the further development of the case, will not let his innocent son suffer but will care for him lovingly and from now on drive away from him for ever all frightening fear of a dark future.*[313]

None of these letters could remove Stanhope's apparent doubts even in the slightest. On the contrary! He noted down each point in Kaspar's favour in order to be able to formulate systematic counter-arguments. How annoyed this work made him is shown by the countless crossings out and additions before he achieved the desired result. Then, on the 15th December 1832 he wrote Hickel a letter containing 43 questions, which were all arranged so that they '...expressed his doubts as to the truth of Hauser's statements about his early imprisonment, with reference to Herr Feuerbach's book about Hauser'.[314]

The ignorance with which the arguments of Feuerbach, Klüber and Schumann were pushed aside forces one to conclude that Stanhope had firmly decided to credit none of these very convincing objections. His foster son was to be driven into a corner.

*

Meanwhile, living in Lebanon was Philip Henry's once beloved half-sister Hester, who in 1801 had made possible his flight to Germany with the help of her many connections to Pitt the Younger, Jackson and others. Since then, the two siblings had become completely estranged from one another, and not only outwardly. On her great journeys through the world, in Syria Hester came across an old prophecy which she thought must refer to herself and which claimed that: 'At a certain time a European woman will come to Mount Lebanon, build a house and gain power and influence like a sultan. A boy without a father will come to her and his destiny will be fulfilled under her protection...' Hester had the 'house' built and she was indeed respected by locals as the true queen of Lebanon, who received friends from all over the world in her rock palace. Among those who did not come but whom she expected due to the prophecy was the Duke of Reichstadt, who died on the 22nd July 1832 at the age of 21. Her doctor, to whom she entrusted her confidences, shared the incredible ideas which moved her all-encompassing mind. When they spoke about secret societies and Freemasons, Hester Stanhope stated that:

> You tell me of secret societies, which have risen up in Europe since the long war. Did not I know all that? I have been bred in the work of revolutions since I was first with Mr. Pitt. How many plots did he crush, within two or three days of their consummation, of which not a syllable was ever known! The great freemasons, doctor, exist all over the world: they know I am the person they want. Many of them have been sent as spies on my actions; but I shall stand in no need of them—it is they who will want me. When the course of events shall have brought things to a point, I shall have assistance enough. All the people who come here after me, are sent to say something: Lord B***, who saw me at Tiberias, was a freemason, and one of those sent.

Napoleon's son, for whom she had waited so long, was now no longer alive, and her doctor wrote in her memoirs: 'It is certain the Lady firmly believed for a long time that the Duke of Reichstadt would visit her and that he was the boy referred to in the prophecy. After his death, she looked to another.'

That 'other'—was he the one with whom her brother had occupied himself and who, like the Duke of Reichstadt, would not live out his 21st year?

*

A view of the events of the year 1832 would be incomplete without mentioning a few key political episodes. Particular hesitations, tendencies and reactions showed clearly in the inner and outer treatment of the Kaspar Hauser Question.

In May 1832 the journalists Philipp Jakob Siebenpfeiffer and Johann Georg Wirth organised a demonstration at the Hambach Castle in the

Palatinate, on the Maxburg hill near Neustadt on the River Haardt. Nearly 30,000 people attended. At the People's May Festival [*Völkermaifest*] the intention was to 'lay the foundation stone of the rebirth of Germany'. The assembly consisting of the banned *Burschenschaften* [students' clubs], liberals and democrats proclaimed sovereignty of the people and the 'United Free States of Germany' in a confederated republican Europe. In the castle courtyard the German national flag (black-red-gold) was unfurled as patriotic songs were sung. 'No eye was without tears, chests swelled proudly, filled with a blessed ecstasy, and from mouth to mouth went the call: "Hail, hail the day when Germany's flag shall unite men from all regions of the country in brotherly concord"' (Johann Wirth). A delegation from Frankfurt presented a 'battle sword' [*Schlachtschwert*] to the main speaker Wirth, who called in his speech for the violent overthrow of the existing order. After Siebenpfeiffer had already called on the 'friends of freedom, who do not value the miserable statelets with their princely crowns higher than the majesty of a great nation', to set aside the German dynasties, Wirth went even further and declared that the King of Bavaria was 'a traitor to the human race'. This act of defiance was rapidly repressed by Field Marshal Wrede's troops, by arrests, prosecutions and the withdrawal of the very recently granted modest degree of 'press freedom', but it nevertheless appeared very similar to the disturbances which had preceded the July Revolution of 1830.

In this climate every prosecution was held to be the misdeed of princes. Were Bavaria to be regarded as taking a public stance that was seen as indifferent in the case of the Nuremberg foundling, the fact could rebound on Ludwig, as it could well be represented as an example of the alleged depravity of the rulers with regard to 'the prince's son Kaspar Hauser'. Under these circumstances, a dispute which affected the fundaments of monarchy, of Bavaria as well as of Baden, could and had to be continued only with the greatest caution.

13. The Death Year

Kaspar Hauser—Anselm von Feuerbach, 1833

The connection between the once much beloved Kaspar and his foster father had shrunk to a pathetic minimum. From this point onwards (Dec. 1832), Stanhope sent only two letters to his disappointed foster son, who had to wait half a year for the first one and a further seven months for the second. The third and last letter (of a total of 13 that Kaspar received from the Earl) Stanhope sent after he had heard the news of Kaspar's death, a fact which gives to their common destiny a curious signature.

His trip to Germany in 1833 took Stanhope to Karlsruhe and Rastatt but no longer to northern Bavaria, the region of Ansbach and Nuremberg. From Heidelberg, where he took up quarters, it would have been a day's journey to Ansbach—nothing by Stanhope's well-travelled standards. But now circumstances had changed, and other problems had to be dealt with. For Philip Henry, the separation had already been fully and irrevocably accomplished.

At the beginning of January Kaspar Hauser set off for Gotha with Hickel. The trip was undertaken on Feuerbach's behest to

142. Ernst I, Duke of Saxe-Coburg-Gotha (1784–1844)

check information relating to the question of Kaspar's origins. The duchy's Police Counsellor Eberhardt was enthusiastically advocating the thesis that a Senior Lady of the Bedchamber, Frau Königsheim, could possibly be the foundling's mother. The whole matter soon showed itself to be groundless, but by then Kaspar was already in Gotha.

Duke Ernst (Fig. 142) received Kaspar Hauser at the palace on the 20th of the month after a visit to the palace theatre together to see *La gazza ladra* [The Thieving Magpie] by Rossini, after which they had a conversation. That could not go unnoticed. Hickel reported it to Feuerbach, and Hauser himself talked about it in Ansbach. Then another bout of extensive correspondence took place between Klüber, Hofmann, and Schumann, with Feuerbach advising in the background, which focused on only one topic: the need for Stanhope to keep to the agreements he had made and to fulfil the terms of the contract he had entered into. A strong impression had been gained that the foster father (Fig.147) wanted to wriggle out of his commitments. Under such circumstances, one could imagine, the translation and publication of Feuerbach's memorandum, which Stanhope had promised everyone he would bring about, was impossible. But it appeared in London in 1833 (Fig. 145) under licence from the Boston edition of 1832 and at the same time in Amsterdam (Fig. 146). We know that Stanhope worked on it after his departure from Ansbach and asked his son for help with phrasing here and there. Near the end of the Preface of the English edition there is the note that the translation is by Henning Gottfried Linberg. Had Stanhope 'bought' the name of this known translator? Or was the text newly and independently translated by Linberg after Stanhope had so evidently moved into opposition? It is reasonable to assume that two diametrically opposed processes—the effort to represent Feuerbach's ideas to the public and the effort to slander him and above all, Kaspar—could hardly be understood to be going on in parallel. Had Stanhope silently hoped to rid himself faster of the whole affair?

Wessenberg's notable letter to Klüber suggesting that Stanhope's monthly payment be reduced and that Kaspar be given a free public education instead of an expensive private one brought a sobering up, which led to the question of whether the noble lord really did want to remain the foundling's benefactor.

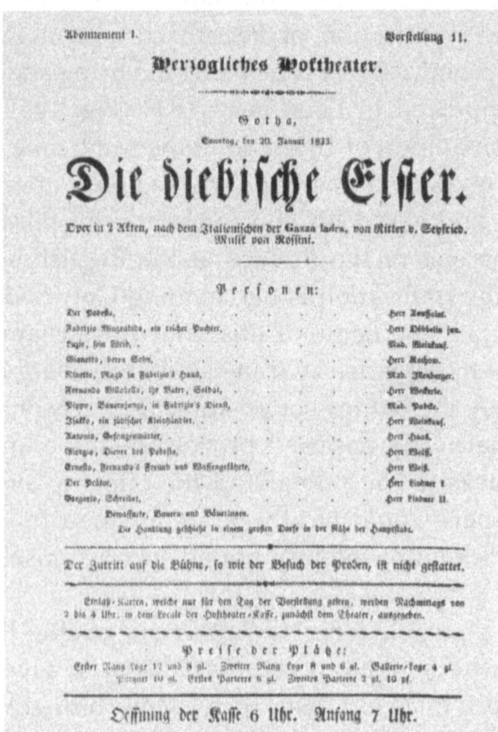

Abonnement I. Vorstellung 11.

Herzogliches Hoftheater.

Gotha,

Sonntag, den 20. Januar 1833.

Die diebische Elster.

Oper in 2 Akten, nach dem Italienischen der Gazza ladra, von Ritter v. Seyfried.
Musik von Rossini.

Personen:

Der Podesta, ... Herr [illegible].
Fabrizio Vingradito, ein reicher Pachter, ... Herr Döbbelin jun.
Lucia, sein Weib, ... Mad. Reinkauf.
Gianetto, deren Sohn, ... Herr Rochow.
Ninette, Magd in Fabrizio's Haus, ... Mad. Ilenberger.
Fernando Villabella, ihr Vater, Soldat, ... Herr Weckerle.
Pippo, Bauernjunge, in Fabrizio's Dienst, ... Mad. Podcke.
Isakko, ein jüdischer Kleinhändler, ... Herr Reinkauf.
Antonio, Gefangenwärter, ... Herr Haas.
Giorgio, Diener des Podesta, ... Herr Wolff.
Ernesto, Fernando's Freund und Waffengefährte, ... Herr Weiß.
Der Prätor, ... Herr Lindner I
Gregorio, Schreiber, ... Herr Lindner II.
Bewaffnete, Bauern und Bäuerinnen.
Die Handlung geschieht in einem großen Dorfe in der Nähe der Hauptstadt.

Der Zutritt auf die Bühne, so wie der Besuch der Proben, ist nicht gestattet.

Einlaß-Karten, welche nur für den Tag der Vorstellung gelten, werden Nachmittags von 2 bis 4 Uhr, in dem Locale der Hoftheater-Kasse, zunächst dem Theater, ausgegeben.

Preise der Plätze:

Erster Rang Loge 12 und 8 gl. Zweiter Rang Loge 8 und 6 gl. Gallerie-Loge 4 gl. Parquet 10 gl. Erstes Parterre 6 gl. Zweites Parterre 2 gl. 10 pf.

Oeffnung der Kasse 6 Uhr. Anfang 7 Uhr.

143/144 The ducal court theatre in Gotha. Duke Ernst I and Kaspar Hauser sat in the middle box on the occasion of a visit together to the theatre on 20 January 1833, at which La Gazza Ladra [The Thieving Magpie] by Rossini was performed.

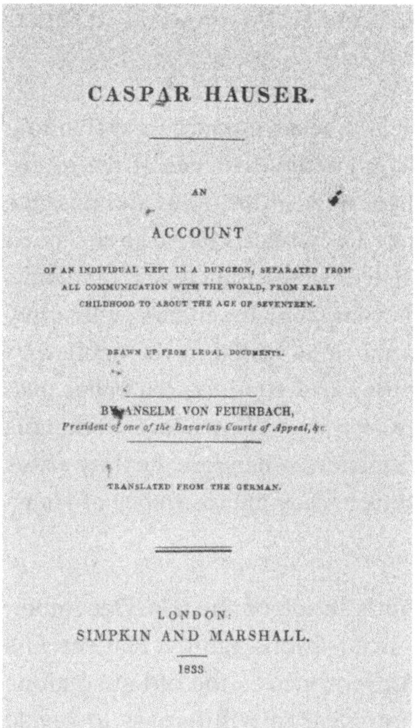

CASPAR HAUSER.

AN

ACCOUNT

OF AN INDIVIDUAL KEPT IN A DUNGEON, SEPARATED FROM ALL COMMUNICATION WITH THE WORLD, FROM EARLY CHILDHOOD TO ABOUT THE AGE OF SEVENTEEN.

DRAWN UP FROM LEGAL DOCUMENTS.

BY ANSELM VON FEUERBACH,
President of one of the Bavarian Courts of Appeal, &c.

TRANSLATED FROM THE GERMAN.

LONDON:
SIMPKIN AND MARSHALL.
1833

145. Cover page of the English edition of Feuerbach's 'Kaspar Hauser - An Example of a Crime Against the Soul Life of Man'.

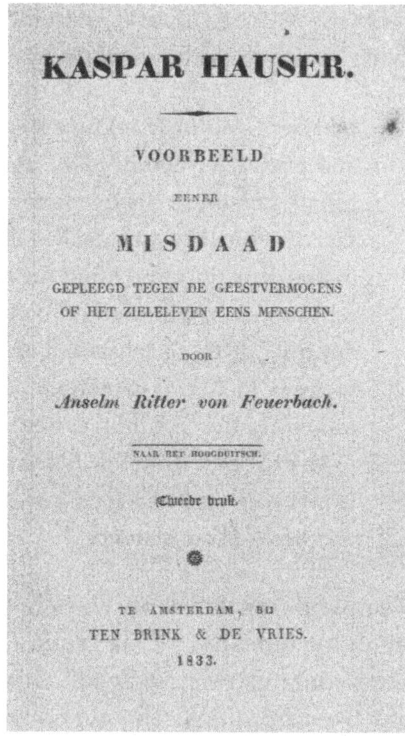

KASPAR HAUSER.

VOORBEELD

EENER

MISDAAD

GEPLEEGD TEGEN DE GEESTVERMOGENS
OF HET ZIELELEVEN EENS MENSCHEN.

DOOR

Anselm Ritter von Feuerbach.

NAAR HET HOOGDUITSCH.

Tweede druk.

TE AMSTERDAM, BIJ
TEN BRINK & DE VRIES.
1833.

146. Cover page of the Dutch edition of Feuerbach's 'Kaspar Hauser - An Example of a Crime Against the Soul Life of Man'.

147. Lord Philip Henry, 4th Earl Stanhope (1781–1855)

On the 7th April Court Councillor Andreas Hofmann wrote to Feuerbach that it would be very necessary

> that here and in Frankfurt there should be a common understanding and thereafter action taken to guarantee the existence of the unfortunate person in the event of changes in basic attitudes and possible vicissitudes. My approaches to State Councillor Klüber have tended in this direction, and I find the content of State Councillor Schumann's reply to be in completely the same vein. Your Excellency will surely approve of these measures, for as much as I trust in the noble convictions of Count Stanhope, as little can I suppress the belief that, following the communication from Herr von Wessenberg, nothing is to be expected from his [Stanhope's] family, wherefore the duty arises firmly to pursue by legal means if necessary the assurance of Hauser's lifelong subsistence.[315]

Meanwhile, in his reply to Schumann's letter of the 21st December, Stanhope repeated all his groundless accusations against Hauser. His letter contains no new arguments and reproduces the old suspicions and fixed opinions. The almost pathological unwillingness to revise the fabricated or misrepresented notion of intentional deception was, however, deliberate. Stanhope stuck to such unproven assertions because, taken as a whole, only they offered the chance of moving the case to the level he desired. It was unreasonable to agree to lifelong support for a fraudster. Hauser was young and in good health and could still easily live another fifty years. That could cost the Earl and his heirs a fortune. Does this indicate *one* possible motive, besides others, that relates to Hauser's early death? One gains the impression that the foster father no longer imagines himself to be standing on grounds of 'social considerations', which, even against his will, would, from quite another perspective, force him to continue with the undertaking so recently embarked upon, and that consequently, he wished to see measures taken that would enable the matter to be concluded as rapidly as possible. In this light, his visits to Karlsruhe and Rastatt, his subsequent trip through Switzerland and Italy, his forty-day wait in Vienna and, most unusual of all, his trip from there to Munich, where he received news of the murder, are further indications of his involvement in the death of his foster son. Here is Schumann's reply to Stanhope, which once again, and more strongly, addresses the situation that had developed. It is all too easily forgotten how short was the period of time between Kaspar's adoption as foster son and his branding as a fraudster.

> Your Lordship not only took up the pitiable Kaspar out of a most noble spirit but also took him out of the hands of the wardship authorities through a formal agreement with the obligation to care for his welfare and education and to provide sufficient assurances for the security of his existence in the future.
>
> This contractual relationship has become generally well-known due to the interest which the whole of Europe has taken in the fate of the remarkable foundling and just as little is it a secret that Kaspar was to follow his magnanimous foster father to England by the summer of 1832 at the latest. However, since he has remained in Ansbach, but there was not the slightest mention of any other provision that Your Lordship might have made with regard to him, and nothing could be said, because Your Lordship really did not send any special instructions here and Kaspar's education was therefore left solely in accordance with the instructions of Herr von Feuerbach, a rumour has spread abroad that there has been a change in Your Lordship's convictions with regard to Kaspar. Since we meanwhile were granted the good fortune to make Your Lordship's personal acquaintance, we were necessarily most strongly convinced by Your Lordship's conduct of the unchangeability of your convictions and were in the best position to form a judgement of the basis of such rumours, and so we have missed no opportunity to refute them.
>
> Your Lordship therefore puts upon my letter of the 21st December an incorrect interpretation when You see therein the expression of some kind of mistrust.
>
> Far removed from such mistrust is rather, as I wrote to Your Lordship, everything deeply grounded in You and in the interests of Your honourable family. Since, in accordance with the law, the wardship authorities in Nuremberg cannot be satisfied with that, and Your Lordship will be caring for Kaspar as long as You live, and since, even more, the authorities are obliged to see that the terms of the formal contract concluded are fully complied with and therefore to ensure that Kaspar's welfare will be guaranteed for the rest of his life, the Nuremberg District Court was sufficiently concerned about this rumour to take official steps to see that Kaspar's situation is ordered securely and to prevent his future from exposure to vicissitude. Official steps by the wardship authorities would cause a greater sensation, as the Appeal Court would be obliged to render legal support

through diplomatic channels, and merely with the intention of precluding such steps, I expressed to Your Lordship the conviction that You would be well advised not to hesitate any longer to insure Kaspar's future against all life's vicissitudes.

In this conviction can lie nothing harmful to Your Lordship, even should You see therein the expression of a wish. In any event, the explanation which I have just given of my intention will reassure You, especially when I tell You that my concern was not without reason, and that the Nuremberg District Court has decided, solely on account of privately conveyed information about the correspondence with Your Lordship, not to proceed with legal action for the present.

When, however, Most Honoured Count, You Yourself in your gracious letter of the 8th of last month, restrict Yourself to an expression of the feelings which my letter aroused in You but pass over the matter itself in silence without even a syllable either to reassure the wardship authorities or to calm the frequently expressed judgements heard in public as to how You think *to guarantee Kaspar's future*, this I can in all honesty only regret.

Conscious that I have done what my concern for good Kaspar as well as the respect which I feel for Your Lordship oblige me to do, I shall hold my peace from now on and modestly recognise that henceforth I have merely to entrust Kaspar's fate to his foster father and to the guardianship authorities.

But Your Lordship will yet allow me to point out most humbly that Herr von Feuerbach, who has not yet quite recovered well enough from his illness to allow him to enter into correspondence has for a long time and will remain troubled in his feelings when he contemplates the mortality of our race until he is assured of how Kaspar's future has been secured. I have arranged for the delivery of the report to the District Court in Nuremberg.[316]

No reply to this letter has survived. How was Stanhope to answer? Wessenberg, however, who had in the interim been recalled home from London, was, strangely enough, the best informed as to how things stood. How could he have gained access to an exchange of letters between Hofmann and Klüber in which Hofmann expressed decided views as to Hauser's capabilities and future possibilities? Hofmann further speculates in this letter about the amount of the 'allowance' *[for Kaspar—Ed.]* and hopes to receive £100 and refers to Feuerbach's idea that he would be satisfied with £60. We find the same arguments and views again, even down to the choice of words, in a letter of the 14th April that Wessenberg sent to Stanhope and in which he now advises going down to £30.

> I understand that the guardianship court in Nuremberg is seeking to demand from you a guarantee of Hauser's sustenance. I believe that the greatest caution is called for on this occasion, especially because it seems to me that the guardianship authorities have been set in motion by Feuerbach. I have been assured that the expectations of being able to fit Kaspar Hauser to a mechanical occupation have not been fulfilled. It is said that neither his eyes nor his hands have the necessary strength for the work. Neither, according to the testimony of his teacher and of experience, is he *at all* suited to a technical training. It follows from this, say Feuerbach & Co., that it can no longer be a question of training and determining this unfortunate for an occupation by which he can support himself, but *only* of his lifelong maintenance, and therefore the time has come for recourse to the declaration and assurance given by the great Stanhope in November 1830 [*sic*—the correct date is 1831—*Ed.*]. The question arises as to whether, under the circumstances, it would not be advisable to respond to a direct demand of the guardianship court by presenting one's own proposal. I should think that a proposal could be made of an annual allowance of £30, which would meet any inconveniences which the Bavarian lawyers could create—the impoverished youngster could certainly not claim any higher amount for his sustenance—if the boy wishes to do no work and contribute nothing to supporting himself, he is all the more unworthy of consideration, especially as long as he refuses to tell of what he certainly *must* know about his earlier fate—I would also advise guaranteeing the allowance in question only as long as his own poverty continues—as for the wording of the proposal itself, I would gladly speak with your new noble friend, for with German jurists one must be damned careful...[317]

That was clear enough. Appeal would be made to the courts if necessary, and on the basis of the evidence, they would doubtless find in Hauser's favour. Stanhope seems to have been somewhat at a loss. His first approach was to write two letters to the King of Bavaria, but they were not sent. What would have made him hesitate to appeal to the highest authority in the land? He must have had reasons for not risking this step.[318]

The fact remains that the letters were not sent, and from Chevening came no word of Stanhope's intent. Did Philip Henry have to gain time by keeping silent in order to clarify another decisive question? To refuse to answer was either in the highest degree offensive or the result of a hopeless situation. He could have confirmed the old arguments in a single sentence. Why did he not hasten to put a few words down on paper?

In this situation Klüber decided on an unaccustomed step which was bound to shake the foster father out of his reserve. Klüber now put the problem before the astounded public, a course of action which went against all precedent but which was seen as the last means of forcing Stanhope to take a position. On the 8th May a note by Klüber appeared in the widely-read *Frankfurter Journal* (Fig. 148):

> The unfortunate young Kaspar Hauser appears to have become even more unfortunate through the magnanimity of an Englishman; for since the wealthy Lord Stanhope prevailed upon the City of Nuremberg to be allowed to adopt him, Hauser is wasting away in an environment he did not himself choose and in the unprotected situation in which the magnanimous lord placed him, far more than he was in his earlier deathly isolation.

That was exactly the kind of thing that Stanhope did not want. All the blame for the foundling's new misfortune was now laid on his shoulders, whereas the plan should have gone the other way. Hauser was supposed to have made himself an unworthy fraudster, and Stanhope could have safely withdrawn his aid without reproach. The later suicide thesis, a veritable tissue of lies, would

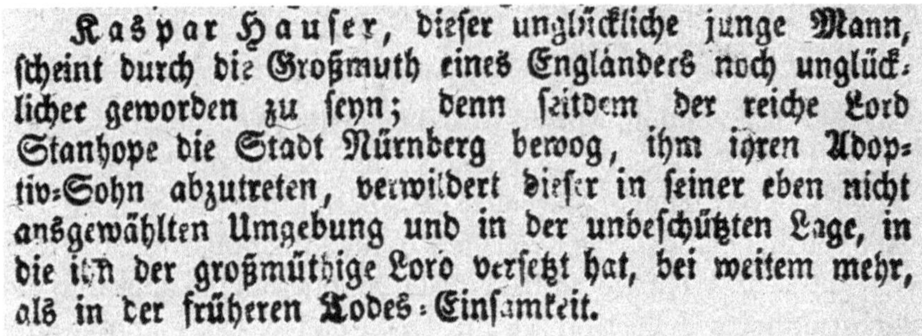

Kaspar Hauser, dieser unglückliche junge Mann, scheint durch die Großmuth eines Engländers noch unglücklicher geworden zu seyn; denn seitdem der reiche Lord Stanhope die Stadt Nürnberg bewog, ihm ihren Adoptiv-Sohn abzutreten, verwildert dieser in seiner eben nicht ausgewählten Umgebung und in der unbeschützten Lage, in die ihn der großmüthige Lord versetzt hat, bei weitem mehr, als in der früheren Todes-Einsamkeit.

148. Text of the news that Johann Ludwig Klüber placed in the Frankfurter Journal *on 8 May 1833.*

have been all the more credible if Hauser had been proven to be a person of no integrity. Klüber's action had placed Philip Henry in an alarming situation which would have to be dealt with as quickly as possible.

The news had appeared in Germany on the 8th May. Stanhope, who subscribed to German newspapers and studied them with the greatest attention, learned of Klüber's note about six days later. What he had to do was immediately clear. Two days later, the carriage was ready. From the 16th to the 17th he made the crossing with Anton Heinrich over to Calais; on the 20th the pair were already passing Brussels and on the 24th, the Belgian-Prussian border at Gennape. On the 28th, they were at Cologne, the 29th Andernach and on the 5th June Schlangenbad. On the 9th June they reached Frankfurt, where Stanhope immediately went to see Klüber.

First, the State Counsellor had some news for him which we do not know how he received. From later comments of Stanhope and from his behaviour, however, it can be concluded that it was with relief! On the 29th, the day Philip Henry was in Andernach, Feuerbach had died not far from Frankfurt in circumstances that have since never been clarified. When something tragic happened in Hauser's circle, Stanhope was always nearby: in 1829, at the time of the first murder attempt, now in May 1833, and then at the end of the year, when the foundling himself met his death.

Feuerbach had gone to Frankfurt to speak to Klüber about some final questions relating to Kaspar's identity, but, as is quite clear from Schumann's letter cited earlier, he would 'remain troubled in his feelings when he contemplates the mortality of our race until he is assured of how Kaspar's future has been secured'.

A few days earlier, Klüber had written to Hofmann:

> State Counsellor von Feuerbach's health continues very well; he commends himself to you most warmly. He told me today that in the last five years he had never felt himself so strong in body as now, and his friends have given him tests enough in this regard. Yet, what more than anything speaks for the strength of his nervous system is a chance event which he himself may well relate to you. It would have been a torrent of blows for the strongest man, but he was hardly shaken, so little indeed, that without the slightest hesitation, he pulled himself together to calm the relatives who were shocked to death.[319]

Feuerbach's biographer, the legal scholar Gustav Radbruch, describes the days before Whit Monday, the 27th May, until the 29th:

> On the 27th May, Whit Monday, Feuerbach went for a walk to Königstein. He was cheerful and light-hearted all morning, and despite the cool weather, breakfasted in a meadow and having arrived at Königstein, strolled around the old castle. On the way back he complained that he was not feeling well and lay down on a bed at the hotel. The stroke came on the way home. His left side was paralysed, he lost the power of speech and could only make himself understood by writing. Hastily he signalled for paper and pencil and wrote the words: 'Oh God, I am going to die.' He wrote several more such notes, all with the greatest accuracy, even with the appropriate punctuation. He was taken into the garden before the All Saints' Gate. On Tuesday evening he suffered for a few hours with convulsions, which in the last two hours completely disappeared, but he retained his consciousness until the end. On the 29th May 1833, at two o'clock in the morning, the last spark of his life's fire went out...
>
> The bereaved members of his family wish it to be known that on one of those notes Feuerbach wrote the words: 'I have been given something.' Feuerbach himself therefore believed that he was dying an unnatural death. The rumour soon spread abroad that Feuerbach had been removed from the world by poisoning in connection with the secret of Kaspar Hauser.[320]

That it was a case of an unusual death is underlined by facts and reactions which move the suspicions that were already being voiced in those days into the realms of possibility.

'Boundless, bordering on rage, was the pain of [his] beloved and kindly daughter at first.' Rage in the face of death? Rage against what or whom? Did this outbreak of feeling have something to do with the observation which Henriette Feuerbach shared in a letter to her son Anselm, which gives rise to the suspicion of poisoning? 'Father had *not* used to vomit when he felt unwell, which sometimes happened in court, nor did he vomit on the trip to Königstein. [It was] a frightful struggle with death; he had frightful pains. He could no longer speak, even when conscious. In death his body was very much swollen.'[321]

'The sad news has deeply shocked poor Hauser,' wrote Hofmann to Klüber. 'He came to me in a flood of tears, which I could only still by comforting him with the certainty that, although he did not know you personally, you would feel called upon out of genuine human affection to show a practical sympathy with his unfortunate story and to shoulder further cares for his safety just as his former protector, Herr von Feuerbach, had done.'

Stanhope received from his son in Chevening a newspaper cutting which had been sent to him—certainly not unintentionally—from Germany: 'According to the newspaper from Hannover, the famous German jurist Feuerbach, who had recently travelled to Frankfurt for the sake of his health, has died, and the general opinion now prevailing is that he was poisoned. He was the kindly protector of the unfortunate Caspar Hauser and the most zealous in his efforts to uncover the criminals behind the case of the mysterious youth.'

'What do you say to this?' the son Mahon asked his father.

On this 29th May Kaspar lost his most influential and active advocate, who had stood like a bulwark against the tide and who perhaps alone would have possessed the strength and power to fend off Stanhope's intrigues in the future. It can thus be assumed that Stanhope received the news of the death more with relief than with any great sadness.

Klüber now came to the point. Stanhope could no longer evade the issue and had to state how he was thinking of carrying out his obligations in the future. How the conversation went is best conveyed by Klüber's letter to Hofmann of the 22nd June. Philip Henry had recognised only too well that he would now have to take the bull by the horns in order to set his strategy in order again and consequently countered Klüber in a most unexpected fashion. After the months of evasive manoeuvres and attempts to defame Kaspar, a truly surprising result was now at hand. The seriousness of his renewed promises had to remain to be seen. The all too smooth and completely harmonious tone of the conversation gives the impression that Stanhope did not at any cost want to make a fuss. The slightest objection or reservation would have been a mistake at this stage. However, we know that his real view, both before and afterwards, was quite different. On the 22nd April 1833, shortly before his journey to Frankfurt, Stanhope had written a letter to his publisher Hodson which included the following:

> Observations on the letters which Kaspar brought and conjectures on the subject have been published in two Pamphlets by Schmidt-von Lübeck, & M. Merker, a Police Officer at Berlin, has also written two to show that there is great reason to suspect imposition. With regard to the cir-

> cumstance which you mention as to the particular nature of the muscles at the knee, I take it to have been the original conformation, & medical persons have assured me that it could not have arisen from long sitting. They are also decidedly of the opinion that he must have been galled by long sitting, & that if it had been continued uninterruptedly for years, his legs must have sunk under him when the attempt was made to set him upright. When he received his first lesson in writing & found his arm seized it is incredible that he did not mechanically turn round & see the person behind him, as this would be done even by an animal under similar circumstances. If the noise made by rolling his wooden horses was heard from without & occasioned chastisement, a noise much louder, such, for instance, as thunder, must have been heard by him within. If he had been wholly ignorant of language, he would not have learned during the journey the phrase '[I want to] be a rider like my father was' or several other phrases found in his own narrative, such as 'boy, show where the Letter belongs'. It is very remarkable that both the persons who first saw him, the Shoemaker who found him, and the Captain's Servant, declared in their official examinations that he spoke to them, & the latter states that he said he knew from whence he came but durst not mention it.[322]

Among the other untruths and half-truths here, this last assertion is the most underhanded. It is a fabrication by Stanhope, who wanted it to underpin the fraudster theory. When the shoemaker, Weickmann by name, was first questioned in 1829, he had not, despite repeated urgings, given any full testimony as to these extremely serious allegations of remarks by Kaspar Hauser, and they had not been recorded on any official statement, but Weickmann did make the allegations for the first time in 1834, after Stanhope had encouraged his willingness to testify with a not insubstantial payment. At the time of his visit to Klüber therefore, Stanhope evidently did not entertain any different views about his foster son, and his character is revealed even more clearly when his letter to Hodson and Klüber's letter to Hofmann are considered together. Stanhope, the master of pretence, must have had pressing reasons to draw attention as far away from himself as possible.

'I did not notice the slightest indication,' wrote Klüber,

> of a cooling in the truly paternal love and warm affection of the noble lord for Kaspar Hauser. He several times assured me most decidedly that although a few doubts had arisen in him recently as to whether Kaspar had revealed everything he knew about his earlier unfortunate fate, these

> had not had the slightest influence on his love and benevolent attitude towards this son of the most pitiful destiny, nor would they ever have, for he had in his conscience completely absolved Kaspar of any blame for possibly, or now even probably, keeping from him [Stanhope] certain facts, in that he believed he had to accept with certainty that Kaspar had only been obliged to maintain such silence with the most frightful threats by, and forced promises to, the 'man with whom he had always been'. Once, with the noble intention of freeing himself conclusively from these doubts, he had written a number of letters to Ansbach and to myself. As practical proof of his intentions, the lord said that he had not only provided, as usual and most punctually, the financial means necessary for Kaspar's maintenance and education, and would continue to do so, but he had also set out in a codicil a solid life insurance for Kaspar in the event of his own death, even though provision for his heirs to care for Kaspar's upkeep in his last will and testament is not regarded as being part of the contractual obligations into which he entered.[323]

That Stanhope made provision for any such life insurance for Hauser then or later is demonstrably untrue, but Klüber, much taken aback, was in no position to confirm this.

The conversation between him and Stanhope must at first have set aside all doubts. Could one declare more solemnly that there were no grounds for doubt? Klüber could feel satisfied. But had the problem, either now or later, altered in the slightest?

After Frankfurt, which he left on the 22nd June, Stanhope did not journey on to Ansbach, which would have been natural, but to Karlsruhe—where, amongst other things, he learned of the death of Dalberg (27th April)—and to Rastatt. Hermann Pies and a number of other Kaspar Hauser researchers were of the view that Stanhope travelled to Stuttgart, which was not the case. Today, we know that the Earl had a very important reason for going first to Heidelberg and waiting there for five days. From there, if he had wanted, he could easily have reached Ansbach in a few hours to embrace his foster son. Why, instead, did he spend so long in Heidelberg? It was only on the 28th that he left the city and made his way to Karlsruhe.

On the 30th June Stanhope arrived in the capital of Baden and stayed there until the 3rd July. In view of the timing and the inner connection of events, his presence there and then afterwards in Rastatt takes on a significance that cannot easily be overlooked. As already described, in Frankfurt Stanhope had to go along with the position described in Klüber's letter without the slightest qualification so as not to lose all credibility and obstruct the course of events just before reaching the final goal and without allowing himself to become the focus of attention. Now, on the other hand, deeds had to be done as quickly as possible that would, from outside and without drawing any noticeable attention to himself, bring the matter resolved upon to its conclusion—deeds that would at the same time result in freeing him from obligations to Hauser that extended beyond his own death.

It is almost certain that discussions on Hauser's future fate took place in Karlsruhe between the 30th June and the 3rd July. Klüber would soon hear of the first results. While Stanhope was in Frankfurt and Heidelberg, Grand Duchess Sophie—as reported in the news bulletin for the Rezat District—was spending time with companions in Ansbach (16–22 June). There were two reasons for her visit. First, she wanted—and so, it would appear, did at least one member of the small group that travelled with her—to observe 'the pretender to the legitimate throne of Baden' close up and get to know his habits, which included taking daily walks in the palace garden. The second and more important reason was a frightening vision from Paris that was oppressing Sophie. Walking about in that city since the 26th May had been clockmaker Karl Wilhelm Naundorff († 1845) from Berlin, who claimed to be Louis XVII [the younger son of the guillotined Louis XVI—*Ed.*]. As remarkably similar was Kaspar Hauser's physiognomy to that of the deceased Grand Duke Karl (his father), so was Naundorff's to the Bourbon. The fact that he suddenly attracted such a surprisingly large number of supporters, especially among the nobility, who were prepared to recognise his legitimacy, could not fail to have made an impression on Sophie. Louis Phillippe's throne was seriously endangered by the sensation that Naundorff created throughout France and beyond. So must it also have appeared to those at court in Karlsruhe. Was it not possible that something similar could happen to Hauser in the future? For the Grand Duchess, such a development in Baden was all too imaginable. The seven-day unofficial visit of Leopold's wife to Ansbach at this point in time was entirely a reconnaissance mission, from Karlsruhe straight to Ansbach and back again.

It now becomes clear why Stanhope did not want to go, or indeed could not go, to Ansbach, and for reasons of caution stayed a few days longer in Heidelberg than Sophie in Ansbach. The travels of both were so well arranged that their conversations in Karlsruhe could take place between the 30th June and the 3rd July.

We do not know what impression of Hauser Sophie took home with her, but there is a drawing (Fig. 149) of him from exactly this period which belonged to Queen Elizabeth of Romania (1843–1916), known under her pseudonym as the poetess Carmen Sylva.[324] It is by the painter Johannes Hitz, drawing master at the Gymnasium (high school) in Ansbach and shows a young man reading, with distinctive, very personal features, who bears no longer any similarity at all to the helpless, staring youngster of 1828. A mature, wilful element can be seen in this 21-year-old that may possibly have given his opponent a certain shock. There is the interesting gesture, also described by Daumer, of the fingers of the left hand, which Hauser would make when he was reflecting or wanted to concentrate. The thumb and index finger are touching as in the self-portrait (1493) by Dürer.[325] The gesture, difficult to interpret, brings to mind the expression that can be seen in meditants and also in the teaching gesture in representations of the Buddha.[326]

149. Kaspar Hauser in his last year of life. Pencil drawing by Johannes Hitz.

It is not impossible that Sophie returned to Karlsruhe with the impression that this person, were he to continue to develop in such ways, could become a great danger to her husband's throne. Was it not only a question of time as to when the unfortunate would begin to make his own moves where possible to claim his own alleged or actual rights before the eyes of the world? Was it not possible that precisely through the death of Feuerbach, who had until then been his protector, his own powers of self-assertion would be set free now in his 21st year, which could have unimaginable consequences? How could all this be prevented?

We learn from Stanhope what at least was planned as the first step. There are strategies which succeed in confusing opponents through their simple directness, mostly with striking success. The action now planned was one such. Kaspar Hauser would simply be brought to Karlsruhe and so placed under the direct control of his enemies or made dependent upon them. In his letter of the 15th July to Klüber, Stanhope writes that he has had the idea of creating 'a very pleasant and very suitable job for Kaspar Hauser as a stable master'.[327] Not long previously, he had written to the King of Bavaria that his protégé was certainly not of subordinate rank; in other words, he belonged to a ruling house. At this point the idea then changed into its opposite, for, with an almost unbelievable cynicism, Stanhope goes on: 'If he were to obtain a position of this nature, it would be a great joy for me to lead him to the place of his choice myself...'[328] Stanhope's intention is that the 'place of his choice' would no longer be the castle of his fathers, but their stable. The letter closes with the remark: 'I had the good fortune to make the acquaintance of your son in Karlsruhe...' Klüber junior was at this time secretary to the grand ducal family.

Klüber senior, however, saw through the plan and the danger for Kaspar Hauser. Once he was in Karlsruhe, there would have been dozens of possibilities of silencing him or making him disappear through machinations of other kinds. To the man who knew all the secrets of Baden, the situation felt uncomfortable, and he began making enquiries in Karlsruhe himself. Since the answers were all negative, his suspicions were only confirmed that the position was not at all really vacant. On the 19th August, Klüber wrote to Stanhope: 'The answers to my queries have revealed that the situation at the grand ducal stables is that there are surplus personnel, and reductions are therefore being seriously considered...'[329] Interestingly, Klüber then comes to his own proposal for Kaspar Hauser's future, which seems far more suitable.

Instead of stablemaster in Karlsruhe, the State Councillor suggests a high position in the chancellery in Ansbach. If Hauser agreed, 'then it would be expedient to continue with his Latin studies in order to fit him for service in the upper chancellery'. That fits more with the image seen in the drawing by Hitz and contradicts the notion that Hauser had reached the end of his capacity to learn.

Service in the upper ranks of the Chancellery at that time called for a consciousness of responsibility, comprehensive knowledge of law and government, decision-making capacities and not least the ability to have an overview of matters. There is also a letter from this period from Prof. Dr. von Tscharner, who wrote to Kaspar Hauser on the 22nd October 1833: 'I would be very happy if you would take the opportunity to attend my lectures, a programme for which I append.'[330] One does not write in this way to someone who is at most cut out to be a stable master. Nothing came from the plan to move Kaspar to Karlsruhe, and it may be that it resulted only in a temporary deferment of the actions planned, which led to the search for a method of getting rid of him that promised more success.

*

In August Kaspar Hauser travelled to Nuremberg to attend the 8th National Festival. He was to be received there by the King and Queen of Bavaria and by the Dowager Queen Karoline. This event has been described and documented many times[331] so, as with many other biographical details in this book, it does not need to be repeated here. At the same time, mention must be made of the enlargement of the state of research made possible by the recently discovered gift which Kaspar presented to Queen Therese and which is documented here for the first time.[332] We know that Hauser had asked the 'Majesties here present' for their personal protection. He requested that 'it be made known that no harm would come to the one who imprisoned him'. That was the only means of preventing an assassination. It can be assumed that this request was also known in Karlsruhe and there led to the suspicion that Hauser would now involve himself in his own cause at the highest level, a probability underscored by his audience with Princess Liegnitz, who was then travelling through the region. The morganatic wife of King Friedrich Wilhelm III of Prussia assured Hauser of personal protection in the King's name.

It can only be speculated as to how far over the previous few months Hauser had in fact seriously imagined himself being able to return to

150. *Drawing in Kaspar Hauser's own hand c. July 1833 and presented to Queen Therese of Bavaria.*

151. *Detail from Fig. 150.*

the environment from which he had originated. There is no record of him making any statements about his origins. He was even silent when Stanhope was blustering about his alleged status as a Hungarian magnate. For the first time, however, on the gift he presented to the Queen (Fig.150), the foundling puts forward a silent request to be allowed to return home. In the upper left-hand corner of the drawing (Fig. 151), like an unspoken thought, is a motif that was perhaps intended as a reminder for the Queen's attention: a wanderer returning home with his staff and his pack on his back crosses the drawbridge into his castle.

At the beginning of his public life Kaspar Hauser's dreams were of his father's castle and of his mother bending over him—as his life drew to an end, it seems that he had gained a real certainty about his origins, which is manifested here in the form of an illustrated message to the Queen of Bavaria. Here too we see a rising self-consciousness that may have been noted and talked about by those who would have preferred a dreaming Hauser. There is a visiting card on the large picture—the last drawing of Hauser's known to us—written in clear self-assured script, a short, final, retrospective public statement from his own hand: 'Kaspar Hauser in Nuremberg'. No homage, no personal dedication. Seated on her throne, Queen Therese, who could now perhaps let her heart be moved—and rather small but not to be overlooked: the actual life question [Kaspar Hauser in Nuremberg]—that is all. Did this picture not correspond to reality, the condition that had been reached, the situation that had developed? How in a single moment the constellation of destiny is captured in outlines? After this event, Kaspar Hauser was silent until shortly afterwards, the time came which Hermann Pies called 'the mysterious last fourteen days'.

*

On the 9th October Stanhope wrote the twelfth, the last letter that Kaspar Hauser received when still alive. The thirteenth was posted when it was already clear that the receiver had already been buried. The twelfth letter, sent from Klagenfurt, is as lacking in content, and full of empty chatter as the letters of the previous seven months. Stanhope writes about 'the repulsive dirt' of the Italians and of the proverb 'there's no accounting for taste' and other such vacuous aphorisms. Only the end of the letter is noteworthy as a typical example of the confusing discrepancy between formal wordplay and reality that is to be found in all Stanhope's letters to Kaspar. 'I need not add that I most fervently do wish you, my dear Kaspar, good fortune and blessings and that I am and remain your truly loving foster father Earl Stanhope.'

The novelist Klara Hofer found a way to describe this trait of Stanhope's that is peerlessly apt. It is 'painful how he [Stanhope] eagerly gathers the brushwood to light the funeral pyre for the one whom he continually commends to the grace of heaven as his most beloved foster son'.[333] Did he never ask himself what his dearest Kaspar could have been feeling or experiencing or how great his affection was? Now, in October, after over half a year, came the second paltry letter, after the truly loving foster father had travelled for a month without Kaspar through Switzerland, Italy, and Austria. A year later, he had a whole book privately published full of imaginary letters for a small circle of friends (Fig.152), all written on his journey through Switzerland, but there is no mention in them of the great love for his foster son.

The question arises: why did Stanhope not take Hauser with him on this trip? Would it not have been a unique opportunity finally to

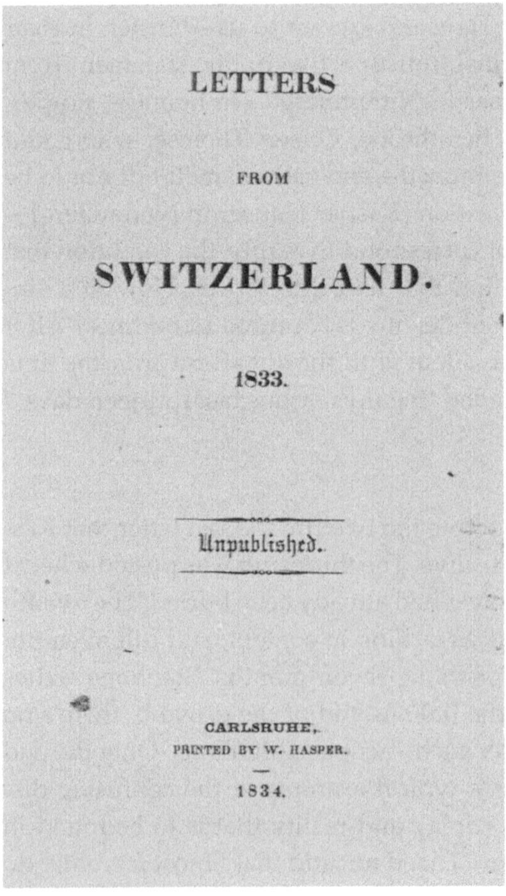

LETTERS

FROM

SWITZERLAND.

1833.

Unpublished.

CARLSRUHE,

PRINTED BY W. HASPER.

1834.

152. Cover page of the privately printed 'Letters from Switzerland' by Philip Henry Stanhope.

achieve what had not been possible in the short weeks at the end of 1831, namely, to really get to know Kaspar himself? Could there have been a better opportunity than this trip to experience him in all confidence, to test his credibility, to recognise his capabilities? Could this not have served at least as a faint equivalent in place of the promised resettlement in England? Would such a trip not have provided the evidence, long overdue, of Philip Henry's 'unwavering love', so emphatically attested to by Klüber and others? In short, the answer to such questions is a decided no! Not one of the actions against Hauser that were now necessary would have been possible in constantly changing locations and certainly not with Stanhope present. On the contrary, all conceivable strikes against Hauser would have to be in Karlsruhe or Ansbach, as the murder at the end of the year shows. Stanhope's final, intentionally delayed letter indeed only makes sense when one assumes that the foster father had at all costs to appear both completely blameless and clueless.

*

Stanhope spent the last days of July and the whole of August in Switzerland. Near Mannenbach, on the Swiss side of Lake Constance, lies Arenenberg Castle, high up with its view of the lake and Mainau island. Since February 1817 it had been the seat of Napoleon's stepdaughter Hortense, daughter of his first wife Joséphine Beauharnais. Grand Duchess Stéphanie often liked to visit her artistically gifted adopted sister who at convivial times would also paint portraits of her, two fine examples of which can still be seen in the castle's Napoleonic collection. Stéphanie does not seem to have been disturbed by the fact that Arenenberg had long been a focus of attention chiefly for the Austrian secret service as a 'centre of the Bonapartist movement'.[334] The Austrians quite rightly saw it as the focal point of revolutionary activities, which more or less amounted to preparing Napoleon's direct descendant for a political career. After the death of her eldest son (1831) Hortense concentrated on the education of the younger, the 23-year-old Louis Napoleon, with whom she even travelled to Paris on the 23rd April with false travel passes and was received by the Citizen King Louis Philippe, even if reluctantly and not according to correct protocol. In June 1831 furthermore, came the significant 10th anniversary of the death-day of the Emperor, which gave to the audience an inevitable political accent. Hortense and her son were even promptly expelled from the country, which appeared all the more necessary as popular wreath-laying ceremonies throughout the country were set for the 5th June, Bonaparte's death-day. When a year later, 1832, the Duke of Reichstadt died in Vienna, Hortense's son Louis Napoleon now became 'eldest offspring of the second generation and thereby a kind of pretender of the House of Bonaparte'.[335]

From the 8th—22nd July 1833 Stanhope took accommodation in Constance and from there began his visits to Arenenberg. In Constance lived as diocesan administrator the widely-known Catholic theologian Baron Ignaz Heinrich von Wessenberg (1774–1860) (Fig.153). Wessenberg was the brother of the diplomat who for years had been Stanhope's ally. At Hortense's court the scholar, among other things, had the position of tutor to the Prince, and since the death of the older son, he occupied himself all the more intensively with Louis. 'You are most welcome, dear Earl,' he wrote to Philip Henry in Stuttgart somewhat later, on the 6th March 1834 in the forlorn hope that Stanhope's route after the murder in Ansbach might lead him again to Constance. The clergyman, who, in opposition to his brother, served the Napoleonids and was as well acquainted with Stéphanie as with all the others who populated Arenenberg, may have had his reasons for welcoming Stanhope.

153. Ignaz Heinrich von Wessenberg (1774–1860)

After it became clear what Philip Henry's intentions actually were, Ignaz Heinrich von Wessenberg was certainly not one of the credulous ones who joined the 'Fraudster!' chanting chorus conducted by Stanhope, but rather, one of the more pensive ones who, on the basis of an intimate knowledge of Bonaparte-Zähringer interrelationships of politics and family tragedies, drew his own, quite different conclusions from Stanhope and his circle. 'The story around Kaspar Hauser becomes more mysterious for me every day,' he wrote to Stanhope.

In July 1833 Stanhope appeared at Arenenberg for the first time, arriving from Constance (Fig. 154). Naturally, it can only be surmised what the intentions and results of his conversations were and how wide the doors were really opened for him. Hortense showed him nevertheless all kinds of momentos of Napoleon: his decorations, a reliquary—a gift from the city of Aachen which dated from the time of Charlemagne—paintings of the members of the family, which included a colossal portrait of the Duke of Reichstadt (Fig. 155), a shawl that Napoleon had worn instead of a sash in Egypt and also his snuffbox. The room in which such receptions were held was arranged like a large war tent like the ones Napoleon used on his campaigns. How after such a short time had Stanhope managed to become privy to such confidences?

154. Schloss Arenenberg on Lake Constance.

155. François Bonaparte, Duke of Reichstadt, Napoleon II (1811–1832). Portrait by E. Billet.

The fact, however, that at this point in time, exactly between the deaths of the Duke of Reichstadt and Kaspar Hauser, the sons of Marie Louise[336] and Stéphanie, Stanhope was frequenting the house in which the last of the conceivable claimants to Napoleon's heritage lived, is most noteworthy. Did Louis Napoleon not also play a dangerous role in Metternich's imagination? Had Stanhope been commissioned to do some investigating at Arenenberg before he was expected in Vienna at the beginning of November? In any event, there was no other comparable location in which political rebellion was so deliberately prepared as Hortense's residence at Arenenberg. Did the news and indications that Stanhope gathered in the two weeks of his stay there bring the men behind the deadly events in the Ansbach palace garden to the final realisation that the Napoleonids were not to be trifled with? Could Stanhope see that since the death of the Duke of Reichstadt, at Arenenberg, the interior of which was closely modelled on that of Malmaison, Hortense gave precedence to her son according to courtly etiquette, thereby clearly demonstrating to whom the Bonapartist succession had passed?

Could it be hidden from him that a Bonapartist colony had developed around the castle? Stéphanie had obtained a property near Mannenbach. The Duke of Leuchtenberg had bought Eugensberg; Colonel Parquin, an old campaigner from the Grande Armée had acquired the nearby castles of Salenstein, Sandeck, and Wolfsburg, the last of which served as accommodation for all the guests at Arenenberg.

Did Stanhope get wind of the military studies and quite concrete plans for a coup, which just at this time Hortense's son Louis, the later Emperor Napoleon III, and his adventurous circle of various conspirators were discussing and soon afterwards—1835 in Strasbourg—actually carried out, albeit unsuccessfully? And if Louis had had better luck in Strasbourg, what position would Stéphanie then have had in the new political order? Would the Kaspar Hauser Question then continue to be addressed, with all the innumerable social considerations that would follow?

In July 1833 Stanhope must have gained the impression that no more time was to be lost. It was no difficult matter to send a hint to Vienna. On the 28th July at Lake Lucerne Stanhope met his 'old friend Neumann', who, having just arrived from England, where he had deputised for Prince Esterhazy at the London Conference for a time, wanted to spend a few days in Switzerland before going on to Vienna. Baron Philip von Neumann (1778–18[52?]), son of the imperial chamber furrier Karl Neumann, had worked his way up out of his bourgeois origins with great tenacity, finally secured a position in the diplomatic service and was raised to baronial status in 1830. His recipe for success was 'to support Metternich's views in all things and from the start, deny his own' and by this means he 'learned how to acquire and maintain a most pleasurable lifestyle', as his colleague Wessenberg sarcastically remarked, and thereafter 'did everything in the diplomatic circles in which he was called to operate, so as to forget his humble origins'. It was certainly a most welcome task for him to pass on to Metternich as quickly as possible news of the machinations at Arenenberg and their possible consequences. For Stanhope, Neumann was not only an old friend, but had also for a long time (1828) been an important go-between.

After he had looked around at Arenenberg, Stanhope travelled on to Italy, but the land that had been to Goethe a lifegiving Arcadia remained closed to the rational spirit of Philip Henry. 'I disliked so much all that I found in Italy, with the single exception of the Lake of Como, that I earnestly hope never to visit again any other part of it.'

> The whole region from Milan to Venice is flat and ugly, an eternal monotony of mulberry trees, corn fields, stunted poplars and willows, very few fruit trees and on the whole boring and without beauty. There is nothing worth seeing apart from a few churches and other buildings, nothing pleasing or enjoyable, only repulsive dirt, a humourless, noisy population, even extremely bad fruit and vegetables which there ought not to be in such a climate, in a word: much that is objectionable and uncomfortable and, to my taste, nothing that could serve as compensation or counterbalance.[337]

So much for our traveller in Italy, who missed no available opportunity to assure his listeners and readers that: 'I am known to be free of national prejudices.'

Why then did he make this journey through such an unbearable country, about which he wrote to his son: 'I disliked so much all that I found'? He certainly did not travel very far in Italy, and perhaps really did not wish to do so. From Ragatz (23.8) the small party went via Chiavenna (25.8) to Milan (5.9) which could not hold him for more than a few days. The cathedral was 'like a lady who should think she improved her beauty by wearing at the same time all the Necklaces, Bracelets, Earrings etc which she found in a Jeweller's Shop. As for the Pictures, they consist almost entirely of martyrdoms, holy families, annunciations & etc for which I have no taste & which tired me extremely.' Padua (24.9) already marked the turning point of the trip.

It is certain that Grand Duchess Stéphanie was in Milan and Chiavenna at just this time. For fear of a malaria epidemic, on the 22nd August she had terminated her stay in Italy which had begun on the 25th September 1832 and had returned to Mannheim by the end of September 1833. Did Philip Henry hear news at Arenenberg of Stéphanie's approximate travel route and want to meet her? The desire for such a meeting cannot be ruled out, but what meaning or purpose could it have had? Apart from the obvious alibi, did the foster father wish to tell the Grand Duchess in passing that he would be staying for a while in Vienna? Such a meeting, so soon before Kaspar Hauser's end and so far from the place of the deed, would fit well with the plan for the coming weeks. Assuming the conversation actually took place, Stéphanie too would have gained definite impressions from it. On the 18th February 1834 the Grand Duchess wrote a warning letter to Hortense, telling her 'that a report is on its way to Vienna according to which Arenenberg is a meeting point for revolutionaries. Louis should be careful.'[338]

Stanhope spent most of October (8th–30th) in the region Pordone—Udine—Klagenfurt. In Innsbruck he visited his 'friend, the governor'. Then finally, he went on to Vienna, arriving there on the 8th November. 'I am here most comfortably established in one of the most admirable Inns which I know, the "White Swan".' That sounds a little almost like an invitation and thanks to a host. The surmise is strengthened by the fact that at the end of his stay in Vienna, his meticulously written list of expenses, which included everything from lamp oil to entry tickets, apart from a small amount of drinks money for the tenant landlord of the 'White Swan', there is no record of expenses for meals and accommodation.

It was around the 18th November that Stanhope first met Metternich again with whom he 'dined and had a very interesting conversation'. Did their ideas and plans revolve around the last act of the Kaspar Hauser drama? Did he recall thoughts that had once occupied him, even 'pained' him, day and night 18 years earlier, in Dresden, and which had led to the idea that only the 'murder' of Bonaparte could guarantee the future of Europe? Such was also *the* solution which at one stroke would remove all problems in the present situation.

Metternich remained a rare guest, and Vienna without Gentz was no longer the place of soirées, huge parties and daily invitations. Stanhope felt lonely. In Gentz's company the weeks had flown by, but now? On the 16th November Stanhope bought himself a black Spitz dog for company, price £2,—'a very beautiful animal', Wessenberg noted, which was given the name Tubby [Dickel].

Philip Henry often went to the theatre accompanied by Count Bernhard von Rechberg (1806–1899), for example on the 20th November and on the evening of his 52nd birthday (7th Dec.). Plays by Raimund were again on the programme. Stanhope visited the poet himself (Fig. 156) once more at his estate Gutenstein near Vienna, probably on the 11th December. On that day he purchased an expensive 'Kaleidoscope for Raimund' which, as Raimund's guest, he presented to him as a gift. The poet was touched and read to his admiring visitor from his latest, then still incomplete work 'The Waster'. That was the last meeting between the two 'unequals'. Everything that Philip Henry himself lacked, the playwright and poet possessed in abundance. Another part of his free time Stanhope spent with a Viennese beauty by the name of Marianne Zillbauer, who occasionally received presents of snuff and later, a snuffbox.

156. Ferdinand Raimund (1790–1836) Lithograph by Kniehuber c. 1835.

The weeks passed by, and Stanhope waited. There were more frequent meetings with Metternich, who occasionally expressed the wish that Raimund would read to him something from his works; otherwise, only a tense silence reigned. Between the conversations of Stanhope and Metternich, Count Bernhard von Rechberg appears to have been the direct and sole intermediary of Metternich's wishes and ideas. The story of his special position is significant.

As a Minister in the Bavarian government, his father Alois had fallen out with King Ludwig so badly that in 1825 he was denied all his previously granted privileges and removed from all offices of State. The reason for this estrangement lay in the two men's differing evaluations of Austria's European policy. As Bavaria's representative at the Congress of Vienna, Count Alois von Rechberg had in the opinion of his king inclined too closely to the ideas of Metternich, so closely that in Bavarian nationalist circles he was held to be a traitor. When Alois's petition for a position in the Bavarian state service for his son Bernhard was refused in 1828, Bernhard turned to Metternich, who promptly found him a post in the Austrian diplomatic service in 1829.

Count Bernhard von Rechberg then served as diplomat for Metternich in Berlin and later in London, where, besides Stanhope, he got to know his future wife, a British aristocrat. Significantly in the present context, he stood very close to Metternich personally, which disposed him in 1848 to save first Metternich's children and then the man himself in his hour of need from the wrath of the revolutionaries. He accompanied Metternich in his flight from Austria through Germany to Holland, and when almost all Metternich's old friends kept away, von Rechberg did not leave the old statesman's side. Metternich's successor, Prince Schwarzenberg, richly rewarded him for these services with high office, and helped his career, which had begun but modestly, to attain unhoped for heights.

Stanhope and the conservative von Rechberg were intimately acquainted with Bavarian and Austrian affairs, and the two men were completely at one on the most decisive issue: the danger represented by France in general and the Bonaparte family in particular. Aside from Raimund, Metternich himself, and Prokesch, Metternich's confidante von Rechberg was Stanhope's only significant discussion partner in those lonely days in Vienna. Philip Henry met him frequently at his estate Schloss Kettenhof near Vienna.

One has the impression that the 40 days in Vienna, which Stanhope endured rather than spent with any pleasure, were essentially determined by the events that lay ahead. Was there still significant information that could determine how the dice would fall in December? Embroiled in the affair in various directions, was Stanhope waiting for the already determined day when the murder gang would now finally strike in Ansbach?

It is demonstrable that Major Hennenhofer and the diplomat Wessenberg were very well acquainted with each other.[339] Did information reach Philip Henry from Wessenberg? The Austrian could certainly be regarded as an intermediary in the complicated question of the date for the deed. This connection would seem to be borne out by the fact that Stanhope called on the infamous Hennenhofer not so long afterwards, in Freiburg on the 13th August 1834. Finally, it should not be overlooked that Baron von Reitzenstein—also on Stanhope's 'gift list'—turned up in Ansbach already on the 22nd December [Reitzenstein himself actually noted that he arrived on the 26th] just a few days after the murder, in order to 'make some investigations at the location', as Bavarian Minister of the Interior Oettingen-Wallerstein put it. From Reitzenstein himself we know that he had previously been to Eppingen to visit the Grand Duchess Sophie who, because of her confession that she had been an accessory to the murder, had been banished there on the orders of Leopold. Why did Reitzenstein think he had to consult with her just before his visit to Ansbach? We know today that the last blow against Hauser must have required some complicated prior organisation. Triggered by the Königsheim case in Gotha, which had come about when a person long since dead had been called up to serve in the army, the prior confirmation of the death of the child Ernst *Kaspar* Blochmann, exchanged in October 1812, was seen to be an urgent necessity. Without these manipulations, the conscription of Blochmann, which was now officially due, could lead to inconvenient investigations into the whereabouts of the *documented* and still living child, as the Gotha case had shown, and this might even uncover the reason for and cause of the crime of 1812. So Blochmann's legal death first had to be organised from Munich, followed by its transfer into the Karlsruhe register of deaths. The murderers then needed a few days to approach Hauser and, using the infamous deceit that they would reveal to him the identity of his father and mother, would arrange the day, time and place of the meeting. All these actions had somehow to be synchronised. What would have happened if Stanhope had suddenly turned up too early in the middle of things? The entire later construction—that Hauser had voluntarily or involuntarily attempted suicide, and had only wanted to pretend to kill himself but had in the attempt fatally gone too far and had arranged the whole thing only to demonstrate to his foster father how necessary it was to keep him with him permanently—all this would have been irreparably ruined. Stanhope and the rest of the affair would only have been served when his innocence was proven by his absence. The historical course of events duly followed in the necessary order.

On the 14th December came the second attempt on Kaspar Hauser's life. A wave of indignation and revulsion spread throughout the civilised world. Having heard the news, Klüber wrote to Hofmann on the 23rd December: 'Truly a real fate was hanging over the beloved Hauser and his persecutors. As the monster was again this time not discovered in the first 4 days after the attack, I now almost doubt that the discovery will be made.'[340] If much had not been lacking, the murderer would perhaps have been caught. By a ditch near the Ansbach post station, waiting for a change of horses, sat Baron von Varnbühler von und zu Hemmingen, then a student (1809–1899), and subsequently a minister in the Württemberg government. Years later, he shared his observations with Prince Eulenburg, who only published them in his memoirs in 1934.[341]

'At the time of the murder,' according to Varnbühler, a figure ran off at a fast pace towards the road leading out of town, which gave him 'cause to think'. The man, who saw Varnbühler sitting by the ditch, realised he had been noticed, and promptly changed direction when he came close by, heading off in the direction of a nearby village. After he had heard about the murder, Varnbühler not only thought again about 'the mysterious runner', but above all about his face, which he remembered clearly from the time they had both spent at court in Karlsruhe: it was Hennenhofer!

*

Two days later, on the 16th December, Stanhope took care of two more things in Vienna. First, he wrote the last of his letters to Kaspar Hauser, who was then already fighting for his life, and secondly, he had a meeting with Count Anton von Prokesch-Osten (1795–1876), who had for many years been the friend and advisor of the Duke of Reichstadt. Prokesch, an intimate friend of the Duke, had witnessed his decline and had pointed the finger at Metternich, accusing him in a small, anonymously written tract of the greatest wrongdoing against Napoleon's son.[342] This mild form of criticism of Metternich's deeds and omissions was the maximum that Prokesch dared to commit to writing, but he knew very well the truth of the matter. 'The cradle and the grave treat you as a king,' he wrote, and his words expressed the reality of the daily existence that Napoleon's son had missed. The Duke died, because the Chancellor had seen no role for him. It can hardly be supposed that Stanhope shared the sentiments of a man who had loved the Duke deeply, honoured him and was perhaps the only one who did so at least for the time the Duke inwardly still held on to life. Thus, there stood together on that 16th December in a very special relationship the two unequal guardians of the two Napoleonids who, born almost at the same time, would neither of them reach their full adulthood. Stanhope and Prokesch would certainly have spoken about the all-too-premature death of the one on the evening before the last day in the life of the other.

On this 16th December Stanhope wrote his last letter to Kaspar Hauser and added to it on that day before Kaspar's death a concluding sentence that was full of promise in that it announced his imminent return to Ansbach:

> A letter which I have received from my wife necessitates that I travel to Munich without delay...Through this change of plan....we shall, as I expect, have the pleasure of seeing each other perhaps sooner than

> would otherwise be the case and hopefully before the end of the coming month. I think I shall prepare this letter for dispatch when I have arrived in Bavaria so that you may have the satisfaction of knowing that you are in the same country as your warmly loving foster father, Earl Stanhope.

On the 18th December, the very day after Hauser breathed his last, Stanhope left Vienna. His departure was recorded indelibly for posterity in the *Wiener Zeitung* (Vienna News) of the 21st December. And what was this journey of which he had written to Hauser that he must undertake without delay?

Until now it had been thought that Stanhope must have taken the regular express coach from Vienna to Munich, which would have enabled him to arrive on Saturday morning, the 21st. It had further been presumed that a single stop had been made in Garching. Research results obtained only recently give a much less favourable picture of the course of the rapid 'homecoming' which had been announced in his letter. Since, as can now be shown, he travelled in his own carriage, Stanhope himself had it completely in his own hands as to when he would arrive in Munich. And that is the decisive difference compared to the regular scheduled journey, which is to be borne in mind when forming a judgement of the mysterious homecoming 'without delay'. The route consisted of eight instead of the necessary three stages:

Vienna to Melk	11½ miles, arrived	Wednesday 18th December
to Stremberg	8½ miles, arrived	Thursday 19th December
to Efferding	8½ miles, arrived	Friday 20th December
to Karpffham	9½ miles, arrived	Saturday 21st December
to PfarrkircheN	3 miles, arrived	Sunday 22nd December
to Landshut	8½ miles, arrived	Monday 23rd December
to Garching	6½ miles, arrived	Tuesday 24th December
to Munich	1½ miles, arrived	Wednesday 25th December

How can this mode of travelling be reconciled with the choice of the fastest route that would get him to Munich 'without delay'? Could Anton Heinrich have driven the carriage any slower? Karpffham, Efferding—(Figs. 157,158) these were tiny little places in those days and certainly not places in which to linger. Dreary post stations with a few farms. Was the weather perhaps the reason why Stanhope did not make faster progress: snow drifts or icy roads? In fact, it was the opposite: 'The autumn of 1833,' according to meteorological observations for this period, 'was very mild...The winter too was uncommonly mild, so that in January several plants were blooming which normally only begin to bloom in March.' In a letter to his son, Stanhope goes even further: in Germany now at the beginning of January the almond trees and cherry trees are in bloom and in the Black Forest flowers were to be seen at 4000 feet which normally bloom only in June. A pleasant trot through the countryside then, and certainly no battle against storms, snow and icy roads.

*

Hauser's wounding on the 14th December was already reported in the Munich newspaper *Bayerische Landbotin* on the 17th. On the 19th the Dowager Queen Karoline wrote to her daughter Elise: 'Therese [Queen of Bavaria] told me Herr von Tann had had the news that Hauser has died!—It is dreadful!'

157/158. The former Efferding post station in Lower Bavaria.

She did not want to tell the King so as not to excite him before sleeping. This news would have shocked him deeply.[343]

The next day, the 20th: 'If only it weren't true! Details about poor Hauser's death are in all the newspapers. So there is no more doubt about it...How awful...There is talk of nothing else...'[344] That evening Karoline noted in her diary: 'This morning the news of Kaspar Hauser's death was confirmed with real pain in all newspapers. Therese had told me about it yesterday, but I had hoped it might not be true...'[345]

On this 20th December, the day of the funeral in Ansbach, readers in almost all south German newspapers learned, as Karoline said, of the foundling's death. Viennese readers were able to follow the drama in the *Ősterreichischen Beobachter* already on the 24th. When did the news reach Stanhope? For him, it was a matter of finding out 'officially' as late as possible. Every day that the gap lengthened between Kaspar's death and Stanhope's own appearance would serve to boost the evidence of his own innocence, which is why the number of waystations and the length of time taken were stretched out as long as possible. The jurist and Kaspar Hauser researcher A. Bartning has therefore stated: 'It therefore seems, desperately, to be the case that he was waiting en route for specific information, namely, for news of Kaspar Hauser's death.'[346] How accurate Bartning's speculation was is borne out by the facts of the actual course of the journey from Vienna to Munich. Post stations were the first places to learn of what was going on in the world. Not perhaps the very small ones, but Pfarrkirchen and certainly Landshut, already in those days a sizeable town just outside Munich, were definitely among those information hubs open to the latest news. News—and especially news of this kind—was not only spread by other travellers. Newspapers were mostly available in such places for travellers to study and were read by them on arrival. Stanhope's daughter, the Duchess of Cleveland later stated: 'My father, who was then travelling, received the news on Christmas Eve at a post station on the road between Vienna and Munich.'[347] Seven days after the whole world knew of the sensation? Even if this incredibly late date be granted, there is still the astonishing fact, of which his daughter was either ignorant or which she forgot, that on Christmas Day her father hurried the 1½ miles from Garching to Munich in order to post his letter to the dead Hauser. In view of the text of this last letter, one would think that after obtaining further information in Munich about the attack, Stanhope would immediately have the carriage readied for the journey to Ansbach so as to reach the grave of his dearly beloved foster son that same day, consult with Meyer, Stichaner, Hickel, Fuhrmann and the doctors, hear about Hauser's last words and thank everyone who had stood by the foundling.

Klüber too in his letter of the 23rd December to Hofmann writes: 'I think that he will hurry to Ansbach.' The purport of the last letter was exclusively to tell Kaspar of the caring Philip Henry's joy that he would soon be entering Bavaria and would then be able to embrace him after their long separation. 'What a show the Lord puts on for us after the death of his foster son!' writes Pies and goes on:

> On the 26th December Stanhope already begins his bitter campaign against Hauser. He hurries to the [Bavarian] Minister of the Interior, Prince von Oettingen-Wallerstein in order to influence him with his 'suspicions' of Hauser, but makes no headway. He tries several times to bring the matter to court in Munich in order to gain an opportunity of blaming Hauser. He calls on various personalities in Munich in order to influence them against Hauser and to collect 'material' against him.[348]

Interestingly, one of these people was the new Prussian ambassador in Munich, Count August von Dönhoff (1797–1874). Did Stanhope intend particular news to reach the King or Merker, in Berlin? He had known the diplomat since 1829, when von Dönhoff had been working in London, eventually as chargé d'affaires.

Stanhope also paid a visit to the Dowager Queen to put before her his newly conceived suicide theory. What was the purpose and the necessity of diverting people away from what was indisputably a case of murder? Had the doctors not confirmed the fact that the force of the wound was such that a suicide could not possibly have inflicted it on himself? But only Stanhope's version, which he now suddenly brought forward, could, if it were believed, disguise the fact that the murder of Hauser was tantamount to proof and recognition of the true origin of the deed. On the 25th December Karoline had a conversation with Prince Joseph Taxis, with whom she spoke 'a great deal about Hauser, because he [Taxis] had seen him in Nuremberg'. The conversation must have confirmed the Dowager Queen in her view of Kaspar Hauser.

'In the almost daily conversations with him [Stanhope] about Kaspar Hauser the Queen's initial warm feelings for this humanitarian soon changed into quite their opposite,' wrote Prince Adalbert of

Bavaria. And on the 3rd January, Karoline confided to her diary the reason for her dislike: '...Always spoke about poor Hauser and Stanhope's new attitude...his shameful suspicion, as if the young man had stabbed himself.'[349]

King Ludwig too wrote of his feelings about the tragedy: 'So that I do not forget. On the 18th last the widowed Queen said that she had seen a picture of Kaspar and found a similarity with her father...' And on the next day, Christmas Eve: 'Truly painful the death of the rightful Grand Duke of Baden, if he was Kaspar Hauser, which is likely...'[350] That Ludwig should only have recognised the fact of the dynastic connection at this point in time, as some have concluded from this very diary entry, is not only unsustainable on account of all his previous tactics, but above all because of the text itself, which nowhere gives evidence of the presumed amazement and ignorance.[351] Ludwig merely bemoans, and quite credibly, the death of the 'rightful Grand Duke of Baden' and again on this occasion confirms his view that the identity is 'likely'. Neither does his regret not to have heard anything from his son-in-law at this time detract from the ignorance he wished to feign: 'I gathered from Therese that our future son-in-law (unfortunately now for the first time) said that when he saw Kaspar Hauser with us on the 27th August at Schmausenbuck near Nuremberg that he noticed such a similarity in the eyes with a cousin from Baden that he (the grand ducal heir apparent) felt the colour leave his cheeks.'[352] If one is to understand this remark rightly, then King Ludwig thought that Ludwig of Hesse, to whom he is referring here, was so shocked on seeing Hauser's face that he blanched. This amounts to a collection of feelings, thoughts, and reflections momentarily suitable for a diary—otherwise nothing. But the fact of the comments itself and the way they were written shows on the contrary more than a superficial cognisance of events. Rather, it signifies an observation and an after-the-event comment of one who knew and who confirmed some truths both for himself and about himself.

*

Kaspar was dead. Some of his last words were for his foster father. Hickel had written them in a letter for Stanhope on the morning after Kaspar's death (18.12): 'He [Kaspar] said he wanted to pray for you, warn you, and be your guardian spirit in eternity.' Another statement by the dying Kaspar, which followed this one, politely did not refer directly to Stanhope, although de facto it did apply to him: 'Sin ruins—can't get free of it. The monster was stronger than me.'[353]

Shock and sadness gripped everyone in these days who heard of the crime. Thousands read of it, passed on the news and held the poor man in their thoughts. Most were probably indifferent as to whether or not he was the Crown prince of Baden. They saw in him the innocent victim of mysterious and complex events. Yet memories now emerged from not a few people, who were rather better acquainted with things, which they communicated to one another orally, in writing, or made available by other means. Elise of Prussia to Amalie of Saxony: 'The portrait of this unfortunate looks really very similar to that of our uncle.' And somewhat later, also to Amalie: 'I did not have the courage to write to Mama about the likeness of the unfortunate Hauser.'[354]

From the French diplomat and Kaspar Hauser researcher Edmond Bapst, who had access to papers of Stéphanie's that are lost to us today, we know that the Grand Duchess travelled to Ansbach incognito in order to see Hauser after Stanhope had not kept his promise to bring his foster son to Mannheim. According to Bapst, on seeing Kaspar taking a walk in the Ansbach palace garden, she almost swooned because he looked so like her dead husband Grand Duke Karl.

Until much later, into the 1860s, King Ludwig concerned himself with the astonishing likeness of the two physiognomies (Figs. 159, 160) and also the striking similarity with other family members. In 1863 he noted: 'Wrote in my diary at that time that if I had seen Princess Marie von Baden, the present Duchess of Hamilton, earlier than Kaspar Hauser, I would have known that he was her brother, so alike did I find him. Most regrettable that that did not happen...'[355] And two years later, there was another comment about this apparently persistent memory:

> At tea yesterday my son-in-law [Grand Duke Ludwig III of Hesse] said of Kaspar Hauser that, as he saw it, he told himself that he was his cousin. Before his death I had seen Princess Marie of Baden—now the Dowager Duchess of Hamilton—between whom and Kaspar Hauser I found such a likeness that convinced me that he was her brother and thus a son of Grand Duke Karl of Baden. I already wrote this in my diary but told it to no-one except my dear departed Therese.[356]

159. Kaspar Hauser. Pencil drawing by an unknown hand.

160. Karl, Grand Duke of Baden (1786–1818)

We know that Grand Duke Ludwig [of Hesse] kept these memories of Kaspar Hauser until his old age. In 1867 he was still telling the French ambassador Count de Reiset—as the ambassador reported in his 'Memoirs'—that the surprising resemblance between Grand Duke Karl of Baden and Kaspar Hauser was for him proof of their family relationship. According to the ambassador, Ludwig of Hesse had no doubt that Hauser had actually been the legitimate heir to the throne of Baden.

The 'Memoirs' of Prince Alexander von Hohenlohe tell a similar story:

> My father (Prince Chlodwig, the Imperial German Chancellor) saw Kaspar Hauser himself, as he often told me. It was in Nuremberg, if I remember rightly, in the summer of 1829 or 1830; my father and his brother Viktor, who were still boys, were sitting with their tutor in a public beer garden when Kaspar Hauser, who was about 16, medium height and slim with blond hair and refined, distinguished features passed by them with his companion Lord Stanhope [it must have been 1831, not 1829 or 1830—*Ed.*]. It was not surprising that they regarded him with particular attention, for he was the talk of all Europe at that time. My father told me that when he had once visited the Grand Duchess [Stéphanie] at Mannheim, he remembered this, and from his [Hauser's] features, it seemed to him not impossible that her conjecture was well-founded.[357]

Finally, Prince Eulenburg. After meeting Josephine von Hohenzollern—Grand Duchess Stéphanie's daughter—he wrote in his diary:

> What excited my particular interest, however, with regard to the old princess, was that when I was in her presence, a portrait of Kaspar Hauser owned by the old Baron Wendelstadt came vividly to mind. There was the same forehead, the same eyes, the same chin. I was actually strengthened by this impression in my view that the unfortunate Kaspar Hauser was the Prince of Baden, who had been robbed of his title.[358]

But back to the year of Hauser's death and the situation at court. Dowager Queen Karoline observed in these days an unusual change in Stanhope, which she shared with her daughter Elise, Queen Elisabeth of Prussia: 'He [Stanhope] seems to me as if he was in a constant high fever...' and 'sometimes [I] find him in a very unquiet, confused state

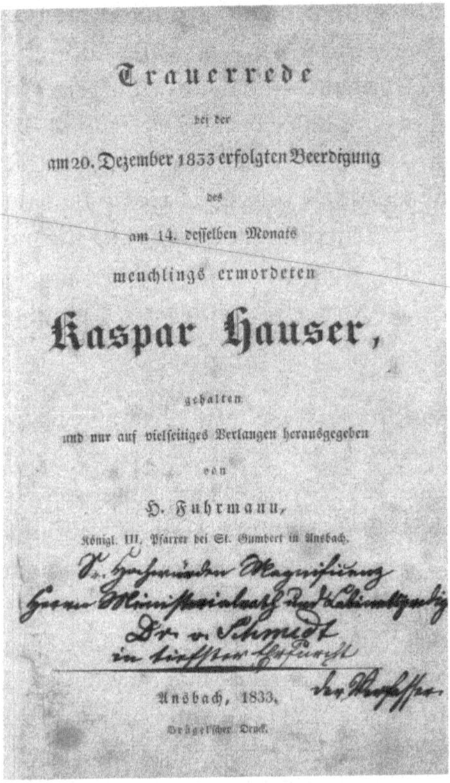

Trauerrede

bei der

am 20. Dezember 1833 erfolgten Beerdigung

des

am 14. desselben Monats

meuchlings ermordeten

Kaspar Hauser,

gehalten

und nur auf vielseitiges Verlangen herausgegeben

von

H. Fuhrmann,

Königl. III. Pfarrer bei St. Gumbert in Ansbach.

Sr. Hochwürden Magnifizenz
Herrn Ministerialrath und Cabinetsprediger
Dr. v. Schmidt
in tiefster Ehrfurcht
der Verfasser.

Ansbach, 1833.

Brügel'scher Druck.

161. Cover page of the 'Funeral Oration…' Example presented by the author, Pastor Fuhrmann, to the Cabinet Preacher Friedrich Ludwig von Schmidt.

162. A lock of Kaspar Hauser's hair.

of mind...'[359] On the last day of the year, Karoline received a letter from her daughter Sophie in Vienna in which Sophie wrote that the 'murder of poor Hauser sent shivers down her spine'. What could have been the cause of such feelings?

*

Pastor Fuhrmann, who accompanied Kaspar Hauser's passing, sent his colleague von Schmidt, Queen Karoline's trusted adviser, a copy of his funeral oration (Fig. 161) and, after the custom of the time, also sent to the Feuerbach family a lock of Kaspar Hauser's hair (Fig. 162).

14. Stanhope Organises the Opponents

Joseph Hickel and Karl Merker, 1834–1835

'It is possible,' wrote G.F. Daumer in his book about Kaspar Hauser that appeared in 1873,

> and happens quite often that the mood, inclination, and opinions of a human being can change; that friendship, love, affection change not only to indifference but even radically into their opposites. The Count [*sic*] was able to believe that he had been tricked by Hauser, and believed himself to have been grossly deceived in his initial enthusiasm; he was able to feel angry about this and withdraw himself [from Hauser]; indeed, such a boy who was lucky enough to fool and lead on an English Earl and Peer of Great Britain to make such public and sensational steps would deserve to go to the devil. That would not be peculiar or unnatural. But the more irritated and ashamed he became about the case, the more he and others should have tried to put it behind them. Instead of this, in an equally open and conspicuous manner, he began again, but this time with a completely different purpose, in court proceedings, in private conversations, and in numerous publications, to express his completely changed opinion and he joined up with an opponent like Merker in Berlin, taking great pains to change the minds of those who still believed in Hauser and draw them to the enemy's side. Everything that this man did was unnatural, not simple or clear or based on any given motives, as anyone will grant who knows and reflects on human nature to some extent.

'What would Daumer have said,' wrote Pies, 'if he had known that almost all of the alleged "charges" Stanhope made against Hauser would on close examination and comparison with official investigation documents dissolve into nothing?'

*

Stanhope remained in Munich at first where he had been drawn, as Prince Adalbert of Bavaria writes, also by the approaching pleasures of the festival of Fasching. As he had left his black Spitz [dog] in Vienna, he now bought 'a very small and very pretty white Spitz' as a substitute.

The new year stood under the influence and in the expectation of Halley's Comet that is said to have an unfavourable effect on earthly conditions. War, catastrophes, fear and turmoil arise as it approaches Earth, which was at least true in this case.

Stanhope's sole intensive efforts in these days were to discredit his former foster son at every available opportunity. At the very beginning of the year, he sought to draw the Dowager Queen Karoline to his side on three occasions, on the 2nd, 3rd and 18th January, and also the Bavarian Minister of the Interior, Prince Oettingen-Wallerstein, who was familiar with all the details of the investigation into the murder.

The Queen very quickly concluded that the humanitarian of yesterday was something other than the man of today, and certainly no protector of a beloved foster son. Her daughter Sophie from Vienna also wanted to know what to make of it all. 'Before the post arrives, I am burning to learn what you would calmly have to tell me ...My God, if it really were true, it would be too awful!'[360]

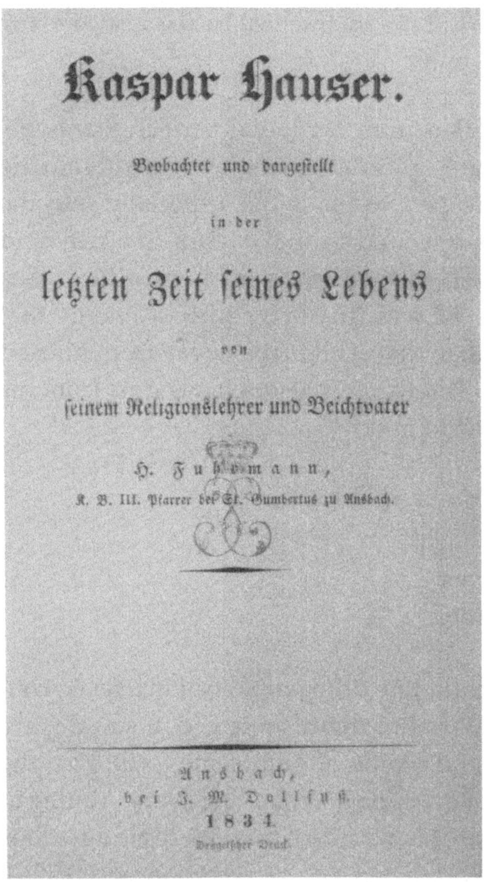

Kaspar Hauser.

Beobachtet und dargestellt

in der

letzten Zeit seines Lebens

von

seinem Religionslehrer und Beichtvater

H. Fuhrmann,

K. B. III. Pfarrer bei St. Gumbertus zu Ansbach.

Ansbach,

bei J. M. Dollfuß.

1834.

163. Title page of Fuhrmann's book. Given as a gift by Queen Karoline of Bavaria to her daughter Sophie, Archduchess of Austria.

We do not know how Karoline replied. Perhaps she spoke with the same openness as she did to Hickel, but she sent her daughter Fuhrmann's book *Kaspar Hauser. As observed and described in the last period of his life by his confessor and teacher in religion* (Fig. 163) and added: 'How can someone with such a character be suspected of suicide, even disregarding the physical impossibility!'[361]

We do, however, know the Archduchess's reply to her mother: 'It is such a horrible story, like something out of the Middle Ages. If only one could uncover this awful mystery—I do not know what I could do for it...'[362] After Stanhope's visits the Queen wrote to her daughter Elise of Prussia, who reported to her twin sister Amalie of Saxony:

> ...I have just received from our dear mother a ten-page letter...I had not heard anything from her for fifteen days. I was longing to hear something from her. She tells me nothing about our new cousin [Grand Duke Ludwig of Hesse] but all the more about Hauser. She is constantly suspicious. It makes my blood run cold when I think about it and tears come to my eyes as in a ghost story. If it were true that he was related to her and she has only now found out![363]

Oettingen-Wallerstein too recoiled from his initial trust in Stanhope. His meetings with the Englishman allow an instructive insight into the state of affairs at court with respect to Stanhope, especially into the misjudgements which Stanhope tended to make. Torn this way and that, with none of the calm, self-assured manner of one who is certain of himself and of his case, he was driven by a hectic energy that appeared to have only one goal: to divert all blame away from himself and place it squarely onto the 'fraudster'. His noble maxims from his time in Dresden no longer came to mind:

> O let me never promise
> What I have not thought through;
> Nor break my word once given
> Because it troubles me so to do.

Things could not have developed more differently. As if in a fever, confused, as the Queen noticed, his gaunt figure appeared at social gatherings and ministerial offices and words of guilt came forth from the depths of his soul. '...dining out every day & spending every evening in company', as he wrote to his son, he provided, through his industrious questioning, probable or actual opponents of Hauser with an exact standpoint from which to argue. 'The information which those people gave to me was in direct contradiction of Feuerbach's statements.' That was what he now wanted to hear and circulate. At any cost, including that of the truth, Feuerbach's position on the Kaspar Hauser Question had to fall; only then could the foundling be convincingly represented as a fraud and a suicide and the actual question thereby be avoided. From all his strange behaviour and the nature of the facts themselves, a whispering began to surround him that would not be stilled. 'Amongst other things,' he wrote to Hickel, 'people say that I had Hauser murdered.'[364] What Hickel did not learn was how this had arisen. The Dowager Queen, namely, had put a question to Stanhope about it! The rumour may have developed from her circle. But: 'No smoke without fire'—that had long been the view, based on experience, of the old criminologist Feuerbach, who had investigated such cases. In his Memorandum to Karoline he had addressed this question more precisely:

> Rumours evidently are only rumours, but are not to be scorned nevertheless; they often flow from very true sources. When it comes to secret crimes, they frequently emerge from such sources as loose talk or carelessness by an accessory to the crime, which betrays him, or because an accomplice seeks to reveal the truth without having to betray it himself, in order to lighten his conscience or to take revenge for disappointed hopes and such like. For these reasons, legal scholars include rumours (*famam publicam*) among the indicators of crimes and their perpetrators and participants.

To his son Mahon, who must have lacked accurate knowledge and insight into the circumstances of the case, Philip Henry wrote on the 29th December the nonsensical idea: 'It appears that he [Hauser] had become very mistrustful of those about him & suspected that they knew & wilfully concealed the secret of his birth.'[365] Who could that have been? The murder was only successfully carried out *because* Hauser was a trusting person.

Then Feuerbach is assigned his share of the blame. Kaspar had found it oppressive to be accompanied everywhere by a policeman, and Feuerbach had relaxed this security or finally removed it. This had happened '...without my knowledge, & was the more inexcusable, as I engaged to take measures for his personal security and was fully responsible'.[366] He did not represent himself in this way without an ulterior motive: 'Please communicate the above to Lord Strangford, Lord Wallace, Sir R. Vyvyan & any other of my Friends who take an interest in the subject, informing them that you are doing so at my urging.' In the same letter to his son, he flattered himself that he had the trust of the Minister of the Interior, 'who, without having previously been acquainted with me, responded to my wishes and granted me access to all the documents in his office pertaining to the case and with whom I am in constant communication'.[367] Or so Stanhope thought.

In her letter of the 31st January 1834 to her daughter Elise, Karoline expressed quite the contrary: 'Wallerstein cannot share all the reports with him [Stanhope] that he receives, because everything he hears, he spreads about here and there just as he does with everything he thinks and suspects...he allows himself to be influenced by every third or fourth person.'[368]

Oettingen-Wallerstein certainly did not allow Stanhope near the documents and certainly none of the important ones, and he had another reason for this, of which perhaps Karoline herself was unaware. Stanhope may personally have been implicated in the investigations, as can be understood from the Minister's letter of the 23rd January 1834 to Stichaner, the president of the local council in Ansbach. At the end of the letter under point 4 of 'factors for further attention' is the passage: 'Finally, the magazine articles against Hauser which for the last two years have appeared and *especially their sources* [emphasis Mayer] on the basis of which Police Commissioner Merker may have gathered the facts to support his doubts about Hauser.' Given the now generally noticed change in the former foster father's position, it was either a foregone conclusion for Wallerstein or else the discovery of the sources was just a matter of time. The Minister's reserve probably resulted from first confirmations of such a suspicion.

On the 2nd February Stanhope was once again with Karoline: 'The news from various quarters that the murderer had been caught, excited me'[369] noted the Queen. Not Stanhope, it seems. Three days later, on the 5th February, he appeared again, apparently invited by the Queen, with whom he dined. This time Karoline noted: 'He too is groping in the dark and has no other thought nor any other interest but this unhappy event.'[370] Meanwhile, Philip Henry was getting anxious about missing correspondence. He told his son to look into it:

> I cannot but believe that several letters are also missing from Butcher & other Agents, for I received a few days ago a letter from him of the 4th

> inst. & the last preceding was of the middle of October. I fear that they may still remain in the Foreign Office, & I shall be very much obliged to you if you will make enquiries about them of the person to whose care they were sent. I do not think that they remain at the Ambassador's as several Letters have been forwarded to me from thence. Pray let me know if they were sent under cover to him or poste restante.[371]

After nothing apparently came of this, a second letter went to England a few days later: 'I need not say that I am extremely anxious to recover them, & I beg that you will make very particular enquiries about them at the Foreign Office.'[372] This characterises the other side of this odd visitor to the Munich Fasching festival. What kind of psychological picture arises when one puts together such observations of Stanhope's behaviour over these days? How did he get into this situation which drove him so hectically?

Let us look again at the reason for his efforts—the organisation of a shift in mood against Hauser's credibility. What was the justified pretext for further procurement and questioning of witnesses after Hauser's death, when his removal meant de facto that there was no longer any dynastic problem? Why could it still have been important whether Hauser was credible or not or whether he had been murdered or committed suicide? Daumer claimed rightly that 'everything that this man [Stanhope] did was unnatural'. Even when quite normal requests were made of him, he declined to comply without giving reasons. Hauser's memory was to be smeared wherever possible. In a letter of the 25th January, Pastor Fuhrmann's publisher Dollfuss in Ansbach asked Stanhope for his permission to include a picture of Kaspar Hauser in the commemorative booklet *Kaspar Hauser. As observed and described in the last period of his life by his confessor and teacher of religion.* But Stanhope declined. Why?

Yet at the same time he invested not an insubstantial amount of money in order to prove that Hauser—who had had no property or means of his own, who had never demanded anything for himself or expressed any pompous intentions, who had simply existed—was a fraud, Feuerbach a falsifier of documents and Daumer a deplorable fantasist.

It was his main aim, if he could, to get those first witnesses of 1828, the ones who had been the very first to see and hear Hauser to make statements that would cast doubt on the foundling's hitherto accepted story. Stanhope wanted to get a new legal investigation underway but one that was prompted by himself and for this reason at the end of February and the beginning of March 1834, he called on the old witnesses. On 27th February he sought with considerable success in Augsburg to get Captain von Wessenig to make different statements. From the 2nd to the 8th March, he tackled the Nurembergers. Daumer (Fig. 164) still remembered Stanhope's visit very well when in 1859 he wrote his book *Revelations about Kaspar Hauser*:

> Stanhope came to me after Hauser's death and tried to get me to testify against him publicly. As the foundling's teacher and most attentive observer, I represented a not insignificant authority, and if this [authority] could be used against him, then things would have gone very badly for him. It was a matter of whether I could be drawn into the shameless plot. The Count therefore paid me several visits, in which he gradually became clearer and clearer as to how matters stood. I became astonished by this and in the innocent trust that I had at first in Stanhope, I did not know where to put myself. Women usually see such things more sharply. It was not I, but my mother who was deeply suspicious, and when I expressed my astonishment about Stanhope to her, she spoke out a word to me which I refrain from repeating. ('Don't you see that this is the...[murderer]?' she cried.) Anyway, that was the end of my trusting

164. Georg Friedrich Daumer (1800–1875) Photo from c. 1830.

> relationship with the sinister man. The last time he was with me, I could no longer suppress my deep ill-feeling towards him; the conversation was painful; he suddenly jumped up and, as if pursued by the Furies, ran down the steps and out of the house and never came back.

Near the end of the same book, Daumer had occasion to speak further about Stanhope's strange visits. As the report contains some additional aspects, the information is illuminating.

> The Count tried very insistently to dispose me against [Hauser] and Feuerbach's view of him, which lit a small spark of distrust in my soul—previously I had been quite unsuspecting and trusting of the Count and had believed everything he had said. When finally, my mother, realising that he was up to no good, swore on the ashes of the unfortunate one, who had once trusted him as his friend and benefactor, that he was certainly no fraud, and asked [Stanhope] very emotionally not to cover him with disgrace—whereupon his Lordship replied that nothing could harm him any more, in that moment the Count showed himself in a light in which it was impossible to see an honourable attitude and a calm noble state of mind. The blood came to his pale face; it was not long before he could any more bear my mood, which probably showed itself too clearly on my face; he jumped up and with strikingly winged steps fled from my house, which has never since had the honour of welcoming him.

After this embarrassing failure with Daumer, with a notable, instinctive feel for the still possible success of his mission, Philip Henry turned to the witness who already in 1828 had been the most controversial and weighty: Georg Leonhard Weickmann (1778–1835), the man who had first witnessed Kaspar Hauser's appearance in Nuremberg, and who Stanhope, unintentionally but comically, kept referring to in his tracts as 'Weichmann' ['soft man'—*Ed.*] Weickmann's statement, which Stanhope had already studied carefully, showed a peculiarity in contrast to all other witness statements, which he could use to his advantage in further developing his plans. He wrote first to Hickel: 'Could you please supply me with copies of the testimony of the shoemaker Weichmann?'

Point 3 of the copy read: 'There are some doubts about Hauser's words: "Regensburg" and "new gate certainly just built". Are you sure about your statement in this case? I remember exactly hearing those words from Hauser's mouth as I described them.'

But that was just what Feuerbach had good reason to doubt. If Hauser knew and could utter as much as Weickmann claimed, then the basis of his long imprisonment and release in Nuremberg was shattered. Feuerbach therefore dealt expressly with this statement in his book *Example of a crime against the human soul*, and Stanhope naturally knew this passage very well. It reads:

> With regard to the details of how Kaspar, with the above-mentioned citizen, got from the Unschlittplatz to the police station and from there to Captain W[essenig]'s house, the documents are partly so full of gaps and unsatisfactory and partly, with regard to the circumstances mentioned, so open to the doubts of historical criticism that I believed I might be able to give a short account of the above. So, for example, that citizen says that after he tried to engage in conversation with K[aspar] on the way and had asked him many things, he finally noticed *that K[aspar] knew nothing at all and had no ideas, so he said nothing more to him*. Thereafter K[aspar] appeared to him just as he did that same evening at Captain W[essenig]'s and later at the police station, then in the following days and weeks. At the same time, that citizen says that K[aspar], in answer to the question where he had come from, replied: 'from Regensburg'. Further, when he came with K[aspar] to the new gate, [Kaspar] said: 'This is certainly just built, 'cos it's called new gate' and so on. That the witness *believes* to have heard this and the like I doubt as little as the fact that K *did not say* it. All the following provides the most irrefutable evidence for this. From Kaspar's constant refrain: 'I want to be a rider like my father', his guide who lent him only half an ear believing him a simpleton, could well have believed he had heard those words. The police documents accumulated in this case are drawn up in such a manner, containing so many contradictions, so much is taken so lightly, and some in their key parts are so terribly *anachronistic* that they can only be used as sources with the greatest care.

Stanhope's plan now aimed directly at getting the weak witness Weickmann to amend or extend his statements on three points. If that succeeded, Feuerbach's reputation would suffer. Such was Stanhope's calculation as can be seen from the legal proceedings of 1834. Weickmann's statements deliberately corresponded to the points Stanhope saw as important and now were recorded as follows:

1. Contrary to the statement of 1828/29 Hauser was no longer said to have tottered on his feet but to have walked in 'good strides', which contradicted the notion of a long incarceration.

2. He could speak sentences in an allegedly respectable fashion and understood essentially more than he let on, from which it can be concluded that he knew how to play his role in the alleged comedy.
3. Weickmann made a recorded statement which read as follows:

> Definitely, ten days after this event Kaspar Hauser was brought to court (thus!), where I had to look at him. But Kaspar did not want to recognise me, and to my question whether he no longer remembered me, he replied: 'No, no'. He spoke these two words in a tone from which one could understand that he was quite 'confused'. When the questions and answers were being recorded, I was always looking at Kaspar Hauser, and when he once noticed that I was looking at him fixedly, he said impatiently: 'Why are you looking at me?'

From this certainly tendentiously interpreted memory of something that had happened six years before, assuming that it did in fact happen and was not perhaps the result of Stanhope's helpful fantasy, two things were supposed to become clear: Hauser's alleged bad conscience that he had been seen through, and Weickmann's unerring ability to judge character; he was supposed to have recognised so early on that there was something wrong with the whole story. In 1873 in his last big book about Hauser, Daumer well recognised the contradictions of the two hearings, the second of which, as already mentioned, was personally inspired by Stanhope, but Daumer did not know concretely the extent to which Hauser's former foster father was the guiding spirit behind such statements. Discussing here the writing of Julius Meyer, the son of Kaspar Hauser's teacher in Ansbach, Daumer wrote:

> The first to see H[auser] in Nuremberg were two shoemakers, Weickmann and Beck; according to the documents mentioned by Meyer, the former testified at hearings in November 1829 and in May 1834; Beck first testified on the latter occasion but not in 1829. His statements are sketchy. Meyer lays great weight on Weickmann's statements. 'In two interrogations years apart, he [Weickmann] gave the same testimony down to the smallest details, clearly and without contradictions.' Nothing could be more incorrect. Weickmann contradicted himself in one and the same hearing; and in the second he spoke otherwise than in the first. In the second [he said] Hauser came down the hill in *good strides*; in the first he said he *tottered* down; that is not the same. In the first, he says that he only read the address of the letter H[auser] was carrying; in the second, he claims to have *looked through* the letter. Another striking

contradiction is the fact that the witness claims to have had conversations with H[auser] and obtained answers to his questions yet also says that H[auser] had not understood the most normal German words and could give no answer to questions that were put to him. 'When I asked him what was the latest in Regensburg, what people were saying there about war and peace, he did indeed repeat the words war, war, but I soon noticed that he neither had any idea of war nor understood what I asked.' It was the same in the second hearing: 'H[auser] retorted: 'war, war' but showed clearly that he did not understand the word.' That is a very important statement. It has entirely the feeling of a genuine recollection; embellishing fantasy and poesy could have had no part in it, for such would create positives, while here there is only the simple negation of a positive. If H[auser] had really not known the word 'war', then obviously the German language was certainly very strange to him and he could not have gone wandering around the country, for everyone who speaks and understands German knows what war is. The alleged conversations can be easily explained by the fact that K[aspar] tried to copy everything that people said to him; the rest was added by the imagination and capriciousness of the witness. So, when he [Weickmann] said: 'We'll go to the [police] station at the new gate', according to Weickmann's statement, H[auser] said: 'Station—station—new gate—surely just built.' One sees here clearly how H[auser] copied the words without understanding them; the expression 'surely just built' or at the second

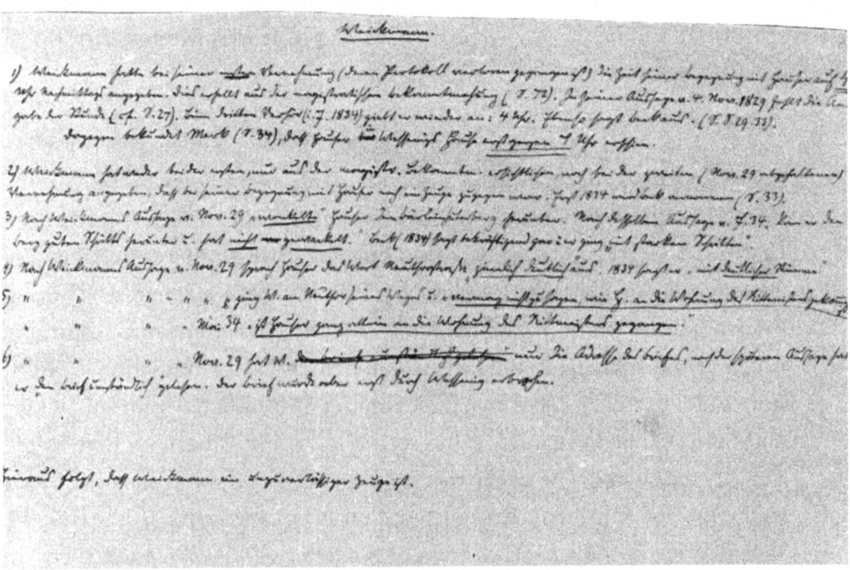

165. Notes by William Pierson about the witness Weickmann.

> hearing: 'just built' is consequently most definitely a false addition. It was the same at the second hearing: When the witness said, 'we'll go to the Captain', H[auser] repeated: 'the captain, the captain'. This kind of repetition, demonstrably documented, is hereby sufficiently confirmed and validated; and that is a very important result for any judgement of Hauser's capacities of speech at that time.

The historian William Pierson also studied the testimonies of witness Weickmann, and after a comparison of his statements of 1829 and 1834 came to the conclusion: 'It follows from this that Weickmann is an unreliable witness.' (Fig. 165)

*

Stanhope had again reached his goal in this case with Weickmann's statement. The hearings of 5–9 May 1834[373] were carried out at his urging. He had previously influenced the direction of all the witnesses' statements, sometimes several times. On the 14th July he wrote from Karlsruhe to Schmidt-von Lübeck:

> You will see in the news that another witness[374] has confirmed the testimony of the shoemaker Weichmann [*sic*] about the first appearance of Kaspar Hauser, and I gather that Weichmann is held by his whole guild to be a very honest man and enjoys their complete trust. The news shows the Feuerbach thesis to be wholly overthrown as well as the urgent necessity to recommence investigations from the beginning and with the greatest circumspection.[375]

This reply was made in connection with extremely critical comments about the witness Weickmann that had previously been expressed by the jurist Schmidt-von Lübeck, who had declared his suspicion of everything that had been stated up to that point. In his letter of the 9th July 1834 to Stanhope, Schmidt-von Lübeck accused the shoemaker of complicity with those behind the crime against Kaspar Hauser.

'So, as matters stand now,' writes the judge,

> the only thing that can still happen is that the very first witnesses be heard once again in Nuremberg and better than before. I cannot conceal that as judge, I would direct my attention especially to the shoemaker Weickmann at the Unschlittplatz in Nuremberg and to his family relationships. The special circumstances at Hauser's first appearance justify

such attention, for the combination of time and place remain extremely striking, especially

1. with respect to the time, that the shoemaker comes out of his house *at exactly the moment* when Casp[ar] Hauser is standing in front of the door or nearby, and
2. with respect to the place, that the shoemaker wants to go precisely to the new gate, thus *to the place* where Hauser is to go. Additionally,
3. that the shoemaker at the hearings has Hauser say all kinds of things that the latter could not possibly have said, and that he therefore carelessly spoke an untruth. Feuerbach on p.3 [of his *Example of a Crime against the Soul Life of Man*] explains this as if the shoemaker merely believed that he had heard this or that, but he did not in fact say so. And finally, was it proved by witnesses' testimony that the shoemaker really found Hauser in front of his door at the Unschlittplatz? Could he not just as easily have picked him up from some hiding place between his house and the police station at the new gate?[376]

Weickmann and Stanhope can be seen as united in a strange way in this mysterious affair. Providing for the second time untrue arguments in the campaign against Hauser, the shoemaker was Philip Henry's strongest instrument in the dark drama of 1834. Was there a connection between the two men which suggested such a prior agreement that would suit their mutual interests?

Weickmann was the only witness who Stanhope thanked with more than words, which is demonstrable in at least one case. In Wiesbaden, where the two men probably met, on the 26th June the 'witness' received the not inconsiderable present of £27 for his services. An entry in Stanhope's travel journal reads:

June 26 | To the shoemaker Weichmann at Nuremberg | 27[pounds] | In Charities

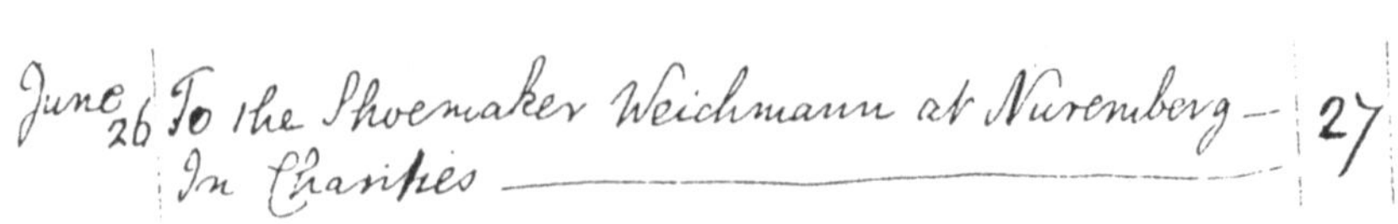
June 26 To the Shoemaker Weichmann at Nuremberg — 27
In Charities

In Wiesbaden Stanhope was expecting the man who would be the main focus of his campaign—the man formerly entrusted with protecting Hauser, Lieutenant Hickel. To get this man on his side, who had known the foundling like no other, who had enjoyed the trust of Feuerbach,

Tucher and Daumer, who the world regarded as an objective unblemished officer, would bring about the decisive turning point in the Kaspar Hauser affair that Stanhope sought. These activities have to be seen and judged in the light of the goals that were being aimed at, in order to be able to recognise that Stanhope was not after a selfless discovery of the true facts of the case but always sought to create the preconditions that would lead to his predetermined result. In the first instance this required changing the judgements and opinions of those who had stood at Kaspar Hauser's side during his life or afterwards.

For this final, completely opposite view of the Kaspar Hauser case, which was intended to fix in the mind of posterity the picture of a cunning scoundrel, Stanhope wrote five defamatory publications, which were all printed and advertised at his own expense or, in some cases, by the banker Haber in Karlsruhe. He also got Merker to publish several hundred pages of disparagements in a second booklet (Fig. 166):

> *Important Revelations about the Kaspar Hauser Story communicated to Police Commissioner Merker by Lord Stanhope*

To arrange all this required Stanhope, who had left Chevening in May 1833, to spend another 21 months in Germany. Only in September 1835—after a stay of 29 months in all —did he return to England.

Again the question arises: why all this expenditure of time and money? There is only one convincing motive. As so often in the Kaspar Hauser affair, it was revealed by Klüber. He was either very near the truth or else he knew it, when on the 23rd January 1834 he hinted to Hofmann that he found it 'very likely that eminent or wealthy persons were involved. I find no satisfactory pointers whatsoever to suicide.'[377] But only when it was established once and for all that Hauser was a fraud and a suicide would the basis for his possible princely status collapse along with Stanhope's own direct responsibility. On the other hand, a verdict of murder would, in the absence of any other motive, render Hauser's relationship with the Zähringers virtually proven and Stanhope too would be accused. Stanhope's effort and expenditure were thus only too explicable. During this period Stanhope strove to gain audiences at Court in Munich, Stuttgart, Karlsruhe, and Mannheim. He started at the beginning of March in Munich.

After he had already tried without much success to speak to the Dowager Queen, 'I was very cordially and graciously received by the King of Bavaria.' The result was, not unexpectedly, meagre. His intention to create another version of the Kaspar Hauser story made no progress. First, he tried to get the King to invite the ageing Raimund to Munich from Vienna, but Ludwig did not want to know. Then he moved on to talk about Hauser, but His Majesty stuck to the foster father's former judgement that Hauser had been 'a good fellow'.

This comment contradicts, incidentally, the common assertion that Ludwig himself entertained no particular picture of Hauser. The King then made it quite plain where he stood on the matter. In Munich, Stanhope reported to his son, '...the whole question is considered as an affair of state, and where I know that one of the Ministers said: "The government chuses [*sic*] [to believe] that Kaspar Hauser shall have been [i.e. must have been—*Ed.*] assassinated & you will take care to repress all contrary reports."'[378]

Stanhope then tried his luck in Stuttgart. The route there would normally have involved a stay in Ansbach, especially the journey via Nuremberg, and in fact, Stanhope had Anton Heinrich head in

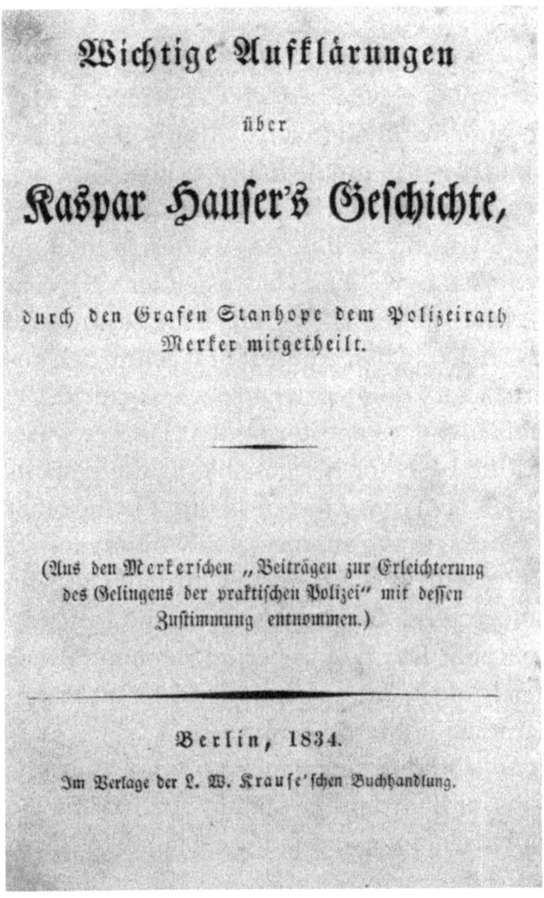

Wichtige Aufklärungen

über

Kaspar Hauser's Geschichte,

durch den Grafen Stanhope dem Polizeirath Merker mitgetheilt.

(Aus den Merkerschen „Beiträgen zur Erleichterung des Gelingens der praktischen Polizei" mit dessen Zustimmung entnommen.)

Berlin, 1834.

Im Verlage der L. W. Krause'schen Buchhandlung.

166. Title page 'Important Revelations about the Kaspar Hauser Story …' by Karl Merker.

that direction. He wanted or had to confer with Meyer and Hickel before going on to the palace in Stuttgart. But—and this is the striking point—he did not wish to be seen in Ansbach, like many others already before and after him. 'I did not like to go through Ansbach.' [i.e. he *chose not to go* there—*Ed.*] He therefore proposed a somewhat distant meeting place. As planned, the three men met on the 8th March: 'I met Hickel and Meyer at one stage [i.e. one post station—*Ed.*] from it [Ansbach] & at a place which was on my road in going from Nuremberg to Stuttgart.' Gunzenhausen post station was 28 km. from Ansbach. The theme of their conference was doubtless Kaspar Hauser and his murder. But why did the meeting have to take place under such conspiratorial circumstances? Why did the three, and especially Stanhope, not wish to be seen in Ansbach? Certainly, it was first of all important to familiarise the two Ansbach men with the view of the Court in Munich, to which neither the teacher Meyer nor Hickel as a Bavarian officer could be indifferent. Then they came to speak of a project which was to become a very significant development for Kaspar Hauser researchers.

First, it is remarkable to see Hickel as a member of this triumvirate at all. Until then, his distance from Stanhope and certainly from Meyer—'my enemy'—was taken as read. Hickel therefore appeared to be half-objective, even as pro-Hauser, which was still the case at least until shortly after the murder, as Hickel's statement to the hearing in Munich on 4.1.1834 made clear: 'I have made the Hauser case a matter of honour; I shall energetically take up and pursue every lead, I shall look into and accurately check rumours and perceptions for and against in order to obtain a satisfactory result and bring light into the darkness.'[379]

Meanwhile, in connection with Stanhope's new efforts with the witnesses, a change in Hickel's stance to the opposite position seems to have occurred, which has not been noticed until now. In Gunzenhausen, the three men spoke of a book project, the authors of which were to be Hickel and Meyer themselves. On the 18th April 1834 Stanhope reports to his son about the work 'which Meyer & Hickel are now writing',[380] and again on the 2nd May, when the plan took on a definite form, which necessitated an interesting conclusion.

Stanhope sent his son his own, freely invented 'letters', which he had directed to Meyer, Hickel, and Merker, and added: 'The three little Tracts [Figs. 167, 168, 169] which I send herewith are Extracts of a Letter to Meyer & to Hickel, & Kaspar Hauser's own narrative of his captivity

& of his Journey to Nuremberg, & they may hereafter be annexed to works Meyer & Hickel are now writing.'[381] During the lifetimes of Stanhope, Meyer and Hickel, nothing of the kind actually appeared, but in 1872 in parts and in 1881 in full, Dr. Julius Meyer, the son of the teacher Meyer published a manuscript alleged to have been left by Joseph Hickel, which raised a storm among those familiar with the Kaspar Hauser case that has continued unabated until the present.[382] By comparing the statements of the historical Hickel with those of the 'Pseudo-Hickel' that had now been introduced into Kaspar Hauser research, Gottlieb von Tucher, Daumer and later, above all Hermann Pies revealed the slanderous character of the alleged letters, which on key points deviated so far from the truth that in general, they could only be described as a conscious falsification. There was a common consensus that probably only Dr. Julius Meyer deserved censure, but not the upright officer Hickel, whom Feuerbach had regarded highly.

In his *Falsifications, False Reports and Biased Accounts* (1973), with regard to the then current state of Kaspar Hauser research on the question of whether Hickel could be the author of the 51 'Letters', and after a prior report on Hickel's documented activities, Hermann Pies wrote:

> From this overview of the conduct and statements of the historical Hickel, one fact emerges with complete clarity: in the whole course of his service in the Hauser case, he was never of the view that the foundling was a fraud. We have got to know him as a keen and conscientious policeman who followed every trail until it disappeared into the sand, without ever allowing the thought that Hauser was a fraud to lame his zeal. Neither did he entertain any such suspicion later, the grounds for which he would certainly have had to report to the authorities.

But Hickel was not the man he was long thought to be. It was at the meeting in Gunzenhausen that the plan was conceived to fabricate letters like those of Stanhope, which would draw their effect, so devastating for the truth, from the fact that the irreproachable Hickel was himself their author! That was indeed a masterly move!

In his conjectures expressed in the *Augsburger Allgemeinen Zeitung* newspaper Gottlieb von Tucher logically asserts: 'All this raises in me the suspicion that these letters were written only after Hauser's death. Hauser was dead and no-one could counter a fiction made up of doubts about the truth of the whole case, but someone could indeed make use of one.' This someone was Stanhope! All the claims against Hauser which he held to be crucial reappeared in Hickel's letters.

According to Stanhope's written consultations in Wiesbaden, Hauser came along 'without trouble or strain' and answered everyone's questions. This went far beyond the recorded statements of witnesses in 1828, who, incidentally, did not include Hickel. Therefore, Hickel already 'knew' on the 7th July 1828 'that the main arguments of [Hauser's] opponents, the number of whom was not insignificant' were founded on exactly these two points: '*walking* and *speaking*'.[383]

Those were just the arguments that Stanhope now needed! Hauser must have staged the first attempt on his own life in just this sense whereby 'his vanity had won a victory over his meaningless pain'.[384] Then Stanhope put his own thoughts in Hickel's mouth. Despite some feeling for the unfortunate, after a few days of [Hauser's] affectation, the aristocrat felt 'distaste'. Nevertheless, 'he was happy to be the provider of assistance on other occasions'.

Then the reader makes the acquaintance of one of the finest men of his time:

> Count Stanhope, Peer of Great Britain, of one of the most noble and oldest English families, from which two other noble families have sprung, the Chesterfields and the Harringtons, is the father of two children, a promising young son, Lord Mahon, and a kind and loving, cultured daughter. The well-known Hester Stanhope in Syria is his stepsister, the powerful Minister Pitt his uncle. He is a tall slim man, 50 years old, of noble bearing and markedly English features. He appears to be good-natured, full of piety and religious, open-minded and a lover of truth. Noble by birth and by service he shows magnanimity in his deeds and in so doing, an attractive modesty.[385]

A few letters later, by contrast, Hickel comes to speak of Hauser's character and shows his new understanding:

'Hauser has the tendency to tell lies and understands the art of impressing his lies with the stamp of truth.'[386] Hickel goes on in this vein for many pages, and the unsuspecting foster father's credulity is naturally ever more shocked. The boldest piece of this Stanhope-Hickel art of deception is a fabricated appearance by Feuerbach himself 'whose eyes are opened to Hauser'. The author (Hickel) has the President say to him:

> You should have seen how the boy really knew how to intrigue. He first came from a distance, moved closer, looked me straight in the eye, only

> little by little showing his intention and finally stepped up with such bold and malicious gestures that I could believe I was looking at a real devil's soul. He stood opposite me as an ingrate, a liar and a slanderer in the highest degree. No—that is not Kaspar Hauser—that is a serpent who wants to crush me—no. With such mischievousness, cunning and finesse he has coiled himself around me so that I am gasping for air and I cannot convey what I have seen or heard. I am in no state to do so. Is that Hauser? No—people will say that old Feuerbach wrote a novel.[387]

The last sentence is an especially perfidious invention which is often cited, without mention of its origin or connections when the attempt is made to suggest that Feuerbach himself had doubts. We are familiar with this last sentence already from Stanhope's letter of the 12th April 1834 and now we find it again with Hickel, word for word. After this point was dealt with, in the 31st letter Philip Henry had his zealous author discuss the question of Hauser's origins.

> You will already have seen in public newspapers that Hauser was suspected of being the Prince of Baden. Here too every trail was followed from the best sources; they were only the slack threads of conjecture based on a ghost that appeared to a sentry in Karlsruhe and a mystical sentence in Feuerbach's book about Kaspar Hauser—they all dissolved like spiders' webs...You see that little glow-worm that has lit up these pages with its light soon disappears again as a result of the probing revelations of the investigation that I have pursued to its bitter end and that terminates in nothingness. It truly has to be taken as utter nonsense that a secretly abducted Prince of Baden would see the light of day in Bavaria after being kept hidden for so long.[388]

Finally, after this prescription, the death sentence had to be pronounced once again. The 48th letter is the longest and cites 19 'proofs' of suicide, agreeing on all points with Stanhope's assertions. 'I am of the view,' Hickel writes to his friendly correspondent, 'that Hauser inflicted the fatal blow with his own hand and I justify my view through a recitation of the grounds that speak against an unknown murderer and for suspicion of an involuntary suicide.'[389]

The claims of Daumer, Tucher and Hermann Pies remain valid as far as they relate to the consciously misleading and fabricated content of Hickel's falsification, but a prize key witness for Hauser's innocence who was hitherto thought to be of solid character must now be reckoned among his secret opponents. How Stanhope created this remains a riddle. There may have been good reasons why the 51 fake Hickel letters, which partly stood in stark contradiction to his official statements and conclusions, no longer appeared during the lifetimes of their author or of his helper, Meyer. Hickel was an officially appointed investigator, and a publication of his letters during his lifetime would have meant that only one of the two versions of the case could be correct—the official record that had been established under his responsibility, or his 'Letters'. Hickel had recognised this problem early on and drawn his own conclusions. If he wanted to avoid an official investigation, the 'Letters' would have to appear only after his death (1862). In which case, Dr. Julius Meyer would, except on a few points, be freed from the accusation that he was responsible for the whole fabrication, and his explanation of its genesis, namely, that he had received Hickel's manuscript from Canon Pflaum in Bamberg, would seem somewhat credible. The suspicion that he [Meyer] had himself fabricated the concoction was nevertheless natural. Hermann Pies thought quite rightly: 'This falsification could only have been put together by someone who had access to official documents. This information from the documents was, however, not communicated to Dr. Julius Meyer until the year 1870.' Since it is established that Stanhope was the original author, it is understandable that knowledge and information from official documents gained from Feuerbach and above all from Stanhope's own wishes should find their way into the collected 'Letters'. Another piece of expert knowledge was provided by Hickel himself, and we know from one of Stanhope's letters where to look for this giveaway morsel. 'Dear friend,' writes Stanhope to Hauser's delegated guardian, 'Could you, when you have an opportunity, obtain copies of the testimonies of the shoemaker Weichmann and of the captain's servant and send them to me via Director Busch at Nuremberg...'[390] Busch complied with Stanhope's wishes, which means that official documents in Nuremberg were accessible to Hickel and Stanhope. The rest, no doubt, was padded out by Julius Meyer from the incomplete writings of his father and of Hickel.

The fact, unknown until now, that Stanhope was from the beginning the inspirer of the whole affair considerably worsens the already confirmed worthlessness of the letters and reveals the author Hickel to be a forger as devoid of conscience as Stanhope and Julius Meyer. Hickel's relationship with Stanhope's family developed thereafter to such an intimate extent that he even composed a poem for the wedding of Stanhope's son. As already mentioned, Hickel spent a while in Wiesbaden in June 1834 working on the letters inspired by Stanhope. From there, Stanhope wrote to his son: 'Hickel, who is now here, intends to write some Verses in German on your Marriage!'[391]

After breaking his journey in Gunzenhausen, Stanhope went on to Stuttgart, where he arrived on the 12th March. His chances were better here than in Munich: he was happy to hear that the King of Württemberg who 'was very gracious towards me' and 'with whom I dined twice recently'[392]—had noted that Stanhope's health had much improved since his last visit. The king 'perceived I only drank water, but that the regime agreed with me perfectly, & that I appeared in much better health than when he had seen me several years before, that is, in the autumn of 1827.'[393] This close relationship to King Wilhelm I (1781–1869) had been going on for exactly seven years, since 1827.

Philip Henry gave his son the task of having a book bound in the national colours of Württemberg as a thank you present for his warm reception. After eleven days, on the 25th March, his tour went on via the south German palaces; it is not known whether Karlsruhe or Mannheim was next on the list. We do know, however, that he did plan to visit Stéphanie. In his letter of the 18th February 1834 Philip Henry had written that his correspondence could safely be sent to Karlsruhe, because before or afterwards he would be going ... 'to Mannheim to visit the Grand Duchess'.[394] It is instructive and characteristic that Stéphanie, who was then in Mannheim for the confirmation of her youngest daughter Marie, did not receive Stanhope. For the Dowager Grand Duchess, who, as her youngest daughter in particular emphatically affirmed her whole life long, had never believed that her first-born son had died in his cradle, it was out of the question to receive a man who had been so close to the death of Kaspar Hauser, the youth whom she regarded as her son.

But the situation was quite different in Karlsruhe. The plans of June 1833 had first envisaged bringing Hauser to the Karlsruhe Court to be a stable boy. They failed due to the intervention of Klüber senior, and far worse ideas were then set in motion. It was quite understandable that the conclusion of the difficult and sensational operation [the murder] would result in a happy reunion for Stanhope—at least with Sophie von Baden. With the troublesome Napoleonid finally silenced, the continuity of the Hochberg line was now assured once and for all. Stanhope was very impressed by the gratitude and respect of his hostess; he lacked for nothing and could have settled down in Baden for the rest of his days. His accommodation alone drew from him the following effusive comment: 'I have a most agreable [*sic*] & comfortable room in the ground floor of the Badischer Hof [Baden Palace], which I find to be an excellent H & which in its situation is very far superior to the others.'[395]

Then he hoped for an invitation to the Court, which kept him waiting a while. Probably Grand Duchess Sophie first had to secure an audience for herself, since her husband found it difficult to speak to her about the solution of the Kaspar Hauser Question, but finally, after some hesitation, he relented and put on a good face with regard to the whole bad business. After the murder, Sophie had revealed to her husband that she had been involved, which shocked Leopold profoundly. Otto Flake has described the situation based on his study of official documents: 'The confession must have been a frightful blow for the Grand Duke. It is out of the question that he planned Kaspar's removal together with his wife. He would never have had the determination necessary for a carefully prepared crime, nor the unscrupulousness that lay in Sophie's character.'

The so-called Court diary helps us determine with some accuracy the date on which she must have told her husband: the 18th December. On the 17th, the diary states: Prince Friedrich of Prussia breakfasted with the Grand Duke and Duchess, Carriage ride, afternoon tea in the Grand Duchess's chambers. On the 18th, departure of the guest. Then a gap between the 18th and the 21st, when the Grand Duke took supper alone without his wife. Until the 29th January the Grand Duchess is only mentioned twice—on the 1st at the New Year's Reception and the 17th January, the great Court Ball.

It is known that she spent Christmas alone in Eppingen instead of with her family. After her confession, which filled him with horror, the Grand Duke undoubtedly demanded that she distance herself and, in order to avoid a sensation, take part only in the two January celebrations. She did not return until the 29th January, when a delegation had to be received [by the grand ducal couple together—*Ed.*].

Sophie, then in her 33rd year, had borne five sons and two daughters in fourteen years of marriage. The relationship had been considered a happy one; from now on, unbeknown to her public, it took an opposite course. When Sophie gave birth to her seventh child, a daughter, in November 1834, there was already talk of a different father. In 1839 she had her last child, another daughter, whose father was openly said to be the banker Haber (see also pp. 320–324). The family relationships at the Karlsruhe Court became fragile; the Grand Duchess made up for it elsewhere, and the Grand Duke took solace in alcohol and gambling. The doctors soon prescribed Marienbad water and already in autumn 1834 the first of many spa cures. To 'recover' from the mineral water, he went to the palace stables and drank with the stable boys. He fell into a deplorable state, tormented by many worries.[396]

Stanhope's meeting with the Grand Duchess took place several months after Hauser's death and a few months before Leopold's first spa visit. Did the Grand Duke act out of a reason of State when he took Sophie back and received Stanhope, who had in the meantime become known as the infamous foster father of Kaspar Hauser? He must have known who was standing there in front of him and wished to avoid a scandal at any cost. It appears to have been so. The warmth of the Grand Duke's welcome was noticeable. Apparently affected by the situation, it was unbalanced and rather exaggerated:

> I was extremely pleased by Carlsruhe, which is the best and most elegant little Town I know... If I were to reside abroad, it would be in the Grand Dutchy [*sic*] of Baden... I dined *en famille* with the Grand Duke, who gave me a most gratifying reception & I have seen other Sovereigns who were affable & gracious, but none who shewed such benignity & kindness of disposition, has personally shown me as much friendliness and benevolence as the Grand Duke… He expressed repeatedly a great wish to see me again when he is at Eberstein.[397]

That was certainly to be seen as a special honour, and there must have been a reason for it. Was Sophie the driving force behind the invitation to Stanhope to the mediaeval castle—and now summer residence—of Scholoss Eberstein, which had been renovated by Friedrich Weinbrenner in 1803. It is hardly credible that Leopold, in a spirit of real generosity and of his own volition, would have invited the very man who was so involved in the Kaspar Hauser affair.* During his stay in Karlsruhe there was still an opportunity for Philip Henry to obtain an extraordinary object for his own use that was worthy to rank along-

*The trip to Scholoss Eberstein in its splendid location high up in the Murg valley went via the little town of Gernsbach that lay in the foothills of the valley. At 1 Amtstrasse in Gernsbach Johann Heinrich David Hennenhofer had first seen the light of day in 1793. Today the rumour still circulates that Hennenhofer hid Hauser for a while in the family home on the way from Beuggen to Pilsach.

side Wieland's golden walking stick. It was a present that Gustav Adolf [the former King of Sweden, Sophie's father] had given to the Duke of Saxe-Coburg-Gotha, a 'very special snuffbox' which Philip Henry used 'continually in the mornings' thereafter.

From Karlsruhe the journey went on to Wiesbaden, where in the meantime Hickel had arrived in order to discuss the letters mentioned earlier which were intended to discredit Hauser and Feuerbach completely. The decisive statements in them with regard to Weickmann's own official statements since 1828 and his revised testimony made this consultation necessary. In Wiesbaden Stanhope met his old 'friend Neumann' again, whom we already know as the bearer of his correspondence from Lake Lucerne to Vienna. Neumann was 'in the worst possible temper, which he vents on "poor me" who am almost his only acquaintance, & this is the more disagreable [*sic*] as we are lodged under the same roof'.[398] This again sounds as if Stanhope were not paying for himself. The instructive brief report on Neumann goes on: 'He pines extremely for England but professes that he would not return there, as he cannot have any communication with Lord Palmerston. I believe, however, that the Grapes are sour, & that the Austrian government will not allow him to return.'[399] This was new information from Metternich who had been informed about the ineffective diplomat.

The years 1816–1828 had been ruled by the search for Hauser. 1829–1832 Stanhope spent binding Hauser to him. From January 1832 began the campaign against Hauser's credibility, and in December 1833 Hauser was murdered. The year 1834 was now, after the visits to the courts at Munich, Stuttgart and Karlsruhe, completely taken up with tireless activity which was aimed at undermining the integrity of the two main figures, Hauser and Feuerbach, both of whom were already dead. For Philip Henry, this campaign of character assassination was of such overriding importance that, despite the pleas of his son [Lord Mahon] to come home at least for his engagement and wedding, he remained unmoved in Germany, which had the grotesque consequence that Mahon himself had to break into the family strong room at Chevening in order to get at the necessary papers for the marriage.

'I shudder when I think of the dangers to which you were exposed in entering by the window my Strong Room, & I hoped that you had too much prudence & good sense to risk your life in such an undertaking...'[400] The family celebration therefore went ahead without the father. He was too busy dealing with the Kaspar Hauser issue. His own writings, the consultation with Hickel—all this needed time. The plan was clear. His own writing would so misrepresent the case of his foster son that the factual background would not even be discussed. The circumspection with which the plan was realised is remarkable, and its partial success considerable.

*

On the 3rd February Hofmann wrote a long letter to Klüber, rich in content, which indirectly aired two main points and involuntarily lifted the veil on the secret conversations and the rules of the collaboration. Hofmann could not help noticing that after his arrival in Munich, without the slightest consultation with or enquiries to the main figures in Ansbach, Stanhope was immediately ready with his judgement on the course of events and the motive of the crime and had declared Kaspar Hauser to be a fraud and labelled him a suicide who was seeking attention with the aim of putting pressure on Stanhope to take Hauser, who needed protection, to the safety of England as soon as possible. One can understand Hofmann being astonished to find on almost the same day that Meyer entertained the very same view of the affair:

> To see how far his [Stanhope's] prejudice reached, I have the honour of sharing confidential copies of his latest letters to Lieutenant Hickel. His real mental confusion can be seen uniquely in his unkind and unjustified judgement of Feuerbach. Herr v. Braumühl, who is mentioned in the letter of the 25th instant is an examiner in the Hauser case at the Ministry of the Interior. In official documents he and the Minister find no satisfactory grounds which uphold Stanhope's opinion. The cause of the long silence which he has maintained towards Your E[xcellency] may lie in the sick condition of his mind, for in a letter to Hickel written in November in Vienna, he says that he will send [Hickel's] report to you and will leave the subsequent decision completely to you, his honoured friend, in whom he places his full confidence. Strangely enough, the schoolteacher Meyer had fallen to a vice similar to that of Stanhope. He explained to me immediately after the deed most determinedly that Hauser was a fraud, had probably inflicted the wound—which he maintained was very slight, because there was little blood—on himself in order to make Count Stanhope believe that he [Hauser] was no longer safe in Germany and thereby to get him to take him to England.[401]

This tone in Hofmann's first assessment could not have been so much in accord with that of Klüber by chance. The course of the increasingly acrimonious dispute between Hofmann and Meyer gave rise to further statements which both characterise the last period of Hauser's life and above all, touch on Meyer's not insignificant role as an accomplice of Stanhope.

Naturally, Meyer's first line of attack was to bring up Hauser's alleged untruthfulness in order to create a framework for the tragedy. On this point, Hofmann refers to a remark of Hauser's which links to a revealing description of the behaviour of his teacher:

> I know that the Count thinks me a fraud; it pained me greatly, I had to cry every night over it. But since I know from my religion lessons that there is a God who sees into hearts, I am calm and weep no more, for He knows that I am no fraud. Also, I am calmed by the thought that I have a father in heaven, even though my first wish is to know who my earthly father is, whether rich or poor, that would be of no account if only I knew him; I do not think about this as do other people.

Then Hofmann goes on in his report to Klüber:

> My observation that sufficient grounds for the acceptance of such a suspicion were entirely lacking, my warnings not to anticipate the course of the investigation, my earnest request not to do Hauser an injustice and not to make a still dubious opinion, which had so much against it, into one that could not be doubted—all this found no entry with him. Rather, Meyer declared himself filled with indignation: Hauser had abused the compassion of the century; what had happened was only an encore to the earlier murder attempt in Nuremberg; there would be no unquiet night tonight (14th December) as there was then at Professor Daumer's in Nuremberg; he had even told Hauser on the way to see where the incident happened, that he deserved a thrashing. Meyer even went so far as to say that, owing to the absence of Herr Hickel, I should throw him out of the house because he no longer wished to look after him. As these unreasonable views were just as unbalanced as the others; I let Meyer know in no uncertain terms of my disinclination so to do and ordered him without further ado to report the incident to the police and the court. This indeed he did, leaving out only the unreasonable opinions he had expressed to me, which—on account of the small amount of bleeding and because the medical examination could not be too intrusive owing to the displacement of the wound, as the autopsy showed, and because Hauser was still able to walk home neither shedding blood nor showing apprehension—put him [Hauser] under suspicion, as is clear from the

> original direction of the investigation, the failure to observe the rules for the possible uncovering of the trail of the facts of the case and for the apprehension of the murderer or for the discovery of evidence leading thereto. Meyer promised to justify himself to me the following day, the 15th December. He came in the morning at 9 o'clock and informed me that according to the doctor attending to the case, Dr. Horlacher, Hauser's condition was perfectly natural and that he was in no danger. His [Meyer's] justification of his suspicion expressed the day before consisted of mere trivialities which happened from time to time with Hauser in lessons, in a few bits of insubstantial information about Hauser, which he had acquired from Nuremberg, and in a few of Hauser's utterances (and Old Bavarian dialect he had picked up), which led Meyer to conclude that Hauser's way of thinking was common and his origins of low rank (Hauser occasionally used a word still used in Old Bavaria or spoke it with the accent of those parts). I found this justification so little convincing that I expressly asked him not to repeat what he had said to me anywhere and to await the result of the investigation, whereby I also gave him notice that Dr. Albert, who I had spoken to about the wounding the night before, had explained that Hauser was not out of danger and was in no state to be conveyed to other accommodation.
>
> On the 18th December, therefore after Hauser's death, Meyer saw me again and brought me Hauser's work and notebooks so as to convince me from such materials of Hauser's carelessness in recent times. I found just the opposite in them and expressed my astonishment at his interpretation, as I saw everywhere in them clear signs of progress. Meyer told me about his end and how he said farewell to him and his wife, which had moved him so much that he wept. Despite this, he stuck to his previous opinion, and as I therefore strongly rebuked him, he remarked in taking his leave that within six months he would be justified before the world. Since then, he has not once crossed my threshold.[402]

What was Meyer thinking at the end of December 1833 when he said that 'within six months he would be justified before the world'? How was Meyer sure so soon that his and therefore Stanhope's innocence would be confirmed on schedule? We see here, suddenly, one of the delicate unintentional fractures in the construction of the conspirators. For a moment, Meyer could no longer sustain the fateful burden and he betrayed one of Stanhope's plans that was yet to be executed. The plan consisted, as explained earlier, of the publication of fake letters later combined with those of Hickel, which would make the 'truth', as Stanhope saw it, crystal clear, represent Hauser and Feuerbach as fraudsters and, as Stanhope had sought to do with respect to his former friend since the beginning of 1834, show Feuerbach's books *Some important documents relating to the unfortunate foundling Kaspar Hauser* and *Example of a crime against the human soul* to be but the works of a writer of fiction.

The King of Bavaria was intended to be the first to learn the 'truth' about the dead Court President. On the 12th April Stanhope wrote to Ludwig:

> Although the end of Kaspar Hauser's life is now a matter for legal investigation, Your Majesty will doubtless have considered that all the circumstances relating to the beginning of his story also require a most careful and critical investigation. Your Majesty will be of the opinion that this is all the more necessary, since the story, as it was reported by Kaspar Hauser himself is hardly credible, and President von Feuerbach of blessed memory wrote as an advocate and not as a judge, and kept back some of the most important facts in his book, in that he showed a great poetic gift with statements that are without any foundation and even contradict witness statements. I have learned that towards the end of his life he expressed doubt in the story and said 'perhaps Feuerbach has written a novel in his old age'. The information which I have recently received from one of the persons who saw Kaspar Hauser immediately after his appearance proves that Feuerbach's portrayal does not correspond with the truth and that the facts call for a more conscious and more grounded investigation than has been made heretofore in order to permit a correct assessment of a story in which great distortions have been prevalent. A very capable, experienced and loyal servant of Your Majesty, the Munich Director of Police, von Menz, can have the honour, if Your Majesty will grant him the opportunity of presenting the view which he has of the matter and the measures which in his opinion could be successfully employed to discover Kaspar Hauser's origins; as I recently heard from one of the persons who first saw him, he crossed the border every day to go to school. If that was the case, then the place where he lived could be discovered towards the southern border of Your Majesty's realm. Your Majesty will, I am confident, with gracious consideration, reflect on the feelings I have modestly expressed in this letter and attribute them to my inmost wish that Your Majesty will also be pleased to throw light on a matter which has long been kept in the dark, and will uncover the truth of a story which has aroused so much attention and unquiet.[403]

In his books Hermann Pies has refuted all the charges levelled against Feuerbach and has revealed them to be nothing but fabrications designed to attack the credibility of Hauser and Feuerbach, which at that point, could have been their only purpose. What Stanhope calls manipulation of the documents has been shown to be documented proof. And then comes the great unknown, which Stanhope affirms in full credulity, namely, that Feuerbach himself towards the end of his life described his own work as fiction. The origin of this formulation is known. It comes from Hickel's 28th letter, which, contrary to Feuerbach's work, must definitely be called fiction. Most revealing is the fact that Stanhope was already using this formula in 1834, which proves that this was a special result of the Wiesbaden 'text conference'. Why does Stanhope not name this important witness? Hermann Pies's thorough research leads him to conclude that the faker was not Feuerbach—but Stanhope!

In April 1834 Stanhope had his own false letters printed, two of them in Karlsruhe by Wilhelm Hasper and the third in Heidelberg by Georg Reichard. It is not known whether the texts were also composed there, but it is very likely because the author spent 68 days in Karlsruhe (26th March—2nd May and 7th July—7th August). That he took care in writing before the appearance of the pamphlet to ensure that the money man of 1831, the banker Haber, should immediately receive a copy suggests that this operation too may have been funded by the House of Haber. And so, Meyer's prophecy was fulfilled on schedule. After six months there it was—in the form of a small separate publication (Fig. 167). Hauser's former teacher could not have wished for anything better:

> 'Extract of a letter from Count Stanhope
> to the schoolmaster Herr Meyer in Ansbach about the death of Kaspar Hauser'

After an introduction that showed Meyer in a very favourable light came 30 arguments against Hauser. 'I was,' wrote the author of this invented letter to his son, 'naturally eager to gather any information about the circumstances of his death...' Conclusion: a fraud and a suicide. At the end of the 'testimony of innocence' for Meyer is written:

> Kaspar Hauser, who about eight days earlier was given a serious dressing down by you 'on account of his great tendency to mendaciousness and had his attention drawn to the consequences of this tendency',

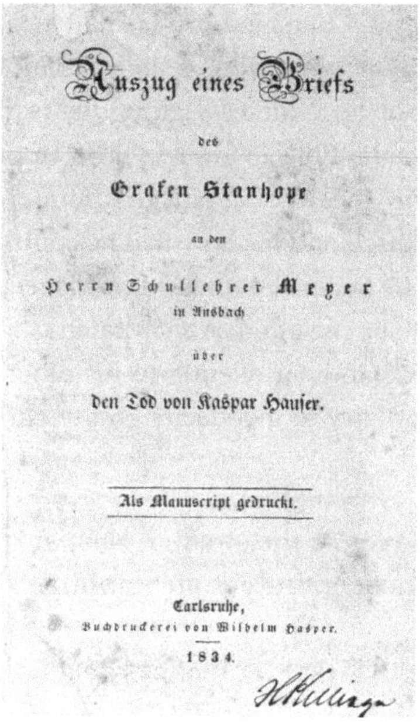
Auszug eines Briefs

des

Grafen Stanhope

an den

Herrn Schullehrer Meyer

in Ansbach

über

den Tod von Kaspar Hauser.

Als Manuscript gedruckt.

Carlsruhe,

Buchdruckerei von Wilhelm Hasper.

1834.

167. Title page 'Extract of a Letter from Count [sic] *Stanhope to the schoolmaster Herr Meyer'.*

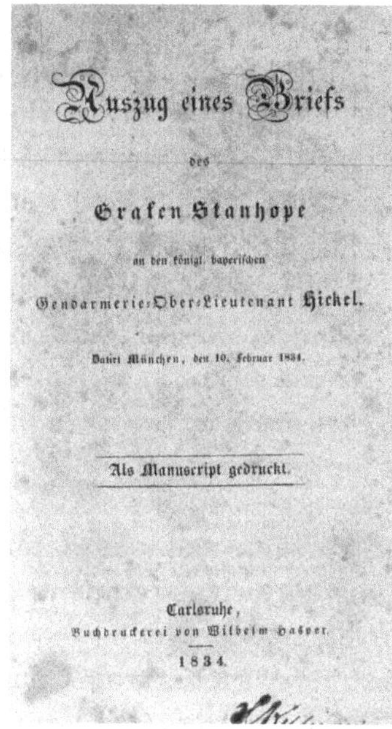
Auszug eines Briefs

des

Grafen Stanhope

an den königl. bayerischen

Gendarmerie-Ober-Lieutenant Hickel.

Datirt München, den 10. Februar 1834.

Als Manuscript gedruckt.

Carlsruhe,

Buchdruckerei von Wilhelm Hasper.

1834.

168. Title page 'Extract of a Letter from Count [sic] *Stanhope to the Royal Bavarian Gendarmerie First Lieutenant Hickel'.*

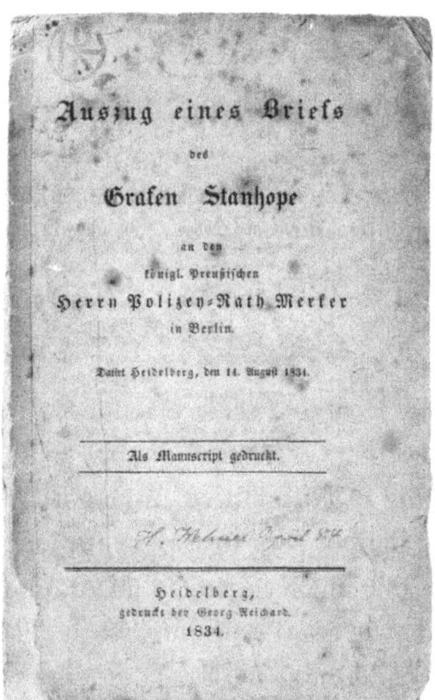
Auszug eines Briefs

des

Grafen Stanhope

an den

königl. Preußischen

Herrn Polizey-Rath Merker

in Berlin.

Datirt Heidelberg, den 14. August 1834.

Als Manuscript gedruckt.

Heidelberg,

gedruckt bei Georg Reichard.

1834.

169. Title page 'Extract of a Letter from Count [sic] *Stanhope to Police Commissioner Merker'.*

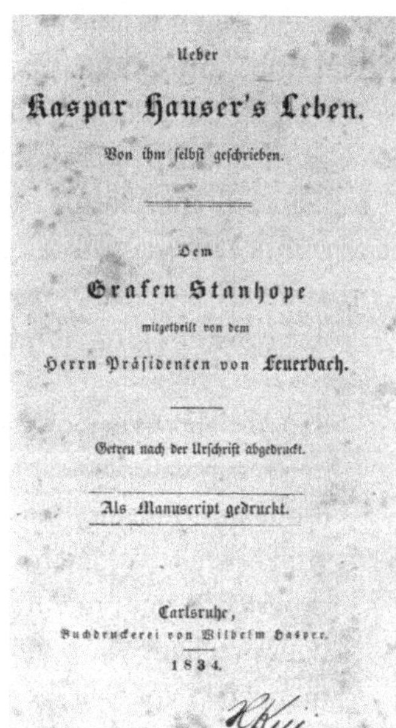
Ueber

Kaspar Hauser's Leben.

Von ihm selbst geschrieben.

Dem

Grafen Stanhope

mitgetheilt von dem

Herrn Präsidenten von Feuerbach.

Getreu nach der Urschrift abgedruckt.

Als Manuscript gedruckt.

Carlsruhe,

Buchdruckerei von Wilhelm Hasper.

1834.

170. Title page 'On the Life of Kaspar Hauser. Written by himself'.

> knew that very many people did not consider him credible. He had also learned from President von Feuerbach that I had doubts about many episodes in his account. He could expect an accurate well-grounded test of all his statements and had perhaps the intentions to impress the stamp of truth and significance onto his story by means of an alleged murder attempt, to arouse further support for himself and to show that he could not live safely in Ansbach but needed to be taken elsewhere. The alleged murder of Kaspar Hauser is in no sense to be regarded as an isolated fact or one related by a credible person, but stands in relation to his other statements and with his well-known tendency to mendacity and to stir up sensations.

With the same methods Stanhope then moves to the story of Kaspar's origins, adducing arguments that stem almost entirely from Stanhope's own fantasy (Fig. 168).

Extract of a letter from Count Stanhope to First Lieutenant Hickel of the Royal Bavarian Gendarmerie:

'Conclusion: If he had lived, I would, with the approval of the Royal Bavarian Government, have had him examined by one of the leading legal scholars in Germany and if this had produced no result, I would nevertheless have proved to him that it appeared quite impossible ever to establish what his family relations were.'

The third anti-Hauser pamphlet (Fig. 169):

'Extract of a letter from Count Stanhope to Police Comissioner Merker of the Royal Prussian Constabulary in Berlin'

repeats all the claims, adds new ones and strikes not least at the now publicly perceptible connection to Kaspar Hauser's earliest, and it must be added, his one serious opponent:

'You know,' begins Stanhope's pamphlet,

> that the discovery of frauds used to be seen as a service rendered to one's contemporaries, but that now those who express doubts about the wondrous fairy tale of the 'Foundling of Nuremberg' are regarded with hostility. You, who were the first man of honour to apply your long experience, your manifold knowledge, your much-respected talents and your excellent sharp mind to an examination of this tale and greatly distinguished yourself therein, have been made into a figure of notoriety.

Stanhope then willingly lines himself up as a comrade in the ranks of anti-Hauser opponents and piles charge upon charge: 'Lies and pretence became second nature to him [Kaspar Hauser]...It has been proven that Kaspar Hauser cheated even those around him and his best friends.' And so it goes on for more than 40 pages, which include a characterisation for posterity of Feuerbach as a falsifier of documents and 'a writer of fiction'.

These three invented letters and a further printed manuscript 'On the Life of Kaspar Hauser. Written by Himself' (Fig. 170) appeared together the following year [1835] from the academic booksellers J.E.B. Mohr in Heidelberg under the title: *Materials On the Story of Kaspar Hauser, Collected and Published by Count Stanhope* (Fig. 171) and in London by James Hodson (1836): *Tracts relating to Caspar Hauser* (Fig. 172).

It may suffice briefly to discuss these ramified activities. Hermann Pies has refuted Stanhope's calumnies in detail. Stanhope and Merker as collaborators—no-one would have thought it possible who had read the police commissioner's book in 1830 and knew of Stanhope's position as foster father since December 1831. First, Stanhope personally sent his writings everywhere, even involving Daumer, who with great audacity, he dragged in as a witness against Kaspar Hauser. This risky

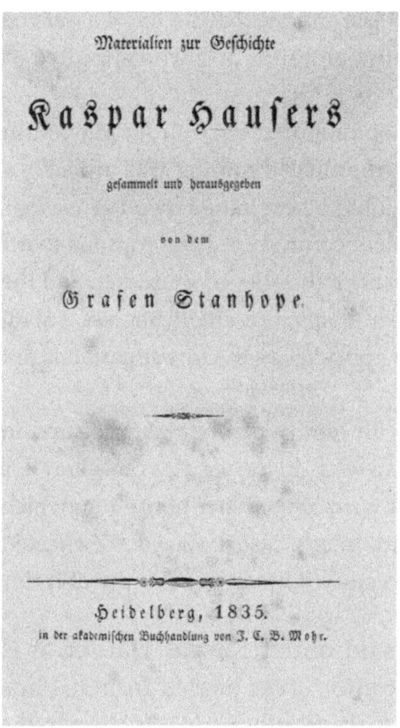

171. Title page of Stanhope's 'Materials On the Story of Kaspar Hauser'.

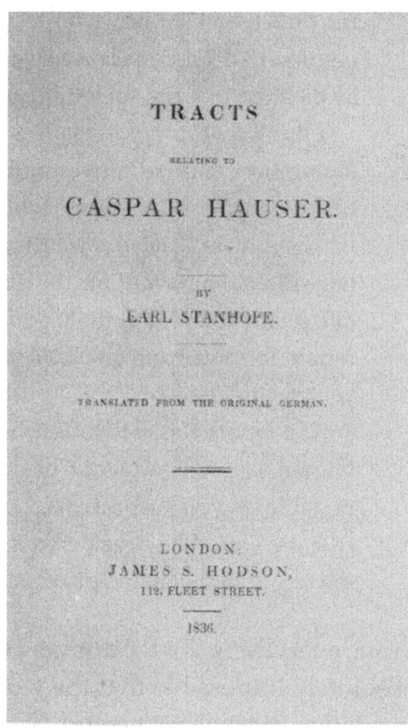

172. Title page of the English edition of 'Materials On the Story of Kaspar Hauser'.

decision, whereby Stanhope put about exactly the opposite of what Daumer actually thought and said, reached a certain peak in a letter of the 12th April 1834 to the jurist and to the novelist Schmidt-von Lübeck, who had written about Kaspar Hauser.

> I have the honour of sending to Your Excellency herewith three small tracts [Figs. 167, 168, 169] which have been 'published as manuscripts' and will later appear as books which are now being written [he means those by Meyer and Hickel]. I hope you will find them interesting, as you yourself have written about the story of Kaspar Hauser, which has been falsified in an unforgiveable manner. The notes which I made from conversations with several witnesses in the past month will, as I expect, soon be communicated to the world and will refute the observations of Feuerbach, which in no sense correspond to the official documents. I have read the two essays which you had published in the literary journals and also your earlier writings more than once, but unfortunately! I have not yet been able to obtain a copy of the first one, and it would be most desirable to procure two copies of it, one for myself and the other for Professor Daumer, who told me last month that he too was of the opinion that Kaspar Hauser was a kind of traitor, and who appeared to be inclined to write something about it.
>
> I think that in it you express the opinion that the murder attempt in Nuremberg was not proven and that the alleged murder was probably a case of 'auto-assassination', which would be explained by other reasons than madness. I have recently publicly contradicted the rumour that I have offered a reward for the discovery of the alleged murderer, and the tale seems to me to contain some very suspicious circumstances. I shall refrain for now from citing the main episodes, as the investigation is not yet concluded.
>
> The letters Kaspar Hauser had with him [when he first appeared in Nuremberg—*Ed.*] say that 'he can also write in the way I write', and it is possible, as you suspect, that he had written the letter himself. In which case, he would be considered a fraud. In any case, however, he cheated the world in the main episodes of his story if not in the entirety of it.[404]

From everything that Daumer ever said about Kaspar Hauser, it is absolutely impossible that the word 'traitor' ever passed from his lips in relation to his former pupil. Grotesquely, Stanhope is referring in his letters to Schmidt-von Lübeck to just that visit that Daumer recalled so well in which the painful notion that he had betrayed Hauser led to

Stanhope's panic-stricken behaviour and his breaking off the conversation by fleeing from the house.

In these days Stanhope's son reported from Chevening on the impression his father's writings had made on the great Sir Robert Peel. 'I think,' Peel is supposed to have said, 'that if Hauser is a fraud then the fraud would be a more extraordinary event than the truth could be.' This surprisingly positive viewpoint was possibly communicated by Mahon out of a very correct insight that there were indeed not a few contemporaries who had great difficulty in seeing Kaspar Hauser as a fraud. Yet Stanhope had already reached the point at which his influence had enabled the 'fraud theory' to take hold. For him, it was now only a case of whether or not Hauser was a fraud, which meant that the actual drama of Hauser's destiny, and especially the dynastic aspect, was removed to another plane, pushed away from all the other facts. In general, by the time he died (1855), Stanhope had succeeded in winning parts of the public over to his illusory picture.

The former foster father had continued his campaign against Kaspar Hauser with all the means at his disposal, including that of friendly protection. Through Baron von Fahnenberg, he sought out and was able to contact the most highly regarded and, after Feuerbach, 'the most internationally renowned legal scholar of his time',[405] Professor

173. Karl Joseph Anton Mittermaier (1787–1863)

Karl Joseph Anton Mittermaier (1787–1863) (Fig.173) in Heidelberg, who was even prepared 'to publish a larger work in German'.

To be able to bring the authority Mittermaier, who was 'enormously well-read, world-famous for his knowledge of foreign law...' (Treitschke), into the lists against Feuerbach would have been a great triumph for Stanhope. But the famous man was still at the beginning of his research into the affair, as he mentioned to Fahnenberg on the 13th May: 'Unfortunately, the riddle has yet to be solved for the earthly eye. I shall go on collecting materials, and as I only want the truth, I shall bring together all the grounds for and against in a non-partisan manner.'[406]

Whether Fahnenberg was filled with the same love for the truth when he asked Mayor Binder for specimens of Kaspar Hauser's handwriting and pictures of him must be open to doubt. Oettingen-Wallerstein was rightly suspicious of Fahnenberg's motives in his (previously mentioned) letter of the 23rd January 1834 to Stichaner, noting: 'The letter of Postmaster Baron von Fahnenberg to Mayor Binder asking for two portraits and original writings in Kaspar Hauser's hand —he is known to be a Karlsruhe man closely connected to the opposition in Baden and his desire for such materials itself would be noteworthy if it proceeded from oppositional tendencies in Baden.'

First—that was the plan—Mittermaier was to publish internationally and make the first results of his Kaspar Hauser research available in the form of magazine articles. But then, some sobering news of great political interest reached him from Paris, which stopped his enthusiasm in its tracks:

> Only a short essay is wanted and in another journal, whose editor my friend contacted, it was made clear that an essay which had the aim of portraying Kaspar Hauser as a fraud, must be regarded as having been paid for by the government of Baden and therefore was not to be accepted or could only be accepted on condition that a notice to that effect be added. Under such circumstances, I do not know what I should do, as I do not care to subject a piece of work to the Paris censor.[407]

This reason for declining is remarkable. If the legal scholar was intending to support the fraud theory, this must be regarded as on commission from the government of Baden. That would certainly not have been written very easily. To be able to adopt such a clear position a few months after the murder certainly required accurate background information. In the meantime, however, Mittermaier had had second thoughts, which he shared with Fahnenberg. First, however, came the astonished question: 'I would like to know who the persons whose testimonies Lord Stanhope recently published appeared before in March 1834, why that happened and whether they had not already testified earlier (as it appears).'[408] This was a very proper question for the legal scholar, who was beginning to sense that this whole scenario had a hidden meaning. He goes on:

> In the interim I have read through again all the writings and articles which have appeared about Hauser and have collected materials in order to publish a larger work in German. I have spoken to several doctors about the wound from which Hauser died, and I confess to you that through all this the conditions for doubt have become still greater. I want to draw your attention to the following:
>
> 1. All the doctors who I spoke to are of the opinion that the wound can only be the consequence of a single powerful blow from the hand of another person.
> 2. The murder attempt perpetrated on Kaspar Hauser in Nuremberg has been so well confirmed that it can no longer be doubted. Only the circumstances relating to the discovery of a specific assailant and which are usually related, are incorrect.
> 3. It is therefore to be concluded that there must have been persons who had a great interest in getting rid of Hauser.
> 4. Information about Hauser's behaviour after the wounding indicates that he did not show signs of a guilty conscience.
> 5. From Daumer's writings, we learn (Vol. 1, p.6) that Hauser possessed exceptional eyesight and could recognise things in the dark that others could not distinguish; this appears to indicate that Hauser really lived for a long time in darkness and thus his eyes gained a special power of sight.
> 6. From the above-mentioned writings of Daumer (p.41) that Hauser tried hard to write his autobiography and on p.42 the beginning of this autobiography is printed, which Count Stanhope has recently republished. These show that in all these attempts at a description there was in his soul a mixture of actual experiences with later images of fantasy and that it was hard for him to clarify the different aspects of his story.[409]

Nothing came of Mittermaier's proposed book. Having acquainted himself more carefully with the details of the case, he no longer let himself be used as an opponent of Hauser.

It is also possible that, having been called on to adopt a position, the scholar made use of his old connections in Mannheim and Munich[410] in order to learn something of the background of this riddle that was as yet unsolved 'for earthly eyes' and in doing so, came across opinions that coincided more with his own observations than the wishes of Stanhope and Fahnenberg. From Bavaria the news was similar to that from Baden.

Mittermaier wrote to Stanhope on the 25th October 1834: 'In Munich I had opportunity to speak to well-informed persons about the story of Kaspar Hauser...Opinion still tends to the view that Hauser did not kill himself, but was killed by someone else.'[411] Mittermaier received such information from 'well-informed persons' from, amongst others, Queen Karoline who not only, while in Karlsruhe in 1832 had had daily conversations with Stéphanie for a week but had also had a long conversation with Mayor Binder on the 6th July 1832, after which she again spent a few weeks with Stéphanie, this time in Darmstadt. Among the many other journals that now took up the Kaspar Hauser Question strongly once more, it was Cotta's *Morgenblatt für gebildete Stände* ['Morning News for Cultured People'] that particularly upset Stanhope. Over the course of several issues, his argument with the paper swelled to nearly 60 pages, of which here only an extract can be cited. There first appeared in Nos. 101–103 a review of Stanhope's publications. Hermann Pies writes:

> The reviewer who cannot imagine that an English lord lies and cheats in such an underhanded manner, gives Stanhope, for example, the benefit of the doubt, when he asserts without any proof that Feuerbach had not wanted to include Hauser's autobiography in his 1832 book about the foundling 'because it would have given rise to doubts', and further, that Feuerbach had 'often said that whoever read the Nuremberg documents would have to think that Hauser was a fraud, indeed these documents should be burned'. And yet one only has to take a look in Feuerbach's booklet to convince oneself of the meaninglessness of Stanhope's fabrications. On the other hand, it occurs to the reviewer that Stanhope expresses his 'convictions now, when Feuerbach and Hauser are no longer alive.'

Klüber responded in Nos. 132–134. That the reviewer agrees with Stanhope on a few points owing to a lack of more accurate information must have roused the well-informed Klüber to action. His criticism of Stanhope and of the case in general is not to be ignored. On Stanhope's role as foster father he writes: 'But his behaviour he showed not only towards his protégé but even to his foster son under legal contract can in ethical and psychological respects be regarded in all impartiality as memorable.'

Then Klüber gets to grips with Stanhope's claims and concludes that

> in no wise do they bring this tangled matter further forward, rather for many they only appear to have tangled it up even more. The thick veil of riddling and mystical unnaturalness which covers the affair remains unchanged. Ethical teaching and law, however, forbid a human being, especially one deceased, to be declared a fraud without firm evidence. Also, the feeling human heart showed itself to be shocked by an individual, who in his physical and mental state showed unmistakable signs of very long helplessness and cruel separation from human society, and who therefore, with very few exceptions, aroused a general sympathy. Yet whoever seeks to study the case for the first time or takes it up anew is urged to separate the main issue, that which is certain—the afore-mentioned signs etc.—from secondary circumstances, which leave open a wide field for doubts and debates. We would, however, certainly not wish to castigate Count Stanhope merely for changing his opinion.

After Klüber, Mittermaier takes up the cudgels—the man on whose international reputation Stanhope had once set his hopes. His final conclusion unambiguously brings Stanhope right down to earth: 'The circumstances made known thus far will move every unprejudiced jurist to the conviction that the manner in which Hauser departed this world affords no grounds of probability that he himself inflicted the wounds by which he died and that therefore, his death can not serve as any plausible reason for deeming him a fraudster.'

Stanhope had not in the least reckoned on any such positions being declared in the reputable and widely circulated *Morgenblatt*. In fury, he turned to the editors. Heading the paper's literary section for a decade, from 1827–1837, and therefore responsible for dealing with Stanhope's complaints was Gustav Schwab (1792–1850), lyrical poet of the Swabian poets' circle, most well-known as a devoted teller of classical Greek and German myths, songs and poetic ballads in Uhland's circle.

On the 26th May therefore, 'Herr Professor Schwab' received the following letter, which amounts to an unconcealed call for the editors to reveal what was behind an interesting rumour that was spreading throughout the country from mouth to mouth. 'You will be so good as to forgive me,' writes Stanhope,

> for reproaching you in these lines about an article which can be found in the *Morgenblatt* (No.123 and 124). It was earlier announced in this journal that some extracts from the small pamphlets which I had had published 'as manuscripts' were to appear therein, but their place is taken by an article which perhaps calls for a rejoinder. I would be curious to know who the author is, or at least, whether the essay comes from Nuremberg or Frankfurt.

The answer to Stanhope's curious question, at least the location of the author would of course have meant exposing the author. Nuremberg would have meant Tucher or Daumer, while Frankfurt would have pointed to Klüber. Stanhope then went on: 'Despite all my efforts, I have not managed to find a newspaper article about a man in Württemberg who claimed that he had murdered Kaspar Hauser, and I would be very obliged if you would be so good as to inform me in which newspaper and of what date this article could be read?'[412]

Schwab replied promptly on the 5th June and after tersely describing both Kaspar Hauser articles as 'commissioned by the editors', he casually provided a superb example of his narrative skill. Relying completely on material evidence, Schwab reveals in a few words the event that had apparently caused Stanhope some worry. Before describing the scene, Schwab insists that: 'The fact has been described to me as true by a credible person.' His report then follows in his famous narrative style:

> In Württemberg on the Bavarian border a local hunter observed a man in the forest whining to himself that he was guilty of the murder of Kaspar Hauser and who made as if to shoot himself with a pistol. When the hunter sprang forward to prevent this, the man fled and could not be stopped. The hunter reported the incident to the nearest authorities, who passed it on to Stuttgart. The incident occurred five weeks ago.[413]

After receiving this charming letter, Stanhope, according to rumour, was at first most reassured that the murderer had escaped from the hunter and was never seen again, but that then seemed to encourage him to pen a still stiffer letter to Schwab. The threatening undertone in its last sentence hinted at serious consequences if things did not go according to Stanhope's wishes. Once again he sought to discover who the author of the article could be, since he did not believe that the editors had written it:

> ...I fear that I expressed myself unclearly in my previous letter, as you appear to believe that the article in the *Morgenblatt* (No. 123 and 124) is the same as was announced earlier, for which it was desired to make use of the three small tracts, and that it stemmed from the editors themselves. If you read this article, of which I would like to receive another copy, you will find that it is nothing but a very distorted and false representation of my conduct with regard to Kaspar Hauser, whereby I wish for no undue praise but in which I certainly do not deserve censure. I am convinced that there are only two or three people who could write such an article, and I was therefore, as I still am, very curious to know from where the article might have come. An answer, though not indeed in my name, was sent to the editors a few days ago, and should it not be taken up by them, it would appear in another journal...[414]

But Stanhope had long had his own and, as we know, false suspicions: 'It was written, I have no doubt, by his earlier guardian, Baron von Tucher...'.[415] The actual author was Klüber!

Meanwhile, in Baden-Baden, where Stanhope had sent his letter to Schwab—Baron Sternberg had arrived. The sponsor of many strange undertakings, he had been at Uhland's in Tübingen with Stanhope, and later in Stuttgart, where Stanhope went for the large sum of money he needed for the coming arrangements relating to his assumption of Kaspar Hauser's guardianship, and it certainly cannot be denied that part of the campaign against Kaspar Hauser that Stanhope organised was discussed with the knowledgeable nobleman from the Baltic. A cornucopia of small presents opened for Sternberg, who just at this time was treated more generously than ever before or afterwards to little gifts of all kinds. In 1834 the still popular aristocrat was moving among the countless salons of the cream of society; this situation would change radically in 1848. Gifts of perfume, eau de cologne, crayons and erasers, eau de Portugal, albums and finally 'a gold ring for Baron Sternberg' testify to the friendly relationship that Stanhope maintained with the international cavalier.

A day later, on the 8th June—Schwab's reply could not yet have arrived—Stanhope took up his pen once more, this time clearly more irritated, as 'the editor', against his express wishes, had named him as the 'author of the contribution'.

> Yesterday I found in the *Morgenblatt* my reply to the article in No. 123 and 124, and the editor states there that he has received it from me. I am never ashamed and never shy away from acknowledging everything that I have written in public. However, it seemed to me unusual as well as unseemly to answer an anonymous attack in my name and for this simple reason I did not sign the essay. The editor had no right to name me as the author and even less so, because he does not name the author of the attack and gives out that he does not know him. He also added the location 'Baden-Baden' to the answer, which is not in the original. In addition, I must point out that the editor neither sought nor obtained my permission to use the three small tracts which were published 'as manuscripts' and which therefore, as he must well know, may not be shared with the world without my consent either in whole or in part. If a further refutation becomes necessary from my side, I shall turn to another editor and not to one who appears to know so little of his duty.[416]

On the 7th July, Stanhope held Schwab's response in his hands, which on the decisive question as to the divulgence of the name of the author, was a cool rebuff to Stanhope's wishes:

> ...I have obtained the different journals in which you will find the essays 1) which I had in mind, from the end of April. This stems from the editorial staff. 2) the one from Nuremberg, included in No. 123 and 124. Herr Haupt, general editor of the *Morgenblatt*, himself does not know the place of origin or the author of this piece. It was written with indelible pencil and bore the inscription of Nuremberg. Whether it really comes from there, Herr Haupt does not dare to wager, but he would nevertheless—as he told me—if he did know it, maintain editorial confidentiality. 3) the essay from Your Lordship, sent via Herr von Fahnenberg, which was taken up...[417]

Stanhope wrote two more times to Schwab. On the 11th July: '...I intend, as soon as I have time, to write a thorough commentary on Feuerbach's text in order to refute it utterly and to show the affair in its true light. However, there are people who remain mired in their prejudiced opinions and who will never see or at least admit that Kaspar Hauser cheated us...'[418] And again on the 16th July of the same month, when he pointed out an 'excellent essay' by a so-called Anonymous in the *Jenaischen Literaturzeitung* which 'is accurately acquainted with the facts'. Did Stanhope really not know that the author was the extremely controversial Karl Heinrich, Ritter [Knight] von Lang (1764–1835) who had made a name for himself as an especially unobjective opponent of Kaspar Hauser and Feuerbach and who could not fail to be known in Ansbach? Lang was the man who had written in the same context to the Bavarian Minister of the Interior Oettingen-Wallerstein, who, for his part, in his letter of the 23rd January to Stichaner, had described Lang as follows: 'The letter of Privy Councillor von Lang, whose commonly recognised tendency is to ridicule the whole affair and to hold off from any further attempts to investigate the deed and trace the murderer...'. In his book *Falsifications, False Reports and Biased Accounts*, Hermann Pies discusses Lang in depth and points out the numerous untruths for which he was responsible.

Stanhope's attention was also drawn to the 'excellent essay' of Herr von Lang by Wessenberg, who wrote in his letter of the 9th July: '...The *Katalog* of Leipzig[419] includes 21 writings on Hauser from which, as the *Literarische Zeitung Halle* puts it, it follows that the famous youth was a scoundrel. It appears that only Prince von Oettingen is of the opposite opinion.'[420]

How could Wessenberg, the man of Baden, diplomat in the service of Austria, know what view the Bavarian Minister of the Interior had of the Kaspar Hauser Question? Did he know from whatever source of that long 16-sided letter of the 23rd January in which Oettingen-Wallerstein set forth to Ansbach local government President von Stichaner his views of Hauser's credibility, Stanhope's 'unstable sensibility', Meyer's 'incomprehensible behaviour' and which concluded:

> ...that anyway, the present grand ducal ruling family in Baden knew nothing of a possible assassination of the children of Grand Duke Karl, that all guilt would fall on the dead Margrave Ludwig and on his advisor, State Councillor Fischer, who was regional administrator in Wertheim at the time of Hauser's birth, and that consequently, any enquiry from Karlsruhe, even if it came directly from the grand ducal cabinet, would never lead to the disadvantage of the present reigning dynasty.

That doubtless went back to the interventions of King Ludwig, who in face of the political situation that had developed, was for several reasons no longer thinking of continuing the old policy. Hauser could no longer be used to apply pressure in the Palatinate dispute. The role which Sophie, wife of the reigning Grand Duke, had played was then hardly visible, and Leopold himself was a man of integrity, so the suspicion that his predecessor, Grand Duke Ludwig, was the actual evil genius was certainly logical. Finally, the cause of monarchy itself in general was not exactly riding high at that time so a public dispute between the two royal houses of Baden and Bavaria could well have irreparable consequences. The July Revolution of 1830 and the Hambacher Fest of 1832 were events of but recent memory.

*

The year after Kaspar Hauser's murder was for Stanhope one of a remarkable activity of correspondence directed at a large, cleverly chosen circle of people who were all inundated with tracts containing the same news about, and accusations against, Kaspar Hauser. Without doubt, Stanhope's plan in all of this was to make the best use of his remaining time in Germany by impressing upon the drama the contours of his own fixed ideas so that he could leave the stage with a carefully arranged image in the final act. His 'direction' of the whole piece proceeded according to this script; Kaspar's opponent did not wish to take his leave without a final swan song to his own innocence and the culpability of his former foster son. The King and his ministers, ambassadors, publishers and publicists all received Philip Henry's near identical letters. On the 18th July 1834 the Director of Police von Mentz in Munich, like all the others, was informed by Stanhope that 'Feuerbach falsified the story', that Hauser had told a stable groom 'that every day he went to school *across the border*' (a complete invention of Stanhope's) and finally, 'that it would contribute very much to the satisfaction of His Majesty and the honour of the Bavarian police if one were to be convinced that that no crime had been committed'!

Such an acquittal would have been invaluable, but Mentz was as careful as the King, who in a letter of the 22nd July 1834—not referred to by [the anti-Hauserian] Striedinger—merely said in relation to the affair: 'I shall tell my Interior Minister about it.' Stanhope maintained the pressure and wrote again to King Ludwig on the 21st August (a letter also unnoticed by Striedinger): '...Your Majesty will note how much the departed President von Feuerbach misrepresented the story of Kaspar Hauser and will excuse me if I express my most earnest hope that careful researches be carried out to discover his origins and better, before it is too late—a discovery which will be cause of satisfaction for Your Majesty and do credit to Your police...'[421]

In impotent rage against 'the slanderer who behind the mask of a friend of truth hunts down the shade of an honourable man...' Feuerbach's son Ludwig, evidently still very hurt, wrote down on a scrap of paper his first answer to Stanhope's misrepresentation: 'This work [Feuerbach's *Memoire* to Queen Karoline—*Mayer*] was composed by father with real love, zeal and steadfast industry at a time when he was still in the fullness of his mental powers; [it was] buttressed by the experiences afforded him by a long practical life and by the results which efforts in the field of criminal legislation in other states have brought to light.'[422]

But King Ludwig was always taciturn when it came to the case of Kaspar Hauser. From Aschaffenberg on the 18th September 1834 he wrote a short note (also missed by Striedinger) to the 'noble Lord' in which he expresses surprise, in a manner that verges on mockery, at his lordship's 'steadfast zeal'. Stanhope's steadfast zeal extended not only to contemporary opinion-formers but also to casual acquaintances whom he met everywhere. He generously gave his writings to whoever wanted them. A young man by the name of Sachs from Karlsruhe was quite taken by Philip Henry's gesture which

> filled [him] with the warmest gratitude for the friendly donor, and this feeling of gratitude is doubled within me when I recall that you did me this honour, a young man whom you had only had an opportunity to see for a few hours. I have read your tract with the greatest attention and its content amazed me, for it is almost inconceivable how a man like Feuerbach would leave unused such proofs as those introduced by yourself and how through the distortion of the facts in the Hauser story a kind of forgery could be perpetrated! One who Everyone concerned with the truth must welcome most warmly the information you have brought forward, for now the fictional element in the affair will disperse, the nocturnal darkness will be lightened, the truth will triumph and Europe, cheated thus far, will be freed from deception...[423]

This was the kind of effect for which Stanhope was striving. C. Sachs's letter of thanks is a graphic example of how Stanhope's modes of argumentation worked on readers who did not have more accurate information at their disposal.

By contrast, Stanhope did not have it so easy in cases where people had some background knowledge or even personal connections to Kaspar Hauser's destiny, such as the wife of the British chargé d'affaires in Frankfurt, Lilly Cartwright, born the Countess Sandizell, who in addition maintained direct relations with the ruling house. Already at the beginning of the year there was correspondence in which the former foster father was searching for a letter of Kaspar Hauser's, which on the basis of a particular suspicion, he thought he could profit from in his campaign, but which on closer analysis proved to be harmless.

Lilly Cartwright wrote at the time:

> ...Here is the letter which Kaspar Hauser once wrote to Mr. Cartwright, which has come into my possession and which I have kept as a momento of that unfortunate young man. I do not remember saying to the Dowager Queen that it was written in order to say that he had not received the payments which you claim that he did say. I am as sure as one can be that I never spoke to the Dowager Queen about this poor young man, but I remember very well that he was spoken of on the day I took my leave of Her Majesty in Biederstein. She spoke to a lady about it who was there in her salon at the same time as myself and who sat near me. When I took my leave of the reigning Queen, Kaspar Hauser was being spoken of, and I said to her that I had had a letter written in his hand in which he complained that he had had no news at all of you and had asked if my husband could let him have such news. As my husband did not have the time to answer him, I asked him to leave it to me to reassure him with regard to yourself, which I did with great pleasure. Despite all my efforts, I cannot recall having said that the letter in question had anything to do with money which you had been so generous as to give to Kaspar. But it could be that in the conversation with Her Majesty I said that Kaspar had for a moment been unhappy about the late arrival there of one of the payments which you were making to him, a matter which someone had told me who had dined with us and who had been told it by Herr Klüber. He will be able to tell you about that better than I, but before I conclude this part, I must admit to you that I was extremely vexed to learn that what I said in Munich was poorly understood and misinterpreted. Would you be so good as to return the letter of Kaspar Hauser? It occupies one of the prime places in my collection of interesting letters...[424]

Stanhope sought to make up for this vexation with a hurriedly dispatched bottle of 'Perfume for Lady Cartwright'. Six months later Lilly

Cartwright addressed herself to Stanhope's tract, which he had sent her, and which was evidently not received as favourably by her as it had been by Mr Sachs in Karlsruhe:

> ....as for what concerns myself, I thank you for the tract which you sent me; I have read it with interest as I do with everything related to poor Kaspar Hauser. You will excuse me, I am sure, for adding the word *poor*, but I feel sorry for this mysterious being; whether he is guilty or not, I cannot give up the interest that his story has awoken in me. This pamphlet indeed shows that Herr Feuerbach was in error in some details of the life of his protégé. Despite everything that still leads me—without me wishing it—to think that he was not completely *perverse*, I beg you to note that I certainly do not share the enmity of the ladies of Karlsruhe and Ansbach...[425]

The most industrious bearers of Stanhope's news and broadcasters of his false reports were his old friends Fahnenberg and Wessenberg, who worked at it incessantly. Both had in the interim gained sufficient time for such activities. Wessenberg had for a few years past found no opportunity for official service, and at the beginning of 1834 Fahnenberg had been retired 'due to ill health'. The large number of partly trivial, partly interesting letters make plain the way in which Stanhope repeatedly sought the assistance of the two men, such as, for example, the expensive 100-guilder necklace for Fahnenberg's wife. In detail, the insubstantial communications reveal no deep insights but they afford a glimpse into the 'workshop' of the agent, who organised an extremely efficient auxiliary service and with its aid, turned his plans into effective action by means of small presents and the personal connections that resulted from the honour of his acquaintance.

A few extracts from these letters[426] will suffice to show how the contacts, news and methods were created.

> Meanwhile a word about Caspar Hauser—have you seen an infamous pamphlet about him that has appeared in Strasbourg and whose author is a man who can know nothing of his story, a certain M. Garnier [Fig. 174] from Rastatt who was imprisoned last year on charges of complicity in demagogic activities? The title of the book is: Contributions to the Story of Caspar Hauser with a dramatic introduction by Jos. Heinr. Garnier—the author explicitly ... makes Caspar out to be the heir to the House of Baden [Wessenberg].

Einige Beiträge
zur Geschichte
Caspar Hausers,
nebst einer dramaturgischen Einleitung
von
Joseph Heinrich Garnier.

174. Title page of the book by Joseph Heinrich Garnier 'Contributions to the Story of Caspar Hauser'.

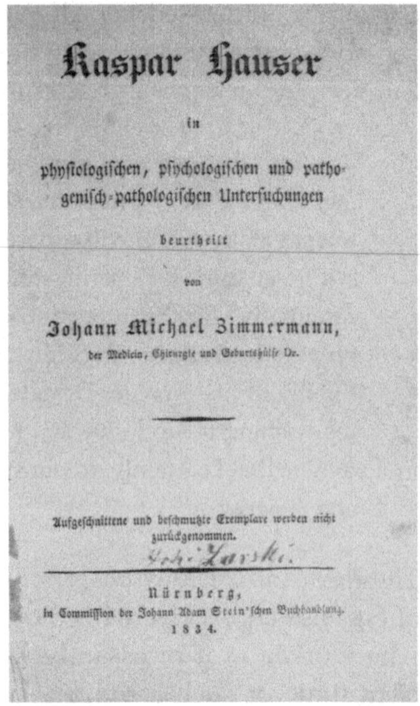

Kaspar Hauser
in
physiologischen, psychologischen und patho-
genisch-pathologischen Untersuchungen
beurtheilt
von
Johann Michael Zimmermann,
der Medicin, Chirurgie und Geburtshülfe Dr.

Aufgeschnittene und beschmutzte Exemplare werden nicht zurückgenommen.

Nürnberg,
in Commission der Johann Adam Stein'schen Buchhandlung.
1834.

175. Title page of the book about Kaspar Hauser by Johann Michael Zimmermann.

Today both of Merker's writings went to the Wessenberg brothers in Konstanz [Fahnenberg].

As I finally hope to see you in the course of *next* week, I shall limit myself today to sending you:

1. the requested numbers of the *Morgenblatt*
2. another proof-reading
3. another article on your writings from a Hamburg newspaper.

I shall get your article in the *Morgenblatt*, but I would have wished that you had *signed* it, as you are now doing something for which you reproach your opponents. [Fahnenberg]

It seems that in Munich people are very angry over the article in the *Gazette* about the bad affairs of Kaspar Hauser. In your place I would let this matter drop for a while in order to see what others will bring. [Wessenberg]

In accordance with your wishes I shall pass this text on to all your acquaintances. Let me know in any case the day of your arrival so that *no* more letters and packets will be sent to Heidelberg. [Fahnenberg]

I shall *immediately* order for you two copies of the new tract about C. Hauser by Prof. Zimmermann. Groos, however, has not received it yet. I would like to thank you for your important post of the 23rd instant, which I found waiting for me on the evening I came back from Baden. I immediately dispatched all the copies of your tract that you sent me. [Fahnenberg]

In accordance with your wishes I immediately sent an imprint of it to the banker von Haber and sent to Ansbach and Altona the copies intended for them. Since Prof. Zimmermann's book [Fig. 175] has not yet arrived, I have not yet been able to send off to Merker the imprints of the *Morgenblatt* intended for him. Rest assured that I shall always most conscientiously complete *all* the tasks you give me. [Fahnenberg]

I thank you also for your last brochure about Caspar—which is of great interest—you will find enclosed an announcement about him which seems odd to me: 'Ansbach, 13 Sept. At the time of the most recent ministerial conferences in Vienna, the sole royal Bavarian Parliament envoy von Mieg, who previously held a senior position of authority, was called to Vienna and took with him all the official documents relating to Caspar Hauser. These documents, as one hears, have not been returned here. There followed soon afterwards the dissolution of the commission of investigation into the Hauser case here, which was thus rendered inactive.' [Wessenberg]

In accordance with your wishes, I shall collect everything that appears on Hauser in your absence...In accordance with your request I opened Merker's package and sent a copy of his paper, together with the *Morgenblatt* in which Mittermaier's latest article is printed, to Herr von Haber. [Fahnenberg]

From my last letter, which has come to you via Herr von Haber, you will have seen that I have dealt with all your requests punctually. Meanwhile, the bookseller Groos has sent me a second copy of Dr. Zimmermann's book about Caspar Hauser. Please be so good as to decide whether I should keep this book until your return or whether it should be sent on to you as soon as possible via H. von Haber. [Fahnenberg]

*

In the second half of the year after the murder of his 'beloved foster son', despite the bad experiences he had been through, Stanhope planned another trip to Italy. Before his departure for the south, he spent once more almost two months in Karlsruhe, from the 7th July to the 30th August. The long stay there, and also in Mannheim, Baden-Baden and Bruchsal, occupies a special place in his travels at this time with respect to Ansbach and Nuremberg.

He was received[427] this time by, amongst others, Margrave Wilhelm von Baden, who was told by Philip Henry on the 24th August that the Kaspar Hauser affair 'had been mystified in a most appalling fashion and that his earlier view that a great crime lay behind it all had been completely erroneous'. Such were the reassuring memories of Margrave Wilhelm, who was content to base his view on Stanhope, Merker, and von Lang and could never understand how Feuerbach, Karoline of Bavaria, Duchess Marie of Hamilton or even Stéphanie could have fallen for the nonsensical and foolish idea that held the foundling to be a Zähringer. Philip Henry spent part of September in Baden-Baden before eventually heading, via Geneva, for Italy.

On the 18th October he stayed a few days in Florence and was in Arrezzo on the 11th November, from where he travelled via Spoleto to Rome. He stayed a month in the holy city—from the 6th November until the 12th December—and the remaining time in the area around Naples. The months before had essentially been filled with an emotional zeal for the persecution of Hauser and Feuerbach, the friends of better days. Both had had to depart this life within a short time of each other and both had been the objects of an unworthy campaign in which Stanhope was only the aggressor. That was not always good for him and his wicked cause. Many just souls now woke up for the first time and resolved, first inwardly and then publicly to speak up for the defenceless dead. Of all people, it was the courageous editors of the *Karlsruher Unterhaltungsblatt* newspaper[428] who addressed themselves to his Lordship's conspicuous change of heart:

> A large section of the public, made mistrustful by Merker's information that roused suspicion, feels that the unfortunate youngster was a fraud who played people false in an incredibly brazen manner. The number of these people has grown significantly as a result of the statements and writings of Lord Stanhope (Kaspar's foster father), who has further confused the judgements of the world about Kaspar Hauser by the three letters he had published in 1834...
>
> He reports that Kaspar did not appear in Nuremberg in the manner described by Feuerbach, for all witnesses who saw him, had said that he could already speak in an understandable fashion, even if not very well. Furthermore, he has caught Kaspar lying and contradicting himself, namely in relation to his time in the cell, his instruction in speaking and writing, and his journey to Nuremberg...Finally, Stanhope claims Kaspar himself had said that there were many things in Feuerbach's published

> book of which he knew nothing. The conclusion thus was that in his old age Feuerbach had written a work of fiction....so much for Lord Stanhope. Although the poor *Unterhaltungsblatt* does not wish to place its authoritative opinion on a par with that of the wealthy lord, in its simple-minded way, it is of the opinion that an even greater fiction would result from explaining Kaspar Hauser as a fraud than it would from seeing him as a hidden prince. For in that case a 16-year-old youth must have played his imagined role as a poor, outcast feral child in such a masterly fashion that he managed for two years to cheat Professor Daumer and President Feuerbach and a great number of the most cultured and intelligent people without giving himself away once. It presupposes such a readiness to lie and cheat on the part of this youth that is perhaps impossible to find a parallel example in the whole history of the world. But there is more! If, as Stanhope suspects, vanity or the desire to cause a sensation are what moved Kaspar the first time to wound himself in the forehead, the second time in the head and the third time a fatal chest wound, all by his own hand, then this half-child pushed vanity further than any man or woman in the world and continued his shameless deception until the moment of his death, where even other liars and hypocrites, even the greatest criminals, try to tell the truth. Every feeling human heart that still possesses even a spark of belief in humanity rises up in indignation against accepting such a suspicion, and we therefore believe that the most flagrant injustice has been done to the good Kaspar in declaring him to be a fraud...

But Stanhope had already loaded so much slander and doubt onto the scales that by the end of that unhappy year it remained uncertain where those who held other views would gain a hearing. They persisted painfully as though lamed and incapable of parrying Philip Henry's adroit moves. He had acted and promoted his view with a restless zeal, written his pamphlets and spread them about to let the whole world know of the great deception and in this manner had carefully drawn many people in his direction. Hauser had previously had a few individuals against him, but the sizeable body of opposition that was now ready to go along with the fraudster theory was the result of Stanhope's work, which has had its effect until the present day. Ludwig Feuerbach was revolted by the change in Stanhope, which so completely contradicted the friendship he formerly professed for Kaspar, and Feuerbach's feelings were shared by many who had witnessed the foundling's years in Nuremberg and Ansbach. Feeling himself called to defend the honour of the dead, Anselm von Feuerbach's son raged with righteous indignation: 'We ask rightly what does His Lordship want, what is the deeper meaning of his short speeches, and we find, instead of the main episodes being attacked and laid open to doubt, only an emotional fixation with trivial details.'[429]

Stanhope too was at first aware of this. He wrote to his son: 'If one of Feuerbach's sons were to write something in memory of his father in which he attacked me, then I intend to write a commentary on Feuerbach's book in order to show how falsely he has presented all the facts...'[430]

That no such commentary appeared speaks for itself. During these months of his continual attacks on Hauser, on Feuerbach and on all who stayed true to the two dead men, Philip Henry's health declined as never before. Again and again, he had to take to his bed with gall-bladder problems, from which he only recovered with difficulty. Health cures in the south were supposed to bring relief.

*

While Stanhope spent all the early part of 1835 in Italy, only returning to Karlsruhe again on the 20th May, Ludwig Feuerbach, the philosopher, who was to publish the secret memorandum to Queen Karoline in 1852 after perhaps hesitating too long, took up once again in the name of his family the defence of the honour of his father and of Kaspar Hauser.

Meanwhile, Stanhope's 'Materials' had appeared. In place of the letters that had been published as 'Manuscripts', they now pushed the public campaign forward in a big way. One can infer from every sentence of Ludwig's Feuerbach's letters and draft replies a struggle to comprehend the inconceivable nature of Stanhope's betrayal, which had come too unexpectedly and too fast. One of the son's draft letters that lacks a salutation or a date—probably intended for a member of the government—first expresses a desire to gain access to the legal documents of the case that at this point in time could not yet have been granted:

> Your Honour will probably have heard that Lord Stanhope has now gone before the public formally and in his so-called Materials has given a summary of his earlier statements in which he so grossly traduced the honour of my deceased father.
>
> An urgent challenge is thereby presented to me and my relatives to speak out in defence of that honour, especially since unfortunately,

those earlier writings, as I thought on a journey in autumn, despite their wretchedness have made a greater impression on the public than one might expect from the healthy sense of the German people. It would be an eternal disgrace for us if we were any longer to look on calmly while that unworthy lord, driven by the most dishonest motives, and behind the mask of a friend of truth, dares to besmirch the ashes of a man who evidently honoured him too highly and undeservedly before all the world.

A defence of my father's reputation is, however, not possible without access to the documents of the Kaspar Hauser case. I therefore take the liberty of asking whether permission for this could not be granted me, especially since, as I understand, the investigation has been closed for some time. It goes without saying that I would respect every indication of the court and would only reveal to publicity those episodes which are uncontroversial and that in all other matters I would hold myself obliged to the strictest confidentiality by the oath that I have sworn as a servant of the state.[431]

Most likely after receipt of a letter declining his request, Ludwig Feuerbach drew up a 'Preliminary Declaration', which was intended for publication but was then held back, as the question must have arisen very quickly as to the most public and effective form in which it could confront Stanhope's accusations—as an announcement in a newspaper or as a flyer? This plan, which could not come to fruition, reveals the weakness of the victimised party, who were forced to recognise that in the Press arena, which was dominated by Stanhope, there was no longer any chance of confronting him on equal terms.

Preliminary Declaration with regard to the Materials on the Story of Kaspar Hauser Collected and Published by Count Stanhope, Heidelberg 1835

Through letters which he had had printed as manuscripts and distributed far and wide, Lord Stanhope, the former foster father of Kaspar Hauser, has for some time sought to spread among the public erroneous views about Kaspar Hauser and to cast a shadow over the character of my deceased father, the former State Counsellor and President von Feuerbach. In a calm and firm trust in the power of truth, which in its own time itself casts off the binding fetters of sophistry, and in the hope that the legal investigation initiated following the recent catastrophe would meanwhile lead to a definitive result, I have until now continued to observe a silence on this matter. Since this hope has not been fulfilled,

> and since His Lordship has once again come before the public and in his 'Materials' communicated a summary of his earlier propaganda, I wish to make a preliminary declaration with the express reservation that what is presented here is borne out with solid grounds: That in the above-mentioned tract facts are partly distorted, significant episodes that speak for the truth of the story of Kaspar Hauser and that must have been known to His Lordship are passed over, that statements are attributed to my father that are either fabricated or interpreted in the most spiteful manner that completely contradicts his character. With regard to all this, as soon as His Lordship gives further cause for doing so, I shall put the facts before the public which will explain his mysterious behaviour and will reveal to those of impartial mind why His Lordship has already spent two years persecuting his unfortunate foster son beyond the grave and has committed an offence against the memory of a man who clearly, if undeservedly, honoured him before all the world.[432]

It is regrettable that Ludwig Feuerbach did not reveal his apparent knowledge of the motives for the persecution of Kaspar Hauser, and it appears certain that the causes of the 'mysterious behaviour' were known only to a small circle of contemporaries.

Would Stanhope have interested himself at all in such moral admonitions if he had known of them? Hardly. On the contrary, he was once again further engaged in his strategy than Daumer, Tucher, Binder, and the Feuerbach family could have imagined possible. On the 16th June 1835 he set out for Berlin, which he reached on the 28th. The actual goal of his journey, however, was not Berlin, but Merker, with whom he had long been in contact. Merker had been Kaspar Hauser's earliest and most determined opponent since 1829 and regarded his attack on the foundling's credibility and his identification of Hauser as a fraudster to be the high point of his career.

The day before his departure for the Prussian capital—15th June—Stanhope discharged another notable obligation. He instructed his Nuremberg bankers Lödel and Merkel (Fig. 176): 'With regard to the 500 *gulden* that I deposited with you in the year 1831, I hereby request you, to pay the same sum to the schoolmaster Herr Meyer in Ansbach, who will dispose of it for purposes determined by myself. Nuremberg, 15th June 1835, Count Stanhope.'[433] Seventeen months after the murder of Kaspar Hauser, his former teacher receives the immense sum of 500 *gulden* for 'purposes determined' by Stanhope! For what intended purpose was Meyer to be so handsomely rewarded and so late after the events

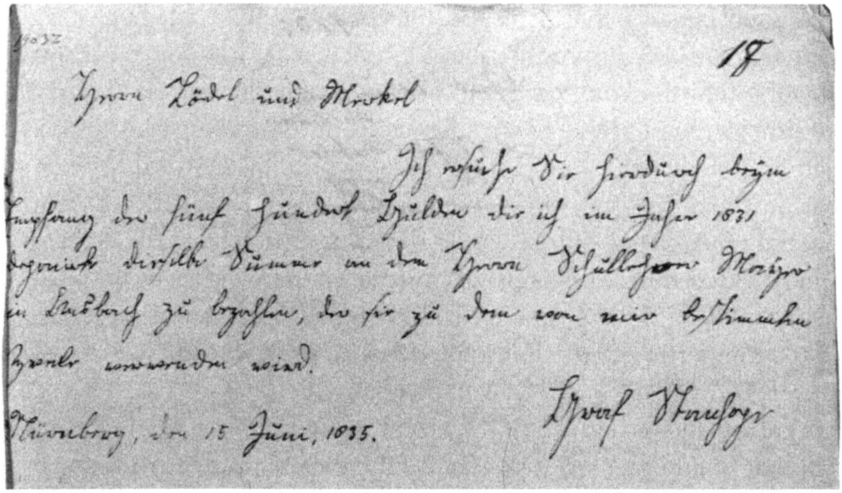

18

Herren Lödel und Merkel

Ich ersuche Sie hierdurch gegen Empfang der fünf hundert Gulden die ich im Jahre 1831 deponirt dieselbe Summe an den Herrn Schullehrer Meyer in Ansbach zu bezahlen, der sie zu dem von mir bestimmten Zwecke verwenden wird.

Nürnberg, den 15 Juni, 1835.

Graf Stanhope

176. Instruction from Lord Stanhope to the banking house Lödel and Merkel.

of 1833? Stanhope's allowances for Kaspar Hauser 1831–33 were paid monthly from the same banking house. The sum could not have been intended as a belated pension payment, so what was it for? Was Meyer much more involved in the demise of his pupil than has previously thought to have been the case? Are there any clues that suggest that the payment of such an extraordinary 'honorarium' by Stanhope was justified? A few examples: Meyer had, as we know from one of Hickel's letters to Stanhope, been collaborating since the beginning of December 1833 in the decision to 'free' Kaspar Hauser from his burdensome protection. Can the fact be overlooked that without Meyer's assistance, an attempt on the life of Kaspar Hauser would not have stood the slightest chance of success? Furthermore, once the murder had been carried out, Meyer, just like Stanhope in Munich, was the first in Ansbach to speak of suicide. From a letter of Henrietta Feuerbach of the 14th February 1872 to Gottlieb von Tucher we know of what then followed:

> ...A few days after the murder, the teacher Meyer, who from the moment of the wounding onwards, appeared to be among the opponents of Kaspar Hauser, came late in the evening to my brother [the surgeon Heidenreich] carrying a piece of veal under his coat and a knife in his pocket. He wanted to try to convince my brother to see for himself that a self-wounding, which my brother, as he saw the matter, held to be impossible, may in fact have been conceivable. This occurred in my presence and the deep shudder that I felt impressed the scene forever on my memory so that I can recall it very clearly.[434]

Is it not absurd that a responsible pedagogue, a teacher charged with the care of the young should specifically ask for a certificate attesting that the youth entrusted to his care had committed suicide? Would suicide not have cast a suspicious light on Meyer himself, as a man and a teacher? Would it not have been more natural for him to seek to prove the opposite? The meaning of this absurdity is simply that only the alleged suicide could divert attention from the fact that a cold-blooded murder was proof positive of the validity of the 'prince theory'. It would have been clear that Hauser's existence represented such a danger to others that to be rid of it, they would even resort to a capital crime.

Against this background, the sizeable amount of the late honorarium that Stanhope paid to Meyer on the day of his departure for Berlin is understandable. Whatever the Kaspar Hauser Question would bring in the future, Meyer was an equal member of the triumvirate that bound him to Stanhope and Merker and was worth his money. Only Gentz and Kaspar Hauser himself had received greater sums from Stanhope.

*

Johann Friedrich Karl Merker (1775–1842) was from 1820 to 1841 Police Commissioner in the Prussian Ministry of the Interior and of Police. He served in Department III at police headquarters in Berlin under his superior, President von Puttkamer, Section 4, the police security office. His predecessor there had been Privy Councillor Falckenberg. Previously, Merker had been private secretary in the royal military cabinet, then—since 1818—commissioner of police in Erfurt, where his first publications appeared on *The Need for the Identity Card in the Maintenance of Public Security...* (Erfurt 1818); in the same year he wrote a *Handbook for Police Officers* and *Suggestions for how a higher level of security would be achieved against robbery, theft and similar crimes through an efficacious use of existing arrangements throughout Germany that are slightly bothersome to the public*. He also collaborated actively in the *News on the Provision of Security Services* and in *Contributions to the Alleviation of the Achievements of Practical Policing* in which he soon established himself as a regular contributor. Both specialist journals were later published by him. He was thus a career official who had early on drawn attention to himself.

The *News on the Provision of Security Services* published by Merker functioned as a circular for all police forces throughout Germany and the neighbouring states, in which wanted posters and reports on murders and crimes of all kinds were communicated in the fastest ways available. Merker was thus one of the most noted and well-known personalities in central European ministries of the interior. Since 1821, on the orders of the Ministry of the Interior, Merker's newsletter had been regularly circulated to all Prussian police stations and border guard posts and within a few years to almost every police station of significance throughout Europe that was concerned with fighting crime. The Berlin police commissioner was thus an internationally recognised expert, whose judgement carried weight. The Czar sent him a diamond ring in gratitude and acknowledgement, and the King of Prussia bestowed on him the Order of the Red Eagle, Fourth Class. Merker's position in the Kaspar Hauser Question in terms of the formation of official opinion was therefore of a significance that could scarcely be overlooked. In view of all this, the question arises within Kaspar Hauser research to ascertain whether Merker took up his position against Hauser out of purely personal reasons or else in the line of his official duties. The question of the validity of his writings, which have hardly been outdone in the copiousness of their argumentation even by later authors, was addressed by Hermann Pies, who in his works took up a clear position against this first and most intelligent of Kaspar Hauser's opponents.

> There is, I believe, no argument, however tentative, that he would not have employed in defence of his sceptical position. None of the later, numerous official and unofficial anti-Hauserians have surpassed him. Indeed, it can be maintained that they all carry on their struggle against the foundling with Merker's weapons, mostly without naming their master or even without knowing of him.

But where in Merker, specifically in this case, are to be found the deeper reasons that led him to report, to argue, and from the very beginning, to build up the fraudster theory so deliberately, far beyond any normal extent?

We know from Julius Eduard Hitzig, a Berlin criminologist, director of the Supreme Court Inquisitors, publisher of Merker's rival journal, the *Journal for Prussian Criminal Administration* and the *Annals of German and Foreign Criminal Administration*, and a supporter of Hauser, that he (Hitzig) had a close relationship to Feuerbach and also to the Prussian Court. Hitzig wrote to Feuerbach: 'Our entire Court takes the deepest interest in the case, and I have been asked by every single member for news of it...'. Nevertheless, in the circle around the royal family—perhaps at the ministerial level or in officers' circles—there must have been those who took a quite different view of the matter from the King and his second wife, Princess Auguste von Liegnitz and above all, later Princess Elise of Prussia. They made use of their excellent contacts to the highest authorities charged with the Bavarian investigation and to its chief, to supply Merker, over the head of the unsuspecting Hitzig, with all the necessary arguments to strengthen him in his continuous lust for writing. 'He does not tire from addressing himself to every argument on all sides and with the keen sense of the advocate, he draws from all of them the best that suits his fraudster theory....' (Pies)

Such zeal was all the more understandable from the Prussian viewpoint, as Prussia began early on to see the Kaspar Hauser case as possibly connected with the House of Bonaparte for whose overthrow Prussia had lined up alongside Russia and Austria in 1814. Obviously, patriotically-minded members of the Court would have had a political interest in the affair from this consideration alone. In 1806 and afterwards, Friedrich Wilhelm III had had to accept the most humiliating defeats at the hand of Napoleon. To convince the King in 1812 of the need for a treaty of neutrality with Russia [Convention of Tauroggen—*Ed.*]—the starting point for the War of Liberation—the Prussian Commander Yorck von Wartenburg wrote: 'As long as Napoleon still has power in Germany, Your Royal Majesty's illustrious dynasty will be endangered. His hatred for Prussia can and will never subside.' There were thus political grounds for employing Merker as criminologist. Feuerbach must have taken note of this special background when he called Merker 'a certain policeman with a sharp nose' and drew attention to the fact that he knew very well why such noises were coming specifically from Berlin. What else could have led, somewhat later, in 1857, the Royal Privy Court Press in Berlin to publish an anti-Hauser tract, 'Four Public Readings', by the Danish Professor of Psychology, Dr. Daniel Friedrich Erschricht from the University of Copenhagen? The translator from the Danish, the Prussian General Consul in Copenhagen, Dr. Ryno Quehl apparently had the same viewpoint as Merker. In this connection can also be included the correspondence of the royal Prussian Privy Councillor G.A. Seyler in Berlin (see p.273), who was linked to A. v.d. Linde and who yet at least at times believed that the deciding breakthrough in the Kaspar Hauser affair would come with the solution of the dynastic question. Merker, Quehl and Seyler, as senior Prussian officials, were obliged to draw their swords for the fraudster theory by the interests of their employer without having had previously to take any personal role in the fate of Kaspar Hauser. The only unofficial characterisation of Merker by a contemporary that has come down to us which tells us of his personality and what an impression the dreaded criminologist sought to make has been left by Mayor Binder. Merker had never seen Kaspar Hauser and visited Nuremberg for the first time in 1837 to pay a visit to the Mayor.

'I therefore can and will never share Merker's views,' reports Binder,

> which, since I have become personally acquainted with the man, have lost all their weight for me. In the half hour that I got to know him, he appeared to me as a man who likes only to speak of himself and of his insights into discoveries and everything related to them, which he then considers as correct. I therefore cannot help but believe that he was not convinced by what he wrote about Hauser but that he only wanted to create a sensation by it. At any rate, I have to regard it as striking that he avoided mentioning even a word about Hauser to me—here, where Hauser had first come into the world, where he [Merker] was standing in front of the man who had returned [Hauser] to civic society.[435]

That Binder considered Merker's motive to have been self-promotion is because he naturally lacked other information. It is important that Binder had the impression that Merker was not basically convinced by his whole theory; this only strengthens the impression that the official had carried out a task that, owing to his position, was bound to be more sustained than others' efforts to cast doubt on the credibility of Kaspar Hauser.

In Merker's circular of wanted criminals one could study the circumstances and read indications as to persons suspected of every break-in, every robbery and murder that had been committed, but when the murder of Hauser shocked the civilised world, it was only in Merker's circular that not a single syllable about the Ansbach crime was to be found. Was the case not important enough, or was it so important that Merker had no interest in apprehending the perpetrator? In the corresponding no. 1511 of his circular, dated 24.12.1833, one could read that on the 17th tin lamps had been stolen from the church at Gerlachsthal and that on the 14th, amongst other things, a grey cloth cap with a lackered peak had been stolen in Züllichau... but nothing about the murder in Ansbach. It was only seven weeks later, that circular no. 1525 (15.2.1834) carried—without comment—the official Bavarian announcement (15th Jan.) of the crime.

*

Immediately after his arrival in Berlin and after securing accommo-

177. Residence of Johann Friedrich Karl Merker in Berlin, Hausvogteiplatz 5; second house from the left.

178. Johann Friedrich Karl Merker's place of work in Berlin, Molkenmarkt 1–3.

dation, Stanhope took himself to Merker's house at 5 Vogteiplatz (Fig. 177), where he was to be a regular guest throughout the following ten weeks. The two men discussed the Kaspar Hauser question in every free hour they had. Merker happily reported to his colleague in Gotha, police commissioner Eberhardt: 'Count Stanhope...spent almost all his evenings and Sundays with me, namely, the time I was free from work. I have therefore also become very clear about the Hauser affair, but not all the items are suitable for the public, and I have put many more aside.'

Sundays were occasionally spent together with Anton Heinrich at Charlottenburg (5th and 9th July: 'Dinner with Merker'). The 12th was spent at Treptow and the 26th and the 2nd August at Pankow. On weekdays the company moved mainly between 1–3 Molkenmarkt (Merker's place of work, Fig. 178) and his residence, about half an hour away via Mühlendamm and Spittlermarkt. Merker was especially interested in gaining an accurate knowledge of the crime scene in Ansbach; Stanhope wrote Meyer a letter on the 6th August which conveyed to him greetings from Merker that sound almost familiar:

> Merker commends himself to you warmly and would like a plan of the palace garden [*Hofgarten*] in Ansbach so he can have it lithographed for his articles. Geometric accuracy is not required, but it should indicate the main points, entrances, paths, artesian fountains, the Uz memorial, the place where the pouch was found, the orangery and the direction of the escape—the Rezat [river]. The Minister of Justice in Munich told me that he had received such a plan, and Herr von Lothagen would probably be able to tell you who prepared it. That person would perhaps be able to give you a copy of the same which Herr von Lothagen would not be authorised to do. The first three copies of the new essays on Kaspar Hauser have already appeared.[436]

The three months of conversation between Stanhope and Merker resulted in almost a hundred pages in Merker's *Mitteilungen* ('Newsletter'). Stanhope's activities here arrived at their peak and their conclusion. With a radical thoroughness not attained by anyone before or since, he worked his way indiscriminately through everything that offered itself, half-truths or lies, in support of a damning verdict of ostracism that was intended to stand for all time as a powerful conclusion to the case of Kaspar Hauser.

In his writings Merker had certainly not taken up everything that

Stanhope had conjured up about his foster son during the course of those several weeks. Many items—as he himself thought—were unsuitable for the public. That may have been a euphemism for 'fabrications', where the cool-headed policeman perceived the mania of the Englishman. At the same time, Merker wanted at all costs to put together facts which could underpin the fraud theory, rather like the following fable which Stanhope spread around in England a short while later:

> Kaspar Hauser had been by trade apprenticed to a tailor or a glovemaker and an inhabitant of a small hamlet on the Austrian side of the [River] Salzach, which forms part of the northeastern border of Bavaria. This hamlet lies opposite the Bavarian towns of Burghausen and Tittmoning, and it is most likely that Kaspar Hauser came by way of Altötting where he received the Catholic objects that he had with him and then arrived in Nuremberg via Neumarkt and Regensburg...Even now his portrait, a copy of his handwriting and that of the letter to the captains in these hamlets could yet lead to a full discovery of the circumstances which had stirred such a rare interest[437]

—as if the portrait and the copy of the letter had not already been widely publicised and made available to all the relevant departments of the Bavarian authorities!

Everything that could testify against Hauser was gathered together indiscriminately into a general indictment that bordered partly on the grotesque but which still gained a power of persuasion thanks to Merker's intelligent style. For his part, Merker was completely convinced that, through Stanhope, he now at last had the real proof in his hands. 'Elucidation of the Story of Kaspar Hauser' was the title of the self-assured general introduction to the series of articles that continued for two years and in which Stanhope's 'evidences' were fully employed.

On the 7th July 1835, after weeks of work on his Kaspar Hauser 'Elucidations', Philip Henry received more unexpected high praise for his efforts. On the occasion of a 'great official dinner' a 'significant personality' in Berlin, whose name we are not told, 'at the end of the event, to my great astonishment, proposed a toast to my health, accompanied by some remarks about my love of truth, as I had shown in the case of Kaspar Hauser. It was all the more flattering in that no other toasts were proposed except to the King and the Crown prince.'[438]

*

On the 20th August Philip Henry left Berlin and after a stay in Germany that had lasted almost two and a half years, made his way back to England, seeking out en route by way of a farewell a few of the key locations of his activities over the years. On the 22nd August he saw Dresden again, Erlangen on the 26th, Ansbach the day after, Karlsruhe on the 30th and on the 3rd September, Heidelberg. On Tuesday, the 15th September 1835, the bells of St. Botolph in Chevening welcomed back the incomparable opponent of Kaspar Hauser who had hurried away in such haste on the 16th May 1833 to reassure Klüber personally of his unchangeable love for his foster son, which the State Councillor had summed up in the words: 'I did not observe the slightest indication, not even a cooling, of the truly paternal love and heart-filled affection of the noble lord for Kaspar Hauser.' That was how Stanhope's journey had begun.

It was just as imperative for him to leave behind that impression at that time as it was inevitable to do the opposite later—the problem of Kaspar Hauser could no longer be dealt with in any other way. In late autumn a Lord Daniel Alban Durtnall [KC, 1792–1843—*Ed.*] appeared in Ansbach, an 'advocate at the Royal Court in London', in order to inform himself. Afterwards—on the 11th October 1835—he wrote to Daumer: 'I am firmly convinced that Kaspar Hauser was murdered. It was all done with bribes. Stanhope had no money and was living off this affair.'[439] Lord Haddington [9th Earl of Haddington 1780–1858—*transl.*] had expressed a very similar view the previous year (2nd Jan. 1834) when he wrote to Stanhope, contrary to the latter's own claims, that 'the poor Kaspar Hauser fell to the hand of a murderer'.[440]

15. The Last Years

Grand Duchess Stéphanie of Baden at Chevening, 1836–1855

In the remaining 21 years of Stanhope's life his interest in Germany declined noticeably. He made seven more journeys outside Great Britain but his destinations were no longer the German states. After a four-year pause, he planned another visit to the Continent, which lasted from 16.7.1838 till the first days of January 1839 but led him mainly to Italy and regions in Austria which were then regarded as German. En route, a few of the old familiar German names did crop up, but he no longer had reason to linger there. These trips appear colourless and yielding little in the way of experience compared to those he made during Hauser's lifetime. As if the significance of his own tragic life had depended on the life of the foundling, his energies for these trips seemed to peter out, and his unplanned urges lacked an aim or a content. Not all at once, but soon after 1836 the environment of the Hauser years receded from Stanhope's life. The Kaspar Hauser affair now seemed to him to belong to the past, or so at least he felt in the context of his own life at the time. There was no more correspondence about the matter. Gentz, Feuerbach, Klüber, Böttiger, Dalberg and many other less significant figures were no longer alive, and neither was the one around whom the whole affair had revolved.

*

On 11th October 1838 Stanhope arrived in Munich from Innsbruck. A few days later, he was already trying to gain an audience at court, but there seemed little inclination there to receive the lord who, as would have been recalled, had obtained little sympathy by his appearances there a few years earlier (see p.448ff) What drove the former foster father nevertheless to seek another meeting? Could he not remain quiet until the last prominent doubter of his fraud theory was converted? The King and Queen were deaf to his wishes. They would not deign to discuss the matter further. A silent agreement continued in force that kept the doors closed to him, his case a taboo and he himself isolated from court circles. Only the Dowager Queen, Kaspar Hauser's aunt, received Stanhope, perhaps from reasons of state. This gesture may have been calculated to ameliorate the apparent affront to the

179. Philip Henry, 4th Earl Stanhope (1781–1855)

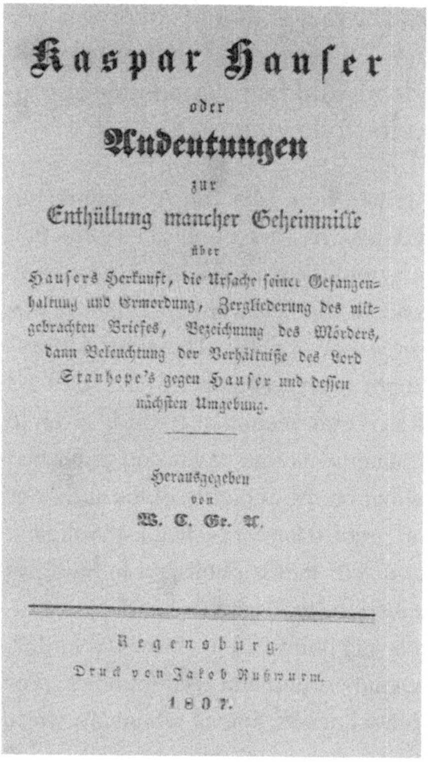

Kaspar Hauser

oder

Andeutungen

zur

Enthüllung mancher Geheimnisse

über

Hausers Herkunft, die Ursache seiner Gefangen-haltung und Ermordung, Zergliederung des mit-gebrachten Briefes, Bezeichnung des Mörders, dann Beleuchtung der Verhältniße des Lord Stanhope's gegen Hauser und dessen nächsten Umgebung.

Herausgegeben
von
W. C. Gr. A.

Regensburg.
Druck von Jakob Rußwurm.
1807.

180. Title page 'Kaspar Hauser or Hints for the Uncovering of Various Secrets'

Englishman. After three weeks, on 31st October Karoline finally granted Philip Henry a short conversation 'without touching in the slightest on the topic of Kaspar Hauser, which we had discussed so much in earlier times'. She dismissed him after a few minutes, as he noted in disappointment: 'She only said: "You look just as you did a few years ago, as if you had been kept in a box"' (Fig.179)—an example of damning with faint praise.

Two days later, on 2nd November, there was a no less notable appearance, at the 'Golden Deer' inn, where Stanhope was staying. The Englishwoman, Countess von Albersdorf, author of a Kaspar Hauser tract (Fig. 180) which subjected Stanhope to incisive criticism, wanted to speak to him; after this, Stanhope was to call for her tract to be censored and banned. Anton Heinrich let his master's compatriot know that he would not be leaving Munich soon. 'But when he reported to his master that I [Albersdorf] wished to speak to him, he suddenly left on the 4th. This unexpectedly rapid departure was noted by his compatriots in Munich and even at the British Embassy people were wondering about it.' Had Stanhope fled from the Countess, who, as the readers of her tract would gather from its title, had in its two volumes and 225 pages principally addressed 'the intrigues played in the course of time' by Philip Henry? The fact is that Munich was not the place where he could handle such a meeting and that only on 9th January 1840, from the safety of England, did he write a letter of protest to King Ludwig, which included the following:

> ...A work which was apparently written by a Mrs von Albersdorf, but which carries only the initials W.C.Gr.A., has been published—the first edition in one volume in Regensburg, and the second edition in two volumes in Munich—in which it is said in the Foreword (p.5) that it was printed with the permission of Your Majesty's police. The work portrays me (pp.32, 87, and 88 in the 2nd edition) as an accomplice in the so-called murder of Kaspar Hauser...As rare as it may seem that credit is given to such calumnies and even to other statements that have been published anonymously and without proof, either on the authority of the author or by the presentation of any manner of proof, it is yet true that Dr. Wolfgang Menzel, the publisher of the *Literaturblatt* that is published in Stuttgart (No. 88, 17th August 1838) recommended the work and that in the constitutional *Staatsbürger-Zeitung*, ['Civic News'] published in Grimma (No. 132, 19th August 1839), it is described as quite sound and well-founded... For my own sake and for that of all those witnesses, among whom are Major

> von Wessenig and the first police officer, who was the first to interview Kaspar Hauser and who at the end of his report stated that he was sly, dissembling and knew more than he said (p.80), and is charged [by Albersdorf—*Ed.*] with behaving towards him [Hauser] with rage and harshness, I should like humbly and most respectfully to ask Your Majesty to allow publication of such extracts [from the interview report—*Ed.*] by a person who is confirmed to have access to the original documents...[441]

The charge against Kaspar Hauser does not appear to have made any great impression. It almost seems that the king even shared the view of Dr. Menzel and the *Staatsbürger-Zeitung*, which described Countess Albersdorf's book as 'well-founded'. Ludwig saw through Stanhope's plan and for a good reason did not respond to his wish for the publication of official documents. In Munich there was only the report of the 1834 hearing, which was partly based on Stanhope's influencing of witnesses and his own testimonies; it therefore contained only the new statements he wanted published. The reports of 1829 and later years were held at Nuremberg and Ansbach; their details were hardly known in Munich in contrast to those of 1834 initiated by Stanhope which re-examined the events of 1829 and in key questions repeated the *new and altered* views of the former foster father. An official publication of the documents held in Munich would mean that Stanhope's accusations would receive the weight of official credibility. The King's officials had to counter the petitioner's cleverly woven plan.

The King therefore wrote back on 10th February 1839:

> My Lord, my envoy Baron Cetto has passed on to me your letter of the 9th January, which deals with certain indications regarding your person contained in an anonymous book about Kaspar Hauser which it is accepted was published by a Mrs von Albersdorf. You request that the government publish the official documents and reports relating to Kaspar Hauser's first appearance and to his mental and physical condition. I immediately gave instructions that enquiries be made as to the suitability of such a publication, and it was found that it would not in fact be right to publish. Consequently, my Lord, I regret that I am not in a position to be able to accede to your request...[442]

It is not unlikely that, following the appearance of Countess von Albersdorf's book, Mayor Binder of Nuremberg remembered her visit in 1831 and sent a written note of it to Munich. Stanhope too knew of this from Binder himself, who had told him about the explosive conversation.

Already at that time the Englishwoman had told her compatriot to his face that he 'had very dangerous plans and intended to do away with him [Kaspar Hauser]'. It can well be imagined that, faced with such an opponent, Stanhope would want to quit the Munich area as quickly as possible. But why did he not go straight to the nearest police station and report Albersdorf for libel and defamation of character? Since the 'delinquent' was in Munich and thirsting for a confrontation, the case could have been decided either way within a few hours. Instead of this, to flee in haste and then from England to write a letter of complaint to the king was already almost an acknowledgement of defeat. In hindsight, Stanhope's stay in Munich in 1838 could hardly have been worse for his position in the still open Kaspar Hauser Question. The renewed attempt to win territory for the fraudster theory was not only without result—more decisively, Stanhope had to admit that as the main representative of the theory, he himself no longer possessed any reputation whatsoever. [This was the situation in Germany, at least; in England, he continued to enjoy a reputation of a different kind in the 1840s as the controversial and eccentric supporter of lost causes in politics—*Ed.*]

Stanhope returned from Germany on 11th January 1839 a tired man, as did Anton Heinrich. He was no ordinary servant and was more a member of the family than the other servants, but he had no children of his own to welcome him after long months away when he came back home to England from Germany, his actual homeland.

The desire for a family of his own must have been so overwhelming that although no longer young, he entered into marriage with a woman who he had perhaps already known for a number of years. In December 1839 the 47-year-old married the 38-year-old Mehetabel, whose family name is unknown. An air of melancholy hangs over the happy event. The lonely Heinrich from faraway Dresden and Mehetabel, whose name also does not sound very English [although many in England had such biblical names in those days—*Ed.*] and who had somehow made herself useful in Chevening, began their life together, even if rather late. The loyal servant received from Philip Henry the rather unusual wedding present of a stuffed bird. Perhaps it had been a wish of the old travelling companion. On 15th July 1840 Mary, as Mehetabel was called, gave birth to a daughter, probably premature. Philip Henry noted outlays of £10 for the baptism in August. But the parents' happiness was not to last long and was finally cut short by sorrow, for the child was not destined for a long life. Their daughter died on the 10th November and was buried on the 16th in the little Chevening graveyard. A large, beautiful gravestone that with the passage of time has become difficult to read still touches the onlooker today:

In Memory of
Sarah Catherine Heinrich
who was born on July 11th 1840
and died on the 10th November
in the same year
This table is placed
by her afflicted parents
Anton Heinrich and his wife

Anton Heinrich is one of those people who in their way are to be counted as belonging to the closer circle of those around Kaspar Hauser. In Nuremberg and Ansbach the two homeless souls often met on excursions and other occasions. There is no evidence of affection between them but there may well have been some. A Saxon, perhaps the son of a respected but impoverished or extinct family,[443] whose spoken German and arduously acquired English one seems to hear of only in the background, a personal servant and valet by occupation, who left home early, slightly stooping and in need of glasses, who lived mostly in the kitchen with his master's dog or else took it for walks, Anton Heinrich is a fascinating figure by the side of Philip Henry, who had a great and lifelong affection for him. Heinrich played a not unsympathetic part in the network of destiny around Stanhope and Kaspar Hauser.

The year 1839 was weighed down by another tragic event. Philip Henry's sister Hester, who had played such a decisive role in his life 39 years earlier in freeing him from the violence of his father, died in June [in faraway Syria—*Ed.*]. And what a death it was! She languished in her final months utterly at the end of her forces, overwhelmed by debt, half-starved and abandoned, and at the end hardly any longer quite of this world, too proud to beg again for the money to which she was entitled. Nothing was to be expected from her own family, something her once so beloved brother Philip Henry had been concerned about. She sent home all those who had served her, had the gates of her Castle of the Rocks walled up and prepared herself for death. Her brother, who owed her much, did not wish to help out in her hour of need, and had wondered whether any proffered help would not merely be squandered.

Five years went by before Stanhope, now 63, found the strength to undertake a lengthy journey again. He wrote to his daughter Wilhelmina that his health was excellent and 'preserved by me with good care', but his many health cures as well as medical prescriptions and notes that exist from this time relating to complaints about his heart, gall and stomach testify that his health was not at its best. He was convinced that he suffered from high blood pressure inherited from his father and passed on to his own son. In addition, he had been plagued for years with rheumatism, which he ascribed to countless days' travelling in autumn and winter. He told his grandson of his aimless daily life: 'I never had the least inclination for sporting, hunting, fishing or farming.' It can therefore be supposed that the 'excellent health' he wrote about to his daughter was, in fact, wishful thinking.

1843 was another sad year. At the age of 57, his wife Catherine Lucy died at Chevening, 'that odd but lively, agreeable and good-humoured wife of an odd but far from agreeable husband', as Lord Glenbervie confided to his diary.[444] For Philip Henry, it is reported, his wife's death was 'a great blow', but the claim that for this reason he never again went to London and kept himself buried in Chevening in deep sadness is contradicted by other facts. He went up to the capital almost monthly until shortly before his death, and his next journey on the Continent was already prepared for the following year, 1844. It began on 27th June that year and ended on 13th June 1845. Once again, he spent most of his time in Italy and Austria, neither of which he cared for. If one recalls his abhorrence of Italy and what an effort travelling there had been for him, the question arises all the more why the old stomping grounds of Bavaria, Baden and Württemberg enthused him even less. Of his 12-month trip he spent only 44 days in German lands, mostly passing through. Only one location—Neumarkt!—stands out alongside the familiar places of Mannheim, Karlsruhe and Heidelberg.

Arriving from Munich, Stanhope stayed in Neumarkt for two days, from 24th to 27th May 1845, before moving on the following day to Nuremberg. Only six kilometres from Neumarkt lies the place where Kaspar Hauser was kept a prisoner for many years—Schloss Pilsach, still completely cut off from all traffic. The owner, as mentioned earlier, was Major-General, Baron von Griesenbeck, commander of the Cadet Corps, then resident in Munich and 58 years old. Griesenbeck himself may have stayed silent as the grave. Perhaps from other directions, however, emerged rumours that related him to the sensational case, which was certainly by no means contrived by him alone. That

Stanhope should have headed straight for Neumarkt after a two-week stay in Munich (9th–23rd May) cannot have been a coincidence. He knew from Hickel, who had taken part in the interrogation of Schrey, sexton at the pilgrimage church of Maria Hilf at Neumarkt in November 1829, that Kaspar Hauser had an appointment there in June 1830, and he knew perhaps from officers' circles or from other informants that people lived in and near Neumarkt who could perhaps reveal a portion of the secret that for Stanhope, still had to do with the fact of the incarceration itself. In the small Frankish town was living the magistrate, who, as Fritz Klee writes, must have known something, but above all, there was Franz Richter, then 57 years old, who was Kaspar Hauser's jailer during his captivity in Pilsach. No more is known about Stanhope's first and last visit to the place. Apart from the Schloss Pilsach manor house, which was beautiful but unused as such since the end of the 17th century, Neumarkt had nothing else to offer that was worth seeing. Why would Stanhope have spent two days there if he had not come for some information or for some meeting or other? Since 1814 Neumarkt had been a garrison town, and light cavalry were stationed there. The letter Kaspar Hauser had with him when he first appeared in Nuremberg in 1828 was addressed to Captain von Wessenig of the same *'chevaulegers'* (light cavalry). It would appear that during these days the restless Stanhope was acquainted with certain things which satisfied him. From this time on, all pointers to his common destiny with Kaspar Hauser cease. Had Neumarkt, or shall we say, its periphery, Pilsach, where Hauser had spent a decisive period of his life, provided for his dark companion, Stanhope, a provisional closure?

*

Meanwhile, on the spot in the Ansbach Hofgarten where Hauser had been fatally stabbed, a stone monument was now standing, for the erection of which, Binder had collected donations years before, in August 1838. He had tried to appeal to Stanhope as a potential donor:

> The enclosed copy of a sketch of the design for a monument that is to be erected at the place where he was murdered shows that now in Ansbach, where he spent his last years, he is not held to be a fraudster, but rather is held in painful remembrance. Ansbach Council chairman von Hartmann, who heads a committee there that, as a result of insufficient funds for the purpose, is collecting contributions for the stone monument, sent

> me an example of the design, from which I have had copies made which I shall use to help gather contributions here also. May I take the liberty of asking you, honoured Count, Hauser's noblest friend and benefactor in life, for a contribution for him in death?

Stanhope, who since 1832 had no longer wished to be known as the foundling's benefactor, certainly did not want to know anything about such a request. He did not answer the letter, and for years afterwards, showed no interest in seeing the monument or even the grave of his foster son, which he did not think worth even a single visit. It may even be that an inner feeling warned him away from approaching the *genius loci* which had meant so much for his own destiny.

The route of his journey went rather directly from Neumarkt back home. Another day, in Nuremberg, where he paid no-one any visits. The next morning, he went on to Frankfurt and from there by the shortest route to the coast. On 14th June he was back in Chevening. Again, for a few years, all his wanderlust seemed to disappear. Since he had left Merker in Berlin, not only had all the main figures in the great drama departed, but the tempo of the age had rapidly altered. The tranquillity, so much appreciated by English travellers, of the little German states, the 'good old backwater, which Kotzebue extols', was disturbed by various protests, above all by the demand for more civil rights and the separation of powers. For a sensitive Tory, the time had come to take one's leave. The violent restructuring of society now announcing itself, with the causes of which all the German states were soon more or less involved, and which found its expression in an ever more self-conscious liberalism, the growing strength of regional assemblies and parliaments, and many other things set in motion by the zeitgeist, created a permanent climate in which a revolutionary element could thrive. Metternich's theories about the suppression of revolutions would have had to prove themselves now. To begin with, it was only a matter of disturbances in southern Europe—Spain, Portugal and even Italy—and then the protesters were at the gates of palaces in Karslruhe, Munich and Vienna. On his penultimate journey, from 27th May to 18th October 1847, which again took him mainly to Switzerland, Italy, and Austria, Stanhope experienced in Karlsruhe (24.6) and on the return journey, in Stuttgart (25.9), something of the mood and forces which, in the following year, would lead to a crossing of the Rubicon. In practise, it soon became clear that Metternich's concept of a common responsibility of governments, of their duty to intervene in the affairs of their neighbours, was impractical when it was a matter of a general symptom and of a similarity of conflicts which, without any notable links between one country and another, had their roots in the daily social life of the respective states. The suppression of reforms necessary since the beginning of the century had thus led to the raising of questions which Marx and Engels would answer with their Communist Manifesto, written in 1847.

Everywhere in the 1840s crises and conflicts between rulers and parliaments were the order of the day, and hardly any of the great or petty thrones could prevail against the revolutionaries in practical politics in the pre-revolutionary mood of the years prior to the 1848 revolutions—on the contrary; the constant general dissatisfaction that resulted from ongoing Press censorship and the prohibition of political parties created the preconditions for an all-encompassing protest movement. Once again, the spark first flew across from France, where in February 1848 the erupting revolution ended the rule of the Citizen King Louis Philippe. A month later, it had spread to Austria and the German states.

In the context of these upheavals the Kaspar Hauser Question hardly figured. It had had its main significance in the early years of the century, a period when the projections of the coming decades were being prepared. Certain answers were now becoming apparent.

On 1st March 1848, the Baden government of Grand Duke Leopold was the first to yield to the pressure of the demonstrators, who were made up of farmers, artisans, townspeople and students. The demands of the liberal opposition were largely met. In Bavaria, King Ludwig I abdicated in favour of his son Max, not only out of personal distaste for the revolutionaries, with whom it seemed to him impossible to come to any arrangement, but above all, because of the campaign organised mainly by the clergy against his relationship with his lover, Lola Montez. Metternich had to flee to England from Vienna with the help of Count Rechberg. That this powerful representative of the old order fled the field so rapidly without a struggle put a perceptible wind in the sails of the revolutionary zeitgeist. The old world, in which the Kaspar Hauser Question had had a political significance, even if limited in its locale, no longer existed. With resignation and perhaps even scorn, Stanhope may well have looked on at the collapse, even the weakness of the monarchies, which had so amazingly given ground at the first sign of revolt. His travels over the past 30 years had enabled him to gather impressions at a number of courts and many insights even into the structure of state and society, and he knew from daily experience the problems of currency exchange at the borders of dozens of small princely states. Yet his experiences did not lead him to discover the need for a customs union; rather, they led him to regret that the superfluity of English goods no longer dominated the markets in Germany's petty states. The idea of a free exchange of goods seemed to him to signify the end of Britain's world trade. He therefore reacted furiously to the Peel government's anti-Protection stance in 1843 by promptly founding a 'Society for the Protection of British Industry' 'in order to obtain full and effectual protection to British Industry, whether employed in Agriculture, Manufactures, Handicraft trades, Mines or Fisheries'. He occupied himself much, as man and Tory, in observing the 1848 revolution; the prevention of such an event had after all belonged to a good part of his own activities over the previous decades. On 25th November 1848, he completed a long, handwritten study 'Reflections on a Future State',[445] probably written on commission for the House of Lords, but also as a résumé of his own feelings and observations. It arrived at a conclusion that perfectly reflects the conservative posture of the British government with regard to the events of 1848. It represents the last visible statement of Philip Henry's views and at the same time it is a document of non-comprehension, and an inability to see where such great events were leading—the same blindness towards essentials as was evident in the case of his protégé.

*

Grand Duchess Stéphanie spent the first two months of 1850 in London at the invitation of Queen Victoria. The two women had met for the first time in the spring of 1845, and Stéphanie felt herself drawn to the liberal climate of the English court. Her stay at that time had been overshadowed by a report in an English newspaper that said that Kaspar Hauser was considered to be her son. Her senior lady-in-waiting, Sophie von Sturmfeder,[446] reported that the Grand Duchess had wept for three days and nights over it and had granted audiences to no-one during that time. Her cheeks had looked like 'raw meat' afterwards. It is not known whether Stéphanie and the Queen spoke about the Kaspar Hauser Question in 1845. It is likely that Stéphanie and Victoria first got to know each better in 1850, so that the Queen first learned in that year about the process of the tragedy. That was to have consequences in the Queen's mind. 'When Grand Duke Friedrich of Baden married Princess Luise of Prussia in 1856, Queen Victoria expressed her displeasure to King Wilhelm, later the first Emperor of the Second Reich (1871) that he should link his daughter with a family, one of whom was widely accused of murder.'[447]

The Grand Duchess's second visit to London was used by the London painter James Swinton for a bust portrait of Stéphanie. Two years later, it appeared as a copperplate engraving by Francis Hall with the inscription 'H.R.M. The Grand Dow. Stéphanie of Baden' (Fig. 184). Stéphanie and Stanhope met one last time on this occasion. She stayed at Claremont Palace—the model for the layout of the Wörlitz estate of the Prince of Anhalt-Dessau—southwest of London, which was also known to Philip Henry. In 1816 Prince Leopold of Saxe-Coburg had lived here (see pp. 143, 293); he had married the British Crown princess Charlotte Augusta, who died at the age of 21, after giving birth to her first (stillborn) child in 1817. Leopold left England in 1831 to become King of the Belgians. Claremont later became a place of refuge for the family of Louis Philippe, the King of France, who had moved in just two years before Stéphanie arrived. Like many others in February 1848, he had seen himself as having no choice but to abdicate and became an exile in England. Stanhope had known him and the former King's brother, the Comte d'Artois (ruled as King Charles X of France 1824–1830) since 1805.

At the end of January, in ice and snow, Stéphanie made the 60 kilometre journey to Chevening, where she stayed at least two days and a night under Stanhope's roof (Figs. 181, 182, 183). What could have been the reason for her visit? It is beyond doubt that more than ever she was at that time firmly convinced that in Kaspar Hauser she had lost her son. Now she was visiting the house of the man who not only disputed that but had also conducted one of the most scornful campaigns against Kaspar Hauser, branding him a fraudster and a suicide. To understand Stéphanie's visit to Stanhope requires some thought. Following her conversations with the Queen, was she hoping to gain further information about Kaspar Hauser precisely from the man most involved? Did she feel herself forced by her own certainty to speak to Stanhope of the insights and feelings that were alive within her and which had led her to quite another view of this still unclear question?

In a small gallery (Fig. 183) of pictures of prominent guests at Chevening hangs the portrait of the elderly Stéphanie with a dedication to Stanhope written in her own hand: 'Souvenir de Stéphanie'. Stanhope had it displayed and thus confirmed that Kaspar Hauser's mother had

181. Chevening House in Kent. View from the park. Present condition [late 1980s].

182. Chevening House. Hall with cantilever spiral staircase to the first floor.

183. Chevening House. Picture gallery, in which the portrait of the Grand Duchess Stéphanie also hangs (see also Fig. 184).

184. Chevening House. Picture of Grand Duchess Stéphanie of Baden. Etching by Francis Hall from a drawing by Swinton, London 1852. Below right, under Stéphanie's dedication of the etching for Philip Henry Stanhope: 'Souvenir de Stéphanie.'

been in Chevening; she had probably said to him what then still had to be said: that it was impossible that the foundling was what Stanhope made him out to be.

In other places in the house hang two of Kaspar Hauser's small paintings of flowers together with his visiting cards. On the back of both are the words: 'Painting and Visiting Card by the foundling Caspar Hauser: died under the knife of an assassin at Ansbach on the 17th December 1833'. It is very unlikely that Stanhope bought the gold-framed paintings (Figs. 185,186) with such an inscription. Were they also a present from Stéphanie?

*

At the age of 72 Philip Henry roused himself for his last journey, and crossed the Channel in August 1853. Via Basel, he went to Naples and Rome, where he stayed almost a month. On the return journey, in 1854, there was a notable long stay of 17 days (5–22 May) in Stuttgart. There, his *General Hymnal*, the product of his years in Dresden, where the first edition had appeared in 1815 under the barely disguised pseudonym of Lord Mahre, was to be published in a second, larger edition, a rebirth at the end of his life.

First, he tried his luck with Baron Cotta, the 'most distinguished and eminent publisher in Germany'. This could not have referred to the friend of Goethe and Schiller; 'the Napoleon of the booksellers' was long since dead. His son, Johann George (1796–1863), no less successful, was now head of the publishing firm. It was no wonder then, that the publisher did not especially warm to Stanhope's bigoted aphorisms and sought politely to send him on his way. The old fox turned to the tried and tested method of praising the work, prophesying a great success for it and recommending a colleague of his to the author.

'He said, after perusing it: *es enthält lauter vortreffliche Dinge* [It contains really excellent things], & he added that it would be very profitable to the Publisher and have an immense Sale. He recommended to me Hallberger ...'[448]

Discussions with his new publisher and the writing of the Foreword were quickly concluded. Stanhope added a sentence to his Introduction that, for those who knew him, was certainly necessary: 'The reader will not expect to find here my confession of faith, the development and representation of which would require a long treatise.'

185. Painting by Kaspar Hauser with his visiting card – from the possessions of Philip Henry Stanhope.

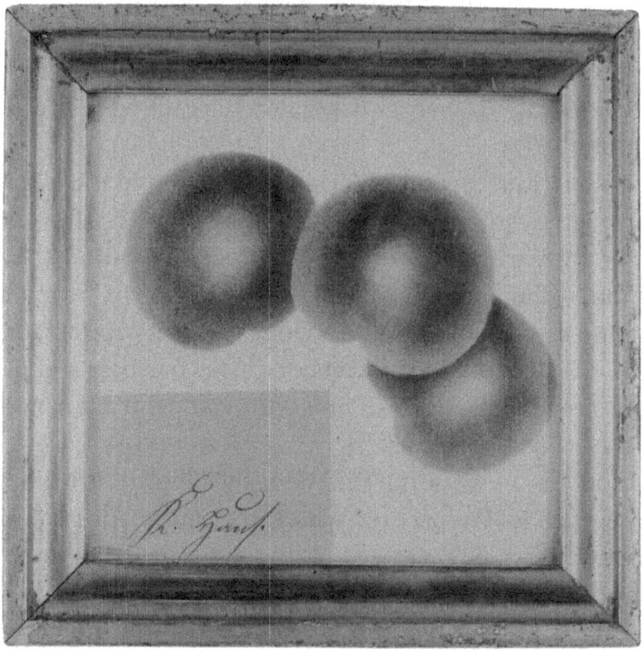

186. Painting by Kaspar Hauser with his visiting card – from the possessions of Philip Henry Stanhope.

One of the added texts, which was certainly not included in the Dresden edition of the then 34-year-old author, was to be found on the last page of the new edition:

When my eyes weep
And yearn for help
So I call out to you, the Lord.
O father, I commend
To you every wish of my soul,
You hear, you help, you bless...

Behind the sentimental tone lay to a great extent his own experience, and so there was truth to the image of 'the weeping eyes seeking for help'.

The manuscript then went to Halberger, who began production of the book 'on the same day'. They had quickly come to terms, as Philip Henry almost made him a present of the manuscript, the rights and the proceeds. 'I, the last undersigned, declare hereby that I make over, free of charge, to Herr Ludwig Wilhelm Halberger, book seller and printer of books in Stuttgart and to his heirs, the right in perpetuity to publish my "General Hymnal", which is to be published by him as his exclusive property. Given in Stuttgart, the 10th May under my signature and the seal of my family crest. Stanhope'.[449] Ten days later, the book was ready. Halberger listed it in his catalogue at a price of 70 pfennigs. (Fig. 187)

Before he left Stuttgart on 23rd May, it occurred to the old dog-lover to take a magnificent specimen home with him to Chevening. This time, unlike the earlier dozens of Spitz dogs, it would be 'a Dog like Löwe ["Lion"—the name of his old, current dog at Chevening—*Ed.*]' 'You are quite right in saying that a Dog is a great comfort to one who, like myself, lives much alone. I consider Dogs our best and most faithful friends, very far superior to most of those who are called Friends amongst the human species.'

With 'Lion', as he was now named, the final return journey first wended its way to Weinsberg, where the aged, almost blind Justinus Kerner (1786–1862) was living and who in that same year was bemoaning the death of his wife. Whether the meeting did not take place for this or other reasons is unknown. But Stanhope wanted to get to know the man who, in his magazine *Blätter aus Prevorst* ('News from Prevorst') in 1832 had published 'a word about Kaspar

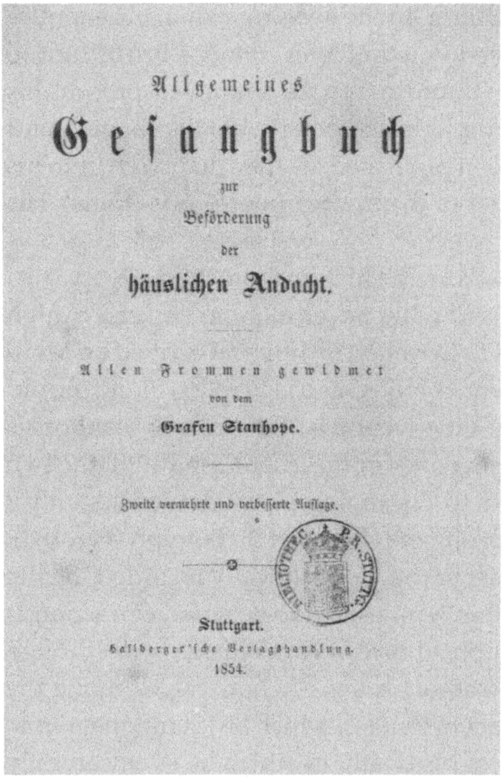

187. *Cover title: 'General Hymnal for the Promotion of Domestic Devotion'.*

Hauser', in which he wrote some of his own observations in relation to Daumer's 'Communications' (*Mitteilungen*) which supported the Nuremberger and contradicted the foster father. Most likely, the seer was little interested in the prospect of a meeting with the man who was so much the opposite of himself and who was possibly accompanied by Anton Heinrich with 'Lion' on the leash. The uneventful journey continued on to the old familiar Mannheim, where he took lodgings for the last time.

Arriving in Koblenz the weekend of the 26th, Philip Henry, who was now frail, had to rest for a week. Apparently, Dr. Soest, a doctor practising there not only made a strong personal impression on him but also rendered such firm medical assistance that remarkably, he was even remembered in his patient's will. He later received that 'walking stick with the golden knob, which Wieland had used for thirty years'. Dr. Soest wrote Stanhope another dozen rules for his health, above all relating to his diet, as well as many remedies for rheumatism.

A few days before he travelled on, Philip Henry saw Wessenberg once more and knew that it was their last meeting 'as I may never again have another opportunity of meeting him'. Wessenberg was on his way from Konstanz to Freiburg. In the evening, when his energies were flagging, 'he always gave to me in the evenings a broad hint to leave him, which I thought extraordinary'. As a farewell present his friend gave him a copy of his unpublished poems, but Stanhope found that they 'ought not to have been published, as they do no credit to his talents, & are, as far as I looked in them, very poor productions'. His time in Koblenz too was now over.

In Calais the carriage that had carried him on more than twenty trips through Germany was dispensed with, never more to be used. Anton Heinrich and his master sailed to Dover on 6th July and arrived on Monday the 10th in the county of Kent. A rented carriage rolled along the old road to London (which at that time went past the walls of Stanhope's estate) to the village of Chevening and for the last time brought the two old travellers, now grey-haired, to Chevening House, which lies only a few metres left of the road opposite the church of St. Botolph (Fig. 188).

The final reckoning of the last journey pedantically recorded 'on the continent 2338¾ miles'. That this ¾ miles had to be noted corresponds to a need that often makes its appearance only in old age and—though often it is a question of how well-off one is—is noticeable among the wealthy. It is the 'painfully exact manner in which he [Stanhope] wrote up his accounts until the day of his death, in which he even carefully noted the copper coins he paid for toys for the children'. Before his

188. The road from Chevening to London. Concealed behind the houses on the left is Chevening House. On the right is the church of St. Botolph with the Stanhope family chapel.

eyes closed for the last time, his letters and thoughts were concerned with his possessions and estates.

Apparently, he was increasingly troubled in the last months of his life with the question of how posterity would judge him and with what consequently would be written on his gravestone. Could he or did he not want to allow the family to speak for him, the family who obviously themselves had seen so little of him? For them he remained more or less as much of a riddle as he was for the servants in Chevening House and for the inhabitants of the small villages around Chevening who saw him coming and going, sometimes only after years had passed.

On one piece of paper is the last of a few previously self-composed inscriptions for his future gravestone. Only the date of death and the age are left out.[450]

SACRED TO THE MEMORY
OF
PHILIP HENRY, 4TH EARL OF STANHOPE
WHO DISCHARGED HIS PUBLIC DUTIES
WITH INTEGRITY AND INDEPENDENCE,
AND WHO IN PRIVATE LIFE
EMPLOYED HIS TIME AND TALENTS
ON OBJECTS OF PRACTICAL UTILITY,
AND ZEALOUSLY ENDEAVOURED TO PROMOTE
THE HAPPINESS AND WELFARE OF OTHERS.
HE DIED ....
AGED .....YEARS

These were his last affirmations. In composing this self-apotheosis, did his foster son come to mind, with whose happiness and welfare he had been entrusted by fate and even by law? Perhaps the unfortunate stood before his inner eye, and the inscription turned out so badly *because* of the insoluble contradiction. He made his last amendments and additions to his will too in these days. His servant Anton Heinrich especially was assured of a simple but carefree life.

*

Early in 1855 a heavy snowfall was followed by inhospitably rough weather, and on Friday 22nd February, in an unheated room adjoining the library, Philip Henry caught a bad cold. Since he had already not left the house for six weeks on account of the snow, with no appetite and with a high fever, he took himself to bed and on the advice of his family doctor, Mr. Adams from Sevenoaks, 'His Lordship's medical advisor' he took two grains of James powder three times every six hours. The next morning he called many times for 'lime flower tea, which is drunk very much in Germany' and afterwards felt so much better that he was able to read for two hours in the '*Fliegenden Blättern*' ['Flying Leaves'; a Munich weekly magazine of humour and satire published 1845–1944—*Ed.*].

After a temporary recovery, on 27th February, his servant George Dyer reported that he was suddenly in 'a most distressing condition' and coughing almost continuously, for which he was given blackcurrant syrup diluted in water. The doctor treating him 'felt uneasy about [his patient's] shortness of breath' and 'he always hoped that when his forces recovered, the symptoms would disappear'. As the illness worsened, the family doctor called for Dr. Paris to be summoned from London, who confirmed the seriousness of the situation and immediately notified Philip Henry's son, who found his father 'wan & weak but in excellent spirits'. Mahon was amazed at his father's cheerfulness, 'having so often seen him in very slight indispositions seriously contemplate & speak of the possible chances of an unfavourable issue. But Dr. Paris assured me that this diversity did not at all surprise him, having often observed it in his practice as distinguishing a slighter from a more serious illness.'[451]

The experienced doctor would be proved right. On the Tuesday night the patient's breathing became still more difficult, so that Heinrich had to sit his master in an armchair, where he tried to find rest until late on into the night. That Tuesday morning,* after a hard night, Philip Henry had thought he heard the sound of the bells of St. Botolph church at an unusual hour and imagined that he was being called. He had his green bound Bible brought to him, from which he apparently wanted to write something down 'with paper & pen for which he had asked, but finding his strength no longer sufficient, he put down the pen and closed the volume, saying: "I cannot do it now."'[452]

*In a letter of 3 March 1855 (now in the Stanhope family archives in Maidstone Kent), the day after Stanhope's death, his only surviving son, also named Philip Henry, who had become the new, 5th Earl Stanhope, wrote in a letter to his sister Wilhelmine informing her of their father's death, that the servant Dyer had later informed him that their father had 'fancied that he heard the church bells toll' (at an unusual time) on *Wednesday* morning. If so, that must have been very early in the morning, as Stanhope died at 1.45 a.m.—*Ed.*

His breathing difficulties returned and worsened as evening approached. After midnight, he was continually fighting for breath, and Heinrich and the young servant George Dyer had to take him to bed. Dyer kept watch alone through the night. 'Peacefully,' the family chronicle records, but 'with fear of hell', as the English historian Elizabeth Evans writes, the 4th Earl died on Wednesday, 2nd March 1855 at 1.45 in the morning at the age of 73 in his mansion at Chevening. The room in which he died, seen from the viewpoint of the main entrance to the house, is located in the room at the righthand corner of the first floor.

On 9th March, 'the mortal remains of the blessed, much mourned Earl Stanhope' were transferred to the small family chapel at St. Botolph's (Fig. 189, 191). In the morning, numerous inhabitants from the surrounding villages of Riverhead, Chipstead, Sevenoaks and Chevening came to experience the last passage of their mysterious Earl. Shops and houses in the area were closed, and suddenly, records the chronicler, it was as if the quietness of a Sunday had spread all around. At 12 noon the funeral procession set out from the mansion, and where

189. Chevening. St. Botolph. Funerary chapel. The second gravestone on the right of the entrance is that of Sarah Catherine Heinrich, and next to it on the right is that of Philip Henry Stanhope's servant Anton Heinrich (see also Fig. 193).

190. Stained glass window in the funerary chapel. In the upper right corner is the coat of arms of Philip Henry, 4th Earl Stanhope.

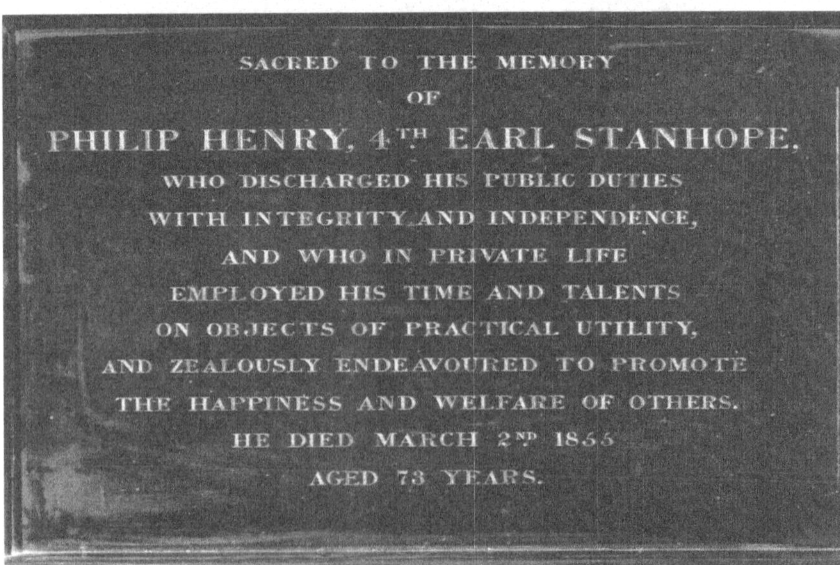

191. Chevening. St, Botolph, chapel. Grave plaque of Philip Henry, 4th Earl Stanhope.

192. Embossed letterhead (enlarged) of the letter of condolence from Anton Heinrich to Philip Henry, 5th Earl Stanhope.

it passed, 'there were many moist eyes and tears fell'. In the first group were the members of the family, following the coffin, and with them, his back deeply bowed, walked Anton Heinrich. At the door of the church, the Reverend T. Sykes awaited the arrival of the pallbearers. The coffin was lifted onto a catafalque in the middle of the nave, and the Reverend spoke the Gospel verses: 'I am the Resurrection and the Life' and 'I know that my Redeemer liveth'. 'Although the church was very crowded, the deepest silence reigned...'

The next day Anton Heinrich learned from the executor of the will how generously Philip Henry had provided for him in the event of his own death. He was to be paid two years' wages immediately and he received further from Philip Henry's son a golden scarf clasp 'which my father always wore' and a 16-volume edition of selected prose writings. In his will Philip Henry had added:

> My servant Anton Heinrich, who entered my service in 1816 and left behind his family and his friends in his country and who has throughout this long period comported himself to my greatest satisfaction and

> always with the deepest loyalty, honesty and zeal and who married a few years ago, is to receive an annual rent of £100, which is to be paid to him, without any deductions, from the income from my lands in the County of Devon for a period of 99 years, if he should live so long. The payments are to be made to him in advance in four regular instalments, and the first payment should follow within a month of my death.[453]

For another 99 years at the most, Heinrich was to be provided for. But who may fathom how deep was the bond of almost 40 years of life together, and how, after the passing of the one, all fell apart, and the streams of life and destiny suddenly dried up? Anton Heinrich could not or did not wish to go on and began to follow his master into death. In the same year, only four months later, he too died.

But who was Anton Heinrich?

There is only a single document in his hand, which in energetic and distinct strokes offers his condolences to the heir of Chevening. The letterhead carries the initials A.H. and above them a crown (Fig. 192).[454]

In an honourable place, before one enters the Stanhope family chapel from the graveyard side, the servant's grave was laid out near

193. Chevening. Graveyard at St. Botolph's church. Gravestone of Anton Heinrich (1792–1855)

the entrance (Fig. 193). Outside the door, but still in the closest proximity and near the gravestone of his own prematurely deceased daughter. On the tombstone of Anton Heinrich, almost illegible today[455], are the words:

Here lies
Mr. Anton Heinrich
A native of Germany
& during almost forty years
the loyal and attached servant
of
Earl Stanhope
by whom he was highly esteemed
and whom he survived
only four months
Died on the July 2nd 1855
aged 63 years

Also of Mehetabel
Widow of the above
Who departed this life
March 29th 1883
aged 82 years

16. 'I was a servant of events'

A 'trail of earthly days' (Goethe, *Faust II*) is the result of every biography. This is clearer in Stanhope's biography than in many others, but the cipher of *these* comings and goings reveals a background that is not easy to penetrate.

How and in what way were the predispositions of Stanhope's life laid out? By what inner laws did he achieve the results that led to the destiny that worked itself out so disastrously for Kaspar Hauser?

Let us consider first the foster father's philosophy of life. We shall look in vain for points of contact with the spirit of the age of Goethe, to the environment of Romanticism which, as far as we can see, Stanhope was able to reflect only sentimentally. He was just as fond of quiet cultural backwaters as he was of the superficial stories of August Lafontaine. Clear exceptions to this are his appreciation of Wieland, if it was genuine and not just a calculation arising from his situation in Dresden, which is more likely, and his interest in Raimund. Still less will one find a bridge to the spirit and content of German idealism. The fact that he was not German certainly releases him in a sense from such considerations. On the other hand, already as a young man he owned and read at least extracts of the works of Voltaire, as we know from a list of books he made in 1803. In Stanhope's youth, the Enlightenment was still the expression of the consciousness of the period, and he had related to that more emotionally, without wide reading. This opens up a first point of access to an understanding of the questions posed above.

'Nothing this man did,' wrote Daumer, 'is clear, simple or based on evident motives...'[456] What motives had Stanhope indicated? His supporters consider that it was first his spontaneous emotion in response to the blind fury of fate which had led him, a man of privilege, to the aid of one who had been robbed of his rights—it was the noble, conscientious motivation of a sympathetic soul. It became the 'noble lord' to trouble himself over the poorest of the poor.

But it was something else altogether that he desired and received. Hauser had to be *handed over* to him, and in these circumstances he committed himself to care for Hauser even beyond the grave. He had named no concrete reasons, motives or anything similar, and yet he did have such.

The hasty willingness of the Nuremberg authorities to release the foundling to him remains surprising and contradicts the preconditions which Stanhope had certainly not fulfilled. To help Hauser would have been possible even without the idea of an almost unconditional handover.[457] What would have been more natural than to renounce all conditions and provisos and become the selfless patron of this poor life?

But on top of everything it was an idea fixed in writing, a condition even, that everything was to be certified and correct *'as long as he remains as he is'*. And what was to happen if this precondition no longer applied—if Hauser were to become more mature, more grown up and more self-conscious? Had the clever contracting party already before the beginning of the enterprise here prepared the decisive precondition that would allow him to turn away from the affair when he wished?

Already after a few weeks it appeared that Kaspar was not remaining as he was. The angelic Kaspar thus became the 'fraud', the upright one became the liar, the murder became a suicide and to these accusations Stanhope added more in the course of time. Then followed the destruction of what from the outside seems like an insignificant life. But was that worth spending most of one's own life and not inconsiderable material resources to achieve? Surely not. And yet, in the way he interfered with Kaspar Hauser's life, Stanhope's biography reveals a vehemence that defies rational explanation. Let us therefore try once again to get at his intentions.

Essentially, there are two key points of personality the understanding of which can unlock the tragic relationship of Stanhope and Hauser. Daumer described the Kaspar Hauser Question as being one of belief, or faith, in the non-ecclesiastical sense, that is, his concept of belief/faith is held to be valid until further notice: 'When we look away,' says Daumer,

> from all the particular relationships and interests that obtain and are possible in the arguments around Kaspar Hauser, we can determine that its significance is that it represents the struggle between belief and unbelief. This, however, requires an explanation and an understanding. When things are put this way, one tends to think particularly only of religious and ecclesiastical positions and their oppositions and negations. This is not the point here; our cause does not concern this; the belief in Hauser, so to speak, appears completely independent of it and not for a single moment has anyone sought to introduce it into the issue... What I

> understand by *faith*, to state it positively at last, is the acknowledgement of what is unusual even if it contradicts what is generally accepted; the devotion to the facts which have been presented and can only be denied by violence; the deep and inner relationship in which things stand to one another; the acknowledgement of things which are not immediately obvious, not to be understood materially and mechanically and yet are true and real, but which the common materialistic understanding feels so antagonistic towards that it seeks to get rid of them at all costs and by any conceivable means. On this faith rests not only all religion but also all *culture* in the full human sense of the word; it is not just at the command of an outward regulation and authority, but a demand of *reason*, of genuine impartial *search for truth* and *science*; and if this does not succeed, then the path which mankind treads—in spite of all the outward benefits of technology, industry and its materialistic-rational direction and activity—will lead to barbarism and the destruction of the whole of man's being, to the loss of man's higher dignity, to the suffocation of all the more delicate and noble feelings of the human heart and of all the deeper insight of the human spirit, to an unbearable impoverishment of man's disposition and life and therefore to a general decay and dissolution, which may not be outwardly visible, but nonetheless is inwardly so, a result and outcome of the process which is recognisable in our time in the most dreadful and sufficiently threatening symptoms today.[458]

From this summary does Stanhope not stand out as the representative, in Daumer's sense, of the 'faithless', for whom rationalist activity at any price is required to set aside the extraordinary? Appeals to a 'higher being' would not make any impression on one to whom the very sphere of existence of this 'being' was foreign. Stanhope, as we have come to know him, was much more a spiritual forerunner of the Industrial Age or, to be more exact, those decades which after the 1848 Revolution, moved consciousness away from the spiritual impulses of German classicism. One such as Goethe, who saw in the coming age of machines the end of a whole epoch for humanity was incomprehensible for Stanhope. On the contrary, Stanhope enthused over his friend Sir George Cayley, the inventor of an unflyable flying machine the 'Aerodiphros', for which he foresaw a great future. 'I have for many years been of the opinion that aerial navigation is practicable and would be of great importance. It will be of inestimable advantage for the rapid conveyance of despatches, and the Government ought to purchase some immediately.'[459]

The invention of the sewing machine, which he already heard of in Dresden in 1815 drew similar comments: 'I do not need to mention the merits of such an invention, which would facilitate a general increase in the sewing of clothes, especially in England, where labour is so expensive.'[460]

That was already a new world, in which belief in Daumer's sense no longer had a place. Progress in this sense therefore found in Stanhope an advocate and a 'radical Reformer', as Lord John Russell referred to his fellow parliamentarian. Characteristically, however, that did not at all prevent Stanhope from adopting at the same time ultra-reactionary conservative positions. From one of Gentz's letters to Metternich we learn that Stanhope had in all earnestness expressed to Gentz that: 'If parliament, jury courts and the freedom of the press are not promptly done away with, England will be beyond saving and will go to the devil.'[461]

Almost directly opposed to this radical conservative worldview was a belief in progress just as radical. A bridging of the opposites or a connecting middle which could perhaps have created a compromise did not lie within his possibilities. Faced with Italian pictures of the Madonna 'consisting of martyrs, holy families, and annunciations', Philip Henry could only state that he found such images 'extraordinarily boring'. Milan Cathedral only drew from him sarcastic remarks. 'Opera means nothing to me...I am very bored there.' This aspect of his character comes most clearly to expression when he confesses: 'Also, I do not dance, I have no sense for what is called musicality.' The most unendurable of all cultural events for him were evening concerts, which he avoided whenever he could. The region of this foster father's heart seemed to be damaged.

That the gentle Hauser, the 'pure angelic being', who was felt to be 'the first human being from Paradise' was not experienced as such by his foster father is a fact of life which requires some thought. It makes one wonder how Stanhope was capable of such betrayal and how he could have adopted the position with regard to his foster son that he did.

Another point is why he entered into an undertaking, the outcome of which was at first certainly unclear but which evidently did not serve any good purpose. The graphologist M. Pulver, who calls him 'a latent criminal',[462] refers to this other problem area which could answer the question about the senseless motive of his actions despite all the external circumstances .

The external meaninglessness, however, did not necessarily imply a lack of inner motivation. This also touches on the question of the lodges. From what is known today about the activities of lodges in the 18th and 19th centuries, it can be assumed that within the widespread lodge network there were groups which had far-reaching political and cultural goals.

Daumer expressed what is meant here: 'One soon came to believe that Stanhope could be seen as an instrument of occult intrigues...and public opinion made him so especially responsible for everything that was secretly directed at his helpless protégé.'[463] That was not nor did it necessarily remain a question of his time. There have been examples in our own day in which certain people have been sacrificed in power struggles of a spiritual kind, because they have, correctly or not, been seen as suspected representatives of certain ideas or social aims. One does not ask after the murderers who, as a rule, cannot name any plausible motive, but rather after those who inspired them to the deed. Jakob Wassermann has one of them say in his novel: 'Hire the knife of a bravo...'[464]—the unfailing recipe as long as it is a matter of an ideological murder. That such initiatives today no longer need to proceed from lodges in the normal sense has nothing to do with it. When the effectiveness of certain people became too great, people who showed a capacity to change social relationships in new directions, their life was put in danger.

It is not necessary in connection with the theme of this study to pose any final questions about the appearance of Kaspar Hauser. His origin and the story of his effectiveness have created such a resonance even down to the present day that out of this fact alone the conclusion that something extraordinary occurred can be drawn. That this is so requires no further evidence than the more than 150 years of Kaspar Hauser research, and the comment of his opponents that the only thing that has kept the public's interest in him alive is the ever renewed occupation with him and his fate, is only unintended confirmation that his existence has been regarded as something extraordinary in each succeeding generation. For is the idea to be taken seriously that a historical process could be artificially maintained in the public mind if it did not contain the necessary substance? A countless number of people have achieved significant things in their time and thereby could be sure that they will be remembered, but they have experienced nothing comparable to what happened to Kaspar Hauser.

*

Hauser's life began in a family situation which perhaps would have opened up for him great possibilities but which at the same time threw him into the midst of a complex dynastic situation due to the sudden extinction of the male line. As the son of Stéphanie, he was counted a Napoleonid, but that was only one, even if the most important, point in the nexus of the discord between the two lines in the House of Zähringen, Bavaria's territorial dispute with the Grand Duchy of Baden, and the view of these facts shared by Metternich and Gentz. Kaspar Hauser's life thus shows itself to have been in danger from the beginning and indeed on several levels which at first glance appear to be unrelated to each other and which yet were so entangled that only a group of strong personalities could have steered through or around the many, almost inevitable conflicts. But such people were definitely lacking.

On what level did Hauser's relationship to Stanhope play out? And was Stanhope, as Wassermann put it, Metternich's paid agent who did not receive his commission to have Hauser disappear from the Chancellor himself but from another quarter before he began 'to become dangerous for us' and was given the instruction: 'Carry out the job thoroughly, or we shall not be served.'?[465]

That Stanhope grew up in a masonic tradition and became a lodge member himself in Dresden can be accepted. But, to press on to the most interesting question: was he a leading mind, operating on own initiative and by his own reckoning? That can, with reservations, be denied. Despite a penetrating intelligence, he had no deeper capacities or insights which would allow such a conclusion. His mental horizons ranged from banalities to the pomposity of common knowledge and nowhere reveal the contours of a great personality. Instead, he had characteristics that made activity in a social no-man's-land attractive for him. Generations had created the predisposition which only required an impulse to awaken the necessary preparedness and the instinctive alertness to the mystery of the case. Not only had unconscious tendencies 'to the mysterious' been inherited from his forefathers but also from that freemasonic family culture which had played a role at Chevening since the beginning of the 18th century. Thus, besides the two known lodge founders of the family, John and Philip Dormer Stanhope,[466] there was also especially Philip Henry's own father, who in his youth in Geneva first became acquainted with Freemasonry through another branch of the family that included the founders of lodges, namely the Hamiltons, and who chose for tutors to his children two men of the same spirit. Thus far were already laid the inner foundations for undertaking of a secretive kind, which can also be observed existing, though in a different way, in the life of his half-sister Hester, who lived in Lebanon waiting for the Duke of Reichstadt and later, it maay be assumed, for Kaspar Hauser. With this background, Stanhope was completely suited to grasp a historical constellation of the kind that lay before him and to make himself more or less consciously available for the settlement of pressing problems out of a yearning to be a participant in a significant historical episode. But how had he been able to embark on such a career?

Here too, with an amazing feeling for the truth, Wassermann may have come quite close when he wrote: 'He moved in the service of high masters and studied the murky mysteries of their antechamber... you are assured of our thanks; we give notice of our thanks with the sum of ... and the sum of...'[467]

There was no written contract, no notice of service, rather, he was a free agent acting on the basis of common interests. At that time, in a certain moment in his life—Dresden and Vienna 1815/16—he found himself in a kind of vacuum shortly before his 33rd year, when everything was open, but when inclination and a lust for adventure made him grasp a 'secret commission', the deeper meaning of which, it would appear, at first he did not realise in full consciousness. That is not to absolve him, but to characterise him and the situation. After that, he was fully and personally involved—enter the sophisticated and passionate 'fellow traveller'. Stanhope's actions nevertheless show him to be Kaspar Hauser's adversary personified. For through him alone, the ever-active one, everything was prepared so that it would be impossible to give to Hauser, who had in the meantime become a self-conscious adult, not only what was dynastically legitimate but also what could have been humanly justified for him in a higher sense. Solidly opposed to this from 1829 onwards, after the crimes against Hauser committed by others, stood his future foster father Stanhope.

Since there are no outer motives for this behaviour, a question remains as to inner ones. What did Stanhope see in Hauser and vice versa? As he lay dying, Hauser said: 'The monster was stronger than me.' I think he was referring to his foster father. Stanhope for his part called Hauser a cunning rogue, 'who was cleverer than all of us', who had 'seduced' him and others and had 'led them by the nose', a fraud and a suicide—positions which in their single-mindedness and accusatory force point beyond the two opponents. Like the mysterious representatives of two opposite poles, Hauser and Stanhope stand against each other, and the victory of the one in life is the defeat of the other in death.

*

In the midst of Kaspar's life's task—perhaps in the political arena, with certain possibilities for the transformation of the social life—obstacles stood in the path of 'Hauser the Crown prince'; the first was the unclarity surrounding his birth, but the second of which was essentially the work of one man.

The complications and dismantlements that Stanhope left behind him on the stage of history resulted from conspiracies which were perhaps impenetrable even to him, but for which he had held himself ready to serve without considering the final consequences. This made him act as he did. The obstruction of Kaspar's life was followed by his murder and finally, the attempt to blot out all memory of him. At this point—in terms of the obstruction—Stanhope in 1829 had taken over the baton in Hauser's biographical decline and through his deeds provided evidence for the significance of his 'opposition'.

This throws up a further question, the justification and necessity of which can give rise to differing viewpoints. Facts are the results of causes, the preconditions of which are of a spiritual nature. Determining causalities can therefore mean two things: finding causal links of a positivistic or metaphysical nature. The former are simpler to access. The latter by contrast risk being too speculative, without any illuminating connection to the facts. A thought of Friedrich Meinecke's agrees with such ideas; he remarks that

> History in general forces one to such actions that every attempt to deal with the stuff of history with exclusively causal means of cognition tempts one to violate the material and to blot out one causal explanation by another if it is carried through with a radical lack of modesty—but when it is undertaken in a mood of tactful modesty soon one must remain helpless before the substance of reality. Only an approach that is no longer purely scientific, that is, a path that is no longer purely causal, can take us one step further into the depths of history; it can indeed never quite reveal everything but an intuitive understanding of them, can make possible, can give us, through lively perception, an empathic feeling for those depths. Science needs to grasp such suprasensory

> means more where purely scientific methods fail rather than using such methods even in situations where their use must necessarily lead to false results.[468]

It is in this sense that at the end of this study of Philip Henry Stanhope, two aspects will be added to the picture gained of his biography—aspects which may remain open to question but which nonetheless open up an outlook worthy of consideration if they are examined without preconceptions.

The one results from his meeting with his teacher Crauford who tormented the boy from the age of 18 in unusual ways. This was the man of whom Hester wrote that he had her brother completely in his power and who began and ended his lessons with curses, who was with his pupil from early to late until he went to bed and even imposed his presence and sinister meditations on the boy's sleep, the man of whom finally even William Pitt warned. The 'villain' as Hester called him, and 'Chrystal Pate' as Mahon dubbed him, had been the first forcibly to imprint something on the boy's soul. The 'Scot' sought and achieved a disposition which—so it seems—had consequences for Mahon's later life.

The other aspect relates to an event of a comparable nature 13 years later in Sicily. Despite their apparent unconnectedness, these two key events—Crauford and Sicily—occupy a markedly significant position in the life of Stanhope. I shall first refer to a comment, only recently questioned but not contradicted, which comes from Count Ludwig Polzer-Hoditz and which he noted down following a conversation with Rudolf Steiner. As I have for a long time known of no counterarguments to the credibility of *the content* of the text, I shall cite it here in the form it was first made accessible to me by Peter Tradowsky from the literary estate of Polzer-Hoditz. The extract that is of interest here is as follows:

> .... South Germany should have become the new Grail Castle of the new Knights of the Grail and the cradle of future events. This spiritual ground had been well-prepared by all those personalities whom we know of as Goethe, Schiller, Hölderlin, Herder and others. Kaspar Hauser was to have gathered around him, as it were, all that existed in the spiritual ground thus prepared. But that was not wanted by those circles (the western lodges and the Jesuits). They could not tolerate a centre that was awakening to consciousness if they were not to relinquish their power

> and designs for power. A spirit such as Goethe's frightened them. Napoleon forced them to unite and form a league for the world domination to which they aspired in the spheres of ideology and commerce. Napoleon had already thwarted their efforts; it was he who fundamentally forced the two currents into an alliance.[469]

This spiritual-scientific communication of Rudolf Steiner's, repeated by Polzer-Hoditz from memory, will first simply be presented here without further elaboration but its connection to the theme of this study will become evident in what follows.

*

In the chapter headed 'Caltabelotta' in his book *Sicily—Island of Cain*,[470] Hans Gsänger considers the effects of the stream of Klingsor. After him, in Sicily '......an occult knowledge [was practised] that was to be carried over to the mainland of Europe'.

On the island the activities of this stream were concentrated around the castle of Caltabelotta, south of Palermo, which, as the crow flies, lies opposite Mount Gargano on the mainland, a site sacred to St. Michael. Caltabelotta 'was the stage for events which deeply affected the internal and external development of the West'.

Klingsor's activity has been dealt with in manifold and differentiated ways, for example by Wolfram von Eschenbach [in his *Parzival*] and by Novalis in *Heinrich von Ofterdingen*; he plays his role in 'The Battle of the Minstrels on the Wartburg' and in Richard Wagner's *Parzifal*. 'The legend of the Grail,' according to Gsänger, 'is no invention, no product of fantasy but the translation into grandiose images of a very real struggle of the Sicilian black magician against the Knights of the Round Table. It was not local history that was made in Caltabelotta but the history of the West.'

Rudolf Steiner refers to the historical figure of Klingsor in his lectures,[471] where, amongst other things, he mentions the fact that effects of Klingsor's Mysteries can still be observed on Sicily. In a lecture of 7th February 1913 and similarly in other places, he said: '...the soul must be strongly armed, even today, when it comes into the neighbourhood of those places from which can emanate all hostile influences related to the Mysteries of the Grail and the advancing evolution of humanity'.

Stanhope ventured into this neighbourhood not only without sufficient self-defences but also with prior weaknesses which had developed in him through Crauford. Gsänger concludes his researches about Caltabelotta with the thought 'that everything opposed to human progress came together in this place'. Such convictions are underpinned by the many facts which relate only to Sicily. It was the birthplace of the underground Society of the Carbonari,[472] also known as the 'Black League', and of the 'noble society', the Mafia, but even necromancers were active here who knew how to draw prophecies about the future from the dead. Certain people were killed for use in such oracles of the dead when the desired information was required from the possessor of a particular kind of consciousness. The notorious Cagliostro was a native of Palermo.

Stanhope arrived on the island and on 9th July 1812 suffered the seizure which he himself described (see p. 91). It is of note that the short fit that he experienced, accompanied by its dramatic symptoms, had no discernible medical effects. After the strong cramps, fearful screams, fear of death and loss of consciousness everything returned to normal, and Stanhope lived on without complications as before. The mere remembrance of the event continued to horrify him for a long time. Neither in his childhood nor in his youth had he ever suffered anything like it. There was therefore no predisposition towards it. The remarkable thing is that Philip Henry describes exactly what specialists today call 'a consciously experienced possession'. There are many such examples these days, and for psychotherapists and psychoanalysts the condition of conscious and unconscious possession is a precisely defined phenomenon. Philip Henry was fully aware of each stage of the process during the attack, whereas normally, experiences of this kind play themselves out more in the unconscious.

Vladimir Soloviev described something very similar in the 'Experience of the Abyss' of his 'Superman' who, 'having already passed his thirtieth year', makes 'cramped jumps, foaming at the mouth' and suddenly runs off into the night, and then falls to the ground, thrown backwards 'as if by an electric shock' and loses consciousness for a moment. 'Do your work in *your* name, not in mine' was the message given in this dark hour. Here too there is no question of medical effects or treatment. Soloviev goes on a little later: 'On the next day not only the great man's visitors but even his servants were astonished by his peculiar, so to speak inspired, appearance.'

A well-known and accepted contrary image is that of Saul on the road to Damascus. It is instructive in this regard to read Emil Bock's account of this.[473] Stanhope experienced near Palermo the exact opposite of what Saul experienced on the road to Damascus. Bock describes how this event struck like lightning and that Saul was admonished not just to consciousness but actually transformed to the very depths of his being. After that, Saul was 'another man'. This destiny did not affect him blindly—*he* was addressed by it, and it was to *his* person that the process that effected the change of consciousness was directed. It brought about his complete initiation, and Saul of Tarsus became Paul.

Such transformations occur mostly between the 30th and 33rd year of life, even if not always with this after-effect, and after prior spiritual and psychological preparation. Countless biographies underpin this fact; the middle of life calls for the step. We see this typically in Paul and in the opposite sense in Stanhope. Following preparation by his 'teacher', Stanhope suffered this consciousness-changing stroke of destiny in his 31st year which did not strike him 'blindly' and an initiation which served the powers 'opposed to human progress'. Stanhope experienced this 'preparation' on Sicily not only on the other side of thirty but notably in 1812, a few weeks before the birth of Kaspar Hauser on St. Michael's Day, which shows the opposing constellation already present in the circumstances of Hauser's birth. In 1813 Stanhope travels 'in haste' back to England; in 1814, at the age of 33, he goes to Dresden and has already been there for two years when, in 1816 in Vienna, he is confronted by the Kaspar Hauser problem. The confluence of two lines of destiny that began so far apart from each other could hardly have proceeded more rapidly. From then on he set himself to track down this individuality, who stood before him first as a Napoleonid, then as the heir to the throne of Baden and finally, as the foundling Kaspar Hauser, pursuing him until his early death—and beyond.

Notes

KA = Kent Archives, Maidstone.

TA = Tucher Archiv, Nuremberg.

1. Heinrich Boos, 'Geschichte der Freimaurerei. Ein Beitrag zur Kultur- und Literatur-Geschichte des 18. Jahrhunderts', Aarau 1906.
2 Ibid.
3. H.R. Calvert, 'The Scientific Work and Inventions of Charles 3rd Earl of Stanhope'. Lecture of 30 November 1953 before the British Society for the History of Science.
4. Philip Dormer Stanhope Earl of Chesterfield, 'Briefe an seinen Sohn Philip Stanhope über die anstrengende Kunst, ein Gentleman zu werden', Munich 1984.
4a. Cf. the very similar constellation in the chart of Adolf Hitler.
5. The Philadelphia Philosophic Society imagined 'the establishment of a republic of scholars spreading out over the whole Earth with its seat in Holland and which, for the good of all, would gradually take over political and economic power in states and set up an order of world peace based on justice. This social imagination, with its utopian goals, has been fruitful not only for the establishment of Freemasonry, but also for modern scientific academies, giving to natural sciences a home base which was often denied them by the old universities. It was precisely these academies that therefore played a significant role as centres of organisation for philosophers in the realm of the "philosophical conjuration" but they appeared—as the Spanish Father Joseph Torrubia already claimed in 1752—to represent disguised Freemasons' lodges'
   (Joh. Rogalla von Bieberstein, 'Die These von der Verschwörung 1776–1945', Frankfurt/Bern/Las Vegas 1978).
6. KA.
7. KA.
8. Eugen Lehnhoff, Oskar Posner, 'Internationales Feimaurerlexikon', Vienna, Munich 1932.
9. Ibid.
10. KA.
11. KA.
12. Allusion to Stanhope's sympathies for the new French constitution of 1795.
13. KA .
14. KA.
15. KA.
16. KA.
17. KA.
18. KA.
19. KA.
20. There was no intention at any time to visit the University of Göttingen, which is so often mentioned.
21. 'Erlangen, Geschichte der Stadt in Darstellung und Bilddokumenten'
   Published by Alfred Wendehorst with the cooperation of Gerhard Pfeiffer, Munich 1984.

22. KA.
23. KA.
24. KA (the entire correspondence Breyer—Jackson).
25. KA.
26. KA.
27. KA.
28. KA.
29. KA.
30. KA.
31. KA.
32. Frederick, Duke of York and Albany was received into the Britannic Lodge in 1787, was then a member of the Prince of Wales Lodge and was created Master of that Lodge by his brother the Duke of Sussex, Grand Master of British Freemasonry. In view of the connections which Hester also had to Freemasonry, it is not without interest to see her in the intimate circle of the Duke.
33. 'Politische Correspondenz Karl Friedrichs von Baden, 1783–1806, Vol. 4, Heidelberg 1906.
34. 'Politische Correspondenz Karl Friedrichs von Baden', Vol. 6. Supplementary volume, Heidelberg 1906.
35. Edmond Bapst, 'A la Conquête du Thrône de Bade', Paris 1930.
36. Ibid.
37. 'Politische Correspondenz', vol. 5.
38. Edmond Bapst, 'A la Conquête du Thrône de Bade', Paris 1930.
39. 'Denkwürdigkeiten des Markgrafen Wilhelm von Baden'. Vol. 1, 1792–1818. Heidelberg 1906.
40. KA.
41. Landgrave Karl of Hesse-Kassel also reports in his memoirs of the visit of Count St. Germain.
42. KA.
43. KA.
44. KA.
45. KA.
46. KA.
47. KA.
48. KA.
49. KA.
50. KA.
51. KA.
52. On the inner structure and goals of Weishaupt's Bavarian Order of Illuminati, R. Koselleck makes the following remarkable statements: 'Masons have nothing to do with politics directly, but they live according to a law that—when it is in force—makes a putsch superfluous. On the one hand, they keep themselves apart from the state, draw themselves away from rulership and form an indirect power that threatens sovereignty, but only morally. On the other hand, their virtue only ceases to be "a crime", that is, ceases to be a threat to the state, when they themselves and not the sovereign determine what is right and what is wrong.'

    Consequently, the rules of the Order were based on a claim to this moral position, which aimed at public influence.

    'Thus were the members of this secular confessional hierarchy formed under the leadership of their superiors into "useful co-workers", ripe for the highest purposes.

'The matadors of the Order declared that in respect of matters of state and religion, "we must (yet) be careful in the presence of beginners"'. Only after an inner probation were the true and actual goals of the Order revealed to the participants with the ongoing process of initiation. 'And at the end came complete insight into the politics and maxims of the Order. The higher council drew up the plans according to which the enemies of reason and humanity were to be gradually disposed of'.The Order of the Illumnati no longer strove, as had most lodges previously, to gain influence in exoteric ways with the support of princes, but rather, without them and against them, it sought to take sole rulership into its own hands.'

Such intentions required not only accurate insight into existing structures but also the corresponding plans together with the logistics needed to carry them out. Koselleck speaks of a real 'Operation Plan of the Ruler' which provides for a silent takeover of actual power. 'If the Order once possesses all the key positions—in Bavaria they reckoned on 600 members as sufficient—then it had the necessary strength and in a place where it wishes, it can be frightfully dangerous to those who do not go along.' The state comes to be steered from the inner moral realm, and thereby the rulership of freedom is assured. The Order then has 'nothing more to fear from the government, which rather, is now in its hands'.

Weishaupt certainly did not restrict his ideas to narrow regional claims but in a comprehensive sense, approached, at least ideologically, the often-ridiculed world conspiracy. In 'The Secret Brotherhood of the Illuminati. Enlightenment, Secrecy and Politics', in: *Freemasonry and Secret Brotherhoods*, published by Helmut Reinalter, Frankfurt 1983, Norbert Schindler writes 'Proceeding from the formation of the character of the individual member of the Order, Weishaupt drew up the organisational plan of an inter-subjective chain reaction of the Enlightenment which, directed through the Order's goal-oriented structural pyramid, would bring nearer the realisation [of the Enlightenment] in a moral rulership based not on authority but only on inner conviction: "A general moral regime must be introduced, a form of government which extends throughout the whole world, without dissolving civic links. Within this, all governments shall continue to operate and be able to do everything they wish, only they must not prevent the great aim from being realised, namely of making Good victorious again over Evil."'

As certainly as Weishaupt's Order of Illuminati captured the special position they sought in accordance with their conception and methodology, is it just as demonstrable that in numerous other connections something comparable was attained on a smaller scale with no less success.

A further example is the deliberate actions of the 'Breton Clubs', which exercised a not insignificant influence over the inner development of the French Revolution. First, W. Schmidt in his essay 'Elemente einer Theorie der politischen Konspiration im 18. Jahrhundert' (in Wolfenbüttler, *Studien zur Aufklärung* Vol. 5) seeks to outline the contours of the initial situation in order to be able to substantiate such calculated plots with some well-documented examples: 'Obviously, this conspiracy was not originally based on some prototype of the politically active secret society, as we know it in numerous forms from the 19th century. Its antecedents were doubtless to be found in all those types of discussion groups and social circles which we know from the second half of the 18th century: academies, reading and correspondence circles, coffee house societies, literary salons, clubs, freemasons' lodges, pansophic and occult associations, student brotherhoods and professors' groups, in short, all the societies of thought that were known to the age. None of these forms of organised sociability in themselves stood for political conspiracy. But every one of them could tend that way when the goals of sociability were linked to the specific need for political participation, whether in the form of a concrete striving for political influence or a share of power, or whether in the form of a general programme which envisaged a change of the structure of the state and society.' As absurd as the conspiracy thesis is in its claim to explain everything, as little should it be overlooked that in concrete situations during the course of the French Revolution decisions were made on the basis of conspiratorial activities: it is generally unknown that the declaration of the Third Estate on 17th June 1789 calling for a National Convention stems from the general staff-like planning of the so-called Breton Club, the club from which the Jacobin Club later emerged in autumn 1789. This Breton Club can perhaps be described as the first parliamentary inside-pressure group on the Continent.

Similarly, the famous storming of the Tuileries on 10th August 1792 was no spontaneous popular uprising but a very organised putsch led by a minority of Convention members in conspiratorial collaboration with the sans-culotte areas of Paris. In both these cases—17th June 1789 and the 10th August 1792—the deliberate aim was certainly to adapt the political circumstances to a new socio-economic structure that had already developed and also to the corresponding mentality of a particular section of the population.

Count Christian August von Haugwitz (1752–1831), Prussian Foreign Minister from 1792 addressed the origins of the Revolution. Himself a former high-grade Freemason who had leadership roles in Prussian, Russian and Polish lodges, Haugwitz wrote a memorandum on the question in 1822 in Verona, at the last of the European Congresses. In it he spoke in similar fashion about 'the insidious poison that seems to threaten mankind more than ever'. First to receive the memorandum was Friedrich von Gentz, secretary at the Congress, as he had been at Vienna, Paris, Aachen, Carlsbad, Troppau and Laibach. Amongst other things, Haugwitz wrote: 'The clandestine machinations, this insidious poison, and serpent's bite which seems to threaten mankind more than ever—these are what I feel called to look in the eye again at the end of my career. Their story stands in such a close relationship with the story of my own life that I can not refrain from raising these issues again and dealing with them here especially.[...] To rule the world—that was the goal of the one [group] with their money and of the other [group] with the all-powerful violence of the spirits. Their aim was to have the throne in their possession and the monarchs as their agents.It was in the year 1777, when I took over the leadership of part of the lodges in the state of Prussia and my office even extended to brethren scattered across Poland and Russia. If I had not experienced it myself, it would appear unbelievable to me today how governments could have been so careless as not to pay any attention to a terrible danger of this kind, which was really a state within the state. The heads did not only constantly exchange letters, using their secret codes, but met each other through their envoys. All stemmed from one and the same emblem but each party seemed to have its own goal. I have already indicated above what I made of it at that time. Later, I came to know another side of it. It was the playful way in which one talks to an infant. The goal was to exercise a ruling influence over throne and monarch [...] at that time I came to the firm conviction that what began in the year '88 and broke out soon after, in the French Revolution, the murder of the king with all its cruelties was not determined solely at that time but had been introduced earlier through associations, oath-swearing, etc. and had existed for God knows how long. My first move was to share all my discoveries and views with Friedrich Wilhelm [Prince of Prussia]. We came to the view that all masonic associations, from the lowest to those of the highest grades known to us were open to every impression, that religious feelings moved in tandem with criminal plans of every kind and that the former could even serve as a disguise for the latter. This conviction, which Friedrich Wilhelm shared with me entirely, led us to the firm decision to forego forever all participation and especially every [masonic] office, but it seemed advisable to the prince not to cut himself off from association with Masonry completely, as he saw the presence of good men in the lodges as a means to stem the influence of treason and to create harmless associations out of the gatherings that then existed. As king later, the prince followed the same path. I hope that there will be no more doubt that the secret network, which has existed for centuries and which threatens mankind perhaps more than ever, is no brain-spun fantasy, that it is real and has an ongoing existence. Cromwell and later Bonaparte knew the system of revolution. Both men used it for their own ends. We know the Tree of Corruption, but it has thousands and thousands of branches. It is easier to cut these off than to find the roots. That calls for more than a Herculean strength.'

53. Friedrich Wencker-Wildberg and Friedrich Kircheisen, 'Napoleon. Die Memoiren seines Lebens', Vienna/Hamburg/Zurich, undated.
54. A contemporary term for English secret agent. Hanover, ruled from Britain with which it was in personal union through the monarch, maintained no ambassadors of its own.
55. Golo Mann, 'Friedrich von Gentz', Zurich, Vienna 1947.
56. Ibid.
57. Ibid.
58. Ibid.
59. Ibid.
60. Ibid.
61. Friedrich Walter, 'Stéphanie Napoleon. Lebensweg und Weggenossen 1789–1860', Baden-Baden, undated.
62. KA.
63. KA.
64. KA.
65. KA.
66. KA.
67. KA.
68. KA.
69. KA.
70. KA.
71. KA.
72. KA.
73. KA.
74. KA.
75. KA.
76. KA.
77. KA.
78. KA.
79. KA.
80. KA.
81. KA.
82. KA.
83. H. Frielinghaus, 'Preussen und England vom Wiener Kongress bis zum Tode von Castlereagh 1822', Cologne 1936.

84. KA.

85. The library director Antonius van der Linde sought in vain during his lifetime to find this 'Hymnal' in a German library. Since he, like many before and after him, did not realise that Stanhope, like all firstborn males of the family, bore the name Mahon until the death of his father and therefore did not know that Philip Henry also thought it necessary at the time to publish under the pseudonym Lord Mahre, his bibliographical searches could not succeed. The correct citations for the publications of Stanhope mentioned by A.v.D.Linde are: 'Allgemeines Gesangbuch zur Beförderung der häuslichen Andacht', by Lord Mahre, Dresden 1814. Only in the second edition, which came out in Stuttgart in 1854, which von der Linde did not know, appear the words 'by Count Stanhope'.

The 'Gebetbuch für Gläubige und Ungläubige, für Christen und Nichtchristen' ['Prayerbook for Believers and Non-believers, for Christians and Non-Christians'], which was published in Leipzig in 1800, has been attributed to Stanhope by Wilhelm Kunze and other researchers, but cannot possibly have been written by him, as he was then 19 years old, spoke only English and was living under the strictest surveillance in Chevening.

86. Hermann Hettner, 'Geschichte der deutschen Literatur im 18. Jahrhundert', Berlin 1961.

87. KA.

88. KA.

89. H. Boos, 'Geschichte der Freimaurerei', Aarau 1906.

90. Example of a secret reading key (see below). Quoted from E.J. Lindner, 'Die königliche Kunst im Bild', Graz 1976.

91. 'Die Freimaurer-Korrespondenz Friedrich Ludwig Schröder—Friedrich Ludwig Wilhelm Meyer 1802–1816'. Selected and annotated by Herbert Schneider, Hamburg 1979.

92. Ibid.

93. KA.

94. KA.

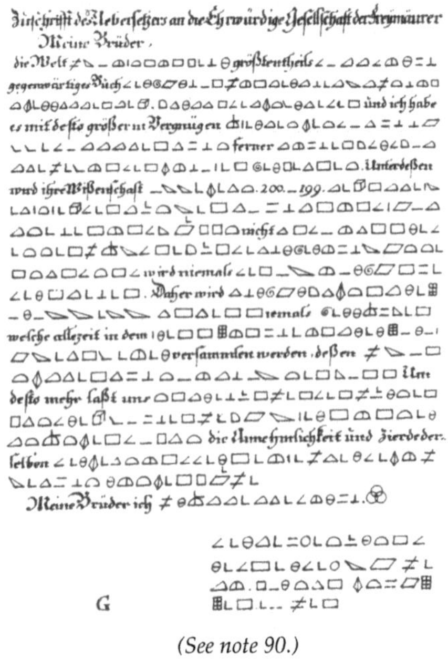

(See note 90.)

95. 'Dresden then and now', Frankfurt 1979.
96. KA.
97. KA.
98. KA.
99. KA.
100. KA.
101. KA.
102. Eduard Vehse, 'Geschichte der Höfe des Hauses Sachsens', Hamburg 1854.
103. KA.
104. See the Introduction to the 'Diaries' of Friedrich von Gentz, 1829–1831, published by August Fournier and Arnold Winckler, Zurich, Leipzig, Vienna, 1920, in which it is stated that dates in Gentz's older diaries were edited by Gentz in the mid–1820s.
105. The first meeting between Stanhope and Metternich, conjectured by F.Walter in his book *Stéphanie Napoleon* [see n. 61] on the basis of a note sent to Metternich by Gentz, took place before 1826. For example, already at the beginning of 1825, Gentz sent Stanhope an invitation to meet Metternich. Like Stanhope, Gentz destroyed all compromising pieces of written evidence. See 'Tagebücher der Fürstin Melanie Metternich' ['The Diaries of Princess Melanie Metternich']. Gentz himself confirms this; on 15th December 1831, he noted: 'Finally got round to revising my papers.'
106. Octave Aubrey writes in his book: *Die französische Revolution*: 'Whether one will or no, this boy is the centre point around whom everything turns. The revolution has him in its power as a hostage and can use him one day as a ransom. Among all the leaders in the different stages of the revolution there was not one who would not have looked upon this child as the main figure on the dangerous political chessboard—the figure one could not afford to let out of one's control. For all men of the age the future of the republic is highly uncertain and questionable, while the principle rooted in centuries past that was represented by this delicate little child's head is so strong that it must necessarily one day rise again.'

    That is the situation. The Committee of Public Safety wants to hold the son of Louis XVI in the interests of the republic, but Madrid's ambassador, d'Yriarte, conveyed to Barthélmy, the representative of France, the view of the Spanish court. 'If you will not hand them [the children] over to us and wish to go on with the war, you will have to slay every Spaniard before you find a single one who will not demand them [the children] from you.'

    Under no circumstances, however, would France hand over the children to the Spaniards yet pressed for peace all the more. In this situation the decision was made to do away with the children and have them 'officially' die. Spain can no longer make demands, and France is saved.

    The parallels of the case with that of Kaspar Hauser are of interest, because Joséphine certainly had more knowledge of the background and ramifications of the case than the historians of her day.

    What had happened? On the 3rd January 1794 the man who had guarded the Dauphin up to that point, the cobbler Simon, was suddenly relieved of his position without any explanation by decree of the Committee of Public Safety. No new appointment followed for the important post; supervision of the child was taken on for a short time by a continuously changing series of municipal officials. After 10 days the prisoner was put into a dark cell and further access to him was forbidden to any of the officials.

The necessary preconditions for his removal were thus arranged: Simon, who knew the boy well, was discharged, the officials who took over did indeed have the real son of Louis under their control, but since in the short time available, they had acquired no actual knowledge of the boy's personality, they could be of no use in the questions as to his identity that would soon follow. A month later, a child was found in the dark dirty cell who bore no similarity to the lively healthy child that Simon had handed over. 'He doesn't sleep, doesn't eat and has frightfully swollen knees.'

The child, who was significantly older, and burdened by an obvious backwardness in his development, made a painful impression: frail limbs, an upper body that was too short and that could not pass as the body of the Dauphin. The sight aroused the suspicions of Harmand de la Meuse, who was sent from the convent. The boy also seemed to be dumb.

Soon afterwards, he fell ill. The Dauphin's sister wants to see her brother, but this is strictly forbidden. The doctor on the case, Desault, is called away after a few days and dies shortly afterwards. The Desault family are certain that a child had been presented to the doctor that 'he had not recognised as the Dauphin'. This child had 'been half-mad', which was quite impossible for the other one, who had been given a royal education in all subjects.

On the 20th Parial the young prisoner dies after experiencing terrible cramps. The cause of death is kept secret until the following morning. An autopsy is carried out, and a report written that is not only highly inaccurate but which also, as in the case of the heir to the throne of Baden, concludes with the empty words: 'the effect of a persistent scrofulous affliction'. The deceased youngster is not identified by anyone who could have known him. His sister, as the most important witness after the cobbler Simon, has been held a floor lower and is not told at once that her 'brother' has suddenly died. Also, the servants Tison, Meunier and Baron—all of whom are held in the Temple and who would immediately have recognised the Dauphin, are kept away from events in the hours before the death. Only doctors and officials who have never had any relationship to Louis XVI's son now confirm his death against their consciences.

The burial of the 'false Louis' took place at the Sainte Marguerite cemetery in Charonne and immediately aroused royalists' suspicions. With the Restoration in 1816 the body was exhumed, which confirmed the deception that had been suspected from the beginning. There was no Louis XVII in the coffin. From the examination of the skull the boy, who had been autopsied after his death, was clearly recognised again, and from the length of the legs and the development of the teeth the experts concluded that: it is absolutely impossible that this skeleton is that of a boy of 10 years and a few months; it can only belong to a child of between 10 and 16.

*

The 'death of Louis XVII' is promptly communicated to the King of Spain, who is now the head of the Bourbon family; but at the same time, he has been robbed of his main means of pressure on the [French] National Convention.

France now presses for new negotiations, which are to take place in Basel, and receives on the 14th Thermidor the peace treaty which had become for it almost a matter of life or death.

The small number of those who actively participated in this state crime must have felt that their political future was now assured through the precautions they had taken. But the others—the members of the Committee—who knew what had happened in the Temple, must have been beset, as in the Kaspar Hauser Question, with the understandable concern about what had happened to the real Louis XVII and when and where he would turn up again. In the course of time several 'pretenders to the throne' did appear, but they were unable to make their claims credible. In Germany the best known case is that of Naundorff. In 1812 in Becêtre, however, one Jean-Marie Hervagault—who in the eyes of not a few French historians was actually the Dauphin—died in suspicious circumstances, and on his deathbed declared 'with a shattering power of conviction the truth of his testimony.'

107. Edmond Bapst, 'À la Conquête du Thrône du Bade', Paris, 1930.
108 Ibid.
109. 'The Emperor of Russia came to me in the course of the day; he was, I believe, 29 years old. Without doubt, the aura of power which surrounded him could blind one's judgement somewhat but like his many charming qualities and his outer appearance, it bestowed a splendour on his high position. He had a magnificent figure, an easy manner, an ingratiating gracefulness and a simplicity which appeared to have forgotten the rank to which the excellence of his person evoked at every moment. He was charming, even warm towards me and treated me just like his sister-in-law and thereby relieved the difficulty of such a situation for an 18 year-old.' (from Stéphanie's diary notes 'Pensées diverses', quoted from Rudolf Haas, *Stéphanie Napoleon*, Mannheim, 1976).
110. Edmond Bapst, 'À la Conquête du Thrône du Bade', Paris, 1930.
111. KA.
112. See Mayer/Tradowsky, 'Kaspar Hauser. Das Kind von Europa', Stuttgart 1984 which discusses the inadequacy of the statements of the French Kaspar Hauser researcher Jean Mistler with regard to the text and origin of the bottle message.
113. Aubrey Newman, 'The Stanhopes of Chevening. A Family Biography', London 1969.
114. Ibid.
115. Ibid.
116. Ibid.
117. Ibid.
118. KA.
119. The insight that the course of life shows such a rhythm comes from Rudolf Steiner. Diether Lauenstein ('Der Lebenslauf und seine Gesetze', Stuttgart 1974) confirms this with examples. For example: 'The drive to sacrifice comes with the second moon node, thus after 36 years. The first node frees the soul partly from the body; the second frees it from the social surroundings. But this liberation is normally felt as a battering. Fichte had to leave Jena at this time where had been more happily and strongly active than was granted him ever before or after. At this critical age Goethe was wise enough to escape to Italy. On his return he found himself estranged from his old circle of friends.'
120. KA.
121. KA.
122. KA.
123. KA.
124. The Kings of France in this period were: 1814/15–1824 Louis XVIII, formerly the Duke of Provence; 1824–1830 Charles X, formerly the Count of Artois; 1830–1848 Louis Philippe I, formerly the Duke of Orléans.

125. Hermann von Pückler-Muskau, 'Briefe eines Verstorbenen. Ein fragmentarisches Tagebuch aus England, Wales, Irland und Frankreich', Stuttgart 1830.

126. Friedrich Walter, 'Stéphanie Napoleon. Lebensweg und Weggenossen 1789–1860', Baden-Baden, undated.

127. K.A. Varnhagen von Ense, 'Denkwürdigkeiten des eigenen Lebens', Vols. 1–12, Leipzig 1871.

128. Prince Adalbert of Baden in: *Der Zwiebelturm*, Monthly Journal for the People of Bavaria and their Friends, 1951, Vols. 5 & 6.

129. In his work 'Kaspar Hauser. Eine Dokumentation' (Ansbach, 1966), Hermann Pies dealt most conclusively with the thesis of an exchange of babies. An essential precondition for this was the research of Fritz Klee ('Neue Beiträge zur Kaspar Hauser Forschung', Nuremberg 1929) which succeeded in providing documentary evidence for the exchange of the infants, and also G.F. Kolb, 'Kaspar Hauser' (Regensburg, 1883). Since nothing of importance has been found to contradict this research for a long time now, it can be concluded that despite numerous avowals that an exchange was an impossibility, it was in fact possible that such a crime had been committed. Otto Mittelstädt, the Imperial State Public Prosecutor commissioned by the House of Baden even sought to attribute crimes in which corpses and children were exchanged to the lower classes only. 'When,' he asked, 'has such a deed ever even been attempted under such circumstances against a reigning royal couple?' Karl Walker's 'Allgemeiner Volkswirtschafstlehre' (Leipzig, 1882, Vol. II) gives numerous examples of such cases, the list of which the author could have extended even for the period on which he was reporting. *Fideicommissum* bequests, which are indivisible in their legal format, contain a considerable number of exchanges for reasons of inherited succession by nurses, fathers, mothers and others with no claim to inheritance and consequently, a number of murders.

In the course of his researches Walker adduces the fact that: 33 princes fell to the hands of murderers; nearly half (14 = 42%) of that group were done away with by members of their own families, 7 (=21.2%) by members of the nobility and 5 (15.1%) by reigning incumbents. It is not enough merely to assert the alleged impossibility in the present case and also when, not just anyone, but high-ranking family members are blamed—to dismiss such cases as court gossip, as Hansmartin Schwarzmaier recently still tried to do in his contribution to the catalogue 'Baden-Württemberg im Zeitalter Napoleons' (Stuttgart 1987). Since crimes of whatever kind have to do not with social origin but with the state of mind that caused them, such objections count not in the least against the arguments raised by researchers from Feuerbach to Pies.

130. The title of the Stanhope speech reads: 'Substance of the speech of Earl Stanhope, in the House of Lords, May 16th, 1820', on his motion 'that a select committee be appointed to consider the practicability and the means of providing employment for the poor, especially in the manufacturing districts'. With notes. Together with his protest. London, J. Harding, 1820.

131. The Blittersdorf ministry was later held to have been reactionary and responsible for the loss of liberal freedoms. Amidst tempestuous cries of 'Away with Blittersdorf!', in the Baden Parliament, his removal was demanded and obtained. In his defence Blittersdorf wrote in the Foreword to his tract: 'From the File of Baron von Blittersdorf' (Mainz 1849): 'So I was held to be the incarnated expression of a system on which a general judgement was passed without any further proof! I belonged to those after whom men shouted "Crucify them!" without troubling to know if the verdict was guilty or innocent.'

132. A particular riddle is evident in Klara Hofer's book *The Destiny of a Soul—The Story of Kaspar Hauser*. On p.256 we read: 'From two completely unimpeachable directions I was informed at the last minute [i.e. just as the manuscript of her book was completed—Mayer] that a deceased imperial prince of middle Germany had revealed that during his lifetime the coffin of the heir to the throne of Baden who had allegedly died in 1812 had been opened and been found empty, from which a number of different conclusions could be drawn.' Confirmation of this information would still be possible today provided that the House of Baden's plan to cover over the grave with a layer of cement does not go ahead. The execution of this plan would amongst other things prevent the kind of ultimate clarification of the case by experts, which has been considered possible. Since the sarcophagi of the stated parents are also located there a confirmation of the blood group could not be ruled out.
133. Alexander von Sternberg, 'Erinnerungsblätter aus der Biedermaierzeit', Berlin 1919.
134. Eugen von Jagemann, 'Fünfundsiebzig Jahre des Erlebens und Erfahrens (1849–1924)', Heidelberg 1925.
135. General Schäffer's name crops up again later (1830) as a participant in the so-called 'State Council Meeting', at the beginning of which he arrested Major Hennenhofer, who was accused of carrying out a *coup d'état* by abducting the heir to the throne (Kaspar Hauser).
136. Heinrich v. Treitschke, 'Deutsche Geschichte im neunzehnten Jahrhundert', Vols. I–V, Leipzig 1927.
137. 'Politische Correspondenz Karl Friedrichs von Baden 1783–1806', Vol. IV, Heidelberg 1876.
138. KA.
139. K.A.Varnhagen von Ense, 'Denkwürdigkeiten des eigenen Lebens', Vols. 1–12, Leipzig, 1871.
140. KA.
141. K.A.Varnhagen von Ense, 'Denkwürdigkeiten des eigenen Lebens', Vols. 1–12, Leipzig, 1871.
142. Ibid.
143. Alfred Ritter von Arneth, 'Johann Freiherr von Wessenberg. Ein österreichischer Staatsmenn des neunzehnten Jahrhunderts', Vols I and II, Vienna and Leipzig 1898.
144. K.A.Varnhagen von Ense, 'Denkwürdigkeiten des eigenen Lebens', Vols. 1–12, Leipzig, 1871.
145. Ibid.
146. Heinrich v. Treitschke, 'Deutsche Geschichte im neunzehnten Jahrhundert', Vols. I–V, Leipzig 1927.
147. '900 Jahre Haus Württemberg', published by Robert Uhland, Stuttgart 1984.
148. Friedrich Walter, 'Stéphanie Napoleon. Lebensweg und Weggenossen 1789–1860', Baden-Baden, undated.
149. KA.
150. KA.
151. KA.
152. KA.
153. KA.
154. KA.
155. The following should be noted with regard to Müller and his story. Whether his assertions are inventions or based essentially on facts is no longer attestable. For

the Kaspar Hauser Question and Stanhope's actions the important thing is that the story was believed at the time, that contemporaries thought it credible and acted accordingly. Only the historical circumstances which provide information as to the conclusions, however inappropriate, that contemporaries saw necessary to draw are of interest, even if, from the perspective of the present day, the basis of judgement would have to be considered as insecure. Müller's statements however, moved the ministries of two states—from Emperor Franz to King Ludwig—and all their envoys into considerable activity and, as even today still seems to be the case, not without reason. See the State Archives in Vienna, Varia Baden, fol. 2–188 (PA VII 40).

156. E. Lehnhoff, 'Internationales Freimaurerlexikon'.
157. KA.
158. KA.
159. KA.
160. KA.
161. KA.
162. KA.
163. KA.
164. KA.
165. This behaviour is reminiscent of that of another family, which thought and acted similarly. The Hungarian Prince Tassilio Festetics de Tolna, a well-known personality in Baden in Stéphanie's time and a frequent guest at her pavilion, knew the story of Kaspar Hauser. His son's wife was born into the Hamilton family, and her mother Marie of Baden was one of Stéphanie's daughters. Festetics inherited Stéphanie's papers, among them those relating to Kaspar Hauser. Jacob Wassermann wrote to Hermann Pies on 10.2.1926: 'All the documents that could reveal everything at one blow are to be found as ever at the original home of the Festetics family in Hungary. As soon as the present prince, the 80-year-old head of the family, has passed on, I shall be the first to be given sight of them. Among those really in the know about the foundling's origins, there is no longer any doubt; the young Count Festetics says so about Kaspar Hauser when the topic comes up, quite uninhibited compared to his great-uncle. The late princess Mary Festetics was born a Hamilton whose mother was one of the daughters of Stéphanie of Baden.' The direct descendant Dr. Georg Prince Festetics de Tolna assured the author in 1984 in Vienna that in his family and among many of his relatives (e.g. the Prince of Monaco) the conviction that Hauser was the heir to the throne of Baden had always been widespread.
166. KA.
167. KA.
168. KA.
169. KA.
170. Some extracts that attest to the content and nature of the correspondence: '7.2.1828. Mylord! Your interesting letter of the 23rd reached me yesterday, 24 hours after my last one, and as another courier is to be sent this evening, I don't have time to write some lines today. You tell me My Lord, of a selection of questions you have relating to the political system of the Austrian cabinet, above all with regard to the oriental affair. All I can tell you is that I am awaiting these with real interest and that I shall reply with the openness and unbound trust that has always prevailed between us.'

'8.2.1828. Most Honoured Count, Your highly esteemed and instructive letters of the 19th and the 23rd January were delivered the day before yesterday. As the

Prince [Metternich] also and perhaps today wishes to send a courier to London, I shall not permit myself to enter into any detailed comments—.

'You will already have gathered from my last letter that I think more or less the same as yourself with respect to the result of the ministerial changes. As I know the individuals most affected rather well, I understand that matters *could not* reasonably have fallen out otherwise than they did. Amongst other things, I thank God that we are saved from the danger of seeing Lords Holland and Brougham in the Cabinet and that we shall no longer have among the Ministers Lord Lansdawne [*sic*] whom I shall not forgive for the abolition of the yeomanry. The attached letter in French will show you with what eagerness I have taken up everything you have written me in relation to Lord Ellenborough. You will note that his name is not mentioned therein, but that everything is so written as if the questions expected stemmed from you alone. I would like to receive the questions as soon as possible, I shall reply in French and hopefully to your complete satisfaction... It is unfortunately true that what one of your friends said appears to be only too well borne out, namely, if things go on this way, "only the actors change while the play remains the same."'

'15.3.1828.The main affair of the moment—for *us* at least—has been rather quiet for the last few weeks. In Constantinople the situation is hopeless; the error—not indeed dead but struck down and despondent. From St. Petersburg I hear virtually nothing, and from Paris only things that are repellent and contemptible to an unexampled degree. From London we have received in the report of the 24th of the month a (rather incomplete) summary of the explanations given by the English Ministry to the Russian ambassador. I have not yet had a really clear and decided report on it. And so far we must be satisfied with mere surmises as to how it will be received in St. Petersburg.

'In the dispatch that goes off today to London, our Cabinet expresses itself with resignation on the single possible measures that could prevent the outbreak of an unfortunate war, which at least will show that even with the firmness of our basic principles we can capitulate when nothing less than *the welfare of the world* is at risk. It would please me if Lord Strangford could read one of the memoranda I have written that belongs to the dispatch. Perhaps he could move Prince Esterhazy to communicate it to him in the closest confidence without, however, bringing *my* name into it. He would find again in the essay the ideas of which we spoke in detail the last time he was in Vienna.'

'5.5.1828. We have meanwhile received the text of the three replies which your government sent to Prince Lieven dated the 6th, 7th and 25th March. The three important texts, which I was ordered to translate into French, have stimulated in me a number of thoughts. I see clearly and fully the thinking, the aim of Lord Wellington and his friends. But to put as much as the direction of foreign affairs (and I would say the same for domestic) into the hands of the partisans of liberalism will only lead in England to a longer struggle between the opposing principles.'

'10.7.1828. Two couriers have just arrived without bringing me any news of you.It has been said here that you are thinking of coming to the Continent. Even this news, pleasant as it is, oppresses me deeply for should I not have had to be one of the first to be informed?'

'19.10.1828. At the same time the courier brought your very pleasing gift for Prince Metternich and me which we esteem highly on account both of its inner quality and of its modernity and curiosity. The Prince has asked me to convey his thanks to you most kindly.'

Incidentally, the exchange of letters did not always go so smoothly.

'2.12.1828. Neumann sent me the letter again which I addressed to you last winter, My Lord. I am assured that, by what fate I know not, this letter has made *a promenade in Brazil*!! However lapsed it may be, I would like you to read it and I do not hesitate to enclose it with the present letter. Mr Newman will therefore be the agent for our correspondence [...] the Prince, who has the highest opinion of you, has asked me to repeat this to you at every opportunity.'

171. KA.
172. K.A. Varnhagen von Ense, 'Denkwürdigkeiten des eigenen Lebens', Vols. 1–12, Leipzig 1871.
173. Michael Dirrigl, 'Ludwig I, König von Bayern', Munich 1980.
174. Alfred Ritter von Arneth, 'Johann Freiherr von Wessenberg. Ein österreichischer Staatsmann des neunzehnten Jahrhunderts', Vols. I & II, Vienna and Leipzig 1898.
175. Michael Dirrigl, 'Ludwig I, König von Bayern', Munich 1980.
176. Heinz Gollwitzer, 'Ludwig I von Bayern. Eine politische Biographie', Munich 1986.
177. Adolf Anton Lieb in: 'Nachrichtenblatt für die Mitglieder und Freunde des bayrischen Volksbundes "Treu-Bayern"', 1951, Nos. 10/11.
178. Ibid.
179. Michael Dirrigl, 'Ludwig I, König von Bayern', Munich 1980.
180. Ibid.
181. G. Friedrich Kolb, 'Kaspar Hauser. Ältere und neue Beiträge zur Aufhellung der Geschichte des Unglücklichen', Regensburg 1883.
182. Adolf Anton Lieb in: 'Nachrichtenblatt für die Mitglieder und Freunde des bayrischen Volksbundes "Treu-Bayern"', 1951, Nos. 10/11.
183. Ibid.
184. KA.
185. Adolf Anton Lieb in: 'Nachrichtenblatt für die Mitglieder und Freunde des bayrischen Volksbundes "Treu-Bayern"', 1951, Nos. 10/11.
186. Michael Dirrigl, 'Ludwig I, König von Bayern', Munich 1980.
187. Karl Birner in 'Volksfreund', Karlsruhe 25/26.1.1927. Publication of correspondence to the bank director Mördes, who passed Hennenhofer's letters on to Countess Langenstein:

    17 July 1837: 'For me it is just that people especially in Karlsruhe do not notice, for a "Royal Highness" had once said that I was always getting money from Mrs von Langenstein!. *But I deserved it for my service to the old Lord!'*

    22 December 1847: 'Because I can say with justified self-assurance that I served Grand Duke Ludwig more honestly, effectively, and unselfishly than almost anyone; that I was equally useful to him as in his capacity as regent and *father*; that I was the one who was there with him *as a man*, when God's representative, *conscience*, led him to make shocking revelations about his own conduct and about that of his father whom he otherwise esteemed so highly [...] and that I dealt with unpleasant discussions that were arising in the Blittersdorf cabinet about property etc [...] because I served through all this and more—of which I have evidence—I made my request!'
188. The complete text in the *Vossische Zeitung* of 2.12.1928 reads: .

    Kaspar Hauser's Genuineness.

    To the editors of the 'Vossische Zeitung'

    The letter titled 'Who Murdered Kaspar Hauser?' awakened youthful memories in me which I should like to share with you.

'Sometime in the year 1898 or 99 I went on a trip to Bavaria with my grandmother. We also went to Ansbach, and she told me something of Kaspar Hauser and his tragic story.

'My grandmother came from a Scottish family which was related to that other Scottish family from which the Countess Montijo stemmed, the mother of the later Empress Eugenie of France. They were not closely related, but the Empress always showed a friendly disposition towards my grandmother.

'At that time in Ansbach she told me that she had been with the Empress and the Emperor Napoleon [III] in Baden-Baden a few years before 1870.

'On that occasion someone in the company of the Emperor Napoleon had expressed his amazement that he could associate so cordially with the court at Karlsruhe even though it was surely known to him that the ruling family there had only come to the throne after the son of Grand Duchess Stéphanie had been abducted and finally murdered. Grand Duchess Stéphanie, née Beauharnais, was related to Emperor Napoleon III through his mother, Queen Hortense, who was also a Beauharnais.

'The Emperor replied, according to my grandmother at that time, that he was well acquainted with the abduction of the child, with Kaspar Hauser and his story and also about his mysterious death, better acquainted indeed perhaps than anyone, but that one could not hold the present members of the grand ducal house responsible for old crimes. They all suffered enough from the awareness that they had a murder to thank for the fact that they had climbed so high. The conversation then went on for a long time on the subject of Kaspar Hauser and all the various conjectures came up.

'The Emperor suddenly said: "No, much was quite different. I know that rather well, for the man who carried out the crime, a Major Ennendorf, sold me the most important documents relating to the case. I read them, sealed them, and locked them away. They are not to be used against the House of Baden."

'This Ennendorf may well be the same person as that Major Hennenhofer of whom Dr. Hermann Hieber speaks in his letter.

'The missing H at the beginning of the name may of course be explained by the fact that, as a Frenchman, the Emperor pronounced the name without an H, thus Ennendorfer [*sic.—Ed.*]. The ending "-hofer" must then have changed in my grandmother's memory to "-dorf".

'It therefore appears very likely that detailed documents relating to the case of Kaspar Hauser could be found in France.

'I also once heard or read something about that but I can no longer recall exactly what it actually was. If I am not mistaken, it was claimed somewhere that such documents would have to be in Brussels in the large Napoleon collection of Prince Victor Bonaparte.

'I have now heard here in Vienna that the Viennese Court was completely convinced of the genuineness of Kaspar Hauser and that no connections existed between the courts of Vienna and Karlsruhe for decades on account of this affair. *Franz Hobarth.*'

189. TA.
190. Ernst Eisenlohr, 'Die Thronfolgerechte der Cognaten in Baden', Heidelberg 1905.
191. Lore Schwarzmaier in: 'Zeitschrift für die Geschichte des Oberrheins', Vol. 134, Stuttgart 1986.
192. TA.
193. Lore Schwarzmaier in: 'Zeitschrift für die Geschichte des Oberrheins', Vol. 134, Stuttgart 1986.

194. KA.
195. KA (and all following notes).
196. The first performance took place in January 1831 titled 'King of the Alps and the Misanthrope'.
197. At the beginning of the 19th century there were three suburban theatres in Vienna: the 'Pimperl Theater' in Josefstadt, the 'Theater an der Wien', and, in Leopoldstadt, the 'Kasperl-Theater' mentioned here.
198. It cannot be excluded that the word 'Hesperus' may refer to Jean Paul's novel of the same name. 'Hesperus' appeared in 1793 and was the second piece of a trilogy, the first part of which, 'Die unsichtbare Loge' ['The Invisible Lodge'] had also appeared in 1793; the third part, 'Titan', followed in 1800.

In his very first novel, 'Die unsichtbare Loge', the hero, Gustav von Falckenberg, was kept for 10 years, at the instigation of his grandmother, a Herrenhuter [member of the Herrenhut Brotherhood, or Moravian Brethren, founded by Count Nikolaus Ludwig von Zinzendorf in 1722—*Ed.*] in underground room in a castle garden, where he was prepared for death by another member of the Moravian Brethren. One day he was told that he was now dead, but at the same time he was released from his confinement to go to the court of the Prince, where at first the youngster who had been estranged from life was unable to find his way in the complex relationships at court. Nevertheless, this unusual young man, who also had to undergo kidnap for many days, was eventually able to advance in his career to the rank of counsellor to a legation. Gustav, who had meanwhile himself become a member of an underground society, is arrested at a secret, meeting. The transgressor is to be trained by a secret brotherhood—the invisible lodge. Here the novel breaks off; Jean Paul himself speaks of his first novel as a 'broken ruin'.

In 'Hesperus' the reader meets a second, rather more mature Gustav. The apparent son of Lord Horion, Viktor by name, is in fact the son of the village priest Eymann, while his foster brother Flamin is actually the son of Prince Jenner von Flacksenfingen. Lord Horion, a freethinking Englishman, shows himself to be the protector and saviour of the princely son but ends up committing suicide despite the disentangling of these unhappy relationships, as he is in reality the secret *spiritus rector* of the intrigues. Jean Paul even puts himself into the plot in that he represents himself in the novel as the Prince's son, who acquires his knowledge of the confusing relationships from a message in a bottle.

In 'Titan' Prince Albano appears—a synthesis of Gustav and Viktor—who, after the deaths of his brother Luigi and his father Gaspard of Cesara powerfully enters into his princely inheritance. He is assisted by shadowy accomplices who strengthen him in his soul so that he is victorious over all his enemies. The freethinker Schoppe finally goes insane, while Roquairol, a self-indulgent hedonist, dissipates himself through his excesses and ends in self-destruction.
199. The above-mentioned letter reads: 'Dear friend, I am really happy to receive your welcome message that I shall meet Lord Stanhope here or in Baden. Herr von W.[essenberg] came back the day before yesterday from Ragatz, where he had not been so well. I shall see him today and I am sure he will be very glad at the news. He thinks very highly of the Count [Stanhope] with whom he is in correspondence. Warm greetings, Your Hennenhofer.'
200. In the course of investigations in the Lessing murder case—a duelling tragedy among March [1848] [political] refugees—correspondence was discovered between Hennenhofer and someone involved in the case. In his book *Kaspar*

Hauser. Old and New Contributions towards the Uncovering of the Story of the Unfortunate (Regensburg 1883), G.F. Kolb wrote as follows:

'These letters, 16 in all, all from the period 31 October 1834 to 5 December 1835 (earlier correspondence is missing) leave not the slightest doubt there was a relationship between Hennenhofer and Sailer that cannot be explained in any simple or natural way. Sailer was the one who had spread Garnier's pamphlet in Baden and elsewhere which directly accused Hennenhofer of the murder of Kaspar Hauser. And with such a man Hennenhofer carried on confidential correspondence; he interceded on Sailer's behalf on occasion with the governments of Baden and Württemberg and repeatedly gave him financial support yet he himself had no abundant resources with which to do this; rather, he even had to sell his library to extricate himself from his own pressing financial predicament. The writing of the letters was contrived in every expression and occasionally cautious, even anxious; none were signed (the authenticity of Hennenhofer's handwriting was clearly acknowledged by Hennenhofer himself at his examination by the Baden District Office at Ettenheim) and the addressee was continually urged to destroy the letters. If Sailer had often told his associates a long time before (in Alsace, Baden, Württemberg and finally in Switzerland) that Hennenhofer had promised him everything possible and how he had done this, so that he, Sailer, was behind the propagation of the old and the declared appearance of a new Garnier pamphlet on the Hauser affair, then, although the letters understandably contained only indirect indications, there can now no longer be any doubt of the correctness of the statement. But other statements of refugees, which had been regarded until then only with the most decided suspicion, were, they believed, confirmed by Sailer's statement: Hennenhofer, they said, had had in his time a secret meeting near Strasbourg with the propagator of the pamphlets which accused him of a treacherous murder (in order to buy his future silence); the deceased Grand Duke's favourite wrote, however, despite all his other caution, "what I said to you in the hut". In such a relationship, no-one would have anything to do with a man who has publicly denounced him as a treacherous murderer unless, driven by a bad conscience, it is to buy his silence. And thereby, in the case, Hennenhofer is not to be considered as acting only in his own name but is to be seen as repeatedly acting in the interests of the Baden government of the time. That government (which had otherwise acted so ruthlessly against its political opponents) had not merely allowed Sailer—who had been handed to them by the French police—to go completely unpunished, the former aide-de-camp of the Grand Duke could also assure this man that the government would even intercede for him with the foreign government of Württemberg; he could even promise to provide him with government money.' Furthermore, Kaspar Hauser gave a detailed description of a mysterious visit to him by two men, one of whom is not hard to recognise as Hennenhofer.

'About six weeks after the murder attempt two strange men visited me, one of whom had a very wicked expression on his face and had a moustache and black sidewhiskers, and he asked me what I was writing there, and I answered: my story, how I was treated in the cell and how the man had brought me to Nuremberg. One of them took it and read perhaps two pages; meanwhile the one with his black moustache asked me about all kinds of things, especially, whether I made a habit of going for walks; I answered, no, for my feet were hurting me then, and whether I was receiving instruction and what I was learning ... and I told him everything. Then he took my story and read it from beginning to end, and then they left and I accompanied them, as I did with everyone else, to the front door. But when I went through the door or down the steps with them, they asked me what this was, and I said it is a wooden storeroom and showed it to them; after I had shown them everything, I asked them where they were from. I received the answer that they were from faraway and that I would not know the place even were they to tell me, and so they went off. Written the 15th June in the house of President Feuerbach 1831.'

His contemporary, Countess Caroline von Albersdorf, who followed Stanhope wrote in her book about Kaspar Hauser in relation to those days and the two characters mentioned by Kaspar Hauser: 'Just at that time, a few days after the murder attempt, His Lordship arrived in Nuremberg for the first time with post-horses and his own carriage, which according to his own account, was somewhat in need of repair, and therefore necessitated a stay of a few days. The following day the two strange gentlemen mentioned in the first part stayed at the same hotel.These two gentlemen soon travelled on as did Lord Stanhope, but three days later the two men returned, stayed overnight at the same hotel and then again journeyed on—'.

201. Hermann Pies, 'Kaspar Hauser. Eine Dokumentation', Ansbach 1966.
202. KA.
203. Johann Sassenbach, 'Die Freimaurerei. Ihre Geschichte, Tätigkeit und innere Einrichtung', Berlin 1905.
204. Ibid. p.55: 'It has been proven that French Freemasons played a significant part in the popular uprisings of the years 1830 and 1848. Louis Philippe, who acceded to the French throne in 1830 was himself a Mason and the lodge had worked towards his advancement; it also contributed to his overthrow. Grand Master Cremieux stated in his lodge: "King Louis Philippe opposed the spirit of the nation; we masons overthrew him, and the one who [now] speaks to them closed behind the disinherited monarch the door of the carriage which carried him into exile."'
205. Egon Caesar Conte Corti, 'Aufstieg der Famile Rothschild', 1949.
206. In her dissertation 'The Ministry of Prince Ludwig von Oettingen-Wallerstein 1832–37' (Munich 1932), Valeria D. Csacsovszka makes clear the role played by the Kaspar Hauser Question in the politics of Baden: 'Cotta had amongst other things rendered special services in the complexities of the building up of the Customs Union [*Zollverein*] and it was through his mediation that on the 27th May 1829 a similarly effective commercial treaty with Prussia was signed, such as he had already brought about in 1828 between Bavaria and Württemberg. Bavaria did indeed at first strive to have Baden join the Bavaria-Württemberg league [...] but as long as King Ludwig pressed his demands for Baden territory, and as long as the riddling and mysterious appearance of [...] Kaspar Hauser [...] increased sensitivities on both sides, an understanding was inconceivable.'
207. G.F. Kolb, 'Kaspar Hauser. Ältere und neue Beiträge zur Aufhellung der Geschichte des Unglücklichen', Regensburg 1883.
208. Pies archives.
209. TA (notes of conversation by G. von Tucher).
209a 'I have never doubted that Kaspar Hauser was a disinherited prince; I only looked for him constantly and not without reason in quite other places than today after I read Linde's mistaken attempt to deny Hauser's princely origins completely. Linde guides us along the trail with much involuntary comedy and yet quite surely. I have now come to the full moral certainty that H. was a son of Stéphanie. This has not yet been proven judicially in public. Linde's speech, by the way, is not that of a cultured man apart from the fact that his emotional remarks which are devoid of all objectivity betrayed a man who was doomed from the start to lose his case before the forum of history. Ferdinand Adolf Gregorovius [1821–1891].'

210. Author's papers.

211. I am very grateful to Prof. Dr. Walther Peter Fuchs of Erlangen for bringing to my attention the correspondence between Kraus and v.d. Linde (Trier City Library).

212. I thank Prof. Dr. W.P. Fuchs of Erlangen for my comments in this note and notes 217 and 218. 'When Eugen v. Jagemann calls the "State Council Meeting" an audacious fabrication, then, formally speaking, he is correct. There is no State Council provided for in the Constitution of Baden and its administrative practice. The meeting of ministers with or without the chairmanship of the Grand Duke is called a "State Ministry". The "State Ministry", the meeting of the highest state authorities in Baden meets irregularly after agreement in a place determined case by case normally under the chairmanship of the "Minister of State"—only *one* Minister is expressly named as such; all other Ministers attend in their formal capacities as "Presidents" of their ministerial departments. If the Grand Duke calls a State Ministry, which happens only very rarely, he naturally takes the chair. Reports of these meetings are never made. As this was a constitutional monarchy, all decisions by the Grand Duke were ultimately recommendations formulated by the State Ministry, because every decree in the name of the ruler required the counter-signature of a Minister who could appeal to a decision of the State Ministry.'

It is contradictory why even Obser speaks of a 'State Council Meeting'. Apparently, it was a case of a customary turn of phrase. Since Obser confirms the meeting as such, Jagemann's objection is reduced to being one of misuse of a technical term.

213. With reference to Widmann's statement, Hermann Pies cast doubt on the authenticity of the Seybold document and paid no attention to it in his researches.

214. Jagemann incidentally used a proven method. When Joseph Heinrich Garnier, author of an 1831 text about Kaspar Hauser that the government of Baden sought to suppress with all means at its disposal, was arrested for the first time on account of it, he declared that 'he had dreamed up [...] the entire content of his text'. Garnier fled to England after his release, retracted his statement and once again was able to put pressure on the government of Baden, and particularly, Hennenhofer.

215. TA.

216. As a comparative example, a test of the style of the Seybold novel, which differs considerably in standard from Rüdt's style quoted in the text: 'Your Highness knows,' retorted Herr Sebastian quietly, 'that I am always silent when I see Your Highness in such a princely rage.'

That allowed Sebastian to remain because he was clever enough to maintain the highest civilities. 'Your Highness is frightening in your wrath that can shake body and soul. I would wish myself faraway in some wilderness and would rather fall into the claws of lions and tigers than stand before Your Highness when you are wrathful, for Your Highness's face then appears so fearfully majestic that one's skin may tremble, the breath die away in one's breast and the marrow freeze in one's bones, have mercy gracious Lord, but it is so, and the honourable old Bastian cannot lie, but must speak the pure naked truth as it is if he is not to incur Your Highness's greatest displeasure.'

'Oh, it is not so bad, you are just an old scaredy-cat!' said the prince, smiling with self-satisfaction and an inner contentment. 'I am not going to have your head even if I am a little angry.'

'Ah, you dear saviour, that means Your Highness is "a little angry" when every Christian must feel his heart tremble in love at the sight of you,' replied Sebastian in lamentable tones and clapped his hands together above his head.

'Now truly, what kind of life are you living? I would not be afraid even if the devil himself were to appear in front of me.'

'Yes, Your Highness and old Bastian, are two different beings. Your Highness knows no fear, as a lord, who, in many battles...' and so on.

217. '"State Councillors" in Baden were men who enjoyed the special confidence of the Grand Duke and were called on by him to give personal advice from time to time. They are neither mentioned in the state constitution nor in the "Court and State Handbooks" that were published at irregular intervals. They are not paid, do not belong to the official bureaucracy and do not even appear as a closed group' (Prof. Dr. W.P. Fuchs, Erlangen).

218. Further notes from Fuchs, Erlangen: 'It is probable that an extraordinary sitting of the highest state authorities took place in 1830 at the accession of the Heir Apparent. However, the meeting had nothing to do with the regular daily "State Council", as Obser later conceded. The themes mentioned in the hearings of Enggesser and Hennenhofer suggest an extraordinary night sitting that ended with the granting of Grand Duke Leopold's permission for a meeting of the State Ministry.

'The remark about the secretary Hacker suggests that the document was first written down long after the 30th March 1830. With regard to his alleged misappropriation, compare the letter of Duchess Alexandrine to her brother Grand Duke Friedrich.' (See p. 569, n.223a.).

219. Count Bogdan von Hutten-Czapski, 'Sechzig Jahre Politik und Gesellschaft', Vol. I, Berlin 1936. The complete extract reads:

'In autumn the following year I spent a few delightful weeks in Baden-Baden. I was often invited by Empress Augusta and by the Grand Duke and Duchess of Baden. I also remember very well a visit to the Duchess of Hamilton, one of the daughters of Grand Duchess Stéphanie of Baden. When I was alone with her at tea, she showed me the picture of a young man with the words: "This is Kaspar Hauser, my unfortunate brother. My mother and I were always convinced that he was my brother." In later years the Duchess repeatedly returned to this question and always answered it with the same certainty. The later General Adjutant von Chelius, my comrade in the Hussars, told me that his father, the old Court Legal Counsellor in Karlsruhe, had had in his library a whole shelf full of books about Kaspar Hauser and was kept very well informed by the reigning Grand Duke, but had always maintained the strictest silence about the case. Prince Chlodwig Hohenlohe once spoke about Kaspar Hauser when I was alone with him one evening. He told me that as a young man he had travelled from his father's castle Schloss Schillingsfürst to Ansbach, where Hauser lived and used to go for walks at specific times. His face had made the greatest impression on him. I told the prince that there was much to suggest that the Bavarian ambassador in Karlsruhe at the time knew much about Kaspar Hauser and had doubtless informed Munich. Hohenlohe regretted that as Minister President of Bavaria he had not had the relevant documents submitted to him. Now the matter would raise too great a sensation. I therefore gained no further insight into the details of the mystery, but on account of many conversations with personalities who were au fait with it and above all with Countess Stéphanie Tascher de la Pagerie, I became convinced that Kaspar Hauser had been the actual heir to the throne of Baden. The Countess, who had grown up at court in Mannheim and was well-acquainted with the affairs of the House of Baden, told me repeatedly that Grand Duchess Stéphanie had been ever more ruled by the idea as she got older that her son had been stolen from her and murdered.'

220. TA.

221. Unfortunately, the result of these long efforts are no longer extant. The Hauser papers, which had been collected and kept secret at the court in Karlsruhe were incinerated at the beginning of 1918 in view of the wartime situation. For more details, see W.P. Fuchs, 'Studien zu Grossherzog Friedrich I von Baden', to be published in the near future by the Commission for Historical Studies of the Land of Baden-Württemberg.
222. Adolf Bartning, 'Altes und Neues zur Kaspar-Hauser Frage'. From the literary estate of the deceased, published by Luise Bartning, Ansbach 1930.
223. Hans Sittenberger, 'Kaspar Hauser'. Der Findling von Nürnberg', Berlin 1925.
223a. I owe the warmest thanks to Prof. Dr. W.P.Fuchs, of Erlangen, for kindly allowing me sight of the manuscript of his chapter 'Kaspar Hauser'. See n.221.
224. KA.
225. TA.

The collection mentioned or used as a pretext, which Stanhope wanted to organise on Kaspar Hauser's behalf in England and for the sake of which he requested and was allowed sight of the official documents pertaining to the case, never took place.
226. TA.
227. KA.
228. Sternberg wrote in his 'Memoirs' that he had got to know Stanhope in Nuremberg in 1831 (n.133).
229. Municipal Archive, Ansbach.
230. Long known from the work of the Kaspar Hauser researcher A.Bartning was the description of the central device of the seal engraving, in which the serpent motif, however, was not mentioned. The reprint of the now missing letter (reproduced in the 'Dokumentation' by Mayer/Tradowsky, p.581) was likely incomplete, so that this detail could not be recognised. In high grade freemasony but also in the cultures of antiquity, this image, stemming from the wisdom of the Mysteries, stood for the final goal of all spiritual cultivation; in masonic symbology the image as such was seen as the beginning of a processional movement which had to be set in motion by contemplation. Whoever looked at the image without involving himself in the process that resulted from this contemplation did not get far on the path of initiation. The serpent that swallows itself from the other end, taking itself into itself again, was an expression of the self finding itself and returning to the Godhead. That is one meaning. Whether it was still so directly construed in the 19th century and with this background is questionable. Another meaning is more simple and corresponds to a popular turn of phrase. If one wanted to make clear the hopelessness of a situation, that a certain intention, a plan would not be fulfilled, because the serpent bites its own tail, then one made use of this image in this sense as a set phrase.

Interestingly, in his book 'Okkultes Logentum' ['The Occult Lodge'] Karl Heise notes that:

'In the final address it is stated how already since the year 929 BC there had been the plan to rule the world in accordance with the principles of the occult league (in 747 BC the spring equinox moved into the sign of the Ram [Aries], which for the masonic brothers was at the same time the significant and actual time when the city of Rome was founded) and according to the Freemason Br. Rebold, King Numa Pompilius set up "the first 131 Freemasons' Colleges", which were also called "brotherhoods".

'The serpent that swallows itself (bites its own tail) was a symbol of this occult rulership: the head represents the initiates; the tail represents the people of "the

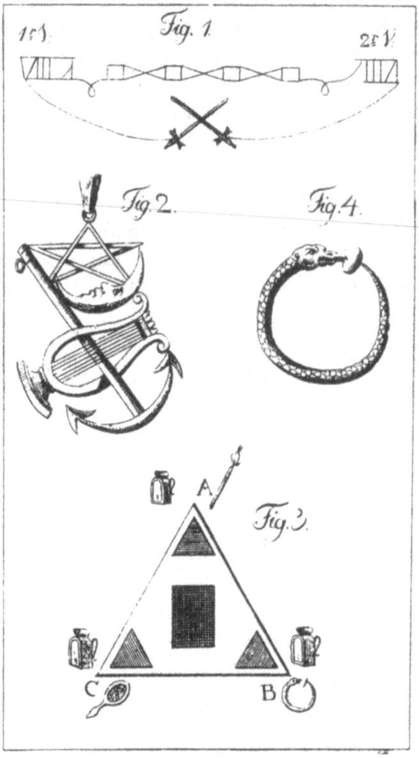

Fig. 1 shows the introduction of the candidates for initiation by both masters (today wardens) who hold their swords crossed. All are linked by a green cord. This comes from a Scottish Rite Lodge or a lodge of St Andrew. Fig. 2 is its insignia and Fig 4 its symbol: the snake with the egg. Fig. 3 represents the order of seating which the three brothers take up with the signalling lanterns. Outside the triangle are indicated the symbols which they carry (cited from Erich J.Lindner, 'Der königliche Kunst im Bild', [The Royal Art in Images] Graz 1976). Higher grades of the Mother Lodge Royal York for Friendship. From: The highest grades of the highly est. GR.M.L.R.Y.Z.FR. Berlin 1804, Joh.Wilh. Schmidt.

brothers". The path of the serpent or the brazen serpent itself consisted of nine stages, parts or "stations":

I. 429 BC, the culture of Greece until the death of Pericles, the Athenian statesman, the creator of the magnificent buildings of the acropolis;

II. the second stage in the rulership of the world lodge continued until the year 69 BC, the time of the Emperor Augustus, Roman culture;

III. the third stage—until the time of Charles V in 1552 and the rising of Duke Maurice against the Emperor in favour of Protestantism;

IV. the fourth stage of world rulership leads to Paris 1700–1793, the murder of Louis XVI and the unleashing of the Revolutionary Terror under the false slogan of liberty, equality, fraternity;

V. the stage of the world power of the lodge: British rule from 1814. Appropriation of all French colonies by Britain. Appropriation of the former Danish territory of Heligoland; the final removal of Napoleon by the Anglo-continental masonic conspiracy.'

231. 'La Fontaine's *Naturmensch und Sonderling* ['Natural Man and the Eccentric],' wrote H. Hettner, 'sees in the world nothing unnatural or foolish; in such a mood La Fontaine's family portraits, even when they raised themselves above thoughtless factory work, could only be only shallow satire or whining sermonising.'

232. Alexander von Sternberg, 'Memories of the Biedermeier Era', Berlin 1919.

233. KA.

234. 'Kaspar Hauser oder Andeutungen zur Enthüllung mancher Geheimnisse über Hausers Herkunft, die Ursache seiner Gefangenenhaltung und Ermordung', pub-

lished by W.C.Gr.A. (Dowager Countess Caroline von Albersdorf), Regensburg 1837; also, 'Kaspar Hauser oder die richtige Enthüllung der bisher unbekannten Geheimnisse...', Vols. I and 2, Munich 1839.

235. Part of the background to the so-called Haber scandal, which became a European sensation in the summer of 1834. It ended with a duel in the Forchheim Forest, two deaths and a third in a following duel and sparked off a storm of popular fury to which Haber's mansion finally fell victim. A crowd of 2000 laid siege to the mansion; there were antisemitic riots and calls of 'Hey! Hey! Jews out!' and finally to the devastation of the estate. Haber was expelled from Baden and in a subsequent criminal action against him sentenced to six months' imprisonment.

236. Note by Ludwig I, 22.3.1861, quoted by Adolf Anton Lieb in 'Nachrichtenblatt für die Mitglieder und Freunde des bayerischen Volksbundes Treu-Bayern', 1951, Nos. 10/11.

237. The well-known author of children's books Otfried Preussler is a descendant of the drawing teacher Preissler.

238. TA.

239. 'Biografie des Doktor Friedrich Wilhelm von Hoven, herausgegeben von einem seiner Freunde und Verehrer', Nuremberg 1840.

240. Ibid.

241. TA.

242. TA.

243. TA.

244. TA.

245. KA.

246. TA.

247. KA.

248. Ansbach municipal archives.

249. KA.

250. KA.

251. KA.

252. TA.

253. TA.

254. KA.

255. For a closer understanding of this characteristic, here is an extract from the graphological report of Dr. M. Pulver of Zurich:

'Even if we wish to make allowances for the Englishman's particular unclarities, as German was not his native language, as I see it, the unclear "R" is related to an unclear pronunciation of the lingual sound "R" so that there are still so many undeniably worrying issues left unresolved that we must see the writer as at least a latent criminal. I certainly think him capable of secretly committing or aiding and abetting a crime.

'The outward pose of an English lord with a conspicuous streak of theatrical vanity. Cool convictions are mixed with a predilection for what is correct and conventional. A tactician, a manoeuvrer, working with a discreet dissembling of facts and information, full of diplomatic falsities and disguises. Apparently open, yet a coldly calculating intriguer, he constantly gives out information in order to hush things up without being noticed. He tries to hide his irrepressible vehemence behind a mask of delicacy.

'Inwardly, completely torn, curt, sentimental and soft by turns, he lives in a fundamental self-contradiction. Love-hate is the typical expression of his soul configuration, which is made still more complex by his secret homoerotic tendencies. One must characterise him as a latent criminal, that is, as the secret supporter and promoter of crimes for which he will not be prosecuted. The murderous refinement of his vindictiveness is to be feared.'

256. KA.
257. KA.
258. KA.
259. KA.
260. Hans Pecht, 'Englands Stellung zur deutschen Einheit 1848–1850', Munich-Berlin 1925.
261. KA.
262. Ansbach municipal archives.
263. Ibid.
264. Ibid.
265. Stéphanie met the third wife of the Director of her Court Theatre, Eleonore Denuelle de la Plaigne (1787–1868) with some reservation, as she had earlier been in a relationship with her adoptive father Napoleon. From that liaison with the Emperor came a son Charles Leon (1806–1881). Did Stanhope approach Count Luxburg with the intention of gleaning information from his wife about Hauser's antecedents?.
266. Cf. Count Bogdan von Hutten-Czapski, 'Sechzig Jahre Politik und Gesellschaft', Vol. I, Berlin 1936.
267. Feuerbach recognises who is now threatened by the existence of Kaspar Hauser. 'The first court involved' was that of the last of the Zähringers, Ludwig. Everything we know today about the first murder attempt went back to him. The 'new dangers' stem from the 'first Hochbergs' who because of Kaspar Hauser were sitting on a very unsteady throne. The activities which led to the second murderous attack point consistently to Sophie of Baden.
268. Imperial Countess Luise Karoline von Hochberg, the second wife of Grand Duke Karl Friedrich of Baden.
269. The four children of the Countess are: Leopold (1790–1852) who ruled as Grand Duke from 1830 and had married Sophie of Sweden in 1818; Wilhelm (1792–1859); Amalie (1795–1869); Maximilian (1796–1882).
270. Grand Duchess Stéphanie of Baden, Kaspar Hauser's mother.
271. KA.
272. Statements of Hickel at the time of his questioning in December 1833.
273. 'Anselm Ritter von Feuerbach. Leben und Wirken. Aus seinen ungedruckten Briefen und Tagebüchern, Vorträgen und Denkschriften', published by his son Ludwig Feuerbach, Leipzig 1852.
274. Born on the 24th January 1764 in Königsbach im Oberamt Pforzheim as the son of a Baden parish priest, he went to the Karlsruhe Gymnasium school. He studied Theology in Jena and gained his first parish in Birkenfeld, the county town of the county of Sponheim in Baden's 'Siberia', the common territorial possession of Baden and Bavaria, over which the dispute between the houses of Zähringen [Baden] and Wittelsbach [Bavaria] had flared up. In 1791 Schmidt got to know the Crown prince Karl Ludwig and his children, Princess Karoline and her brother Prince Karl, later Grand Duke and Kaspar Hauser's father. In 1792 Karl Ludwig appointed the esteemed theologian minister at the Court Chapel in Karlsruhe. 'He (the Crown prince) remained until his death my honoured and beneficent patron,' Schmidt wrote in his memoirs. This position at Court and his confidential relationship with Princess Karoline was to determine his destiny.
275. C. J. Röpcke, 'Die Protestanten in Bayern', Munich 1972.
276. 'Blätter für bayerische Kirchengeschichte', Nos. 4,5,6,7,8, Rothenburg ob der Tauber 1888.

277. Some evidence only a few months older supports the closeness to the Kaspar Hauser Question. It comes from Hauser's teacher of religion H.J. Fuhrmann. He sent one of the first copies of his funeral oration, which had already appeared on the 22nd December 1833, to Schmidt with the dedication:

    His most worthy Magnificence.
    Herr Ministerial Counsellor and Minister to the Cabinet.
    Dr. von Schmidt.
    with the deepest respect of the author.
    [See also Fig. 161.]

278. Quoted from L. Feuerbach, 'Anselm Ritter von Feuerbach. Leben und Wirken. Aus seinen ungedruckten Briefen und Tagebüchern, Vorträgen und Denkschriften', Leipzig 1852. Complete copy in Hermann, 'Kaspar Hauser. Eine Dokumentation', Ansbach 1966, and Mayer/Tradowsky, 'Kaspar Hauser. Das Kind von Europa', Stuttgart 1984.
279. Prince Adalbert of Bavaria in: 'Der Zwiebelturm', Monatsschrift für das bayerische Volk und seine Freunde, 1951, Vols 5 and 6.
280. Ibid.
281. Ibid.
282. Ibid.
283. Ibid.
284. The existence of such a report was unknown for a long time. Where was Hickel's record kept? Was the document removed from Feuerbach's papers by an interested party after his unexpected death? Had the Court President had this report with him in Frankfurt when he had a last conversation with Klüber about the Kaspar Hauser case?
285. Feuerbach had apparently received concrete indications which went far beyond the suspicions expressed up to that point. At any rate, it must have concerned information which touched so centrally on the Kaspar Hauser that it did not appear advisable to Feuerbach 'without great danger' to commit to his letter.
286. Feuerbach never saw Stanhope again after his one stay in Nuremberg and Ansbach in 1831–32.
287. KA.
288. TA.
289. 'He is just right for this position at such an important moment', Metternich had written to the Emperor on the 19th September 1830. Metternich had chiefly impressed upon him the importance of two things on his way to England: to put a stop to the further spread of the revolutionary spirit in the Belgian provinces which had disturbed them so much following the July Revolution in neighbouring France, and to ensure that there be no weakening in the line of defence against France from the Rhine to the North Sea. With regard to the first point, everything possible must be done to prevent the victory of the revolutionary party.
290. TA.
291. Ansbach municipal archives.
292. KA.
293. KA.
294. KA.
295. The translation and publication of Feuerbach's book 'Beispiel eines Verbrechens am Seelenleben des Menschen', Ansbach 1832.
296. KA.
297. KA.
298. KA.

299. KA.

300. The lack of revealing documentation, confirmed and regretted by Prince Adalbert of Bavaria and Karl Obser, on Klüber's actual position on the Kaspar Hauser Question may be remedied by these letters to Stanhope. See also pp. 488, 398, 422 & 484.

301. KA.

302. That this was very possible was shown by the medical reports of Preu and Osterhausen, who on the basis of their findings had hit on this one sole possible cause. Lacking an extensive vocabulary at the time, Hauser was unable to clarify the matter. Also, at Pilsach he was able to move within narrow confines. The distance to the ceiling and the very small amount of light may have made it necessary for him to sit or lie down.

303. The present condition of Schloss Pilsach confirms Hauser's statements almost completely. The cell, which was hemmed in by outer walls partly over 2 metres thick was covered only by a light wooden ceiling. This fact explains without doubt the apparently contradictory acoustic phenomena Hauser described.

304. No-one had disputed that he could, within the very small range of words known to him. At this point, however, Stanhope wants to spread the idea that Hauser had given very reasonable answers and spoken well-connected sentences, which should prove that he was only deceitfully dissembling, which is completely contradicted, chiefly by Hiltel, Tucher, Daumer, Feuerbach, and the doctors Preu and Osterhausen. That Hauser's linguistic capabilities had been noted by two or three witnesses was a fabrication of Stanhope's.

305. KA.

306. KA.

307. KA.

308. Ansbach municipal archives.

309. Statement of Hauser's about Stanhope's letter to him: 'The other is nothing but uninteresting stuff. I know this already.'

310. KA.

311. Only the few sentences cited by A. van der Linde from this letter were known until recently. The full text reads: .

'22 Dec. 1832.

'I only received Your Excellency's honoured letter of 10 November with the enclosed letter from Count Stanhope, dated 6 October, on the 16th of the month.

'Since Your Excellency, in the interests of the family of Count St. regarding...? ... expressed to Kaspar Hauser against me, it would please me very much if I could succeed in persuading His Excellency to make some reassuring disclosures about that relationship. I would be very far from passing an unfavourable judgement that Count Stanhope, after his return to England, could have changed in any essentials the view of Kaspar Hauser which he had gained after long and most exact personal examination of all the circumstances of location and place, without some other factual circumstances having determined him to do so. *Guinio hominis, ut voluntas ambulatorem est usquam ad mortem* said an ancient Roman familiar with the ways of man. As I would like leave to allow such an alteration the respect it deserves, I have only a single query to add to the serious grounds I have for my own view of the matter which I have already summarised for the Count in my reply of the 2nd August this year. Let it be accepted with a certain probability that quite independent of his earlier history and of all differences of opinion about the consistent veracity of his statements is the incontestable fact that he found himself in Nuremberg in a situation of utter helplessness, in consideration of which the city authorities took on the responsibility to care for his maintenance and education until he was in a condition to provide the necessary . . . means for himself; that Count Stanhope completely on his own initiative took over this responsibility from the city through legal contract after long examination of the circumstances and after a struggle with the—[?]—guardian of the helpless [Kaspar] and took upon himself incontrovertibly the fact that Kaspar was still not in a position to provide the means for his own upkeep. Even were Lord Stanhope to have changed his mind completely about the veracity of the facts as related by Kaspar Hauser, or to have doubted them, or were he to have regretted entering upon his contractual obligations, or, which is scarcely to be believed, is reluctant to follow the inclination of his heart to this charitableness, he could nevertheless still now speak in terms merely of *fulfilling* the contractual obligations which he has undertaken.

'Added to this must be the fact that Kaspar has not in the slightest fashion made himself unworthy of the magnanimous charity of his new benefactor and rather, only does him honour. All observers are agreed that Kaspar has continually shown only the purest childlikeness of feeling and the highest degree of peaceful goodness without the slightest trace of pretension or mischievousness. Lord Stanhope has never spoken to me about this other than with delight. It is all the more understandable that the noble lord—?—where—?—as the eyes of the entire German people were earlier fixed on such a generous deed [Stanhope's assumption of guardianship—*Ed.*] they now therefore look forward to the certain fulfilment of the duty of education and have made it into a matter of honour.

'Abuse of the goodness of the noble Count who has taken on the role of father must not occur. To my knowledge, no-one has outdone the Count's own—?— No-one is expecting a glitteringly expensive education, on the contrary, such would be considered most unsuitable for the young man and detrimental to his welfare. All the good wishes of his friends and patrons are focused on the prospect of him being put in a position to earn his own upkeep as a useful, fruitful member of human society.'

312. KA.
313. KA.
314. Text of a statement by Hickel at his questioning in December 1833.
315. TA.
316. KA.
317. KA.
318. KA 'First draft:

'When I engaged to care for the maintenance and education of Kaspar Hauser, I stipulated no fixed sum nor was I required to set one for this purpose, and the reckoning must naturally be determined in accordance with other considerations and circumstances such as his behaviour and the large or small steps he makes in his studies. Even in the case of a father, who stands under a moral and religious, as well as a legal duty to support his children, the law does not require the sum to be set which is to be spent in such a case and leaves it to him to fix this sum, thereby supporting his control.'

'Second draft (extract, not sent):

'Sire, the condescension and friendliness with which Your Majesty graciously deigned to note the services I have rendered to Kaspar Hauser, give me to hope that I will be allowed, in all deference and humility to put before Your Majesty the following declaration. Following my indications the sum of 60 florins a month will be paid regularly every month in favour of Kaspar Hauser, who remains in Ansbach in order to pursue his studies and receive that instruction which appears indispensable for him, whatever the future prospects for his life may be. As I have undertaken constant duties with regard to him which I did to the relief of many, and after I showed on many occasions my zeal for his welfare, which I promoted with much effort, I learned with sorrow and surprise that my conduct has not been judged correctly, that an unjust and unfounded suspicion of me has arisen and that the Municipal Court in Nuremberg intends to demands that I stipulate a fixed sum for the period of Kaspar Hauser's life. As the Municipal Court acts in the name, and with the authority, of Your Majesty, I have the greatest respect for it, but if Your Majesty notices its proceedings in this particular case, you will, I am convinced, lend Your additional approval and agreement to this mistrust that is raised against me although my character and my conduct ought to instil trust. Your Majesty will allow me to note that if Kaspar Hauser receives a stipend from me, the amount of which cannot be altered by me in accordance with his conduct and which could then be made independent of my life, the duties which I would have to fulfil as a foster father would then be completely illusory and their exercise would lie outside my power. Under other engagements into which I entered was that of caring for his maintenance until my death, but without Your Majesty deigning to wish it, the Municipal Court ought not to demand from me that I make known the provisions for him in respect of my will.

'Your Majesty's wisdom and sense of justice will, I modestly hope and confidently expect, allow me to refuse to fulfil demands that are unjust and in themselves unreasonable, which from all viewpoints of this case would have to be regarded as an ungrateful reversal of my freely given services to Kaspar.

'Your Majesty will, I trust, forgive this request with forbearance and recognise the motives which have led me to put it present it for Your Majesty's gracious consideration.

'I am with the greatest respect.

'Your Majesty's most obedient, trusting and most devoted servant.

Stanhope'

319. TA.
320. Gustav Radbruch, 'Paul Johann Anselm Feuerbach. Ein Juristenleben', Vienna 1934.
321. Pies Archive.
322. KA.
323. TA.
324. Queen Elizabeth of Romania (Carmen Sylva), born Princess zu Wied, was convinced that Kaspar Hauser was the son of Grand Duke Karl. The mother of her husband (King Karl I of Romania) was the previous Princess Josephine of Baden (1813–1900), daughter of Grand Duchess Stéphanie von Baden. The Queen of Romania requested the picture by the painter Dora Hitz—daughter of the artist Johannes Hitz—who lived at the Romanian Court from 1878–1882 and created the frescoes at the Sinaia Castle near Bucharest. Johannes Hitz wrote to his daughter: 'With regard to Kaspar Hauser, it gives me satisfaction if my work pleases Her Royal Majesty and I shall try to give a faithful and true likeness.' It has often been noted that Kaspar Hauser again strongly changed towards the end of his life. Stanhope wrote to the Ansbach lithographer of the 'Royal Court of Appeal for the Rezat District' C.Oertal, the court artist in modern parlance, on 15 January 1834: 'Two weeks before his tragic end I suggested to Kaspar to have an etching of himself done on stone, because the earlier paintings of him which still exist no longer resemble him.' Oertal, who on account of his office, had very sharp powers of observation therefore regarded the well-known engravings and pictures as no longer comparable to how Hauser's face looked in December 1833.

325. Self-portrait of Dürer, 1493 (formerly Lemberg, Lubomiski Museum).

326. Cf. W. Zwalf, 'Buddhism Art and Faith', 1985 published by the British Museum Publications Limited for the Trustees of the British Museum and the British Library Board, Figs. 128,131,141,156,161,167,169,185.

327. KA.

(See note 326.)

328. KA.
329. KA.
330. TA.
331. Cf. Mayer/Tradowsky, 'Kaspar Hauser. Das Kind von Europa', Stuttgart 1984.
332. The drawing, from Hauser's own hand, is based on a subject by the Munich Court painter Joseph Stieler (1781–1858). As the drawing shows itself to be the wrong way round compared to the painting, it may have been a matter of traces of a popular reproduction of Stieler's painting, which was analogous to the size of Hauser's drawing (35 x 39 cm). Hauser reproduces the general composition and a few iconographic details but gives the work a more inward mood through his own small painstaking modifications, for instance, of the background, and the handling of the perspective has a charm typical of his artwork.

    The representation of a castle (upper left) appears to have been done without a model. It comes from his own imagination or memory and raises questions about the possible location. No convincing explanation has yet appeared. Perhaps the reproduction in this volume will lead to some indications.
333. Klara Hofer, 'Das Schicksal einer Seele. Die Geschichte von Kaspar Hauser', Nuremberg 1924.
334. Rudolf Haas, 'Stéphanie Napoleon', Mannheim 1976.
335. Mario Marquet, 'Geschwister, Marschälle, Minister. Die Spitzen des napoleonischen Reiches'. Vienna-Cologne-Graz 1983.
336. Marie Louise of Austria (1791–1847), Napoleon's second wife and mother of his only son, the Duke of Reichstadt.
337. KA.
338. Rudolf Haas, 'Stéphanie Napoleon', Mannheim 1976.
339. TA.
340. TA.

Queen Therese of Bavaria (left). Lithograph based on a painting by Joseph Stieler. Photo: Munich City Museum.
Therese, Queen of Bavaria. Lithograph by Schreiner. Photo: Munich, Bavaria.

341. Prince Philip zu Eulenburg-Hertefeld, 'Das Ende König Ludwigs II und andere Erlebnisse', Leipzig 1934.

'At the time of the tragedy in the Ansbach palace park in 1833, the Prime Minister Baron von Varnbüler* (the father of my friend Axel), who has recently died, found himself a student in Berlin.

'I was told by him personally when I once in Hemmingen turned the conversation to the unclear story of the unfortunate Caspar Hauser.

'In his student days at the beginning of the Christmas holidays the minister used to travel from Berlin to Hemmingen by coach; it always made a stop at the post station on the highway above Ansbach. Varnbüler used this time for a little walk in the ditches by a field where one could have a long view over towards the town and the palace garden. Suddenly, he saw a man running along a footpath partly hidden by the slopes in the direction of the highway and so quickly that it made Varnbüler think. The man had not seen him, as only Varnbüler's head protruded above the ditch.

'In the moment when the man came towards the ditch close by Varnbüler, he realised that he knew him but could not recall who he was. The man turned his head to the side and when he turned again towards Varnbüler, the expression on his face changed completely, whereupon the strange man ran towards a nearby village. Soon afterwards Varnbüler had to return to the post station to continue his journey to Stuttgart and Hemmingen.

'A few days later the newspapers were carrying the news which caused great commotion everywhere that the poor Caspar Hauser had been murdered in the palace park at Ansbach. Naturally enough, Varnbüler thought of the mysterious runner but always without being able to remember of whom his face reminded him. Only much later, when certain secret investigations into the [Hauser] case were revealed that named Captain von Hoinninger [actually Hennenhofer], did he suddenly realise that this had been the individual of whom the man running in Ansbach that day had reminded him. Varnbüler had often been in Karlsruhe, had seen the Captain several times there and even got to know the man fleetingly, who was generally avoided because of his character and the strange stories about him everywhere. He also remembered having heard that the man possessed great gifts of deception and disguise.'

342. His obituary that appeared in Freiburg, published by Herder in 1832:
'Letters to the Duke of Reichstadt from one of his friends' was, at Metternich's orders, only allowed to be published anonymously and begins with a sentence that uncovers something of the reality of the Duke's destiny: 'You desire, you expect from me a few words about the youth who departed so early, who was born, from the [union of] the daughter of the oldest imperial house and the most powerful man of the age, to the mightiest throne of Europe, who appeared through his birth to guarantee the hopes, the desires, the glory and the power of a new dynasty and with it the re-enlivening of the most important elements of order, and who, surviving the collapse of this throne and the destruction of the Empire, the exile and death of his father, the fall of his own family, poor in fact, rich in memories and hopes, broke like a flower in the middle of its blossoming, and expired like the last spark of a giant fire, like a bright star in the clouded sky.'

At the end, after a sensitive appraisal of his life, comes the apotheosis:

'You have returned home, noble Prince! The cradle and the grave treat you as king. I behold your father standing before the dark portal of the grave and

*Baron Axel von Varnbüler—until 1918 envoy of Württemberg in Berlin.

stretching out his arms to you in the bright land of freedom where all time is the present. I behold the great warriors of all peoples and ages greet you as one of their own, the uncountable crowds who history knows not who press towards you from light to light—the mighty heroes of Greece and Rome, the bold Phoenician, who amazed you so often and his great-hearted conqueror—the crowned forms of the Habsburgs, the worthy shadows of those who received the crowns of Germany and France at Aachen—Wallenstein and Gustavus Adolphus—Eugen and Frederick!—Step into your own company. There is a crown more splendid than all those made of gold and jewels. Who does not know from what it is made? You yourself wore it! Your unblemished image floats before us like that of a saint. History draws it on her purest pages.'

343. Prince Adalbert of Bavaria in: *Der Zwiebelturm*, Monthly Journal for the People of Bavaria and their Friends, 1951, Vols. 5 & 6.
344. Ibid.
345. Ibid.
346. Adolf Bartning, 'Altes und Neues zur Kaspar-Hauser-Frage'. From the literary estate of the deceased, published by Luise Bartning, Ansbach 1930.
347. 'The True Story of Kaspar Hauser. From Official Documents'. By the Duchess of Cleveland, London 1893.
348. Hermann Pies, 'Kaspar Hauser. Fälschungen, Falschmeldungen und Tendenzberichte', Ansbach 1973.
349. Prince Adalbert of Bavaria in: *Der Zwiebelturm*, Monthly Journal for the People of Bavaria and their Friends, 1951, Vols. 5 & 6.
350. Ibid.
351. When Prince Adalbert of Bavaria writes in his essay that 'The fact is, that King Ludwig is showing interest in Kaspar Hauser only now [December 1833] ...' and in other places: 'Thereby the assertion is contradicted that King Ludwig had known that Hauser was the rightful Grand Duke of Baden ...' (he means again the time before Hauser's murder), it is hard to credit.

Compare here the anonymous letter to Binder, which Feuerbach sent to King Ludwig in which Kaspar Hauser is indicated to be a prince of Baden. That was in

THE TRUE STORY

OF

KASPAR HAUSER

From Official Documents

BY

THE DUCHESS OF CLEVELAND

London
MACMILLAN AND CO.
AND NEW YORK
1893

All rights reserved

(See note 347.)

July 1828. Cf. also n. 206 which relates to the years 1828/29, and also Feuerbach's letter to the king of *8.4.1840*, in which he writes: 'the foundling is a princely son of the Grand Duke Carl of Baden and Stéphanie, who has been abducted, exchanged for another and set aside, and consequently, is no less a person than the—from this time on—actual Grand Duke of Baden'.

On 23.12.1831 Ludwig wrote to Stanhope a letter in his own hand about Kaspar Hauser (cf. n.258), which says, amongst other things, that Kaspar Hauser was 'certainly not born in that darkness in which he was placed by his enemies...' on which Stanhope comments *without contradiction* in his reply, which apparently did not exist in the Bavarian State Archive at the time: 'All circumstances of the case prove with incontrovertible clarity... that he [Kaspar Hauser] is of very high rank... and more than [a] subject' (cf. n. 259). And how is Feuerbach's formulation to be judged, which he writes to the Cabinet preacher von Schmidt (n.273): 'Confidence in the sacred royal word gives me a secure guarantee.' The 'royal word' could hardly stem from Karoline who could not give this of herself nor could guarantee the assured protection. Only Ludwig could give such a word, or at most his wife Therese in his place, but not the widow of the previous King of Bavaria. Feuerbach is therefore indicating Ludwig here who had probably recommended him to handle the matter with Karoline, which corresponds to the known position that Kaspar Hauser was not to be acknowledged *officially*. In 1834 King Ludwig maintained in his conversation with Stanhope that Hauser had been 'a well-disposed fellow'. It is improbable that Ludwig would have acquired this knowledge only a few days after Hauser's murder.

The assertion postulated above by Prince Adalbert can hardly be designated as 'fact'.

352. Prince Adalbert of Bavaria in: *Der Zwiebelturm*, Monthly Journal for the People of Bavaria and their Friends, 1951, Vols. 5 & 6.
353. KA.
354. Prince Adalbert of Bavaria in: *Der Zwiebelturm*, Monthly Journal for the People of Bavaria and their Friends, 1951, Vols. 5 & 6.
355. Ibid.
356. Ibid.
357. Alexander von Hohenlohe, 'Aus meinem Leben', Frankfurt 1925.
358. Prince Philip Eulenburg-Hertefeld, 'Das Ende König Ludwigs II und andere Erlebnisse', Leipzig 1934.
359. Prince Adalbert of Bavaria in: *Der Zwiebelturm*, Monthly Journal for the People of Bavaria and their Friends, 1951, Vols. 5 & 6.
360. Ibid.
361. Ibid.
362. Ibid.
363. Ibid.
364. KA.
365. KA.
366. KA. Stanhope keeps silent about the fact that he has already known for a whole month—from Hickel's letter of 18.12.1833—that 'Meyer, my opponent ... was himself in favour of the removal of the accompaniment' [by the police officers]. That is not at all unimportant, as Kaspar Hauser's teacher was in ongoing correspondence with Stanhope and was following Stanhope's instructions to the letter.
367. KA.
368. Prince Adalbert of Bavaria in: *Der Zwiebelturm*, Monthly Journal for the People of Bavaria and their Friends, 1951, Vols. 5 & 6.

369. Ibid.
370. Ibid.
371. KA.
372. KA.
373. Von Wessenig, Weickmann, Beck, Merk, Hacker, Lemarie, Wüst, Hüftlein, Blaimer, Hiltel, von Rumpler were all questioned again.
374. Referred to here is the shoemaker Beck, who was not questioned in 1829.
375. KA.
376. KA.
377. KA.
378. KA.
379. Hermann Pies,'Kaspar Hauser. Fälschungen, Falschmeldungen und Tendenzberichte', Ansbach 1973.
380. KA.
381. KA.
382. 'Caspar Hauser'. Manuscripts of Joseph Hickel, found after his death, published by Dr. Julius Meyer, Ansbach 1881.
383. Ibid.
384. Ibid.
385. Ibid.
386. Ibid.
387. Ibid.
388. Ibid.
389. Ibid.
390. TA.
391. KA.
392. KA.
393. KA.
394. KA.
395. KA.
396. Otto Flake, 'Kaspar Hauser. Ein Tatsachenbericht', Mannheim, undated (1949).

(See note 382.)

397. KA.
398. KA.
399. KA.
400. KA.
401. TA.
402. TA.
403. KA.
404. KA.
405. Gustav Radbruch, 'Paul Johann Anselm Feuerbach. Ein Juristenleben', Vienna 1934.
406. KA.
407. KA.
408. KA.
409. KA.
410. 'At the court of the intelligent and highly cultivated Grand Duchess Stéphanie in Mannheim, he [Mittermaier] was a constant guest and met there with diplomats in complete security.' (A. von Sternberg, 'Erinnerungsblätter aus der Biedermaierzeit', Berlin 1919).
411. KA.
412. KA.
413. KA.
414. KA.
415. KA.
416. KA.
417. KA.
418. KA.
419. Just as he had done in the *Jenaischen Literaturzeitung*, the tireless Lang had already taken sides—contrary to the truth—against the foundling's supporters in the 'Blättern für literarische Unterhaltung', which appeared in Leipzig on 4.1.1834, again with reference to the 21 contributions to the Kaspar Hauser Question.
420. KA.
421. KA.
422. TA.
423. KA.
424. KA.
425. KA.
426. All the following texts KA.
427. Stanhope's meeting with Wilhelm of Baden is described by Lore Schwarzmaier in 'Zeitschrift für die Geschichte des Oberrheins', Vol. 134 in which for the first time, at least the parts relating to Kaspar Hauser from the second part of the long unpublished 'Erinnerungen' [Memoirs] of Margrave Wilhelm of Baden (1819–1847) are quoted.

    It is noteworthy how Lore Schwarzmaier (Karlsruhe) attests to the credibility and objectivity of all the opponents of the prince theory and how, naturally, Merker, Stanhope, Lang and others are introduced as serious witnesses or interpreters without further question. From this perspective, memories and speculations become worthwhile sources, while Kolb, Welcker and others merely shared in general court gossip. The assassination attempt of 1828 is 'alleged' to have happened and the assurances of Margrave Wilhelm as to the impossibility of an exchange of infants is described as 'utterly reasonable' (see n.129). The Kaspar Hauser affair is therefore treated as a 'legend'.

428. *Karlsruher Unterhaltungsblatt*, 1835, Nos 7 & 8.
429. TA.
430. KA.
431. TA.
432. Ibid.
433. Nuremberg City Archive.
434. TA.
435. KA.
436. Photo of the missing letter (Pies archive).
437. KA.
438. KA.
439. G.F. Daumer,'Kaspar Hauser. Sein Wesen, seine Unschuld, seine Erduldungen und sein Ursprung', Regensburg 1873.
440. KA.
441. KA.
442. KA.
443. The 'Neue allgemeine Deutsche Adelslexikon' by Heinrich Netschke, Leipzig 1859–1870 includes a Court Counsellor J. G. v. Heinrich (†1831) who is listed as belonging to the Saxon nobility. 'But in the many pieces of information available to the editors on Saxon ennoblements and elevations in the peerage there is no indication of a corresponding certificate.' There is no evidence that Heinrich was a member of this family (see n. 454).
444. Diaries of Sylvester Douglas Lord Glenbervie, London 1928.
445. KA.
446. TA.
447. Friedrich Welcker-Wildberg, 'Rätsel der Weltgeschichte', Berlin 1944.
448. KA.
449. KA.
450. KA.
451. KA.
452. KA.
453. KA.
454. By the use of a crown above his initials Anton Heinrich points to a social position that is not easy to understand. Situated in heraldic terms between a king's crown and a duke's hat, it corresponds to no known correct form; an earl's, baron's or other noble's crowns, which are defined by the number of their pearls, are therefore ruled out in this case. Yet Stanhope tolerated the use on the letterheads of his servant (a fact in itself most unusual), an attribute that was reserved only for the aristocracy or nobility. It is unlikely that Heinrich allowed himself this presumption, so a possible conclusion would appear to be that he was entitled to use the stylised device. It is possible that he had been an illegitimate child from the circle of the numerous demonstrable royal offspring at the Saxon court.
455. The existence of the gravestone at Chevening was also unknown to the vicar of St. Botolph's. As an interment at the cemetery was likely, the attempt was made on all the weather-beaten gravestones to decipher the passages of text, the legibility of which could actually be made out. Selection resulted in the indication of the gravestone which revealed itself to be the one that was sought. Work on the surface of the stone under suitable conditions of light brought the text out to the point where the words could be deciphered.
456. G.F.Daumer, 'Kaspar Hauser. Sein Wesen, seine Unschuld, seine Erduldungen und sein Ursprung', Regensburg 1873.

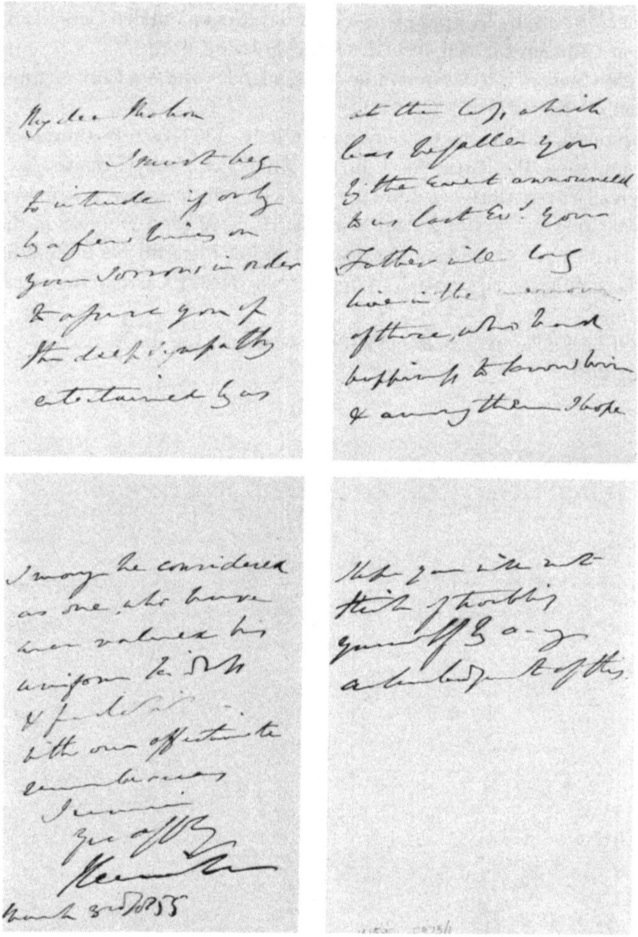
My dear Mahon
I must beg to intrude if only by a few lines on your sorrows in order to assure you of the deep sympathy entertained by us at the loss, which has befallen you by the event announced to us last Ev.g Your Father will long live in the memory of those, who had happiness to know him & among them I hope I may be considered as one, who have ever valued his uniform kindness & friendship with our affectionate remembrances I remain Yrs affly [signature]
March 3rd 1855

I hope you will not think of troubling yourself by any acknowledgment of this.

457. Cf. the letter of 21.12.1831, n. 294. *Letter of Condolence from Anton Heinrich (n. 454), Kent Archives, Maidstone.* (Facsimiles above.)

458. G.F.Daumer, 'Kaspar Hauser. Sein Wesen, seine Unschuld, seine Erduldungen und sein Ursprung', Regensburg 1873.

459. KA.

460. KA.

461. Friedrich Walter, 'Stéphanie Napoleon. Lebensweg und Weggenossen 1789–1860', Baden-Baden, undated.

462. Cf. n.255.

463. G.F.Daumer, 'Enthüllungen über Kaspar Hauser', Frankfurt 1859.

464. Jakob Wassermann, 'Caspar Hauser oder die Trägheit des Herzens', Stuttgart-Leipzig 1908.

465. Ibid.

466. Philip Dormer, Earl of Chesterfield, 'Briefe an seinen Sohn Philip Stanhope über die anstrengende Kunst, ein Gentleman zu werden', Munich 1981.

467. Jakob Wassermann, 'Caspar Hauser oder die Trägheit des Herzens', Stuttgart-Leipzig 1908.

468. Friedrich Meinecke, 'Zur theorie und Philosophie der Geschichte', Stuttgart 1959.

469. Peter Tradowsky, 'Kaspar Hauser oder das Ringen um den Geist', Dornach 1960.
470. Hans Gsänger, 'Sizilien, Insel des Kain', Freiburg 1968.
471. Rudolf Steiner, 'Die Mysteriendes Morgenlandes und des Christentums', Dornach 1960, (Collected Works GA 144).
472. Carbonari, Italian secret society, mainly active 1800–1820. Its third and final grade of initiation, the 'Great Elect' or the 'Knight of Thebes', demanded an oath to be ready to sacrifice one's life for the victory of the cause, if necessary. The Laibach Congress occupied itself with the rising of the Carbonari in the Kingdom of Naples in 1820 against Ferdinand I and at Metternich's urging, the rebellion was completely suppressed. On the 24th March 1821 Austrian troops marched into Naples.
473. Emil Bock, 'Paulus'. 'Beiträge zur Geistesgeschichte der Menscheit', Vol. 7, Stuttgart 1954.

Stanhope

(excerpt)

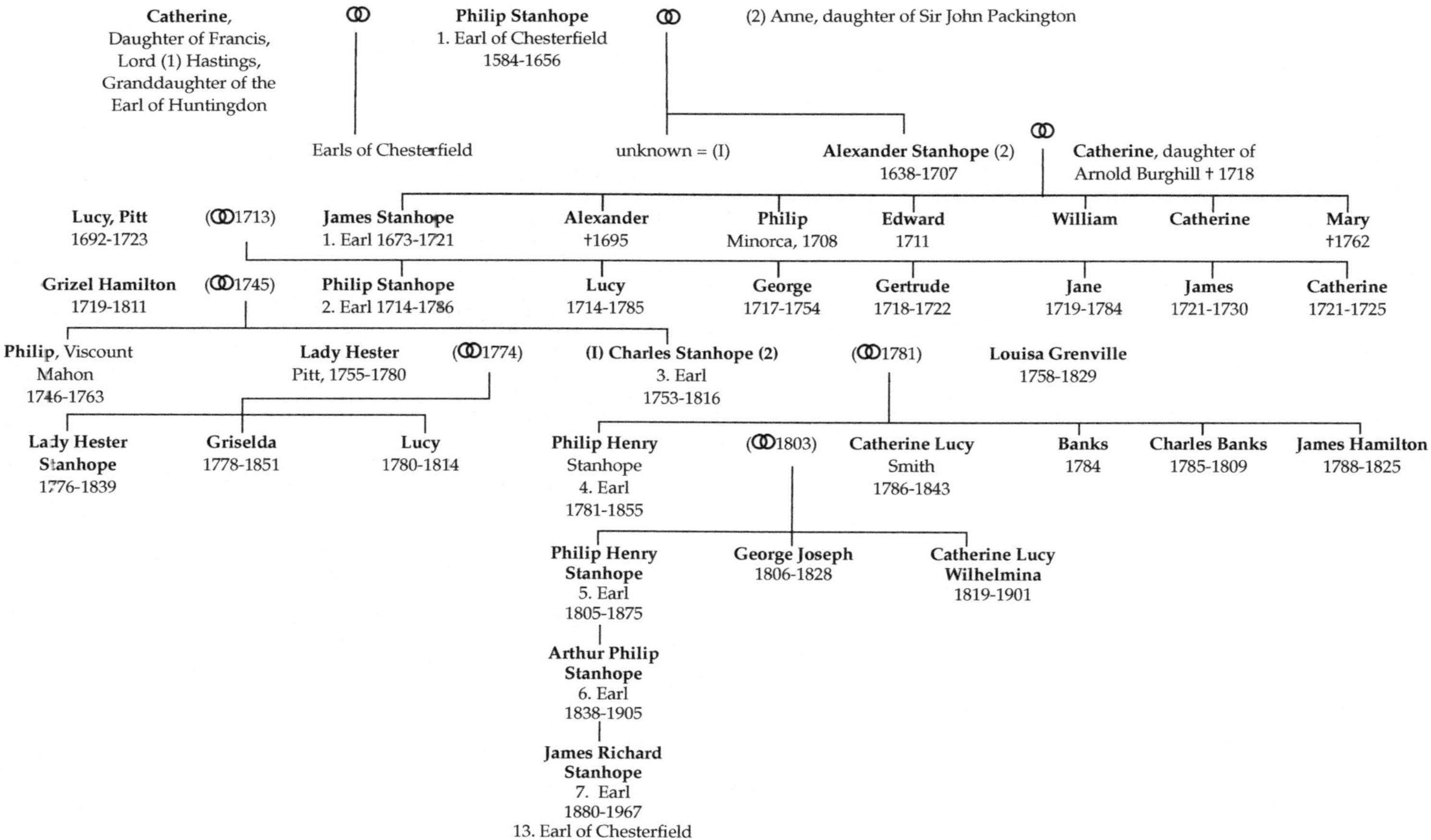

Pitt and Stanhope

Kinship relationships
(excerpt)

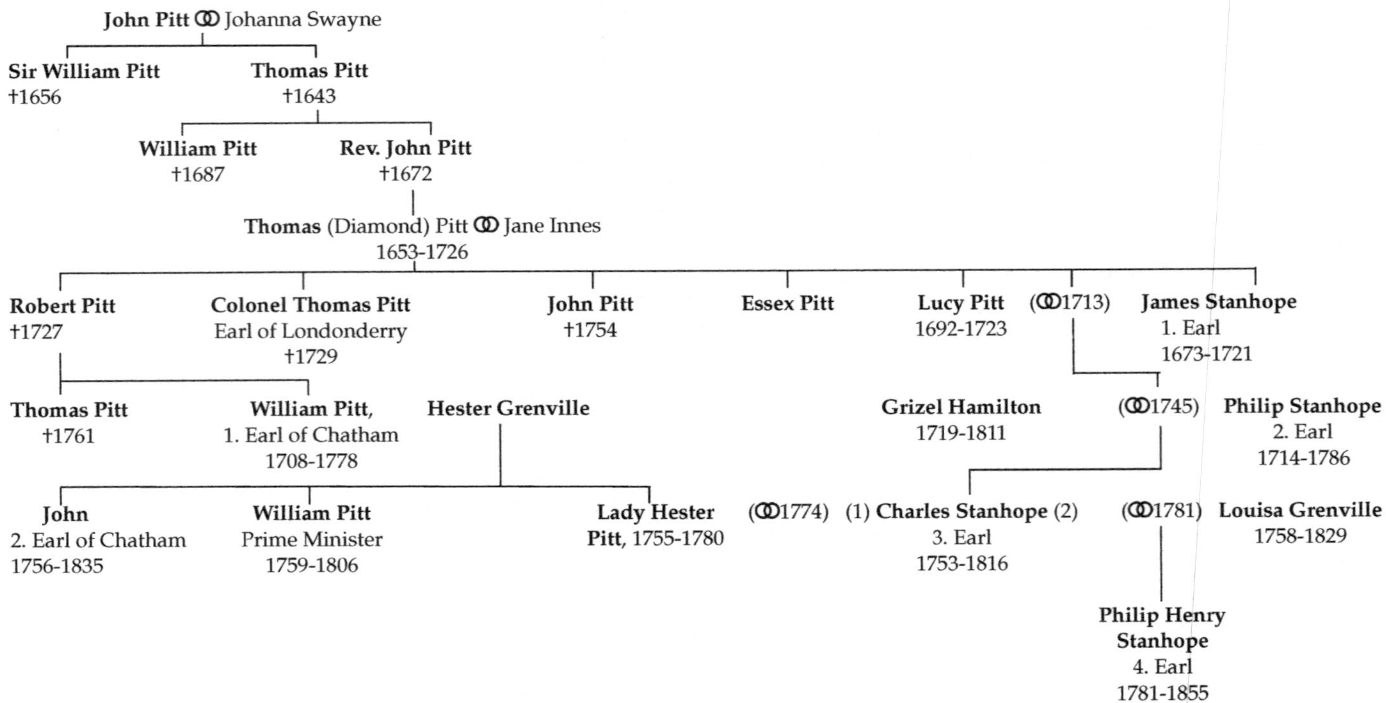

Bourbon Kings of France

(excerpt)

Henri IV
1553-1610

Louis XIII
1601-1643

Louis XIV
1638-1715

Louis, Grand Dauphin,
1661-1711

Louis,
Dauphin, 1682-1712
Duke of Burgundy

Louis XV 1710-1774

Louis,
Dauphin, 1729-1765

- **Louis,** Duke of Burgundy 1751-1761
- **Xavier** Duke of Aquitaine 1753-1754
- **Louis XVI** 1754-1793 Duke of Berry ⚭1770 Marie-Antoinette, Daughter of Emperor Franz I 1755-1793
  - **Louis** Dauphin 1781-1789
  - **Ludwing XVII** 27.3.1785-8.6.1795 or 17.9.1803 until 1792 Dauphin Charles Louis, Duke of Normandy
- **Louis XVIII** 1755-1824 until 1795 and 1814 Stanislas Xavier, Count of Provence
- **Charles X** 1757-1836 until 1824 Charles Philippe, Count of Artois
  - **Louis** Duke of Angoulême 1775-1844, Dauphin (Louis XIX)
  - **Ferdinand** Duke of Berry 1778-1820

The Line of Orléans

(excerpt)

Philippe I
1640-1701
Duke of Orléans
Brother of Louis XIV

Philippe II
1674-1723
From 1715, Regent of France

Louis
1703-1752

Louis Philippe I
1725-1785

Louis Philippe II
1747-1793
'Philippe Égalité', voted for
the death of his cousin Louis XVI in 1792
and was guillotined himself the following year

Louis Philippe III
1773-1850
1810-1948 Louis Philippe I,
King of the French

Beauharnais and Bonaparte

Kinship relationships
(excerpt)

Senior Line
From 1756, Marquis de Beauharnais

François
Governor of Martinique
1714-1800

Alexandre
1760 Martinique
guillotined 1794 in Paris

⚭ 1779

Joséphine Tascher de la Pagerie
1763-1814

⚭ (2) 1796

Napoleon Bonaparte
1769-1821
1804-1814 Napoleon I,
Emperor of the French

Eugène
1781-1824
Adopted by Napoleon
1806 m. Auguste of Bavaria
Viceroy of Italy,
From 1817, Duke of Leuchtenberg

Hortense
1783-1837
adopted by Napoleon
1802 **m. Louis Bonaparte**
1806-1810 King of Holland
1815 Comte de St. Leu

Junior Line
From 1756, Comte de Beauharnais

Claude
1717-1784

Claude
1756-1819
Lieutenant in
Royal Lifeguards,
later, Senator
of the Empire

⚭

Claudine-Adrienne-Gabrièle de Lecay-Marnesia
1768-1791

Stéphanie-Adrienne-Louise
1789-1860
1806 Adopted by Napoleon I
1806 m. Karl of Baden 1786-1818,
Crown Prince,
From 1811, Grand Duke

Bonaparte
(excerpt)

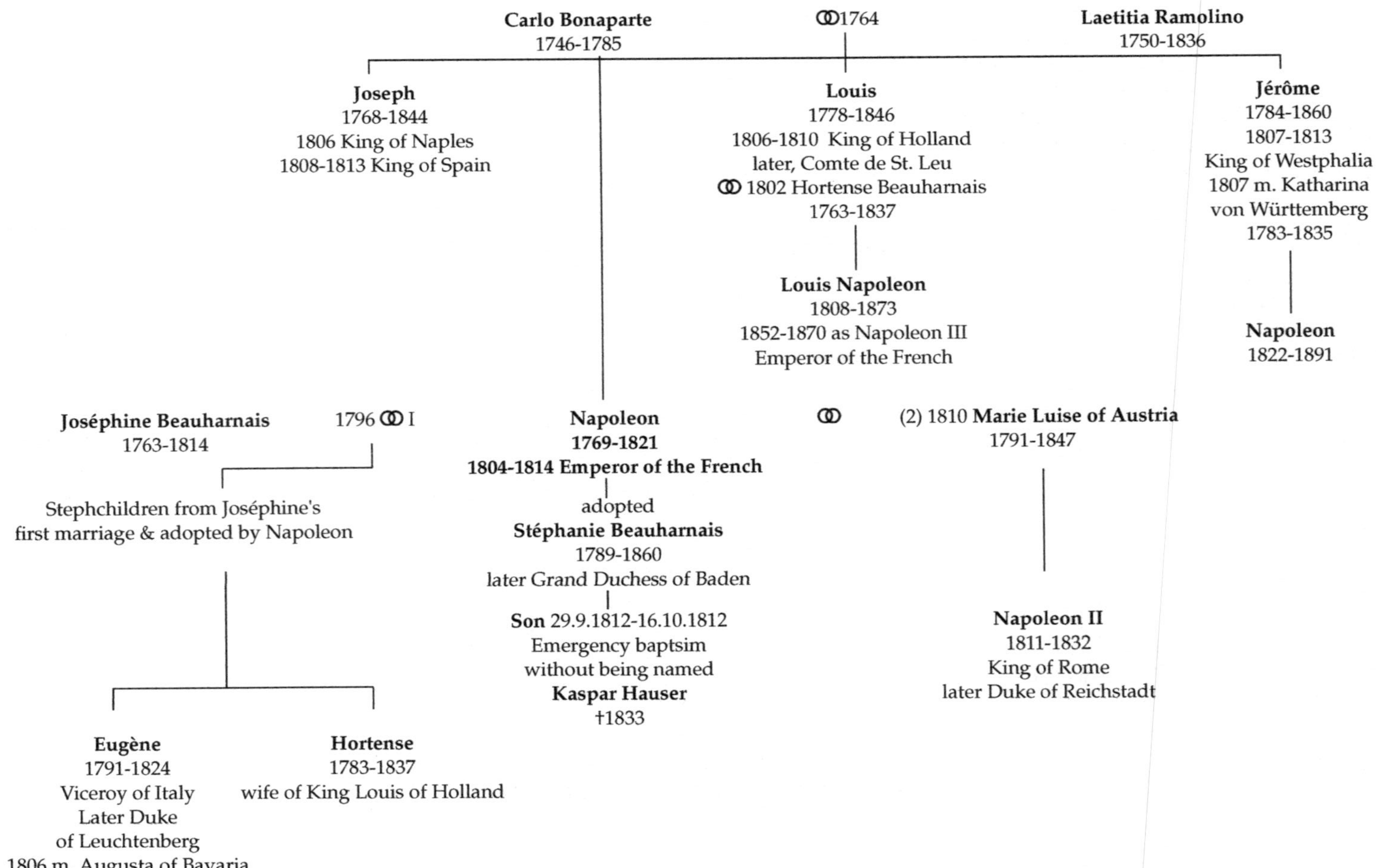

Wittelsbach
Bavaria
(excerpt)

Royal Line

Maximilian (IV) I Joseph
1756-1825
Count Palatine 1795-1799, Prince-Elector 1799-1805, King 1806-1825
m. (1) Auguste Wilhelmine Maria von Hessen-Darmstadt
m. (2) Karoline Friederike Wilhelmine von Baden

1	1	1	1	2	2	2	2	2
Ludwig I 1786-1868 King 1825-1848; m. Therese von Sachsen-Hildburghausen 1792-1854	**Augusta** 1788-1851 m. Eugène de Beauharnais, Duke of Leuchtenberg, Prince of Eichstätt 1781-1824	**Charlotte** 1792-1873 m. (1) Wilhelm von Württemberg; 1781-1864 divorced 1814 m. (2) Franz I of Austria 1768-1835	**Carl** 1795-1875 m. (1) Sophie von Bayrstorff; m. (2) Henriette von Frankenburg; d. 1866	**Elisabeth** 1801-1873 m. (1) Friedrich Wilhelm IV of Prussia 1795-1861	**Amalie** 1801-1877 m. Johann of Saxony 1801-1873	**Sophie** 1805-1872 m. Franz Karl of Austria 1802-1878	**Maria** 1805-1877 m. Friedrich August II of Saxony 1797-1854	**Ludovika** 1808-1892 m. Maximilian, Duke in Bavaria 1808-1888

Children of Ludwig I:

Maximilian II 1811-1864 King 1848-1864 m. Marie of Prussia 1825-1889	**Mathilde** 1813-1862 m. Ludwig III of Hesse 1806-1877	**Otto** 1815-1867 King of Greece, 1832-1862 m. Amalia von Oldenburg 1818-1875	**Luitpold** 1821-1912 Regent (of the Kingdom of Bavaria), 1866-1912 m. Auguste of Austria 1825-1864	**Adelgunde** 1823-1914 m. Francesco V of Modena 1819-1875	**Hildegard** 1825-1865 m. Albrecht of Austria 1817-1895	**Alexandra** 1826-1875 Abbess of the Convent of St Anne, Munich	**Adalbert** 1828-1875 m. Amalie of Spain 1834-1905

Zähringen – Baden

(excerpt)

Carl Friedrich
1728-1811
1803 Prince-Elector, 1806 Grand Duke
m. (1) Caroline Luise von Hesse-Darmstadt 1723-1783
m. (2) Luise Geyer von Geyersberg
(Countess Hochberg)
1768-1820

1 — **Karl Ludwig** 1755-1801 **m. Amalie von Hessen-Darmstadt** 1754-1832

- **Amalie** 1776-1823
- **Karoline** 1776-1841 m. Maximilian, King of Bavaria 1756-1825
- **Luise** 1779-1826 m. Czar Alexander I of Russia 1777-1825
- **Friederike** 1781-1826 m. King Gustav Adolph IV of Sweden 1778-1837
- **Marie** 1782-1808 m. Friedrich Wilhelm, Duke of Braunschweig-Wolfenbüttel 1771-1815
- **Karl** 1786-1818 1811 Grand Duke, m. **Stéphanie Beauharnais** 1789-1860
  - **Luise** 1811-1854 m. Gustav of Sweden 1799-1877
    - **Carola of Vasa** 1833-1907 m. King Albert of Saxony
  - **Son** 29.9.1812-16.10.1812 Emergency baptism without being named. **Kaspar Hauser** †1833
  - **Josephine** 1813-1900 m. Karl Anton, Prince of Hohenzollern-Sigmaringen 1811-1885
    - **Leopold** 1835-1905 m. 1861 Antonia of Portugal 1845-1913
    - **Stephanie** 1837-1859 m. 1858 King Pedro V of Portugal 1837-1861
    - **Carol I** 1839-1914 King of Romania, m. 1869 Elisabeth von Wied 1834-1916 (Carmen Sylva)
  - **Alexander** 1816-1817
  - **Marie** 1817-1888 m. William, Duke of Hamilton 1811-1863
    - **Marie** 1850-1922 m. (1) 1869 Prince Albert I of Monaco, marriage annulled 1880 m. (2) 1880 Tasziló 1, Prince Festetics de Tolna 1850-1933
- **Wilhelmine** 1788-1836 m. Grand Duke of Hesse 1777-1848

1 — **Friedrich** 1756-1817 m. Luise von Nassau-Usingen 1776-1829

1 — **Ludwig I** 1763-1830 1818 Grand Duke

2 — **Leopold** 1790-1852 1830 Grand Duke **m. Sophie of Sweden** 1801-1865

- **Ludwig II** 1824-1858 1852 Grand Duke (non-regnant due to illness)
- **Friedrich I** 1826-1907 1852 Prince-Regent, 1856 Grand Duke m. Luise of Prussia 1838-1923
  - **Friedrich I.** 1857-1928 m. Hilda of Luxemburg 1864-1952
- **Wilhelm** 1829-1897 1863 Marie von Leuchtenberg 1841-1914
  - **Prince Max of Baden** 1867-1929 m. Marie Luise of Hanover and Cumberland

2 — **Amalie** 1795-1869 m. Karl Egon, Prince von Fürstenberg 1796-1854

2 — **Wilhelm** 1792-1859 m. Elisabeth von Württemberg 1802-1864

2 — **Maximilian** 1796-1882

Picture Credits

Newbery Smith Associates, London: 1, 3, 5, 7, 8, 9, 10, 13, 15, 16, 22, 55, 66, 67, 85, 147, 152, 179, 182, 183, 184, 188. Author's archive; Photo: Newbery Smith Associates, London: 189, 190, 191, 192, 193; Andy Williams, Guildford: 111, 181. The Tate Gallery, Millbank, London: 2. Kent Archives, Maidstone: 4, 11, 88, 185, 192. Author's archive: 6, 30, 38, 43, 46, 60, 75, 80, 81, 101, 104, 105, 120, 122, 123, 134, 139, 145, 157, 158, 173, 177, 178, 180; Photo: W. Krafft, Stuttgart: 45, 47, 53, 54, 59, 70, 82, 87, 90, 94, 96, 106, 107, 108, 109, 110, 121, 122, 125, 126, 149, 150, 151, 161, 163, 166, 167, 168, 169, 170, 171, 172, 174, 175. British Museum, London: 12. National Portrait Gallery, London: 14, 17, 68. R.H. Love Galleries Archives, Chicago: 18. Essex County Library, Harwich: 19. Historisches Museum am Hohen Ufer, Hannover: 20. University Library of Friedrich-Alexander University, Erlangen-Nürnberg: 21, 23, 25, 28, 79. Erlangen City Archive: 24, 26, 27, 29. Napoleonmuseum, Arenenberg: 31, 140, 154, 155. Private possession; Photo: W. Krafft, Stuttgart: 32, 72, 73, 74, 112, 116, 129, 130, 131. Staatsarchiv Nürnberg: 114. Stadtarchiv Ansbach: 97, 135. Stadtarchiv Ansbach; Photo: W. Krafft: 57, 65, 98, 113, 115, 119, 138. Private possession; Photo: W. Schmidt, Karlsruhe: 33, 34. Department of the Environment, Walmer: 35, 36. Goethe-Museum, Düsseldorf: 37. Wien Museum (Vienna): 39, 100. Kunsthistorisches Museum, Vienna: 40, 41. Prussian Heritage Image Archive: 44, 52, 58, 69, 92, 93, 117, 156. The Saxon State Library, Dresden: 48, 49, 50, 51. Tucher-Archiv, Nürnberg; Photo: T. v.d. Borne: 56, 102, 118, 132, 136, 165. Landesdenkmalamt Baden-Württemberg: 61, 62. Institut für Zeitungsforschung, Dortmund: 64. Badisches Generallandarchiv, Karlsruhe: 71, 76, 99, 124, 153. Landesbildstelle Baden: Verkehrsamt Bad Griesbach: 77. Reiss Engelhorn Museum, Mannheim: 78. Südwestdeutsche Verlagsanstalt, Mannheim: 83. Bildarchiv der österreichischen Nationalbibliothek: 86. Stadtarchiv, Innsbruck; Photo: Murauer: 89. Bayerisches Nationalmuseum, Munich: 91. Bayrisches Armee-Museum; Photo: Scheuerer, Ingolstadt: 95. Schiller-National-Museum, Marbach: 103. Martin-von-Wagner-Museum, Würzburg; Photo: Gundermann: 127. Stadtmuseum, Ansbach; Photo: Beer, Ansbach: 128. Stadtbibliothek, Nürnberg: Photo: T. v.d. Borne, Nürnberg: 130, 131. Germnisches Nationalmuseum, Nürnberg: 133. Münchner Stadtmuseum, Munich: 141. Schlossmuseum, Gotha: 143. Forschungsbibliothek, Gotha: 144. The Institute for the History of Frankfurt: 148. Frankfurt University Library, Frankfurt: 164. Stadtbibliothek, Nürnberg: Photo: T. v.d. Borne, Nürnberg: 176. Württembergische Landesbibliothek, Stuttgart: 187.

Index of Names

Index of Places

A note from the publisher

For more than a quarter of a century, **Temple Lodge Publishing** has made available new thought, ideas and research in the field of spiritual science.

Anthroposophy, as founded by Rudolf Steiner (1861-1925), is commonly known today through its practical applications, principally in education (Steiner-Waldorf schools) and agriculture (biodynamic food and wine). But behind this outer activity stands the core discipline of spiritual science, which continues to be developed and updated. True science can never be static and anthroposophy is living knowledge.

Our list features some of the best contemporary spiritual-scientific work available today, as well as introductory titles. So, visit us online at **www.templelodge.com** and join our emailing list for news on new titles.

If you feel like supporting our work, you can do so by buying our books or making a direct donation (we are a non-profit/ charitable organisation).